Communicating for Better Health

Communicating for Better Health

A Guide Through the Medical Mazes

Christina S. Beck

Ohio University

Allyn and Bacon

Boston • London • Toronto • Sydney • Tokyo • Singapore

Executive Editor: *Karon Bowers*
Editorial Assistant: *Jennifer Becker*
Senior Editorial-Production Administrator: *Joe Sweeney*
Editorial-Production Service: *Walsh & Associates, Inc.*
Composition Buyer: *Linda Cox*
Manufacturing Buyer: *Megan Cochran*

Copyright © 2001 by Allyn & Bacon
A Pearson Education Company
160 Gould Street
Needham Heights, MA 02494

www.abacon.com

Library of Congress Cataloging-in-Publication Data

Beck, Christina S.
    Communicating for better health : a guide through the medical mazes / Christina S. Beck.
      p. cm.
    Includes bibliographical references and index.
    ISBN 0-205-30777-9
    1. Communication in medicine. 2. Medical care—Social aspects. I. Title.
    R118 .B43 2000
    362.1′042—dc21   00-058272

Printed in the United States of America

10 9 8 7 6 5 4 3 2 1   04 03 02 01 00

For Brittany, Chelsea Meagan, and Roger

CONTENTS

PREFACE

From August 1996 to December 1997, I struggled through a difficult health care experience. Although I had studied health communication for nearly a decade, that stressful saga cast a strong light on the complexities of contemporary health communication. As I suffered through misdiagnosis after misdiagnosis, miscommunication after miscommunication, I grew increasingly confused and frustrated. Who should I trust, I wondered? What should I do? How should I proceed when the passageways of my medical maze darkened and denied a prompt escape?

In *Communicating for Better Health: A Guide Through the Medical Mazes*, I chronicle my quest for wellness as I discuss important considerations for all health care participants—health care professionals, health care seekers, and support system members. Through my auto-ethnography of that health care ordeal, I offer a raw peek at the physical, emotional, and spiritual implications of and for contemporary health communication. Woven throughout the book, my narratives enable readers to grasp the intensity and the consequentiality of interlocking health care relationships and issues for the enactment of health care and health communication.

Featuring the most current scholarly research and issues from the popular press, the book captures the health care industry in light of the chaos of continual change. Further, the book situates health care challenges in light of the fragmentation of contemporary life, exploring the splintering of social support networks for sustaining good health. Through artfully chosen, relevant examples, the book highlights how health care participants strive to discern the "best" course of action, the "best" decision about health, amid alterations in the health care industry and families, the advent of technology, increasing awareness of diversity issues, and loudening public dialogues about health.

This book boasts no easy answers, no "top ten list" to surviving health care episodes. Instead, I hope that the stories and discussion of issues spark insight within the unique context of individual situations, whether you picked up this book as someone who wants to get better health care, someone who wants to help loved ones who may be captured in a health care crisis, or someone who works in the health care industry.

ACKNOWLEDGMENTS

Communicating for Better Health: A Guide Through the Medical Mazes would not exist if not for the efforts and support of some very important people. Karon Bowers, my editor at Allyn & Bacon, convinced me to undertake this project, and her endless encouragement empowered me to develop the book into its current form. Teri Thompson (University of Dayton), Elaine Jenks (West Chester University), and Rajiv Rimal (Texas A&M University) offered invaluable advice, wisdom, and support throughout the review process, and I am grateful for their strong suggestions.

As I detail throughout the book, my colleagues at the School of Interpersonal Communication at Ohio University constitute an incredible support system, personally and professionally. I am grateful to Sue Dewine, David Descutner, and Raymie McKerrow for the availability of resources as I endeavored to meet my deadlines. To Roger C. Aden, Sue Dewine, Claudia Hale, Anita James, Kathy Krendl, Gayle McKerrow, Raymie McKerrow, Dan Modaff, Wanda Sheridan, Candice Thomas-Maddox, and Ray Wagner, I extend my deepest possible gratitude for their kindness during my illness. Much of my personal knowledge of social support stems from their unceasing generosity during a time of need.

In her role as research assistant, Catherine Houghtaling pursued background sources with zest and professionalism for two quarters. Zabedah Saad worked tirelessly on the reference list, entering citations and verifying information. In addition, Debbie London, John Schriner, and Subrata Dass identified and collected possible resources for the book. Further, students in my Interviewing classes conducted interviews with health care participants as a part of their coursework, and some excerpts from those interviews appear in this book. I appreciate the contributions of these undergraduate and graduate students to *Communicating for Better Health*.

I thank Sarah Beck, George and Elizabeth Groscost, Robbie Beck, and Teresa and Jeff Kane for their support, as well as my friends, Corinne, Carolyn, Michelle, and Shari. Further, I owe a great debt to my friend and mentor, Dr. Sandra L. Ragan, for introducing me to health communication and for constantly encouraging me in my scholarly pursuits.

I could not have completed this book without the love and understanding of Brittany and Chelsea Meagan, my wonderful daughters, who uplifted me during my illness and throughout the writing process. I remain forever grateful to Roger for never letting me give up and for never giving up on me. I am so blessed to have each of you in my life.

Without the Grace of God, I literally would not have lived to tell this tale. I praise Him for a wonderfully abundant and fulfilling life and for the opportunity to learn through all of our health and other challenges.

1 Introduction

I slumped back against the cushions of the couch and felt very frustrated. It was August, and the sun was spilling into my friend's living room. I wanted to be outside, running from side to side on a tennis court somewhere, dashing to nail a cross-court backhand. I could almost feel the rush of whipping my racket back and banging the ball to the opposite corner, just clipping the line, just out of my opponent's reach. Unfortunately, as I turned my head to savor my great shot, I saw my laptop computer. I've really got to concentrate, I told myself. Ah, I had thought that I would be able to concentrate here.

I looked around at the mess that I had made of Roger's living room, with papers in stacks around the edges of the couch. I was in the process of finishing my book (ironically, on women and health communication), and I felt so far behind. I had already requested and received one extension, and I was not going to ask for another one.

I stretched my arms in the air. The wrist that I had broken in a fall about eight years before had started to hurt every time that I tried to type. As I stopped stretching and shook out my hands by my sides, I yearned once more to be outside and for my wrist to stop throbbing. Great, I thought. I've not only lost the summer to the book; I'll possibly have to get my wrist treated for carpal tunnel, so I'll lose tennis playing in the fall as well.

As I started to pick up my papers and return to typing, I happened to look down at my wrist. I saw a lump. I studied it for a moment; I had never noticed the lump before. It's possibly nothing, I told myself. It can't be anything that I can't deal with later. I turned my attention back to the book and tried to put the pain and the lump and my tennis fantasies deep in the back of my mind.

Our Medical Mazes

My preteen daughter, Brittany, and her friends like the words of a song about irony by Alanis Morissette, often shouting (more than singing) the words, "isn't it ironic, don't ya think?" I found it ironic that I was finishing a book manuscript that focused on interactions between women patients and their health caregivers when I made that fateful discovery that would prompt my own health care encounters. However, as I will detail throughout this book, the ironies of contemporary health care and health communication stretch well beyond me, my book, and my particular illness.

At a time when health care facilities are more diversified and dispersed than ever before, fear about the availability of health care is increasingly prevalent. At a time when more resources are invested in medical research than ever before, skepticism about scientific conclusions being absolute answers for health care concerns continues to grow. At a time when individuals have more access to information than ever before (on the Internet, television, magazines, etc.), confusion over contradictory claims and mixed messages continues to mount. At a time when health care has become more specialized, cynicism about "experts" who enact care compartmentally, rather than holistically, continues to climb. At a time when health care options and alternatives abound, rhetoric about "truth" and "quackery" continues to surge. At a time when medical advances offer high-tech solutions, questions about culture, religion, and personal choice continue to arise. At a time when globalization makes disease a concern of all in the world, appeals for appreciation of diversity and individual choice continue to swell. At a time when we can theoretically search for more information and connect with more individuals who share our situations via the Internet and when we have a plethora of alternatives with regard to approaches to care, we lack the time to pursue those resources, due to our chaotic contemporary lives. Indeed, isn't it ironic, don't ya think?

The purpose of this book is not to offer a guide for health care participants. I can offer no answers, no easy directions. In fact, I am pretty sure that no one can. I have incredible respect for members of the health care industry, for doctors and nurses and and all of the other health care professionals who attempt to help those who suffer. Yet, I feel strong empathy for people who try to make sense of health care options amid the frenzy of their lives. We live in a world with too many answers, not too few, too many conflicting voices from diverse cultural, political, economic, intellectual, and, of course, medical perspectives. In such a world, communication becomes a critical component of health and wellness. Communication constitutes the core of enacting optimal health care.

Communication and Health Care

Health care concerns never fit easily into our schedules or our lives. From the common cold to more major health concerns, the acknowledgment that "something is not quite right" forces busy people to deal with symptoms, treatments, options, appointments, and emotions amid all of the other responsibilities and commitments of their cluttered lives. Stepping across the line from suspecting a problem to determining one can be analogous to stepping on the elevator at the Tower of Terror at DisneyWorld—a surreal free-fall ride, something that we enjoy at amusement parks but not in our efforts to navigate everyday life.

Dr. Jane Hanscom, a general surgeon for the Spence Center for Women in Chevy Chase, Maryland and a specialist in breast surgery, discovered the lump on her breast while doing her monthly examination in the shower. During her work with cancer patients, she had reflected on how she would handle breast cancer personally—she would opt for a mastectomy and then reconstructive surgery. According to Glatzer (1998, p. 79), "It seemed like the least fussy method. She'd do it instantly, as soon as she found out about the cancer. Simple, quick."

Yet, when she actually discovered the lump, she tried to push it from her mind. Although, as a doctor, she knew the risks of waiting to remove the growth, as a wife, a mother, and a woman, she shifted her focus to upcoming vacations. Glatzer (1998) explained:

> Summer was in full swing, and Dr. Hanscom had vacation on her mind. She and her husband, Doug (a lawyer) and their two sons, Gregory, 11, and Jeffrey, 12, were planning several trips. There was so much to do, so much to look forward to; there wasn't any time to worry about cancer. So she tried not to think about it. . . . Once she announced she was ill, there would be no more pretending nothing was wrong. The longer she kept the secret, the more afraid she became of revealing it. (p. 79)

Of course, Dr. Hanscom did eventually reveal her discovery to her husband and her partners. Because of her professional connections, she found a surgeon whom she could trust with relative ease, and her knowledge of breast cancer and cancer treatments enabled her to approach her decisions with relative confidence. She did choose a mastectomy with reconstructive surgery, as she had thought that she would. However, despite all of her prior understanding and reflection on the subject, Dr. Hanscom resisted making that initial admission of "something wrong," an admission that would distinguish her from being a "well" person who could travel to Maine to being a "sick" person who must struggle with the emotional turmoil and medical consequences of "illness," to becoming a woman who would have to journey back to "wellness," rather than one who could take wellness for granted. As Musa Mayer, another breast cancer survivor, explains, that journey can be dark and isolating. Mayer (1993) details:

> Somewhere out there in that darkness are hundreds of thousands of women like myself. . . . In one moment of discovery, these lives have been transformed, just as mine has been, as surely as if they had been plucked from their native land and forced to survive in a hostile new landscape, fraught with dangers, real and imagined. (p. 5)

In my own situation, I managed to live with the pain and some uncertainty until I shipped my manuscript safely to my publisher, about three weeks after I discovered the lump on my wrist. However, my subsequent efforts to discover answers about the lump and the pain launched me into a convoluted medical maze of conflicting and inaccurate diagnoses, diverse treatment recommendations, and multiple disparate medical approaches to problems that, at least for a time, only seemed to send me from the frying pan smack into the fire.

As I struggled through my own health care saga, which will be described throughout this book, and as I researched this volume, I have realized that prescriptive approaches to health care and health communication fail to prepare us for life and health situations which are far too complicated for a simple "how to" list to solve. Although Dr. Hanscom "knew" about breast cancer from a clinical perspective, her medical background did not prepare her for the emotional saga of breast cancer and for the impact that it would have on her life, her identity, her family.

In my case, my surgeon and I practiced many of the communicative behaviors that are recommended for practitioners and patients/clients. Yet, I almost died because of a missed

diagnosis. Despite my best efforts to gain information and to sort through options, I was trying to do so when my mind was blurred and my body was weakened due to illness. I kept
hearing subtle hints that certain health care professionals really weren't making the right
diagnosis or didn't really have the background or authority to offer insight. I found myself
questioning and doubting, like a traveler who suspects (but cannot confirm) that some
prankster switched road sign directions. I couldn't get perspective, perspective about recommendations and decisions nor even perspective about who I had come to be. Despite the kind
efforts of friends to help me, I kept trying (and failing miserably) to enact who I was when I
was "well" so I could fight my way back to being "mom" and "friend" and "professor," to
return to "me." I had not just lost my way; I had somehow misplaced myself.

As I will detail throughout this book, through communication we socially construct conceptions of "illness," "disease," and "wellness." Through communication, we co-determine
the relevance of "disease" or "wellness practices" for us, as individuals and as co-culture
participants. Through communication, we co-create what counts as "legitimate" treatment.
Through communication, we co-define our relationships with various health care practitioners
and social support network members. Through communication, we discover, pursue, evaluate,
and share information from an array of sources. Through communication, we prioritize that
information individually, in our social support networks and with our health care practitioners.
Through communication, we co-construct our identities as individuals, not just as "well" people or "sick" people. Through communication, we co-define "normal," in terms of approaches
to health care and our individual identities as people in society.

Throughout this book, I will emphasize the importance of communication in enacting health care relationships and in struggling with health care issues. Especially as we
begin the new millennium, the consequentiality of communication for health care has never
been more at the forefront of a public dialogue about health and wellness.

The Case of Public Health Concerns

As a world community, we seek answers about disease and disease prevention. According
to the Committee on Labor and Human Resources (1998), "More than 17 million people
will die this year as a result of infectious diseases, nearly 50 thousand every day" (p. 82).
In the case of HIV/AIDS alone, the figures are staggering. A December, 1998 UNAIDS
report revealed that " . . . the epidemic is frankly out of control in many places "(UNAIDS,
1998a, p. 2). Although economic, political, environmental, and technological factors play
significant parts in addressing the spread of infectious disease, communication is at the
heart of enacting solutions (see MAP, 1998; UNAIDS, 1998b).

For example, Randy Shilts argues in his powerful book, *And the Band Played On:
Politics, People, and the AIDS Epidemic* (1987), that the lack of communication about
AIDS in the United States hindered positioning of the disease as relevant to all, dwelling
instead on the implication that AIDS was just punishment for a few. Communicative
choices by members of the media and the government literally cost lives by muting voices
that cried for the sounding of a national alarm for awareness and prevention about HIV and
AIDS (Shilts, 1987). Shilts (1987) stresses that silence stifled early intervention in the
spread of AIDS, noting that the United States " . . . failed because of ignorance and fear,
prejudice and rejection" (p. 601).

In the case of the AIDS epidemic in the United States, the failure to share information or to cast it as relevant did kill. In this instance in particular, political muffling of concerns proved deadly for multitudes who received tainted blood or who continued to engage in risky behavior without appreciating the danger. Notably, *Healthy People 2000*, a document produced in 1990 by the U.S. government specifying health-related goals, acknowledged the need for "new strategies" to address the spread of HIV, three years after the publication of *And the Band Played On.*

Certainly, communicative efforts can impact wellness and, in some cases, the quality of life for entire communities (see Piotrow, Kincaid, Rimon, & Rinehart, 1997). From infectious disease to family planning to cancer awareness, communication can provide the vital bridge from scientific discovery to impacted lives. In *Healthy People 2000: National Health Promotion and Disease Prevention Objectives*, the U.S. Department of Health and Human Services (1990) heralds the potential of health promotion and disease prevention, arguing that "the Nation has within its power the ability to save many lives lost prematurely and needlessly" (p. 6). The continued commitment to broad-based public health communication efforts echoes throughout the web-based draft of *Healthy People 2010*, especially as it acknowledges that the "public" actually constitutes diverse collections of individuals throughout society.

Posted on the Internet in order to solicit feedback from individuals and organizations across the United States, *Healthy People 2010* argues that *Healthy People* offers a simple but powerful idea: "provide the information and knowledge about how to improve health in a format that enables diverse groups to combine their efforts and work as a team" (see http://web.health.gov/healthy people/2010fctsht.htm). Linked with the World Health Organization's "Health for All" program, this phase of the Healthy People initiative emphasizes the elimination of health disparities (e.g., in terms of availability of care, diverse health-related needs, and propensity for illness). In so doing, the plan pushes diversity in the United States (in terms of factors such as racial or ethnic background, socioeconomic status, age, gender, educational level, geographical location, or sexual orientation) to the forefront of health-related discussions.

As I will elaborate on later, complex, interrelated issues influence enactments of health communication and health prevention. For public health officials and members of the general public, a sincere appreciation for and understanding of communication with increasingly diverse health care participants will endure as essential for the accomplishment of public health objectives.

The Case of Managed Care

A 1998 Harris poll, entitled "The Future of Health Care," revealed that "about 55 million Americans believe the overall quality of health care they receive has gotten *worse* in the past five years" (Harris & Associates, 1998, p. 9). In fact, the survey found that "large majorities of the public"(p. 1) anticipate a continued decline in availability, accessibility, and affordability of health services.

The public dialogue in the United States about health care and health care reform continues, despite the failure of President Clinton's health care reform package in the mid-1990s (Coile, 1997b; Rosenau, 1994). Although Congress and the Clinton administration could not come to consensus on ways to control the spiraling cost of health care, their lack of movement did not impact the quakes that have erupted throughout the health care industry during the 1990s and into the twenty-first century. The high cost of health care, combined with the emergence of national health care organizations, has prompted a widespread reconceptualization of care and care management, with managed care organizations emerging as an increasingly prevalent option for cost control (see Coile, 1997a, 1997b, 1998; Emanuel & Dubler, 1997; Gold, 1998; Nieves, 1998). Josephine Nieves, Executive Director of the National Association of Social Workers, recalls:

> Managed care swept with unprecedented speed through our institutions, our medical community, and our work places. A radical, historic shift in society's health care process took place before our astonished eyes, driven totally by market forces and entirely outside regulatory management. (1998, p. xiii)

The rumblings throughout the health care industry persist as everyone who is involved, from third party payer organizations to health care consumers, tries to determine how health care will and can get enacted. As Gold (1998) explains, "This dramatic growth in managed care has challenged policymakers, consumers, the press, and all those involved in the healthcare industry to understand the proliferation of organizational models and products it has spawned" (p. 5).

Theoretically, the notion of "managing care" makes sense. With a focus on preventive medicine (see, e.g., Schamess & Lightburn, 1998), Gelber (1998, p. 85) explains that managed care organizations strive to "reduce cost" as well as work to coordinate care efforts, control quality, and improve efficiency and services. While such goals seem consistent with consumer desires to gain the best services for the least possible cost, the communicative enactment of "efficiency" in health care services poses serious consequences for the way that health care participants can approach health care.

On political, organizational, interpersonal, and cultural levels, communication emerges as a core component of how people can muddle their way through this economic and political labyrinth. While legislators and lobbyists debate the merits, ethics, and economic consequences of "patient rights," individual health care seekers make appointments with health care professionals. Before an individual even drives to the health care professional's office, he or she may need to gain permission to see that particular professional, if that professional is not on the list of participating providers for the health care seeker's third party payer (see Emanuel & Dubler, 1997).

During the middle of my own health care saga, my employer shifted to a managed care plan that excluded my surgeon. For reasons that will become clear throughout this book, no other doctor would take my case at that point in my treatment, and I had to present an argument to my third party payer about the necessity of continuing care with my surgeon. Although those interactions were relatively free from confrontation, the need for those exchanges added one more barrier within my medical maze, one more obstacle that I had to deal with and somehow get around.

As health care seekers, we go to health care professionals, seeking assistance for some health care concern and requesting expert counsel. While interactions between health care professionals and health care seekers are often difficult in and of themselves (see Chapter

Three on health care professional-seeker interactions), the advent of managed care invokes a new voice, a third voice, into dialogues and decisions—the third party payer (see Emanuel & Dubler, 1997; Gold, 1998; Schamess & Lightburn, 1998). Individuals in the United States are still in the midst of public and private arguments about the enactment of that third voice.

The 1998 Harris poll concluded that "nearly three in four physicians (71%) believe that pressures to limit the number of services to patients will increase in the next five years" (p. 8). Further, 78 percent of physicians who were surveyed feel that "the trend toward managed care will *harm* the quality of health care" (Harris & Associates, 1998, p. 11). For example, the public outrage over "drive-through deliveries" (in which new mothers and their babies were limited to just 24 hours in the hospital following "normal" births) constitutes just one example of concern about the role of third party payers in health care decisions. Notably, the very vocal reaction of health care seekers and professionals to situations like "drive-through deliveries" has compelled managed care organizations to consider perspectives of health care participants more proactively in their policy making (see related arguments by Coile, 1998; Schamess & Lightburn, 1998).

Yet, the perpetual debate over options and issues continues, contributing to the constant state of change. The reshuffling of the health care industry in the United States shows no signs of settling into a state of "this is how things are going to be." With the unfolding of the daily paper, new notions of managing the cost of health care get tossed into the mix. For example, MacStravic and Montrose (1998) offer an alternative to managed care—"demand management," which promotes the philosophy that individuals are "able to take the right actions if given the right options, information, resources and support" (p. xiv).

This affirmation of the consumer voice is heartening; however, the challenge for health care seekers and professionals stems from how the participants attain voice and participate in the co-construction of "acceptable" ways of managing care—indeed, in the co-definition of "acceptable." With the challenges of accessibility for marginalized groups, freedom of choice of providers, flexibility of diagnostic and treatment options, and so on, communication remains critical to sorting through this national puzzle. As that sorting ensues, health care seekers, especially our ever-aging population, continue to watch and listen anxiously as others make decisions that impact their very access to care (see Millenson, 1997).

The Case of Fragmented Support Networks

In the movie *Steel Magnolias* a young woman, portrayed by Julia Roberts, tells her mother that she is going to have a child. The mother, played artfully by Sally Field, dissolves into tears, agonizing over her daughter's choice to have a child despite the health risk due to complications from diabetes. After her initial frustration and fear, the mother supports her daughter. Although the daughter gives birth to a healthy baby, the pregnancy takes a tremendous toll on her body. The mother stays by her daughter's bedside in the hospital and holds her hand as she dies.

In the case of this movie, mother and daughter lived in the same town, talked daily, and interacted with a common circle of friends, a circle of friends who subsequently supported the grieving mother. With ever-intensifying efforts to reduce costs, social support for health care participants has never been so critical nor so problematic.

People who struggle with illness have always needed family and friends for emotional support; however, with increasing emphasis on outpatient surgery and home rehabilitation, individuals leave hospitals earlier than their counterparts from yesteryear. According to Havas (1998, p. 80–81), medical staff "rely on family and friends to provide care that formerly would have been provided in hospital. Even in the hospital . . . outsiders provide care that previously would have been provided by nursing staff."

Last summer, one of my little neighbor girls crashed her bike in front of my house. One of her brothers frantically rang my door bell, pointed to his sister, and then ran to get his mom. I dashed across the yard to see Laura in a heap, with blood gushing from her mouth. I applied pressure on her jaw, but I couldn't even see the source of the blood. It just spewed from her mouth. Her mom, who had just had a baby, drove up in her van and took Laura to the local emergency room. After calling to make arrangements for my younger daughter to be picked up from preschool, I drove to the hospital to check on Laura and to see if I could help in any way.

Laura's oldest brother was in the waiting room with the newborn. Not wanting to stick my nose where it didn't belong and yet wanting to help with the baby, if necessary, I popped my head in the examining room and asked if I could do anything. Laura's mom was holding a compress on Laura's jaw, waiting for the doctor to return. Laura's face was bloody, but not tear-stained. She is one tough little girl. After visiting for a few minutes, Laura's mom realized that the baby needed to be fed, and she asked me if I could hold the compress.

I didn't mind holding the compress. I was all too glad to be able to help—Laura goes to my church and does activities with my girls. However, I was stunned that I never saw a nurse or someone to assist the doctor in Laura's care. Even when the doctor came in to examine her, he told me to keep holding the compress, "just like that."

As hospital staffs continue to be slashed due to budget cuts, responsibility for care will increasingly shift to people who happen to come to support ill or injured parties, or that care may not happen at all. Disturbingly, these economic and organizational shifts unfold as social support networks continue to fragment, due to the realities of contemporary life. Unlike the cozy community in *Steel Magnolias*, contemporary life consists of fragmented family relationships, nomadic geographical movement, and multiple roles beyond the home—lifestyles that hinder caring for ill or elderly relatives or getting involved in the lives of people who happen to live in our communities for a few years (see related works by Bellah, Madsen, Sullivan, Swidler, & Tipton, 1985; Elkind, 1994; Gergen, 1991; Gibson, 1998; Roots, 1998; Segalman, 1998; Shorter, 1992). According to Hogan (1998), "The signs of stress and fragmentation appear everywhere . . . in all of the various communities that define our social lives—our families, our neighborhoods, our towns and cities, our professions, and our social and cultural associations" (p. xii).

In his edited volume *Reclaiming the Family*, Segalman (1998) bemoans the splintering of family relationships. He points to divorce, remarriage, single parenting, absentee parents, women who choose (and who are economically compelled) to work outside of the home, geographically distanced families, and devaluing of family responsibilities as challenges for accomplishing "family" in contemporary society. To be sure, "families" have never been "perfect" or statically defined (Coontz, 1992; Elkind, 1994), and efforts to depict the perfect mother and father with a daughter and son and a dog in the 1950s may well be glorified, as the movie *Pleasantville* suggests. Yet as Elkind (1994) observes, the ideal of the nuclear family "had boundaries that were legally, geographically, and biologically explicit" (p. 27), enabling roles and responsibilities to be clear and defined.

Through the shift to a postmodern treatment of "family," individuals may define kinship relationships more flexibly and fluidly; role differentiation may blur responsibilities and lines of authority (see Elkind, p. 35). As Elkind (1994) explains, "the postmodern permeable family . . . mirrors the openness, complexity, and diversity of our contemporary lifestyles" (p. 1). Such reconstructions of family life, combined with the cluttered, chaotic schedules of contemporary living, make extraneous issues such as illness difficult to integrate in the frenzy of everyday life. With more women working outside of the home, families struggle to care for children during brief illnesses; caring for a relative with a long-term illness adds considerable pressure to families as they search for solutions (see Elkind, 1994; Roots, 1998).

As the population in the United States continues to age (see Roots, 1998; Wacker, Roberto, & Piper, 1998), care for our nation's elderly is a concern in the context of the uncertainties of managed care and of fractured families. According to Wacker and colleagues (1998), the ever-increasing complexity of family relationships "might reduce the number of potential family caregivers and increase role ambiguity of adult children within divorced and blended families" (p. 4). Further, as people live longer and as more individuals wait until later in life to have children, the potential of caring for elderly relatives becomes one more piece of an unsolvable time and resource riddle—caring for parents as well as for children while balancing career, house, personal health, and sanity (see Roots, 1998).

Hillary Clinton's (1996) book *It Takes A Village* prompted both cheers and chuckles. In our ever-individualized and ever-isolated lives, the idea of relying on a "village" approach or even building "community" seems distant. Best and Kellner (1991) explain that assumptions of "social coherence" are inconsistent with postmodernity, abandoned "in favor of multiplicity, plurality, fragmentation, and indeterminacy" (p. 4).

When Laura had her accident on her bike in front of my house, I marveled that I was home. I am never home. I'm always at the office or in my car commuting kids from dance lessons to basketball practice to church youth group meetings, and so on. On that particular day, I had happened to come home to get something before running back to pick up Chelsea Meagan from preschool and then dart off to dinner in town. Like nearly all of the other people in my little neighborhood, my house gets lit at night when I come home to sleep.

As we dash around in our everyday lives, we take little time for "being neighborly" or for becoming invested in "community," in the lives of others. Muller (1999) argues that "to be unavailable to our friends and family . . . to whiz through our obligations without time for a single mindful breath—this has become the model of a successful life" (p. 4).

How can we know when someone else is ill or if someone needs help when we are never home to see? During my life-threatening illness, with home health care workers coming three times a day, none of my neighbors stopped by. Most of them didn't know about the illness. The few who did were busy, just as I had been too busy to keep up with them. As we nomadically move in and out of neighborhoods and lives, just as we tear in and out of our houses in the frenzy of daily existence, the potential for connectedness and community dwindles.

As I will detail in the chapter on social support, communication is critical in this era of increasingly fragmented social support networks. The ways in which we share our needs and seek support impact our potential for physical, emotional, and even spiritual wellness. Yet, juxtaposing health care and social support demands with our contemporary lived realities requires artful communication with family members, employers, and friends. With the advent of the Internet, some have turned to e-mail to rebuild connectedness with relatives in remote areas, breaking down the barriers of geography, time, and resources. Others have transcended geographical boundaries and extended interpersonal networks to include virtual strangers who happen to struggle with similar issues (see Coiera, 1997; Harris, 1995; McKenzie, 1997; Sharp & Sharp, 1998). Although certainly restricted to those who may easily access technological resources, the communicative accomplishment of virtual support fits as a postmodern response for increasingly fragmented families and communities.

The Case of Medical Uncertainty

In her book, *It's Always Something*, Gilda Radner (1989) described her efforts to seek relief from symptoms that were later diagnosed as stemming from ovarian cancer. As she battled to discover the nature of her illness, she anxiously pursued someone who could help her, someone to believe her. Radner recalled:

> Then a new symptom appeared—an aching, gnawing pain in my upper thighs and in my legs. It started slowly, then increased and would not go away. The gynecologist and the gastroenterologist could find no reason for it. My blood work showed nothing wrong. I continued to keep a chart of everything I was eating, and I started to take Tylenol to ease the intense leg pains. . . . (p. 65)

However, the pain and frustration continued, and Radner pursued health care providers beyond the bounds of Western medicine. As she noted, "At least he [the holistic doctor] and the acupuncturist were taking me seriously" (1989, p. 66). Still seeking help, relief, and answers, Radner detailed:

> On October 13 the acupuncturist stuck needles in my swollen stomach and gave me a special abdominal massage. Two days later, the holistic doctor suggested I have a colonic to clean out the bowel. I insisted that would be too weird for me. The next day, I saw my internist. He did blood work again—I was running a low-grade fever. He gave me a gamma globin shot, which was working on some patients with this Epstein-Barr virus. He felt my stomach and told me I was literally "full of shit," and gave me a prescription for laxatives. He told me to come back in a week.
>
> Suddenly, I began to wonder how to please so many people. Do I take the magnesium citrate? What about the coffee enema? Do I do both? Do I do the abdominal massage or the colonic? Do I tell the doctors about each other? East meets West in Gilda's body: Western medicine down my throat, Eastern medicine up my butt. (p. 67)

Truly, if anyone has ever been lost in a medical maze, it was Gilda Radner. Time after time, she was told that "it was nothing." Time after time, she was told "not to worry."

Time after time, she left a health care professional's office without answers. After struggling to find someone to believe her, someone to help her to find the cause of her symptoms, she eventually learned the source of her suffering. The doctors removed a grapefruit-sized tumor as well as her reproductive organs. After battling to fight the cancer for two and a half years, Gilda Radner died on May 20, 1989.

As I read Ms. Radner's book, I found myself crying and asking how so many doctors and tests could have missed such a sizable tumor. However, after reading Gene Wilder's (Ms. Radner's husband) account in his book with Dr. M. Steven Piver, I was even more stunned to learn that the doctors failed to pick up on a key part of Ms. Radner's medical history. Her grandmother had been diagnosed with "stomach cancer," her mother with breast cancer, her cousin with ovarian cancer. As Wilder acknowledges, "truth to tell, even if some doctor had made the connection in Gilda's family history, that same internist or gynecologist might not have known what to do with the information in 1986" (Piver & Wilder, 1996, p. 32).

Since Gilda Radner's death, Mr. Wilder has been a staunch advocate for awareness about ovarian cancer, promoting a more widespread use of the blood test, CA125, to detect ovarian cancer. His goal is to help "other Gildas and pull them out of the woods" (Piver & Wilder, 1996, p. 32).

Can "other Gildas" be pulled "out of the woods"? I sat at my keyboard staring at that question for several minutes. The answer would have to be—it depends. Certainly, as we begin the millennium, more information is available about ovarian cancer; however, despite the onslaught of press about ovarian cancer immediately after Gilda Radner's death, publicity about the disease has paled in comparison to AIDS and breast cancer, which command considerable media attention through the pressure of activists (see related work by Batt, 1994). Certainly, more gynecologists realize the importance of family history, and yet, expensive tests such as CA125 may not be ordered routinely for early detection due to economic constraints and third party payer restrictions. Certainly, well-educated and well-located women may know questions to ask and tests to request, but lack of education, geographical location, economic status, and co-cultural background may hinder many women from learning about the disease or pressing their doctors for information or testing. Certainly, some "Gildas" have been spared Ms. Radner's fate, but almost certainly, some continue to tear through their own thick forests, looking for answers, for someone to believe, for someone to help.

In a 1997 letter to "Dear Abby," Marsha Newman, a member of an ovarian cancer support group, explains that ovarian cancer has been dubbed "the 'silent killer' because the symptoms are vague, often ignored or minimized by both patient and physician," hindering the likelihood of detection and treatment. Sadly, she adds her personal testimony that "there are three women in my Ovarian Cancer Support Group at SHARE in New York City who had breast cancer and complained of ovarian cancer symptoms and were not diagnosed until an advanced stage" (see Van Buren, August 22, 1997).

One of the most frightening revelations over the past two decades of American medicine, for both health care seekers and for health care professionals, is that health care practitioners don't just absolutely know what to do (see Bursztajn, Feinbloom, Hamm, & Brodsky, 1981). "They" don't have the market on "the" truth. "They" might not ask the "right" questions or order the "right" tests. "They" might make mistakes (see Berg, 1997;

Bogner, 1994; Keyser, 1993; Lantos, 1997). In fact, a 1999 Institute of Medicine report affirms that medical mistakes account for nearly 100,000 annual deaths, the eighth leading cause of death in the United States (see Gallagher, December 3, 1999; Page, December 7, 1999).

When I finally decided that I needed to pursue the source of pain in my wrist, I made an appointment to see my family practitioner, Dr. S. Dr. S. is a doctor of osteopathic medicine, and he exemplifies the patient-centered philosophy that constitutes the heart of osteopathic medicine. He observed that I was likely suffering from carpal tunnel syndrome, and he recommended a doctor in a nearby town who specializes in nerve damage. Because Dr. S. didn't seem to notice the lump, I didn't press the issue. I wanted to believe that it wasn't a problem.

On the following Friday afternoon, I arrived for my appointment with Dr. J. I was taken into an examining room and greeted by a person whom I perceived to be either a resident or a medical student. He was a resident. I asked if he would be conducting the test, and he looked surprised and said, "Well, yes." I explained that the test was important to me and that I really wanted Dr. J. to do the test. The resident said, "Well, Dr. J. will be supervising the test." At that point, Dr. J. entered the examining area. An older man, very assertive to the point of abrasive in his demeanor, Dr. J. immediately looked at the way that the resident had hooked up all of the wires on my arm and described the nature of the test to me. In essence, the test would determine whether my nerves respond to the electronic signals that would be sent through little electrodes.

As I sat on the bed with the testing wires hooked onto my arm with little pads, I again asserted my desire to have Dr. J. conduct the test. Dr. J. said, "Well, I'm right here." He instructed the resident to continue the test. With every shock, my arms reacted, and they kept increasing the voltage until I was literally almost shocked off the table. At that point, I asked the doctor about my condition and the treatment for carpal tunnel. "You don't have carpal tunnel," he bellowed. "What?" I asked. "You don't have carpal tunnel, and your nerves are responding fine," Dr. J. noted. "Okay," I said, "then what could be causing all of this pain?" Dr. J. stared at me and suggested, "You know, pain is a relative thing. I think we overexaggerate pain a lot." He then proceeded to note that he had written an article on the overexaggeration of pain and asked for my card. He sent me the article a week later. I had absolutely no desire to read anything that he had written.

I returned to Dr. S. He commiserated with me about some physicians' insensitivity to pain and took another look at my wrist. This time, he noticed the lump. It had become even more pronounced during the previous two weeks. He grew very concerned and sent me down to x-ray. I dutifully sat for the x-ray—the first of many—and then carried the film back upstairs to Dr. S. "You know," he said, "I think that this is getting out of my league. I think what you might have is a small tumor on your wrist, and I am not . . . I don't really know what we could do about it; I am not an orthopedic specialist. I think I need to refer you to an orthopedic specialist who would have a little more expertise in this area." One of the very best things about Dr. S. is his willingness to admit when he doesn't know, or at least is not certain, about something. As I came to discover, more health care practitioners should develop that characteristic.

Dr. S. referred me to Dr. C., a colleague of his in another department, and he was able to see me right away. I picked up my x-ray and went to the first floor. As I went down to Dr. C.'s office, part of me thought that I should be a little bit worried about the possibility of a malignancy. The other part of me remembered all of the work that was waiting for me back at my office. I sighed deeply and waited to see Dr. C.

Dr. C. entered the room and very respectfully asked to see my x-ray. He observed the possible tumor on my arm and suggested that I obtain an MRI so that he would have more information. When I told him about my pain and my visit to Dr. J. (and Dr. J.'s outright dismissal of my possible carpal tunnel), Dr. C. said, "You know, I have a problem with that guy. I really don't send any of my patients to him because I really don't trust any of the results that he sends back." Even though I didn't say anything at the time, I was surprised. I didn't like Dr. J.'s style, but I thought that the test was pretty standard, and Dr. J. was supposed to be an "expert." However, Dr. C., another medical professional, questioned his expertise and professional judgment.

Dr. C. provided me with a brace to stabilize my wrist and to help alleviate the pain a bit. His office staff scheduled the MRI in Columbus (about an hour and a half from my town, Athens) for the following week. The MRI ruled out any kind of malignancy.

Back at square one and in Dr. C.'s office, Dr. C. reviewed my MRI and x-rays and observed that two of my bones seemed to overlap and that the MRI did not indicate any signs of carpal tunnel. He suggested that my "lump" stemmed from a bone that was out of place, rather than a tumor.

While I was excited that I did not seem to have a malignancy, I started to question the process. Why couldn't Dr. C., an orthopedic specialist, figure out that I had two overlapping bones from an x-ray? How could a MRI rule out the possibility of a malignancy? I was too busy for this. I had two conference papers to send out in a few weeks. I had to give comments to my 100 interviewing students on their interviews. Impatiently, I asked for my options. Dr. C. said that we could do the carpal tunnel release or that I could go into physical therapy for the pain, assuming that it came from carpal tunnel, or that I could get the malunion problems corrected—a more major surgery. I wondered why Dr. C. proposed a carpal tunnel release or physical therapy when the MRI and Dr. J.'s test did not reveal carpal tunnel. I wondered why I had to hurt so much every time that I moved my arm . . . why it was so hard to just get answers?

I should have been happy with the way that this interaction unfolded. I had just written a book on partnerships in health care. Dr. C. gave me very little direction, empowering me to make my own decision. However, I didn't feel as though I had the knowledge or the expertise to make the decisions that were necessary. Without that knowledge, I chose the less aggressive option—physical therapy—even though I did so with the sound of a mental time-suck clock ticking very loudly in my mind. How many appointments would this mean? How could I integrate this new commitment into my schedule? Dr. C. gave me a referral to a physical therapist and told me to come back in a week.

By the time that I got to the physical therapist's office nearly 48 hours later on Election Day, my wrist was really hurting. The slightest touch or bump resulted in agonizing pain. Even a touch to my shoulder sent waves of pain through my arm. I thought of Dr. J., and I really wanted him to feel this. The physical therapist began by taking measurements of my movement ability, and she was concerned by my lack of mobility in my right hand. She really didn't know what to do because she didn't want to hurt me, but she wanted to do something. I mentioned that Dr. C. had recommended ice packs, and she gave me one. I felt as though I should help her out because she felt so bad for me. Nothing made much sense any more.

Although she was hesitant, I encouraged her to keep doing something if it could eventually help. After she worked on me for about half an hour, she stopped and said, "Does Dr. C. realize how much pain that you're in?" I said that I had tried to express it to him. She said, "I've never seen anybody with carpal tunnel to this extent. If this is really carpal tunnel, this is the worse case I've ever seen." As we talked further, I really began to question Dr. C.'s assessment of my situation. Perhaps this could just be the very worst case of carpal tunnel that anybody had ever experienced. However, none of the scientific data supported a carpal tunnel conclusion. Could the malunion of my bones cause this much physical distress? The physical therapist said that she would call Dr. C.'s office and describe her concerns to him; however, she emphasized several times that "I am not a doctor. I don't profess to be a doctor. But yet in my experience (i.e., with her realm of expertise, her knowledge, what she had come in contact with), this would have to be a very, very bad case of carpal tunnel for you to be in this much agony."

From my perspective as a health care seeker, this depiction of my condition constituted another instance of questioning of recommendations, assessments, and so on, according to each "expert's" realm of knowledge. As a child of the sixties, I was brought up to believe that doctors have knowledge. They go to school. Their textbooks are like cookbooks that give them the recipe to fix us. Yet, on two different occasions thus far, health care providers had questioned another provider's evaluation, based on their own experience and their own understanding about what does or does not ring true.

I went back to the physical therapist two days later. She recommended that I use a Tens unit to alleviate the pain. "Will this device cure my wrist?" I asked. "No," she said, "it will only tell your brain that the pain is not there." It was November 7, the day before Britti's (my older daughter's) birthday, and my mother was coming for the party. I would try anything to get through the weekend.

The Tens unit was a royal pain to hook up, and it wasn't solving anything. My patience was running thin, and my students were really starting to hate me. I couldn't write comments on their interviews; I was walking into class hooked up to wires, and I snarled at everyone. To make matters worse, I couldn't even pick up my own baby—little Chelsea Meagan was only two, and her mommy couldn't hug her.

I stormed into Dr. C.'s office and demanded "answers." I got the name of a Dr. T. in Columbus, a wrist specialist. I made an appointment for mid-December, dropped off my Tens unit at the physical therapist's office, and prepared to go to a conference in San Diego in the third week of November. I felt confident. I was tired of fiddling around with my health, and two people had recommended this specialist as a guy who could "fix things." Yet, I felt more than a little anxious and confused by the nearly three months of diagnoses and tests and treatments that I had experienced to this point. How could I legitimize knowledge? How could I tell who was "right"? How could I thirst so for truth when I had argued in my previous book that no one truth exists? I wanted absolutism. I yearned for certainty. I had found neither.

The Case of Postmodernity and Pluralism

Gergen and other proponents of postmodernism suggest that a characteristic of the contemporary era is relativism (see Anderson, 1995; Gergen, 1991; Seidman, 1994) or, at least, ambiguity (Ritzer, 1997). As Seidman (1994) suggests, "Postmodernity is characterized by a loss of certainty" (p. 5). A consequence of postmodernity for health care is that health care seekers are increasingly aware that health care professionals do not "own" some external, static truth (see Gordon, Nienstedt, & Gesler, 1998; Kolata, 1994; Lewinsohn, 1998).

Our questioning emerges from, first, the plethora of medical choices for mainstream approaches to health care alone—not to mention the wealth of nontraditional methods of health care (see, e.g., Kolata, 1994; Lerner, 1994). For example, in his book on alternatives for cancer patients, Lerner (1994) explains that even

> . . . within the mainstream of conventional medical approaches, opinions and recommendations can differ considerably in critical areas such as diagnosis, prognosis, and treatment among different physicians and surgeons, different subspecialists, and in different countries. (p. xii)

Beyond the abundance of alternatives, a second reason for our uncertainty emerges from a more general questioning of authority. Meyrowitz (1985) maintains that "authority rests on information control" (p. 160), and even as early as the mid-1980s, health care practitioners no longer held information captive (see Freimuth, Stein, & Kean, 1989). Contemporary health care seekers watch *ER*, read *Cosmopolitan*, scan the Internet, and purchase popular press books on wellness practices, problems with physicians, and alternative medical choices. Meyrowitz (1985) argues, "high status is protected through special and exclusive access to information. Once authorities 'give away' their information, their expertness and status may dissolve" (p. 166).

Williams, Gabe, and Kelleher (1994) point to a "loss of faith in expert systems" (p. 186) that extends even beyond the medical community. They suggest that "we are witnessing the most recent manifestation of what has been happening for at least a century: the questioning of objectivity and the undermining of authority" (p. 186).

Adherence to the biomedical model by many health care professionals and seekers in the United States has reflected a widespread commitment to medical absolutism and institutional authority. The growing use of alternative medicine has chipped at the biomedical model's facade as "the way" that health care should be accomplished, sending ripples of doubt about the effectiveness of biomedicine throughout some segments of our society (see, for example, Gordon, 1996; Gordon et al., 1998; Kelner & Wellman, 1997; Lerner, 1994; Lewinsohn, 1998). Consistent with postmodernism, as our society now looks at the Western emperor of health care, some see a fully clothed image with all of the answers; others see an image that has been stripped naked and exposed for its imperfections; many likely feel that they can't get a good enough look to know for certain either way. In any case, because "truth" has grown more ambiguous and elusive, more options now seem viable. Framed as almost endless possibilities, alternative medicine can inspire hope for hurting people who have found traditional methods lacking. Eisenberg and colleagues (Eisenberg, Davis, Ettner, Appel, Wilkey, Rompay, & Kessler, 1998) report in the *Journal of the*

American Medical Association that "alternative medicine use and expenditures have increased dramatically from 1990 to 1997" (p. 1575).

Medical pluralism, common in a global context (see Baer, 1995; Baer, Singer, & Susser, 1997), permits choice and fits with contemporary consumerism (see Gesler & Gordon, 1998) as well as our postmodern preference for embracing cultural diversity in health care (see, e.g., Airhihenbuwa, 1995). Consistent with the fluidity of postmodernism, according to Kelner and Wellman (1997), people may select

> . . . specific kinds of practitioners for particular problems. It is misleading to assume that people will choose one kind of health care. For example, they choose chiropractors for backaches, naturopaths for colds, and Reiki practitioners for emotional stress. (p. 211)

Yet, shifting between medical paradigms is not as simple as selecting different laundry detergent at the grocery store each month. Even if we envision all of our options as part of a health care buffet, our choices come with consequences that are far more serious than heartburn. We must make comparative decisions—what will work best and why? We make such selections in light of our individual identities and preferences as well as our desires for co-cultural consistency. A woman might want a midwife to help with the birth of her child but hesitate while wondering, "what will my mother and family think?" Just as we consider what "goes well" together in terms of food, we pick portions of the health care buffet that fit with how we approach health and who we are as individuals and as part of collectives.

Similarly, we know enough to realize what approaches might "clash," at least in the eyes of some outsiders. Blurring boundaries of medical paradigms to sample help in different forms is fraught with medical incompatibilities and relational challenges. For example, like Gilda Radner, Americans struggle with revealing their use of alternative medicine to their traditional health care providers. According to Eisenberg and colleagues (1998), "less than 40 percent of the alternative therapies used were disclosed to a physician in both 1990 and 1997" (p. 1575). The nature of disclosure can impact health care and health care relationships. Telling might be awkward, confrontational, or threatening. Disclosing might imply doubt or lack of trust, potentially jeopardizing future interactions with health care professionals.

In a recent editorial in the *Journal of Clinical Oncology*, Dr. John R. Durant, a member of the American Society of Clinical Oncology, reaffirmed his skepticism about unorthodox treatments, especially given the lack of clinical testing to support claims of effectiveness. However, Durant (1998) also asserted that physician–patient relationships could be damaged if alternative treatments could not be discussed in an open and nonjudgmental manner. Durant recalled one such experience with a cancer patient who decided against a recommended procedure:

> He went home and did three things of which I self-righteously disapproved. First, he stopped his maintenance therapy. He then got married and, worst of all, went to a faith healer. I predicted only disaster. It is almost 25 years later, and he is fine. What is not fine is that my behavior broke the relationship. (1998, p. 2)

The Case of Ambiguous Medical Roles

In this time of medical plurality and questioning, the enactment of relational and medical roles during health care encounters becomes more tenuous for participants. Health care participants co-construct medical "authority" through mundane communicative choices, choices that influence their relationships with professionals, social support networks, and even health care organizations and third party payers. Even the simple, often taken-for-granted selection of labels to describe health care participants resounds with implications for how those participants treat each other during health care encounters (see related arguments by Lupton, 1996; Rinehart, 1991; Sharf & Street, 1997; Williamson, 1992). For example, in keeping with the Western biomedical model, the term "patient" implies a passive recipient who "ought to" comply with recommended treatments and tests (see Sharf & Street, 1997). The term "client" permits a more participatory role for those who seek health care, suggesting a possible collaboration, a partnership, with a health care practitioner, whereas the word "consumer" reflects a preference for a more service-oriented health care model (see Lupton, 1997). The choice of term, whether introduced by the person seeking or person offering medical assistance, is communicative and consequential. Each alternative reflexively makes relational and personal statements—"I trust you/myself *this* much; I believe in your/my knowledge *this* much."

Consistent with postmodern resistance to categorization and "pigeon-holing," however, self-positioning and preferences for legitimizing someone else (or self) as "expert" may blur and fluctuate (see Lupton, 1997). Thus, health care participants continually struggle with negotiating preferences for "authority" and working through medical uncertainties. The communicative treatment of "authority" and "knowledge" flavors the very nature of the interaction between health care participants and how decision making gets accomplished.

An acknowledgment that caregivers do not "own" the truth opens the door for individuals to participate more actively in their own care (Sharf & Street, 1997; Williamson, 1992). However, as in my case, health care seekers can grow frustrated when answers do not come from their "expert" counsel, especially when they expect communicative practices from caregivers that are consistent with the Western biomedical model (i.e., giving directives, offering recommendations) (see also Lupton, 1996).

Marcy Olmsted was on the verge of completing her residency. Busy with interviewing for jobs and preparing for the birth of her first child, she found the lump on her breast during a monthly exam. Her midwife agreed that it was "possibly nothing" and encouraged her to pursue it further after giving birth. A new mother to daughter Melissa, Olmsted mentioned the lump to her doctor during her follow-up visit, noting that she was about to leave the country to start a new job. She received a handwritten note with the results of the subsequent pathology report—"ductal carcinoma of the breast." Olmsted (1994) recalls:

> That week was a whirlwind of doctors' appointments and decisions about treatment. Mastectomy, lumpectomy plus radiation, chemotherapy. Side effects, risks of treatment, risks of recurrence. Oncologists, radiation oncologists, plastic surgeons. They quoted statistics until we were dizzy with options, but they gave almost no opinions.

The doctors kept saying it was up to me. No one understood that I wasn't a statistic, that this was my life and that these were awful decisions. . . . I kept wondering if I was being treated differently because I was a doctor. Were my doctors skipping significant details because they assumed I already knew them? (p. 74)

As I will discuss throughout this book, the co-definition of medical roles impacts health care relationships and, perhaps more importantly, discussion of diagnoses and treatment alternatives. Notably, roles rarely remain simple—we are not uni-dimensional individuals who abandon the multiplicity of our identities in the world in order to participate in medical encounters (either as health care professional or health care seeker). Olmsted came to her health care interactions as a mother, a wife, a doctor, and a professional as well as a seeker of health care services. Olmsted's concern that her status as "doctor' flavored details by her doctors exemplifies the complexity and possible contradictions of often ambiguous and multifaceted health care participant role enactments.

A Case for the Consequentiality of Communication

A plethora of implications emerge from these discussions of public health issues, managed care debates, fractured support systems, medical uncertainty, postmodernity and medical alternatives, and ambiguous medical roles. As I will detail throughout this book, diverse philosophies of medicine, cultural enactments of "health" and "illness," and masses of information dramatically influence how health communication occurs and how health care ensues. However, the consequentiality of communication is even more evident upon realizing that communication permits and facilitates the enactment of philosophies, cultural and interpersonal relationships, and the sharing and evaluating of information. Truly, communication constitutes the core of the interconnected complicated relationships and issues that are critical to contemporary health care.

Plan of the Book

The combination of scattered lives, diverse perspectives, and conflicting information can be paralyzing and devastating to individuals who try to work their way through their personal health care problems. Yet, individuals can gain power through understanding how health care relationships and micro and macro health issues fit together and are implicit to contemporary health communication. *Medical Mazes* will strive to spark reflection, hopefully enabling health care participants to find their own ways more insightfully. This book seeks to challenge health care participants to apply ideas to their own lives, their own health, their own communicative practices with health care practitioners, friends and family, and health care organizations. As particular topics become especially interesting, given your own life and health circumstances, I encourage you to pursue the referenced books, websites, and organizations on your own in a more indepth manner.

Throughout this book, I will explore the complexities of relationships that are related to health care (health care professionals and seekers, social support networks, and health care industry participants), and I will delve into difficult issues that impact health care interactions (such as the advent of technology, preferences for efficiency, diversity of health care participants, implications of the ever-increasing public dialogue about health, and challenges of power and decision making for health care participants).

Although the writing process requires some degree of linearity, I encourage readers to search for the interrelatedness of topics and the multiple concerns that stem from every example. As I pursue this analysis of aspects of contemporary medical mazes, I hope that the book provides each reader with a hand-held lantern, enabling each to see more clearly while striving to find his or her own way.

2 Social Construction of "Normal" Health Care Relationships

I slowly stirred my daiquiri with a straw. I don't usually drink at lunch, but I thought that I would treat myself. I watched as the water spilled from the top of the waterfall, causing tiny ripples in the small pool. We had decided on lunch at Don Pablo's, a Mexican restaurant in Columbus, which was near Dr. T.'s office, and despite the lunch rush, we ended up with a table in the middle of the room, right by the statuesque stone pool. I peeked through the falling water at pairs of people dining at intimate tables on the other side of the restaurant. Smiling, laughing, nodding—clearly, they were enjoying a lunch out at a fun place with their cares safely back on their desks at work.

"Explain what he said again," my friend Roger requested, drawing me back to our table, to my troubles. I inhaled deeply and said, "Okay. He basically told me that he has to reconstruct my wrist, that he needs to straighten out my bones, fuse them together with a bone graft, and build me an artificial joint to enable me to move my wrist from side to side." I looked down at the sketch that the doctor had drawn for me. I pointed to the recommended place for the artificial joint and noted, "He will cut a hole about here in my one bone and then wrap muscle or something around so that I can move. Otherwise, because of the bone graft and all of the screws that will hold my bones together and in place, I won't be able to move."

As I spoke, I heard my voice, and I could have been describing someone else, some distant acquaintance who had had an unfortunate accident, and commenting how awful it was that she would have to have this procedure—a bone graft and fused bones, can you imagine? However, I was talking about myself, not some nameless, distant person, and I needed to decide whether to trust this stranger, whether to entrust my wrist to a doctor who seemed so self-assured that he knew just what to do to fix me. "Why do you have to have the bone graft and the screws?" Roger asked. I took a drink of my daiquiri and replied, "Apparently, I have managed to destroy cartilages and joints and stuff, and my bones just won't stay without all of the hardware." Hardware, indeed.

I took a deep breath again, trying not to get really upset. I couldn't believe that I had come to this possible solution. I thought back to all of the other things that I had tried, a splint, physical therapy, the Tens unit. None of those options had relieved my pain nor addressed the problem. How could I know if this option would work?

From the moment that Dr. T. had entered the examining room, he spoke with author- ity and confidence. Shadowed by a resident, he positioned my x-rays and MRI pictures on the lighted board and pointed to the malunion and the parts of my wrist that were destroyed. Respectfully, he talked to me and asked me about my level of activity and what I liked to do and needed to do in life. I told him about my passion for running and tennis. Without telling him what I researched—revealing an interest in women's health communi- cation could cause some apprehension, I reasoned—I shared my love for writing and for researching, which require considerable time on a keyboard.

He recommended the reconstruction of the wrist, contending that such a reconstruc- tion could best enable me to return to the activities that I love without pain. If I continued down my current path, I would likely develop arthritis, and I could lose the ability to use my wrist effectively. I would be crippled. Images of dashing for my beloved backhand flashed through my mind. He then explained the risks of the surgery and asked me to sign a waiver that acknowledged those risks—paralysis, infection, pain, perhaps even death.

As I glanced up at the resident who had been left waiting for me to sign the sheet, I rationalized that the odds of any of these potential ramifications must be remote. They do this kind of thing all of the time. I would be at the best hospital, with a specialist in ortho- pedics. What are the odds that any of these possibilities might actually happen to me? The resident glanced at the clock and then the door, and I realized that I had been hesitating for a few minutes. I signed the paper. What choice do I really have? I thought.

The resident took me to the receptionist, and I scheduled the surgery right away, aim- ing for a time in the next two weeks before the end of 1996. Because I had already met my deductible for my insurance, I wanted the surgery to happen in that calendar year. As I sat at the receptionist's desk, listening to her make the necessary calls to arrange "the proce- dure," I tried to reassure myself by remembering that I could think it over and cancel before the surgery. I could always back out of this, if I decide to do so.

"What are you going to do?" Roger asked. The daiquiri was almost gone now; I needed to catch that waitress' eye to get her to bring me another one. "He wants to cut a hole in my bone. For the rest of my life, I would have a hole in my bone, screws in my arm. For the rest of my life . . . " I couldn't stop thinking that I shouldn't be talking about the rest of my life at 35 years old. Suddenly, I felt very old.

"So, what do you think that you will do?" he asked again. I looked at the water spilling from the waterfall, the laughing people in the other world just beyond me. "I don't know," I said, "I don't know."

In his work on the social meaning of surgery, Fox (1992) notes that "because surgery is a human activity, conducted by human actors in social contexts, it is not 'just' surgery, just a 'technical intervention' " (p. 2). As I sat at the table in the restaurant that day and as I struggled with my decision throughout those next few days, I realized that Dr. T. viewed my surgery as a logical procedure, a way of enabling me to accomplish my "activities of daily living" (a phrase that I would hear a great deal during my recovery), a "normal" route to restoring a "normal" life. From the numerous people who filled the chairs of the waiting room outside of his office, I understood that Dr. T. saw a lot of individuals with wrist injuries, his area of specialization.

Even though Dr. T. expressed great concern for how I wanted to use my wrist, I could not help but contextualize my situation more in terms of "what ifs" than in terms of "what could bes" as I considered the surgery. I know that I am more than a "wrist." I yearned to really care for Britti and Chelsea Meagan. I wanted to swing my tennis racket and ride my bike and play on my computer. I longed to reach out once again to my Girl Scouts, without holding my arm back in fear of pain. I'm a mother and a professional and a scout leader and a Christian and a friend; I am not simply one part or another of my body, not just a "procedure." To me, the surgery was not just about fixing a problem, sending my body to a "people garage" to replace a broken part. My surgical decision depended on who I could be after the surgery and what I could be if it never occurred.

As I visited over the Christmas holiday with friends and family members who know my heart and mind and dreams, I came to appreciate that they could not even fathom the seriousness of this decision for me. I also began to realize that they did not view my situation similarly. Some could not grasp the extent of my pain; others did not comprehend the extensiveness of the proposed surgical procedures. Some likely wondered why my wrist had to be "such a big deal" or if the injury or surgery had been "blown out of proportion." Although all of the players in my health care drama shared some common realities, our realities were not static nor predetermined nor completely consistent. Instead, we engaged in the continual process of striving to co-construct relational, individual, and medical meanings.

Whether we are seeking care or attempting to offer assistance as a professional or a social support system member, the ways that we present ourselves and treat others matter, especially in terms of how we accomplish health care. Communication should not be viewed as simply some "nicety" or extra. As scholars in medical anthropology and medical sociology observe, issues of health, wellness, illness, disease, medical roles, and individual health care participant identities gain significance through ongoing social negotiations (see discussions by Atkinson, 1995, 1997; Emerson, 1970; Fox, 1992; Good, 1994; Kleinman, 1978, 1980; Nettleton, 1995; Wright & Treacher, 1982).

Throughout this chapter, I will discuss how health care participants (from health care professionals to social support system members to health care seekers) socially construct the meaning of "normal" in terms of health-related issues and roles through artful communication practices in their complex relationships. After providing a brief overview of social constructionism, I explore the implications of the social construction of "normality" for achieving individual and relational identities, for enacting culture, and for defining preferred approaches to medicine.

Social Constructionism: An Overview

I paused at Chelsea Meagan's crib. She lay like a beautiful baby doll, with her blonde curls across her face and her arms around her favorite "blankie." She has such long lashes, I marveled. I adjusted the book bag on my back and glanced around the room. Okay, I thought, I have everything; I'll only be gone overnight.

I had decided to have the surgery. The benefits seemed to outweigh the risks, and Dr. S. and Dr. C. had indicated during my subsequent visits with them that the procedure seemed to make sense. The always hurried holiday visits to grandparents' homes in

Virginia and Indiana had been physically grueling for me this year, and I realized that I didn't have a lot to lose. From driving the car to holding Chelsea's hand in line for the annual picture with Santa, every jolt, every minute movement, thrust waves of pain up and down my entire arm. I could not not *have the surgery.*

Peeking once more at Chelsea in her crib and Brittany in her bed, I tiptoed into the living room and looked at the clock. It was 2 A.M., December 31. It was Grandpa's birthday, I realized, as I hoped that I had remembered to send his card. Shutting the door behind me, I started the two-hour trek to Columbus.

I fought to stay awake as I navigated my Neon down the near-empty streets. I am always afraid of oversleeping if I have to be somewhere early, and after tossing in bed for fifteen minutes around midnight, I showered and left early. After some rather heated discussions at home about how I would get to the hospital at 6 A.M., I resolved to drive myself. I could handle all of this on my own, I thought.

Safely in Columbus at 4 A.M., I pulled the car into the hospital parking garage, grabbed my bookbag, purse, and briefcase, and walked toward the front entrance. A few people in hospital garb passed by me, and I overheard one refer to an after-Christmas sale. The congestion of crowds pushing and shoving to secure the best deals amid the lingering holiday decorations seemed so distant now.

The front hallway was empty, the greeting station abandoned. I walked slowly through the hall on the first floor, hoping to find the cafeteria or a waiting area. I discovered two employees, likely security personnel, who asked if I needed help. I smiled and said, "I need to go to outpatient surgery," starting to dig for the paper that I had received from Dr. T.'s office. One of the men responded that "no one is there. It's only 4 A.M. They don't usually start prepping until around six." I tried again. "I've come from out of town, and I was nervous about the drive. I needed to be here at six. I know that I'm way early, but I was hoping that it would not be a problem for me to go on up to the floor." I hoped that I looked confident yet just pathetic enough that he would give me permission. "Fifth floor," he said with a shrug of his shoulder, gesturing to the elevator.

My footsteps echoed loudly throughout the otherwise silent corridor as I stepped from the elevator. I glanced into the nurse's station and found two male staff members who were sitting in an inner portion of the area. After I acknowledged once more that I was "way early," they directed me to a tiny waiting area, and I pulled out my copy of Parents. *I tried to focus on the wisdom of the writers, but the words just jumbled on the pages. It was the middle of the night; I was virtually alone on the floor of a strange place, a hospital to boot; a stranger was about to operate on my wrist (and my hip for the bone graft) for around six and a half hours. I would wake up, and I would go home tomorrow to start the new year. I stared at the scrambled words on the page.*

Like actors arriving early to set up their props before the play, the staff appeared around 5:45 A.M. and started sorting papers and preparing for registration. They moved with confidence as they separated charts and readied rooms; they knew their routines. To them, this morning was just the start of another day, nothing special, nothing out of the norm. Without a word, I watched, feeling like an intruder on the rituals of backstage behavior.

At 6 A.M., a family converged in my waiting area, complete with a woman, a man who held the woman's hand and rubbed her back, an older man and woman who chatted with the younger woman and man, and two adorable little kids who placed pillows, blankets, and small bookbags on the couch beside me. One of them caught my gaze, and I looked away, realizing how much I missed my girls. Health misadventures rarely fit neatly into our lives. Wade, the girls' dad (to whom I was still married at the time) and I were having serious difficulties. He had pretty much refused to drive me up to Columbus, arguing that I really didn't need the surgery and that a two-hour drive in the wee hours of the morning would be too difficult. Such a drive would not be fair or convenient to him or the girls. Tears of loneliness and hurt swelled up in my eyes as the other woman's daughters gave her good luck kisses before she left for her prep room. That's how a family should be, I thought.

In my own room, I changed into a hospital gown. After shoving my sweats into my bookbag and climbing up on the bed, I could feel my sense of control and identity eking away. I held out my arm for the IV, dutifully answered questions about my medical history, cautiously explained that I had a cold, and timidly asked for one more clarification of risks. The nurse inquired about which family member had come with me, and I made some joke about the value of making time for oneself. Because I didn't have anyone to watch my purse and bookbag, she offered to hold them behind the nurse's station. As she carried my belongings out of the room, I leaned back against the bed and felt a strong desire to call someone. They wouldn't be awake at this hour, I reasoned, resisting my urge.

At twenty minutes to seven, the nurse who took my history checked on me and noted that the unit had a lot of patients this morning. She shared her frustration that the floor was understaffed due to the holiday. What holiday, I wondered? Oh yes, it was New Year's Eve, a time for Dick Clark, festive excursions, and fancy dresses. I made another trip to the bathroom in my bare feet and sheet-like frock.

As I came out of the bathroom, Dr. T.'s resident entered, and I grabbed for the open back of my gown, awkwardly clumping the sides together in a lame attempt at modesty. I tried to get into bed gracefully while he explained that Dr. T. wanted to change part of the surgical procedure. Apparently, Dr. T. had decided to wrap tendons somewhere to make the artificial joint instead of doing something else that I couldn't remember at the time. My body ached for sleep now, and I fought to make myself concentrate. I asked the resident why Dr. T. reconsidered the original plan. "Because Dr. T. thinks that this will work better." I pumped him for information, "Are there any additional risks for this particular surgery?" "No," he answered, "but I will have to ask you to sign another release form noting the change." I quizzed him again, "And the reason for this change is just that he thinks it will work better?" The resident sounded like a broken record by responding, "Yes, upon reflection, Dr. T. believes it would work better this way."

He held out the paper and pen, looking incredibly matter-of-fact. Clearly, he treated this substitution as standard, something that should not be problematic or unexpected. From his perspective, such adjustments happen all of the time.

In ten minutes, the anesthesiologist would come, and the surgery would commence; I could hear the sands gushing to the bottom of the hourglass. How could they nonchalantly change the rules now, as I lay isolated, nearly naked, and exhausted in a foreign place? They thought that it would work better. I thought that he knew the "best" plan in his office. What if he thinks wrong?

I shivered beneath my paper-thin scrap, pushing the call button for a blanket as I watched the resident leave with my signature on the new consent form. I didn't have any information. I would not be afforded the opportunity to talk to Dr. T. directly; he sent only his scripted messenger. Yet what else could I do, but just trust. I couldn't sweep the cobwebs from my mind to get perspective. My head felt heavy on the bed, and I gained comfort from the heated blankets that one kind nurse brought to me.

I attempted to figure out the pattern of the ceiling tiles as they wheeled my gurney through the corridors, trying not to see any stares from family members in the now congested waiting room, trying not to look at others as they bided time on their own portable beds in line for "procedures." I broke my gaze at the ceiling only to turn my head to cough and then happened to find my eyes locked with a set of steel blue ones. Her eyes were sad, and the woman's face was wrinkled. I grew curious about her story. Why was she here? What was she feeling? Was she alone too? What had her life been like and what would it hold for her in the future? I couldn't learn her story, though, as the patient care associate pushed my bed past her and through the shiny grey doors into the surgical area. I squinted at the bright lights above me and realized that she would not discover my story either, nor would the people in white coats and blue pantsuits who bustled to prepare the equipment. This moment, this drama, would be what we would share.

Co-Construction of Meaning

Building on the work of Berger and Luckmann (1966) and Schutz (1962), proponents of social constructionism maintain that social actors engage in the continual process of co-defining their social realities (see, for example, Dreitzel, 1970; Garfinkel, 1967; Gergen, 1991, 1994; Goffman, 1959, 1963, 1967; Potter, 1996; Sarbin & Kitsuse, 1994; Shotter, 1993). As opposed to taking a more macro-oriented view of social life (see discussion by Knorr-Cetina & Cicourel, 1981), a social constructionist perspective suggests that meaning emerges through interaction and that interpretations and activities are temporally bound, not pre-scripted and a priori (also see related work on hermeneutics by Gadamer, 1976). Dreitzel (1970) explains:

> . . . the relevance or meaning of social situations and actions is not, as in the normative paradigm, settled once and for all in a preestablished world of shared symbols, but is subject to reformulation on every new occasion, i.e., an ongoing accomplishment. (p. xiv)

Communication enables everyday people who engage in health care interactions, whether as health care professionals, seekers, or social support system members, to accomplish multiple important interpretations and activities (see Atkinson, 1995, 1997; Eisenberg & Kleinman, 1981; Grainger, 1993; Hahn & Gaines, 1985; Kleinman, 1978, 1980; Nettleton, 1995; Wright & Treacher, 1982). At the most rudimentary of levels, Schutz notes (1962), "In order to communicate with Others I have to perform overt acts in the outer world which are supposed to be interpreted by the Others as signs of what I mean to convey" (p. 218).

As those "Others" respond and indicate affirmation of shared meaning, though, they necessarily go beyond simply understanding words in a sentence; they rely on social interaction to facilitate co-definitions of "what is going on here," "what does this interaction mean for us, as participants," "what is 'normal' for us now." When Wade balked at the idea of transporting me to the hospital, he forced me to face the surgery alone. His refusal symbolically reified the state of our relationship and his status as a resource for social support. Unfortunately, such treatments of our relationship had become quite usual, and especially in this scenario, I yearned for what would likely be "normal" for many other spousal and family interactions in this type of situation.

When the nurse asked me questions before my surgery, we were not only in the business of interpreting words. We were striving to make sense of questions and to offer viable responses. We co-constructed the nurse's legitimate authority to inquire about personal issues, and we co-defined what counted as "acceptable" for an answer. When she asked me about previous surgeries, I wondered whether it would be relevant to disclose my two Cesarean sections. What could that type of operation have to do with my wrist? However, in doubt, I posed a clarification question, and the nurse emphasized that it was important to disclose all information, regardless of whether I thought that it might be relevant. Thus, the co-construction of meaning between social actors is not simply some accidental overlap that is limited to a grasping of language. As Garfinkel (1967) contends, social actors need to perform some "operational structure" (p. 31) (such as my clarification question, in this case) to facilitate the multiple social activities that can occur in and through the talk.

Our interactions, our everyday talk and treatment of each other, enable us to co-construct "social artifacts, products of historically and culturally situated interchanges" (Gergen, 1994, p. 49). Extending from our respective experiences, goals, desires, and understandings, we communicatively reveal where we were, where we are, and where we want to go, revelations that can hint at any number of issues—including culture, religion, gender, demographics, education, and even fear. Our emergent co-accomplishment may be a product of similarity or separation, depending on shared visions, common understandings of "what we are doing, here and now" (see related work by Burke, 1969).

The co-production of "social artifacts" simultaneously and reflexively includes the co-construction of social structures, social roles, and social rules (see, for example, Boden & Zimmerman, 1991; Dreitzel, 1970; Drew & Heritage, 1992; Garfinkel, 1967; Goffman, 1959, 1963, 1967) as well as social relationships (see related works by Burke, 1969; Watzlawick, Bavelas, & Jackson, 1967) that lurk in the constant state of becoming. As Gergen (1994) contends, "The degree to which a given account of world or self is sustained across time is not dependent on the objective validity of the account but on the vicissitudes of social process" (p. 51). The health care professionals at the hospital, from security guards to surgeons, attain authority to direct behavior and offer recommendations as they interact with those who seek care. As I positioned for permission from the security guard and obligingly offered answers to the nurse, I participated in the co-construction of emergent co-definitions of social roles and rules. Notably, that process of co-construction integrated our respective taken-for-granted assumptions and our emergent verbal and nonverbal treatment of each other.

Co-Construction of Legitimacy

Social constructionists acknowledge that individuals bring their own preconceived ideas to interactions (see, e.g., Garfinkel, 1967, Schutz, 1962). In fact, Garfinkel (1967) suggests that "members take for granted that a member must at the outset 'know' the settings in which he is to operate if his practices are to serve as measures to bring particular, located features of these settings to reasonable account" (p. 8). Yet, like other proponents of social constructionism, Garfinkel (1967) emphasizes that social interaction permits people to display their taken-for-granted understandings of their roles, preferences, and conceptions of activities as they stumble through everyday life and coordinate their actions with others.

When I went into the hospital for my surgery, I had a preconceived notion of what types of behaviors might "count" as "legitimate" for a "good patient," and I tested those preconceptions during my interactions with the staff. Only when I revealed that I did not sleep during the previous evening did the staff question the appropriateness of my behavior. The nurse commented that she would have to report my lack of rest to the people in recovery and noted that "this (the lack of sleep) will make it hard to wake you." When the anesthesiologist entered the room, the nurse informed him that "she (me) chose not to sleep" and shook her head as she left. Clearly, the staff positioned my choice to drive up early as a "mistake" that would make their jobs more difficult. I could have challenged their treatment of my choice (i.e., by sharing my life circumstances and reminding them about the length of my drive to Columbus and the change in my surgical schedule), but I remained silent. I refrained from demanding to see Dr. T. when my procedure was altered at the eleventh hour. I did not want to be taken as an "Elaine," a character on the sitcom *Seinfeld* who made a medical "mistake" in one episode and then became branded and ostracized by doctors who labeled her as "difficult."

In light of the fragmentation and multiplicity of contemporary life (see Gergen, 1991), though, how can social actors "know" what is reasonable and what is "normal," especially in the health care context? How can they juxtapose their assumptions with other social actors while presenting themselves as intelligible and informed about what one ought to do in specific settings? More than in many other social arenas, possibilities abound for enactments of roles, rules, and relationships in the health care context. With a plethora of information about medical advances, alternative medicine, and consumerism (to name just a few subjects), health care participants must struggle to co-define what counts as "legitimate," what counts as "expert," what counts as "expected," what constitutes "good" professionals and seekers, and what counts as "normal behavior." In so doing, they must necessarily juxtapose individual a priori expectations and assumptions with the ways in which participants treat each other during specific interactions (see related work by Cicourel, 1970; Garfinkel, 1967; Goffman, 1959).

As Garfinkel (1967) suggests, even when we think that we know the rules or directions, our taken-for-granted understandings fall short of complete certainty and knowledge. For contemporary health care participants, the social construction of health care realities and "normal" is increasingly consequential and problematic for the accomplishment of health and health care.

Constructing "Normal"

Borrowing from general systems theory, Watzlawick and colleagues (1967) argue that social actors co-construct relational systems through their ongoing verbal and nonverbal exchanges. Their interactional choices enable them to co-define the meanings of the system, the implications of those systemic meanings for individuals within and beyond the system, and the interrelatedness between system members (i.e., if one is a "legitimate" member, how should that person perform that role? what should that person do in relation to others?). As in other systems (e.g., religious, fraternal, organizational), participants in health care system(s) take part in the emergent co-definition of values, knowledge, and social activities, rules, roles, and relationships. Through their verbal and nonverbal communication, they indicate and reify what "should be" normal in terms of how they approach health care and each other.

However, the challenge for contemporary health care participants is the fragmentation of "normal." Would "normal" family members enact support differently than my family did? Was I "normal" to feel apprehensive about the last minute change? Did members of the health care team treat me reasonably, "normally"? How did we come to our understanding of what "normal" meant for us and the experience? How did we co-define a "normal" way to proceed? These types of questions reflect issues of relational and medical cultures, specialized systems that are reflected in and perpetuated through interactions between system participants. For health care professionals and seekers, an understanding of the social construction of "normal" in terms of identity and relational and medical cultures, in particular, has never been so important, given the fragmentation and temporality of medical relationships.

Social Construction of Culture

Our understandings of societal expectations and stereotypes impact how we approach our health care experiences and, potentially, how we pursue health care outcomes, thrusting forward the notion of "culture" and/or co-cultural involvements as an important dimension of enacting "medicine" and "health care" (see Airhihenbuwa, 1995; Baer, 1987; Baer et al., 1997; Ehrenreich, 1978; Eisenberg & Kleinman, 1981; Finkler, 1991; Lupton, 1994; Spector, 1996a; Stein, 1990). Spector argues:

> . . . health and illness beliefs are deeply entwined within the cultural and social beliefs that people have. To understand health and illness beliefs and practices, it is necessary to see each person in his or her unique sociocultural world. (1996a, p. xii)

For health care seekers, that unique world may involve commitments to deep cultural traditions and societal obligations, all with related health beliefs and logistical or religious constraints.

Traditionally, "culture" has been conceptualized as something to be inherited and "passed on" (see B. Hall, 1997; Helman, 1984; Purnell & Paulanka, 1998). In fact, as Helman (1984) contends, "to some extent, culture can be seen as an inherited 'lens' through which the individual perceives and understands the world that he inhabits, and learns how to live within it" (p. 2).

An alternative perspective to conceptualizing culture as something static to be "passed on" consists of treating culture as a temporally bound construction, something in process (see work by Carbaugh, 1990; Philipsen, 1992). Through artful communicative practices, individuals co-create ever-emergent constructions of what it is to be a legitimate member of this culture and what members of this culture should/can do at particular times and in particular ways (see Basso, 1990; Carbaugh, 1990; Fitch, 1998; Philipsen, 1992). Such enactments of culture harken back to and reflect the past; however, they get performed within the here-and-now, unique symbolic co-creations melded by historical and current influences.

The frenzy and chaos of contemporary society has further muddied streams of continuity and connectedness, as individuals embrace alternatives to traditional societal structures (such as family, religious organizations, and ethnic communities), and the very definitions of those entities and their role(s) in everyday life. Indeed, the advent of technology, the shrinking of global boundaries, and the splintering of previously take-for-granted structures has contributed to confusing conglomerations of cultural influences (see Barnlund, 1997; Gergen, 1991, 1994).

Especially in the United States, the vast array of co-culturally based options and influences resembles a massive buffet, rather than a simple dinner of meat and potatoes. Individuals may select from a plethora of religions, traditions, activities, and rituals that reflect historical/cultural roots and/or newfound preferences/approaches. Some people may always make the same selections, ignoring the choices just beyond the periphery of their focus; others may scan the entire assortment of possibilities and engage in endless sampling; still others may choose consistently yet change their habits when former ways no longer fit their needs or interests. An individual's world view may even reflect fragmented pieces of multiple cultures and co-cultures, just as one might fill a smorgasboard plate with spoon-size portions of assorted foods that spill against each other on the way back to the table. As Martin (1997) suggests, our identities are "dynamic and context-related," noting that "I am not just a female, a professor, a white German American. I am all of these, and any one identity may be highlighted or suppressed depending on the situation or context" (p. 55).

For health care participants, the challenge involves understanding fluctuating identities as well as increasingly complex and diverse orientations to the world and, ultimately, health care and health care relationships (see Hare, 1993; Huff & Kline, 1999; Ritchey, Yoels, Clair, & Allman, 1995). Additionally, the very nature of the health care experience may shatter a priori assumptions that an individual holds about his or her place or role in the world (or even how his or her world functions). For example, a compelling study by Becker (1994) on responses to infertility argues that participants (all U.S. citizens) assumed order and consistency prior to the infertility diagnosis. Becker observes:

> The predominance of Western scientific and philosophical thought in cultural notions of order was obvious in women's and men's statements about their efforts to make sense of the disruptive effects of infertility on their lives. They struggled to find a fit between the cultural model and their own experience. (p. 391)

As individuals wrestle to make sense of their already complicated lives in light of the added challenge of a health care event, they interact with health care professionals who come to interactions within the context of their own unique worlds. For health care professionals, that world encompasses their own cultural and spiritual frameworks as well as particular perspectives of how health care should ensue, such as a faith in bio-medicine or alternative medical practices—or even some blend of multiple medical ideologies (see related works by Airhihenbuwa, 1995; Baer, 1987; Baer et al., 1997; Coreil, 1988; Eden, 1993; Eisenberg & Kleinman, 1981; Gevitz, 1988; Gordon, 1996; Gordon et al., 1998; Hare, 1993; Kleinman, 1980; Lock, 1990; Raso, 1994; Rothman, Marcus, & Kiceluk, 1995.) When health care participants come together to address health care issues, their respective cultural orientations (and degree of co-orientation) flavor the extent to which they can understand each other's goals for how health care should occur and for how they should proceed in a manner that coincides with their multiple cultural, social, and institutional preferences (see Finkler, 1991; Ritchey et al., 1995).

Medical Culture

Kleinman (1980) argues that "we can view medicine as a cultural system, a system of symbolic meanings anchored in particular arrangements of social institutions and patterns of interpersonal interactions" (p. 24), much like religion or kinship relations (see also Atkinson, 1995, 1997; Bury, 1986; Ehrenreich, 1978; Good, 1994; Kleinman, 1978; Lupton, 1994; Nettleton, 1992; Zola, 1983 as well as related work by Whaley, 2000 on explaining illness and by Geertz, 1973, on cultural systems). As doctors (whether allopathic, osteopathic, or chiropractic), nurses, professionals in allied health fields, and health care seekers engage in health care encounters, they strive to present themselves as legitimate participants of specific medical cultures (see Adams with Mylander, 1998; Atkinson, 1997; Bosk, 1979; Good & Good, 1993; Klass, 1987; Shapiro, 1995). They work to learn "the code" (i.e., what they must do and demonstrate to be taken as "legitimate" members of those particular communities), while trying to be true to their own goals and visions of medicine (see Wieder, 1988).

Implications of Acculturation

In her book about her own allopathic medical school experience, Perri Klass (1987) remembers wondering "by the time I finish, will I still remember any of what I originally wanted to be? When I am through with my training, will I have any way of knowing what kind of doctor I have actually become?" (p. 40) For medical students, in particular, learning the rules and interacting as a viable system member has traditionally been essential for their treatment by others in their profession (and, to some extent, by patients) as "one of us," a "real" doctor.

Professional Distance   As dramatized in the 1998 motion picture bearing his name, Patch Adams decided to attend an allopathic medical school with the goal of helping people. As Patch Adams observed the way in which his professors talked to and about patients, he became increasingly frustrated with the impersonal, medicalized approach to health care, an approach that stemmed from their commitment to principles that underlie much of bio-medicine. In his book, *Gesundheit!*, Adams recalls:

> People were called by the names of their diseases, as if the disease were more important than the human who suffered from it. We were taught to ask the patient quick, penetrating questions in order to ascertain which tests to order and which medications to prescribe. . . . All other facets of the patient's life—family, friends, faith, fun, work, integrity, nutrition, exercise, and much more—were considered virtually irrelevant to medical practice. (Adams with Mylander, 1998, p. 10)

Howard Spiro, M.D. (1992) maintains that "medical schools squeeze empathy out of our students as we take them 'backstage' in the body. . . . During medical education, we first teach the students science and then we teach them detachment" (p. 843). Mack Lipkin, Jr., M.D., an internist and a professor at New York University School of Medicine, also commented in an interview with the *New York Times*, "Most of the incoming students are very idealistic. But by the end of medical school they have learned to look at symptoms, not people. The role models they see are inadequate in this domain" (Quindlen, 1994, p. A21).

When the hit television drama *ER* first aired, John Carter, a medical student, started his shift in the emergency room of a busy Chicago hospital. Through his eyes, viewers peeked into the heroism and the chaos of emergency room medicine. As he attempted to learn the rules of medical school, surgery, and life in the ER, viewers obtained a close look at the transformation of an idealistic medical student into a competitive residency candidate and then into a more emotionally removed resident. Carter's metamorphosis from medical student to resident reflected his own emergent enactment of "doctor," in light of his incarnation of medical, social, and personal values and practices.

As depicted in *Patch Adams*, Adams started to sneak into patient rooms at the hospital and ingratiated himself with the nurses (who skeptically told him that he will be "just like the rest of them" one day) by playing with the pediatric patients and truly talking with adult patients. Despite overt disapproval of his conduct by his professors and amid the threat of expulsion from the medical school, Adams refused to amend his approach to patients throughout the movie. To this day, Adams continues to strive for more holistic health care in his Gesundheit Institute, "a community that embodies to the extreme the philosophy that art, fun, and connectedness are as important to health as CAT scans and IVs" (Adams with Mylander, 1998, p. 119).

Communication and Caring   Similar to other cultural systems, language comprises the core of creating and perpetuating shared values, norms, and practices in medical systems. Good (1994) suggests that the language of medicine is "a rich cultural language, linked to a highly specialized version of reality and system of social relations . . ." (p. 5).

Klass (1987) explains that learning medical jargon and abbreviations as a medical student permitted her to talk "like a real doctor"; however, she disliked dismissive positionings of patients that occurred through those linguistic choices. When one of the residents with whom she was working used the phrase "CTD" to describe a person with terminal pancreatic cancer, Klass asked for clarification. Klass (1987) recalls, "The resident smirked at me. 'Circling the drain.' The images are vivid and terrible. 'What happened to Mrs. Melville?' 'Oh, she boxed last night.' To box is to die, of course" (p. 74). Unfortunately, Klass found such comments to be treated as "normal" and expected by "legitimate" members of the residency program.

Unlike Patch Adams's medical school experience in the early 1970s, more contemporary medical schools do include training on patient interviewing, psychosocial influences, and empathetic listening (see, for example, discussions by Boorstein, 1995; Charon, 1986; Evans, Stanley, & Burrows, 1992; Quindlen, 1994; Reid-Wallace, 1992; Sharf & Poirier, 1988; Sullivan, 1992; and texts by Mengel & Fields, 1997; Stewart, Brown, Weston, McWhinney, McWilliams, & Freeman, 1995). Courses consist of role-playing, video analysis, and a host of other creative pedagogical tools to prompt student reflection on communication issues. For example, Sharf and Poirier (1988) describe a course that introduces medical students to the importance of communication through literature-based examples, and Charon (1986) suggests the potential of humanizing the medical experience by asking students to write fiction based on their cases. Good and Good (1993) contend that Harvard Medical School students work actively to co-define "competence" and "caring" and to balance both as priorities. According to Good and Good, the case-study-based curriculum enables students to "experience a culturally distinctive configuration of contradictions as they attempt to maintain qualities of 'caring' while encountering the world of medical science" (p. 91).

Notably, though, the notions of "competence" and "caring" still get positioned dialectically and, at least to some extent according to Good and Good, as "contradictory" at Harvard and likely many other allopathic medical schools. Such treatments work to perpetuate medical cultural values and rituals that reflect "how medicine gets accomplished best." Yet, conversely, the concepts of competence and caring are framed as more analogous in nursing programs or osteopathic medical schools.

Implications of Cultural Positioning

As Patch Adams came to realize, the adoption and enactment of biomedical ideology and practices constitute one way of approaching health care—not the only way. Those who learn (through formal training or through lay experiences) and behave according to any model of medicine enact roles, rules, illness, and healing through intricate symbol use and patterns of behavior (see Gaines & Hahn, 1985). Although distinctive, various medical cultures share some similarities with each other, and medical cultural systems certainly evolve (note the shift in allopathic medical school training from the 1970s to the 1990s suggested above). Yet, economic and political concerns and diverse orientations to medicine contribute to divisiveness in the greater medical community. Despite the advent of interdisciplinary team orientations to health care as well as the plethora of alternatives to biomedicine, especially in the United States, the rhetoric from training programs and professional organizations in health-related fields (and from individual professionals to health care seekers) tends to be more targeted toward division than pluralism (see Baer, 1995; Durant, 1998; Lawrence, 1991; Miller, 1998; Oberst, 1995). For example, Miller (1998) documents the difficulty that osteopathic medicine has had in establishing credibility as a profession, and Lawrence (1991) details the legal wars between the American Medical Association and chiropractors.

Such rhetorical jousting works to create and perpetuate aspects of medical cultures. Particularly in the case of proponents of variations on the biomedical model, advances in popularity by other medical models impact the social construction of biomedicine as dominant and authoritative, as the "normal," "legitimate," and "traditional" approach in the United States (see Baer, 1995; Baer et al., 1997; Gordon et al., 1998 as well as commentary by Nettleton, 1995). For economic, political, ethical, and cultural reasons, the social construction of opposition between various health care professionals ultimately becomes consequential for people who seek help.

When I visited with a chiropractor to gain assistance with back pain, I did so because my regular doctor, a doctor of osteopathic medicine, was out of town. I told the chiropractor that I usually see a D.O. for my back, and the chiropractor proceeded to interject comparisons with the D.O. throughout the rest of the encounter. He went so far as to say that "medical doctors miss things that we don't" and "Chiropractors are the only doctors who can tell you what's wrong." If I continue to see this guy, I thought at the time, I certainly won't tell him when I visit Dr. S., even if it is for something unrelated. Moreover, the chiropractor's claims of opposition and absolutism made me question his credibility and openness—I wonder about anyone who purports to have the market on the truth.

The postmodern challenge for people who seek, obtain, and provide health care involves determining how to position themselves when they might well juggle multiple allegiances, understandings, and ideas. Especially in the United States, individuals value choice and flexibility (Bellah et al., 1985; Gergen, 1991), but medical pluralism becomes difficult in light of conflicting systemic values, rituals, core beliefs, and relational definitions. We live in an era of increasing globalization, multicultural awareness, and overabundant information (see Gergen, 1991), and individuals must find ways to juxtapose personal convictions, religion, co-cultural involvement, education, economics, politics, and experiences in order to make choices that are consequential to their own health care orientations as well as to their emergent relationships with others.

Social Construction of Medicine

At a time when health care professionals are increasingly recognizing the implicativeness of co-cultural allegiances and influences for enabling patients to enact proactive health care, those professionals will likely wrestle with the consequences of considering their own medical and co-cultural orientations amid diverse approaches to health care. How do we enact "normal" when "normal" can mean so many different things throughout society and yet be so ingrained and rigid for particular collections of people? As I will detail below, the theoretical orientations of medical cultures can differ significantly in terms of conceptualizing and accomplishing medicine and health care relationships.

Medicine as Art and/or Science?

In Chapter 1, I shared part of Marcy Olsted's story. A new mother and medical resident, she discovered a lump on her breast near the end of her pregnancy. During her efforts to discern the nature of the lump and to decide on a course of action, she was stunned to learn that health care professionals made critical blunders on her case. Olmsted laments:

But what really shook us was our total loss of faith in doctors. Several of them had reviewed my mammograms and missed the calcifications, and two pathologists had misread my slides. It was frightening to realize that if my husband hadn't pushed for a second opinion, I would have been misdiagnosed and mistreated with life-threatening consequences. (1994, p. 77)

In a December 21, 1999 cover article in *USA Today*, Rubin reports that mammograms "invite unrealistic expectations" (p. 1A). As Judy Perotti, the Director of Patient Services for Y-Me National Breast Cancer Organization, stresses, "The public's perception is that mammography is a foolproof system. Women are absolutely shocked when you tell them how many breast cancers are missed" (Rubin, December 21, 1999, p. 1A).

Prioritizing Scientific "Facts"

Dr. Olmsted, like Gilda Radner and perhaps millions of other health care participants in the United States and other Western countries, put their trust, their faith, in the science of medicine. The dismay of learning that a doctor could be wrong or that a test could be inconclusive stems from a socially constructed (and biomedically oriented) treatment of medicine as a science, complete with certainty and absolutism (see, e.g., Hunter, 1991).

Zussman (1992) argues that "medicine used technical expertise not only to carve out an area in which physicians could act independently but also to establish grounds on which lay people would accept their jurisdiction"—the promotion of a belief in the merits of science (p. 225). Although Lewinsohn (1998) notes that a modern emphasis on medical science ". . . has only existed for little more than two generations" (p. 1261), she also stresses its dominance in the United States, claiming that "modern medicine has come to arrogate to science, technology and bioengineering, to the detriment of any other approach . . . " (p. 1267).

With the rampant advances in technology and medical research (as well as proportional private and federally funded sponsoring of such developments), such an orientation to medicine-as-science is not surprising. According to E. Cassell (1991), "The American public embraced the wonders of medical science and technology, further enhancing the reputation of medicine as a science and of doctors as medical scientists" (p. 23). As Arney (1982) argues in his description of the field of obstetrics, technological advances have deeply impacted the way in which doctors enact their relationships with patients and the way in which birthing a child, a very personal experience with social, relational, and cultural meanings and implications, gets co-produced by the participants.

Jordan and Irwin (1987) offer an account of a pregnant African woman who was living with her American husband in the United States. The woman rejected the possibility of a Cesarean section, despite her slow progression through delivery. The hospital pursued a court order to mandate the Cesarean section even though the woman vehemently opposed the surgery. The judge was willing to issue such an order. Apparently, the refusal of the c-section could not be construed as "normal" or "reasonable" by the judge when c-sections are quite routine in the United States. For that woman, though, opposition to the surgery seemed quite logical (although, I am sure, very difficult). As opposed to the United States, c-sections are far less routine in her native nation, and she feared that this c-section could jeopardize her future ability to have children when she moved back to her native nation. Ultimately, the woman began to progress and delivered the child without surgical intervention; however, this example amplifies the implicativeness of technological advances for treatment dialogues—scientific "facts" frequently dominate decisions (see also account of the intensive care nursery by Wiener, Strauss, Fagerhaugh, & Suczek, 1997).

Whereas non-Western societies highlight religion and folk culture as part of health care (see, e.g., Farquhar's, 1994, work on Chinese medicine; Finkler's, 1985, 1991, research on health care in Mexico; Logan's, 1991, exploration of Brazilian herbalists; Warry's, 1998, analysis of aboriginal health practices), Western societies have tended to separate medicine from other aspects of culture in the United States (see Gaines & Hahn, 1985; Gordon, 1996; Lewinsohn, 1998; Rhodes, 1990; Romanucci-Ross, Moerman, & Tancredi, 1991; Williams & Calnan, 1996). Gaines and Hahn (1985) suggest that, in non-Western societies, health care is much more "explicitly associated with religion, politics, economics, and social relations, themselves closely intertwined" (p. 5).

Unlike the potential (and perhaps perceived) ambiguity of more religious and folk-cultural approaches to healing, a focus on medicine-as-science gained stature and capitalized on "a faith in the benefits of material progress, and in man's capacity to analyze and devise solutions for all the problems that confront him" (Gordon, 1996, p. 21). As I will detail in the chapter on public dialogues about health, advertisements even highlight scientific findings in their efforts to persuade consumers to purchase particular products. For example, in a magazine ad for Cellesene, a dietary supplement to aid in the reduction of cellulite, readers are encouraged to "accept only the clinically researched formula," even though the ad admits that Cellesene lacks approval by the Food and Drug Administration.

The prevalence of the biomedical model in the United States flavors typical treatment of medicine by health care professionals, seekers, and related marketers as something that involves "facts" driven by "scientific" conclusions (see Rhodes, 1990). Indeed, Stein (1990) argues that "in biomedical environments, 'facts' are the most highly valued category of information" (p. 13).

However, two key problems for a biomedical treatment of medicine-as-science remain the lack of clarity about what counts as "facts" and what living, errant human beings do with those "facts." As Turner (1992) explains, in postmodern society, ". . . there is no longer a single coherent rationality, but rather a field of conflicting and competing notions of the rational: thus we live in a fragmented, diversified and decentralized discursive framework" (p. 142).

Determining "Facts"

In the same month that Gilda Radner died (May, 1989), Anne Frahm received the news that she had stage IV breast cancer (Frahm, 1993, 1998). Like Dr. Marcy Olmsted and Gilda Radner, Frahm started her saga with a consequential misdiagnosis. With a family history of cancer, she had diligently monitored her body and immediately reported her discovery of a lump. After a mammogram, her doctor concluded that "there was nothing to worry about" (Frahm, 1998, p. 80). Yet, she did have reason for concern.

Following months of suffering and confusion, her doctor finally validated her fear—cancer. Frahm underwent a mastectomy (removing a tumor that was nearly the size of her breast), intensive chemotherapy, an autologous bone marrow transplant, and blood transfusions. As her doctors prepared to release her from the hospital following the transplant, Frahm (1993) remembers that "basically what they told me was to go and live life to its fullest. I knew that behind their words was the unspoken prognosis that my time was short" (p. 23). She picked up her bags, left the hospital, and started her own fight.

Frahm decided to try a nutritional approach to battling her cancer. During a regular follow-up visit to her oncologist about five weeks later, she explains, "I told him about my nutritional program. I will never forget his reaction. He looked at me, then his chart, and said, 'Your cancer has nothing to do with nutrition' " (1998, p. 83). Nearly a decade later, Frahm is cancer-free and runs a nonprofit organization, HealthQuarters, with her husband. The organization's publication, *HealthQuarters Monthly*, heralds nutritional importance and ways of enhancing functions of the body naturally.

Would Anne Frahm's oncologist acknowledge the viability of nutrition in light of her incredible success story? Would the advocates of medicine-as-science elevate nutrition to "fact" status? Regardless of the answers to those questions, the critical component of this discussion lies in its relational and medical implications (see related work on explaining illness by Whaley, 2000). Like the oncologist in Chapter 1 who dismissed an alternative approach to health care as "not scientific enough," Frahm's oncologist also treated her turn to nutrition as a last resort of desperation, something not "normal" because it lacked consistency with the biomedical preference for scientific proof. Perhaps she was searching for some strands of hope, even if the approach seemed "off the wall" to her doctor. Yet the doctor's construction of "facts" as based only on "scientific evidence" worked interactionally in both cases to hinder conversations about options.

However, dismissal of alternate perspectives by medical "authorities" does not always halt hope—nor the potential of adding something new to "science." When little Miles Seroussi's doctor diagnosed him as autistic, his mother, Karyn, rejected the grim prognosis—a life without normal social interaction (Seroussi, 2000). Desperate, she searched for information and discovered another mother's belief that her child's autism developed from a milk allergy. Miles consumed a lot of milk, Karyn thought, and his problems seemed to unfold after the move to cow's milk from soy formula. Karyn removed all dairy products from Miles' diet, and as she notes, "what happened next was nothing short of miraculous" (Seroussi, 2000, p. 120).

After sharing her story with an Internet support group, she found an "overwhelming" number of others who made the link between autism and dairy allergies. However, Seroussi (2000) also encountered skepticism, noting that "even though dietary intervention was a safe, noninvasive approach . . . until large controlled studies could prove that it worked, most of the medical community would have nothing to do with it" (p. 123).

Given the socially constructed preference for prioritizing "scientific facts," it is not surprising that health communication research has tended to treat compliance gaining as the "normal" preferred outcome of health care encounters. Researchers have emphasized, in particular, how doctors can work to gain compliance from patients and how public health campaigns can compel people to behave in ways that are preferred by doctors and agencies (see, for example, Elliott, 1992; Eraker, Kirscht, & Becker, 1984; Fisher, 1992; Hunt, Jordan, Irwin, & Browner, 1989; Kreps & Query, 1990; O'Hair, O'Hair, Southward, & Krayer, 1987; Paskett, Carter, Chu, & White, 1990; Phillips & Jones, 1991; Piotrow et al., 1997; Steele, Jackson, & Gutmann, 1990; Stone, 1979 as well as related discussions in subsequent chapters on public dialogues about health and medical decision making). Implicitly, such research and orientations to health communication reflect a prioritizing of a static set of "facts" or "truth," widely based on "scientific" conclusions—doctors and agencies "know" *the* way to proceed; thus the focus of communication should be on ensuring patient compliance.

Because of diversity issues and individual lifestyles, though, how can only one way exist? How can we treat health care as a one-size-fits-all endeavor, especially since people react differently than others (physically, psychologically, spiritually, etc.)? Jordan and Irwin (1987) suggest that "facts are always constructions, always suspect . . . " (p. 186), yet health care participants (both health professionals and health seekers) have not traditionally treated them that way, leading to confusion and frustration when individual cases result in dispreferred outcomes. As Lewinsohn (1998) contends, "A great deal of the disappointment with modern medical practice may be owing to the dashed hopes of an exaggerated faith in scientific medicine. . . " (p. 1266).

Ultimately, people come together for health care interactions, and they must share information, interpret literature and disclosures, and collaborate on possible outcomes. Certainly, mammograms get misread; symptoms go unreported, and people forget to take their pills. In our society of litigation, someone gets blamed, perhaps even sued. Humans do err, and such mistakes are devastatingly tragic. However, another piece of the puzzle becomes important when people perpetuate the assumption that medicine-as-science involves static recipes for curing disease—if someone had just known "the facts," then the patient could have been spared through some prescriptive and pretested treatment.

Balancing Science with Art

As a number of health care commentators now argue, medicine may be reconceptualized as an art and a science, thus enabling the health care participants to acknowledge the necessity of interpreting and juxtaposing diverse medical and personal sources of information, contextualizing medical problems in light of unique health care participants and circumstances, and enacting more creative, dialogic approaches to health care (see Arney & Bergen, 1984; Berg, 1997; E. Cassell, 1991; J. Cassell, 1991; Eisenberg, 1988; Gadamer, 1996; Hunter, 1991; Millenson, 1997). E. Cassell (1991) for example, refers to surgery as "an art, a craft, and a science. . ." (p. 9). Hunter (1991) maintains that "medicine is an interpretive activity, a learned inquiry that begins with the understanding of the patient and ends in therapeutic action on the patient's behalf" (p. xx).

While the introduction of medicine-as-art or medicine-as-art-and-science counters the traditional Western enactment of medicine-as-biomedicine, perhaps invoking images of faith healing or acupuncture, even the Hippocratic Oath (see Edelstein, 1943) refers to "this art" of medical practice. Regardless of the positioning of medicine as either art or science or a combination of the two, that enactment by health care participants simultaneously and reflexively impacts and constrains what becomes "normal" for the emergent relational system and how all of the aspects of that system become possible—the co-definition of medical culture, individual identities, social rules and social roles, essentially, the nature of interactions between all health care participants.

Medicine as Reductionistic and/or Holistic?

In her 1986 book, Sue Fisher describes her experience in seeking treatment for an ovarian mass. Because she had been researching and writing in the area of women's health for some time, she anticipated the drill. Fisher (1986, p. 1) explains, "I knew I would be referred to a physician who would most probably be male. I knew the medical task would be to rule out the possibility of invasive cancer. I knew what tests would be performed for diagnosis and the likelihood of surgery for treatment." Over child-bearing age at the time, she realized that her surgeon would likely recommend a total hysterectomy, a procedure that she was not convinced was necessary.

Fisher's assumptions proved correct. Her doctor informed her (not suggested to her) that "he would conduct the necessary tests one day and perform a total hysterectomy the next day" (Fisher, 1986, p. 2). She sought a second opinion. That doctor also recommended a total hysterectomy. She finally obtained the doctor's agreement that he would "remove only what was medically necessary" (1986); however, she writes, "I was left with an echo: 'It could come back'; 'You could need surgery again' . . . cancer . . . cancer . . . cancer . . ." (p. 3). For Fisher, as well as many other women in similar situations, the surgery was positioned as the only alternative, the only reasonable option. If she did not conform to the doctor's definition of "normal" (in terms of how a "good" patient should respond—i.e., comply—as well as how a rational person would see a "less than functional" organ), she put herself at more risk. The decision could be hers, but the doctors clearly framed that decision as "out of the ordinary" and, thus, not preferred. Because they concentrated on the cancer, they could not understand how Fisher's response could possibly be a reasonable one.

Disease-Centered Focus

As numerous scholars on women's health in the United States argue, the prevalent practice well into the 1990s was to perform complete mastectomies and hysterectomies when such surgeries might not have been medically necessary at all (see Finck, 1986; Fisher, 1986; Keyser, 1984; Kolata, 1993; Laurence & Weinhouse, 1997; Nechas & Foley, 1994; Smith, 1992; West, 1994). As in Sue Fisher's case, many surgeons view such organs as unnecessary or disposable, especially when women are past child-bearing years. Those organs lack any "normal" function so the routine response makes the most sense.

However, the positioning of an organ as disposable or unnecessary by a health care professional shifts the focus of discussion from the person to the disease, interactionally making the personal, relational, social, and cultural orientations of the individual less important, less of a central concern. Such a shift is consistent with a more scientific, biomedical approach to medicine, an approach that tends to distinguish the disease from the person who suffers from it (see Arney & Bergen, 1984; E. Cassell, 1991; Kleinman, 1978, 1980; Lantos, 1997; Mishler, 1984; Stein, 1990). As Stein (1990) contends, in this medical model, "the physical body and its constituent parts are the units of clinical discourse" (p. 13). For Fisher, for the African woman in labor noted earlier, and countless health care seekers as well, preferences, identities, co-cultural and religious allegiances, and so on get dropped and trampled on the cutting room floor by professionals who produce the emergent medical drama. As Stein (1990) argues, the very act of reductionism works to perpetuate implied power—"I get to direct you. I get to choose what we discuss. I get to define what is 'normal' and 'useful' and 'routine'."

Determining Relevance

Notably, mundane behaviors serve to facilitate the co-construction of what counts as relevant during medical interactions. As with Fisher and the African woman, doctors prioritized parts of the body in nondiscussions about courses of action; they did not open doors for other issues to become relevant. As Patch Adams discovered, watching his professors and fellow medical students refer to patients by their diseases, people faded in favor of procedures. Those professors and students typically classified patients by parts. Notably, the very act of labeling or talking about a person in terms of a disease reflexively works to socially construct that person as reduced to that particular problem.

Lantos (1997) remarks that "doctors all opine that it is wrong to abstract the person into the disease, to blur the uniqueness and the humanity of the person who is our patient" (p. 173; see also Mishler, 1984). Harvard Medical School is almost certainly not alone in contemporary emphasis on "care" along with "competence" (see Good & Good, 1993). Yet, how does that humanity get addressed? How do co-participants enact "care"? How do the co-participants prioritize the person over the problem when the problem remains the rationale for the interaction? Rolling into surgery on that December morning, I glanced into a woman's eyes, yet I wanted to know more. With busy surgical schedules, how did that woman's health care providers have an opportunity to learn any more about her than I did that day?

The patient care associate and one of the nurses helped me to roll from my gurney to the surgical table. Another member of the surgical team saw me shiver again and covered me with another heated blanket. The surgical team and I engaged in light-hearted small talk, and I told them that they were much friendlier than the team who participated in my cesarean section at the same hospital. They laughed. The anesthesiologist entered the room, asked if I had any questions, and started a gradual drip in my IV. The sounds of their voices and then the music drifted further away. Someone took my right arm and stretched it out at a 90 degree angle away from my body. I cuddled deeper in the blanket. I felt the brightness of the light against my eyelid, and I considered lifting my arm to shield my eyes, but I couldn't move either of my limbs.

The nurses greeted Dr. T. as he came into the room, and I forced myself to open my eyes to see him. I squinted as the lights grew more intense. "Dr. Beck, how are you this morning?" he asked. "Fine, thank you," I answered like I would in the stairwell of my school to a passing student. "I understand that you approved that last minute change, and we're going to do a great job. We're going to take good care of you," he seemed to whisper now. Darkness started to descend as I heard him say, "I'll come by and talk to you in recovery after you get out of surgery."

Through his comment to me that "we're going to take good care of you," Dr. T. reassured me and displayed concern for me while reasserting his competence as a physician. Yet that brief snippet also worked to gloss the potential panic prompted by the last minute change. Notably, he did not apologize for shifting his game plan (nor even for failing to tell me about his rethinking in person). He did not offer an explanation for his altered opinion. In so doing (and through my own lack of comment or question), he implicitly reified his authority to make those decisions as the "expert" about that portion of my body. He knows hands and wrists, and his enactment of the decision confirmed that my wrist was his focus, much as an automotive mechanic might only adjust the brakes of a car if a customer complained of a squeak upon stopping. That mechanic would not likely look further than the brakes for the source of problems with the car.

Achieving Holism

Critiques of biomedicine point to reductionism as a major relational and medical flaw, heralding "holism" instead (see, for example, Altenberg, 1992; Eisenberg & Kleinman, 1981; Gordon et a., & Gesler, 1998; Walters, 1992; Weil, 1995). Altenberg (1992) suggests that "holism is . . . an approach to the patient that acknowledges . . . each of us is greater than the sum of our individual parts. . ." (p. 12).

Often rhetorically positioned in opposition to the Western biomedical model of medicine, a wide range of "alternative" medical models suggest that a disease-centered model cannot account for the complexities of people (see Altenberg, 1992; Eden, 1993; Gordon et al., 1998; Walters, 1992; Weil, 1995 as well as chapters on diversity and decision making). Dossey (1998) explains that "alternative therapies fit the spiritual beliefs of individuals who use them . . . there's a prevalent attitude that orthodox medicine has become remote, technical, and cold" (p. 6D). For the traditional "ill person" (in a Western, biomedical conception of "patient"), the passive acceptance of Parsons' sick role results in ". . . having the particularity of his individual suffering reduced to medicine's general view" (Frank, 1995, p. 11).

Notably, all or nothing dichotomies tend to gloss over much more complicated continuums and complex configurations of health care philosophies. Individual medical doctors certainly orient to patients in a wide array of ways, depending on their medical school training, personality, co-cultural allegiances, religious beliefs, and so on. Dr. T. treated me with dignity, orienting to my status as a "doctor" (of philosophy, not medicine, but a doctor, nonetheless) and reassuring me that they would "take good care" of me. He did not ignore me or talk over me (at least until I fell asleep). However, the biomedical emphasis on reductionism and disease-centeredness cannot be ignored as an influence on how medical doctors orient to patients. Although I appreciate the time that Dr. T. took to talk with me and gain insight into my lifestyle and activity preferences before recommending a procedure, as a hand and wrist specialist, his focus was on my wrist. Biomedical reductionism serves as a philosophical underpinning for the contemporary fragmentation of medical care into medical specializations that concentrate on individual body parts.

Mainstream Holistic Approaches

Although nursing is not usually associated with the holistic medical movement that stems politically from more nontraditional approaches to medicine, prevalent philosophies of nursing underscore the importance of overall care of patients and issues of patient education and communication with family (see, for example, use of systems theory in nursing text in Joos, Nelson, & Lyness, 1985 and discussion of nursing roles in Orem, 1995 as well as Aroskar, 1991; Engel, 1980; Kristjanson & Chalmers, 1990; Latham, 1996). According to Engel (1980), "Nightingale was intensely aware of the interaction between emotions and physical health. Today, this is hailed as 'holistic health'" (p. 53).

In her research on interactions between nurse practitioners and patients, Fisher (1986, 1993, 1995) reports that nurse practitioners employ artful means of permitting providers and patients to present themselves more holistically (see also related work by Beck with Ragan and Dupre, 1997). According to Fisher (1993), "Nurse practitioners argue that the problems patients bring to examining rooms cannot be separated from the complex social and psychological lives people lead."

Osteopathic medicine and chiropractic medicine also constitute, at least philosophically, more holistically oriented approaches to care. According to one of their brochures, the American Osteopathic Association (1991) maintains that "D.O.s practice a 'whole person' approach to medicine. Instead of just treating specific symptoms or illnesses, they regard your body as an integrated whole" (p. 2). (See related writings on osteopathic medicine by Gevitz, 1982, 1988, 1996; Hruby, 1996; Walter, 1993.) Walter (1993) reveals that, even in the development of osteopathic medicine, founder Dr. Andrew Taylor Still emphasized "the study of the health of man as an individual and as an integrated unit" and believed that ". . . the heritage of osteopathic medicine is the humanization of the physician's relationship to his patient" (p. 5).

Chiropractors hold a similar underlying commitment to holism, although they focus their treatment on spinal subluxations (see, for example, Haldeman, 1992; Koren, 1997a, 1997b). According to Koren (1997a), "As in the creation of disease, so in the healing of disease do we see that same unique combination of physical, emotional, spiritual, cultural, nutritional, genetic and other factors that make us, indeed, unique" (p. 2).

Time pressures, cultural diversity, economic mandates, and political agendas can complicate the co-construction of health care interactions, especially in terms of reductionism and/or holism. (The argument can be made by contemporary overcommitted providers and patients that it is quicker and more efficient to just "cut to the chase.") However, the way in which health care interactants approach disease and wellness shapes and constrains their emergent relationships and treatment options. Reductionism can stifle discussion of issues that may be branded "irrelevant" (remember the oncologist's reaction to Anne Frahm's turn to nutrition—"Your cancer has nothing to do with nutrition"). Conversely, holism can also hinder attention to specific medical complaints.

An Argument for Pluralism
Because of the medical cultural values and ways of enacting health care, people who seek/provide care can be trapped in pigeon-holes while preferring the flexibility to seek/ provide multiple avenues of care. Although difficult due to clashes in core values, in the spirit of postmodernism, health care seekers can be liberated from either/or choices of medical paradigms by health care professionals who embrace a both/and approach, art and science, reductionism and holism (see discussions of integrating "traditional" and biomedical approaches to medicine by Cavender, 1988; Coreil, 1988; Lock, 1990; Van Blerkom, 1995). For example, Engel (1980) argues that "caring is the essence of nursing. This does not understate the science of nursing. Rather, nursing has identified the science of caring" (p. 53). Van Blerkom (1995) describes the work of the Big Apple Circus Clown Care Unit, a group that approaches healing much as "shamans" do in non-Western cultures. Van Blerkom (1995) explains, "One cannot deny the efficacy of physicians compared to shamans, but integrating doctors with complementary practitioners such as clown doctors may render Western medicine even more effective" (p. 163).

In their research on midwifery, Davis-Floyd and Davis (1996) discovered that "postmodern midwives" blend understandings of intuition and technology, enabling women to integrate their own personal resources and beliefs while ensuring that the birthing process proceeds safely. Davis-Floyd and Davis (1996) contend:

> . . . even the most holistic of midwives, in this postmodern era, is likely to have attained a high level of competence in using the technocratic tools of birth, and to be able to explain and defend her actions in scientific, linear, and logical terms. The praxis of postmodern midwifery entails, in many ways, the careful exercise of inductive and deductive reasoning even as it continues to rely for its primary ethos on the enactment of bodily and psychic connection. (p. 241)

Through such a creative combination of medical cultural and co-cultural traditions and values, health care providers can avoid forcing health care seekers to choose between two orientations of what is a "normal" approach to health care. In so doing, as I will detail in the chapter on medical decision making, health care participants can begin to explore the complexities of health care and the potential for participatory, discussion-based decision making.

Sources of Healing

> Now when Jesus returned, a crowd welcomed him, for they were all expecting him. Then a man named Jairus, a ruler of the synagogue, came and fell at Jesus' feet, pleading with him to come to his house because his only daughter, a girl of about twelve, was dying. As Jesus was on his way, the crowds almost crushed him. And a woman was there who had been subject to bleeding for twelve years, but no one could heal her. She came up behind him and touched the edge of his cloak, and immediately her bleeding stopped. "Who touched me?" Jesus asked. When they all denied it, Peter said, "Master, the people are crowding and pressing against you." But Jesus said, "Someone touched me; I know that power has gone out from me." Then the woman, seeing that she could not go unnoticed, came trembling and fell at his feet. In the presence of all the people, she told why she had touched him and how she had been instantly healed. Then he said to her, "Daughter, your faith has healed you. Go in peace." While Jesus was still speaking, someone came from the house of Jairus, the synagogue ruler. "Your daughter is dead," he said. "Don't bother the healer any more." Hearing this, Jesus said to Jairus, "Don't be afraid; just believe, and she will be healed." When he arrived at the house of Jairus, he did not let anyone go in with him except Peter, John and James, and the child's father and mother. Meanwhile, all the people were wailing and mourning for her. "Stop wailing," Jesus said. "She is not dead but asleep." They laughed at him, knowing that she was dead. But he took her by the hand and said, "My child, get up!" Her spirit returned, and at once she stood up. (Luke 8:40–55)

In this powerful passage in the Gospel of Luke (New International Version), Jesus heals two individuals. As a Christian, through faith, I believe that Jesus worked miracles for many during his time on Earth. Those crowds that swirled around Jesus during His Earthly ministry also believed in His ability to heal their physical concerns. In his novel, *The Prodigal Daughter*, Jeffrey Archer (1973) tells the story of a powerful woman in politics who discovers that her husband has been injured in a terrible traffic accident. Archer (1973) writes, "In times of helplessness one suddenly believes in God. Florentyna fell on her knees and begged for her husband's life" (p. 339).

Although members of our contemporary global community enact faith and belief systems in diverse and multifaceted ways, contemporary health care seekers still find themselves searching for their own solutions to health care challenges. As health care participants, from health care professionals to social support members to health care seekers, strive to co-construct relational and medical cultural systems, everything comes back to the question—what will work and how? Based on her research in Mexico, Finkler (1985) contends, ". . . people judge the treatments they are given by their effects. They look toward those who provide them with the best medicine for a given sickness episode" (p. ix).

Professionals' Knowledge of Science as Source

As health care seekers scrutinize options, their views of how health care works and their prioritizing of science, religion, relationships, fears, and so on flavor where they turn and how they interact with others in health care interactions (see chapter on diversity). Treatments of medicine by all involved parties as science and/or art and reductionistic and/or holistic link directly into how "healing" (and emergent health care relationships) get co-constructed by health care participants.

In the Western biomedical model, the notion of "healing" ties into socially enacted performances of medicine as science and as reductionistic. Earlier, I referred to my frustration with the process of determining the nature of my wrist problem, and I bemoaned the doctor's inability just to go to his books, tell me what is wrong, and fix me. Given his inability to do so, I questioned his knowledge, interpreting his indecision to a lack of competence. I grew up with the phrase, "Take two aspirin and call the doctor in the morning." Like Dorothy in *The Wizard of Oz*, I simply had to skip down a street to the wizard, and the "wise and wonderful" wizard would solve my problems and send me on my way.

The enactment of biomedical values and practices by health care participants permits many to perpetuate what has become traditional within Western health care relationships—doctors assert, and patients comply. Healing occurs unidirectionally—take this medicine, have this procedure, follow this plan. Ironically, like Dorothy, I usually fight my own battles and strive for my own journeys over the rainbow. Bellah and colleagues (1985) suggest that Americans, as a whole, take pride in their independence and self-determination. However, also like Dorothy, I pursued my wizard because I wanted to believe that someone could know what to do, and I grew disappointed as I discovered that the person behind the regal curtain was just an educated man, not an "all and powerful wizard."

Why did I agree to the last-minute surgical change, a change that reflected a choice by the doctor to rethink his initial position of "the best option"? I could have yanked out my IV, yelled at the resident, and sauntered straight out of the hospital. However, I didn't know what else to ask or where else to go, and Dr. T. seemed to possess the knowledge about possibilities. The resident was less than convincing as errand boy, but I kept remembering Dr. T.'s confidence when discussing my MRIs and my situation. Borrowing from Foucault's writings on links between knowledge and power (1972, 1994), through my consent to the revised surgery, I legitimized the doctor's knowledge and authority to direct what would occur. I perpetuated treatment of the change as "acceptable," if not "normal."

Self-Knowledge of Science as Source
As I have shared thus far, though, the postmodern tendency toward distrust of authority and static knowledge has prompted more people to peek behind their own curtains; however, it has not necessarily turned them away from a commitment to science as a source of healing (see Stein, 1990). E. Cassell (1991) suggests:

> During this last generation the scientific knowledge of medicine has become increasingly accessible to laypersons and the public has shown a voracious appetite for scientific information. . . . Knowledgeable patients do not believe that they are doctors; the belief is that a piece of knowledge the same as their doctors' will do the same work in their hands as their doctors'. (p. 23)

The media bombards us with encouragements to take our health care into our own hands. Advertisements urge us to "ask our doctor about _____," citing "the latest research findings" from television shows to websites. Companies and advocacy groups continually herald scientific research as a source that should be trusted. As I will discuss in the next chapter, armed with such information, many health care seekers feel empowered to treat themselves and to seek the compliance of their health care professional. Manning (September 22, 1997) contends that "patients today demand a quick fix . . . and will search until they find a physician who will give them what they want" (p. D1).

Frank (1995) offers a compelling description of the "post-colonial" patient who defies definition by others' authority. According to Frank (1995), "Post-colonialism in its most generalized form is the demand to speak rather than being spoken for and to represent oneself rather than being represented or, in the worst cases, rather than being effaced entirely" (p. 13). Like Anne Frahm (who started HealthQuarters with her husband after her struggle with cancer), post-colonial patients can reject efforts by health care providers who attempt to lock them into one paradigm or another; they can liberate themselves to find their own voice, their own identities, their own ways of accomplishing health and wellness.

Thus, although the extremes of passive acceptance of objectification (on one hand) and passionate reclaiming of voice (on the other hand) get socially constructed by health care participants, Frank's description of a post-colonial patient reflects a person who asserts individuality, desire for choice, and willingness to participate as a partner in health care decisions (see related work by Beck with Ragan and Dupre, 1997; Lambert, Street, Cegala, Smith, Kurtz, & Schofield, 1997; Lupton, 1997; Rimal, Ratzan, Arntson, & Freimuth, 1997; Shaffer & Sherrell, 1995; Sharf & Street, 1997; Stewart et al., 1995).

Trust in Spirituality and Folk-Healing as Source
In her research on health care in Mexico, Finkler (1985) argues that "biomedical symbols lack efficacy outside Western industrial society because illness not subject to speedy recovery is resolved not by biomedical symbolic manipulation but by culturally meaningful symbols" (p. 8). For those individuals who prioritize other aspects of culture above science, a focus on science (whether trusting one's physician or some other conglomeration of sources and/or oneself) rings less true (see, in addition to previously identified works on alternative medicine, Farquhar, 1994; Finkler, 1985, 1991, 1994a, 1994b; Gevitz, 1988; Stein, 1990).

In her compelling descriptions of medical practices in Mexico, Finkler (1985, 1991, 1994a, 1994b) explains how biomedical doctors and spiritualist healers and their patients work to symbolically co-construct the healing experience. According to Finkler (1994a), "While biomedicine attempts to refashion the patient's view of his or her body, spiritualism alters the person's experience of his or her body" (p. 189). For example, Finkler (1985, 1991, 1994a, 1994b) discovered that biomedical doctors in Mexico attempt to offer explanations that draw from biomedicine and folk knowledge. In so doing, though, biomedical doctors still practice reductionism with a focus on disease while "spiritualistic healing can gradually transform the person's existence by incorporating him or her, and sometimes the entire family, into a religious community" (Finkler, 1994a, p. 188–189).

Sources of Healing: Summary

Notably, the notion of "healing" is not some static concept to be associated with only one medical culture or another. For interactants, the challenge becomes socially constructing legitimate sources of healing and approaches toward healing. Consistent with social constructionism and general systems theory, healing constitutes an emergent, temporal process of co-determining shared meanings of social roles, rules, relationships, and so on. Clearly, orientations toward "healing" impact how health care participants treat information, prioritize rituals and procedures, and make decisions.

Social Construction of Health Care Identities

"Christie . . . Christie . . . Dr. Beck . . . Man, this one's really out, huh." "Yeah, they said that she didn't sleep last night. Smart, huh?" "Dr. Beck, can you hear me?" The voices echoed through the tunnel. I could hear them over and over again, like they stuck their heads in the Grand Canyon and yelled really loud. I was glad that they weren't yodeling. Those people can be so annoying in their little outfits. "Christie . . . "

"Dr. Beck." A different voice . . . Wait, that's Dr. T. Why is he with the yodelers? "The surgery was a success. There will be somebody from occupational therapy to come talk to you. I'll see you in the morning." I wanted to scream for him to wait, but I couldn't move. I couldn't even open my eyes. I couldn't respond. Why couldn't I talk? Why couldn't I just concentrate hard enough to open my mouth and move my tongue?

I fought to move, but I couldn't, and I realized then that I couldn't breathe. Who took the air out the canyon? Where were those voices, the yodelers? Why couldn't I breathe? I just wanted to breathe. I wanted someone to help me to get air. I tried to scream, but my mouth wouldn't budge.

"All right, she's ready to go up to her room." I could gasp now, but I couldn't catch a breath. I tried to will my body to sit up; I always breathe better when I sit up, but those yodelers kept shoving me down.

I pried my eyes open. The yodelers abandoned me in my room, and I started to remember. Hospital, surgery, tired . . . darkness . . . The treacherous torrents pulled me under, and I couldn't breathe again. Waves of water engulfed me; I fought to fling my arms around to swim, but I couldn't move. Why couldn't I reach for the surface? "Help, help,"

I gasped. "What?" I heard a voice. "Drowning . . . help, help," I struggled for air and willed my eyes to open. I couldn't catch my breath again. I was suffocating, and no one could help. I felt Roger's hand on my shoulder and recognized his voice, "It's just a dream. Just a dream."

Clawing my way back to reality, I finally relaxed and regained some level of consciousness. Roger looked really scared. He had come to Columbus to visit me. It was New Year's Eve, and his Huskers would play that night. I rewarded his kindness by freaking out on my cocktail of remnant anesthesia, morphine, and Percocet. What are friends for? I faded back into the darkness . . .

Hot . . . The room felt so stifling, and I had trouble inhaling again as I awakened. I looked at the chair by my bed, but Roger must have already left for home. I heard moaning, and I glanced at the bed on the right side of the room. I had requested a private room, but I got stuck in a semi-private, with a whining roommate who wanted to recuperate in a sauna. She kept begging the nurses to crank the heat. Why couldn't they just bring her another blanket? The heat overwhelmed me as I fought for a breath of air.

I needed to go to the bathroom. My left arm was hooked up to the IV, and my right arm was in a football size cast from my fingertips to about two inches below my shoulder. My hip incision ached. Figuring that I needed help, I pressed the call button. As the nurse tried to help me out of bed, pain shot through my leg. "Well, this is crazy," I said. "Dr. T. said that in a few days I could even run. Is it supposed to hurt this bad?" The nurse stared at me like I was either stupid or naive. "Yes," she answered, "when you have bone grafts taken from your hip, it hurts."

My frail-looking older roommate turned out to be a smoker. Recovering from surgery, in the dead of winter, she demanded that the patient care associate haul her outside for a cigarette. Great, I thought. She'll really be cold by the time that she drags her sorry butt back inside. I shot her a glare as she left in the wheelchair. Where was the part of me that used to try to be nice? Back home, I thought, along with the part of me that used to be comfortable.

I had to go to the bathroom again. The same two male nurses who had been on duty the previous evening entered the room. After they helped me back into bed, it occurred to me that I didn't care what they saw or how they helped me. Desires for modesty diminished as I focused on the bare essentials of shuffling one foot in front of the other while trying not to trip over my IV poll or bump my cast. I made no effort to close the gap of my gown to guard my nakedness, to summon some shred of dignity. I felt removed from the fragments of my identity that involve individuality, sexuality, and modesty. They didn't matter at all now.

I worried about managing at home with the girls. How could I take care of myself and the girls? How could I possibly be released the next day in this much pain? The nurse asked if I wanted to watch Dick Clark. It was 11:45 P.M., New Year's Eve. I said, "no," punched the morphine drip, and drifted into a drug-induced slumber as others toasted the ball descent in Times Square.

Vanderford, Jenks, and Sharf (1997) emphasize that "the patient's experience of health and illness is inherently bound to the individual's identity" (p. 15). I would go further to argue that health care participants engage in the ongoing process of socially constructing their multifaceted identities as they interact with each other, their surroundings, and their circumstances (see related work by McNamee, 1992). Notably, the notion of "identity" is consequential beyond the individual; emergent identities impact (and get perpetuated or redefined through) a plethora of health care relationships (see subsequent chapters on health care professional-seeker interactions, social support systems, and industry relationships) and health care outcomes.

Enacting Identity

When Nancy, a character on the television drama *thirtysomething*, learned that she had ovarian cancer, she told her husband, Elliot, and then committed him to silence. She wanted them to handle the situation alone; she didn't want anyone else to know about the cancer. Like the breast surgeon in Chapter 1, Nancy clung to her identities as wife, mother, friend, and artist, resisting further fragmentation as a "sick person." Beyond her doctor and Elliot, Nancy just wanted to be "normal," "regular" Nancy. Sitting on their bed, Nancy looked intensely into Elliot's eyes and insisted that "this is just us, Elliot, just us." Not able to keep the secret, though, Elliot told his business partner, Michael, who then confided in his wife, Hope.

While playing with Hope and their respective daughters at Hope's house, Nancy caught Hope looking at her sadly over their tiny toy teacups. Almost immediately, Nancy realized that Hope knew. Angry at Elliot for violating her trust, Nancy tried to explain her desire to keep the cancer separate, something not to be made relevant to her relationships beyond Elliot. Revealing the cancer constrained how she could legitimately present herself and interact with Elliot and now Hope and Michael (i.e., could she really still answer "fine" to a "how are you?" by knowing others?). While the cancer diagnosis did not define her, she could no longer ignore it as part of her identity (especially in relation to knowing others); it became another fragment of an already complicated life.

Facework

Consistent with social constructionism and postmodernism, scholars suggest that individuals may accomplish multifaceted identities through their interactions with each other (Beck with Ragan & Dupre, 1997; Carbaugh, 1996; Dreitzel, 1970; Gergen, 1991, 1994; Goffman, 1959, 1967; Grodin & Lindlof, 1996; Katovich, 1986, McNamee, 1996; Shotter, 1984; Shotter & Gergen, 1989). In his classic works, Goffman (1959, 1967) argues that individuals engage in artful social performances of who they are in relation to others and, in so doing, of how they want to be treated by others. This interactional positioning enables individuals to display and discern their orientations to each other as individuals and as relational partners (see related works by Carbaugh, 1996; Garfinkel, 1967; McNamee, 1996; Sanders, 1995; Shotter, 1993). As Goffman (1959, 1967) suggests, individuals engage in artful performances of their own respective "faces" and the "faces" of others.

For health care participants, the construction of "face" is critical to health care relationships and health care outcomes. Professionals must be taken as "legitimate" providers of information and recommendations; to "pass" as a professional, the professional must behave in a manner that rings true to the seeker (and vice versa) (in terms of overall approach and interpersonal style). Social support system members must also perform in a manner that gets treated as "acceptable" or "normal" for both parties. When someone threatens a given face (i.e., "good" professional, "good" family member), the participants must struggle with issues of politeness (see Brown & Levinson, 1987; Cupach & Metts, 1994; Ting-Toomey, 1994; Tracy, 1990). As Goffman (1967) contends, a person "tends to conduct himself during an encounter so as to maintain both his own face and the face of the other participants" (p. 11).

Incompatibilities and Identity

However, a postmodern challenge for contemporary social actors stems from the absence of absolutism (see Gergen, 1991). Our a priori expectations about accomplishing role identities point us in general directions but often fail to serve as more concrete road maps amid our abundant, ambiguous alternatives. Although organizations and institutions (including the family) have historically enforced particular ways of enacting their respective cultures, increasing individualism and diversity foster fragmentation, fracturing and testing taken-for-granted assumptions of how things are, how things should be, what is a "normal" way of proceeding (see, for example, Wieder & Pratt's 1990, work on becoming a "real" Indian). One static option does not exist for behaving as a "real" doctor, a "real" patient.

Moreover, can we ever just conceptualize ourselves as "just" a doctor, "just" a patient? Individuals dabble in a plethora of pockets of society, blurring disparate activities and random relationships (see Gergen, 1991, 1994). Despite ancestrial commitments to a culture and a family, our contemporary, cluttered lives compel us to splinter our selves, enabling us to slide in and out of communities, relationships, and obligations. Unlike their foremothers, women become "Super Moms" who master juggling career, home, and social commitments. More than driving the van and posting reminders on the refrigerator, though, enactments of our multifaceted identities challenge us to become chameleon-like in our abilities to morph from aspect to aspect of our selves—professional, parent, friend, lover, and so on (not to mention all of the diverse components of those more global clusters of our identities).

The multiplicity of our identities does not get discarded or simplified during illness. As in Nancy's case, discovering the cancer prompted another chipping of who she could be—wife, mother, friend, artist, and now all of the complexities of co-defining her enactment of illness (e.g., cancer patient, cancer victim, cancer survivor, patient, participant, person who needs encourage others, person who yearns to be encouraged, etc.). When I went in for surgery, I did not (frankly, could not) put the rest of my identities on a shelf and become a "patient." I worried about how to care for my children and how to do my job. I thought about how I would be able to turn the steering wheel of my car with my dominant right arm in a huge cast. I longed for my friends to be with me, and yet I did not want to bother them or to reframe our relationships to include focus on my illness. All of these fragments of my identity swirled around me throughout my journey through confusing medical mazes; I was never just a body with a cast and an IV.

In the comic strip *Funky Winkerbean*, the character of Lisa gets diagnosed with cancer. Like Lisa, Musa Mayer, another cancer survivor explains, ". . . cancer invades the entire context of a life, disturbing its balance, heightening its struggles" (1993, p. 6). As Lisa reflects in one strip, the experience of cancer is "like you've been shifted to some cold, dark dimension where only you exist." She sadly comments that "you can still see everyone in the other dimension going about their same boring routines . . . but you're not a part of it any more." Wistfully, Lisa wishes, "what I wouldn't give right now for those same boring routines" (Batiuk, February 7, 1999).

The paradox of postmodern identity emerges with the possible incompatibility of identities. Our society continues to debate whether a female professional can also be a "good mom." Health-related problems can also contribute to paradoxical identities—can one be an effective worker, a strong parent, and a caring partner while ill? Can a person be "normal" while living with a chronic or mental illness or a substance abuse problem? Of course, the answer is not simplistic nor absolute. However, the important issue here is not physical capability but rather the ways in which illness and identity get co-constructed can work to confirm or to disconfirm concurrent identities beyond that of "ill" person.

Determining "Normal"

Described as "a hard-driving, popular student who was president and one of three valedictorians of her 1995–1996 senior class at Wissahickon High School" (Hubbard, O'Neill, & Cheakalos, 1999), Sara Hunnicutt traveled a path that was strikingly similar to many other successful young women. She went to college, joined a sorority, earned good grades, and gained a little weight during freshman year. As she returned for her sophomore year, she started to diet. After Sara's weight fell just below 100 pounds, her mother cautioned her about her weight loss. As Sara explained, "In my mind, anorexics ate a leaf of lettuce a day and were stick thin. That wasn't me" (Hubbard et al., 1999, p. 56).

Sara eventually received medical and psychological assistance with anorexia nervosa, discovering that her desire for control and her commitment to success (even in terms of dieting) constituted classic characteristics of people with anorexia. The emergent co-definition of what is normal and what is exceptional echoed throughout her enactment of herself during this time. Like others, Sara positioned her dieting as "normal," something that most college girls do. While "normal," Sara recognized that she seemed to diet better than others; she excelled at losing weight. As Sara admitted later, "I was a damn good anorexic" (Hubbard et al., 1999, p. 57).

Although other authors have pursued the psychological and symbolic underpinnings of anorexia nervosa (see, for example, analysis by Lester, 1997), I want to focus on the implications of Sara's casting of her situation as "normal" for her interactions with others and her identity. Because she envisioned her dieting as "normal," she distinguished herself from "real" anorexics who "have a problem." Given that she did not have a medical concern, in her view, she could honestly downplay her dieting (and related medical consequences) to her mother, doctor, and friends, thus potentially avoiding possible negative constructions of herself by denying the existence of a "situation."

Sara's denial put people who cared about her in a difficult position. If they chose to accept Sara's version of reality, they could uphold her face and confirm that reality—nothing's really wrong; everything's okay. However, this nonconfrontational approach would work to perpetuate the anorexia, not to help Sara move toward recovery. If her loved ones chose to disconfirm Sara's presentation of self, those loved ones risked pushing her away by threatening her face (see related work on confirmation and disconfirmation in Watzlawick et al., 1967 as well as descriptions of family interactions about bulimia in Beach, 1996).

As many of the stories in this book will attest, the advent of illness introduces an alien aspect to already chaotic lives, especially when we position it in a dialectical relationship with "normal." As I worked on this chapter, I happened to receive my June 1999 issue of *Parents* in the mail. The front cover highlighted an article titled "Is Your Baby Normal? A First-Year Checklist." Although the article emphasizes that "there's actually a wide range of normal development" (Graves, 1999, p. 165), it also acknowledges that many parents express concern about their babies' development as they compare it to "normal." As a mom, I understand that concern; however, dubbing development as "normal" sets up the automatic polar opposite—"not normal," a phrase fraught with meaning and physical and psychological implications. The social construction of "normal" contributes to a co-definition of a key fragment of individual identities, especially in terms of how we get treated by (and treat) others. Those identities impact and are perpetuated/reshaped by social interactions with health care professionals, social support system members, and others in the world.

Identity and Health-Related Stigma

Brown and Levinson (1987) argue that face threats are socially acceptable when the benefit of challenging face outweighs the cost. In Sara's case (as in the case of a number of other health situations), the health condition warranted intervention, but the potential face threat was considerable. In his book *Stigma*, Goffman (1963) discusses the interactional consequences of being "normal" and being "stigmatized" (see also related work by Williams, 1987). Because anorexia is a psychological illness, an acknowledgment of it can result in possible shifts in perception by peers and family (thus, opening the door for alienation). Sara could no longer be considered "normal" in this aspect of her life. Paradoxically, because Sara now viewed dieting as "normal" and "routine," seeking treatment would mean an end to the preferred act of dieting and the inconsistency with how she had come to react to food.

Williams (1987) suggests that "there is a real need to give systematic attention to the social, personal, and emotional dimensions of 'stigmatizing' illness conditions and to address the problems of personal adjustment and adaptation . . . " (p. 159). Indeed, the co-orientation to a condition or illness as something other than "normal" can impact health-seeking practices and health care relationships.

Implications for Health-Seeking Practices
As in the case of Sara and the millions of other women and men who have or will battle anorexia and/or bulimia, individuals who struggle with alcoholism and drug abuse face similar relational and medical challenges. Meg Ryan offers a passionate portrayal of a woman who is an alcoholic in the motion picture, *When a Man Loves a Woman*. The character continued to deny her alcoholism until she collapsed in the shower. Her young child discovered her in a pool of blood and broken glass and called his stepfather at work, saying "Mommy's dead." The woman agreed to get help; however, the road to recovery was rocky. The acknowledgment of alcoholism forced the woman to take on a dispreferred identity—alcoholic, not someone who likes to drink; someone who needs help, not someone who enjoys a good party.

To admit an illness that has been societally constructed as "unacceptable" or "dispreferred" (such as mental illnesses, addictions, sexually transmitted diseases, etc.) drains an individual of social options and, particularly, of his or her preferred face (i.e., as a person who makes reasonable choices that society may endorse, a person who should not be ostracized). Thus, as I discuss in the next chapter, the potential of stigma may prevent people from seeking help or submitting to tests that could confirm a "worst case scenario."

Implications for Identity as "Normal"

The diagnosis and disclosure of a disease, particularly a chronic illness, forces reflections on "what can be normal now" and "who am I now" (see Conrad, 1997; Frank, 1995). As Toombs (1995) argues, "diagnoses are permeated with cultural and personal meaning. The dread diseases—cancer, heart disease, AIDS, multiple sclerosis—carry with them a particularly powerful symbolic significance" (p. 6).

Diagnosed with Parkinson's disease in 1991, actor Michael J. Fox (*Family Ties, Back to the Future, Spin City*) spent years hiding his illness. Just before winning a Golden Globe award in 1997, Fox ordered the limo driver to keep circling the block until his medicine started to work, easing the shaking of his left arm and leg (Schneider & Gold, 1998). Despite the supportiveness of his wife and the close friends and associates who shared his secret, Fox chose to guard the news closely for years. As Schneider and Gold (1998) report, Fox became a "master of concealment" (p. 130). Fox notes, "There are a billion tricks I can do to hide [the symptoms]" (see Schneider & Gold, 1998, p. 130). Notably, after Fox revealed his news to *People Magazine* in December 1998, a *USA Today* article stated that "Fox plans to continue acting" (Davis, November 27, 1998, p. 3A). Ironically, Fox picked up a second consecutive Golden Globe award for best actor in a television sitcom (*Spin City*) in the following month, yet that sentence in *USA Today* implies that *not* acting may have been viewed by some as a possibility—can people with Parkinson's disease continue to function "normally"? What is a "normal" enactment of life with such a disease?

For people who live with chronic illness as well as their friends, family, and co-workers, the social construction of "normal" is emergent and temporal. As Toombs, Barnard, and Carson (1995) explain, "To live with chronic illness and disability is to live a certain kind of life" (p. xi). Toombs, Barnard, and Carson (1995) argue that "the enduring nature" of chronic illness "requires a personal and social response that is different in kind from that which is called for by the temporary disruption of acute illness" (p. xi).

Tom Hanks received an Academy Award for his performance in *Philadelphia*, playing a lawyer who learns that he has AIDS. After his physical symptoms become apparent, Hanks' character is terminated by his law firm even though he was on the brink of being named a partner in the firm. His character was clearly stigmatized for revealing this particular disease; his employer positioned Hank's character as someone who could not now present the firm (and its clients) credibly and effectively. As Williams (1987) explains, "Stigma is a societal reaction that 'spoils' normal identity" (p. 139). In addition to battling the disease, Hanks' character launched a legal fight for his rights and his very identity as someone who could still contribute as a professional.

Implications for Relationships

In *When a Man Loves a Woman*, the husband continued to pledge his love and support, yet the relationship started to diminish due to the wife's difficult search for a redefined identity—"who I am now" as opposed to "who I used to be" as well as periodic "slips" in terms of her self-definition as an "alcoholic." As Dindia (1998) explains, the choices to admit or deny, to conceal or disclose, are spiral, not linear.

The revelation of a medical situation to co-workers, health care providers, and romantic partners can prompt uncertainty (and even fear), bringing identity and relational issues to the forefront for clarification and potential reevaluation (see, for example, Capitanio & Herek, 1999; Derlega & Barbee, 1998; Devine, Plant, & Harrison, 1999; Herek, 1999; Herek & Capitanio, 1999). How can relationships be "normal" now? How will others (knowing and unsuspecting) respond?

In the first season finale of *Sportsnight* (a sitcom about a sports show similar to ESPN's *Sports Center*), the character of Isaac (portrayed wonderfully by actor Robert Guillaume) visited the set after he is discharged from the hospital following his stroke. (In real life, the actor also suffered a stroke.) One of the staff members approached him and asked loudly and slowly, "Would you like to watch the show in your office?" Isaac turned to another co-worker and inquired, "Does she think I'm deaf?" A few moments later, the male anchors of the sports show teased Isaac about being a "cheese danish" because he took so long to return to the show. Isaac smiled and stated, "You're looking good, boys." The anchors nodded, and one responded, "You are too, sir."

This brief snippet exemplifies the interactional work done to co-define "normal." Would a stroke necessarily mean hearing loss? Conrad (1997) notes that "after all, illness may call personal competence and interactive capacity into question, creating the possibility of being seen as (or seeing oneself as) as less than a whole person with a blemished self . . . " (p. 11). Whereas the first staff member approached him as different (perhaps slower) than he once was, the anchors positioned Isaac as the "same old Isaac," not less than whole. Their good-humored bantor resembled interactions prior to the stroke. Isaac's response affirmed those attempts to define "normal" as what was "normal" before.

Just before her thirtieth birthday, S. Kay Toombs received devastating news. The doctor told her that she had multiple sclerosis. Upon diagnosis, her enactment of self and her interactions with others changed dramatically. Toombs (1995) recalls:

> Though multiple sclerosis does not carry the stigma of diseases such as AIDS and cancer, from the moment I was diagnosed people treated me differently. Even though I had no overt physical signs or symptoms, I was encouraged to "take it easy," to relinquish projects, to cut down on activities, to circumscribe my goals. (p. 6)

After her condition grew more serious, Toombs became wheelchair-bound. Although she notes that her friends and family have come to see the world (especially in terms of accessibility issues) from the perspective of someone with physical limitations, reactions by strangers to her now-visual disability contribute to a social construction of her identity as "less normal," "less able." For example, Toombs (1995) reveals that "whenever I am in my wheelchair, for instance, strangers tend to address themselves to my husband and refer to me in the third person. 'Where would SHE like to go?' 'What would SHE like to drink?' " (pp. 16–17). Brooks and Matson (1987) report similar struggles for MS participants in their research. According to Brooks and Matson (1987), "Being stared at, receiving overly intimate questions from strangers, or being excluded from social occasions are examples of stigmatization which had become familiar to many" (pp. 90–91).

Importantly, illnesses and identities should be treated as social constructions amid all of the other simultaneous aspects of relational identity that emerge through ongoing interactions. For example, Thorne, McCormick, and Carty (1997) discuss the implicativeness of gender construction in light of chronic illness, and Charmaz (1997) details the identity struggles for chronically ill men. As Charmaz (1997) explains, some shove the "sick" (and stigmatizable) dimension of their selves to the side, disguising the consequences of their conditions by avoiding social situations in which they could be revealed:

> An executive maintained a policy of not socializing with business associates. By not attending cocktail or swim parties, he hid his restricted diet and his dialysis shunt. A craftsman with emphysema hid how hard walking had become. He lagged behind anyone who might observe him struggling to climb a few stairs. Later, as his coughing and spitting fractured ordinary conversation, he refused social invitations and reduced his work to a few projects that he could complete alone at home. (p. 56)

CLOSING THOUGHTS

We seemed to hit every bump on Highway 33 on the way home. My hip hurt, and my arm ached. I slumped against the back of the passenger side of the Saturn. After learning that hospital policy prevented me from leaving without someone to drive me, Roger agreed to take me home. Another friend came up to Columbus to pick up my car.

I looked out of the window at the light snow on the ground as we drove through the rolling hills of southeast Ohio. My eyes worked to adjust to the brightness of the world beyond the hospital walls. Ugh, another bump, I thought, as the car nailed another pothole. As the car careened further and further away from Columbus, I thought about what had occurred and what was yet to come.

Not being able to move my fingers on New Year's Day, the day after my surgery, Dr. T. rushed me in for an emergency procedure to release pressure on my nerves. Although I still felt groggy from the first day of anesthesia and pain killers, I was aware enough to ask for a private room after the procedure. I entrusted another kind nurse with my bags and prayed that Dr. T. could just fix me this time.

I woke up to another semi-private room with a noisy roommate, more pain, and missing bags. My roommate cranked the volume on her television set, blasting the Ohio State game. Thankfully, the nurses responded to my pleas for quiet and insisted that she wear earplugs. This time, I got the nasty look.

I hated the smell of the hospital by now, and my new room was even more cramped than before. I couldn't get comfortable on the narrow cot, and I kept shifting to gain space for my heavily casted arm. My roommate kept coughing and calling for the nurse. The drape between the beds was transparent, and I watched the shadows of the staff as they attended to the woman. Whatever she has, I thought, she must be very sick.

Ugh, I think that they should outlaw potholes, I thought, as I looked back out of the window of the Saturn. In only a few days, I had been through so much. . . . I found out that my second roommate needed to be quarantined because they discovered that she had an infectious disease, and I had to fight to get information about what she had and risks to me. Images of my babies barrelled through my mind as I feared spreading disease to them. I didn't come to the hospital to get sick; I came to get better. What had I done? Had I made things worse? I felt powerless in my gown with my arms bound with the IV and the cast as I begged staff members for information and reassurance.

The road sign said ten miles to Athens, ten miles to home. I touched my purse, and I thanked God that a staff member finally located my bags. I couldn't get anyone to help me. I cringed as I recalled the nurse's shrug and comment that she didn't know anything about them. I looked at Roger as he held the wheel, and I felt so grateful that he came to visit me on that second day and that he managed to get someone to track down my bags. What would I have done without an advocate?

We passed by the exit for The Plains, and I closed my eyes. I had no strength, and my body ached. Had I positioned myself for the best care, I wondered? I had gone through two surgeries, two intolerable roommates, lots of drugs, lost personal belongings, fear of catching an infectious disease, and countless people who had poked and prodded my exhausted body. I opened my eyes to the roof of the car—had I prepared myself for what was to come?

CHAPTER

3

Communication Between Health Care Professionals and Health Care Seekers

I walked into my office and sank into my seat. Moving a mound of papers aside, I cradled my head in my arms, and my cheek brushed against the surface of my desk. When I was in grade school, we used to play a game called "Heads Up Seven Up," and I loved to feel the cool wood of my desk against the side of my face as I hid my eyes. I used to feel so young then, I thought, as I wondered how I could muster the strength to rise, re-enter the classroom, and return to lecturing after break.

The calendar caught my eye as I shifted to get more comfortable—January 24, 1997, three weeks since the surgeries. According to Dr. T., all of the procedures had been a success. Ah, then why did I feel so lousy?

Ohio University had resumed classes on January 6, four days after I left the hospital, so I jumped immediately into the frenzy of a new quarter of teaching. I hobbled into classes to greet my new students for Winter Quarter, lugging my arm in the massive cast and limping because of my still-sore hip. I wanted to press on, to resume my life. According to Dr. T., I should have been able to go back to everything that I did before with relative ease. I needed to respond to the copyeditor's queries on my book manuscript and to share information with my students, not to mention caring for my girls and working with the scouts. I yearned to go for a nice long run around the indoor track at our campus recreation center.

When I called to make sure that I was progressing "normally," Dr. T. encouraged me to pursue my regular activities, although he cautioned me against falling or getting in a wreck. I wondered if he really understood what was "regular" for me, but he expressed pleasure that I wanted to exercise and rehab my wrist. Dr. T. kept saying that my physical condition and desire to get better combined to make me an ideal candidate for a successful recovery. Yet I seemed locked in slow motion. Before the surgery, I could clip an eight-minute mile during my daily runs. At two weeks post-op, I barely inched around the one-eighth mile track once in fifteen minutes and then stopped, exhausted by the effort. The bone graft from my hip had been positioned as a minor surgery; however, the one incision in my hip bothered me more than the three in my arm, and I just felt fatigued all of the time. I understood that my hip and arm would require rehabilitation time, but Dr. T.'s initial predictions about my rehabilitation period missed the mark entirely.

I resolved to probe for information during my follow-up visit on January 16. How long would my hip take to heal? Would I always walk with a limp? I began to fear a ramification from the surgery that had clearly been downplayed during prior discussions—possible damage to my hip.

We arrived for that appointment on the 16th to find a packed waiting room. Roger had volunteered to take me, and I groaned as I saw the overflowing waiting area, dreading the delay and regretting his wasted time. After Katie, the head nurse, beckoned me back into the examining room corridor, I could see Dr. T. and his resident, Dr. A. (who had started her rotation with him on my last day in the hospital), visiting with another patient in one of the cubicles. Katie ushered me into the large casting room and informed me that the doctor would see me next. As she left, I looked around the room at the considerable equipment and materials, and I wondered about the volume of people that this group of physicians must treat in order to justify such a storehouse of resources. I closed my eyes and sighed. I am fortunate, I thought, to have found doctors with so much experience, so much credibility. I opened my eyes and glanced out in the hall. Leaning back a bit, I observed Dr. T., Dr. A., and the other patient. The teenage boy in the baseball cap sat expectantly as Dr. T. examined the boy's wrist on the table between them. I shut my eyes again and relaxed. I'm in good hands, I reflected. They do this all of the time.

"Tired?" Dr. T. asked, as he came into the room with Dr. A. and Katie. I smiled and said, "Actually, I'm generally tired these days. Could this have anything to do with the surgery?" Dr. T. shook his head and stated, "Not at this point. You did have a lot of anesthesia, but the residual effects from that should be about over." He picked up my football-size cast and queried, "so how is your arm doing? Are you ready to get in your permanent cast?" I responded, "Yes," and before I could draw the conversation back to my exhaustion and hip, Dr. T. began to talk about the new cast. Dr. T. touched the existing cast and commented, "I think that we're going to put you in an experimental cast. You're doing great, and that cast will allow you to move more than traditional casts. I think that you'll like it more." Flexibility did sound good. I had not even been able to get my right arm through most of my shirt sleeves.

I felt like a favorite toy to be tinkered with as I heard Dr. T. give Katie quick instructions on how to construct my cast. I bet that Dr. T. built model cars as a child. He turned his gaze to me and said, "I brought you something. I thought that you would be interested in reading research reports about the procedures." I grinned at him then. He really did enjoy playing with wrists, I smiled as I glanced at the article titles—"Midcarpal Instability Caused by Malunited Fractures of the Distal Radius" (Taleisnik & Watson, 1984) and "Correction of Post-Traumatic Wrist Deformity in Adults by Osteotomy, Bone-Grafting, and Internal Fixation" (Fernandez, 1982). Although I knew that the articles would soar right over my nonmedical head, I appreciated the gesture—a sign of respect from one professional to another, one doctor to another, even though I was "just" a Ph.D.

Dr. T. moved toward the door and said, "I'll stop in to talk with you before you leave." Looking at Dr. A., he suggested, "You're really into this case, so why don't you stay and watch?" Dr. T. smiled at me again and nodded toward Dr. A. "Dr. A. presented your case this morning." The resident responded, "It is a very interesting case. A real success story." "Suck up," I thought to myself, trying not to chuckle.

I watched Dr. T. leave the room and then returned my gaze to Katie and Dr. A. Katie charged into action, retrieving the materials for the cast from the shelf and handing them to Dr. A. With the efficiency and precision of a drill sargent, Katie prepared with confidence. She spoke of the materials and the cast construction process with authority. Her hands worked swiftly to remove the existing cast. "Dr. T. likes bulk," Katie commented. "He likes bulk a lot." She twisted the scissors in her hand as she tore through the cast. "Your new one will be a lot easier. . . . I'm not sure why he wants to put the experimental one on you. The other one would work just fine and give you more stability." "Well," I began hesitantly, "he might be thinking about my activity level." Katie responded, "Oh, you would do just fine in the other one. He just likes bulk and being different."

Dr. A. spoke for the first time without Dr. T. Dr. A. observed, "Her case is fascinating." She started to rattle off all that Dr. T. had done to me, emphasizing the complexity of the procedures—corrective osteotomy at the distal radius, iliac crest bone grafting, distal radial ulnar joint fusion with a screw, osteotomy of the distal ulna, distal ulnar stabilization with a free tendon graft. (I recaptured the names of the procedures from a copy of my operative report; the words pretty much flew past me at the time.)

Out of the corner of my eye, I caught Katie shaking her head quickly, and I wondered about my "case." Perhaps, my "procedures" were not as common nor as clearcut as I had believed. Had I convinced myself of that, or had I misunderstood? Why was it "interesting" enough to be presented at a major medical school? Did Katie shake her head because she thought that Dr. A. was naively blowing my procedures out of proportion or because she did not think that Dr. A. should be discussing them in that manner? I felt drained even trying to make sense of the seemingly mixed messages.

Katie removed the last piece of cast from my arm, and I slowly shifted my head to see my wrist for the first time since the reconstruction. "It looks shriveled," I said, noting the wrinkled skin that clung loosely to my bones. "Well, when you don't use it even for a few weeks, you lose muscle tone," Katie said matter-of-factly. She touched her stomach. "Look, it's 2 P.M., and I haven't had anything to eat yet. This new cast will take about an hour to put on. I think that I'm going to go grab something to eat real quick before getting started." She smiled, "You don't want to listen to my stomach growl for an hour, do you?"

I tried to lift the sides of my mouth, but I really didn't care if her stomach growled or not. She certainly didn't seem to care that I had not eaten lunch yet or that my friend was on a tight timeline to get back to Athens before his class. Moreover, my arm appeared so precarious, as though a strong wind might just blow it away and destroy all of our efforts thus far. I did not want to wait; I wanted her to begin the new cast right away. However, by the time that I worked up the nerve to protest, they were gone, and I was left alone with my now bare and vulnerable wrist. I sat on the cot, not daring to move. I didn't want to mess anything up. I had been through too much to risk anything more.

"Dr. Beck?" I hoisted my head from the coolness of my desk. I must have drifted off to sleep, and I fought to orient myself. My computer, my degrees on the wall, oh, and a student at the door. "Yes?" I answered, still struggling to figure out where I was and what I should be doing. "I just thought that I should check on you because, well, it's been a while," the student explained. Oh, no, I thought, my class had been on break. I cringed as I imagined them waiting on me in the classroom. I sat up straighter and said, "I'll be right

in." I had never fallen asleep during a class break before—how embarrassing. . . .
I inhaled deeply and ran my hand through my hair. The student still seemed concerned as
she hesitated at the doorway. "I'm all right," I said. "I'm all right."

As I stood to return to the classroom, I wondered if I was telling the truth. During that
visit on January 16, Dr. T. had seemed much more interested in the artistry of my recon-
structed wrist than my other concerns. He had assured me that I was fine; nothing was wrong.
Feeling still worse just the previous day (January 23), I had road-tripped up to Columbus
again by myself—I was sick of bogging down other people with my problems. After dragging
myself all the way to the big city, Dr. T. had met with me for five minutes to emphasize once
more that my hip was fine and that my fatigue and confusion did not stem from the surgery.
He was starting to look at me as though I simply wanted attention. Oh, maybe I was just sub-
consciously trying to milk this, I had thought on my way back to Athens, maybe. . . .

Waves of dizziness swept over me as I wobbled toward my office door back to my
waiting class. "I'm fine," I told myself. "I am going to be fine."

For a host of reasons, my interactions with health care professionals throughout this
health care saga were consequential. Although those interactions occurred within the context of other relationships and issues that I will discuss in subsequent chapters, the importance of professional-seeker interactions merits special consideration. Notably, I chose
these labels with care. For example, dubbing professionals "health care providers" or
"health caregivers" can be misleading; after all, they are not the only ones who provide
or give care—health care seekers certainly help themselves as well as receive assistance
from support system members. Further, the use of "provider" or "caregiver" (as opposed to
"health care professional") implicitly puts health care seekers in a more passive role of
recipient of some service, rather than active participant in enacting health and wellness.

For the purposes of this book, "health care professional" refers to all individuals who
have received training to offer particular health care services, including a range of individuals from midwives to obstetricians, chiropractors to allopathic medical doctors, family
practice doctors to surgeons, dentists to psychologists, home health care nurses to nurse-
practitioners and advanced practice nurses who perform specialized duties in hospitals, and
of course, occupational therapists, physical therapists, x-ray technicians, and so on. Depending on the particular medical situation, any or all of these types of professionals could participate in care and contribute to health outcomes. Health care interactions do not just involve
doctors (as opposed to all of the other types of health care professionals who might well participate in cases).

Similarly, health care interactions do not just involve "patients." I use the term
"health care seeker" to indicate individuals who want to improve their health through some
form of health care. As I discussed in Chapter 1, labels such as "patient" and "consumer"
reflect specific ways of orienting to health care situations by individuals in those situations.
However, in this project, I want to avoid taking the static position that all individuals fit in
a certain category—such as "patients" or "consumers"—when nothing could be further
from the truth. People approach health care interactions differently, and individuals may
even fluctuate in their own preferences for working with health care professionals. Given
the fragmentation of contemporary society and selves, health care seekers may well come
to health care encounters with a conglomeration of mixed (and perhaps even contradictory

and shifting) roles, identities, expectations, fears, and goals. The type of health care situation and emergent relationships with various health care professionals also contributes to fluid identities and goals. Thus, I hope to avoid pigeonholing people into a particular paradigm of pursuing health care by using the more generic term of "health care seeker."

In this chapter, I explore the complexity of interactions between health care professionals and seekers. First, I describe the importance of professional-seeker interactions, and second, I detail the types of goals that health care professionals and seekers tend to bring to those interactions. After discussing the implications of communicative choices for achieving individual and mutual goals, I conclude the chapter with an argument for caring communication through identification.

Importance of Professional-Seeker Interactions

In his analysis of health care seeker memories of health care experiences, Ruben (1993) discovered that patients remembered more about interpersonal issues and information sharing by caregivers than about clinical matters, policies, or facilities. According to Ruben (1993), personal treatment/interpersonal communication and quality/quantity of information "accounted for 52.5% of reported experiences across the six study sites" (p. 105). Notably, those recollections stemmed from interactions between health care seekers and a wide array of health care professionals—not just physicians. As Ruben (1993) argues, ". . . a variety of health care staff groups play a role in creating the experiences that are most critical and memorable to patients" (p. 106).

I remember Katie's brisk yet pleasant efficiency, Dr. T.'s excitement about the possibilities of my reconstructed wrist, Dr. A.'s eager efforts to position herself as an expert, a doctor, and a "good resident." I remember Dr. T.'s coming back into the casting room on January 16 and changing his mind about the experimental cast, opting for the traditional cast instead. "Given everything that you've had done," Dr. T. had told me, "it makes more sense to support the wrist as much as we can and to immobilize the elbow." I recall the frustration of uncertainty about another change and his lack of focus on my fatigue and hip pain, but I also recollect my dissonance with that frustration—he had been so nice, respectful, and concerned about my wrist. The images remain vivid, even though this visit constitutes only one in a series of even more consequential encounters. From that chilly day in January, I remember limping through the icy parking lot, climbing into the car, and driving home with feelings of fear and dismissal and confusion. Perhaps most of all, though, I retain powerful memories of my resolve to regain my life by proceeding as though those symptoms really were not there because they had been brushed aside.

However, interactions between health care professionals and health care seekers do not just influence memories; the nature of those interactions contribute to critical components of the health care process (including, for example, how health education, health care decision making, and health care identities get co-constructed by the participants) (see, for example, literature reviews by Beck with Ragan & duPre, 1997; Kreps & O'Hair, 1995; Kreps & Query, 1990; Ong, DeHaes, Hoos, & Lammes, 1995; Stewart & Roter, 1989; Thompson, 1998).

For example, relational issues are not mere "niceties." They reflexively impact the co-accomplishment of multiple other educational and medical goals. Kreps (1988) argues that ". . . interpersonal communication relationships established between health care providers and consumers have a major influence on the level of success of health care treatment" (p. 351). Lazare, Putnam, and Lipkin (1995) contend that relational work during health care interactions "facilitates several clinical objectives" including:

> (1) the patient's willingness to provide diagnostic information, (2) the relief of physical and psychological distress, (3) the patient's willingness to become an active and cooperative participant in the diagnostic and treatment process, (4) the successful termination of the relationship (or transfer of care to another health care provider), and (5) patient and clinician satisfaction. (p. 11)

Awareness of Medical Educators

Increasing integration of communication training into medical school curriculums (albeit to varying extents) attests to growing appreciation for the importance of interpersonal communication between health care professionals and health care seekers (see related work by Evans et al., 1992; Mengel & Fields, 1997; Parle, Maguire, & Heaven, 1997). According to Schrof (1998), in a 1997 survey, 60 percent of doctors claimed that "medical school had poorly prepared them to talk with patients" (p. 66). In an attempt to respond to such concerns, the University of Pittsburgh School of Medicine even recently announced the creation of the nation's first endowed chair to concentrate on "the patient-doctor relationship and patient-centered care" (AAMC STAT, July 5, 1998). As Cousins (1988) argues in the *Journal of the American Medical Association*, ". . . the physician's communication skills need no longer be regarded as theoretical assets" (p. 1611).

Growing Public Doubts About Medical Care

For increasingly well-schooled and consumer-oriented health care seekers, realizations about the importance of communication skills by health care professionals could not happen too soon. As I detail in the chapter on public dialogues about health, the popular press abounds with magazine articles, newspaper columns, television programs, and self-help books that focus on "getting the most from your doctor" or "improving your relationship with health care providers." From newsstands on the street to the nightly news on television, individuals in contemporary society routinely get bombarded with warnings about problems stemming from health care service and suggestions about ways to improve communication between health care professionals and health care seekers.

Why are we so concerned about health care interactions at this point in history? One key reason may be one that I alluded to earlier—*uncertainty amid constant change.* As health care professionals and health care seekers meet together to discuss health-related concerns, they do so in light of intensifying personal and cultural paradoxes with regard to diverse medical paradigms, growing ambiguity about authority, skepticism of scientific "facts," tales of malpractice and medical mistakes, and general absence of clear choices and directions. Out of the murkiness of postmodernity, health care seekers in Western societies (especially the United States) may realize that they can choose their doctors, approaches, and treatments, but they may not possess the background to assess alternatives. Health care seekers may well know enough to understand that health care professionals do not "own" the truth, but they may lack sufficient information to evaluate claims and sort through diverse (and often contradictory) material. Health care seekers may desire a "personable" and "well-qualified" professional, but they may struggle with defining those attributes and finding health care professionals who meet all of their needs. Health care professionals may understand their patients' desires to question and to pursue alternatives—after all, health care professionals also become health care seekers in times of illness—but they may wrestle with positioning their "expert" recommendations amid differing preferences for information and direction by various health care seekers. Health care professionals have a stronger appreciation for caring communication than ever before, but large case loads may dramatically limit time for dialogues and for follow-up interactions. As their medical mazes keep morphing into ever-changing and confusing configurations, health care participants have grown increasingly aware of the need to attend more carefully to each other and to collaborate in their efforts to find their ways.

Goals for Health Care Interactions

During health care encounters, health care professionals and health care seekers strive for individualized and co-constructed health-related outcomes. In earlier works, I argued that health care professionals and health care seekers bring a range of *relational goals* (e.g., desires to be taken/treated in particular ways by interactional partner), *educational goals* (e.g., desires to obtain/share certain information), and *medical goals* (e.g., desires to make/obtain effective diagnoses and to advance/discuss options for accomplishing wellness) (see previous reviews of goal work in health care interactions in Beck with Ragan and duPre, 1997; Ragan, Beck, & White, 1995). Although the linearity of writing requires me to list one of these types of goals before another, I want to emphasize, first, the interdependence and reflexivity of the goals. Relational activities impact and constrain the nature of educational efforts and medical tasks. Educational activities impact and constrain the nature of the relationship and the possibility of some medical procedures. Medical procedures can flavor how participants treat each other and share information. Consistent with social constructionism and systems theory, I contend that the multiple goals and activities that get advanced during health care encounters affect a multiplicity of other aspects of those encounters. As Roter and Hall (1992) suggest, " A patient's very motivation to get well can be seen as springing from the quality of exchange with the doctor" (p. 5).

Second, I must stress that individuals prioritize relational, educational, and medical goals differently, even from situation to situation, moment to moment. For some individuals, a doctor's ability to empathize becomes more important than his or her ability to give information. For others, the opposite may be true. Still other people may just want a diagnosis and a prescription. Even criteria for what constitutes "effective" relational communication or education shift from person to person, health care episode to health care episode. In light of the ambiguity and temporality of "ideal" outcomes for health care encounters, relational, educational, and medical goals have grown increasingly challenging to define and ever critical for health care participants to strive to accomplish.

Relational Goals

In an interview (see Appendix A), one health care seeker, Ann, referred to initiating a relationship with a new doctor:

> Definitely, when I first met him, I knew what his references were, but I hadn't actually talked to him. I didn't know how he was as a person, as far as being personable. So I was very cautious when I first met him. I answered his questions, but I didn't come right out and tell him about things that were in my life, personal things about me, but over time, I began to like him, and I established a relationship with him. I started to trust him, began to trust him. Of course, that takes time. You can't just walk into a doctor's office, meet a doctor, and establish, you know, the perfect doctor–patient relationship. You have to take the time to get to know the doctor, and sometimes the personalities do clash, and you may not want to take that time to get to know the doctor, but if you do like the doctor at first, you should hang in there. Eventually, you will establish the trust relationship.

Relational goals refer to how health care professionals and health care seekers want to position themselves as individuals and in relation to each other. Both health care professionals and health care seekers bring individualized preferences and perspectives about "what should occur," "what is normal," and even "what is sincere" to their interactions, preferences that may fluctuate depending on the health care situation, individual identities, philosophies of/approaches to health care, and culture, gender, occupation, age, race, and so on (as I will discuss in the chapter on diversity). For example, as Strauss, Fagerhaugh, Suczek, and Wiener (1985) note, "one person's authentic gesture can be judged as wholly inauthentic by the other or simply inadequate to the occasion, or it may seem completely inappropriate" (p. 149).

Such assumptions about "normality" and "authenticity" stem from (and work to reify) individual inclinations for face and relational roles. Especially in this era of managed care, professionals and seekers must clarify where the particular professional fits into a seeker's situation—for example, primary physician or specialist, one-time consultant or possible long-term doctor or home health care nurse, and so on (see Lipkin, Putnam, & Lazare, 1995). Face and role enactments influence how the participants treat and perceive each other as well as the types of educational and medical activities that may occur during the encounter.

Preferred Face

As I noted in Chapter 2, "preferred face" refers to the ways in which individuals want to be taken as and oriented to be others (see especially, Brown & Levinson, 1987; Cupach & Metts, 1994; Goffman, 1959; Ting-Toomey, 1994). Although desires for a particular face may stem from internal visions of self, constructing face constitutes a social and emergent process. Consistent with the description of social constructionism that I offered earlier, facework involves artful communicative practices by co-participants as they present themselves and orient themselves toward their interactional counterparts (see Goffman, 1959).

For health care participants, facework is both critical to and problematic for other activities during health care interactions. Because of societal commitments to face and politeness, threats to preferred face jeopardize trust, confidence, security, understanding, and mutual concern—all central to relational, educational, and medical goals. However, the accomplishment of face can be difficult for health care participants due to disparities in ways of enacting concern, displaying knowledge, and so on. Interactants can also struggle with facework because affirming face for one participant constrains possible face accomplishments by other participants—for example, who gets to be "most knowledgeable"? "most trustworthy"?

As I describe possible face desires for health care seekers and then for health care professionals, please note that such desires get asserted, advanced, achieved, and perceived on a continuum. Individuals can be more or less serious, more or less knowledgeable, rather than extremely serious or knowledgeable or not at all, and such enactments may be more or less important for presenting oneself (and being treated by others) as a "good professional" or a "good health care seeker."

Health Care Seekers   Clyde bemoaned how one doctor treated him:

> I had a very small breakout, and I freaked out and went to see [the dermatologist] . . . I think he treated me as if he didn't have to spend very much time with me. He looked me over for about ten minutes, and he didn't let me speak and just said "this is what you need." He wrote me a prescription up really fast. I don't feel like he spent due time on me, and I got the medicine home, and I started using it, and within two days, I had a horrible rash. I called him, and he claimed that the only reason he prescribed it in the first place was because a lot of kids come in there with "mental-like" disfigurements. The whole thing had nothing to do with the physical so I ended up spending over sixty dollars for something he felt was a little mind thing I was playing. Then, I had to pay an extra thirty dollars to get the cream to take away the rash.

Although health care seekers certainly vary with regard to preferred face during health care encounters, prevalent propensities include the desire to be taken seriously, the desire to be treated as knowledgeable about one's body, and the desire to be considered as a complex, multifaceted person. In Clyde's view, his doctor did not orient to him as a person who had a genuine health problem nor as a person who knew his own body. Because of the doctor's implicit dismissal, Clyde could not advance his preferred face, thus hindering the accomplishment of his educational and medical goals.

In my case, Dr. T. treated me with the respect of a fellow professional. He legitimized my status as a fellow scholar. Certainly, he affirmed my complicated lifestyle through his surgical recommendation. Yet when I came to him with symptoms that did not fit his orientation to me—a model patient with an ideal opportunity for a swift and full recovery—he dismissed me. Through that dismissal, he did more than imperil my health; he implicitly rejected my preferred face as someone who knows her own body and who yearns to be taken seriously.

Health Care Professionals   When asked about her goals for a good health care interaction, Maggie emphasized, "Two key areas are the confidence in his work and the rapport with you." Deb concurred, noting that "I think that one of the most important things you could have with your doctor would be a trusting and open relationship." For Maggie and Deb, confidence and trust emerge from the relationship, not from credentials on a wall or even references—does the professional indicate a genuine interest in the seeker? Does the professional seem to care about the person who is ill, not just the source of the "problem"?

For health care professionals, preferred face may include the desire to be taken seriously and to be treated as a trustworthy expert, someone who possesses knowledge about medical issues and procedures. As I detailed in Chapter 2, what constitutes a "legitimate" health care professional comes largely from particular medical cultural philosophies. Behaving as a "real doctor" may necessitate reliance on medical terminology and an emphasis on the medical "problem." Whereas such professional distancing may coincide with medical acculturation, it can clash with connecting and caring that constitute other aspects of preferred face.

As I discuss next, facework flavors relational roles. If a health care seeker gets treated as knowledgeable, what happens to the health care professional's status as "the" legitimate authority, "the" real expert? If a health care professional talks like "an average person" who can "feel our pain," can that professional then assert him- or herself as calm, rational, and perhaps even "machine-like" enough that he or she won't make "human" mistakes?

Relational Roles

Through their verbal and nonverbal behaviors, health care participants co-construct the nature of their relational identity—who they are as individuals and who they can be to each other. The definition of roles within health care interactions emerge from cultural understandings of appropriateness as well as from situated co-constructions of particular dyads (see related work by Goffman, 1959, 1967; Watzlawick et al., 1967). Because of the latter, I would argue that we can conceptualize relational roles as power-based continuums and as artfully framed accomplishments.

Power-Based Continuums   Larry asserted:

> When I go to the doctor, I always feel uncomfortable as it is anyways so I'd rather have them just be real nice and just try to make me feel at ease and just talk to me and listen to me and have me explain what's wrong with me. I don't want them to cut me off or talk to me like I'm five years old.

Interestingly, Larry seems to blur biomedical and consumer-oriented medical models in his ideal health care interaction. To begin, Larry feels uncomfortable with medical appointments, for some unstated reason. Notably, he puts the bulk of responsibility for reducing that discomfort on the shoulders of the doctor. Larry wants the doctor to "make me feel at ease." Yet, despite deferring his control over comfort to the physician, Larry wants the physician to listen and to treat him as an adult in order to put him at ease.

Relational roles of health care participants range from rigid doctor–patient dichotomies (see Parsons, 1951) to health partnerships (see Beck with Ragan and duPre, 1997; Veatch, 1991) to consumer-oriented models (see extended discussion in the next chapter), with a vast variety of configurations in between (see related work by Cichon & Masterson, 1993; Gerhardt, 1987; Wolinsky & Wolinsky, 1981). Regardless of position on the continuum, though, the performance of relational roles reflects and reifies respective power bases of health care participants. If Larry interactionally defers to his doctor, he implicitly empowers him to determine what happens during the health care visit. When I did not persist in probing Dr. T. about my exhaustion and hip pain, when I did not object to Katie leaving to eat lunch before constructing my cast, I enabled them to walk through the examining room door without giving me answers or addressing my unspoken concerns.

Framing of Multiple Roles   Building on the work of Bateson (1951, 1972), Goffman (1974) argues that social actors cue each other about "what is going on here and now" through artful metacommunicative devices. For example, individuals can indicate if they are kidding around or being serious. In the case of health care encounters, framing activities constitute an important part of the social construction of individual and relational identities, the "normal" course of events during the encounter, and even the nature of symptoms, diagnoses, and treatment discussions (see, e.g., Evans, Block, Steinberg, & Penrose). As I detail later, the ways in which we participate in health care encounters work metacommunicatively and reflexively to frame our health care relationships and activities.

Especially given complicated contemporary lifestyles and the confusion of interacting with a plethora of diverse health care professionals and seekers, health care participants rely on interactional framing to co-determine what aspects of their respective identities should be highlighted during health care encounters. What role should a particular health care professional take—counselor, leader, consultant? What fragments of a health care seeker's identity should be addressed and affirmed during particular parts of examinations and decisions? How could health care participants frame procedures and decisions to reduce face loss and to make discussions mutually productive?

When Bruce Mitchell learned that he had colorectal cancer, he visited a surgeon (Mitchell, August 23, 1999). The surgeon explained his recommended procedure and checked to see if Mitchell still wanted to obtain a second opinion or if he planned to proceed with the surgery (i.e., how did the health care seeker view his role in his health care saga?). Mitchell liked the surgeon, but he stressed his desire to schedule the surgery immediately. Mitchell told the surgeon that "if I have to wait a month, I've got to keep looking" (August 23, 1999, p. 16). According to Mitchell, the surgeon "explained that the cancer was growing very slowly and waiting a month wouldn't affect the outcome" (August 23, 1999, p. 16). Yet, Mitchell persevered, noting that "I understand, Doc, but I got a family to take care of and a business to run. I can't be walking around on the beach, enjoying a vacation, with this cancer inside me. I can't think about anything else" (Mitchell, August 23, 1999, p. 16).

In his discussion of dialectics in health care interviews, Mishler (1984) suggests that the traditional biomedical model has worked to mute the voices of those who seek care, particularly in relation to their selves beyond the medical context. Through interactional framing, health care participants can make emotions, external commitments, and commonalities relevant or irrelevant to health care discussions. When the surgeon acknowledged Mitchell's concern and agreed to perform the surgery soon, he implicitly enabled identities to emerge beyond a limited focus on the specific medical issue (such as Mitchell's "slow-growing" colorectal cancer).

Educational Goals

Laura's observation exemplifies an important educational goal:

> The older I get and the more knowledge that I have, it is easier to communicate with health care providers. I want to be educated about what illnesses are out there that may impact my life. I guess that I feel that if you are educated and your health care provider is educational, it makes for a much more productive patient/provider relationship.

Educational goals refer to desires for sharing and seeking information that are held by health care participants (including health care professionals, health care seekers, and social support system members). Grueninger, Duffy, and Goldstein (1995) argue that "patient education . . . is often as important as any prescription or surgical procedure in restoring or maintaining a patient's health." Indeed, Lipkin and colleagues (1995) contend that education is one of the three core functions of any health care interaction (see also Lorig, 1992; Redman, 1997; Weston & Brown, 1989).

Although Samra (1993) suggests that "in the last fifteen years, with the campaign on preventative medicine, a new breed of patient has emerged" (p. 341), health care seekers are far from generic, and their educational goals (and those of health care professionals) lack static definitions. However, individuals do know what it important to them, and the extent to which their educational goals are realized during health care interactions impacts decision making and reactions to information (or lack thereof). Patient education can facilitate uncertainty reduction, professional credibility, and medical activities.

Uncertainty Reduction

Steptoe, Sutcliffe, Allen, and Coombes (1991) argue that health care seekers deal with the potential stress of health care situations by approaching information differently. They suggest that some people reject details while others, like Jen, actively search for information to reduce their uncertainty about health concerns (see also Whaley, 2000). Jen explained:

> Well, when I went to him [the doctor], I originally wanted to know what was wrong with me because I didn't know specifically what was wrong with me. I also wanted to know, since it was mono, what to do and how to deal with the emotions I would go through, and how to deal with all of a sudden having to put my life on hold and not do anything but rest.

For Jeremiah, unresolved uncertainty about a prospective laser surgery on his eye prompted him to turn to another health care facility. Although the initial health care facility was "world renowned" for its success with that particular surgery, the health care professionals failed to meet his educational needs, needs that he could not even express because he did not have the background to know what to ask. Jeremiah recalled:

> . . . the first time I had gone to the [health care facility]—world renowned place—and the communication was completely lacking. Um, they did a very poor job on just educating me as a patient. You know, for the laser surgery I was getting done, I kind of needed to know what I was getting into, so I went elsewhere to a place called [name of facility], and they were wonderful. They sat down with me for approximately an hour, answered all of my questions, explained the procedure to me, showed me a video, that kind of stuff.

After the interviewer asked Jeremiah if he questioned the staff at the first facility about the surgery, Jeremiah continued:

> If you knew enough about the procedure to ask the questions, they would answer the questions, but I didn't know enough to ask certain things. . . . so because [name of second facility] showed me a whole tape of everything about the procedure then that allowed me to come up with questions I had. We kind of had the same knowledge base about what was going to happen.

When health care professionals take the time to explain health care situations to seekers (and their family and friends), the educational process can reduce fear of the unknown and work to validate the need for information as "normal" and "legitimate." Bert explained that his mother had battled cancer for years. He credited a concerned nursing staff for their efforts to attend to his anxiety about his mother's condition on one specific occasion. Bert remembered:

> My mother had a major operation, and I was very young at the time. I was very young at the time and very scared. It was just the two of us because my father had died several years prior, and I was terrified, and the nurses we had gotten to know really made it possible for me to understand what was going on. They could explain everything that was happening, and they would go to the doctors and tell them that I was very scared so they would explain things to me so I would understand and so she would understand. That really helped.

Professional Credibility

The ways in which health care professionals share information can also influence their credibility with health care seekers. For example, Max visited three different health care professionals about his foot. The three professionals varied widely in their approach to providing information, flavoring Max's perception of their effectiveness as doctors. Max contended:

> Yeah, it is very important for a doctor to communicate as much as possible with their patients. You know, I had this injury, and when I left [name of facility], I didn't have the slightest clue of what was wrong with my foot. Then I went to Doctor @@, and I had a pretty good idea of what the extent of my injuries were, but I didn't know how severe it was until I visited Doctor **. He made me understand it so much better. He sat me down and

made a 20 year old college guy that doesn't have a damn clue about injuries and x-rays understand. It's to the point now that I can look at my own x-rays and read them and tell you what is wrong. That doctor is doing one heck of a job.

Max's third doctor presented information in a manner that Max could understand, thus building his credibility with Max. Such credibility can contribute to trust and confidence in future recommendations about medical alternatives.

Medical Activities

Mathew enters health care encounters with the primary goal of sharing information with the health care professional so that she or he could best help him:

> I feel that I should be able to go into a doctor's visit and that I should be given the chance to explain why I'm there, whether it is for a regular check-up or it is because I am sick. I want to explain to the doctor what is going on, and if I am allergic to things and go through the whole list, you know, the whole procedure so he is aware of everything that is going on. Maybe I could tell him a few things about myself that may be important or critical to the treatment I'm going to get. If I'm active, then a certain kind of cast may be inappropriate if I had broken a leg, or something like that. That's my main goal.

The mutual sharing of information enables health care participants to collaboratively achieve medical activities. Although health care professionals work in a familiar environment, performing procedures that may be all but rote, health care seekers can lack an understanding of what is happening, what is going to happen, and what all of the medical tasks mean for them and their health. Danielle described her frustration with her dentist:

> My dentist would always just come in and be in a big rush to get through the day and through the appointment. He would just tell me to open up my mouth, and he would immediately begin to look things over. You know, scratching at things with those utensils, and he would never explain what he was doing. He never explained any of the thoughts that were going through his head at that time or anything. It was really bothersome to not know what was happening.

Medical Goals

Angela's goal for her interactions with health care professionals reflects a central priority for contemporary health care seekers. As Angela argued, "If a doctor is able to communicate well for the most part, you'll know what's wrong with you, why that's wrong with you, and what you can do to fix that. That's the reason you go to a doctor." Denise concurred, "Well, I think that any time you go to see a doctor, not any time, most of the time, you know, other than like normal appointments, something's wrong, and you want to make it better."

Medical goals refer to all medical activities that occur during or as a result of health care encounters, including assessments of the health care situation, conducting necessary tests/procedures, determining the diagnosis, discussing treatment options, and so on.

According to Lazare and colleagues (1995, p. 4), "the most commonly acknowledged function of the medical interview is to determine the nature of the problem, or to 'make the diagnosis.'"

While health care seekers and professionals might well agree that the accomplishment of medical goals constitutes a core component of measuring a "successful" health care encounter, the nature of medical goals likely depend on medical philosophies and a host of diversity issues for both professionals and seekers. Notably, the definition of "success" stems from orientations to medical goals, such as professional preferences for "patient" compliance and consumer desires to be "cured," often on their own terms.

"Patient" Compliance

When health care professionals invest their time and resources in the care of particular health care seekers, they want those endeavors to be worthwhile. From a biomedical perspective, for example, medical goals often become linked with compliance (see, e.g., Feinberg, 1988; Lewis, 1994; Parrot, 1994). Wadsworth (1976) contends that "from the doctor's point of view success or failure of consultations has been judged in two ways: whether or not patients carried out instructions, and how well they remembered advice, instructions and the diagnosis" (p. 4).

Compliance with Medical Examinations   To even get to the point of diagnosis, though, health care professionals require information, data that can only come from health care seekers' willingness to respond to questions and to permit a physical examination. As I note in *Partnership* and, to some extent in the discussion of stigma in Chapter 2, questions or procedures that threaten the preferred face of the health care seeker (such as revealing culturally taboo information or displaying otherwise private body parts) may lead to seeker silence, anxiety, or apprehension (see especially Emerson, 1970).

For example, Healy (1997) reports that, of the 15 percent of women who conversed with health care professionals about STDs, only 3 percent raised the topic on their own. Likewise, in a letter to the editor of the *Journal of the American Medical Association*, Drs. Squire, K. Huss, and R. Huss (1991) argue that "physicians may incorrectly believe that information of such obvious importance [smoking] will be volunteered, or at least not withheld" (p. 2702). However, a 1997 Genecom survey for the Association of Reproductive Health Professionals indicates that "about 75 percent of women smokers say they don't volunteer that information to their doctors." Additionally, individuals might refrain from revealing information that could point to stigmatized health concerns, despite the likely benefit of gaining treatment/assistance (see Healy, October 5, 1998; Jezierski, 1994).

Especially with gynecologic, breast, and prostate examinations, as well as discussions of mental health issues or addictions, health care professionals and seekers struggle with framing the encounter as "normal," and "not a threat" to preferred identity (see Beck & Ragan, 1995; Beck with Ragan & duPre, 1997; Emerson, 1970; Ragan et al., 1995; Ragan & Pagano, 1987). The interactional framing of health care encounters as a safe, nonjudgmental context is essential to the sharing and seeking of information (see, e.g., Jezierski, 1994). As I detail later, health care participants can reframe such potentially embarrassing and distressing disclosures and examinations; however, without such reframing, health care seekers may choose to avoid sharing relevant information or to refuse necessary examinations.

Compliance with Treatment   Neil recalled his experience with a medical procedure that became more serious after all participants started to react adversely (see related work by Cousins, 1988):

> I think that doctors should be able to understand that parents are going to panic; patients are going to panic, and they [doctors] should be able to deal with the problem. I don't think that he [the doctor] dealt with that very well because my mother and I were panicking. He sort of panicked and just tried to get the tube down my throat and suck everything out. I think that basically he saw us getting on edge, and he got on edge because of that.

In *Partnership*, I tell the story of Mallory, a girl who arrived in the emergency room after swallowing a bottle of sleeping pills. As an ethnographer in the small examining area, I watched the two nurses as the emergency technicians briefed them on Mallory's situation. They focused on setting up equipment, only speaking to Mallory when she had to lift an arm or sit up. I grew increasingly angry as I observed the frightened little girl in the hospital bed. Only the doctor interacted with her when he informed her that the nurses needed to pump her stomach. When she asked if it would hurt, the doctor acknowledged that "it's not comfortable." When she asked for something for the pain, the doctor noted that "I think that you've had enough."

The nurse prepared to insert the tube in Mallory's nose, and Mallory sat up straight and screamed. The nurse said only that the procedure had to happen and that Mallory needed to cooperate. Again, Mallory fought the tube insertion. Then, and only then, did the second nurse explain the procedure to Mallory, offering tips about how to make it easier and gently massaging her arm. The first nurse then inserted the tube in her nose without resistance from Mallory (see Beck with Ragan & duPre, 1997).

Given fear of pain and the unknown, health care seekers may struggle with complying with treatment, even when they originally agree to some course of action. For example, Mark explained his last-minute resistance to a surgery during his struggle with cancer of the larynx:

> [I had] good experiences with my doctor "Hancock" in [a major eastern city]. He's my laryngologist, the specialist, the one that did the laryngectomy. I'm just . . . real compatible with him. I feel like he is a compassionate, caring person. He's always willing to spend time talking things over with me, and that's what I need a doctor to do to help me get through this because I had a lot of fear about going into this surgery. That morning of my surgery, I almost canceled out because I had so much fear. I asked to speak with him before my surgery, and he made it a point to come up and talk to me. He just assured me that I was young enough and healthy enough to go through that surgery and that it was the best thing for me. If I did have the surgery, he couldn't guarantee it, but he thought it was curable if I had the surgery. And I just feel that he was very compassionate and reassuring, and I like that in a doctor.

For seekers who adhere to a more biomedical approach, satisfaction may depend on compliance. Lochman (1983) suggests that ". . . reports of satisfaction were positively associated with adherence to treatment plans" (p. 91). As Sternberg (January 12, 2000) suggests with regard to treatment regimens for HIV, failure to comply with specific prescribed plans hinders health outcomes, thus impacting satisfaction with care.

The difficulty for health care participants stems from the multiplicity of conflicting preferences for medical goals. Health care professionals may strive to gain compliance because they sincerely believe that they know the best course of action for accomplishing wellness. Yet, recommendations may not fit with health care seeker identities, beliefs, lifestyle, family, professional, or social commitments, and so on.

Implications of Consumerism

In our busy lives, we rarely have time to waste. Health care seekers go to a health care professional when we need to do so, perhaps neglecting to do so even after we get bombarded with warning signs. Thus, when health care seekers do schedule appointments, sit in the waiting and examining rooms, and justify spending money as well as time, we want that effort, money, and time to be warranted.

With the advent of consumerism and the explosion of information that is available to health care seekers, though, seekers may believe that they know the "best" way for health care professionals to proceed. Some seekers face the challenge of asserting their own beliefs and preferences (thus implying their own expertise) while depending on the professional (with his or her own expertise) to implement the seeker's plan.

Michael went into the emergency room with the assumptions that "the doctor would thoroughly look me over, x-ray my ankle, and thoroughly examine and go over the x-rays and give me the proper diagnosis." As in Michael's case, Joe became frustrated when the doctor did not comply. Joe recalled:

> The doctor came in and said "How are you doing?" I was like I'm in some pain, damn it. I was really pissed. They [the doctor and nurse] look at me. The doctor looked at my ankle. Obviously, it is in pain. He touched it anyway, though. He said, "We're going to have to get some x-rays." I was like "we can administer some pain medication. Just give me a shot of Demerol. Let's get this underway." I wasn't really nice to the doctor. There wasn't much reason for me to be nice to him up to that point. He proceeded to tell me my alternatives anyway. I told him again, "I just want a shot of Demerol, and that would be fine." I knew that my leg was broken. I thought I was going to have to have surgery. I'm a pretty good judge of medicine. I knew it was broken as soon as I did it. So he came back in. They gave me that shot of Demerol. That kinda sent me out. It made the pain go away. I never had a shot of Demerol before, but when people are in serious pain, that is what they get. It took my mind off of it [the ankle injury] for a little bit. They didn't seem to, like, warm up to me. Maybe because I was kinda frank with them. I can't say that they didn't deserve it. So, they wheeled me into the x-ray room. They took a couple of different x-rays. They put my leg in a couple of different positions. They wheeled me out of the x-ray room. They took me to another room. They just left me in there basically. The doctor came in there a while later. In the meantime, the Demerol put me to sleep. They came in and showed me the x- rays. I looked at them. You could see that my ankle was shattered. I thought, what worse place could I be

with an ankle this bad? All of the bad things you hear with [name of health care facility]. They're almost all true. They really are. They proceeded to wrap it up. I was kinda mean with them again. He did a couple of things to see if it hurt. He did the same thing over two or three times. I told him, if he did it again, I would hurt him. I'm really not a violent person. He was really testing my patience. They proceeded to wrap it in a temporary cast. They gave me something else to put me to sleep just because they didn't want to deal with me.

Joe wanted pain killers because he was in considerable agony due to his injury. The relief of pain became his primary medical goal, yet he also wanted to ensure effective treatment of his leg. Although the health care professionals needed to perform certain tests to determine the extent of his injuries (and thus, to accomplish their primary medical goal of making a correct diagnosis), Joe expressed his goal of pain reduction in a manner that likely conflicted with the health care professionals' ability to ascertain his condition. Given Joe's attitude about the particular health care facility, perhaps Joe's goal of pain relief outweighed his desire for long-term treatment. He might have discounted any proposed diagnosis or treatment by the health care professionals at that facility. In any event, the way in which Joe spoke to the health care professionals (and vice versa) flavored the emergent health care relationship and, potentially, medical outcomes.

For health care seekers and health care professionals, the compatibility of medical goals underlies the extent to which they can work together in realizing those goals. For example, April shared her own decision to switch to a homeopathic doctor who pursued medical goals more holistically. April detailed:

My baby is seeing a homeopathic doctor up in Lancaster. He gives him different remedies when he's [the baby] not feeling well. He's informally diagnosed him with an asthmatic condition, probably from a lot of ventilator use when he was young and that was really intruding on his lungs. A lot of babies that are on ventilators have asthmatic conditions. So he gives him different remedies and tries different things out on him. One remedy has worked really well with him. When we give it to him, it works great. His doctor's viewpoint, like we came in and we had been dealing with a lot of [name of health care facility]'s traditional health care. Then we come to him [the homeopathic doctor], and we're like "okay, our kid's got this genetic syndrome, and this is the problem this is what's going on." He says, "Okay," and grabs all of the information and puts it aside. He was like "so tell me about your pregnancy." He just took a very holistic approach. He's just like taking in every perspective on everything. A little bit from here, a little bit from there, to draw a whole picture instead of just knowing the symptoms.

While April clearly appreciated the holistic approach of the homeopathic doctor, I doubt that she would continue to explore that health care alternative if the baby's treatment did not "work great." Perhaps more than any other goal, individuals want relief from symptoms, an opportunity to return to their "normal" lives. Tina detailed her bout with TMJ:

I can recall one time I had a problem with my jaw. I went to my orthodontist to see what he could do about it, and he diagnosed me with TMJ. It is a ligament problem, and he said he could make a mouth guard that I could wear at night, and it would take care of everything. It would relieve a lot of the stress and pain. The thing is supposed to cost $500. It was just a little piece of plastic you put in your mouth, like a mouth guard, and I wore it for a least a year. It didn't really work, and I still have a problem with it to this day, and the insurance company really wouldn't pay for a lot of it. I found out it was really a waste of money. I was disappointed with that. I have been seeing that doctor since I had braces. I trusted him a lot, and he showed me he didn't really handle that too well.

Summary of Goals

When my wrist started to throb in the late summer of 1996, I sought answers. When I could not shake my fog-like state after my surgery, I reached out for help. For me and the many people who I have discussed or will describe throughout this volume, medical goals motivate us to seek a health care professional's counsel. For the health care professionals whom I have discussed or will discuss, medical goals guide their time with us. However, our mutual concern in terms of seeking and offering help does not always mean that we share philosophies of how medicine "should" work, nor that we manage to share/obtain all of the information that we necessarily need to facilitate care. While medical goals constitute the reason that we go to health care professionals, relational and educational goals permit us to attain our objective to return to "normal," to take back our lives as "well" people.

Accomplishment of Multiple Goals

I pulled the car into McHappy's drive-thru for my daily dose of doughnut power on Monday, January 27. As I sorted through my purse, I couldn't quite figure out where my money was. I thought that I had cash, but I couldn't think right. The objects in my purse blurred together.

I got lucky and pulled a green bill from the depths of my cluttered bag. I handed the dollar to the lady who takes my order almost every morning, and I realized that I didn't know her name. Why didn't I know her name? I looked up and saw that she was staring at me. I glanced in my rearview mirror and noticed three cars behind me. I have got to start concentrating, I said to myself.

I felt so hot and nauseous. I had spent a lot of time in bed over the weekend. Wade had given me quite a hard time about going to bed so early on Friday night, but he finally had agreed to watch the girls for a bit so that I could get some rest. I glanced at the clock as I pulled out of the McHappy's lot—8:00 A.M.; I needed to get to the office. However, as I passed the medical center, I slowed the car down, hesitating while deciding whether to stop. I knew that I just had the flu and, as such, Dr. S. couldn't really do anything for me, but I felt so sick. I had to try something. I turned the car into the parking lot, picked up my doughnut bag and a can of pop, and wobbled through the cold winter air to the front door of the physician office building.

Sick people don't drag doughnuts and Diet Coke around at the doctor's office, I thought, rebuking myself for making a senseless stop when I needed to get to the office. Hey, I'm kind of hungry, I retorted to myself. If I have to wait, I can save time by eating now. Realistically, I wondered whether I could even get in for an appointment on such short notice. I limped to the counter, plunked down my casted arm, and explained my symptoms to the receptionist. She agreed to fit me into Dr. S.'s schedule and turned to prepare the insurance papers. "Have you met your deductible yet?" she inquired. I laughed, nodding and noting that I had also reached my out of pocket limit for the year as well. I can't believe that it's only January, I thought, taking the papers from her outstretched hand.

As I rode up on the elevator to the third floor, I propped myself up against the wall of the elevator. It's just the flu, I thought, chastising myself again for wasting time at the doctor's office when I had so much to do at work. The elevator bell clanged, and I wished that I wore a watch as I checked in with the nurse. I had to be in class by 10 A.M. I hoped that I would not have to wait long.

Fortunately, the nurse worked me in right away. Dr. S. had not seen me since the surgery. As he entered the examining room, he looked at me, with my cast and pale face, and I commented that he should see the other guy. "What's up?" he asked. I overviewed my symptoms, emphasizing my lay diagnosis of the flu and apologizing in advance for taking his time for "nothing."

I stretched out on the cold cot as Dr. S. examined me. I had a fever, and I felt chilled. My hip throbbed, and my head ached. I just wanted a blanket and a pillow and about a thousand hours to sleep. I cuddled deeper in my sweats. (My other pants had not fit over my bandaged hip since the surgery.)

Dr. S. removed the bandage on my hip, and I looked at it with him. "Is it supposed to look like that?" I inquired. My skin bulged around the hip area, red and swollen. "No, no, it's not," Dr. S. responded slowly. He put his hand on my shoulder and told me that we needed to get a blood test immediately. A nurse entered, drew blood, and left me alone once more in the examining room.

Slowly chewing my doughnut, I opened my bookbag and tried to work as I awaited the results. Why couldn't I concentrate? What could be wrong? Images of my second roommate at the hospital flashed through my mind, and I prayed that I did not have some awful disease. Hadn't I been through enough with this process already?

When Dr. S. returned with my results, he seemed concerned. He said, "Your blood counts are very high, and that suggests an infection. You need to get to Columbus to your surgeon immediately." I looked at him, dumbfounded. "I've been to him," I said. "He doesn't believe that anything is wrong with me. I just saw him on Thursday, and I felt this bad then." I realized that I was starting to whine as I continued. "I don't think that he will believe me now either, and I don't have time to keep driving to Columbus just to hear that nothing is wrong with me."

Dr. S. stepped closer to me. "With a blood count like this," he said, "he cannot deny that something is wrong. If he has any questions, he can call me, and we can discuss what's going on with you."

"Can't you just prescribe something?" I asked. I felt so incredibly tired, and the prospect of driving to Columbus was more than I could stand. I didn't know how I would stay awake to get there, and I had a class to teach, a book manuscript to proof, and a Girl Scout meeting at 2:45 P.M. Surely, I could just get a prescription of something to get me through the day.

"Christie, he is the expert on this, and since he handled your surgery, he should be the one to take charge of the case now." Dr. S. shook his head. "Besides," he said, "I think that the infection might have to be surgically drained. You should go prepared to stay the night."

The girls were at school; I was supposed to meet with twelve fifth and sixth graders in six hours; I had class in 45 minutes, and I had nothing with me, nothing packed. I wanted to cry about the possibility of an infection, but I almost dreaded the likelihood of Dr. T.'s denial of my symptoms even more. Was it worth it to drive to Columbus, only to be disconfirmed once more?

Dr. S. made me promise that I would go to Columbus immediately. I wanted to wait until after the scout meeting, but he stressed the need for me to go and "go now." "Keep me posted," he said, as I got up to leave, tossing my now empty doughnut bag and pop can in the trash as I left the room.

I pulled into the parking lot by my school, and as usual, I could not find a parking space. Not thinking about the impact that it might have on other traffic, I drove my car into the alley beside the office building, locked the car, and limped in the door. Sue, the school director, had to know about the new turn of events, and I needed to con Wade into covering the scout meeting for me.

Sue arranged for one of our staff members, Gayle, to drive me to Columbus. Dr. S. had said that he would call up to Dr. T.'s office to let him know that I was coming and to share his concerns and the blood test results. As we traveled up Highway 33, I wondered what would happen when we arrived.

Although the waiting room was packed, Katie took me back to an examining room as soon as we entered the office area. I felt groggy and apprehensive as I waited for Dr. T. and Dr. A. Would he think that I had gone behind his back to another doctor? Would he think that I was taking his time for "nothing"? Would he believe that something was amiss? What, if anything, was really wrong?

"Hi, Dr. Beck," Dr. T. said as he came in the room, shadowed by Dr. A. "What's going on?" he asked. I explained my visit to Dr. S., emphasizing that I had thought that I had the flu but that Dr. S. had conducted this blood test that indicated an infection. Dr. T. said, "Well, at this point, I doubt that you have an infection, but let's take a look."

He removed the bandage from my hip, shook his head, and said, "This did not look this way the last time that I saw you. When was that?" I responded quietly, "Thursday." He sighed. "And your blood count was what?" Dr. T. queried. I couldn't remember. "He said that it was high, but I don't remember the number," I answered. He sighed again and said that he would have to determine the cause of the swelling. Dr. T. told Dr. A. to see if she could extract some type of fluid from my hip area. Apparently, if she could draw a particular type of fluid, I had an infection. If not, perhaps, the problem could be something else.

Before Dr. A. inserted the long needle into my hip area, I thought that the needle would hurt. However, my head started to swim, and I felt nothing. As I looked away toward the opposite wall, I heard her sigh and say that I definitely had an infection in my hip. I needed to go to the hospital immediately to be scheduled for emergency surgery and started on IV antibiotics.

Gayle helped me back into the car, and I shook my head. The clock clicked on to 2:00 P.M. as we drove over to the hospital. The whole day had been surreal. It began with my ordinary routine of grabbing doughnuts and ended with a spot on the surgical schedule. We arrived at the hospital, and I thanked Gayle for the ride. Automatically, I wished her a safe trip back to Athens. I adjusted my bookbag on my shoulder and hobbled into the building alone.

Like other health care seekers, I brought a multiplicity of goals to my visits with Dr. S. and Dr. T. As in other interactions between health care professionals and health care seekers, the ways in which we communicated with each other impacted how we co-defined and co-accomplished our respective individual and mutual objectives for the health care encounter. In particular, each of the following communicative practices works to reflect and reify relational, educational, and medical goals: directives, questions–answers, assertions of knowledge, attempts to legitimize knowledge and perspectives, listening, and disclosures.

Directives

From the moment that the health care professional enters the room to initiate the health care visit, a careful collaboration begins with regard to how relational, educational, and medical activities can occur (see, e.g., Robinson, 1998). As I have discussed earlier (see Beck with Ragan and duPre, 1997), the examining room usually gets treated as the professional's turf wherein health care seekers likely obey preliminary directives to get undressed, to sit here or there, to do this or that, and so on (see, e.g., Mulholland, 1994).

Now undressed and in need of medical attention, health care seekers tend to comply with subsequent instructions, thus implicitly, perpetuating the health care professional's "right" to direct the encounter. To do otherwise, the health care seeker might jeopardize an opportunity to gain health care in a timely manner. He or she does not likely want to "screw anything up" or hinder the process. According to Stacey (1996), "Encounters with doctors—and sometimes with nurses and technicians as well—tend to reduce us to childlike status: anxious to please, afraid of seeming silly, intimidated by authority" (p. 78).

In my case, nurses directed me to examining rooms; the doctors directed physical examinations by telling me to position myself in particular ways at specific times. Notably, I affirmed the health care professionals' "right" to take charge of our interactions by simply complying with the instructions.

Although health care seekers come to the encounter with knowledge about their bodies and their convictions, fears, and insights from other sources, they are relative aliens to the medical office territory. Through the process of mutual framing, in many cases (see Platt, 1995), they tend to get treated (and present themselves) more as polite guests than as active participants in the foreign, sterile confines of examining room walls. Like other health care seekers, I watched as health care professionals prepared equipment, examined me, and talked to other health care professionals. When I heard Dr. T. tell Katie how to construct the cast, I caught myself looking at them, and I diverted my gaze—"polite" guests do not eavesdrop, even when they are the subject of conversation by nearby others. As I shifted my eyes to the opposite wall, I did more than turn my gaze; I took myself out of that interaction. Like Dr. T. and Katie, I perpetuated my status as a passive, rather than active, participant in that talk by avoiding eye contact and by failing to make my voice relevant to the conversation. They seemed to have everything under control.

Questions–Answers

Research attests to the desires of health care seekers for sharing and seeking information (see Beisecker & Beisecker, 1990; Clark & Mishler, 1992; Fisher, 1995; Helman, 1985;

Johnson, 1997; Siegal, 1988; Waitzkin, 1984, 1985, 1991; Waitzkin & Stoeckle, 1976). In fact, according to Putnam, Stiles, Jacob, & James (1985), "Patients want to be understood sometimes even more than they want to be cured, yet numerous studies have documented how rarely physicians allow patients to express their concerns" (p. 75). Watzkin (1984) also suggests in the *Journal of the American Medical Association* that "doctors tend to underestimate patients' desire for information and to misperceive the process of information-giving" (p. 2441) (see also Beisecker & Beisecker, 1990; Cegala, McNeilis, McGee, & Jonas, 1995; Goldberg, Guadagnoli, Silliman, & Glicksman, 1990; Helman, 1985; West & Frankel, 1991).

The practice of question-asking and answering during health care encounters is particularly indicative of asymmetrical framing. As numerous scholars suggest, professionals (especially medical doctors) ask many more questions than the health seekers who come to them with health-related concerns (see, e.g., Aronsson & Satterlund-Larsson, 1987; Frankel, 1984, 1990; May, 1990; Roter, 1984; Tabak, 1988; ten Have, 1991; West, 1984a, 1984b, 1993a; Wolinsky, 1980). Notably, asymmetrical interaction patterns do not inherently equate lack of caring or power plays on the part of health care professionals; as in my case, those patterns could reflect what is "normal" and "acceptable" for individual professionals and/or seekers.

Differential in Obligations

Certainly, some of the asymmetry stems from diverse background knowledge about what issues might be relevant in a given situation, that is, the professional requires particular information in order to ascertain the health concern, and the seeker would not necessarily know what issues might pertain to making a diagnosis or recommended course of action. I did not know anything about cast construction or possible infections. I assumed that the professionals did. I did not know what to ask, and I liked to believe that, as professionals, they would ask questions to gain the information that they needed. However, this position reflects the asymmetrical starting point—the professional implicitly "ought" to determine what "counts" as relevant during health care discussions because of assumed medical knowledge and expertise.

Particularly for people (both professionals and seekers) who behave in a manner that is consistent with the biomedical model, the health care professional should assume the lead without relying on seeker questions; accepting such a position interactionally works to frame the asymmetry as a "normal," "legitimate" part of health care professional responsibilities. For example, Joel explained his belief that "good" health care professionals will automatically provide any necessary information without being asked to do so:

> Good doctors don't—I think good doctors don't wait for a patient to ask the questions; they tell the patient. Like um . . . I know my pediatrician was the nicest man ever. He was one of the ones who would take like the stethoscope and warm it up before he uses it. He was one of those guys. But with him, it was never a question of "What are you going to do with that?" "What's that for?" "What's this test mean?" Because he would tell me before he'd do it, and he was honest too. It wasn't like, "Oh, you know, this isn't gonna hurt at all." He'd tell me, "This is gonna hurt."

Margaret agreed, commenting:

> When I go to the doctor, I'm already sick, so I don't feel like I should have to ask questions about my treatment as far as my medication or my prescriptions or how many days I'm going to be sick. So, I need them to tell me these things, and sometimes they don't, and I don't feel like I should have to ask them because I'm not feeling well at the time.

Differential in Authority

Margo explained that "I've learned to ask specific questions because I get sick so often. So, if I ask specific questions so I don't get sick as much, because I want to know what is going on and why." Limited research indicates that health care seekers do pose more questions when they come prepared to ask (see, e.g., Greenfield, Kaplan, & Ware, 1985; Roter & Hall, 1992; Tabak, 1988; Thompson, Nanni, & Schwankovsky, 1990).

Typically, health care professionals begin health care encounters with their questions. Yet, especially when one or both participants subscribe to a more biomedical model of medicine, the pattern of question–answer, question–answer (with the professional asking and the seeker answering) constrains seeker ability to initiate questions—to break that pattern might be construed and treated as "rude" or an interruption (see Aronsson & Satterlund-Larsson, 1987; ten Have, 1991). Even if seekers try to advance questions tentatively to avoid sounding impolite—for example, "I'm just kind of wondering—this pain couldn't have anything to do with my surgery, could it?"—the question might not be treated as seriously as the underlying concern (see Beck with Ragan and duPre, 1997; duPre & Beck, 1997), prompting frustration by the health care seeker who leaves without a definitive answer (see Roter, 1984).

Even when questions do not get completely ignored, health care professionals and seekers can construct their questions and answers in a manner thaat implicitly discourages future questions and/or positions the inquiries as somehow "inappropriate" or "not something I would normally do," particularly within the context of other professional directives (see West, 1984a, 1984b, 1993a; West & Frankel, 1991). For example, I complained about my hip pain, and Dr. T. shifted the focus of the discussion from my hip to my wrist. The question was interactionally negated.

Depending on the specific relationship between health care professional and health care seeker, health care seekers might opt to silence themselves, deciding that the desired answer is not worth the risk or interactional discomfort. Emily noted that she posed questions:

> . . . if I feel comfortable with asking him questions. Sometimes, doctors are really rushed, or if they are not taking me seriously, I just don't feel comfortable. I just won't say anything. So, it just depends on how approachable they are, or like how bad I want to get out of here, or you know, if I don't like the doctor, I'm not really going to ask too many questions.

Assertions of Knowledge

From that first visit in Dr. T.'s office through my first stay in the hospital, I pretty much accepted Dr. T.'s expertise. Although I asked cautious questions, I empowered him to tell me what he thought that I needed. I did not know how to participate. He seemed to have everything under control.

However, when I started to feel sick, I did have something to contribute. I could share my knowledge of my body, my gut feeling that something was amiss. I knew that I hurt and that I kept falling asleep. I knew that "something" had to be wrong. Yet, when I tried to introduce that topic, I failed. What happened?

Here was a doctor who wanted to involve me so much that he copied research articles for me. Even though I lacked the medical background to grasp the terminology, the fact that he gave me the articles made me trust him even more. He obviously knew what he was doing if he was willing to share research articles with me. Here was a doctor who respected me so much that he referred to me as "Dr. Beck."

Why did I have to work up the nerve to raise the topic with him? Why did I accept his treatment of my concerns and questions, rather than pursuing more information? Why did I downplay my fears even when I visited with my regular doctor, Dr. S., calling my situation "possibly nothing"?

At least part of the explanation can be attributed to my prior interactional patterns with Dr. T., in particular. I permitted him to direct our exchanges, deferring to his medical knowledge, knowledge that I lacked. Only when I really started to get frustrated during the entire process did I violate what we had interactionally co-constructed as "the normal way that we proceed"—an asymmetrical pattern wherein the doctor dictates and I accept.

Importantly, I played a critical role in that co-construction process—I did not pursue information beyond initial expressions of a topic, and I even discounted my own concerns as I revealed them (i.e., maybe I kind of have a problem . . . I feel sorta sick . . . .). I felt more than a little odd about "changing the rules" midstream. Extending from Watzlawick and colleagues (1967), my shift in communication patterns disrupted the carefully constructed system, forcing both of us to address potential alterations in our relational roles and dyadic system.

In her book, *Caring: A Daughter's Story*, Diane Rubin (1982) details her mother's struggle with cancer. At one point, her mother was very uncomfortable and wanted to check with her doctor. However, she wrestled with the decision to call him. Diane overheard her mother on the telephone to Diane's sister, saying " 'I don't want to bother Dr. Daniels, Barbara,' I heard Mother say. 'But I know he's going away and I think he ought to know I'm very weak and coughing and I'm tired' " (Rubin, 1982, p. 124). Ultimately, the other sister (Barbara) did call the doctor so that the mother could describe her symptoms. The mother spoke with the doctor and repeatedly expressed her gratitude for the call. Rubin (1982, p. 124) recalls that she "shrieked" to her mom—". . . stop groveling!" Her mother paused and attributed her approach to a lifelong pattern of interactions with physicians; her apologies to the doctor permitted her to display a preference for the assymetrical relationship, despite her "presumptuous" assertion of knowledge.

As in the case of Betsy Lehman, an award-winning reporter for the *Boston Globe* who focused, ironically enough, on health issues, the failure of health care professionals to respond to such assertions can prove fatal. While undergoing chemotherapy, she sensed that something was dreadfully wrong. According to Stacey (1996), Lehman " . . . begged doctors and nurses to look into it. No one listened. One of her last acts was to leave a message on the answering machine of a social-worker friend . . . , pleading for help in getting her doctors' attention" (p. 78). After her death, investigators discovered that Lehman " . . . had mistakenly been given a massive overdose—four times the prescribed amount of a powerful chemotherapy drug designed to kill off cancer cells" (Stacey, 1996, p. 78).

Through their dismissal of Lehman's concerns, the health care professionals interactionally disconfirmed the validity of her fears and her legitimacy as a source—That is, "we know better therefore she can't be correct." Such positioning of assertions can be relationally and medically critical.

Attempts to Legitimize Knowledge/Perspectives

Notably, health care seekers and professionals may discount or prioritize particular types of information, invite or discourage the perspective of their interactional counterpart, and explore or deter certain options, depending on their respective approach to medicine, time limitations, personality (and perhaps gender and age). For example, consistent with a more biomedical approach to health care encounters, some doctors might even structure "patient" education to encourage compliance with specified recommendations (see, e.g., related work by Grueninger et al., 1995). Melissa reported her doctor's persuasive efforts:

> We wanted more information on vaccinations because we weren't for sure about vaccinating our young, not fully healthy kid yet. She [the doctor] was really for it [vaccinations]. She was like "if anybody needs it, he needs it now." And we weren't into putting, directly putting, poison and sickness into our unhealthy kid and taking that risk. So we asked for information. They brought us some so-called information. I called it propaganda more than anything else. It didn't have any facts or statistics or anything, and that's what I was looking for. And, um, I don't know, she called children's services on us to make sure that we were, um, good parents and taking care of our kid, and he was getting fed and all that stuff. It wasn't a neglect call. It was just like children's services needed to see what was going on.

When Melissa expressed a different opinion of the information than her health care professional, her parenting skills were investigated. When I read this account, I was amazed. Admittedly, I wasn't in the room during the encounter and much more might remain to the complete story; however, I was astonished by the apparent lack of appreciation for Melissa's position. I happen to think that vaccinations help to prevent the spread of disease, especially to innocent little children. Yet, having made that admission, I can still understand Melissa's perspective as a mom with a sick child. I will never forget my reaction when a nurse asked me to sign a waiver for a Hepatitis B vaccination for my newborn, only two hours after her birth. I stalled, called my friend Carolyn (who works in the health care field) long-distance during the day, and checked with my pediatrician before authorizing a vaccination on my precious tiny Chelsea Meagan. I wondered if I should inject a live virus into a little baby who seemed so defenseless.

Although I can appreciate the doctor's perspective—sick babies can be the most susceptible to other illnesses—the doctor rejected the legitimacy of Melissa's position, thus threatening her face and hindering her desire for information. The doctor dismissed Melissa's concerns as "not normal," questioning even her ability to be a "good parent" just because she did not share her doctor's view of the "evidence."

Although the popular press and Internet websites abound with encouragements to empower ourselves by taking initiative (see, e.g., Hittner, 1992; http://www.ahcpr.gov/consumer/surgery.htm), our cultural preferences for politeness also limit our willingness to threaten the face of health care professionals. Only when I was at the end of my rope with frustration and fear later in my case did I refuse to affirm a health care professional's face as knowledgeable and authoritative, and I had just written a book that advocates a partnership approach to health care.

The framing of information as unimportant or even irrelevant impacts the ability of participants to attain particular relational, educational, and medical goals. In *Partnership* (Beck with Ragan and duPre, 1997), I tell the story of "Ellen," a Native American woman who is seeking care for her pregnancy as well as her cough. Ellen introduces her concern about the cough by stating, "She told me um to tell you also about the cold that I've had. I've had it for almost three weeks now." The physician's assistant says, "Okay," and Ellen continues with "started coughing up little blood last night." The physician's assistant responds with "Okay. Birth date?"

In this excerpt, Ellen tries to legitimize the information about the cough by referring to an authority figure (the nurse who took her history), citing the length of time of the cold (almost three weeks), and indicating seriousness of the cough (coughed up blood). The physician's assistant only answers with "okay" twice and moves on to another topic. As Beach (1995) observes, the use of "okay" may enable professionals to "keep the interview 'on track' with 'official' business at hand—a focus on issues treated by clinicians as important that, apparently, patient-initiated actions . . . can essentially sidetrack" (pp. 282–283).

However, by treating this disclosure as a "sidetrack," the physician's assistant diverts discussion about something that could prove critical to what the physician's assistant marks as the primary reason for the visit—the pregnancy. During the conversation, Ellen refers to her cough again; however, on the second occasion, she happens to mention that she has been taking her mother-in-law's prescription cough syrup to resolve the cough. As the physician's assistant explains to Ellen, prescription medicine can hurt unborn children. The physician's assistant then attends to Ellen's educational and medical goals for information and for help by framing her disclosure as "legitimate" and "relevant" to the encounter.

When I wrote about Ellen in my prior work, I was disturbed by Ellen's lack of assertiveness and by the physician's assistant's implicit dismissal of Ellen's information. After my own health care experience, I understand Ellen's position a bit better. Although she obviously felt that something was wrong, she did not trust her information over the health care professional's, at least enough to pursue the matter directly. I will never forget walking into Dr. S.'s office and apologizing for taking his time to tell me that I had the flu. I just assumed that I must have the flu and that nothing else could be wrong because my situation had been treated as "nothing" by Dr. T. As Gilda Radner and Anne Frahm and others have discovered, "nothing" can be a frightening and contradictory casting of information for health care seekers who fear that "nothing" is truly "something."

As health care professionals and seekers frame health care interactions more holistically, they broaden the definition of what types of information might be construed as "relevant" or "legitimate" for health care interactions. Further, both health care professionals and seekers need to co-define what information is really needed and what is "legitimate" to seek and share. As Mathews (1983) argues, "the extent to which patients and practitioners successfully exchange information is affected by the degree to which their realities are mutually compatible" (p. 1371).

In *Partnership*, I argue for a dialogic approach to education (see Beck with Ragan and duPre, 1997 as well as related work by Anderson, Cissna, & Arnett, 1994; Arnett, 1992; Baxter & Montgomery, 1996; Geist & Dreyer, 1993; Hellstrom, 1998). To accomplish a dialogue, participants must construct issues by facilitating mutual input. For such an approach to work, both participants must (1) truly want to hear the other person's concerns and perspectives, (2) truly believe that each person must contribute to the accomplishment of the multiple goals of the encounter, and (3) truly work to frame the encounter so that both 1 and 2 will be evident.

Listening

According to Rowland-Morin and Carroll (1990), ". . . within limits, greater silence time would generally be associated with greater information transfer, more positive patient feelings of being well understood, and lower levels of physician dominance" (p. 181). One of our interview participants, Jessica, received a prescription from her doctor that contained medication to which she was allergic, after making it a point to tell her doctor about her allergy. He apologized, noting that he did not "hear her."

Jane argued that health care professionals need to listen to health care seekers and to affirm the knowledge and insights of health care seekers:

> . . . when I was about nine years old, my appendix ruptured, and my mother was an EMT (emergency medical technician) so she figured that was the problem. And she went into the emergency room and told them that, and the doctor on call said, "no, it's just the flu." They left me in the hospital for twelve hours or so. By that time, it was like ruptured, gangrene, and I practically died because this doctor did not listen to what my mother was saying. I mean, he just expected that my mother was stupid, and she just didn't know. And when my actual doctor from home came in, he said, you know, immediately, get this girl to surgery.

Disclosures

The practices of seeking and sharing of information contribute to how a wide range of relational, educational, and medical goals get framed and realized by the participants (see, for example, Hensbest & Stewart, 1990; Wartman, Morlock, Malitz, & Palm, 1983). For example, as Clark and Mishler (1992) maintain, the encouragement of patient stories provides rich opportunities for developing the professional–seeker relationship, fostering chances for clarifying issues, and facilitating care within the context of the seeker's lived realiy. Kim felt that her health care professional missed an opportunity to understand her situation by focusing on her foot injury. Kim recalled that "the doctors and nurses didn't talk to me. All they did was look at my foot. They didn't really care what or how it had happened."

By compartmentalizing Kim's problem, the health care professionals missed an opportunity to contextualize the "problem" (as well as any proposed "solutions") in terms of her life. Further, as in similar situations, the health care professionals miss the chance to cast themselves more widely than "just a doctor"; they could enable health care seekers to peek beneath the doctor role to get a glimpse of the person who enacts the role.

In earlier works, I contend (see Beck & Ragan, 1995; Beck with Ragan and duPre, 1997; duPre and Beck, 1997; Ragan et al., 1995) that disclosures by health care professionals permit professionals to communicate commonality with health care seekers, contributing to a common ground (see Burke, 1969). Joel mentioned that he did not mind revealing information to his doctor because "he [the doctor] is a very personable man. I know about his personal life. I know about his family—his children. Things that are going on in his life—his interests, and we often share these during office visits."

As Joel's account indicates, reciprocity of information sharing (as well as information seeking) enables health care professionals to broaden their relational frame beyond rigid traditional medical roles. In so doing, the offering of personal stories and experiences by health care professionals impacts relational goals as well as educational and medical ones, especially if health care seekers feel more comfortable as a result.

Caring Communication Through Identification

Throughout my health care crisis, I tried to ask good questions and to sort through information. Because I experienced a number of different types of relationships with diverse types of health care professionals, I spent a lot of time trying to discern what is appropriate and what was normal in particular scenarios—what can I ask? How far can I push for answers? How much expertise did the particular professional possess in certain areas? How was I expected to act? How should I expect particular professionals to respond to me? How could I get others to affirm my concerns? How could I best seek care?

When I arrived at the hospital, I limped into admissions and told them that I had been sent over by my doctor's office for emergency surgery. The admissions lady was sympathetic, saying "oh you poor thing." She worked with me to get a private room and found me a wheelchair.

I felt tired, but calm. They had discovered the problem, I thought. They would clean out the infection and send me on my way. As I reflect on my experience now, I marvel that I was not angry or more frightened. Although I was not happy to discover that I had an infection, in a strange way, I felt relieved to know that I wasn't crazy. I hadn't imagined my symptoms; something had really been wrong.

A patient care associate wheeled me to my room, as I held my bookbag and purse once again on my lap. I sighed in relief as he pushed me into a spacious private room with a window. He wished me well. I sat in the wheelchair and realized that I should call someone. No one knew that I was about to have surgery other than Gayle. I should call my mom, I thought. I should check in at the office. Wade had agreed to cover the scout meeting so he possibly wouldn't be home yet, I figured, struggling to concentrate on the numbers on the clock. When the nurse came in to prepare me for surgery, I asked to make some calls first. The events of the day started to overwhelm me. I remembered that I had not eaten since that doughnut. The realization brought hunger. Maybe I can get something to eat after I come out of surgery, I thought. I knew that they could not feed me before.

I lay on the bed and picked up the phone. Mom freaked. My co-workers already knew about the surgery because Gayle had updated them upon her return. I had just left a message on Roger's machine and the machine at home when the nurse returned. I had to hurry, she said. They wanted to take me down to surgery right away.

As the patient care associate wheeled me through the corridors, I looked up at those ceiling tiles again. How incredibly surreal, I thought. Unlike the frenzy of early morning surgical schedules, the surgical floor was quiet. The patient care associate placed my gurney against a wall and told me that they would be with me soon. I tried to relax, and the ethnographer in me started to think about the wonderful data collection opportunities that I had been afforded—the ultimate participant observation. I turned my head to look up and down the hallway. Except for a rare surgical team member, the corridor was empty, except for me. I listened to the silence and tried to think about data, rather than my hunger and fear.

I continued to wait. I lacked a watch and could not see a clock. I felt chilly, and I wanted to go to the bathroom before the surgery. No one came by. I started to get the weird sense that everyone had gone home and forgotten about the skinny girl from Athens with the infected hip who lay alone in the hallway. After a while, that sense spiraled from a passing thought to a real fear. It had been so long since I had seen someone. Okay, I thought to myself. If I don't see someone in the next few minutes (as though I had any way of knowing time), I would heave myself off of the gurney and drag my hip and IV to find someone.

As I strategized my plan, someone entered the hallway from one of the operating rooms. "Hi, I'm Dr. X.," he said as he walked toward me. "I'm sorry that we're backed up in the OR. It'll be a little bit still." Like I had anywhere to be, I reflected—I was just pleased to see another person on the floor. "That's okay," I said.

He had a reason for checking on me. "I'm going to assist with your anesthesia," he said. He asked me the typical questions about allergies and so on, and somehow the conversation turned to me, where I was from, what I did. We talked about Ohio University for a while because he graduated from the College of Osteopathic Medicine and then decided to pursue a speciality in anesthesiology. The cost of private practice as a family doctor had been too high, he explained. See, I thought to myself, a great data opportunity—wonderful information about the inner workings of the health care industry. I should almost be grateful for the turn of events . . . almost.

Dr. X. left, and I happened to see a patient care associate down the hall. I flagged him down and asked if he could help me to a bathroom somewhere. Ironically, he recognized me from my earlier surgery. He had assisted in my care on the second day. "What are you doing here?" he inquired. "Well, it seems that I have some sort of infection in my hip," I replied. "Oh man, that sucks," he said. "You wouldn't believe how often that happens. I am so sorry. You must be ticked." I smiled at him as he helped me down from the gurney, and I tried to grab the back of my gown together while managing the IV pole and my sore hip. "I'm not mad," I said. However, as I eased into the bathroom, I realized that it was nice for someone to think that I had a right to be.

"Caring" as "Empathy"

According to Montgomery (1993), health care professionals need to be in the business of "caring." However, what does it mean to "be caring"? A traditional conception of "caring" involves attending to the emotional needs of others. For example, like Montgomery (1993), researchers have emphasized "empathy" as a key part of "caring" by health care professionals (see Hornblow, Kidson, & Ironsides, 1988; Olson, 1995). In perhaps the simplest terms, to empathize is to sympathize with another person's perspective. To not empathize is to dismiss or disconfirm another person's perspective. Jodi engaged in a negative interaction when her health care professional rejected her reactions to pain:

> He basically told me that I was a wimp and that cramps really aren't real and that I need to suck it up, and I need to take um I need to take aspirin or something like that. And I told him, I said, well, you don't get it. You're a guy, you know. You don't know what cramps feel like. And he . . . he was just . . . he was pretty much a jerk about it. He didn't think I had cysts, and when I told him that most women have cramps when he asked me how it felt, I was like, well, you know most women have cramps. He's like "not all women have cramps and a minority of women have cramps." And I was like "you don't know, you know, you're a doctor" and he was like "fine. I'll check, you know. I don't think you have anything bla bla bla." So he went and got one of the nurses, and we just had like a basic check, a female check, but he was a complete jerk about it. He would, like, throw things around. He was just really ticked that he had to do anything with it. And then he sent me . . . he sent me to go get some pills and that was about it. He was just pretty much a jerk.

Need for Mutal Understanding

Clearly, the health care professional did not work with Jodi to frame the complaint as "normal," nor did he engage in behaviors that would facilitate face preservation during the examination. In fact, given Jodi's account, the health care professional overtly discounted Jodi's complaint and made the examination physically and emotionally uncomfortable for Jodi. He did not attempt to offer Jodi an "out" for her physical and emotional concerns, and he chose not to acknowledge her pain, even if he did not believe that the pain stemmed from cysts. Cassell (1999) argues that "making a diagnosis of suffering . . . differs from the usual diagnostic process . . . because suffering is an affliction of the person not the body" (p. 531). For multifaceted, complex individuals, the onset of physical challenges can be painful as well as terrifying, disconcerning, and annoying, perhaps interfering with work performance, family commitments, and overall enjoyment of life.

When Doctor J. dismissed my wrist pain, he did not just hinder my treatment. He disregarded my frustration that I couldn't hold Chelsea, that I couldn't grasp a pen, that I could think of little else. Like Jodi's doctor, Dr. J. just didn't get it; he didn't try to understand. As Cassell (1999) contends, "it is the nature of the person and the specific threats to their personhood that determine the nature of suffering" (p. 534). Somehow, health care participants must co-accomplish a common understanding of and orientation to the health care concern and its impact on life tasks and medical options (see related work by Thompson, 2000; Whaley, 2000).

Impossibility of Complete Understanding

Jodi attributed the health care professional's approach to the fact that he was "just a man" who "could not understand" a female condition. As I will detail in the chapter on diversity, some scholars suggest that female health care professionals can identify more readily with female health care seekers than male health care professionals can with female seekers (see, e.g., Fisher, 1993; Todd, 1993). For example, female health care professionals can refer to "our problems," "our cycles," and to any number of common physical issues when those issues become relevant during discussions with female health care seekers (see examples in Beck & Ragan, 1995; Beck with Ragan and duPre, 1997; Ragan et al., 1995). Through such pronoun selection, professionals can indicate a common ground—"we are both females, and I can understand and identify with your concerns and needs. Because of that connectedness, I can care for you and about you."

While that pronoun selection, for example, works to create and perpetuate "commonality," though, individuals can never completely share realities (see Burke, 1969). Burke (1969, p. 22) argues that the inherent *division* between individuals necessitates the accomplishment of *identification*. Through artful communicative practices, individuals can transcend divisiveness, despite ongoing distinctions between them. Burke (1969) maintains that "A is not identical with his colleague, B. But insofar as their interests are joined, A is *identified* with B. . . . In being identified with B, A is 'substantially one' with a person other than himself" (p. 20).

Even in the case of health care participants with the same sex, those individuals may enact gender differently. Although gender research indicates some patterns, the postmodern splintering of social roles and self-presentations hinders static (or even consistent) co-definitions of "what a normal or legitimate female will do in this situation" (see Haraway, 1995). Further, the health care participants are not simply females. They come to health care encounters amid a plethora of influences (co-cultural involvements, fear, diverse knowledge bases, mixed ideas about "how things should work here," etc.) and a conglomeration of identities—female, professional/seeker, mother, and so on. Because female professionals are both professionals and females, their respective enactments of "female" as "professional" (or vice versa), combined with their many other identities, frames how they will perform "being a female," "being a professional," and so on. They make connections with health care seekers in some areas but lack orientation in others.

Given such diversity, couldn't we make the legitimate argument that no one can truly "understand" our individual feelings and reactions because no one is "like us"? At a time when individuals feel increasingly fragmented, empathizing with others becomes more difficult. We can't really know what someone else experiences. We can't know what they feel, emotionally, physically, or spiritually. Outside of my skin, no one else could feel my wrist or hip pain. Until something could be seen or felt, it could be discarded or discounted by others as "not there" or "not that bad."

Thus, accomplishing complete mutual understanding, a solid common ground, may prove elusive. Acculturation in medical cultures may work to exacerbate distinctions or enhance connectedness, depending on the social construction of health care relationships. For example, the extent to which health care participants share understanding of medical terms and procedures impacts the achievement of common ground (see Hadlow & Pitts, 1991; Thompson & Pledger, 1993; Whaley, 2000). Issues of diversity and fragmentation complicate the ability to understand varying perspectives and needs.

Reconceptualizing "Caring"

Hallstein (1999) suggests that traditional conceptions of "caring" focus on emotional connections—"I feel your pain," to borrow from President Clinton. However, just as we know that people can and do feel for us and for our health care sagas, we also know that those well-meaning health care professionals cannot truly know "our pain." Diseases, people, and circumstances simply differ too much.

If we can't rely on empathy alone for caring in postmodern health care, how can we frame health care encounters as "caring"? Borrowing in part from Hallstein (1999), I believe that "caring" necessitates an artful combination of affirmation and empowerment. Grounded in postmodern theory, Hallstein (1999) argues for adding reasoning, narrative, and argumentation to empathy for a more comprehensive conception of caring. As I read Hallstein's (1999) assertion, I wondered about the role of argumentation in caring and, especially, in health care encounters. As Jodi, the woman who experienced dismissal of her complaint about cramping, discovered, an argument would be about the last thing that someone needs when she or he is ill. I am unsure of Hallstein's exact intent in choosing the word "argumentation"; however, I will use it in this book to suggest that "caring" professionals enable health care seekers to struggle with both sides of issues. They can serve as facilitators for health care seekers by encouraging them to debate the merits of health care decisions as well as the ways in which they decide to live with their health situations. In the end, caring should involve enabling others to frame their health care experiences in a productive and proactive manner.

Notably, the process of co-constructing "caring" necessarily involves participation by both health care professionals and health care seekers as needs get displayed and affirmed and information gets introduced and discussed. Health care professionals cannot "just know" that health care seekers hold particular beliefs or prioritize certain information. While health care professionals need to ask artful questions, they cannot inquire about everything, and health care seekers need to collaborate by sharing information and posing questions, even when they lack words to articulate specific issues of interest. Moreover, both health care professionals and seekers should show "caring" by taking information seriously, even when they disagree on the merits of that information. Mutual "caring" comes with mutual "respect." Ideally, the framing of health care interactions should permit health care seekers to gain perspective and to feel affirmed and liberated to participate in the process.

Enacting "Caring"—Humor as an Exemplar

Increasingly, health care professionals utilize humor to facilitate such framing (see e.g., Beck with Ragan & duPre, 1997; duPre, 1998; Pizzini, 1991; Ragan, 1990; Saunders, 1998; Sparta, January 28, 1999; Wloszczyna, January 4,1999; Wooten, 1998a, 1998b). From micro-level verbal play during gynecologic exams (see Beck with Ragan & duPre, 1997; Ragan, 1990) to the outrageous antics of hospital clowns like Patch Adams (Adams with Mylander, 1998; Sparta, January 28, 1999; Wloszczyna, January 4,1999), advocates argue that people react to humor physically and emotionally.

Humor accomplishes more than just a good laugh, though. Through humor, health care professionals can demonstrate their concern for patients as people while permitting them to reframe their orientation to given situations. In a *USA Today* article, Dr. Dizzy (aka Tim Anderson), a clown from the Big Apple Circus, notes that parents of seriously ill children have told him—"I saw my child not as someone who is sick. I realized for the first time he's still there" (Sparta, January 28, 1999, p. 8D).

In an article about the hit movie, *Patch Adams*, Wloszczyna (January 4, 1999) refers to a "pool of noodles," "an enema bulb," and "angel wings" (p. 4D) when describing how Patch prompted laughter from people who didn't have a lot to chuckle about in their lives. As Adams emphasizes in his book, laughter enables people to embrace life, even during difficult circumstances (Adams with Mylander, 1998).

However, even humor requires an artful sensitivity to the needs, preferences, orientations of the other. A successful enactment of humor demonstrates affirmation of the other person while reflexively offering an alternative perspective. Humor reflects "caring" because the other person takes the time to listen to expressions of needs, to provide a humorous possible reframing of fears and other realities, and to adapt to the other's reactions.

Certainly, humor is not the only way to accomplish caring interactions between health care professionals and health care seekers. However, humor constitutes a good example of "caring" that goes beyond simple acknowledgment of a concern or expression of sympathy for situations. Humor involves collaboration between health care participants as they co-construct the instance of laughter in relation to the potential laughable. Humor offers emotional and physical relief to the health care seeker, and perhaps most important, humor enables the participants to frame their health care encounters, their relationships, and their health care experiences in creative and unique manners. Humor permits health care participants to co-accomplish "caring" in often sterile and uncaring places.

CLOSING THOUGHTS

As I was working on this book and reflecting on my health care experiences, I reviewed all of the information that I had requested from the doctors and hospitals. My operative report, dated January 27, 1997, detailed the operative findings:

> The incision was opened up. In the deep tissues between the iliac crest bone graft and the hip musculature, the patient had a large absess. This abscess was sent to cultures of antibiotics. . . . The patient will be admitted for IV antibiotics. She will be started on triple antibiotics including Flagyl, Vanco and Gentamicin. Once the culture results are back, she will be placed on the appropriate single dose antibiotic. The plan is she will have antibiotic whirlpools to that hip area. Planned hospital stay until the erythema resolves.

To this day, I do not know how I developed a post-operative infection. Until I started this research, I had no idea how common such infections are nor how dangerous they can be. Although the risk of infection was revealed but downplayed by the doctor and the resident (i.e., I just needed to give a "quick signature" on the "standard form"), the Centers for Disease Control and Prevention report that 1.8 million hospital patients contract an infection, resulting in approximately 70,000 annual deaths (see Yoffe, November 14, 1999). In my case, I had developed a staphylococcus aureus infection, a serious post-op infection with a fatality rate of up to nearly 60 percent (see Blot, Vandewoude, & Colardyn, 1998).

As I look back on this chain of events and the ones that I will continue to describe, I do not think that communication could have prevented the staph infection. However, I do believe that the ways in which all of the health care professionals and I interacted during my health care saga impacted my ability to pursue and realize important relational, educational, and medical goals.

Importantly, my health depended on the ways in which health care professionals and I co-constructed our conversations (as well as our respective roles during interactions), the ways in which we legitimized/discounted information, and the ways in which "caring" was displayed. My concerns over hip pain and fatigue did not get treated as priorities (and, to some extent, realities) because the focus of my interactions with Dr. T. was on my wrist, the presumably primary health care concern.

Although I was surprised at the lack of attention to possible infection (especially given the frequency of post-operative infections) by my surgeon, I can understand his tunnel vision. I had hired him to rebuild my wrist, and he had spent considerable time in surgery, carefully crafting my new wrist via complicated and artful procedures. The hip was just a donor site—a means to a greater end and not a subject of focus.

In this era of specialization, care has become compartmentalized, resulting in missed symptoms by health care professionals who simply are not equipped to recognize problems beyond their area of expertise and/or who take a narrow perspective on their role in the care process—just a surgeon, just an anesthesiologist, and so on. As my family practitioner, though, Dr. S. knew me well enough to know that something was wrong. He validated my concerns by exploring them, not dismissing them.

However, my situation was, of course, not that simple, nor were these very complicated health care relationships. Consistent with the literature on health care seeker preferences (see Hjortdahl & Laerum, 1992; MacStravic, 1994; Rost, Roter, Bertakis, & Quill, 1990), I would have preferred to work with one health care professional whom I could trust throughout the entire saga so that I could ensure continuity of care and holistic understanding. I would have preferred to avoid delays and long trips to Columbus. I would have preferred to share my concerns with health care professionals who affirmed my perspectives and who acknowledged my pain. I would have preferred to seek health care options, rather than fight through red-tape and institutional hierarchies.

My desires for health care experiences resemble those of many other health care seekers—simple, clear, collaborative. Yet, as I will continue to detail throughout the book, and especially in the next chapter, the complexities of postmodern health care relationships preclude simplicity, clarity, and occasionally, collaboration. Because health care seekers must often meet with multiple health care professionals (perhaps from disparate philosophies of health care) on diverse health issues, especially with the advent of managed care and medical specializations, health care professionals and health care seekers face great challenges in constructing their health care encounters so that both parties can attain their respective relational, educational, and medical goals.

4

Industry Relationships— Movement to Managed Care

Like a frightened little girl, I frantically pushed the buttons on the phone. "Mom?" A groggy voice responded with "Yes?" and then "What? What's wrong?" When I was in college, I competed on the speech and debate teams, and I would call Mom as soon as I got home from trips to report the tournament results. She used to be able to tell how well I did from the sound of my voice. I doubt that I ever woke her then with the tone of terror that I did on that Tuesday night/early Wednesday morning from my bed in the hospital.

"Mom, my whole arm is turning black and blue. I don't think that she knows what she is doing. No, no, I KNOW that she doesn't know what she's doing, and I'm all alone, and they're going to put a tube in my throat, and I'm sure that they don't know what they're doing. I don't know what to do. Mom, I don't know what to do, and I can't understand what's going on. Mom, they don't know what they're doing at all." I rushed the words as though my very life depended on forcing them from my lips into the phone.

"Christie, what is going on there? What's happening?" Mom pressed me for information. Earlier that day (Tuesday, my first full day of fighting the infection in the hospital), I had dismissed her concerns and discouraged her impulses to race to my bedside from her home in northern Indiana. I was doing fine, I assured my worried mom. I simply needed some antibiotics, and I would soon be as fit as a fiddle. Only hours later, I was too caught up in my own emotions to care about positive, optimistic reassurances for distant others, even my poor mom.

I gulped air and choked out words. "My IV got clogged or something and stopped around 7 o'clock, but my friend Roger had just arrived from Athens so I asked if we could start it again after his visit. The nurse said okay. All right, well, he left about 9:30 or so, and I buzzed for the nurse to come back and start the IV."

I started to cry again, and my entire body shook. I hadn't slept much at all, and I had only had a bit of food much earlier that day, and I was hungry. I could feel the start of a good caffeine headache to boot. I wanted to go home. I yearned to get out of bed, swing through a McDonald's drive-through for a super-sized Diet Coke with a quarter pounder with cheese extra value meal, go home to my girls, and sleep for a month.

"Christie, honey, what happened? What is wrong?" My poor mother pressed again, searching for the source of trouble in my broken and rambling telephone SOS.

"Okay," I started again. "I waited and waited, and this nurse finally came in, but she wasn't the nice nurse who had said that she could start it again after Roger left. She was this different nurse. I guess that the other lady got off of her shift or something. I don't

know. They're all in and out of here, and I never know who's going to come through that door next, or who is working or . . ." I buckled over in my bed as waves of sobs overtook me. I clutched the phone like a life preserver.

"Christie, Christie, are you there? What is wrong?" My mother waited for a minute, hearing only uncontrollable crying on my end of the line. "Do I need to come over there now? What is wrong?"

I lifted the receiver back to my mouth and fought for words. "So, this nurse comes in, and she looks like that awful nurse in One Flew Over the Cuckoo's Nest, *and she starts fiddling with the needles." I struggled to stop shaking and to get through my account. "She tries to insert a needle to start the IV, and she can't get a vein. Mom, I have GREAT veins. I run; I work out. EVERYONE ELSE says that I have great veins. I NEVER have a problem giving blood, and no one else EVER has a problem starting an IV on me. Well, this lady says that I have lousy veins. Mom, she kept blaming it on my veins." Tears flooded down my face.*

"She kept blaming WHAT on your veins?" Mom asked.

"Mom, she kept jabbing me and jabbing me, and she couldn't get the IV started. I was patient at first, but she tried until around eleven and couldn't get it, and my arm was start-ing to hurt. So, I looked at her, right? I tried to suggest that she go in at an angle, like all the other people do. She was trying to get the IV started by plunging the needle straight down at my arm. Can you believe it? I was telling HER how to do it." Anger and frustra-tion with the nurse's apparent incompetence overwhelmed me. I leaned my head back against the pillow. I felt so very tired, physically exhausted and emotionally spent. I wanted to go home. I wished that someone could come and take me home.

I inhaled deeply. I craved control and perspective, but calm evaded me. My trembling hand vibrated the receiver as I finally continued, "You know what she said? She said that she didn't see why the hospital had to get rid of the people who used to come around and do the blood work stuff. She said that she wasn't equipped to deal with people who had veins like mine. Mom, veins like mine? Mom, I have GREAT veins. EVERYONE says that I have great veins."

"All right, well, did the nurse get the IV started?" Mom asked.

"NO, no, she kept trying and trying. She kept blowing veins and saying, 'Well, that vein won't work now.' Mom, my whole arm is turning colors, and I have to preserve at least one good vein in case I have that line thing, and I only have TWO veins left. I wasn't going to let her take a chance on that second vein. If they blow all of my veins on my left arm, and they don't have my right arm, they're going to have to put a tube down my neck. Mom, they're going to cut open my throat, and they don't know what they're doing!"

"Okay, why can't they use your right arm for the IV?" Mom asked tentatively.

"BECAUSE I HAVE THE CAST ON THAT ARM, DON'T YOU GET IT?" I screamed into the phone. No one "got it." No one could help.

"Please try to settle down," my mom responded. "I'm just trying to understand. Now, what is this about a line thing?"

"Dr. T. thinks that I need to have something called a PICC line so that I can have IV antibiotics at home for eight weeks," I answered. Steady, I tried to coach myself—try to relax and think.

"Oh my goodness, is this infection that serious?" Mom asked.

"Oh, Mom, I don't know. On the one hand, they all seem to treat this like it's not a big deal, just a routine thing. And then Dr. T. suggests this line, like it's important so I don't know. Anyway, that's not the point. The point is that I don't want to have a tube down my neck because people don't know what they're doing because the hospital is trying to save money by not having blood people doing the blood work. How could they get rid of the blood people? I don't even know if that nurse has been trained or not. She didn't know what she was doing."

"How did you get her to stop?" Mom inquired.

"After so long, I got her to give me a break for a bit. It was almost one in the morning! When she came back into the room, I basically told her that I knew that she was trying, but that she obviously didn't know what she was doing and that I needed to preserve those veins and that she needed to send in someone who knew what she was doing." I took a long, deep breath. Calm, I thought, be calm. *"She wasn't happy, but she left."* I paused, and despite my best efforts, tears started to swell in my eyes again. *"She hurt me so bad. Why couldn't she admit that she didn't know? Why couldn't she have called for help? Why doesn't anybody know anything here?"* I felt dizzy and drained; however, I was mostly terrified. What if no one could get an IV to work on me? What if they needed to cut open my throat to do a main line? How had I come to this point from a wrist surgery?

"Do you want me to come over or to call someone?" Mom was starting to sound stressed now, and I certainly did not want her to make a four-hour drive from Indiana in that condition, especially not during the middle of the night. Her offer to call *"someone"* was nice and well-intended, but it helped little. After all, who would she call? I was right there in the hospital, and I couldn't even figure out who was in charge or who would know what to do. Mom couldn't help. *"No,"* I answered. *"I'll figure it out here. Thanks for listening to me rant like a lunatic. I just needed to get it out."*

I slowly hung up the phone after promising that everything would be all right. Would it? Not even my mom could assist me now—not so far away, not at two in the morning. She didn't know anything about IVs or infections or hospitals. I guess I knew when I placed the call that she couldn't do much for me from Indiana, except to listen. I felt so lonely. If nothing else, the call enabled someone to be with me during my crisis for at least a few precious minutes. I closed my eyes and waited. I tried to remember stuff from Lamaze to quiet my nerves. Breathe in, breathe out, focus on something, some happy thought, a peaceful place. Breathe in, breathe out . . . ocean sounds . . . dolphins leaping in and out of the mist of sparkling waves. . . .

Footsteps—I felt my body stiffen and my heart start to race as I heard people approaching—so much for Lamaze. I watched as a different nurse entered, followed by the one who had been working on me. I could only imagine what the second nurse had been told by the first one—*"the patient in Room 510 is really difficult. She even threw me out of her room. She was totally uncooperative."*

The second nurse and I exchanged greetings while the first nurse and I pointedly avoided eye contact. The first nurse spoke only to the second nurse. *"Her veins roll,"* the first said to the second. The first nurse continued, *"If she had lain still, I could have gotten it. Then, she got tense, and it made matters worse. I could have gotten the IV started, but she demanded that someone else try. Apparently, they are trying to get her to do a PICC line. If she had agreed to that procedure today, none of this would have happened tonight."*

I lay still. I decided not to speak in my own defense. I only wanted the second nurse to start the IV. I couldn't offend her. At nearly two in the morning or so, I had already lost around seven hours of IV drugs, and I didn't know who would be available to start the other type of IV, if this new nurse could not access one of the veins on my left arm. The second nurse looked at me. I wondered if she could see the fear and frustration in my eyes. "Thank you," she said to the first nurse. "If you can check in on Room 521, I'll see what I can do here."

I extended my arm and prayed. Please let her find a vein . . . please let her be able to get it started . . . please don't let her hurt me. . . . "

"I got it," the second nurse said after her first attempt at inserting the needle. I opened my eyes and watched as she bandaged the area around the IV needle and checked the fluid bags. "Your veins do roll a little. That can make it tough to do sometimes," the second nurse noted. "Yeah," I replied, barely daring to move or speak. She encouraged me to agree to the PICC line and bid me a good night. "If you need anything else, just call," she said as she left. Just call, I thought. I longed for such simplicity. For the rest of the night, I concentrated on lying motionless, and I prayed that I would do nothing to jar the needle that allowed the vital drugs to flow into my vein and through my weakened body.

In this chapter, I begin by discussing our societal quest for efficiency and then describing the implications of a McDonaldized enactment of health care. I close with an analysis of our redefined health care industry relationships, particularly with regard to the impacts of consumerism and economics for health care participant relational dynamics.

Our Quest for Efficiency

Throughout my sagas with my wrist and then the staph infection, I just wanted to get well. No, to be honest, I did not *just* want to get well. I wanted to get well in the most efficient manner, with the least pain, the least cost, the least time, the least hassle. Throughout my ordeal, I assessed my health care professionals on their ability to get their jobs done swiftly and effectively. I watched them skeptically to determine if they "really" knew what they were doing by the ways in which they treated me and performed procedures, and I carefully noted how the professionals referred to and spoke with each other. Could Doctor XX or Nurse YY be trusted? Did she or he seem to be respected and respectable?

I quickly grew wary of those who did not demonstrate knowledge and competence rapidly. In the incident with the IV insertion, I believed that, if the nurse truly "knew what she was doing," *then* she would surely be able to start the IV. Because that first nurse failed to start the IV promptly (or even to employ techniques that I recognized from my lay experiences) and the second nurse inserted it on the first try, I concluded that the first nurse "obviously" did *not* know what she was doing. The second nurse's comment that my veins did "roll a little" seemed to be an awkward excuse for the first nurse's incompetence.

Granted, my evaluation of the first nurse might not have been fair or necessarily correct. Nonetheless, that judgment impacted my emotions and my reactions to that situation as well as to that particular nurse. My desires for and expectations of certain types of health care service flavored how I viewed that encounter (and others during my bout with the wrist and staph infection) as well as how I responded to various professionals during our interactions.

I would argue that I am not alone in my quest for efficient treatment from doctors, nurses, therapists, insurance agency representatives, and so on. Sister John Gabriel wrote in 1935 that "still under the strain of an abnormal, sensitive, emotional state caused by his sickness and his new environment, the patient will scrutinize [health care professionals] very carefully, and perhaps very skeptically. . . ." As I suggested in Chapter 3, health care seekers are more consumer-oriented than ever before.

Similar to other aspects of our overcommitted lives, we want the best quality health care for the least possible cost and time. Our lives charge forward like an uncontrollable freight train, and we dare not pull the cord to stop. A great friend of mine recently told me that she was more frustrated than frightened by her bout with melanoma because the stitches from her surgery kept her from pitching in an important softball game. I took my book manuscript into the hospital with me during my staph infection treatment so that I could try to get some work done and beat a deadline. Herzlinger (1997) describes one of her friends who phoned her excitedly with news of a time-saving pharmacy. The friend, who juggles demands from family and work, praised the pharmacy for its delivery service, easy renewals, and cost-effectiveness, noting that the pharmacy works "on my schedule not theirs" (Herzlinger, 1997, p. 3). Like everything else, we'd like to order our health care to go and to resolve our problems on our way to the next stop in our schedules.

At the same time, professionals in the health care industry continue to struggle with providing care amid economic-driven cutbacks in personnel and financial reimbursements. What care can be provided quickly? How can more people be served with less staff? What incentives exist for long days, lengthy paper trails, and more bureaucracy/less freedom? How can professionals with diverse perspectives work together to reconcile potentially incompatible viewpoints about providing care?

The critical communication challenge for all health care participants comes from the clash of individual (and often diverse) ideas about what constitutes "efficiency," especially when "efficiency" gets juxtaposed with simultaneous (and often contradictory) notions of what counts as "acceptable" and "quality" care. These conceptions of (and desires for) "efficiency," "acceptability," and "quality" greatly influence relationships between various industry personnel and between health care professionals and health care seekers.

McDonaldization of Health Care

I love to eat at Olive Garden. I relish the rare occasions during which I savor tasty pasta with romantic Italian-sounding music in the background. I enjoy relaxing conversations and lingering over scrumptious bread sticks and salad. However, I don't have the money or the time to eat at Olive Garden often. Tossing two bucks per Happy Meal to the drive-through attendant enables me to feed my kids quickly. I have learned the fine art of ripping into ketchup packets as I maneuver the van out of the drive-through lane and back on the road to soccer or softball fields. Cheeseburger or chicken nugget Happy Meals provide Britti and Chelsea Meagan with enough energy to "get by" until we carve moments for meals at home or allocate resources for an evening at a finer place like Olive Garden. Given our lifestyle, a Happy Meal is an efficient meal—certainly "good enough." With the exception of Chelsea's occasional pleas to eat inside (i.e., to play in the McPlayground), we don't even really see fast food as a sacrifice; it's more of a reality of our priorities in terms of time and money.

Ritzer (1996) suggests that our societal preference for a particular type of service has been greatly influenced by the economic and cultural success of McDonald's. In his book, *The McDonaldization of Society*, Ritzer maintains that key characteristics of McDonald's mirror priorities in contemporary society. Borrowing from Ritzer (1996), I contend that relationships in the health care industry have been greatly flavored by a gradual "McDonaldization of society," due to consumer, government, and industry professionals' interests and goals. Indeed, as I reexamine my plight with the first nurse, I can easily recognize the characteristics that Ritzer (1996, pp. 9–10) advances as "dimensions of McDonaldization"—efficiency, calculability, control, and predictability.

Efficiency

I was frustrated by the lack of *efficiency* during my encounter with the nurse. According to Ritzer (1996, p. 9), "efficiency" is the "optimum method for getting from one point to another." Ritzer notes that "for consumers [of McDonald's], this means that McDonald's offers the best available way to get from being hungry to being full" (p. 9). In the case of this health care incident, the prompt and painless insertion of the IV needle would have been "most efficient." In my other experiences with IV needles, the nurses or technicians had been able to hit a vein on the first one or two tries, certainly within around five minutes of attempts. I viewed the repeated failures by the first nurse as most *in*efficient, and thus, frustrating. I had come to expect quicker and less traumatic starting of IVs, and this encounter could be compared with a two-hour traffic jam in a drive-through on a hot summer day—unexpected, distressing, and disheartening. In health care scenarios, though, frustration becomes magnified by fears about lack of competency and physical anguish.

Calculability

I became distressed by a concentration on *calculability* during my time in the hospital and especially during this incident. Ritzer (1996) describes "calculability" as "an emphasis on the quantitative aspects of products sold (portion size, cost) and service offered (the time it takes to get the product)" (p. 9). Quantity has become equivalent to "quality." From an organizational or third-party payer perspective, calculability has become a huge component of health care dialogues. How many people can be treated and released? How quickly can patients be sent home? How can increases be made to product and output? In what ways can costs be minimized?

After a few days in the hospital, I struck up a conversation with a friendly patient care associate, whom I will call "Lamar," while he transported me to x-ray. Lamar explained, in his view, that the hospital was trying to cut corners and save money and that the reorganization from scale-back efforts resulted in more duties for fewer employees. According to Lamar, remaining employees resented the extra work, and some even lacked skills to do the additional tasks. Of course, Lamar may have been suffering from sucking on a few too many sour grapes; however, my experience with the first nurse's inability to insert the IV offers at least some lay support to Lamar's claim. My nurse was an older one, certainly from the prior-cut-back era wherein specially trained technicians from the lab collected blood and inserted IVs. I suffered personal consequences from the cost reductions, particularly given my expectations (based on prior IVs) about the time and pain that this service would entail.

Control

I yearned for *control*. I could not control who would care for me in the hospital, and I would have little choice about home health care providers. I had gone to such great lengths to prescreen physicians and to seek second opinions (within the constraints of my preferred provider plan) prior to my initial surgery, but once in the hospital, I lacked the power to choose my caregivers. Only after I asserted myself forcefully did I persuade the first nurse to obtain help. In the nurse's defense, though, I doubt that she enjoyed jabbing me time and time again. That nurse's failure to start the IV (and my request to get another nurse) catapulted that nurse into an embarrassing, face-threatening exchange with another nurse when she went for help. The first nurse had been expected, by management and by her peers, to handle a relatively mundane task, and her inability to perform jeopardized future control during peer and patient interactions. As I will detail later, my subsequent experiences in the emergency room became even more frustrating because control constitutes a coveted commodity for all health care participants, one not easily surrendered nor gained during health care interactions.

Ritzer (1996) explains, in the McDonald's model, that carefully crafted control mechanisms work to enforce managerially preferred employee and customer behaviors. According to Ritzer, "The people who eat in fast-food restaurants are controlled, albeit (usually) subtly. Lines, limited menus, few options, and uncomfortable seats all lead diners to do what management wishes them to do—eat quickly and leave" (p. 11).

The red tape of third-party payers, the bureaucracy of health care organizations, the institutionalized hierarchies of health care professionals and seekers, the artfully learned practices of enacting preferred face during health care interactions between professionals and between professionals and health care seekers—each of these characteristics of contemporary health care works to facilitate and constrain control by the various health care participants, even to the point of forcing consumers to receive care quickly and empty hospital beds for other people and other procedures. The emphasis on control in health care certainly resembles efforts by the powers behind the Golden Arches.

Predictability

Moreover, I became disturbed during the IV situation because of my desires for *predictability*. Ritzer (1996) suggests that:

> McDonald's offers *predictability*, the assurance that their products and services will be the same over time and in all locales. . . . The success of the McDonald's model suggests that many people have come to prefer a world in which there are few surprises. (p. 10)

My grandparents like to eat out. From time to time, they find a place that they particularly enjoy, and they come to expect certain standards of quality in terms of food, selection, and service. If the restaurant does not uphold that level of expectation on a given afternoon, my grandparents become disappointed. Although they may have visited that restaurant on numerous occasions without an unpleasant incident, one poor meal or sloppy server tends to gloss over all of those other positive memories. My grandparents value predictability.

Interestingly, during that Tuesday in the hospital, I had experienced wonderful treatment by an assortment of caring professionals—a very attentive day nurse, a therapist who talked and joked with me while supervising my antibiotic whirlpool, and a number of extremely competent and respectful patient care associates (including Lamar). Prior to my IV trauma on Tuesday evening, other nurses had performed blood-related procedures without a problem. Yet, in my conversation with my mom, those professionals faded as I argued that "*none* of *them* know what they are doing."

Such a claim certainly constituted an exaggeration; however, my dispirited glossing was not simply an overstatement. In this era of managed care and interdisciplinary team approaches to health care, interactions between individual health care professionals and health seekers (and between various types of professionals) can no longer be viewed in isolation—either from each other or from the wider institutional and societal influences on professional and seeker roles, responsibilities, expectations, and perceptions.

My surgeon's dismissal of my concerns . . . the misdiagnoses . . . the staph infection . . . the nurse's inability to start the IV. . . . Each of these incidents contributed to how I spoke with, questioned, and even directed subsequent health care professionals, and my experiences with various health care professionals affected their exchanges with each other as well. As I noted earlier, all components of a system impact (and are impacted by) each other (see Watzlawick et al., 1967). Because she was part of the hospital (and someone performing a certain procedure), memories of the first nurse haunted me as other nurses at the hospital approached me to draw blood and start IVs. I could no longer just assume that a simple needle stick would do because it had always been that easy before. I lost chunks of confidence in the staff because of that grueling and unpredictable evening.

Desiring and Demonizing McDonaldized Health Care

As Kellner (1998) observes in his 1998 response to Ritzer (1996), "the phenomenon of McDonaldization . . . interpreted as a set of processes geared at increasing efficiency, calculability, predictability, and control is more complex and ambiguous" (p. x) than focusing on service providers with such an orientation. As I have suggested, individuals in the health care industry and health care seekers alike may find aspects of a McDonaldized approach to be appealing. Although McDonald's reaps great financial success from its emphasis on standardized mass production, people who count on McMeals gain as well. Kellner (1998) explains:

> There are times when one wants what Ritzer calls McDonaldization, when efficiency and various modes of instrumental rationality are particularly beneficial and when one wants to avoid their opposite. . . . Likewise, there are some products and services that one wants to be as rationalized, predictable, and instrumental as possible . . . (p. x)

Yet, borrowing from Gergen (1991), contemporary social actors tend to pursue seemingly incompatible desires. In the medical arena, such incompatibilities might include the desire for individualized attention mixed with the desire for consistency and "standard approaches," the desire for personalized (and potentially lengthy) interactions balanced with the desire to avoid delays in waiting or examining rooms, the desire to pay less juxtaposed with the desire to obtain more, the desire to trust others during health care interactions juggled with the desire to position oneself, to guard face, and to listen to personal instincts.

In short, we might praise McDonaldization of health care when we choose to use urgent care facilities (especially as we dash from one commitment to the next), but we may condemn such a trend as we realize that we lack intimate relationships with health care providers. We might be grateful for our low-cost HMO until we get sick and learn that our coverage fails to blanket our expenses. Villanizing the McDonaldization of health care (as does Helen Hunt's character in the award-winning motion picture, *As Good As It Gets*, during her diatribe on HMOs) may be as easy as bashing the nutrition level of a Big Mac. However, both consumerism and economics have contributed to the emergence of contemporary health care, and the reshaping of relationships within the health care industry stems from a complex (and often conflicting) mix of individual, health, and financial priorities.

Redefining Health Care Relationships

I have to remember to take all of the flowers, I thought, scanning the various floral arrangements that adorned the dressers and table in my large hospital room. As I slowly shifted my head on the pillow, I noticed the window in the middle of the far wall and wondered about the view. I made a mental note to walk over and check it out before I leave. Roger should be here soon to pick me up.

I closed my eyes, exhausted from even this simple visual journey around the perimeter of my room. I drifted into the silence that was interrupted all too soon by the tapping of footsteps and the clinking of dishes on a tray. Reluctantly, I reopened my eyes as the cafeteria person entered and declared "lunch time." I got a whiff of the food and started to feel sick again. Uhhhhh . . . gross. How I would manage at home, I wondered? I hadn't eaten since Tuesday, and the most minute movement or smell prompted vomiting and then dry heaves. "I'm really queasy," I told the cafeteria person. "Please take it away." She hesitated, then shrugged and left with the tray.

As I watched the door close, I felt so weak and lost. How would I handle home life? I had been in the hospital for five days, and I felt frailer than I had ever imagined that I would in my life. After coming to the hospital and having the surgery on Monday, I thought that I would be well on the road to recovery. I figured that I would leave the following day or so, with a prescription and a caution to take it easy. Thus, when Dr. T. told me on Tuesday that I needed a PICC (Peripherally Inserted Central Catheter) line for eight weeks of interveneous antibiotics, I suspected that he was overreacting or, at least, being overcautious with the rest of my care. Certainly, I didn't need to have some tube stuck into my arm and chest. I had the surgery to remove the infection, right? I couldn't be that sick.

Yet, after a night of sleeplessness with the IV incident on Tuesday evening, I started to feel very ill on Wednesday morning. When the student nurse and patient care associate came to transport me to one of my twice-daily sessions in the antibiotic whirlpool, I threw up as I climbed out of bed. Nausea, dizziness, and disorientation overwhelmed me, and I clung to the tin pan in my lap during the wheelchair ride to another floor. I sat in the whirlpool, felt the chemicals spiraling around my open hip wound, and turned my head over the side of the tub while I vomited until only I had nothing left.

Where did this reaction come from, I wondered? I have a cast-iron stomach, and I had not thrown up in ten years, not since I was pregnant with Brittany. The whirlpool treatment ended. I looked up at the therapist as he carefully leaned over the tub to help me to a standing position. He took my left hand and elbow, trying to avoid jarring my IV tubing. I anxiously watched the fragile IV in my left arm as I lifted my casted right arm away to avoid splashes. I felt like a sick, drowning rat, with my dripping gown and dry heaves. The therapist assisted me out of the steel basin, and the student nurse propped me up as the therapist dabbed around my hip and toweled over my nearly naked body. I don't care what he sees, I thought. I don't care . . . , I mused as my legs started to buckle. They eased me into the wheelchair, and I gestured again for the tin pan. What did my body want to reject that was no longer there?

I kept gagging as the student nurse pushed me through the corridors and on to the elevator, and I bowed my head and let my hair veil my face as I noted the disgust of visitors who shared part of our ride up to my floor. They moved to the back of the elevator, and from the corner of my eye, I saw a few cringe as my shoulders shook and my throat made the most awful of sounds. A distinguished-looking visitor in a classy suit and matching shoes held her gentile nose as she looked purposefully away. Better not mess up your makeup, I chided mutely.

The equally disgusted student nurse aided me as I scrambled awkwardly into bed. "I'll send Joan in to replace your hip dressing," she said, hurrying from the room, and I wondered if I would be the reason for her to ditch nursing. "A regular Florence Nightingale," I reflected aloud.

That afternoon, Dr. T. again urged me to agree to the PICC line, and once more, I waffled. I didn't want something like that. No matter how bad I felt, I couldn't really be that *sick. Further, the description of the PICC sounded dangerous, and I just didn't feel competent to make a decision like that. I couldn't think. He would just have to wait until I got better and managed to concentrate more clearly. Alone in the hospital except for brief nightly visits by co-workers, I desperately longed for someone beyond hospital personnel to enable me to find perspective, to know what to do, to help me to understand everything that seemed so jumbled because I could not bring myself to focus well enough.*

I was right to distrust my awareness (or lack thereof). Hearing my fear and confusion about the PICC line during one of our telephone visits, Roger contacted a patient care advocate at the hospital to make sure that I was getting information. By all accounts, staff members described the PICC line procedure to me on two occasions, but their explanations must have vanished into the abyss that had become my mind. The dry heaves had pushed me past the point of exhaustion, and I fell into a fog by late Wednesday afternoon. I just couldn't think.

Emotionally, I felt like an old rag doll, limp and lifeless in a dark, ill-defined corner of an overwhelming maze of voices, vomiting, and procedures. I simply wanted all of them (the continual stream of nurses and patient care associates and cafeteria people and occasional residents and rarer doctors) to go away, to let me sleep and remain still so I didn't have to keep battling the now-constant nausea. They kept interrupting me, and I wanted to hide under the covers. Why did solitude seem so elusive? Stop pestering me, I thought as staff revolved through my door.

I refused to go to my antibiotic whirlpool, opting instead to drift back into nothingness. I didn't care. I couldn't care. Caring took energy, and I expended all of my remaining might into heaving drips of drool. Time passed, and the room grew dark. At last, I gained silence. Blessedly, I slept.

All too soon, though, still another nurse entered. This nurse had been really nice to me earlier, and I felt bad for wanting her to leave, but I did. Just go away, I thought, please just go away. She didn't. I peeked at her as she checked my vitals and then turned to the IV. Avoid eye contact, I thought, she'll finish sooner. I closed my eyes, but not quickly enough—she caught me. She adjusted the IV fluid bag and turned to look at me. Gently, she laid a hand on my right shoulder and asked me about the PICC line. I mumbled that I wasn't sure, that I couldn't think well enough to decide.

Her words were like a beacon from a distant lighthouse heralding a lost ship to the shore. "Don't you get it?" she asked. "The PICC line will allow you to get drugs without being restuck every few days as your IVs go bad. If you don't have IV therapy for weeks, you will die."

Die? I had an infection; people don't die from infections, I silently scoffed. People take pills and get better. As bad as I felt, I never thought about dying. How could I be that sick? Was I that sick? The nurse's warning cleared just enough of my fog for me to start to grasp the seriousness of my situation.

I finally consented to the PICC line, and two specially trained nurses inserted it on the fourth day of my hospital stay, Thursday. As they donned surgical masks and prepped me for the procedure, I was terrified that this IV would cause more problems than it would solve. What if they punctured a vein? What if they missed and ripped into my heart? How could they know where the line was going as they pushed it through my vein? I lay motionless but apprehensive, still struggling with dissonance about the necessity of this type of procedure and fear over the nurses' competence to accomplish it.

Yet, if I had to have IV antibiotics for eight weeks in order to battle the infection, at least the PICC line permitted outpatient (and less expensive) treatment than inpatient hospital care. With the PICC line, home care became an option for treating the infection.

Home . . . I peered at the door where the cafeteria person had just exited. Roger would soon come through that door to drive me back to Athens. Home . . . as much as I wanted to see Britti and Chelsea Meagan, I could not imagine functioning at home when I could barely stand. With the cast on one arm and the PICC line in the other, I could not take a shower or wash my hair, even if I could summon the strength to balance my body upright. I sighed and pressed the call button to get help to go to the bathroom. Besides, how could I figure out this whole home health thing, I thought as I waited for the nurse to respond. Who could I call? How could the service be arranged? Would I be able to get my dosages scheduled for tonight at such short notice? I had no idea how home health care works, and the prospect of figuring out a new system seemed far too daunting. I closed my eyes and waited for a nurse to come.

The accomplishment of health care and health care relationships in the 1990s and into the new millennium has been influenced greatly by two pivotal issues beyond medicine—

consumerism and economics. As I reflect on the PICC line decision, I realize that much of my frustration stemmed from my inability to obtain and process information. As a "good" consumer, I am accustomed to pursuing data from a variety of sources and getting multiple opinions. I usually give much thought to major decisions. However, given the circumstances, I could not be a "good" consumer, and I felt very uncomfortable with agreeing or not agreeing to the PICC line as a result. Further, I understand now that the PICC line was important for economic reasons as well. Although home health care is expensive, lengthy hospital stays become much more costly to third-party payers. Only 24 hours after I received the PICC line, I was discharged to home care, thus saving the vast expense of keeping me in the hospital for eight weeks. Both consumerism and economics constitute tremendous factors in the movement for more "efficiency" in health care and, to some degree, a McDonaldized health care system, a movement that has greatly redefined contemporary health care relationships.

Relationships Redefined by Consumerism

As several scholars suggest, we live in a consumer society in the United States—we want what we want and when we want it (see Goodwin, Ackerman, & Kiron, 1997; Herzlinger, 1997; Keat, Whiteley, & Abercrombie, 1994; Lury, 1996; Miller, 1995). In fact, a consumer society corresponds with spending options and general affluence (see Goodwin, et al., 1997).

Of course, most of us cannot access unlimited resources—even our Visa cards limit our spending power. Yet, the power in consumerism stems from the selectivity of consumption choices. Shoppers at the turn of the twenty-first century pursue information and compare services and benefits from products. Indeed, as Abercrombie (1994, p. 44) suggests, "in more and more aspects of their lives people are expected to behave as consumers and it is similarly expected that they will be treated as consumers."

With that selectivity, consumers carry the force of the dollar. With more products to purchase than money to spend, consumers do more than "shop smart." Their selections implicitly communicate priorities, preferences, and self-definitions. Miller (1995, p. 30) explains that "consumption is simply a process of objectification—that is, a use of goods and services in which the object or activity becomes simultaneously a practice in the world and a form in which we construct our understandings of ourselves in the world." Abercrombie (1994, p. 51) concurs, noting that "struggles between producer and consumer are not, therefore, only about what is produced and at what price, but also about meaning and the commodification of meaning."

While our purchases certainly communicate something about our values, priorities, and self-definitions, the ways in which we consume are also powerfully symbolic. Our shopping practices reflect who we want to be and how we want to be treated.

When the title character on *Murphy Brown* learned that she had breast cancer, she doggedly pursued information. Murphy visited doctor after doctor after doctor; she sought studies and written resources on the subject. She refused to accept the first (and even the second and third) "expert" recommendation because she wanted to discover the "best" option. Moreover, Murphy could not just agree to the initial treatment option because such a passive approach to her cancer would have been contradictory to the usually aggressive way in which she lived her life in other realms. As an investigative reporter, Murphy defined herself by her ability to sniff out details, to leave no stone unturned in researching a story.

Although most of us are not investigative reporters by trade, the advent of our consumer culture has prompted many of us to join the ranks of "smart shoppers." We want to get the "best" deal, the most "bang for our buck." People may be taken as "frivolous" if they don't compare prices or justify the value of their more expensive purchases.

Consumer Control of Health Care

Herzlinger links consumer desires for quality and efficiency in health care with similar consumer behaviors in other industries. Herzlinger (1997) explains:

> The consumer revolutionaries want their health care system to provide them with the same kinds of convenience and mastery that they've found with Home Depot, *Consumer Reports*, and Nordic track, so that their health status and costs will improve even further. (p. 4)

However, the consumeristic message of buyer awareness that resonates over the Internet and in volumes written during the seventies, eighties, and nineties emphasizes more than getting the best buy; it encourages taking charge of health care encounters to optimize outcomes (see, e.g., Cyr, 1998; Halvorson, 1993; Illich, 1976; Jones & Phillips, 1988; Millenson, 1997; Shaller, Sharpe, & Rubin, 1998; Starr, 1982; Williamson, 1992). As early as 1976, Illich warned that "the medical establishment has become a major threat to health" (p. 3). Two decades later, in his book *Demanding Medical Excellence: Doctors and Accountability in the Information Age*, Millenson (1997) argues that health care consumers should challenge and question their health care professionals, as opposed to assuming that those professionals have absolute answers. As Millenson (1997) and others contend, health-conscious consumers can bring their own stock of information to health care interactions, and they should participate more equally than ever before.

Increasingly, the media instruct us to question and to demand quality service from health care professionals and managed care organizations. Kaplan (1998) describes the shock of one health care industry lobbyist while viewing *As Good As It Gets*—wherein a mother blasts her heartless HMO—at the movie theater with his family. According to Kaplan (1998, p. 58), ". . . his fun came to a sudden end . . . [Hunt's] words were *really* scary, Kahn recalls with a shudder. 'I do not have horns,' he says meekly."

Despite Kahn's protest, the demonizing of aspects of the health care industry (especially managed care organizations) continues. Even former United States surgeon general C. Everett Koop offered the following advice in the U.S. Airways publication, *Attache*: "Under the present health system, you had better take charge of your health because no one else is going to do it" (Cyr, 1998, p. 40). Hamilton Jordan seized such control:

> Hamilton Jordan vividly recalls the moment back in 1985, when, diagnosed with non-Hodgkin's lymphoma and lying in a hospital bed feeling sorry for himself, he received a visit from a doctor friend. His friend spoke bluntly. "You've got to take charge of your own health care. Nobody has more at stake in this than you do." With that, the former chief of staff in the Carter administration recalls, "I got up, got someone to help me into a wheelchair, went down to the medical library, and began to research my illness . . ." Jordan per-

sonifies a new type of health care consumer: educated, interested, aware, and very active in charting the course of his or her own health care. (Hagland, 1996, p. 25)

Industry Response

Jordan's story is inspiring; however, the source of the account is also interesting. Hagland contributed the article to *Hospitals & Health Networks*, a health care industry publication. In an industry that has thrived on institutionalized power and control, industry professionals have carefully watched and overtly discussed the trends toward consumer activism and assertions of consumer control (see also Hibbard & Weeks, 1987; Liner, 1997; Messner, 1993; Ostasiewski & Fugate, 1994; Sharf, 1988; Ware, 1994; Wiles & Higgins, 1996) amid industry-wide transformations. Messner (1993) contends in an *American Journal of Nursing* article that "with practically everyone shopping for quality these days, health care is now taking its cues from industry . . ." (p. 38). Messner emphasizes that ". . . it's not enough to provide excellent quality medical and nursing care if the patient doesn't *perceive* it as such" (p. 38), and consumer advocates and government officials pounce on suggestions about cracks in safeguards (see AP, October 9, 1999; December 7, 1999). Craig agrees, writing in 1987:

> Twenty-five years ago, hospitals were political sacred cows. Today, public officials accuse hospitals of waste and inefficiency. Twenty-five years ago, health care professionals were regarded as dedicated people who made personal sacrifices for the well-being of others. Today, patients, and their attorneys, routinely question treatment decisions, outcomes, and motives. (p. 19)

Some facilities have tried to reach out to consumers and to proactively address needs and concerns. Noting the desire of many parents for an intimate and comfortable child birthing experience, some hospitals feature state-of-the-art birthing centers—single rooms with birthing beds and soothing decor (Somerson, October 2, 1999). However, even more upscale options exist for other patients, especially those who have the resources to pay. According to Rundle and Binkley (August 27, 1999), "At least 10 medical centers have built entire luxury floors or corridors with everything from chefs and concierges to high-end beauty products in the bathroom." Although the medical centers contend that care resembles less plush units in their facilities, the centers hope that elegant accommodations will attract people who can afford the extra daily premium of $170 (Cleveland Clinic in Cleveland, Ohio) up to $2800 (Memorial Sloan-Kettering Cancer Center in New York), offsetting income reductions from patients who rely on managed care and Medicaid (Rundle & Binkley, August 27, 1999).

However, appeals to potential patients also extend to those of us who cannot afford such surroundings. For example, Ostasiewski and Fugate (1994) describe the efforts of one hospital to include customer voices in improving care through an adoption of "quality circles" for patients.

While the "patient circle" idea constitutes a creative response to including non–health care professionals in hospital improvement, the tangled mazes of contemporary health care should not be viewed simplistically as "us" and "them," "consumers" and "industry members." Indeed, the greatest challenge for health care seekers and professionals might well be in discerning who to contact and how to battle through tangled and confusing medical mazes to get answers and authorizations. As I detail next, in this era of hospital takeovers and mergers and insurance conglomerates, control over decisions may no longer remain with primary physicians or individual hospitals (see e.g., Gold, 1998; Gray, 1991; Herzlinger, 1997; Schamess & Lightburn, 1998). Health care seekers and professionals often need to negotiate treatments and reimbursements with third-party payers over the telephone in distant cities. Hagland (1996) even writes in bold print in his article for hospital and health executives, "In a world where managed care is a misnomer, is it any wonder that consumers are taking charge of their own destiny? After all it's not like they can rely on their doctors to do it for them" (p. 25). In this era, doctors might just find that their hands are tied.

Relationships Redefined by Economics

Dr. Wolfhard Baumgaetel began his medical practice in the tiny village of Albany, Ohio in 1955. Although he only works part-time now, Dr. Baumgaetel still makes house calls (Holbert, October 26, 1998). Doctors who make house calls seem more easily linked to frontier doctors on nostalgic television shows (such as *Dr. Quinn—Medicine Woman* and *Little House on the Prairie*) than to contemporary practices. Quite simply, costs constrain what doctors can do. As Baumaertel reflects, "The administrative details have gone overboard. Medicine is being organized by insurance companies . . . which diverts attention from the patient" (Holbert, July 8, 1998, p. 5).

In a Scripps Howard News Service column, Hilton (July 8, 1998) recalls a childhood doctor, Doc Devine. Heralding back to 1939, Hilton observes that Doc Devine didn't need to be concerned with many of the issues that clutter contemporary health care. As Hilton notes, "Nobody would want to go back to the medicine of 1939; before antibiotics, CPR, and kidney dialysis. But you can't help envying the independence with which Doc Devine was allowed to practice his craft" (p. 4).

According to Hilton (July 8, 1998), people paid Doc Devine what they could for his services, sometimes "a side of mutton or a bushel of rutabagas." Somewhere between the times of Doc Devine and Dr. Baumaertel and the times of managed care, health care became about money, about compensation, about profit. From the simplicity of country doctors emerged highly specialized physicians who seek large fees for services to repay skyrocketing costs of medical school and advanced training. In the film, *Doc Hollywood*, Michael J. Fox portrays a doctor bound for California and a high-paying job as a plastic surgeon. Perhaps only in Hollywood could a twist of fate end with such a specialist selecting to serve as a small-town doctor who accepts cows for compensation.

In his book, *Gesundheit!*, Patch Adams describes an idealistic health care community that refuses to purchase malpractice insurance or to accept payment. Discouraging the conceptualization of health care as a commodity, Adams (with Mylander, 1998) suggests that too many individuals in the health care industry get caught up in greed and profitability. As for the Gesundheit Institute, Adams (with Mylander, 1998) asserts that "we hope to eliminate the factor of debt entirely from the healing interaction" (p. 53).

In this contemporary era of health care, wherein many (if not most) focus on funding and reimbursements, Adams' notion of a community hospital that promotes a fun-loving, caring philosophy of medicine struck a nerve with motion picture ticket buyers in late 1998; however, such an approach contrasts sharply with the prevalent economic emphasis of the contemporary health care industry. In fact, the opposite of Adams' vision appears to be more possible—economic and logistical "realities" of health care in the 1990s continue to motivate critical decisions about health care delivery. Even rankings of hospitals place emphasis on economic efficiency of care delivery (see Vergano, December 13, 1999). In 1993, Halvorson bemoaned the state of health care in the United States. He charged:

> . . . as the actual delivery of health care and the treatment of given conditions has become much more complex—often involving several caregivers in the care of a single patient—our organizational models for providing health care have basically been locked into the ineffi- cient, splintered, nonsystem approaches of the 1940s—with a million separate and fiercely independent caregiver profit centers competing with each other for their piece of the health care dollar at the expense of both efficiency and care quality. (p. 4)

Making Health Care Affordable
Soaring expenses of staffing, drugs, procedures, hospital stays, and specialists during the 1980s and 1990s have progressively pushed hospitals, practitioners, third-party payers (including government programs such as Medicaid and Medicare) and companies that pay health benefits for employees to tighten purse strings and to pursue more cost-effective options of providing care (see Bronstein, 1996; Coile, 1997b; Ginzberg & Ostow, 1997; Gold, 1998; Gray, 1991; Halvorson, 1993; Herzlinger, 1997; Kassirer, 1997; Keyser, 1993; Ogles, Trout, Gillespie, & Penkert, 1998; Rosenau, 1994; Rother, 1997). Further, as costs continue to mount, the burden shifts to companies and then to employees who face a new bottom line.

Porter (January 16, 2000) reports that "on average, insurance premiums are rising eight percent in 2000, the largest increase since 1993" (p. G1). Ironically, as the price tag for employee contributions bound upward, coverage wanes. According to a *USA Today* editorial on health care cost for workers, employee contributions for single coverage have escalated 284 percent in the eight year period of 1988 to 1996, with a 146 percent jump for family coverage (Jurgensen, October 23, 1998, p. 10A).

When Ohio University switched to a PPO (preferred provider organization), I became quite nervous. A PPO contracts with networks (health care practitioners and hospitals who band together to bid on contracts with managed care organizations) to provide care. How- ever, my wrist surgeon was not a member of one of the specified networks. I had to nego- tiate to get coverage for my continuing struggles with my wrist because I could not simply transfer to another doctor at that point—my case was too complicated and advanced. Although the PPO was designed to save money for my employer, my fellow employees and I lost our free health care, some provider options (especially in terms of specialists), and a good chunk of income from our monthly checks.

Perhaps more importantly, though, as I realized through my health care experiences (and especially during my conversations with health care professionals like Lamar), eco- nomic decisions of the 1990s have impacted more than the bottom line. Economic factors have catapulted health care participants (health care seekers, practitioners, and nonmedical industry members alike) into radically revised interpersonal and power relationships. Indeed, as Capron (1996) contends, "The rapid evolution of the health care system is radically reshaping the relationships of hospitals and other providers, physicians, nurses, and other professionals, insurers and payers, patients, and government" (p. 23).

The Third Voice in Health Care Interactions

As I pen this book, *managed care* has emerged as the health care industry response to reduction of health care costs. According to Coile (1997a), "The trend toward cost-management by employers, HMOs, and health plans is loosely defined as 'managed care,' an aggressive cost-management effort by healthcare purchasers and insurers to limit their health spending" (p. ix). Ogles and colleagues (1998) agree, defining "managed care" as "a collection of business management strategies used to make health care delivery more efficient and cost effective" (p. 254).

Restricting Resources   One example of a managed care management strategy involves *utilization management*, a review process to eliminate unnecessary services and to ensure the most cost-effective means of providing care (see Boyd, 1997; Gray, 1991). As MacStravic and Montrose (1998) explain, this strategy positions third-party payers as gatekeepers that can restrict access to care. Before I went into the hospital for my wrist reconstruction surgery, my insurance company required me to obtain a "preauthorization." One of my surgeon's nurses called the insurance company with a description of my case, and I received authorization for the procedure, along with a restriction about number of days in the hospital. After I experienced complications with the first surgery, my surgeon had to request (and obtain) permission for me to remain in the hospital after I exceeded the original number of approved days.

Many managed care organizations have also turned to *capitation* as a means of controlling costs and reducing unnecessary procedures. Coile (1997a) provides this explanation of capitation:

> Under capitated contracts, HMOs and insurers pay physicians and hospitals a fixed amount per month for each health plan member, regardless of whether a member makes 20 visits, has open heart surgery, or never sets foot through the providers' doors . . . . (pp. 41–42)

As Coile (1997a) suggests, capitation effectively shifts the responsibility for cost-containment to health care providers—if those providers commit unnecessary resources, they pay. If those providers minimize costs (through eliminating tests, procedures, hospital stays, etc.), they profit. Coile (1997a) argues that "providers assume the position of insurer—they become both risk holder and risk manager" (p. 42).

In essence, capitation pushes primary physicians into a gatekeeping capacity (see Bodenheimer, Lo, & Casalino, June 2, 1999; Grumbach, Selby, Damberg, Bindman, Quesenberry, Truman, & Uratsu, July 21, 1999; Halm, Causino, & Blumenthal, November 26, 1997; Kerr, Hays, Mittman, Siu, Leake, & Brooke, July 23–30, 1997). While physicians acknowledge efficiency-related success of capitation, the response to gatekeeping in terms of relational consequences for professionals and seekers remains mixed (see Bodenheimer et al., June 2, 1999; Grumbach et al., July 21, 1999; Halm et al., November 26, 1997).

Mihalik and Scherer (1998) note that ". . . capitation created the incentive and need for organizations to establish specific mechanisms by which to control utilization and create delivery systems that made accountability possible" (p. 1). Of course, as Mihalik and Scherer assert, "The premise guiding these efforts is that members do not always access the appropriate types of services and that control of access can direct members to appropriate care" (p. 12).

Coordinating Resources   Theoretically, managed care constitutes a solid solution to the difficult dilemma of making health care services more affordable and available to health care seekers, thus addressing concerns about industry fragmentation (see Coile, 1997b; Halvorson, 1993). Ideally, with a managed care approach, care becomes more coordinated, and both the health care industry and consumers save time and money. Coile (1997b) points to accomplishments of managed care such as the "reduced excessive use of testing and ancillary services" (p. 1). Kassirer (1997) explains in an article in the *Journal of the American Medical Association*:

> The inherent virtues of managed care have manifested themselves in many salutary improvements to the system that might otherwise never have been made. These include attempts to eliminate waste and redundancy, a greater focus on health promotion and disease prevention, more attention to the management of chronic diseases, a focus on the accountability of physicians and health plans and on the quality of care, lower hospitalization rates without an obvious decline in the quality of care, heavy investment in patient-information systems, and—at least for the present—control of employers' health care costs. (p. 1014)

Controlling Resources   Despite these benefits of managed care, the reshaping and rethinking of how health care gets accomplished has challenged health care seekers and practitioners to adapt to less flexibility in terms of health care options. For health care consumers, Rother (1997) explains that ". . . the price of this progress is the necessity . . . to be more informed, to take a more active part in medical decisions, and to be more sensitive about the need to use medical services appropriately" (p. 89). For health care professionals, Dr. Patti Tighe argues, "everything about managed care—being told how many minutes to spend with each patient and what medicine and what treatments to use—is contrary to the role of the consistent, nurturing healer" (Stapleton, 1998, p. 26, as well as related work by Flocke, Stange, & Zyzanski, 1997).

Health care professionals can even be told which drugs are off limits when managed care organizations deny coverage (see Gallagher, December 21, 1999) or which medical materials to recycle despite potential health risks (Gallagher, November 30, 1999). Both health care seekers and practitioners have been forced to adjust to the reality that managed care involves "closely controlling the practice patterns of hospitals and physicians and . . . limiting the choices available to their enrollees" (Ginzberg & Ostow, 1997, p. 1020).

In a controversial move, Kaiser Permanente, a huge managed-care company, extended its control even further. According to Appleby (August 24, 1999), "This is the next evolution of managed care: Insurers, who already dictate what medications are covered and how long patients will stay in hospitals, now want to oversee emergency services" (p. A1).

Although the state of Maryland passed a law to prohibit services that compete with 911, Kaiser anticipates that this emergency program will spread to other regions of the country, just as other managed-care policies dictate the practices of health care professionals in nonemergency medicine.

Kaiser contracted with Colorado-based American Medical Response to screen calls before directing individuals to 911 for emergency service. Ideally, the program could reduce the number of individuals who require ambulances, saving money for the HMO and preserving the limited resource of ambulances for people who truly need them. Unfortunately, the program could also waste time for ill or injured patients or intimidate others from calling 911, especially if some fear that their HMO will refuse to cover the expensive ambulance ride (see Appleby, August 24, 1999, p. A2).

That fear is not based on paranoia—managed care organizations have already been reported to deny benefits for emergency treatment if patients do not first gain authorization. Gallagher (May 4, 1999) tells the story of a woman from Seattle who sought emergency assistance for significant chest pains.

> Early last year, a Seattle woman began suffering chest pains and numbness while driving. The pain was so severe that she pulled into a fire station seeking help, only to be whisked to the nearest hospital, where she was promptly admitted. To most that would seem a prudent course of action. Not to her health plan. It denied payment because she didn't call the plan first to get "pre-authorized," according to an investigation by the Washington state insurance commissioner. (p. 12A)

Struggling for Resources   With all of the sweeping consumer and economically driven changes in the contemporary health care system in the United States, one central question remains unanswered: Who gets to decide whether efficiency or acceptability should be prioritized? However, even that question oversimplifies the problem for health care professionals and health care seekers because two underlying issues lack resolution: Who gets to decide what counts as "efficient"? Who gets to decide what counts as "acceptable"?

In the early 2000s, that battle continues to roar, from the halls of Congress to the front pages of the daily papers to water fountain talk between co-workers to scholarly and professional debates (see, for example, Erbe & Shiner, July 16, 1999; Ignagni, June 28, 1998; Keyser, 1993; Mitchem, June 28, 1998; Schamess & Lightburn, 1998). Among others, one state representative candidate in Ohio campaigned on the claim that "HMOs that focus on profits, not patients, threaten our health." According to Sternberg (November 23, 1998), "Millions of Americans believe the nation's health care system is fatally flawed and would vote for candidates bold enough to reform it" (p. D1).

A report in the July 14, 1999 issue of the *Journal of the American Medical Association* that for-profit HMOs rank lower than their nonprofit counterparts fueled the fire for change (see Appleby, July 14, 1999; http://onhealth.com/ch1/briefs/item, 45081asp). HMOs fired back, launching a $9-million-dollar ad campaign to counter their negative public image (see AP, July 2, 1999 as well as discussion by Appleby, October 29, 1999). One health care insurer even reduced its control over physicians amid fears of public backlash (see Appleby, November 9, 1999). In an editorial in the *New England Journal of Medicine*, Angell and Kassirer (1996) argue:

... the quality of health care is now seriously threatened by our rapid shift to managed care as the way to contain costs. Managed-care plans involve an inherent conflict of interest. On the one hand they pledge to take care of their enrollees, but on the other their financial success depends on doing as little for them as possible. ... We have embraced a financing and delivery method that rewards doctors, sometimes quite directly, for doing less for their patients. Most doctors are now double agents—working for their patients but also for their companies. And despite the lip service, the financial interests of those companies are not the same as the health interests of their enrollees, a truth underscored by the gag rules some MCOs have imposed on their doctors. (pp. 883, 885)

In an industry that overflows with desires for power (from consumers to professionals to third-party payers to government officials) and with a multiplicity of agendas (from cost and effectiveness of care for consumers to profitability of facilities and services for third-party payers), the struggles over resources resemble children squabbling over a treasured toy. Like those young people who turn to their mom to settle disputes, each group—consumers, professionals, and third-party payers—has appealed to the government to see its side and to tell the others to let it have its way (see AP, July 12, 1999, July 13, 1999; Appleby, July 29, 1999; Merline, 1996; Welch, July 12, 1999, July 14, 1999). In one judgment, a court awarded $51.5 million to a widower who lost his wife to cancer. Anthem Blue Cross/Blue Shield of Cincinnati denied treatment coverage to Esther Dardinger, a denial that purportedly contributed to her death (see Price, September 26, 1999). In this case, the legal process decided care issues of access, responsibility, quality, and efficiency.

In the end, what counts as "good enough" in terms of expense for a particular patient or in terms of effort for that patient? The dispute over reimbursement for the impotence drug, Viagra, stems from quality/enjoyment of life as a "good enough" reason to count as a "medical necessity" (see Rubin, June 22, 1998). Are managed care organizations' practice guidelines "good enough" (see Jurgensen, December 7, 1998) to emphasize over the expertise of individual professionals who visit with individual patients?

Fighting for Voice   The struggle over defining "good enough" care resonates strongly with health care professionals. According to a random survey of 1053 doctors and 768 nurses conducted by the Kaiser Family Foundation and the Harvard School of Public Health (see www.kff.org), a majority of doctors report that their patients have received denials of coverage requests (87%).

The prevalence of this third voice in medical dialogues has become so pervasive that some medical schools now prepare students to interact with third-party payers (Brink, 1997; Marwick, 1996). Although one study indicates that medical faculty present managed care negatively to medical students (Simon, Pan, Sullivan, Clark-Chiarelli, et al., 1999), at least a few schools have taken the more proactive route of developing special programs for equipping future doctors with the communication skills to adapt to managed-care demands (Brink, 1997; Marwick, 1996). Yet, even with such programs for professionals, for many health care participants, the advent of a foreign third voice has shaken a priori expectations and prompted serious redefinitions of how health care gets accomplished. Indeed, in his book on reengineering strategies for medical practices, Hultman (1995) argues that "... the loss of autonomy and other negative changes accompanying managed care have created an environment where doctors feel helpless and no longer enjoy practicing" (p. 2).

Further, with their lives and health on the line, consumers also want a voice in the efficiency/acceptability war—a way of cutting through bureaucracy and regaining some of their own power lost to managed care organizations. Although various versions of a "Patient's Bill of Rights" cycled through and were rejected by Congress (see AP, April 9, 1999, April 11, 1999; Welch, June 19–21, 1998, June 25, 1998, July 17, 1998), one finally passed in late 1999 (see Welch, October 8–10, 1999). Although some discovered loopholes in the law before this legislation (see Cerminara, 1998; Pear, August 15, 1999), health care seekers may now legally appeal decisions of managed care organizations, especially when care gets denied.

Echoing the denial tales of frustrated health care professionals (who are not great fans of litigation themselves), advocates of legal recourse for health care seekers point to denials of care. One woman told the story of her son who was born with cerebral palsy during an episode of the *Montel Williams Show* (January 28, 1999). Although the woman's HMO initially agreed to reimbursements for physical therapy, it stopped payments when her son was one and a half years old. If the son continued the therapy, he could learn to walk; if he did not, he would be wheelchair bound for the rest of his life. As the woman queried, "They were telling me that they had the right to tell me whether or not my son could walk?"

An HMO denial contributed to the death of Terry Johnson's daughter, Melody. Melody suffered from cystic fibrosis, and her mother sought a referral from her HMO to a specialist. The HMO did not immediately grant the referral and then overruled the specialist's recommendation (Welch, June 19–21, 1998).

For Joseph Plocica, a denial also led to death. Although his hospital psychiatrist argued that Plocica's suicidal depression required continued treatment, the health plan claimed otherwise. On the night of his release, he committed suicide by drinking antifreeze (see Gallagher, July 13, 1999).

Mayer (1993) describes the legal battle of a fellow breast cancer patient to get recommended (albeit experimental) treatment:

> Claiming it was not "medically necessary," Metropolitan Life denied Pat's predetermination request for a second high dose chemotherapy (HDC) with stem-cell harvest and reinfusion, using different and more effective anti-cancer drugs. . . . Pat's oncologist testified that, in his estimation, the repeat procedure should give her a 15 to 20% chance at long-term survival or cure. Without it, he stated flatly, she would die in a matter of months. (p. 165)

In their fight for a voice in their patients' care, some health care professionals grow desperate to secure preferred means of treatment. In fact, research indicates that physicians feel forced to lie or exaggerate symptoms in order to qualify individuals for recommended care (see Freeman, Rathore, Weinfurt, Schulman, & Sulmassy, October 25, 1999; Jurgensen, November 11, 1998; Kisken, November 9, 1999).

A Good Steward   I cannot imagine the terror, the frustration, that must come from knowing that hope lurks around the corner, but a gatekeeper prevents passage. In the flux of these power struggles, though, some managed care organizations are trying to be more dialogic and more open and responsive to concerns and consumer interests, prompted by watchdog organizations such as the Agency for Health Care Policy and Research (AHCPR), the

National Committee for Quality Assurance (NCQA), the Joint Commission on Accreditation of Healthcare Organizations (JCAHO), and the Foundation for Accountability (FACCT) (see Lieberman, 1999; Schauffler, Brown, & Milstein, 1999; Shaller et al., 1998). Nearly 450 health plans submit data to a database called "Quality Compass" (see www.ncqa.org), coordinated by the NCQA. In its publication, "The State of Managed Care Quality," the NCQA details the performance of managed care plans in preventive health and member treatment.

Notably, the NCQA argues that "accountability drives quality" (1999, p. 32). As Spragins (1999) reports, some health plans may release data to Quality Compass and yet refuse to allow the public to access the information. According to Spragins (1999), of the 447 health plans who submit data, 155 plans requested that their data be concealed from public view. In response to the plans that withhold information from the public, the NCQA emphasizes:

> The differences in performance between accountable and unaccountable plans are not only consistent, in most cases they are large as well. Substantial gaps separate accredited and non-accredited plans and publicly reporting and non-publicly reporting plans across essentially all performance measures. . . . It is important to remember that even a 1% difference may translate into hundreds of cases of blindness prevented, hundreds of cardiac deaths avoided or millions of dollars in medical costs saved. (p. 32)

With the efforts of organizations that emphasize public accountability and the highly publicized cases of health consequences from coverage denials, the struggle for control over access is far from resolved. Indeed, the public rage over "drive-through deliveries" (wherein women were expected to leave the hospital within 24 hours of childbirth) prompted legislation and third-party payer policy reform (see AP, June 10, 1999; Somerson, July 18, 1999). However individual cases and situations get resolved, though, one thing is clear—the conflict over efficiency and acceptability cuts to the core of power-based interpersonal relationships between participants in the health care industry.

Survival of the Biggest— Grouping Individual Professionals

When I gave birth to my oldest daughter, Brittany, in 1986, I selected a pediatrician. Actually, I chose a group of pediatricians—Physicians for Children. As a new (and inexperienced) mom, I felt safe with the knowledge that a pediatrician was always available at the state-of-the-art center, just in case. When I cut baby Brittany's finger while trimming her tiny fingernails, I picked up the phone and called a nurse at 11:30 P.M. on a Sunday night. When I couldn't get the bleeding to stop (and promptly overreacted), I drove to the center to consult with the waiting pediatrician. Of course, the bleeding ceased as soon as I crossed the threshold of the facility at midnight, but the kind doctor made certain that Brittany was okay, reassured me that I had done the right thing by bringing her in for a small finger cut, and even rechecked her ear infection, all for the cost of an office call. I hated to move away from Physicians for Children when we left Roanoke.

Strength in Numbers

My current pediatrician for Brittany (and now for Chelsea Meagan) operates a solo practice, and he cares for many community children. Although well regarded, he is only one person, a person who needs to take vacations, sleep at night, and occasionally, get sick himself. Recently, Chelsea developed a high fever in the middle of a weekend night, and we made yet another trek into the emergency room of our local hospital. The admissions clerk asked me for the name of my pediatrician. I told her and joked that "of course, he possibly doesn't remember her because Chelsea only gets sick on nights and weekends."

Fortunately, my insurance company usually picks up the tab for these late night adventures to the ER. Although I do not always know the doctor who helps us in the ER, I have been generally comfortable with the care. As a mom, I have not really been impacted by my shift from a group pediatric practice to a solo one.

However, the tightening economic forces that compel many health care professionals to link with other professionals (see Capron, 1996; Coile, 1998) impact those practitioners greatly. *Group practices* involve a collection of practitioners who share administrative expenses and support staff. As Coile (1998, p. 7) suggests, some physicians' groups have combined into *mega-medical groups*, a business maneuver that permits such groups to garner more attractive managed care contracts and to reduce expenses. Health practitioners may also opt to work for health maintenance organizations or health care institutions, receiving a salary rather than fee-for-service reimbursements.

Losing Control

When health care professionals commit to group practices, HMOs, hospitals/institutions, and/or HMOs, those professionals make a choice that impacts their autonomy, scope of practice, and financial compensation for services (see MacStravic & Montrose, 1998; Posner, Gild, & Winans, 1995). For medical doctors, in particular, authority and autonomy herald from a long tradition of institutional power and control (see Feldman, Novack, & Gracely, 1998; Flocke et al., 1997; Freidson, 1975; Grumbach, Osmond, Uranizan, Jaffe, Bindman, et al., 1998; Parsons, 1951; Starr, 1982; St. Peter, Reed, Kemper, & Blumenthal, 1999; Strong, 1979).

Unlike many of his counterparts who partner with other physicians, my pediatrician can set his schedule, hire his staff, dictate his policies, and choose a certain number of patients. Solo practitioners avoid potential interpersonal and power conflicts that may result from debates over organizational policies or procedures. For example, groups of practitioners who make capitation agreements with third-party payers may struggle with advancing individual agendas while making group decisions (see Coile, 1997a, 1997b; Posner et al., 1995).

Yet, the cost of autonomy continues to mount. Even with an established practice, escalating administrative expenses and reimbursement limitations hinder the profitability and feasibility of solo practices. According to Hultman (1995), "The entrepreneurial skills that brought success in the past will not lead to success in the future. That is why so many [doctors] are now willing to become employed by HMOs" (p. 6). With employers turning to managed-care organizations (who favor capitation-based, rather than fee-for-service reimbursements) for their employees' health care benefits, solo practitioners scramble for a diminishing market of people who are not forced into particular practices or institutions. Some solo practitioners strive to compete for managed care contracts, while retaining autonomy, by joining together legally to bid on contracts with managed care organizations as independent practice associations (IPAs) ("Putting Managed Care in its Place," January 5, 1998).

The economic downside of signing a managed care contract is the need to accept lower payments for services or alternative fee structures (such as capitation-based). Certainly, some professionals who require fee-for-service payment ". . . gain financially by ordering tests and performing procedures that may not always be in the patient's best interest" (Emanuel & Dubler, 1997, p. 501; see also Holleman, Holleman, & Moy, 1997). However, as Emanuel and Dubler (1997), among others, note, the managed care system may constrain what a professional can do (in terms of testing, procedures, etc.), given lack of available reimbursement.

Resistance Through Connection

Even if health care professionals can afford such fee structures, the eking away of autonomy is a consequence of the third voice that many cannot accept. Dr. Melvin H. Kirschner, a doctor in Van Nuys, California, wrote in a letter to *USA Today* on July 1, 1998:

> As a physician in family practice and a longtime patient advocate, my medical decisions frequently were impeded by HMO delays or denials. Long before the HMO explosion, I practiced frugally, always seeking the best and most cost-effective ways to treat my patients. I finally resigned from the HMOs, a move which significantly reduced the volume of patients and the size of my income. I did this because my patients and I were frustrated by HMO restrictions, and there was nothing we could do about them.

Although Burdi and Baker (1997) found that participation in health maintenance organizations (i.e., by seeking contracts or by working directly for the HMOs) did not reduce perceptions of physician autonomy, some key members of the American Medical Association see the widespread turn to HMOs and managed care as a major threat to a doctor's ability to treat his or her patient. Citing "undue second-guessing, disincentives to care, prescription controls, and limits on advocacy," Gallagher argues in a June 25, 1999, *USA Today* editorial that "managed care's emphasis on cost-cutting has been so ruthless that even $160,000-a-year doctors look sympathetic" (p. 14A).

In a bold and ironic move, members of the American Medical Association (AMA) recently pushed to assert their collective "strength in numbers" as a means of regaining control and individual autonomy (see Eisler, December 7, 1998). If members of the AMA win critical legislative battles, ". . . hundreds of thousands of independent physicians [would be able] to unionize against health maintenance organizations and other managed care plans" (p. A1). Although federal law already permits employees of health care institutions (such as HMOs and hospitals) to unionize, the self-employed doctors cannot unionize unless they receive exemption from federal antitrust laws (AP, June 24, 1999a). Through unionizing, those physicians could win the best of both worlds—economic survival on their own terms. One doctor explains:

When I entered the practice 15 years ago, unionization was thought of as totally unprofessional, unmedical and un-American. But there's a growing feeling that we're losing control—losing control of patients, losing control of the health industry. (McKinlay & Stoeckle, 1997, p. 186)

Survival of the Biggest— Grouping Individual Hospitals

Similar to the advent of physician groups, larger organizations (such as hospitals) have grappled with the notion that size equates survival for individual hospitals and profit for huge conglomerates (Craig, 1987; Gray, 1991; Herzlinger, 1997; McKinlay & Stoeckle, 1997). For example, according to Limbacher (1998), "Today stand-alone rural facilities are up against managed care and Medicare pressures and sometimes need to partner or be acquired to survive . . . " (p. 68).

Residents of Barberton, Ohio (a town near Akron, Ohio) resisted efforts by larger health care systems to take over their small community hospital. Yet, in 1996, according to Lore (July 15, 1997), "residents overwhelmingly approved the sale of Barberton Citizens Hospital to a Tennessee for-profit hospital chain and Akron's Summa Health System" (p. A1). The hospital could no longer operate under the economic pressures of managed care, and residents could no longer withstand the temptation of strong financial gain. The profits from the sale of the hospital were enough to enable the community to build a new high school and to start a foundation (Lore, July 15, 1997).

The purchasers of Barberton Citizens Hospital will likely see rampant returns on their investment. Indeed, the growth explosion of some industry players (such as Columbia/HCA Healthcare Corporation, currently the largest for-profit health care chain) has propelled health care into a service that can produce profits, not just healthy lives. According to Craig (1987), "Twenty-five years ago, private enterprise saw few opportunities to enter the hospital business" (p. 19). Yet, as McKinlay and Stoeckle (1997) note, ". . . many multinational corporations, with highly diverse activities, have become involved in all facets of the generally profitable business of medical care . . ." (p. 182), and large health care companies continue to sniff the market for individual institutions that are particularly vulnerable, such as independent rural hospitals (see Limbacher, 1998). In a larger system, such institutions can become profitable acquisitions.

Craig (1987) argues that "today, the health care delivery system is on the threshold of megahealth corporations, which combine insurers, suppliers, and providers" (p. 19). As Fischer and Coddington (1998) maintain, such integrated heath care systems can provide "value-added" health care, resulting in better services for consumers at less cost. For stockholders, effective systems can be very profitable. Herzlinger (1997) observes:

Today, managers who believe that big is beautiful are rushing to integrate the fragmented health care system. Many of the stand-alone providers that characterize the sector have been cobbled together into chains of horizontally integrated hospitals, nursing homes, home health providers, and physicians' practices, among others. (p. 130)

Shifting Power Relations

With mega-growth comes mega-change, particularly in terms of relational dynamics between professionals within organizations. Historically, hospitals, as institutions, have reflected and reified the power structure of the medical profession—doctors in charge and others accepting a taken-for-granted chain of command. In his study of Pacific Hospital, Bosk (1979) describes how surgical staff members perpetuate implicit hierarchy through their social interaction and, through their positions within that hierarchy, perform tasks and respond to errors (see related work on social construction of medical errors by Paget, 1988). J. Cassell (1991) explores how certain surgeons present themselves (and how others in the hospital orient to them) as part of *the* "fellowship of surgeons" (p. 60), noting that the surgeons who were part of her study overtly claimed:

> . . . that outsiders—laypersons, patients and their families, even internists—were unable to understand, and consequently evaluate their behavior. The implication was clear: only surgeons (especially colleagues, who understood the personal, social, and professional forces that constrained their actions) could judge surgeons. (p. 66)

Turner and Samson (1995) explain that "the hospital is . . . symbolic of the social power of the medical profession, representing the institutionalization of specialized medical knowledge" (p. 153). However, the more widespread societal and economic shifts have quaked the very foundation of power relationships in contemporary hospitals. Quite simply, the organizational context for health care interactions contributes to the nature of exchanges between health care professionals and between professionals and health care seekers. With the new emphasis on economic efficiency, hospital administrators (and subsequently staff members) thrust the organizational focus to issues such as *accountability* (ensuring that individuals are responsible to management for efficient accomplishment of institutional and medical goals) (see Gray, 1991) and *case management* (ensuring that teams assess patient needs, establish clear goals, and identify specific means of attaining those goals for patients and for departments) (see Togno-Armanasco, Hopkin, & Harter, 1995 as well as Tweet and Gavin-Marciano's 1998 work on benchmarking). By shifting the emphasis to administrative concerns (and away from physician-based, medical-specialty concerns), the power base also gravitates toward administration and away from doctors.

Dr. Cynthia Wilkins, RN, Ph.D., a vice president for human resources for a healthcare system in southeastern Ohio, argues that *healthcare systems* (conglomerates of different entities that provide a variety of services—such as primary care, rehabilitation, psychiatric care, home care, acute care—to patients) are increasingly replacing traditional hospitals and hospital power hierarchies (Wilkins, 1998). Wilkins (1998) describes contemporary health care as a three-legged stool. The legs include the doctor, the healthcare system, and the payer/insurance company. The patient sits upon the stool. Notably, in this model, the doctor interacts with the health care system, but the doctor no longer controls the direction or decisions of the system.

Shifting Cultural Values and Practices

The roles of health care professionals, the mission of the institution, the values, beliefs, standards, and goals of organizational participants (from the person who sweeps the floors to the person who performs an operation to the person who makes tough staffing decisions)—each of these components contribute to the emergence of organizational culture within health care facilities. Dimensions of organizational culture, whether well-defined or ambiguous, do not just impact the place of the company picnic; they shape how work gets done and priorities get set. For example, in their 1998 investigation of Canadian hospital cultures, Rondeau and Wagar explain that the culture of particular hospitals frame perspectives on effective performance. Notably, the larger hospitals tend to focus on innovation and growth while the smaller hospitals concentrate on human resources and community involvement (see Rondeau & Wagar, 1998).

Culture also impacts staffing decisions. When economic factors became more prevalent, administrators at the hospital where I had my wrist surgery made decisions about staffing and staff roles and responsibilities. Those decisions influenced patient care (at least, they did for me!), staff morale, and staff cohesiveness. Bloom, Alexander, and Nuchols (1997) suggest little economic benefit for hospitals to decrease nursing staff and to rely on temporary help during peak times, and the cultural and care consequences of economically driven staff reductions hinder interpersonal relationships between staff. In the case of nursing, the enactment of "dispensable nurses" has even discouraged newcomers from entering the field (AP, February 28, 1999; Strofolino, February 23, 1999).

In another example of economically driven staffing, some hospitals contract with groups of practitioners (such as physician groups) to provide certain chunks of care. With these specified subgroups, notions of cohesive organizational culture become even more remote, and members must juggle multiple organizational and individual allegiances. Posner and colleagues (1995) investigated the interaction between two physician groups at a teaching hospital—cardiothoracic surgeons (funded by a division within the Department of Surgery) and cardiothoracic anesthesiologists (funded by the Department of Anesthesiology). Posner and colleagues (1995) explain:

> Both the cardiothoracic surgeons and anesthesiologists received remuneration based on a complex piecework formula. The largest portion of their hospital income derived from their base salary. Nevertheless, the contribution of "piecework" (number of procedures) was substantial. For example, anesthesiologists might increase their base salary 25 percent by spending extra time in the operating room and from other clinical activities. The funds to pay their salaries derived from income generated almost entirely by patient fees. (p. 479)

The groups faced a dilemma when the hospital needed to renegotiate its contract with a major insurer. Ultimately, the insurer and the hospital agreed to a contract that resulted a major budget cut—nearly 15 to 20 percent reductions for reimbursement for surgical procedures. Posner and colleagues (1995) note:

> Although hospital administrators had the legal authority to negotiate contracts with insurers, thereby determining the source of patients for physicians and setting the price of services,

they had limited cultural and social authority to dictate clinical practice changes to those physicians. (p. 480)

In the delicate negotiations that ensued between surgeons and anesthesiologists about revised protocols and pay for services, both groups of doctors struggled with issues of physician autonomy, physician authority, decision making, and bureaucracy. Moreover, the difficulty stemmed from their fragmented roles—individual practitioner, physician group member, organizational member. Notably, these professionals affirmed strong respect for the positions of others—acknowledging the importance of each profession and the distinction of clinical and economic issues. Posner and colleagues (1995) contend:

> In this case study the historically embedded social relations between anesthesiologists and surgeons within the economic and power structure of the hospital had ramifications for their clinical decisions. One could easily imagine that, if surgeons had clear authority over anesthesia consultants, changes in clinical practice in response to reductions in reimbursement might have taken a very different form. Likewise, if the hospital administration had direct authority in clinical decisions, perhaps the economic goal would have been more directly and effectively addressed. (p. 488)

Losee (1998) contends that "hospitals have become battlegrounds between the bottom line and humanitarianism" (p. 5). As hospitals develop into health care systems that incorporate diverse professionals and professional groups and that advocate an array of services and interdisciplinary teams (Wilkins, 1998), the battle lines become much more fuzzy and indistinct than simply choices between profit or people. Especially when we draw mergers and acquisitions into already muddy cultural waters, conflicts over central goals and values leap to the forefront of difficulties during economic transitions.

Before she ascended to vice presidential ranks with a health care system, Cindy Wilkins said that she could write a dissertation on the trials and tribulations of hospital organization transitions. I encouraged her to do just that. In her doctoral dissertation, Wilkins (1996) details the cultural trauma that confronted staff in two hospitals during a "joint venture" (and subsequent merger) between a Catholic, nonprofit hospital and a non-Catholic, for-profit hospital in one city. Suddenly, cultural values and traditions of each hospital that had once been assumed were now negotiable—staffing, services. Delivery services were evaluated in terms of efficiency and cost effectiveness (Wilkins, 1996). For example, although reproductive services, such as abortion, were not debatable by either hospital during this particular merger, Wickham (1998) reports that mergers between Catholic and non-Catholic hospitals in other areas have resulted in discontinued reproductive services in nearly half of such merger agreements.

Of course, not all of the mergers and joint ventures involve facilities that do not share similar organizational cultures (see Bellandi, 1998); however, the emergence of mega-structures adds another layer to the medical maze for health care practitioners and seekers who must work within the organizational hierarchy and constraints of the greater network, not to mention the confines of insurance limitations.

CLOSING THOUGHTS

Lamar, the patient care associate who had helped me during both of my hospital stays, assisted me into the wheelchair as the nurse handed my discharge papers to Roger. She pointed to something, but I couldn't concentrate enough to comprehend her instructions. I can't think—how can I be going home? I closed my eyes, yearning to go back to sleep, but as I felt the chair start to move beneath me, I forced my eyelids to open.

"Wait," I said. "Do I have everything?"

I moved my eyes to search the room as Roger assured me that we had all of the flowers and my bookbag and purse. Yet, as much as I wanted to check for belongings, I also needed to take one more look at this place, this room. Memories flooded my mind . . . that first day . . . the phone calls from frantic friends and relatives . . . Roger had been so sweet to check in and to help with the patient care advocate . . . He's been a good friend, I thought as I looked up at him.

I glanced once more at the bed before Lamar began again to push me from the room, and images of the nurse and the IV disaster and the PICC line and the portable x-ray machine and the vomiting, lots of vomiting, swept through my mind. I closed my eyes as I felt the chair bump over the bar between the memory-filled room and the hallway to freedom. Every ounce of energy had been drained from my body, my strength sapped. I thought of the maple syrup festival that I'd visited as a child. How do the maple trees stand so strong after getting stripped of their syrup, I wondered?

I felt the chair move around a corner, and I pried my eyes open to peer at the huddle of nurses around a counter—the nurse's station, I realized after a few seconds. Did I recognize any of them? Would any of them know me? They busied themselves with their work, unaware of my stare, not acknowledging my departure from a week under their collective care.

Lamar artfully backed my chair into the elevator, and I prayed that I wouldn't vomit as it descended. I smell, I realized. Grease practically spilled from my hair, and I imagined my ghastly image as strands fell around my pale face. What a sight I must be, I thought, as the doors to the elevator opened to the busy lobby of the hospital.

"You take care now, Dr. Beck," Lamar said as he prepared to help me into Roger's awaiting car. I strained the sides of my lips to shape a smile.

"Thanks," I replied. He had been so kind. Perhaps more importantly, he had been there nearly every day of my stay, caring for me, pretending not to be disgusted by my vomiting, sympathizing with my situation. I had seen him more than anyone else—doctor, nurse, friend, or relative—all week. In a strange way, I would miss him.

"You don't come back here any more," Lamar admonished me. "You don't want to be comin' back here no more."

I watched him turn and wheel the chair back into the hospital and out of the chill in the late January air. How surreal to drift in and out of his life, I reflected as I realized that I would likely never see him again, nor the nurses, other patient care associates, the x-ray techs, the anesthesiologist from OU, the whirlpool guy. How bizarre that they could play such a significant part in literally saving my life, and yet, we really just brush each others' paths, remembering only exceptional incidents or conversations.

"Do you want some crackers or something?" Roger asked gently after we merged on to the highway toward Athens.

I repositioned my head on the back of the seat so that I could see him. He had been so nice to come and retrieve me, yet I had barely uttered a word since we departed from the hospital. I felt very disconnected from the brightness of sun upon the snow, and casual conversation seemed suddenly unfamiliar. Other than answering brief medically related queries, I hadn't had much occasion to speak since that fitful call to my mom on Tuesday night.

"No," I said, closing my eyes as we hit a bump on the road. Please don't let me throw up, I prayed. "Thanks for getting them, though," I remembered to add.

I'll be better now, I thought. I'm going to gain strength to speak, stomach to eat. My mind started to cloud as I imagined home—my bed, my television, my remote control, my favorite chair, my girls, my cats, my dog. The hospital drifted further away, and my dreams lifted me home in advance of the car.

5 Industry Relationships— Movement to Team-Based Care

*R*oger helped me into my pink chair, and I stretched my legs and gingerly propped up my arms. Before I moved to Ohio, I purchased a huge bed-like chair from a former neighbor in Kingston, Pennsylvania, and I loved to curl up in it with a good book. The former neighbor had purchased the chair for her bad back because the chair featured a vibrating device as well as a switch for adjusting degrees of reclining. As I leaned my head back on the familiar chair, I looked around my living room. Brittany fixed her eyes on me and sat tentatively on the couch. Chelsea Meagan, only a toddler, gazed timidly at the strangers in her house as Wade interacted awkwardly with Roger and the two other co-workers who helped us to get my car home as well.

I caught a glimpse of the nightly news. Andrea something-or-other was giving another perky health update, and I remembered channel-surfing past this station on Tuesday before the IV incident. I shifted my gaze back to the four people who were conversing just beyond me in my living room. The hospital in Columbus seemed worlds away from this one, and yet, I couldn't compel myself to be part of my old life yet.

What was that life, I struggled to recall? My smiling face peered from frame after frame with the family on the walls, and I attempted to imagine the energy to run five miles and to keep up with fourteen fifth graders during a sleepover. How had I shifted into a shadow of my former self in just five days? This fragile shell belongs in the hospital, I thought, not in this place, not in this room, not with my girls and cats and dog and responsibilities.

I thanked my colleagues as they departed. Although I could still hear the news on the television in the background, the silence from the absence of voices in the house was deafening. Now, I felt like the stranger, the intruder, in the house. After a few minutes, Chelsea Meagan came up to me and tried to touch my "boo-boo" (her name for my IV). I tried to guard the IV with my casted right arm from Chelsea's efforts just as Sunni, our Sheltie, attempted to charge on to my lap. I couldn't move, and I felt too drained to protect myself. Wade yelled at the dog and directed Chelsea toward the television. "You're not in isolation," he said. "What did you think was going to happen when you came home? We have cats and the dog and kids. The whole world can't stop for you to be able to function."

What DID I think was going to happen? I didn't know how to be at home without serving as a mom, without walking to the bathroom or to the refrigerator, without keeping Chelsea Meagan and Sunni out of near-constant mischief . . .

I turned my head and noticed boxes along the entryway by the door. How did I miss those boxes as I entered the house, I wondered? "What are those?" I asked Wade, nodding toward the packages.

"Oh, and that's really great," he responded. "Some guy delivered those this afternoon. Those are the supplies for the home health nurse. I don't even want to know how much all of this is going to cost."

"Wade, the insurance will cover the nurse," I said, hoping that I was right.

"You and your insurance. With the hospital stay and the home nurse, you're driving up insurance costs for everyone," Wade continued.

"I really don't want to fight right now," I responded, wanting to sleep. The people at the hospital said that I would be able to sleep better at home without all of the interruptions of the hospital.

"How often does this nurse need to come? The agency called and said that she would be over around seven tonight, which is just great because the house is a wreck. I've been with the kids all week without any help, and I haven't been able to clean or anything." He paused. "I can't believe that you have nurses coming to our house and that you let all of those people from the office come over here now. The house is trashed and. . . ."

He kept talking, but I closed my eyes and strived to slip into slumber. Wade truly hated for anyone but kids to see our house, and I should have thought about his reaction to the home health people. Of course, given the situation, I don't think that I had much of a choice but to agree to professional care in my home.

I never imagined that I would benefit from home health services. As I made the decision to have the wrist reconstruction in the first place, I primarily concentrated on finding a good surgeon who knew what he was doing. Although I had interacted with physical therapists, x-ray technicians, and nurses prior to deciding who would perform my surgery, I viewed my surgeon as the single most important piece of the puzzle. The surgeon should know everything about everything, I thought. The others were simply supporting players, people to hand the scalpel or assist in minor ways.

Yet, with the staph infection, I found myself in a situation in which I had to trust strangers; I did not know their qualifications, and I did not have the opportunity to get second opinions and to investigate my options. My desire to be a good consumer and to participate in my health care could not be satisfied because I was too ill to assert myself, to ill to interview home health care agencies.

Moreover, I was too ill to understand that I had never truly understood the inner workings of contemporary health care. Perhaps more frightening for me than losing control was the realization that I felt trapped in a terrifying maze of people who, as individuals, did not possess all of the answers. I didn't know that I was wrong to assume that doctors call all of the shots and that they necessarily know "everything about everything." I didn't know that multiple health care professionals participate in providing health services and in coordinating care.

I left the hospital with the surgeon's orders for IV therapy, but the home health care nurses had to rely on their own expertise, knowledge, and judgment to facilitate my care at home. As I discovered time after time during my health care struggles, the empowerment of professionals beyond medical doctors comes with a double-edged sword—more individuals with legitimate perspectives and, at least occasionally, more confusion for people who seek care. With so many voices beckoning from around the maze, I often did not know which sound to follow nor which way to turn.

For industry professionals and consumers, the trend toward team approaches to health care has necessitated reconceptualizations of authority and role relationships. After discussing the negotiation of team roles and the emergence of home and community-based care, I close the chapter by outlining relational consequences of team approaches for health care participants.

Negotiating Team Roles

With the emphasis on integrated care in the managed care movement (and the de-emphasis of ultimate physician authority), health care facilities have turned to interdisciplinary teams as a way of working efficiently and treating patients holistically (see Barr, 1997; Beck, Dries, & Cook, 1998; Cott, 1997; Faulkner, 1985; Resnick & Tighe, 1997; Sheer, 1996; West & Wallace, 1991; Zimmermann, 1994). In fact, as Felton, Cady, Metzler, and Burton (1997) detail, "The Joint Commission on Accreditation of Hospitals is including as a standard the expectation that nurses and physicians collaborate on coordinated practice teams" (p. 123).

Ideally, health care professionals on interdisciplinary teams pool their "different knowledge and observations to patient care," and the patient benefits from integrated, thoughtful care (see Escaf, 1995, p. 19). In a less-than-perfect world, individual team members perform their duties, fail to communicate effectively, and the health care seeker lacks coherent information about what to do and how care will occur.

Interdisciplinary teams and health care seekers handle health care concerns with a careful balance between clear role expectations and rigid separations between duties (see Barr, 1997; Cott, 1997; Zimmermann, 1994). For example, as Cott (1997) noted, teams do not prosper from a "we decide, you carry it out" approach; instead, "the ties that assume most importance for collaborative teamwork should be problem-solving, planning and helping each other with work" (Cott, 1997, p. 1417–1418; see also work by Lamb & Napodano, 1984). However, even if that ideal joint problem solving and decision making occur, team members face the challenge of discerning how to prioritize perspectives and how to communicate team roles to health care seekers and their family members (see related work by Sheer, 1996; R. C. Smith, 1996; Zimmermann, 1994).

Traditional Role-Related Responsibilities

Agreeing on a shared vision and clear roles for an interdisciplinary team (or other less formal collaborative working arrangements between diverse health care professionals) can be difficult to attain, especially given traditional roles and power bases in the medical hierarchy (see related work by Anspach, 1997; Atkinson, 1995; Bosk, 1979; Butterill, O'Hanlon, & Book, 1992; J. Cassell, 1991; Drass, 1988; Ellis & Miller, 1994; Morse & Piland, 1981; Paget, 1988; Peterson, Halsey, Albrecht, & McGough, 1995; Thompson, 1984). For example, nurses have historically served as support staff to doctors and as nurturers of patients (see Bulecheck & McCloskey, 1992; Joos, Nelson et al., 1985; O'Connor, 1996; Orem,

1995; Pinkerton & Schroeder, 1988). Especially in institutional contexts, the nurse has tended to be the one who spends time with people who seek care and their families and who facilitates and monitors progress. As such, nurses can develop different perspectives of patient care than their counterparts in other medical areas.

In her book on interdisciplinary teams in neonatal intensive care units, Anspach (1997) offers the example of Robin, a premature baby with major respiratory problems. Robin's mother essentially abandoned Robin in the hospital and ultimately left her to the care of the increasingly discouraged nurses. When the team met to negotiate future care for Robin, Anspach notes:

> The attending doctor and the nurses who participated in the conference not only articulated contrasting conceptions of Robin as a patient, but had differing visions of the central dilemma. For the attending, the dilemma was one of profound prognostic perplexity. Torn between continuing to treat a patient who might be doomed and ending the life of a patient who might otherwise recover, he steered a middle course that spared him from confronting either alternative. For the nurses, the dilemma was one of continuing to care for an infant whose "unsocialized" behavior provided them with few rewards and who, in addition, may have even been damaged by their own neglect. (pp. 75–76)

Okay, I admit that I was a bit stunned to read about this response by the nurses to a tiny, helpless infant. The reaction of the nurses in this situation seems harsh and uncaring, to those of us who get to lurk as Monday morning quarterbacks. Surely, we would have been able to feel more compassion; certainly, we would have wanted to do anything, to try anything, to help that little baby to live and to grow and to prosper. Yet, as I reflected on this account and tried to conceptualize the lived realities of these nurses, I started to understand (although possibly not agree with) their collective view of the child. They had watched the baby, day in and day out. They had heard her tears, and yet, they could not comfort her. They had watched her linger on the brink of death, and yet, they could not help her. They had cleaned her and cared for her, and yes, possibly cried for her, and yet they could do nothing for her suffering but to watch helplessly. Over time, their emotional defenses prompted them to detach and to grow numb to Robin's anguish.

Indeed, nurses cannot separate themselves from human emotions of hurt and anger any more than they can make all of their multiple roles compatible. As the story of one oncology nurse suggests, the multifaceted role of "nurse" prompts deep (and sometimes conflicting) allegiances. That nurse felt torn between the patient's (an elderly male cancer patient) desires, the family's needs, confidentiality issues, and her professional obligations to others in the medical community.

The nurse recalled that, during one treatment session, her patient "turned to me and said, 'I don't want to miss my daughter's wedding.' There were tears in his eyes, and I knew he realized that he would not see June" (Gilligan, 1988, p. 16). Referred by the oncologist to the nurse, the man's daughter called to ask if treatment could accommodate the wedding in June. The nurse responded by encouraging the daughter to " 'plan an earlier wedding.' She knew immediately what I was saying" (p. 16).

Tears welled up in my eyes as I read this moving account. The daughter did move the wedding date, and the father was able to share the wonderful occasion. I respect the nurse's decision to tell the daughter to move the wedding if she wanted her father to attend. However, notably, the nurse's response to the daughter's call varied sharply with the oncologist's response. Although we do not know what the oncologist told the daughter, the nurse's story indicates that the doctor revealed little beyond specific medical information, if that. If the daughter had gained all of the information that she wanted from the oncologist, why would she make the second long distance call? We do not know if the oncologist's reaction would have been different if he would have understood the context better or if the patient would have told the doctor about his desire to be at the wedding. If nothing else, commitment to doctor–patient confidentiality likely prevented the doctor from telling the daughter about the patient's condition.

We certainly cannot know how other nurses would have reacted to a similar situation. However, the nurse's decision to consider the patient's needs beyond the medical arena (and the oncologist's decision to share minimal information with the daughter) exemplifies a substantial philosophical difference between these types of medical professionals (see related work by Bourhis, Roth, & MacQueen, 1989). Although I was very fuzzy during my PICC-line decision process, I do know that the nurse who had come to know me best was the one who presented me with the harsh bottom line. I never had a clear idea from my doctor about the seriousness of my situation.

Menikheim and Meyers argued in 1986 that "as attitudes change, the caring orientation of nursing will be seen as equal to the cure orientation of medicine. Nursing is different than, rather than less than, medicine" (p. 86). While Menikheim and Meyers may be correct in their assertions, differences in care philosophies and in real or perceived institutional hierarchies contribute to communication problems between diverse professionals (and between those professionals as they collaborate on interdisciplinary teams) (see related work by Cunningham & Wilcox, 1984).

Role-Related Conflicts

When a variety of individuals, bringing diverse health care philosophies, perspectives, and priorities, intersect, how do decisions get accomplished? In my case, time after time, health care professionals disagreed, breeding dissension and causing confusion. Clay, an interview participant, offered a similar story:

> I was in the hospital because I had a lot of symptoms for [medical condition]. There were two doctors who were reviewing the case. One doctor wanted to operate, and the other did not. Basically, they got into an argument at the foot of my bed. One doctor said "let's just give him a bag of peanuts and see if it explodes." That bothered me.

In this scenario, the doctors likely held similar status, as consultants on the case. Although that similarity contributed to subsequent conflict (i.e., who is going to "win"? who is going to convince the other or back down?), both doctors apparently oriented to each other's opinion as something that should be legitimized with a response. Their respective roles as "doctor" commanded mutuality in terms of face-to-face conversation about the medical situation.

Conversely, role differentials can exacerbate conflict in a deeper way—through silencing. Davis (October 19, 1998) reports, for example, that "the culture of the operating room sometimes works against warnings to surgeons or anesthesiologists. Nurses, who may have the best overall view of the procedure, are not always encouraged to give doctors advice" (p. D1).

When I was doing field research in a hospital, a few nurses told me about an obstetrician who induced labor or performed c-sections to ensure that he delivered babies prior to his vacation. The nurses bemoaned the health risk to the baby, yet when I pursued an explanation for their unwillingness to challenge the doctor about this potentially unethical and medically risky practice, they noted that "you don't do that"—that is, call the doctor on the validity/acceptability of *his* or *her* medical decision. As I will detail, deference to my orthopedic surgeon abounded on the part of team members (such as the nurse who worked in his office and the occupational therapists), even when they believed that he was making serious mistakes in terms of diagnosis and treatment.

Case of Expanding Role of Nurses

In the wake of team-based approaches to health care (and of advanced training and legislation that permits more autonomy for nurses), the rules for the doctor–nurse game (see Stein, Watts, & Howell, 1990) have shifted, making formerly clear lines of subordination ambiguous (see Fagin, 1992; Katzman & Roberts, 1988; Stein et al., 1990). In their comparison of physician–nurse roles from 1967 to 1990, Stein and colleagues (1990) contend:

> The image of nurses as handmaidens is giving way to that of specialty-trained and certified advanced practitioners, with independent duties and responsibilities to their patients. Physicians increasingly depend on nurses' special expertise in prestigious settings such as emergency departments, specialty clinics, and intensive care units. Such strong nursing roles are reinforced by contemporary television series such as *St. Elsewhere* and *China Beach*. . . . New roles for nurses in utilization review and quality assurance directly threaten physicians' authority in clinical decision making. (pp. 265–266)

For physicians who are also losing power due to organizational restructuring and managed care mandates, the blurring of boundaries between nursing and physician domains may be difficult to watch silently. When the Health Care Financing Administration initiated a proposal to permit nurse anesthetists to practice without supervision by a doctor, physician organizations balked—loudly. In a May 21, 1998 editorial, *USA Today* took the position that a physician anesthesiologist and a nurse anesthetist should administer anesthesia together (see Jurgansen, May 21, 1998). In his "opposing view" response, Scot D. Foster (May 21, 1998), president of the American Association of Nurse Anesthetists, argued that the paper's stance ". . . promotes traditional dogma that the only good health care in this country is that provided under the watchful eyes of physicians, regardless of the facts to the contrary" (p. 14A).

In fact, as Foster (May 21, 1998) continued, in many areas of the United States, any physician (even those without training in anesthesia) may supervise a specially trained nurse anesthetist—in his view, the rule could enable hospitals to legitimately staff people with training in the area. In her letter to the editor of *USA Today*, Linda Jeffries, CRNA (certified registered nurse anesthetist), pleads, ". . . Check out the educational requirements CRNAs must meet to administer anesthesia. We're not 'just nurses'; we're specialists in anesthesia. We know what we're doing, and we take pride in our profession. Nurse anesthetists are specialists, not just 'nurses'" (1998, p. 14A).

Regardless of which side might be "right" or "wrong" in this political struggle, the dispute exemplifies tension over turf, authority, and legitimacy. In these types of situations, the strain can stretch into the inner workings of a team and into the artful process of role negotiation and legitimate authority to perform particular duties and to make certain decisions. For example, Laschinger and Weston (1995) discuss the link between role perceptions and collaborative decision making between medical students and nurses. Johnston (1992) argues that inappropriate comments and behaviors by medical faculty toward medical students interfere with work and learning and that awareness of the problem has prompted special training programs for doctors. One medical facility has even started coordinating multidisciplinary rounds so that all of the team members can participate in "information sharing and ongoing communication" (Felton et al., 1997, p. 122).

Patient-Centeredness

Interdisciplinary team role conflicts can be resolved through effective communication that emphasizes patient-centeredness (see Beck et al., 1998; Escaf, 1995; Eubanks, 1992; Faulkner, 1985; Gage, 1998; Zimmermann & Applegate, 1992). As Gage (1998) contends, ". . . the adoption of the client vision as a focus for the work of the team may create a transcending purpose for the team" (p. 22).

Noting the importance of examining both mental health and physical health services, the Collaborative Family HealthCare Coalition advocates interdisciplinary teams of doctors and psychotherapists (see Peterson, 1998). When included in health care discussions, social service staff members also contribute significantly to holistic and patient-centered care (see Thompson, 1984). Resnick and Tighe (1997) describe the Vine Hill Community Clinic:

> The clinic, which is located in a public housing development in Nashville, is staffed by a multidisciplinary team of family nurse practitioners, mental health clinical specialists, a medical social worker, a community outreach nurse, a medical assistant, a business manager, a janitor, and a receptionist–secretary. Physician preceptors include an adult primary care specialist, a pediatrician, and a psychiatrist who are on call for consultation and who review charts weekly (p. 92). . . .
>
> After recognizing the psycho-social needs of their clients (low to middle income urban residents, including some who have mental and physical disabilities), the clinic team increased its use of the clinic social worker to assist in screenings and medical/community referrals. . . . In fact, through the social worker's connections, the clinic has become a "partner in community health as opposed to a mechanism for the diagnosis of individual pathology." (p. 95)

Resnick and Tighe contend:

> Interface between the clinic social worker and social agencies enhances provision of services to the Vine Hill Community. Together, the clinic social worker and community agencies address the need for food, transportation, prescription medications, and employment. This

cooperative effort continuously expands, and networking now includes community religious organizations and community action groups. . . . Creating and maintaining a continuing dialogue between the clinic and the community has been one of the outstanding features of the Vine Hill Community Clinic. (p. 95)

The interests of individual health care seekers—people who come to the clinic with needs—lie at the heart of that ongoing interaction. Especially with the explosion of home and community-based care, the effectiveness of interdisciplinary teams contributes to how individual health care seekers strive toward wellness.

The Emergence of Home- and Community-Based Health Care

Recently, I was walking my dog on the bike trail along the Hocking River and something flew into my eye. After unsuccessfully trying to wash out the "something," I stumbled into the UrgentCare unit of our local hospital, which is located just off of the bike path. The UrgentCare unit shares space in the hospital's emergency room, but the unit offers care for less critical injuries and illnesses for a few hours each day (and at a lesser cost than the ER). Although I felt a little silly for seeking attention, my eye really hurt, and I feared that I had been stung by an insect in the eye. One of the doctors in the UrgentCare unit examined me, flushed the eye, and gave me instructions to purchase an over-the-counter eye drop. The visit cost over $150, but fortunately, my insurance paid most of that fee. If I had been treated in the emergency room unit (after the hours of the UrgentCare unit had ended for the day), the cost would likely have been doubled. Even so, the pricetag was still much higher than a visit to my eye doctor would have been in the morning.

Given the expense of hospital staff and materials, health care in hospitals has become cost prohibitive for individuals and insurers. In fact, the hospital portion of my bills for the staph infection totaled thousands of dollars, for five days of care, drugs, and materials, in addition to charges for the surgery and anesthesia. My home health care was not cheap—each visit cost a little less than $100, not including drugs and materials. However, home health care does offer one alternative to lengthy (and more expensive) hospital stays. As Dr. Anthony J. Grieco (1998) noted in a newspaper column on home health care, "Home is where the heart is. These days, it's also where more and more patients are as well. In the 1990s, home medical care for the acute or chronically ill has expanded dramatically and successfully" (p. D3).

Home Health Care

My home health care agency resembles other such organizations in its range of available services, including general nursing, various therapies (IV, physical, occupational, speech), nutritional counseling, and attention to other physical needs, depending, to a large extent, on physician referrals. (Exceptions include laws like Ohio's Advanced Practice Nursing Act, which authorize some nurses to provide patient care without direct supervision from physicians—see Reed, 1999). As the National Association for Home Care's web site (www.nahc.org) attests, home care services abound. Notably, the various home care professionals collaborate on care, offering a holistic (rather than fragmented) approach to recovery.

Although most home care agencies feature nurses and therapists, at least a few doctors have abandoned their waiting rooms to venture into homes. According to the American Academy of Home Care Physicians (see aahcp.org/aahcp), doctors can build lucrative practices around home care (especially given the Medicare reimbursement policies of the mid-1990s), with significant benefits to patients.

Dr. Felix Obregon works with Mobile Doctors, an organization that serves more than 7,000 individuals in three states (see Uzelac, July 23–25, 1999, as well as company website—mobiledoctors.com). According to Dr. Obregon, "This is about proactive medicine. You're taking care of the patient as a whole" (see Uzelac, July 23–25, 1999, p. 4).

The choice of home care as a health care delivery option stems from both economic and medical necessity, not just a more holistic approach, however (see, for example, www.medicarerights.org for restrictions and requirements on home care). In my case, home care made more financial and medical sense than hospital care because the same medically necessary IV therapy could be provided to me at much less cost at home.

Of course, like the rest of the health care industry, the economic viability of home health care rests on the willingness of managed care and Medicare to reimburse adequately for services. A little more than a year after my illness, four agencies in my area were impacted by the federal Balanced Budget Act of 1997, which slashed Medicare reimbursements for home care. Cutbacks due to that bill resulted in the closure of two agencies in my region and dramatic staff and service reductions in two others (Gibson, July 9, 1998).

Hospice Care

Especially for individuals who suffer from serious illnesses, the absence of home care would force many into nursing homes or other care facilities (Gibson, July 9, 1998). Hospice care, a form of home-based care, enables people to receive medical attention on a long-term basis for less expense than hospital care. In so doing, hospice permits individuals to choose home care instead of care in more institutionalized settings, permitting them to enjoy the comforts and familiarity of home during a difficult physical and emotional period of life.

Charles Wicks, a father, grandfather, and great-grandfather, decided that he did not want to return to the hospital after doctors informed him that he had a malignant brain tumor. His wife had died in a nursing home, and he was determined to leave his earthly life in his own home. According to a profile on Wicks in one hospice newsletter ("Hospice helps keep families together," Spring, 1998), "Thanks to a loving family and hospice nurses, home care aides, social workers and volunteers, Charles Wicks lived out his final days exactly as he wanted" (p. 1).

Community-Based Health Care

Community-based health centers, community nursing organizations (CNOs), and nursing centers also allow individuals (especially those who are underserved) to obtain care that meets their particular needs at affordable costs (see Clear, Starbecker, & Kelly, 1999; Dievler & Giovannini, 1998; Gerrity & Kinsey, 1999; Kinsey & Gerrity, 1999; Kristjanson & Chalmers, 1990; Lundeen, 1999; Schraeder, Lamb, Shelton, & Britt, 1997). Such community-based facilities offer important and creative options to community members, especially in the areas of preventive medicine and health promotion. Kinsey and Gerrity (1999) emphasize that "nursing center models and other community-based and focused health enterprises support the proposed vision for *Healthy People 2010* (HP 2010), which is 'Healthy People in Healthy Communities'" (p. ix). In fact, Gerrity and Kinsey (1999) argue that ". . . such a nursing service model is proving to be a linchpin in planning and providing optimal health care to diverse populations in community settings" (p. 30).

In Philadelphia, for example, staff members of the LaSalle University Neighborhood Nursing Center (LSUNNC) reach out to people who cannot access care because of financial, location, time, or transportation barriers (see Gerrity & Kinsey, 1999). Health promotion programs include immunizations, prenatal care, cancer awareness, and lead poisoning prevention, in addition to other health care services in a variety of settings. Student nurses and staff members stretch more traditional clinic boundaries by providing services at churches, day cares, community centers, and other facilities within the heart of urban neighborhoods.

Notably, such service-learning approaches to the education of health professionals have emerged as components of medical and nursing curriculums across the country as well as pivotal parts of community-based health care delivery. At the osteopathic medical school at my university, the Ohio University College of Osteopathic Medicine (see www.ohiou.edu), service-learning includes similar visits to tiny rural communities in Appalachian Ohio. Students and staff members offer preventive care for women (such as screens for breast, ovarian, and cervical cancer), immunizations, and sports physicals. They also provide health information at wellness fairs at local malls, and other such activities.

While nursing centers, in particular, strive to serve comprehensively (rather than programmatically), community nursing organizations concentrate even more on developing personalized partnerships between health care seekers and nursing professionals. In the case of CNOs, specially trained nurses work as case managers with individuals in order to maximize health outcomes. Schraeder amd colleagues (1997) explain the roles of health care seekers and "nurse partners" in CNOs:

> At its core, the CNO model depends on individual choice and empowerment. Each CNO member is actively involved in determining health care priorities and the level of personal commitment to selected goals. Professional nurses are available to coach enrollees and facilitate the process, rather than simply to ensure patient compliance. (p. 64)

Although the proliferation of home- and community-based care constitutes important care options, such delivery systems also jar traditional power relationships and views of enacting health and wellness. In the case of home health/hospice care and CNOs, nurses serve as case managers who contact resources, facilitate physician recommendations, and educate health care seekers (see McHann, 1994). They function in a delicate balance of coordinating care yet remaining aware of limitations on their authority and training to practice medicine (McHann, 1994). Given the status of managed care and the advent of diverse contexts for health care, the interpersonal and power relationships in interdisciplinary teams of health care professionals has never been so critical nor so challenging.

Lingering Relational Problems

I looked at the IV pump and then the clock. "Only a few minutes to go," my home health care nurse, Pam, said. I glanced at Roger and then back at the clock. "We'll be okay," he said.

I closed my eyes and leaned back. After coming home on Friday evening, I had started to feel better by Sunday afternoon. I could finally eat bland foods, and the nausea subsided. The home health care nurses came at 8 A.M., 4 P.M., and midnight, after we managed to start a schedule on Saturday morning. They had been great about explaining things to me, and they took care of administering drugs, changing my hip dressing, and charting my vital signs. People from work were kind enough to bring over food. On Sunday, Wade took Chelsea Meagan and the dog to his mom's house in Virginia so that we wouldn't have to worry about Chelsea and Sunni around the IV wires. I even got one of the hairstylists at Penny's to wash my hair, nasty from nearly a week without shampooing, on Sunday afternoon. Yet, late on Sunday evening, I started feeling very tired again. When I told Pam about my fatigue during her midnight visit on Sunday night, she gently reprimanded me for "overdoing it."

I awoke on Monday morning to new symptoms—pain in my neck and left shoulder. Upon her arrival, I dutifully reported my new symptoms to Pam. She affirmed my concern, noting that everything had potential importance during this critical time. As she started the pump and began to change my hip bandage, Pam told me to be sure to tell the surgeon during my scheduled check-up in Columbus that morning.

I opened my eyes and looked at the clock—8:30 A.M. We were supposed to be in Columbus by 10 A.M., and Roger had to get back for his night class that night. I had booked the girls' favorite babysitter, Jenna, to run the scout meeting for me and to bring Britti home, but I didn't know how late she could stay.

I looked at the IV pump as it buzzed. Pam removed the pump and reminded me to ask the doctor to look at my neck. "It is a bit red and swollen," she said. "It didn't look this way last night." As she packed her bag, she turned to me and noted that one of the head nurses would meet with me at 4 P.M. to do an intake and to talk about how I could do the pump myself. Right, I thought. With a cast on one arm and the IV in the other, I'm NOT going to be very self-sufficient.

We drove up Highway 33, and I thought about making that same trip just a short week before. The snow gently tipped remnant pieces of grass on the side of the road, and two horses peeked out of their barns. We passed a yellow school bus that was jammed with laughing children. One of them made a face at me as he caught me staring at the commotion. They must be on some sort of field trip, I thought. Amazing, how life goes on, richly and abundantly, for others while mine seems to have ground to a screeching halt.

We pulled into the parking lot, and Roger stopped the Saturn in front of the building. He helped me to step out of the car and to limp across the icy pavement. I wondered why an orthopedic medical facility would lack the good sense to scatter salt. Good for business, I thought cynically.

Once again, the waiting area was packed, filled with casted arms and legs, the old, the young, people with companions and those who sat alone, some with magazines and a few who watched a game show on television. I hobbled to the desk, figuring that I would have to wait, but the receptionist directed me to an examining room. Roger took a seat in the crowded waiting area.

When I re-entered the waiting area, though, he was gone. I peered into the hallway and then moved toward a chair by the door. "What are you doing out here so fast?" he asked. "Well, Dr. T. checked me over and said that I'm doing fine," I responded.

"What about your neck and shoulder?" Roger inquired. "Well, Dr. T. said that it was possibly nothing and that I'm doing fine," I reported. I was so tired.

"What do you think?" he pressed. He had heard the "it's nothing" line before.

"Oh, I don't know. What are the odds that anything else would go wrong?" I tried to joke, but somehow, none of this seemed remotely funny any more. I didn't know what to think; I didn't know when to be concerned and when to dismiss the aches and pains of everyday life. My home health nurse seemed concerned. Dr. T.'s nurse seemed concerned. Dr. T. couldn't have looked less concerned.

"Do you think that it's the PICC line?" Roger asked. "Oh, I don't know," I said. "They did x-rays when they put it in, and they said that it was in the right place. I felt some discomfort when it went in, but the nurses just said that I was nervous. They even did another x-ray here, just to be sure, after I told Dr. T. about the neck pain. I don't know what could be wrong. It really is possibly nothing," I continued. I must not have sounded convincing.

Roger looked at me. I'm not very good at masking my feelings. I wanted for nothing more to be wrong, and I was willing to accept his word and leave. Yet, I feared the worst—even though I had no idea what "the worst" might be—hadn't "the worst" already happened?

"Let's go talk to him," Roger said, and we walked down the hallway to the rear receptionist desk.

We caught Dr. T. between patients. If a person can groan without making a sound, Dr. T. did it then. He had appointments stacked up in the waiting room; he was running way behind, and I had already consumed considerable time. He assured us that nothing was wrong, and yet, when Roger pressed him on possible complications of a PICC line, we learned that Dr. T. knew very little about PICC lines. Members of a specially trained PICC line team install them, and people don't seem to have problems. Apparently, surgeons rarely get involved in this state of infection treatment.

Dr. T. tried to be helpful. He asked his receptionist to get the name of a PICC line person who could answer our questions. We stood in the hallway, waiting. I felt faint. I wanted food and caffeine. The clock kept ticking—noon, 12:30, 12:45. Finally, the receptionist told us that she could not identify who could respond to our questions. The nurses referred all queries to the surgeons (despite the latter's lack of expertise), and the surgeons didn't have the training to respond. Someone brought me a chair, and I sank down, wondering where to turn.

"Well, I'm not sure what to tell you," Dr. T. said. "People really don't have problems with PICC lines. I'm sure that the neck is unrelated to everything else. Take some ibuprofen and see your family practitioner if it keeps swelling. Go home and get some rest, and

I'll see you in a week." He smiled at me. "Pretty soon, you'll be out of that big cast and on your way."

I tried to smile back as I stood to leave. Dr. T.'s nurse stared at me as I turned to walk down the narrow corridor. What a strange look, I thought, as we entered the elevator.

Roger helped me into the car. "What do you think?" he said before starting the engine. I didn't know what to think. Surely, nothing else could be wrong. Dr. T. had to be right on this one. Even if something was amiss, though, where would we go? How could we have time to figure it out when we had to get back for that nurse to do her intake with me and for Roger to teach his class? I was hungry, and I just wanted to go eat and sleep.

"To the hospital?" Roger asked, not letting the subject drop.

I sighed, knowing that he was right. I nodded. "To the hospital," I agreed.

With all of the changes in contemporary health care, communication between health care professionals and between professionals and health care seekers has become increasingly critical and increasingly complicated. With the advent of specialties, we gain highly qualified individuals in particular areas, but we lose the "big picture." With the advent of McDonaldization efforts such as cutting costs, we eliminate redundancy and waste, but we muddy the waters of individual and institutional power. With coordinated care, we put a number of "great minds" together to help people, but we lose the focus of a family doctor and the understanding of who addresses which problem. With interdisciplinary teams, we gain holistic care, yet we add complicated communication and confidentiality concerns.

Flow of Information

From home health care nurses and community agencies who depend on hospital discharge information (see Smith, 1996) to physicians who depend on details from home health and community agency staff to health care seekers who yearn to understand and to participate in decision making, contemporary health care participants rely on effective, clear, and concise information. Health care professionals, in particular, require details in order to provide continuity of care and to facilitate progress toward wellness, especially when health care seekers move from facility to facility or from one type of professional to another.

When more than one professional offers assistance, the quality of information greatly impacts health care seekers and their respective ability to maneuver through his or her medical maze (see Gerteis, 1993). At a most fundamental level, seekers need clarification about which professional can contribute the best insights about which aspects of the situation, how the professionals fit together, and the extent and limitations of their expertise, power, and authority. For example, Gerteis (1993) describes a woman who believed that her surgeon was "in charge" but discovered, in the hospital, that her oncologist had taken over primary responsibility for her case without her knowledge. As I learned during my struggle with the PICC line, distinctions in the areas of expertise, power, and authority become especially important (and potentially ambiguous) when health care seekers pursue answers to complicated questions. I grew increasingly frustrated with blurred boundaries between types of health care professionals that trapped me in a web of vague responses and unclear lines of responsibility.

The communication process can also be hindered by some third party payer arrangements. The Clinton administration has initiated steps to remove the Medicaid HMO gag clauses, clauses that prohibit doctors from telling patients about uncovered tests or treatments (see Aston, 1997; Meyer, 1997). However, until legislation passes, such "gag orders" constitute another communicative dimension of the relationships between providers and third party payers and another huge factor in the freedom of professionals and health care seekers to interact about options.

Confidentiality Issues

Angela, a *doula* (a person who caters to a woman during the birthing process), encourages parents to strive for their "dream birth" (see Frenchmeyer, October 20, 1999). Parents discuss their plans with physicians; however, Angela does not interact directly with doctors (as a fellow professional and certainly an important part of the birth plans), citing trust and confidentiality issues.

As the number of participants on a case grows, confidentiality becomes problematic for professionals and for seekers. During my wrist reconstruction, the doctor who referred me to Dr. T. and my family doctor were both copied in on notes in my patient file. Such copies ensure the flow of communication; however, do they constitute a violation of my confidentiality? When doctors share bits of patient conversations with the rest of the interdisciplinary team, do those disclosures interfere with confidentiality? When a nurse offers an explanation of her position by referring to a patient's fear or lack of resources, does such an explanation violate confidentiality principles? No easy answers exist; however, with the advent of integrated care, health care seekers should ask pointed questions about how health care professionals share information and when confidences may be preserved.

Given the increase of computer databases and large-scale health care organizations, health care seekers risk additional violations of medical privacy by providers or payers who make patient information available to others (see Gallagher, June 11, 1999; Jurgensen, July 13, 1998). The consequences of leaked information can be devastating for health care seekers. Gallagher (June 11, 1999) explains:

> The result can be embarrassment and worse—lost jobs, lost opportunities and poor-quality care. More than a third of Fortune 500 firms, for instance, reported checking medical records before hiring or promoting workers. Another report found 206 cases of discrimination because of outsiders' access to patients' genetic information. (p. 25A)

Summary of Relational Issues

The frenzy and confusion of contemporary life often force us to clutch at the fragments of our lives like a desperate attempt to hold on to a stack of papers in a windstorm. Amid the whirlwind of our lives, we just try to cling to as many things as we can, realizing the impossibility of keeping all of the loose ends together.

As health care seekers strive to sort their ways through health care situations, in the most efficient manner, they do so in the context of their chaotic everyday lives. When they work with one doctor to treat an ear infection or obtain annual physical examinations, the integration of medical care seems relatively simple—just another slot taken on a daily schedule. However, when a health care issue becomes something more, when a child does not respond to antibiotics for ear infections and then requires tubes or when a physical uncovers a questionable mass, health care seekers suddenly plunge into a maze of multiple health care professionals, time-consuming appointments, and questions about how everyone fits together, what tests mean, and what way is best. Who can be trusted more? How should one behave to avoid being lost in the shuffle of the increasingly complex medical world?

As health care professionals work with health care seekers, they do so in the context of escalating demands on their time and restrictions on their resources and options. External forces command them to do more in less time, yet collaborating with other professionals requires time; explaining options takes time; guiding seekers through the saga of the system and their personal health care struggles demands time. How can they give time to Person A without robbing it from Person B? How can they delineate lines of responsibility without accepting or yielding too much of their authority?

In this era of fragmentation, questioning of medical authority, managed care and, yes, litigation, health care participants face significant constraints on their ability to communicate. Yet, the need to share information in terms of medical details and lines of responsibility/expertise and the need to preserve trust have never been so vital for accomplishing health and wellness.

CLOSING THOUGHTS

When we arrived at the hospital, we really didn't know where to go. Did the PICC-line nurses have an office, a department? Should we talk to the patient advocacy contact that Roger had made during my hospital stay? The hospital had not seemed so big from my bed, and the patient care associates had artfully navigated my wheelchair through the maze during my trips to x-ray and whirlpool.

I felt a little nervous; Dr. T. had told me to go home. I didn't want to upset him—I still had a long way to go with my arm after I got better from the infection. He possibly won't even find out, I reasoned.

We decided to check in with the woman in admissions. As we entered the reception area, I scanned the room. Had it really only been a week since I came to this place and climbed into the wheelchair? Would I need to stay here again?

"Hi," I said to the admissions representative. "I'm not sure if we're in the right place or not, but we're hoping that you can help us . . ."

I explained about the infection, the PICC line, the PICC-line nurses' assurances that they would provide assistance if I had any trouble at all, the inability of Dr. T.'s receptionist to discover who to contact here. I wondered if I was making sense. My story kept getting more complicated, with the wrist and the infection and now the PICC line.

"So, Dr. T. sent you over?" the admissions representative inquired. I looked at Roger. I felt like a little girl who had been caught crossing the street without her mom's permission. Roger evaded the issue. "Actually, we were just hoping to get some basic information from the PICC-line nurses before we head back to Athens," Roger explained.

"Well, let me call Dr. T.," she said, waving us to nearby chairs.

I slowly turned and went to a chair. "We're in so much trouble now," I said. "He's going to tell them that he didn't send us, and we're not going to get to see anyone because he doesn't think that it's necessary. Uggggggh . . ." I sighed, leaning my head back against the chair. "I don't want to make him mad. What if he says he can't trust me so he won't treat me? I am so screwed." I felt exhausted and so very hungry. Even though I had just sat in a car and walked into two buildings, I had exerted myself more than I had, well, since before last week.

Roger put his hand on my knee. "We're going to be fine. We haven't done anything wrong. The PICC-line nurses said that they would help, and Dr. T. admitted that he didn't know much about them so this could be the problem."

I wasn't convinced. I watched the admissions representative end her conversation and go to a back area. I kept trying to imagine the look on Dr. T.'s face when he got this phone call about his problem patient. I inhaled deeply and closed my eyes.

"Christie," Roger said. I opened my eyes, and the admissions representative stood before us.

"We're waiting for a call back from his office," she said. "In the meantime, I have asked for one of the PICC-line nurses to come and speak with you."

We thanked her and settled back in our chairs. We sat in silence as the hands of the clock moved to 3 P.M. Roger would need to leave for his class soon; I had to return home for Brittany and that lady from home health. Darn, I thought as I rechecked the clock. With a two-hour drive, I knew that I could not make the 4 P.M. meeting with the home health lady. What about my 4 P.M. medicine, I wondered?

Roger had returned from calling the home health agency (and grabbing some quick junk food) when the PICC-line nurse entered. The admissions clerk gestured to us, and the nurse sat down beside me.

"What can I do for you?" she asked.

"Well, I'm sure that it's nothing, but I have this pain in my neck and shoulder, right about where the PICC line is. My home health nurse said that it's red and swollen and that I should have it checked out," I said.

"You really need to talk to your doctor about this," the nurse explained.

"Well, we did, and the surgeon didn't seem to know too much about it," Roger said.

I peered into the nurse's eyes. "The lady who installed this thing said that you all were available if I had problems," I said.

"I'm not sure—you see, I'm not a doctor, and I really don't know what I can tell you. I am not qualified to offer medical opinions," she said.

Tears of frustration started to well up in my eyes. I felt tired and sick and hungry and completely passed around like a hot potato. "Who can help?" I asked. "My doctor doesn't know anything about it, and I thought the PICC-line people would know because they are specially trained. . . . Who can help?"

She inhaled and glanced away and then back at me. "Okay," she said. "I'll take a look." I smiled. "But, I can't give you advice or anything, okay?" the nurse said.

I nodded and then walked with her to a small area off of the admissions room. I took off my shirt and felt her fingers on my arm and my neck. "Have you had an x-ray to confirm that it is in the right place?" the nurse asked.

"Yes, I had one on Thursday after the procedure and one this morning." I answered.

"Well, it feels like it's in the right place to me, too. I can't really say anything about the swelling or the redness. I am not a doctor." The nurse was starting to sound defensive.

"*I understand,*" *I said, as I tried to get my shirt on over the IV and my cast.*

We re-entered the admissions room, and the nurse reiterated that she couldn't offer medical opinions or advice. She couldn't be responsible for figuring out any possible complications with the line. We thanked her for her time and watched her leave.

I looked at Roger. "Well, what would you like to do now?" he asked. "We could go to the emergency room or . . ."

I cut him off. "No, let's just go on home. You have class, and I've had two people look at me today and not see anything wrong."

"The one person didn't know anything, and the other person wasn't going to say anything. That doesn't mean that nothing's wrong. I can even see the swelling in your neck now," Roger said.

I leaned down for my purse, and I noticed the admissions representative coming toward us as I stood straighter. "Good, you're still here. We reached Dr. T.'s office." Oh no, I thought, I'm going to lose his trust over a totally worthless two hours in the hospital admissions area.

"Dr. T. is glad that you're here, and he wants you to go to the ER immediately for tests," the admissions representative continued.

"He does?" I asked, hoping that I didn't look as shocked as I felt.

"Yes, he wants to rule out the potential of a blood clot before you head back to Athens," the admissions representative explained.

Roger and I walked out of the room. Where had the blood clot possibility come from? Why would I be at risk for a blood clot? If I was at risk, what would he have done if I'd already headed back to Athens? Who would know anything about my condition in the ER? How could I even know the questions to ask in order to find the right person to help me?

We continued through the winding hallway toward the ER in silence. Both of us hungered for food and for someone to give us clear authoritative answers and solutions. After a day of frustration, we longed to escape the maze.

6 Social Support and Health

*"*M*om?" Brittany said as we walked in the door. "Is everything okay?"*

"Yeah, honey, everything's fine," I responded weakly. You are just a bundle of re-assurance, I thought to myself, as Roger helped me to the pink chair.

Jenna, our favorite sitter, turned the corner from the dining room into the living room. She glanced at me and then at Roger and at Britti. "I can stay," she offered. "Just in case, well, if you need anything . . ."

"Thanks, Jenna." I smiled at the pretty blonde-haired college student. "You have been such a lifesaver anyway." I took a deep breath. "It's late. You need to go on home." I shifted my gaze to Roger and added, "you too. You've both gone above and beyond the call of duty today."

They stared at me. "I'm fine," I said. "Everyone in Columbus says I'm fine." I was so tired. "I have my heating pad and my chair and my Britti." I tried to will the corners of my mouth to turn upward as I shifted my gaze to my daughter. What was that expression? Fear? Concern? Uh oh, I thought. Britti wasn't buying the "I'm fine" line any more than Roger and Jenna. Still, Roger had missed teaching his class, and Jenna had altered her evening plans in order to take care of us. I couldn't impose any more. Brittany and I had to manage ourselves now. I looked at Roger and Jenna again. "We're fine, and the nurse will be here later anyway." I said. "You guys go on."

While Roger and I were en route to the emergency room from the admissions area, evidently, Dr. T. had contacted a colleague in the ER and expressed his concern, a concern that seemed to come straight out of the blue—the possibility of a stroke. His nurse, Katie, had looked especially concerned. Could she have said something, suggested something?

After a sonogram of my neck (that revealed no blockage) and another x-ray, the doctor could find no reason for the swelling and redness and no foundation for fearing a possible blood clot. "Take some ibuprofen and use a heating pad on your neck and shoulder," he recommended after nearly two hours of testing and waiting. "You'll be fine," he said.

Brittany closed the door behind Roger and Jenna, and I motioned for her to sit beside me. "How was the Scout meeting?" I asked. "Fine," she responded. Everything just seemed to be "fine" today.

"How was the Lark Quartet?" I asked. Prior to my illness, I had arranged for a group of women professional musicians from the university to come to the Scout meeting and talk about their work.

"They were good." Britti paused. "Why were you in Columbus for so long? Are you okay?"

"Brittany, I have been picked and prodded more than a pig at the county fair," I said, trying to look positive. "You don't need to worry. We don't need to worry about anything." I patted her leg. "Thanks for being so sweet and so brave. Tell you what—let's try to add 'obedient' to the list. Let's see if you can go to bed without an argument." She hesitated, and I added, "Go on, off to bed now."

Defining Social Support

When I decided to write this book, I knew that I wanted to explore the complexities of contemporary health communication. I also realized that I desired to reflect on my own medical mazes, my own struggles to communicate with all kinds of people and professionals during my journey toward wellness. Sharing the story, I thought, might enable readers to conceptualize principles from the book more effectively. In addition, though, telling my tale has contributed to emotional healing from the ordeal, a voyage which has taken longer than its physical counterpart. As DeSalvo (1999) argues, writing about difficult experiences can liberate us from our demons and facilitate our ability to cope and to move on with our lives.

Further, as I discovered during my illness and re-realized throughout my reflections, aspects of health (from wellness to death and all of the gray layers in between) are social as well as individual. Although, on many occasions, I bemoaned my feelings of isolation and separation from the rest of my world, I could only feel "lonely" because I had also known connection—I had experienced "social support."

For the purposes of this project, I define "social support" as the communicative process of enabling, empowering, and facilitating the ability of another person to meet his or her physical, emotional, and/or informational needs, borrowing from the works of Albrecht, Adelman, and Associates (1987); Burleson, Albrecht, and Sarason (1994); Duck with Silver (1990); Gottlieb (1988) and Pilisuk and Parks (1986). This definition broadens the scope of more traditional conceptions of social support, which have tended to focus on assistance during times of problems (see Duck with Silver, 1990).

Indeed, we do think about helping others during a crisis. When a tornado strikes a town or a flood devastates a community, many want to reach out and to help. Kaniasty and Norris (1995) contend that "disasters elicit outpourings of immense mutual helping" (p. 95). Certainly, as Miller (1989) explains, health-related trials also constitute stressful life events, and I can think of numerous occasions when our minister has called for members of the congregation to take food to a person who had just returned from a hospital stay or to assist with transporting ailing individuals to appointments.

Although those times of hardship spring to mind when we conceptualize "support" simply as "help," supportive practices and attitudes expand beyond instances of "helping." Kaniasty and Norris (1995) suggest that victims of disasters experience feelings of loss because their social relationships have been disrupted as well as their physical surroundings.

As I discussed in Chapter 2, identity emerges through social interaction and social relationships. We co-produce our selves with others as "well" people, "happy" people, and "fulfilled" people through our interactions and activities with those others. Together with particular others, we co-create relational definitions (i.e., "this is who we are together") and rules (i.e., "we treat each other this way, not that way"). In so doing, we construct a relational culture with another person or group of individuals that permits sharedness in terms of mutual understandings and expectations (see Wood, 1997)—we know the extent to which we can count on those others for various (often mundane) activities/behaviors at certain times. For example, I know that my friend Shari in my hometown will always hold last minute get-togethers at her house, that my friend Michelle in Indiana will always remember my birthday, that my friend Carolyn in Illinois will always tell me that she loves me innumerable times during our conversations, and that my friend Corinne in Texas and I will always talk on the phone for hours about our kids, houses, and lives. Our friendships focus on lifting one another up, albeit long distance, regardless of our moods or situations.

During times of illness or tragedy, though, the ability to perform expected role-appropriate behaviors diminishes to some extent. When I was ill, I could not care for my children or interact with my friends as I usually did. I could not enact those aspects of my identity (i.e., "mom" or "friend") as I wanted, much to my despair, because my illness stole my energy and my awareness and many of the attributes that comprise the well me.

Also in times of illness or tragedy, our constantly emerging relationships get redefined (albeit potentially temporarily). In contrast to how others in our lives served as enablers, empowerers, and facilitators of our needs and dreams prior to the trauma, those others shift to share our attention on the source of trouble. On such occasions, dyads highlight the ailing/assisting aspect of their relationships, and other fragments of their lives, identities, and relationships fade in importance.

As I argue in the next section, the accomplishment of social support during health crisis situations impacts and often contradicts the plethora of relational and individual identities that relational partners bring to already complicated contemporary relationships. Amid the strains of distance, fractured family ties, disconnected communities, and a host of activities and commitments competing for attention, the enactment of social support in health care situations has never been so necessary nor so problematic.

Incompatible Roles and Social Support

As I noted in Chapter 1, contemporary lifestyles hinder connectedness with others. Individuals wrestle with contradictory desires for less and for more, for simplicity and for adventure, for familiarity and for risk, for commonality and for individuality (see Gergen, 1991). We move from community to community to secure better jobs and more opportunities, bemoaning our loss of civic and family connection while appreciating our gain of money and/or experiences (see Bellah et al., 1985). For a range of reasons (from economics to guilt), we take on more roles at work, home, church, school, and various other organizations, but no matter how efficiently we manage our time, God only gave us 24 hours per day and seven days per week. We can dabble in all, but we can specialize in few. We become experts in the art of juggling. When "wanting it all" becomes the goal, compromising conflicting wishes becomes unacceptable yet inevitable, especially in terms of relationships and social support.

Conflicting Role Demands

Deborah Pryce, a Republican congresswoman from Ohio, balanced her work in the United States House of Representatives and her relationships with her husband and 8-year-old daughter, Caroline. When Caroline was diagnosed with cancer in September, 1998, Pryce told *USA Today*:

> Everything just came to a screeching halt. There was no way I had the desire or the inclination or even the energy or emotional fortitude to concentrate on anything besides her. There was so much to do. All these decisions had to be made. And the distress of seeing her so ill, in a wheelchair, not able to walk—nothing really went through my head except that I was going to be with her. (Lawrence, November 17, 1998, p. 18A)

Even though the House of Representatives was struggling with its monumental decision about a Clinton impeachment inquiry, Pryce focused on finding medical options for Caroline. When the time arrived for a vote on proceeding with the Clinton impeachment process, Lawrence (November 17, 1998, p. 18A) observes that "there was only one House member not present for the historic moment: Pryce." Despite the attention of the nation on Clinton and impeachment, though, Pryce noted that "everybody realized that to talk to me about something like that in light of what we were facing was really not appropriate" (Lawrence, November 17, 1998, p. 18A). According to the *Columbus Dispatch* ("Cancer claims life of Pryce's daughter," September 5, 1999), "Even after returning to her congressional duties, Pryce, 48, and her husband spent much of their time caring for Caroline" (p. D1).

Sadly, although Caroline seemed to be doing better and her mother had returned from her two-month leave of absence from Congress, her condition worsened in August 1999, the day after she started the third grade. Caroline died on September 4, 1999, almost a week after turning nine years old ("Cancer claims life of Pryce's daughter," September 5, 1999).

For individuals who become ill and for loved ones who assist in their care, the regular routine of life—work, activities, family outings, outside commitments, and so on—blends into a blur of doctor appointments, sorting through information, caring activities, and waiting. Although that "regular routine" can be stressful, the advent of illness cannot easily be juxtaposed with nor integrated into other simultaneous roles and obligations.

"Women's Work"

When I was in high school, I participated in a production of *Inherit the Wind*. In one scene, the defense attorney questions a potential juror, inquiring about his religious convictions. The juror responds that "my wife tends to the religion." When the defense attorney probes further about what the juror does, he exclaims, "I tend to the feed store!"

Although the role of women in society changed a great deal during the twentieth century, the role of women in contemporary families still includes very traditional activities—caring for children, cooking, cleaning, and often, spiritual leader. In fact, in their study of housewives who were hospitalized, Giovannetti de Jesus and Bergamasco (1998) report that "the hospitalization of the wife/mother affects families and ruptures the view that women have of themselves as being the responsible person who takes care of everything and everybody" (p. 392).

Multiple Obligations

Even if Giovannetti de Jesus and Bergamasco's (1998) data reflects perceptions from only women participants, the women in that study likely struggled with similar issues as I did during my illness—communicating with others to ensure that children received care (including meals, baths, medicine, general supervision) and were transported to school, appointments, and activities; rearranging obligations and obtaining substitutes for civic commitments. Yet, my illness hindered my ability to interact with others about what needed to be done, exacerbating my feelings of frustration about my absence from my roles in the home (see related example by Swingle, January 12, 2000).

As a working mom, I am used to juggling—to sacrificing family some weeks to meet work demands and to sacrificing work obligations during 4-H judgings and hectic scout and dance recital times. Despite the "unmanageability" of my everyday life, though, I manage.

However, my illness threw me—I couldn't function as much more than a sick person, a person who had to send one child away to her grandmother's house and to rely on other people for help with the second. As a woman and a mom, I wanted to do much better for my family. Almost primally, I felt as though I should "at least" be able to care for my children, no matter how ill I became. For one of the first times, I eventually had to acknowledge that I couldn't "do it all," despite my fervent desire to do so.

Gender Differences

Although women continue to increase their number and status in the work force, their families count on them to "do it all" by serving as primary family caregivers (in addition to their other multiple roles) in times of illness (see Abel, 1991; Abel & Nelson, 1990; AP, July 1, 1998; Marshall, Barnett, Baruch, & Pleck, 1990; Orodenker, 1991; Parrott & Condit, 1996; Stein, Bauman, & Jessop, 1994; Wood, 1994). In her excellent book, *Who Cares?: Women, Care, and Culture*, Julia Wood (1994) describes her father's response to her query about hiring help for his increasing health needs:

> Rejecting this proposal, my father said musingly, "It's funny, Julia. I used to wish I had sons, but now I'm glad I have daughters, because I couldn't ask a son to take this kind of time away from his work just to take care of me." (p. 6)

A well-published scholar on gender issues, Wood sacrificed her health and professional and personal interests to care for her father and then for her mother. However, as she notes, her decision to provide care for her father and mother mirrors her father's (and society's) expectation about which gender *should* tend to ill family members. Wood (1994) details a conversation with colleagues wherein she explained that she would have to leave a meeting early in order to attend to her mother. Wood recalls:

Immediately they supported me with comments such as "I know it really matters to her that she's living with you"; "You're right to make time for her now while you still can"; "Taking care of your mother is certainly more important than this meeting." (p. 8)

However, when one of her male colleagues mentioned that he had to put his own mother into a nursing home, given his professional responsibilities, Wood (1994) notes, "Again, there was a chorus of support for his choice." Comments included:

"You have to live your own life, as hard as that can be"; "Well, she surely understood that as busy as you are with your work you couldn't be expected to take on that responsibility"; "It's true, you can't do everything; you had to put your work first." (pp. 8–9)

The two diverse sets of reactions exemplify equally opposite gender expectations with regard to social support, especially in terms of health care. In her analysis of this exchange, Wood concludes:

Both my male colleague and I were given certain allowances and deprived of others. . . . Had he made the choice that I had, he would have been judged differently—as unprofessional, which is to say, unmanly. Had I made the choice he did, I would have been judged as uncaring, which is to say, unwomanly. Both of us were the prisoners and the beneficiaries of social expectations of women and men. (p. 9)

Indeed, for Jenny, a college student who participated in Gilligan's feminist research on moral development, her mother constituted an ideal individual because "she would do anything for anybody, up to a point that she has hurt herself a lot because she just gives so much to other people and asks nothing in return" (Gilligan, 1982, p. 136). Especially for women who care for ill family members, in combination with work and other family and civic obligations, the cost of caring can be high. According to Marshall and colleagues (1990), women who expend time, energy, money and other resources and who invest themselves personally in others' difficulties ". . . are at high risk for psychological distress, poor health, and reduced well-being" (p. 275).

The Sandwich Generation

From early childhood, many young people are taught to follow the fourth commandment in the Christian faith: "Honor your father and your mother, as the Lord your God has commanded you, so that you may live long and that it may go well with you in the land the Lord your God is giving you" (Deuteronomy 5:16, NIV). Like mama and papa birds who raise their little baby birds, ideally, parents nurture their children, gain their respect and trust, teach them to test their wings, and then gently push them into the world. In this scenario, boundary lines for roles get etched quickly and deliberately—parents instruct, children listen; parents command, children obey.

Role Reversal
However, with ever-expanding lifespans, more adult offspring face a return to the nest, this time as caregivers for their elderly parents (see Abel, 1991; Angel & Angel, 1997; AP,

July 1, 1998; Briar & Kaplan, 1990; Gibson, 1998; Kahana, Biegel, & Wykle, 1994; Orodenker, 1991; Painter, July 13, 1999; Palomo, March 8, 1999; Roots, 1998; Sawa, 1992). This second season relationship often involves a role reversal wherein the adult offspring assumes a position of authority and the parent trusts that offspring for care (see Abel, 1991).

Time reporter Cathy Booth cared for her mother, who ultimately died from Lou Gehrig's disease, and then for her father, who suffers from dementia. Booth describes her "descent into elder-care hell" as "a personal journey for which there are few reliable road maps and precious little reassurance" (August 30, 1999, p. 50). As a team of Stanford University researchers discovered, the revised relational dynamic can prove stressful, given uncertainty about new role expectations and limitations, impacts of the new role on other family relationships, and coordination of the new role of parent caregiver with other roles (work, family, etc.) (see AP, July 1, 1998).

Yet, the terrain will grow increasingly familiar during the opening decades of the twenty-first century. Like Booth, millions of other baby boomers will assume responsibility for older parents as they can no longer care for themselves (Booth, August 30, 1999). According to Census Bureau statistics, the percentage of Americans who are 65 years or older will steadily mount through the first thirty years of the new millennium (see Greenwald, August 30, 1999).

Relational Complications

Roots (1998) dubbed adult offspring caregivers as the "sandwich generation," individuals who might be thrust into caring for elderly parents while raising their own families, establishing their own careers, building their own financial security, and so on. As Armour (August 19, 1998) explains, the responsibility for an elderly parent, in addition to other life roles, can result in depression, workplace stress, competing demands between children, parent(s), and work, and even isolation (see also Painter, July 13, 1999; Palomo, March 8, 1999).

The challenge for some adult offspring might be compounded by their childhood relationships with parents (see Booth, 1991; Elkind, 1994; Hall, 1997; Roots, 1998; Segalman, 1998). Busy working parents, some married, some divorced, some single, raise their children in a wide variety of ways—some engaged, some quite detached. With rampant technological diversions, children can control their environments with remote controls, MTV, and Nintendo, occasionally as diversions from domestic violence, alcoholism, and drug abuse. Many homes get ripped to shreds by nasty divorces with endless verbal attacks and accusations. For children, disruptive family lives during formative years may lead to individual acts of violence or to future relational problems (see Elkind, 1994; Segalman, 1998).

In the New International Version of the Bible, the Apostle Paul admonishes parents: "Do not exasperate your children; instead, bring them up in the training and instruction of the Lord" (Ephesians 6:4). Indeed, the book of Proverbs advises parents to "train a child in the way he should go, and when he is old he will not turn from it" (22:6, NIV). When parents inadvertently train their children to engage in inappropriate treatment of others (through the parents' own improper or even abusive behaviors), those parents may ultimately suffer when the caretaking roles are reversed.

A. Hall (1997) reports, for instance, that parental drinking problems continue to plague their children, even as they reach their college years, in terms of their ability to cope and to develop self-esteem. In such cases, parents may not be able to offer support in the form of role modeling or nurturing, and children withdraw from parents who drink, reducing their own support of parents. As Roots (1998) observes, children who grow up in dysfunctional families wrestle with reconciling their exasperating (if not anguishing) memories of neglect and abuse with the obligation to care for a now elderly mother or father. According to Roots (1998), "it becomes apparent that many of our families are dysfunctional, showing little regard for offspring. It comes as no surprise, therefore, when adult children often show a lack of interest and concern for elderly parents" (p. 45).

Of course, every family co-creates its own unique culture, with its own sets of relational dynamics and emergent relational and individual identities. As family members age and health needs become more prevalent, family members face the challenging task of redefining and clarifying roles, identities, expectations, desires for independence, and health-related limitations, especially in the context of physical and/or emotional distance.

Independence/Dependence

I love soap operas. In fact, I wrote my master's thesis about young soap opera couple relationships. Unfortunately, my schedule usually denies me an opportunity to watch "my stories" (*Guiding Light, As the World Turns, Young and the Restless*, and *Bold and the Beautiful*) anymore. On some particularly hectic days before my illness, I used to fantasize about being confined to bed and doing nothing but watching my soaps and catching up on sleep.

After I came home from the hospital, that harmless daydream turned into an actual nightmare. During the day, I could barely move from the pink chair, and the hours between visits from the home health nurse stretched endlessly. I had never known that time could pass so slowly. Fortunately, from 12:30 to 4 P.M., I could click on the remote control and watch people who struggled with more problems and plot complications than I had.

Becoming "Dependent"
Kim Hughes, a character on *As the World Turns*, faced her own health care drama around the same time as my illness. Kim, an active professional woman, is a committed pillar of the community. She works full-time, volunteers, encourages her physician husband, helps her elderly mother-in-law, visits with friends, assists her alcoholic son in his twenties, and nurtures her preteen son, not to mention always entertaining in her beautiful (and clean) home.

Given her hectic life, Kim initially discounted some discomfort in her chest that she was experiencing; however, she inevitably confided her pain to her former husband, Dr. John Dixon, a world-renowned cardiologist. John examined Kim and, after some testing, concluded that she had a heart problem and that she needed an operation.

As I lay in my pink chair, with my remote control and cordless telephone, I watched Kim respond to her own surgery. Because she is a wonderful person, people bound to her side to assist her. One friend, Lisa, took over Kim's television show and much of her work schedule. Kim's mother-in-law, Nancy, cared for Chris, the preteen son. Her husband, Bob, and Lisa and Nancy assured Kim that every detail of her life had been delegated and covered—she had nothing to worry about during her recovery. According to her loved ones, Kim should "just focus on getting better."

Yet, as she watched her concerned and well-intentioned friends and relatives whispering around her, Kim grew despondent. Every time that she tried to do something for herself—even attempting to pour a cup of coffee in her kitchen—someone would jump in to help, even gently rebuking her efforts and telling her to "take it easy."

Kim didn't want to take it easy, though. She yearned to recapture her life, to refuel her spirit, to return to normal as a functioning, contributing, viable member of her family and community. Kim desperately missed her relationships with others as well as the person whom she could be with them. Although in kindness, her family and friends treated Kim as a dependent and, in so doing, forced her into relational and self-definitions that were most incompatible with her preferred identities as a free-spirited, independent, caring professional, wife, mom, friend, and so on. Thus, she felt lost and out of place in her own home.

Identity Implications

I could identify with Kim. On the one hand, I truly appreciated all of the help that I received during my illness—drives to and from the hospital (sometimes in the middle of the night), meals for me and Britti, assistance with my work obligations, and so on. My wonderful boss pursued medical information on my behalf and considered seeking a power of attorney to help protect my interests, if my condition worsened. As soon as I went into the hospital, she arranged for colleagues to teach my classes and, ultimately, for my medical leave for the quarter. Because of her generosity and concern, I did not have to worry about my job.

I could not have asked for more supportive colleagues during my time of great need. Yet, on the other hand, I felt a little uncomfortable with the identity implications of that support (and more than a little guilty about feeling awkward about that discomfort—after all, my colleagues were being incredibly kind and caring) (see related work by Sass & Mattson, 1999). Why was I uncomfortable with such helpfulness?

At a most surface level, the illness thrust us in a very different relational dynamic than "normal." Whereas only family usually see me at my worst (i.e., with greasy hair and bedclothes), my illness forced me to permit more people "backstage" (see Goffman, 1959) and to reframe our relationship beyond professional interactions (see Goffman, 1967). To be honest, I truly had little energy for modesty or embarrassment about my appearance when I returned home from the hospital. However, I didn't quite know how to juxtapose our relational enactment during my illness with the way in which I still wanted them to see me—sharp and professional.

At a more pervasive level, I became increasingly frustrated by being treated as "sick." Certainly, I was quite ill and I needed help. Yet, ironically, despite my prior silly daydreams about being trapped in bed and despite the seriousness of my medical condition, I resisted being bedridden. I fought to go back to work; I tried to call into the office; I arranged to hook up my e-mail in my home so that I could communicate with the outside world. Even though I experienced dizziness and fatigue by merely standing, I begged to go to Britti's basketball games and to an Ohio University basketball game. I knew that I was ill, but I didn't want to define myself that way. Like Kim, I yearned to regain my life and the multiplicity of complicated relational and individual identities that encompass me. Like Kim, I came to realize that that kindness and support can be paradoxical—I knew that I needed help, but I could not easily reconcile that assistance with how I desired to position myself in relation to others.

In their book, *Surviving Dependence: Voices of African American Elders*, Ball and Whittington (1995) describe the dilemmas of seven African American senior citizens who struggle with health care needs and desires for independence. Ball and Whittington explain:

> Despite an ideology that values independence, the real world of these participants often is of ever-increasing dependence, and, for some, the ensuing angst is only sharpened by these memories of their former lives in which they were fully independent people accustomed to "doing." (p. 111)

However, as Brown (1990) observed in her ethnographic study of a rural community, some dependence actually facilitated independence. For citizens of Germanville, isolation increased the risk of ill health (and, ultimately, one's home) when individuals rejected social connections (such as prayers, companionship, and mutual concern) (see Brown, 1990).

Affliction of the Seeker or the Supporter?

Lisa, the character with breast cancer in the comic strip, *Funky Winkerbean*, awakes to find her husband sitting and staring out of a window. She knows that he is upset about her illness, but as she admits to him, "I wish I could help . . . but I can't be strong enough for both of us" (Batiuk, February 21, 1999).

Northouse (1988) found that husbands reported inadequate support from friends and health care professionals during their wives' bouts with breast cancer. Stetz, McDonald, and Compton (1996) reported that family caregivers of marrow transplant patients felt ill-prepared in terms of availability of information and additional role demands as well as "ineffective" during interactions with health care professionals. Similarly, vom Eigen, Walker, Edgman-Levitan, Cleary, and Delbanco (1999) discovered carepartner frustration when health care professionals did not involve them actively in treatment and discharge decisions.

The desire to be involved and consulted—and even cared for—reflects a relational and situational definition of "our" illness, rather than just the health care seeker's illness. Clearly, the impact of illness spans beyond the health care seeker, but the research indicates that health care professionals may not attend to that carepartner definition, either due to confidentiality issues or unclear communication. When the supporter's preferred role in care does not get enacted, further pain and emotional distress likely result.

Puddifoot and Johnson (1997) conducted an investigation of partners' experiences during miscarriage. Although both parents lose a child during a miscarriage, the men in this study did not easily find a distinct role for themselves during the health care crisis.

. . . men may find their own role to be relatively unstructured and the expectations of them to be quite minimal . . . the male partner may feel to an extent caught in a double-bind. If he were to openly discuss his feelings with his partner, it may be suggested to him, subtly or otherwise, that this will be upsetting for her, and that after all it is his role at this time to support rather than to grieve with his partner. But if he does not show his feelings, he may be seen as uncaring. (p. 844)

Indeed, one of the greatest trials for supporters may be the handling of intense emotions—emotions of grief, frustration, anger, despair, and so on—honestly while remaining sensitive and attentive to the needs of the health care seeker (see examples in Pearson, 1995). Notably, the ways in which these emotional needs get managed dramatically impact the emergent relational definitions and role expectations of the health care participants.

The play *The Shadow Box* features three groups of health care seekers and their loved ones. In each of three cottages, health care seekers and their loved ones wrestle with unresolved emotions about their relationships and the illnesses that will soon end those relationships.

Agnes, the daughter of a woman in the late stages of cancer, tells the Interviewer about her efforts to make her mother happy by writing letters to her mother, letters from her dead sister, Claire. The Interviewer tries to steer the conversation toward Agnes' well-being, but Agnes recurrently shifts the focus back to her mother, arguing that the letters cheer her mother—"It means so much to her. It's important to her. It's something to hope for . . ." (Cristofer, 1977, p. 70). Agnes buries her resentment of caring for her mother amid her mother's longing for Claire. Agnes silently drafts letters from Claire and listens to her mother's constant insistence on wanting to see Claire instead of expressing gratitude for Agnes' care and companionship.

Summary—Incompatible Roles

Especially in this time of geographically dispersed and emotionally scattered families and friends, the dilemmas of incompatible roles impacts health care and interpersonal relationships (see related work by Pilisuk & Parks, 1986). Health care situations thrust health care seekers and their supporters into new, convoluted relational dynamics, and the lack of consistent or clear ground rules or expectations can burden relationships, intimacy, the accomplishment of health activities, and even the offering/accepting of various types of social support.

Types of Health-Related Social Support

Researchers herald the importance of social support during health-related situations (see Aaronson, 1989; Gjerdingen, Froberg, & Fontaine, 1991; Gottlieb, 1988; Kelsey, Earp, & Kirkley, 1997). For example, Kennell, Klaus, McGrath, Robertson, and Hinkley (1991) discovered that women who are accompanied by "supportive" companions during the labor process tend to require fewer c-sections. Taylor, Falke, Mazel, and Hilsberg (1988) noted that cancer support groups can provide a mechanism that facilitates patients' abilities to cope with cancer. Researchers at the Cooper Institute in Dallas, Texas claim that social support constitutes the key to motivating individuals to commit to daily exercise (AP, June 21, 1999). In fact, Pilisuk and Parks (1986) claim that ". . . integration in a supportive network makes a difference in our ability to resist breakdown, and that social psychological factors affect the workings of the immune system" (p. 46).

However, what exactly counts as "social support"? In her book, *It's Always Something*, Gilda Radner recalls a critical fight that she had with her husband, Gene Wilder. At the point of the argument, Radner and Wilder had been caught up in the saga of diagnoses and treatments and waiting and all of the emotional and physical ramifications of battling cancer. Both were exhausted, Radner from the strain of illness and chemotherapy and Wilder from the stress of supporting his tense and fearful wife.

They had just climbed into bed when Radner, once again, expressed her fear and begged for help. According to Radner (1989), for the first time since she became ill, Wilder snapped:

> I can't help you—I'm tired of helping you. Why don't you worry about something besides yourself? Worry about me—worry about the dog. Just get off yourself; I can't help you any more. You're mean and cranky and inconsiderate all day and then at night you get in bed and you get frightened and panic and you want me to make everything be all right and I can't. (p. 197)

Radner hesitated for a moment and then fired back, ultimately asking "You can leave me—leave me if you want—or are you afraid to leave someone who is dying of cancer?" (p. 198). The pair grew quiet, then held hands and fell asleep. However, from that terrible fight, Radner gained more strength than she had experienced in a long time—she was no longer afraid.

> It was so good that Gene yelled back at me. It made me feel like a real person. If Gene thought I could take it, then I wasn't dying. People whimpering and hovering over me made me feel like I was dying. People yelling at me made me feel alive. (p. 199)

Can yelling and arguing count as "support"? Just as relational and individual identities are multifaceted and emergent, the meanings and functions of communicative activities get co-constructed by the participants during interactions. Surely, Wilder thought that his prior actions (sitting by his wife's bedside, comforting her through procedures, helping her to gain medical help) were more likely to be interpreted as "supportive" than his frustrated comments. Like the examples that I provided from my own experience and from that of the soap opera character, Kim, the Radner–Wilder interaction points to two serious challenges for health care participants—discerning what type of support that an individual needs and then collaborating on the best way to satisfy that need (an issue that I will take up in later sections). As I detail the following types of support, please note that they are not mutually exclusive. Physical and informational support can certainly also constitute emotional support. Emotional support can provide information, and so on.

Physical Support

Physical support involves attention to logistical and/or bodily needs. Logistical needs might include transportation to and from a medical facility, food, or assistance with paying bills or housecleaning. Bodily needs might include changing dressings, giving medications, or assistance with other aspects of medical care.

However, recent medical and technological advances have enabled some individuals to extend their physical support even further. Organ donation has permitted individuals with weakened body parts to live rejuvenated lives after a successful transplant. Although organ donations usually occur after one individual dies, relatives with matching blood types have donated body parts to other family members who need a transplant.

USA Today reporter Scott Bowles has an even more unique situation. In a series of columns for the newspaper, Bowles offers a peek into his struggle with diabetes. After battling diabetes for twenty years, the 33-year-old learned in December 1998 that he needed a kidney transplant (Bowles, March 29, 1999). Bowles describes his wife, Julie, as his "full-time nurse, taking my temperature, feeding me juice, calling my parents with updates" (p. 5D).

In February, 1999, Bowles' medical team encouraged him to seek an organ donation from a family member, rather than waiting for another match. As he said, "How do you even broach the subject? . . . 'Hey, I was wondering what you're doing with that spare kidney of yours?' " (p. 5D).

However, he didn't need to even ask his friend, Spencer Tirey. The best man at his wedding and former co-worker called and offered to be evaluated as a possible suitable match. Bowles stressed the seriousness of the surgery, and Tirey reiterated his offer. "I thank Spencer over and over, a gesture that seems pitifully small. He tells me to shut up, that of course he'd do this. We're friends" (p. 5D). Ultimately, though, the friend was not able to provide the transplant. On January 13, 2000, Bowles benefited from an unknown donor, a 21-year-old who lost his life in an accident (Davis, January 14, 2000). The friend's generous offer and the accident victim's unselfish gift constitute excellent examples of physical support.

Emotional Support

Emotional support involves attention to needs for connecting and for coping. For example, in her book, *Care Packages*, Dana Reeve offers exemplars of the thousands of messages that her family received after announcing the news about her husband Christopher's spinal cord injury. From religious insights to trips down memory lane, the notes communicated concern and served as a source of inspiration (Reeve, 1999). Wellness efforts and illness can be isolating, and Pilisuk and Parks (1986), among others, stress the importance of social connections for optimal health outcomes.

Oxman and Berkman (1990) suggest strong ties between social support and elderly patient health outcomes (see also Litwin, 1996). Although Ball and Whittington (1995) note that their African American elder participants did not desire to be dependent, they also emphasize a link between social interaction and health. However, as Ball and Whittington (1995) acknowledge, "the situation is complex and multidimensional, and a number of factors now present in their lives unite to create this social deprivation" (p. 73).

The seven African American elders in the Ball and Whittington study share key similarities—their physical limitations, combined with social conditions such as poverty and neighborhood violence, constrain their ability to leave their homes and to open their doors to relatives and their remaining friends. Ball and Whittington (1995) explain:

> For some people these obstacles fuse with attitudes and beliefs—some life-long and some born out of the deterioration of their bodies—to contribute to further isolation. Although not every participant is alone or lonely, everyone's social world is diminished. (pp. 87–88)

The lived realities of individuals with illnesses and/or disabilities combines with the hectic, almost frantic, lifeworlds of the rest of the world. Well people continue to be busy with activities and obligations that also consumed less able others until they were forced to the sidelines (and, occasionally, out of the stadium) with health-related afflictions.

As soon as I went into the hospital, I left my classes for the quarter, but the students kept right on going, with another instructor. Colleagues went to meetings, and neighbors went to work. People at my church continued to go to services and to Sunday School. The scouts had meetings without fail. Brittany attended school and brought home papers. Life went on, even though I stopped.

Despite my dissonance over blurred roles, inability to communicate and concentrate, and poor personal appearance, I coveted connectedness. I can't remember the details of my phone conversations with my friends or my grandparents late in that week in the hospital, but I know that I clung to the phone as much as I did when I talked with my mom on that difficult Tuesday. When one colleague visited me on Wednesday evening and another on Thursday evening in the hospital, I faded in and out of our talks, but I recall watching them leave and wishing that they could stay with me for just a bit longer. To borrow from a wistful little mermaid, I wanted to be a part of their world, and because of their emotional support, I could connect with that world again for a snippet of time.

Emotional support also can facilitate coping with an illness. In the earlier example, Gilda Radner gleaned hope from her husband's willingness to take off his kid gloves and talk to her frankly—he would not talk that way to someone who was dying, she reasoned. In that particular instance, she needed to be treated as strong in order to achieve strength to continue to cope.

Perhaps more often, though, the need for help with coping is met through encouraging reassurances. For example, in one of the early strips in the *Funky Winkerbean* series on breast cancer, Lisa's husband attempts to reassure her by noting "just because they spotted something on your mammogram doesn't necessarily mean that it's something bad" (Batiuk, January 31, 1999). Lisa responds with "You sure know how to say the right thing at the right time . . . You've convinced me!"

Emotional support need not "convince" health care seekers about the potential of particular outcomes. The crux of this type of support is attentiveness to the seeker's individualized desires to put his or her world and illness into a preferred perspective.

Informational Support

Informational support involves attention to needs for information (see Beck with Ragan & duPre, 1997). As I detailed earlier, individuals in an increasingly consumer-oriented society seek details and insights so they can make informed choices. When I struggled to make the initial decisions about the surgery and then about a variety of issues, including the PICC line, I desired information. A core difference between the decision about the surgery and the decision about the PICC line, though, stemmed from the disparity in my ability to obtain and process opinions on my own. Especially in the case of the latter, I could not gather and weigh options without assistance from others.

When I felt that I could not obtain enough information or perspective in order to understand the PICC line, I became frustrated. Yet, the lack of this type of support can also be emotionally crushing.

Before I had Chelsea Meagan, I carried two little babies whom I named Brianna and Caitlyn. Like too many other babies who are lost due to miscarriage, they died far too soon. I had had trouble becoming pregnant after Brittany, and I was incredibly excited to hear the positive pregnancy test result in February 1992. Wade and I took 5-year-old Brittany to Chi Chi's and announced that we would be blessed with another child. A week later, as I headed out of the door for a Saturday afternoon at the mall, I started to bleed, and I called my doctor immediately.

After six days of testing, waiting, hoping, and praying, the doctor told me that tiny Brianna was gone. My first question was "Why?," followed very closely by "What went wrong?" My faith buffered the terrible loss. I know that Brianna is with God and that God has ultimate control. Yet, as I walked through the waiting room that was filled with beautiful, pregnant women on that terrible yet sunny Friday, I kept wondering about how my body malfunctioned, about the whiff that I got of paint fumes in the hallway at my office, about the argument that Wade and I had had the night before the bleeding started, about what I could have, perhaps should have done, or not done. I needed to know what I could do to change for next time, if I would have a "next time."

I happened to flip on the *Young and the Restless* during lunch as I was writing this chapter. Megan was comforting her older sister, Tricia, a twenty-something character on the show who just suffered a miscarriage. Like me, Tricia's initial response was to cry and ask "why?" and then, more specifically, "why didn't I know that something was wrong?" Megan gently inquired if Tricia posed those questions to her doctor, and Tricia replied, "She said that some things just weren't meant to be." Such a response might be true, but also quite unsatisfying to someone who thirsts for understanding. Laura Cooper (1999) wrote the following letter to the editor of *Parents*:

> Thank you so much for printing "Miscarriage Myths." I had a miscarriage a few months ago, just one day short of completing my third month, after trying to get pregnant for a year and a half. I was and still am very sad. You answered a lot of my questions, in some cases better than my doctor did. (p. 25)

Certainly, contemporary health care seekers can tap more information sources than ever before. Unlike the days of relying on Grandma's lay remedy for the common cold (see Blaxter & Paterson, 1982) or a physician's recommendation, individuals can turn to independent publications for particular audiences (such as parents), the Internet, and organizations (including support groups) for alternative insights. Churches have even been tapped into partnerships with health care organizations to disseminate health information to members (see Hatch & Vookorst, 1992).

AIDS activists have been particularly proactive in obtaining and disseminating information, for example. From tiny, rural organizations in southeast Ohio (such as the Athens AIDS Task Force) to the AIDS-related magazine, *POZ*, AIDS activists focus on sharing information with a societally marginalized community. Targeting another traditionally marginalized group, the National Women's Health Network also works to distribute information about women's health issues (see *The Network News*, January/February, 1999 as well as http://feminist.com/health.htm).

Sources of Support

I had the strangest sense of deja vu. I felt awful, but I was fine. Dr. T. told me that I was "fine"; the ER doc dubbed me "fine." I must be "fine." Yet, why did my neck throb? Why did my head ache so? Why couldn't I think? Could something else really be wrong but slink through the tests undetected?

My alarm rang, and I reached to shut it off with my IV arm. Pain ripped through my shoulder. I looked toward the ceiling and then, oh so cautiously, at the clock. Okay, I thought, Pam will be here soon for the eight o'clock visit. I need to get up and help prepare Brittany for school.

I called for Brittany to get up, and I sat up slowly. Waves of dizziness swept over me, and I stood, trying to concentrate on putting one foot in front of the other. I remembered some childhood song about that . . . let's see . . . oh yeah, one foot in front of the other . . . Christmas video . . . Santa Claus Is Coming to Town . . . the wizard who turned out to be nice . . . one foot in front of the . . .

"Mom, are you okay?" Brittany asked.

"Yeah, I'm fine. I just bumped the wall. I'm fine." Brittany came and took my arm and assisted me to the pink chair. I closed my eyes.

"Mom, will you be okay today while I'm at school?" Britti pressed.

I opened my eyes. She was so cute to be concerned. "Yeah, Pam will be here soon," I replied. Britti hesitated and then turned to finish getting ready for school. I closed my eyes.

I pulled my blue blankie up to my nose while I cuddled in the pink chair. I forced my eyes to open. Something sounded really annoying—buzzing, banging, something . . . I saw Pam at the window, and I called for Britti to let her in the door. Britti didn't come. I called again. I paused. She must have left for school. Did I watch her get on the bus? Did I get up to see her off?

Pam banged on the window. The door seemed so far away, and I felt so tired. Okay, I thought. Just get to the door . . . get up.

I turned the doorknob, and Pam charged through the doorway. "What's going on?" she demanded. "Are you okay?"

I looked at her while I concentrated on keeping my knees from buckling. "I don't know," I answered, as she helped me back to the chair.

The Importance of Support Networks

As several authors argue, social support can stem from a multiplicity of sources, depending on an individual's collection of family members, friends, co-workers, church family members, acquaintances from clubs and school, support group members, internet contacts, and health care professionals (see Baker, 1998; Biegel, Tracy, & Corvo, 1994; Cain, 1996; Duck with Silver, 1990; Litwin, 1996; Pilisuk & Parks, 1986; Smith et al., 1997; Stewart, 1993; Suominen, Leino-Kilpi, & Laippala, 1995; Wacker et al., 1998; Zarit, Pearlin, & Schaie, 1993). The conglomeration of various (and varying) relationships constitutes a network of potential resources for individuals as they proceed through daily life, in times of trouble and in times of triumph. Albrecht and Adelman (1987) explain that "the network system that embeds the individual has numerous functional and dysfunctional potentialities because of the possibility of interconnectedness (or 'density') among all contacts" (p. 41).

I mentioned Dr. Marcy Olmsted in Chapter 1. Just after giving birth to her first child and preparing for a new job, Dr. Olmsted discovered that she had cancer. After finishing chemotherapy, Olmsted (1994) contends:

> Emotionally and physically I'm ready to move on. What has helped me get through this so well? The encouragement of family and friends, particularly my husband, has been the foundation, and support groups have allowed me freedom of expression in our cancer-phobic society. For eight weeks I met with 10 women and discussed the specific losses caused by breast cancer . . . It has been a relief just to be in a room where I wasn't the only one with cancer or the only woman with an abnormal or absent breast. (p. 81)

In her book, *Healing the Child: A Mother's Story*, Dr. Nancy Cain offers a riveting account of her son Alex's battle with E. coli. I read the entire book in one night, partly because I found myself thinking, "there but for the grace of God go I," and partly because each page prompted me to be more admiring of the family's courageous and creative use of human resources.

On his fourth birthday, Alex started to get sick, and, according to Cain (1996), "in the space of forty-eight hours, he went from a healthy child to a child near death" (p. 13). Yet, E. coli kills without discrimination or compassion. Cain noted that she and her husband were told that only one child out of thirteen children who had been as ill as Alex had lived.

Cain and her husband pressed on, talking to Alex even though he lay unconscious, willing him to live, promising him a puppy (his heart's desire) if he kept fighting. Cain (1996) recalls:

> Our careers as writers allowed us to put our lives on hold so that we could stay at Alex's side. We took turns sitting at his bedside. We talked to him, we told him silly stories, and we read to him. Sometimes we were so physically and emotionally exhausted that we just held on to him and dozed in a rocking chair beside his bed. We quizzed the nurses on every detail of his care and questioned every specialist who visited him. We asked for reading material on his illness, and we talked openly with his medical team. (pp. 17–18)

Yet, after three days, they experienced a parent's worst nightmare—they were told that their son would not live. They visited him for what they thought would be the final time. They called family members with the tragic news, and they awaited what they expected to be the inevitable. Fortunately, Alex proved them wrong. According to Cain (1996), "His steadfast will to survive so amazed his medical team that he was nicknamed 'the Miracle Child' " (p. 19).

The moving account does not end with the blood clot that halted the bleeding in order to spare his life. Cain (1996) heralds person after person who contributed to Alex's recovery and to the family's ability to care for two sons, Alex and his little brother—extended family members, medical team members, the "cashier lady" in the hospital cafeteria, the "tray lady" who delivered Alex's food, the kind nurse who encouraged her to hold Alex despite his wires, prayer partners from around the country, internet support groups, community members. Cain's account of Alex's struggle truly serves as a testament of the importance of physical, emotional, and informational support and the vital need for a diverse and interconnected support network.

Support Network Links

Thump, thump, thump . . . I slowly started to lift my eyelids. Louder now . . . thump, thump, thump . . . Something was banging, possibly the cats . . . Still louder and more insistent—THUMP, THUMP, THUMP... It's nothing, I thought. Nothing's wrong, nothing's here . . . nothing . . . THUMP, THUMP, THUMP, THUMP, THUMP . . .

Okay, okay, I thought. I'll try. I'll try to figure out the noise. I raised my head a sliver above the back of the pink chair. My neck throbbed. I wanted another Percocet. Could I take another one now, I wondered? THUMP, THUMP, THUMP, THUMP, THUMP.

I pried my eyes the rest of the way open and saw Pam on the porch. I have to let her in; I have to make one leg move and then another leg . . .

"Christie, what is going on?" Pam said urgently as I finally let her in the door.

"Weren't you just here?" I asked.

"That was at eight. It's four now. What has been going on today?" Pam pressed as she helped me back to the chair.

"Well . . ." I tried to remember. I felt so foggy, just like that Wednesday in the hospital only without the vomiting. "Okay, I know that Roger called sometime." I paused and then panicked momentarily—"Brittany is supposed to be"—I caught myself. Brittany and a friend must be playing in the other room. They must be . . . I couldn't think.

"Have you eaten today?" Pam asked. I couldn't remember. I couldn't think of moving from the pink chair since Pam left that morning. Come to think of it, I couldn't recall when Pam departed.

"Ouch, that hurts." I cried as Pam tried to examine my neck.

"That's it," Pam said as she stood abruptly. "Something is definitely going on with you. I don't care what the people in Columbus said yesterday. Something is terribly wrong."

Pam reached in her bag and retrieved Dr. T.'s number. She dialed the number and asked to speak with him—now. I bet that he's going to love this, I thought. Pam used to be in the military, she had told me when we met. Hhhhhhh, I exhaled and closed my eyes. I'm glad that she's on my side, I thought as I drifted to sleep.

"Christie," Pam said. The woman needs to let me sleep, I thought. "Yeah?" I responded.

"I left messages for Dr. T. and for Dr. S. I'm going to wait to see if they call me back before I take off. I'm very concerned," Pam reported.

"They said it was nothing yesterday. I'm sure it's nothing . . . I really just want to sleep," I muttered.

Dr. T. called back first. He was sure it was nothing. I wearily looked at Pam. "See," I said. Pam pleaded her case—"I've got a patient with a swollen neck and who is increasingly lethargic. Something is wrong." I eavesdropped for a few moments and then shut out the conversation. They can figure it out, I thought. I started to drift . . .

"Christie, Christie, come on, wake up," Pam said.

"Don't you have other patients to see?" I whispered, half asleep.

"Dr. S. is on the line," she ignored my question and pushed the receiver under my right ear.

"Hi," I uttered groggily. "What's up?"

"I just talked to Dr. T. on my car phone, and we think that it's best if you go up to Columbus and have someone in the ER check you out," Dr. S. said.

"We did that yesterday . . . There's nothing wrong. Everyone says that I'm fine—Dr. T. and the guy in the ER and the PICC line lady. I promise. I just want to sleep for a little bit now," I answered.

"Christie, I want you to go up to the ER now," he said.

"Okay," I said, clicking the off button.

"What did he say?" Pam asked.

"I'm supposed to go up to Columbus," I answered and closed my heavy eyelids once more.

"Let me know if you need anything," she said. "I want to know what happens." She told me her schedule for the night as I cuddled up with my blankie and started to sleep . . .

Ring, ring . . . Ring, ring . . . Ring, ring . . . I reached for the phone. With my eyes shut, I muttered, "hello?"

"Christie? Christie?" I heard Roger's voice on the other end of the line.

"Yeah?" I replied.

"Are you all right?" he asked.

"Yeah," I said again.

"What did Pam say when she came at four?" Roger sounded concerned.

"They want me to go to Columbus," I answered, my eyes still closed.

"Why?" he asked. He had been there with me yesterday. He knew the drill—the waiting and the testing and the ultimate conclusion that I'm fine, just fine, always fine.

"I don't know," I answered.

"Well, do you want to go?" he inquired.

Do I want to go, I thought? The question stirred me a bit. Do I want to go? Even if I thought that it would be worth my time to drive all the way up to Columbus, in the dark, in the cold, in the snow, I didn't have the strength to drive. I didn't even have my car—I had left it at Roger's house after I started feeling bad on Sunday. I couldn't think to drive, and I had no one to take me. Wade was in Virginia; I had already gone to the well with my colleagues so much that I couldn't, wouldn't, ask any of them. Roger had been so kind, but he had a life. I couldn't keep asking for favors, especially when the trip would be a waste of time. Someone would just dub me "fine" and send me home.

"No, I don't want to go," I replied. "I just want to get a little bit of sleep, and I'll be fine."

I hung up, and I heard a knock on the door this time. A colleague dropped off Kentucky Fried Chicken . . . I couldn't eat, but Brittany and her friend, Deb, dove into the food . . . Another knock at the door . . . Brittany and Deb opened the door for Deb's mother.

Deb's mom looked concerned. "Why don't I take Brittany home with me? I'll make sure that she gets to bed early. She can ride the bus from our house in the morning and home with Deb tomorrow afternoon. In fact, you can pick her up after Awana. Just give me a call when you know more about what's up with you," she suggested.

"Oh, we're fine," I replied.

"You might be able to get more rest. Why don't we do that?" she paused. "Christie, let me take her for you tonight." She sounded worried.

"Please, Mom," Brittany begged.

"It's a school night," I hedged.

"Please, Christie," Deb begged.

I agreed, mostly to quiet them, and they left. Sleep, now I could sleep . . . Ring, ring . . . ring, ring . . . ring, ring . . . I almost didn't answer, but I knew that I should. What if it was Brittany? She might need something. My hand felt for the phone, and I clicked the on button.

"Hello? Hello? Christie?"

"Hello?" I whispered.

"Why are you still there?" Dr. S. demanded. Why shouldn't I be here? Why was he calling me? My head and neck throbbed, and I couldn't think. Why couldn't people just let me sleep? I didn't hurt so bad in my dreams.

"Um . . . I'm just getting some rest. Everything will be better after I sleep," I answered.

"They have an ER team waiting to look at you in Columbus. I was hoping that you'd be gone by now. This could be something very serious," Dr. S. said.

"I was waiting for my car to get back. My car is over at a friend's house. I was waiting on my ride," I said. However, I really wanted to scream that I didn't have anyone to take me tonight and that I knew deep in my heart that I couldn't drive myself. It's the middle of the night, and I don't want to go until morning, I mused. Who was in charge here anyway? No one can make me do anything, I said to myself.

"You need to be seen immediately." He sounded worried, but I couldn't bring myself to care.

"They are only going to say that it's nothing. I blow things out of proportion, and I'm sure that this is nothing," I tried to reassure him.

I couldn't imagine driving, and I didn't want to ask anyone. Maybe they should just send a cute little chopper for me, coming right down in my big side yard. The neighbors would get quite the kick out of that. None of them had even been over to visit me since I came home from the hospital. What if the chopper got there and found me on the floor and the guys would have to break down the door and then what would the cats do, if the emergency guys forgot to shut the door? They would have to remember to shut the door. I wouldn't want my cats to get loose for nothing . . . There's nothing wrong . . . cats all over the neighborhood . . . cars . . . neighbors . . . dog barking at the chopper . . .

"Well?" he repeated.

Focus, I thought, I've got to remember the question. Oh yeah, will I go? "All right," I responded, *without a clue about how I would keep my word. Dr. S. seemed bound and determined to force me to make a pointless drive.*

I clicked the off button. Now what? I wondered. I just want to sleep . . . I promised that I would go . . . I picked up the phone and tried to decide who to call. No one from my church had been by to help . . . None of my neighbors knew me well enough to impose . . . I didn't have any family nearby . . . My good friends were in other states . . . My colleagues had families and needed to work the next day. By the time that we would leave, it would be at least eight, and I had no idea when we would get back . . . I could only think of Roger, but I had bothered him enough . . . I paused and then dialed his number. Thankfully, he was gone. Good, now, I won't have to bother him. I left a quick message and hoped that he had gone to a movie.

I tried, Dr. S., I thought as I arranged my blue blankie. I just need some sleep . . . I don't care anymore . . . I can't care . . .

Ring, ring . . . ring, ring . . . ring, ring . . . "Hello?" I said *as I brought the receiver to my mouth. My neck ached as I moved my head to position the phone.*

"Hi," Roger said.

"Hi," I replied.

"What's up?" he asked.

"About what?" I said.

"You called me," he reminded me. *Oh man, I did. I didn't want you to be home, I thought. I shouldn't have left a message. I really don't want to bother you again.*

"It's nothing now," I replied.

"What's up?" he pressed.

"Where'd you go?" I asked, *changing the subject.*

"To the store . . . What's up?" he repeated.

"Oh, Dr. S. called, and he kind of wants me to go up to Columbus, and I need my car," I responded. *I didn't want to make him feel obligated to help.*

"Why?" Roger asked.

"I don't know . . . Pam called him and Dr. T., and they talked, and now they think that I might have internal bleeding or be on the verge of a stroke or something, but I'm sure that it's nothing," *I didn't do a very good job of downplaying this, I thought as I finished.*

"Do they think it's serious?" Roger *tried to get specifics.*

"Well, kind of. Can you believe it? I really just need my car," *I tried to make it a joke.*

Roger wasn't laughing. "I don't think that you are in any condition to be driving to Columbus."

"Well," I responded. "I really don't want to impose on anybody else any more. I am tired of imposing on people, especially you. You've already done enough. They will only say that it's nothing. I'm tired of bothering people for nothing. You wasted your whole day yesterday for nothing. I just want to SLEEP."

Roger sighed. "Why don't I take you up to Columbus?"

"No," I said firmly. "Everything will be better in the morning, and I can take care of it myself anyway. We're not driving up there in the middle of the night. I just need to sleep and to get my car."

"I'll be right over," Roger insisted.

I slowly hung up the phone. I felt so sick and so scared. My neck pulsated with pain. I appreciated Roger's willingness to drive me to Columbus, but I viewed my situation as a huge imposition. I closed my eyes, but I couldn't sleep now. I wondered what would happen to me in Columbus. I wondered what was happening in my body—was I bleeding? Would I have to go back into the hospital? What would Britti do? I was supposed to be responsible for her, and I didn't know how quickly Wade could return. Would I die? Would I be alone? I opened my eyes and stared into the darkness of the living room around me, and I waited for another knock on the door.

As I discovered during my health care saga, each link in my health care network impacted my ability to realize physical, emotional, and informational support, sometimes positively, sometimes adversely. The following general descriptions of three general sources of support highlight how collections of individuals can contribute to the composite of support for a health care seeker. Notably, any health care seeker may turn to one or another type of source during a particular health care crisis (as I came to count on my colleagues for help), and certainly, individuals from a source group may offer more assistance than others (as my friend and colleague Roger did for me). As health care seekers tap into each source of support (and turn to individuals who constitute that source of support), health care seekers likely experience diverse benefits and relational consequences/implications, depending on the relational contexts which were co-constructed prior to the health care episode.

Family as Source of Support

When Bruce Mitchell, the newspaper publisher whom I described earlier, discovered that he had cancer, his first reaction was disbelief. Upon affirmation from the doctor that the tests were conclusive, his thoughts turned to his family, especially his little boys. He told the doctor, "But doc, I've got two little boys. I can't have cancer . . ." (Mitchell, August 19, 1999, p. 1). Later, with his wife by his side, he listened as the doctor recommended the specialist and informed them that a convention trip and a vacation should be canceled, at least for now. Mitchell recalls: "Susan (his wife) and I looked at each other in disbelief. Reality was now slapping us hard. It wasn't until that moment we both realized that in the last 30 minutes, our lives had changed forever. We were both very, very scared" (p. 11).

In times of joy and in times of sadness, we turn to family for social support (see Bass, 1990; Cicirelli, 1992; Ell & Northen, 1990; Silverman & Huelsman, 1990; Yelsma, 1995). From elder care (see Kosberg, 1992; Silverman & Huelsman, 1990) to chronic illness (see Cole & Reiss, 1993; Unger, Jacobs, & Cannon, 1996) to rehabilitation from accidents (see Smith & Godfrey, 1995) to cancer (see Baider, Cooper, & De-Nour, 1995) to issues like bulimia (see Beach, 1996) and HIV prevention (see Austin, 1995; Winett, Anderson, Moore, Sikkema, Hook, et al., 1992), the relational context of family dynamics can offer a safe haven from the storm of health threats (see also related research on proactive health behaviors by Franks, Campbell, & Shields, 1992).

Diverse Definitions of "Family Support"

Even though my mom was hours away in Indiana, I called her from the hospital during my IV scare. I worried about Britti and Chelsea Meagan, and I wished that I had the type of marital relationship that could offer support during such a trauma.

While I was conducting my research for this project, I found an article about Nancy Reagan. The wife of the former president carefully attends to her husband, Ronald Reagan, who is suffering from Alzheimer's disease (Benedetto, July 7, 1998). Even though the former president's health has steadily declined, Nancy Reagan commented during a trip to New York that "a week is too long to be away [from home]. I miss waking up with Ronnie next to me" (Benedetto, July 7, 1998, p. 11A).

As a romantic, I love my ideal of family—the two parents with children, dogs, cats, and a house with a basketball hoop on the garage. When I think of family, I still dream of hot chocolate by the fire at Christmas and the sense of tradition from strong extended, supportive family members who live just down the block. Yet, like so many other contemporary families, my own family has been splintered by alcoholism, divorce, geographical distance, and a host of other illnesses and afflictions.

As I did, many move beyond their individual "ideals" to craft family support within the context of their own complicated family relationships. For example, the motion picture *Stepmom* features Susan Sarandon as the mother of two young children who is forced to confront her impending death and to forge a bond with her likely replacement, her ex-husband's girlfriend, portrayed by Julia Roberts.

Assistance with Medical Care

One real-life single mother turned to her young sons for support during her battle with cancer. Lynn Sandlin, of Columbus, Ohio, heralds her sons by stressing "the caring and selflessness of these young men is at a level many adults never attain—such heavy burdens for shoulders so young. This is why they are my heroes" (Sandlin, December 20, 1998, p. 21).

Especially in this era of managed care, family members may need to provide medical care. Judy Pearson, an expert in family communication, describes one couple who cared for two daughters. Until the daughters eventually died from complications of their genetic disorder, Pearson (1995) details:

> The living room and kitchen were set up with an oxygen machine, a breathing treatment machine, and a suction machine. The couple learned to read the various machines, and they became better acquainted with the meaningfulness of the girls' vital signs than did the physicians. (p. 115)

Whether tending to a loved one with a life-threatening illness or cradling a child with a cold, family members facilitate health and wellness through participating in care. In my case, the lack of a loved one forced me to depend on others when I couldn't drive, cook, or make good decisions.

In some contemporary families, distance, circumstances, and miscommunication in contemporary families may hinder actual and perceived assistance. For example, a study by the American Association of Retired People that was released in November 1998 indicates that older parents and their adult children disagree on the quality of their communication about health-related issues (see "Independent living: Do older people and adult children see it the same way?" November, 1998). According to Peterson (January 28, 1999), "Adult children may be providing help that parents don't think they need and therefore don't give their kids credit, while the help parents do want isn't there" (p. 1A).

Informal Non-Kin Sources of Support

Anne Norman benefited from similar non-kin support. After her breast cancer diagnosis, Norman's friends filled the void that she faced because she lacked nearby family and "didn't connect" with a support group (Baker, 1998, p. 37). Norman emphasizes, "The way people rallied around touched me most of all . . . If I'd been lonely, I think it would have affected my recovery" (pp. 37–38). As Lisa, the character with breast cancer in the comic strip *Funky Winkerbean*, commented to a friend, "You know, they gave me some pills to help calm me down . . . but what really helps is having good friends like you, Funky" (Batiuk, March 21, 1999).

Facilitating Everyday Life

When Bill Johnson, a father of three and frequent community soccer coach, discovered that he had kidney cancer, he also learned about the incredible kindness and supportiveness of others in his small town. According to Lenhart (February 28, 1999), Bill, 36, and his wife Michelle, 35, have a wall chart in their kitchen with "a list of 60 or so neighbors and strangers, town residents and colleagues from her school and his company, who have offered to get groceries, take the kids [ages 9, 6, and 2] to school or just pick up the phone and check in."

Michelle's colleagues at the elementary school where she teaches donated one sick day each so that she could help with Bill's care. Bill notes that members of the community have "come over and sat with me, offered to put up the Christmas lights, shovel the snow . . . I've had people call and say, 'I'm going to Price Club, do you need anything?'" (Lenhart, February 28, 1999). Even individuals in Bill's parents' retirement community in Ocala, Florida contributed prayer from a distance. According to Lenhart (February 28, 1999), "Congregations of Baptists, Jews, Lutherans, and Presbyterians have added him to their prayer lists."

In our splintered society, these wonderful examples of unified small town communities and close personal friends may be anomalies rather than certainties (see Gergen, 1991, 1994). As in my case, support came from co-workers, not intimates from nonwork related settings such as civic organizations nor, ironically, a "church family."

Contemporary Conundrums

Although I had been very active in church life in my previous churches, I had grown distant from my local church. My attendance became irregular as I struggled to finish my earlier book by working on Sundays. At the time, I didn't share ties with other church members beyond going to the same church, and I lacked a strong connectedness with other attendees/ members. Our paths intersected for only a fraction of time each week, and all of us were caught up in our own frantically paced lives, complete with children, work, and activities.

When I fell ill, I was easily missed. Wade disliked the pastor and the church, and he refused to call the church office to let them know about my hospital stay. When I went home, one of my home health care nurses happened to be a woman from our church, and I asked her to let the minister know about my situation. However, no one came. No one called. I fell through the cracks of a support system because people (including me) routinely get swept up in the frenzy of life—messages did not get relayed; individuals ran out of time to share or become pressed for information; too many activities distract from attention to one fringe community member.

Especially during my times of fear, I would have appreciated support from others who share my faith in God and my religious beliefs. As Patch Adams (1998), "It is amazing how effective drawing on faith can be even if the patient has rarely practiced it. . . . If patients are very ill it can be comforting to read to them from the texts of their faith" (p. 106).

I did not necessarily need reassurance. I knew that God was still there and that He would control the outcome, but I yearned for someone who shared those convictions to minister to me on a spiritual level, particularly given the seriousness of the situation. More-over, I wanted to know that others in my church cared, and I hoped that they would demon-strate that concern by coming to visit.

In retrospect (and after discussions with the church staff), I understand why I lacked support from the local church as I battled the staph infection. In fact, that absence of support has made me all the more aware of the challenge for health care seekers in remaining con-nected in a fragmented world. Because we are a society of "scatterers," we drift in and out of each other's lives as we change jobs, move, or float into other activities and relationships. Although my world stopped for the infection, the rest of the universe kept on spinning, per-petually altering our relational definitions and ability to link, albeit momentarily.

Fortunately, I recovered. My rejuvenated health allowed me to become more active in the church. However, even though I now direct holiday drama productions and work with youth ministries, I am not sure if someone would come to my door or call me up if I missed four weeks of services in a row—others could attribute my absence to an out-of-town trip or work on another book or a conflicting kid function. Unless someone would call the pas-tor and emphasize the seriousness of trouble, my absence could go unnoticed again.

Our transient, uncertain, chaotic world permits people to lose contact, deterring the prevalence and likelihood of non-kin social support from some aspects of their social net-works. From elderly people who can no longer drive to couples who become consumed over an ill child, from individuals with stigmatizing diseases to those who grow embar-rassed about their afflictions, isolation may result from a fractured contemporary society, especially in terms of informal non-kin support.

Structured Supports of Support

Faye and Todd Wilson embraced their strong religious faith and the support of family and friends since their son, Alexander, was born with a rare heart defect (see Holbert, October 26, 1998). They have also benefited from links with structured sources of support, such as the Make-A-Wish Foundation and support groups. After four surgeries, Alex's condition stabilized enough for him to take a dream trip to Disney World, compliments of the Make-A-Wish Foundation; however, no cure exists for his particular heart ailment. Faye continues to gain support from participation in an on-line support group and hopes to spread hope and encouragement to others through her web page (www.peoplecity.com/health/thealex) and a local support group for heart patients (see Holbert, October 26, 1998).

Charitable organizations, such as the Make-A-Wish Foundation, and health-related community organizations, such as Planned Parenthood, offer physical, emotional, and informational support to health care seekers and their families. For example, through Ronald McDonald House Charities, parents like Bill and Lynn Statler, of St. Louis, Missouri, can stay near their children during out-of-town hospital stays. When their baby, Janet, arrived prematurely during a visit to relatives in central Ohio, the baby was admitted to Children's Hospital in Columbus. Bill and Lynn needed a place to stay. They discovered the Ronald McDonald House to be a source of physical lodging as well as emotional support. According to *Ronald McDonald House Charities* ("In the Blink of an Eye," 1998), ". . . the emotional support they derived from sharing similar experiences with the other families at the Ronald McDonald House has been like 'therapy'" (p. 1).

Facilitating Inclusion

Individuals who face potential marginalization from other strands of society may reap the most from structured social support. My local community has a crisis hotline, Careline, for individuals who suffer sexual assault, as well as Health Recovery Services, for individuals who battle substance abuse issues. Wacker and colleagues (1998) describe community resources that target the needs of the elderly, and Frey, Query, Flint, and Adelman (1998) detail social support within a residential facility for people who are living with AIDS.

Adelman and Frey (1997) offer a compelling account of Bonadventure House, a residential facility for PWAs (people with AIDS). Adelman and Frey (1997) argue:

> Considering the physical devastation, uncertain symptomology, and omnipresent sense of impending death associated with this disease; the loss of significant others to AIDS and the fragile social networks left behind for those still living with it; and the societal stigma associated with AIDS that often results in the loss of social support; no other group of people may have more need for community than those affected by AIDS. It is not only the marginality, but the fragility of everyday life of PWAs that makes the creating and sustaining of community so compelling in this particular context. (p. 5)

While the social stigma of AIDS enhances the potential for social isolation, the advent of support groups for a host of diseases and situations suggests that feelings of isolation due to illness are not limited to those that have been stigmatized by society. Individuals seek an opportunity to obtain social support by connecting with others who share their health-related situation. Although support group members may have little else in common, the health-related situation constitutes a link that may be more powerful than actual kinship. Support groups can offer individuals an opportunity to highlight an aspect of their respective identities that may lack an outlet in other parts of their respective worlds.

For example, support groups like Sidelines National Support Network (www. sidelines.org) and Pillows of Support enable women who struggle with complicated pregnancies to avoid social isolation from extended time in bed. As Swingle (January 12, 2000) explains, "pregnant women say someone who's been through the same isolation can offer a level of understanding and encouragement that most friends or husbands can't" (p. 8D). Through phone calls, emails, and sometimes personal visits, volunteer "veterans" of the experience eleviate some strain from an inherently stressful time of worrying and waiting for the birth of a hopefully healthy child.

A scan of a Sunday edition of the *Columbus Dispatch* reveals over two hundred support groups in the Columbus, Ohio area alone. Nationally based support programs exist for people dealing with alcohol abuse—such as Women for Sobriety, Inc. (see http://www. mediapulse.com/wfs), Adult Children of Alcoholics (see http://www.adultchildren.org/), Al-Anon and Alateen (see http://www.al-anon.alateen.org)—to cancer—such as SHARE (self-help for women with breast or ovarian cancer—see http://www.sharecancersupport.org as well as cancer.med.upenn.edu). In their investigation of an HIV/AIDS support group, Cawyer and Smith-Dupré (1995) suggest that support group messages " . . . are about coping with loss, fighting for individual rights, reviving amidst adversity, and finding peace in a sometimes unjust and cruel world" (p. 248). Leavitt, Lamb, and Voss (1996) argue that individuals with brain tumors treated their support group as a "safe haven" in which:

> . . . participants found acceptance, understanding, and a shared critical relevance to one another because of their shared circumstances. The safe haven was evident in remarks such as "Something happens here that you can't get anywhere else." Patients removed their hats and wigs in the group. Feelings of isolation and stigma were counteracted in the safety of the group. (p. 1251)

Building Connections
Lisa Sperry (December 20, 1998) explains that her breast cancer support group enabled members to connect as fellow breast cancer patients while asserting their individual identities that spanned beyond the diagnosis of cancer:

> . . . we shared our cancer stories, our tears and our laughter. We shared jokes that no one else understood. We questioned everything there was to question and even imagined that, in our talking, we might find some answers. And woven into the stories of our cancer were the details of our lives: who we were, and who we still hoped to become. (p. G1)

With the increasing availability of the Internet, individuals can seek connectedness with others on-line without needing transportation and without some of the emotional implications of face-to-face interactions (see Bly, July 14, 1999; Nichols, 1999; Oldenburg, January 7, 1999; Weinberg, Schmale, Uken, & Wessel, 1996). For example, Nichols (and her on-line group of MS sisters) describes a collection of women who live with multiple sclerosis and who communicate in an online chat group, dubbed the "Flutterbuds' Group." The women contribute resources, insights, and reactions in their messages via round-robin on-line letters. Nichols' (1999) book, *Women Living with Multiple Sclerosis*, features excerpts from postings about issues from family to fatigue to sex to spirituality.

Support for Supporters

As the many stories in this chapter suggest, health care seekers turn to a variety of sources for vital physical, informational, and emotional support. However, the emotional/relational, physical/financial, and social costs and consequences of providing that support can be devastating for supporters (see Carter with Golant, 1994; Clipp & George, 1990; Snyder, Omoto, & Crain, 1999).

In her book, *Helping Yourself Help Others: A Book for Caregivers*, Rosalynn Carter describes her mother's commitment to caring for her husband (Rosalynn's father), and subsequently, for her father-in-law (Rosalynn's grandfather). Partly because of her mother's efforts, Mrs. Carter assisted in founding an organization for caregivers in Georgia, CARE-NET, as well as the National Quality Caregiving Coalition (Carter with Golant, 1994). Especially with managed care initiatives that have thrust patients out of health care facilities more quickly, the need for support for supporters has become increasingly obvious.

Some supporters turn to like-others for support. Internet websites enable supporters to write about their loved ones who are ill and to exchange supportive messages (see, for example, http://www.thriveonline.com/health/herhealth/herhero/contest2.html). Tardy and Hale (1998) found that "stay-at-home moms" sought health information from other mothers during structured play groups. Roman, Lindsay, Boger, and colleagues (1995) discovered that individuals who have had children in neonatal intensive care units constitute invaluable resources for parents with currently hospitalized children. Similarly, Dawson (1997) heralds the success of a "parent-to-parent" program that offers support to parents of special needs children.

In the case of programs like Adult Children of Alcoholics, Alateen, and Al-Anon, individuals seek assistance in responding to loved ones with drinking problems as well as in handling their own emotional challenges that have resulted from the drinking environment (see, for example, http://www.adultchildren.org). SHARE, an organization that facilitates self-help for women with breast or ovarian cancer, also offers assistance to men. A SHARE brochure (1998) provides the example of a man named Michael. The brochure notes:

> Michael's wife was always the emotional foundation of the family. Since her diagnosis of ovarian cancer, she cries at anything. Michael is distraught, he finds himself losing his patience with their kids, becoming distracted at work, and unable to see a future. In SHARE's men's support group, he can talk with other men who share his struggle, whose lives have also been undeniably changed by their wives' diagnoses.

Summary—Sources of Support

Clearly, sources of support vary greatly from family and friends, government-sponsored organizations, on-line commitment, and others. With each of these incarnations of support comes the core issues of access and personal fit. If individuals do not know about resources or lack the ability to access them (i.e., no transportation, funds, or technology), those sources of support cannot benefit individuals with needs. Further, if individuals do not have the communication abilities or the emotional strength to participate in such support structures, they may feel even more isolated.

For example, in their investigation of communication and social support in elderly support groups, Query and James (1989) note that ". . . interpersonal communication competence appears to be associated with social support satisfaction" (p. 178). Additionally, as Sperry went on to explain in her account about the breast cancer support group, members may celebrate support as well as suffer great loss because of their mutual support and concern. Her fellow support group members never anticipated the pain that a member's death might bring. According to Sperry (December 20, 1998), "We had been a continuing source of support for one another, but we had allowed ourselves to get too close. The friendships that we had formed early on and then lost had begun to take a toll" (p. G1).

Accomplishing Social Support

Diana Douglas wanted a baby. She had the perfect husband, the perfect house, the perfect job, and she now desired the perfect baby to fill that last void in her life. Her husband, Andy, also desired children, but he felt less stressed about their inability to conceive immediately than Diana.

Although Diana's "perfect" life with the potentially fatal flaw (infertility) made for a classic Danielle Steel novel, *Mixed Blessings*, Diana's passion to conceive and her commitment to checking ovulation and scheduling lovemaking rang so true to me, given my experiences in trying to have Chelsea. Perhaps even more real, though, was Steel's depiction of Diana's reaction to her family and to her beloved Andy as she went through the infertility tests. When her sister Sam called, Diana was devastated by the reminder that Sam was pregnant and that she never would be:

> Don't, Diana whispered to herself as she hung up the phone . . . don't call me again . . . ever . . . don't tell me how fat you are . . . how pregnant you are . . . about your children or your baby . . . "Who was that?" Andy walked in just behind her. "Sam," she said tonelessly. "Oh." He understood immediately. "You shouldn't talk to her. Don't answer the phone any more. I'll tell her you're out." But Andy's brother, Greg, was no better when he called them that night and asked when they were going to have a baby. "When you grow up," Andy joked with him, but the remark hurt even him. And it would have killed Diana. (Steel, 1992, pp. 141–142)

Diana and Andy chose not to tell anyone about her infertility after the final tests returned; Andy assured her that it didn't matter—they could always adopt. Yet, Diana grew depressed. She exploded at her sisters during Thanksgiving dinner, provoked by innocent table talk about babies that would have been insensitive if the others had any idea of Diana's plight. When she called later to apologize, her parents said that they were there for her, and the topic of babies (even her sister's newborn) became taboo around Diana without further discussion (Steel, 1992).

As I have stressed throughout this chapter, contemporary life complicates social support. The transience and technology of this era enable us to disconnect and to reconnect at rapid paces. Even so, certain confounding factors may have always hindered social support—family tensions (such as parental preferential treatment of offspring or sibling rivalry), embarrassment about health issues, feelings of personal failure, dissonance over conflicting emotions or goals, or uncertainty about expression.

Because individuals, situations, and relationships vary dramatically, I cannot offer a checklist of specific utterances that can constitute "support" across the board. However, core communication considerations, such as facework, identification, and interactional framing, underlie the extent to which individuals can co-accomplish social support.

Facework

Karas (1998) advocates "focused listening" as a means of enacting social support and personal empowerment. In his book, *Housecalls*, Patch Adams (1998) recommends that individuals who visit their ill friends and loved ones ". . . can offer a great service simply by doing conscious listening. Let your friend talk freely. Show a keen interest in everything without being impatient" (p. 107). As relational partners demonstrate their attention to each other (through eye contact, head nods, summary statements, etc.), they display mutual concern and respect for their respective orientations to a situation, each other, and themselves. Adams suggests, "In a friendly way, ask questions that may have come up for you, either from what you know about your friend or from your natural curiosity. These moments will draw you closer . . ." (p. 107).

As I discussed in Chapter 2, each communicative action works to reflect and reify self- and other-definitions and face preferences (see Goffman, 1959). Notably, "supportiveness" can be weighed in terms of individualized face implications of utterances and actions. Within the context of diverse relationships, messages may be interpreted quite differently than in other relational and situational dynamics. For Gilda Radner, her husband's frustrated response reflected his treatment of her as strong, not fragile. For others, constant suggestions might work to threaten preferred face, especially in terms of the health care seeker's ability to make decisions independently and to engage in optimal health care practices.

Goldsmith (1992) emphasizes that "supportive interactions are potentially problematic because they entail multiple goals" (p. 269). Goldsmith explains:

> . . . the kinds of communication acts that typically convey support (e.g., giving advice, offering to help, providing information, expressing caring, etc.) may threaten the face of both parties . . . threats to face and face-work strategies suggest an explanation for the behaviors that receivers of support perceive as helpful and unhelpful. (p. 269)

Nordenberg (1997) offers the account of Lisa, a woman who was struggling to get pregnant. According to Nordenberg (1997), Lisa reported, " 'Everyone gave me advice,' she says. 'My mother said I should just go to church and pray more. My friends said, 'Try to relax and not think about it' or 'You're just overstressed. You work too much' " (p. 1). Such statements worked implicitly to indicate that Lisa might not be religious enough or that she might not be handling the situation well emotionally—each a potential threat to Lisa's face and a deterrent to enacting social support. As Goldsmith (1994) argues:

> . . . threats to face are not merely unwanted side-effects in the support process; they threaten the very outcomes that are believed to link supportive interactions to physical and psychological well-being. (p. 36)

Identification

DEAR ABBY: My husband and I wanted so much to have this child, and we almost made it, but I miscarried a baby boy in my sixth month and he couldn't be saved. This tragedy was heartbreaking enough, but some of the "comforting" comments from well-meaning friends made it even worse. Abby, will you please ask your readers NEVER to try to comfort a woman who has lost a premature baby with any of the following comments . . . :

*"Cheer up, you're still young. You can try again."
*"You have one child already. Be thankful for what you have."
*"It was God's will. Praise the Lord."
*"You could have been lucky; it might not have been normal."
*"Don't be so downhearted—it isn't as though you lost a child."—GRIEVING

DEAR GRIEVING: To the above well-intentioned but inappropriate comments, I can repeat some advice I have frequently offered: To the parents, a miscarriage is the loss of a child . . . . If a friend loses a child through miscarriage, express your feelings of sorrow as though she had lost a "living" child. Because she has. (Van Buren, January 26, 1999)

As I detail in Chapter 2, "identification" involves connecting with another via some common ground. When the would-be supporters of this couple tried to say "the right thing," they failed because they did not establish common ground on the core issue—the couple's enactment of their loss as a real, painful death in their family. Even though well-meaning supporters may not be able to identify completely with the plight of their loved ones (or perhaps, even agree with the orientation of their loved ones to an illness or death), sensitivity to the lived reality of the health care seekers is essential to the enactment of social support. One "Sad Father in Connecticut" offers this reaction:

DEAR ABBY: We just lost three perfect little boys, our triplets. They were born prematurely. Many people have been kind to us, yet we have been stunned by the insensitivity of others. The day our triplets died, a doctor went to my wife in the hospital and said, "Look, it wasn't meant to work out. People aren't supposed to have litters." My wife's hairdresser, on hearing the news, said "Who would want three babies anyhow?" To such people, I'd suggest they think of the three people they care about most in the world, and then imagine them all dying in front of you.—SAD FATHER IN CONNECTICUT (Van Buren, May 12, 1999)

In this letter, the father points to individuals who do not even seem to try to be supportive. The doctor and the hairdresser lack consideration for the orientation of the parents, and thus, counter it. Not only do they disregard a need to connect with the parents on some common ground, they also implicitly threaten their face. "Who would want three babies?"—those parents would have given the world for them. Through their reactions, the doctor and the hairdresser treat the babies as dispreferred, thus alienating the parents and destroying any prior common ground on this topic.

Framing

In *Mixed Blessings*, Diana's husband, Andy, attempted to recast their situation by referring to adoption possibilities. In so doing, he endeavored to broaden the couple's (and especially

Diana's) vantage point on the disappointment of infertility. Andy noted that they were both young and healthy and successful and that their marriage could survive this trial (see Steel, 1992).

Initially, Diana refused to shift perspectives, even growing angry at Andy's efforts to "make everything all right." In fact, because identification and facework are implicitly interwoven into the enactment of interactional framing, Diana felt that Andy could not understand her emotions and reactions to the test results. She pushed him away.

Dana Reeve, however, persisted in her efforts to enable husband Christopher to reframe his situation. Dependent on a ventilator, unable to move or run or embrace his wife and son, Christopher felt depressed and desperate. Dana's words—"You're still you"—recast his situation. He was still a husband, still a father; he still had wonderful reasons to live.

Goffman (1974) argues that interactants utilize communicative resources to co-define how utterances will be treated within the context of conversations and relationships. The framing of talk about health care situations by health care participants dramatically flavors topics and tone of subsequent interactions (as well as emergent social support and understanding of the health care situation).

Particularly in difficult health care discussions, framing shapes what can and cannot legitimately be said, given face needs and preferences for identification with others. For example, Cline, Johnson, and Freeman (1992) found that sexual partners did not engage in safe-sex talk due to fear of embarrassment or shift in mood. In their review of research on HIV/AIDS risk behavior among college students, Lewis, Malow, and Ireland (1997) also report that partners perceive safe-sex talk to be awkward.

The choices to raise safe-sex issues (or not to initiate such discussions) reflect on assumed social support from partners for talk about precautions. If a person feels that she or he faces a potential face risk from inquiring about a potentially life-saving precaution, that person questions the supportiveness of the partner.

In two intriguing articles, though, Adelman (1991, 1992) suggests that interactional framing can permit the partners to conduct the conversation in a manner that reduces potential face risks. For example, Adelman (1991) contends that partners may socially construct safe-sex talk as play:

> . . . joking about the condom serves three functions. First, it provides a release from the tensions raised by the woman's request that the couple practice safe sex. . . . Second, joking about the condom serves to circumvent embarrassment for both the participants about the object itself. By acknowledging the condom's object qualities as a "thing," the man displaces negative attributes associated with its use or his character (e.g., prevention, questionable health). . . . Third, joking transforms the condom from an object of tension to an object of pleasure. (p. 151)

As Adelman notes, framing enables the would-be sexual partners to minimize awkwardness and to facilitate the use of precautions against sexually transmitted disease. Beyond the sexual arena, though, framing permits health care seekers and would-be supporters to accomplish supportive interactions which attend to preferences for face and identification.

CLOSING THOUGHTS

As we drove into the oval in front of the hospital emergency room, I instinctively said to Roger, "Please don't let them keep me here." I knew that he couldn't promise, and I felt cowardly for my reaction. Yet, as I looked at the lights of the hospital glistening against the tiny layer of snow on the ground, I felt fear more profoundly than I had before.

Roger eased the car to a stop, and I shut my eyes and tried to take a deep breath. How could I be more terrified now than I was for the wrist surgery? I tried to visualize the person who drove herself to the surgery, who read Parents *in the waiting room in the wee hours of the morning. How could I be more terrified now than I was as I entered the hospital for the staph infection? When Gayle dropped me off and when I got wheeled to my room, I felt relatively calm. Not now . . .*

Roger opened my door, and I opened my eyes and shivered as the cold February air engulfed me. Gently, he helped me to climb out of the Saturn, and I fought to stand. Waves of dizziness and now a bit of nausea hindered my stance, and I leaned against Roger as we entered the waiting room. I paused as we passed triage and asked the nurse if she was expecting me. The same lady was on duty as the previous day.

"Weren't you just here?" she asked.

"Yeah," I answered. I pressed heavier against Roger as she sorted through papers and finally found a note with my name.

"Yes," she said. "We've been expecting you for some time. We've been expecting you since around six."

Had Dr. S. and Dr. T. really expected me to just call someone at a moment's notice and jump in the car so that more people could tell me that I'm fine? The lady directed me to a chair. I needed to wait to register. I cuddled in my sweats in the chair as I scanned the room—why were others here? Ahhh, why was I here? Who would really know something and be able to figure out what's wrong?

The registration lady called my name. She could not have looked any less excited to be working. She verified my address, phone, and insurance. "They haven't changed since last night," I responded.

I didn't care if I sounded flip or rude. I felt like a broken record, endlessly repeating a seemingly never-ending saga. I was so tired of telling my story to staff members and to doctor after doctor, nurse after nurse, technician after technician—surgery on December 31, surgery on January 1, staph infection discovered three weeks post-op, drainage surgery on January 27, PICC line installed on January 30, released from hospital on January 31, home care, neck swelling, seen in ER yesterday, back again . . . As the nurse led me back to an examining room, we passed a group of residents, and I wondered how many of them would hear my story that night.

Laying on the narrow examining room cot, I looked up at the ceiling and listened to the sounds of vomiting and talk of IVs in nearby areas. I felt so tired . . . I wanted to get to the bottom of this . . . I wanted to get fixed and go home.

A resident walked in to take my history. I tell my story again—Reader's Digest style, and I asked, "Are you an internal medicine resident?"

"No, I'm a psychiatry resident," he answered.

I just looked at him, then at Roger, and then the ceiling. I'm just an exercise, I thought. This boy has no clue about how to help me. He has no clue at all. He doesn't know anything but how to spot a nut, I said to myself.

The resident wrote frantically, trying to capture every detail. Maybe I am a nut, I thought. The x-rays confirmed that the PICC line is in the right place; the ultrasound verified the PICC line placement and the absence of blood clots. I have no good reason for pain and swelling—I am just a nut, and they know that I'm crazy so they sent in the psychiatry resident. Tears started to well up in my eyes from desperation and frustration and exhaustion. . . . The psych resident left with his chart of notes.

Another resident entered, took information, and left . . . The clock continued to tick . . . I wanted my blankie . . . Roger sat by my bed, mostly reading.

A doctor entered with the psychiatry resident and another resident. The doctor greeted me and ordered more blood work . . . We waited . . . Midnight neared . . . The doctor returned to tell me that he was leaving and that someone else would take over.

"Well, we're ruling things out. We're trying to figure out what the situation is. To be honest with you, you've stumped us. We don't know what's going on with you," he informed me.

"Is it likely that I'll be admitted tonight?" I asked.

"I don't know. I really couldn't tell you," he answered.

"What can they do for me here?" I inquired, not really knowing who "they" might be.

"Well, we could just wait until morning and have somebody who is an expert at PICC lines take a look at you," he suggested.

He left, and I stared at the ceiling. Who could help? We had tried to find a PICC-line expert yesterday, but the nurses who know something didn't want to take the responsibility and no doctor was truly in charge. As I looked at Roger, tears streamed down my face, and I felt frustrated and terrified. They didn't know anything; they didn't know anything at all, and I kept feeling worse. What was going to happen to me?

Even though I had experienced fear during the IV episode at the hospital, nothing matched my terror in the ER that night. I listened to the sounds of sirens, vomiting, and hushed voices around me as I realized that I could do nothing but wait—nothing but wait and apologize to Roger for dragging him up here in the middle of the night without any idea of when we could return home.

Roger came closer to the bed, and he asked me how I was doing. "Fine," I responded with a weary smile. I wasn't, but neither of us could do anything about it—nothing but wait.

CHAPTER

7 Technology and Health Communication

"*What time is it?*" *I asked.*

Roger lifted his shirt sleeve and looked at his watch. "Around 12:30," he answered.

I cringed. We'd been in the ER for over three hours, and I'd just missed my midnight dose of antibiotics. "We're trapped in a really bad episode of ER," I said.

"Yup," he agreed.

The main ER doctor had left for the evening, and an internal medicine resident took his place on my case. He entered and introduced himself as Doctor A., but I didn't care. I was getting tired of being tired, spent from serving as someone's science project gone wrong. Leave me alone, I wanted to spit at him. Call someone who knows something or let me go home.

"All of your blood levels are normal. There's no indication of any infection. What I'd like to do is, I'd like you to bear with me for just a few minutes. I'd like to give you a thorough examination," Dr. A. said.

Roger stood up and caught my eye. He nodded. I glared. I didn't care about being nice; this guy didn't know anything more than the rest of them, and I no longer wanted to be a living cadaver to be tested and examined. Just leave me alone, I thought. Yet, I grudgingly nodded consent. What I wanted no longer mattered.

Dr. A. began talking about the PICC line. I interrupted—"All of the tests indicate that it's in the right place."

"Give me five minutes. I'd just like to look you over and see if we can make any kind of assumptions," he said. He recognized the look of total discouragement in my eyes, I'll give him that, I thought.

He started with my eyes, then moved to my ears and throat, head to toe. He proceeded to the PICC line area. "You know, when it goes up here by the collarbone, it just seems to disappear behind the bone."

"Well, yeah, that's consistent with what they found on x-ray and ultrasound yesterday, especially on ultrasound where the technician said she had a hard time seeing it," I responded. I could talk the talk with them, I thought, even if I didn't understand how all of the new procedures and technology worked exactly.

"Shouldn't it disappear behind the bone?" I probed.

"Well, it depends on where your vein is. But I don't know why it would just disappear like that and then reappear. That's a weird thing," Dr. A. seemed to be talking to himself aloud.

Dr. A. moved into the corridor and brought back two more residents, including a guy whom I called "Attitude." Attitude had been advocating the more extreme reactions to my condition throughout the night—"pull the line," he had said. Now, Attitude argued, "I think we ought to insert dye and see exactly where it is."

I glared at Attitude. "No dye—I'll lose the line. If I lose the line, there's no other vein, and I'm not going to get well. I'm not doing that," I stressed. If only that other nurse hadn't blown all of those veins . . . if only I'd agreed to the PICC line before we used up the remaining veins with temporary IVs . . . if only . . . a thousand "if onlys" . . . Roger moved closer; he knew that my breaking point broached nearer.

Dr. A. touched my neck again. "I think that the line popped into your vein and then popped out."

I disagreed. "The x-ray shows it straight across and in the vein. You would not believe how many people have looked at my x-rays and concluded that it's in the right position."

"Well, the problem is on x-rays, you don't exactly see the vein, you see the bones. So this could be showing as very near the bone exactly where it needs to be; however, it could have popped in the vein and then popped out of it, hence causing internal bleeding and your neck to swell," Dr. A. hypothesized.

I froze, staring at him. As peculiar as his idea sounded, somehow, it made sense.

"The odds of something like this happening are so extreme," he continued.

Hmmmph, I snorted. What are the odds? What are the odds that all of these things, any of these things, would happen to me? I felt so exhausted and now even more afraid. "So, what do we do?" I asked.

"We could pull the line," Dr. A. answered.

"I can't. I need IV antibiotics for at least seven more weeks," I asserted.

Dr. A. looked at me and down at the floor. "All right, well, let me think about this for a few minutes." He patted my leg and walked into the corridor.

What was I going to do, I wondered? What could I do? If I could just get some rest, I'd be able to think. I couldn't think; I couldn't make major decisions.

Yet, just then, Attitude popped around the corner of my cubicle. "Okay, we decided that we're going to pull the PICC line and just install a local IV," he announced.

"WHAT?" I said loudly.

A big male nurse took my PICC line arm and turned it. I jerked it away and tried to rise from the bed. I looked at Roger and said, "I'm leaving." Yet, I felt too dizzy to move quickly so I kept talking. "You are not pulling this line. This is my only way of getting better. You are not pulling this PICC line." Roger wouldn't move out of the way to let me up. I was trapped. I wanted to kick and claw and scream my way out of this dungeon of procedures and gadgets and needles. LET ME OUT OF HERE—I screamed in my mind.

Attitude said, "Well, it's easy enough to install an IV line every two or three days. All it would mean is that you would get stuck all those times."

"YOU KNOW, YOU GET STUCK. YOU GET STUCK. I'M NOT GETTING STUCK. I AM LEAVING. I AM OUT OF HERE. GET AWAY FROM ME," I kept screaming. I didn't care if I made sense or if the psychiatric resident came back to commit me. I had reached my limit—I wanted to go home and to be left alone.

Roger grabbed my left hand and right shoulder, and I wanted to hit him. Are they paying you or what? If you care about me, help me escape . . . please just help me, I thought as I started to cry.

"Just a minute," Roger said calmly. How could he be calm? How could he be rational? "We need to relax," he continued. "Nobody's doing anything to you until you give them permission to. You have the power."

I searched his face. How could he think that? My body would not budge from the bed, like a flea flinching yet fatally fatigued in the invisible chains of a spider web. No energy, no clothes, no options . . . I possessed no power; I shoveled it away when I signed in at the start. They could do as they wished.

Tears flowed as I refocused on the mad scientists, the ones with the tests, the needles, the authority. I was just the poor girl who happened to walk in the wrong place at the wrong time. Frankenstein and Mr. Hyde owned adjoining rooms. Desperately, my eyes darted around at the lights, steel, machines, and then I fixed my gaze upon Roger again—please just let me go home, I pleaded silently. I sobbed, but couldn't speak. Someone stole my voice.

"Would you give us a minute, please?" Roger asked the nurse and Attitude. I peeked at them, and they appeared disgruntled. Yet, they left. Thank God, they left.

Roger breathed deeply and said, "All right, this is what we're going to do. Nobody's going to do anything to you until you give them permission to do so. I'm going to go talk to people and find out what I can. I'll be right back."

I watched him leave, and I shivered. I couldn't get warm.

With medical advances that permit at-home tests and dramatic life-preserving surgical procedures, technology has changed the way that individuals orient to the health care process. Bronzino, Smith, and Wade (1991) contend:

> The contemporary American health care system is a far cry from the structures that provided care at the turn of the century, which often consisted of little more than a rural doctor with few surgical techniques and a drug cabinet almost devoid of effective remedies. (p. viii)

More than any other time in the history of man, humankind can tap a plethora of resources for facilitating health and extending life. During my wrist experience, I had an MRI, countless x-rays, a few sonograms, and an array of other tests, procedures, and apparatuses for various aspects of my recovery process.

As individuals seek and communicate about technological resources, they collaboratively co-accomplish artful social constructions of their experiences with and through technology. Notably, the ways in which health care participants co-define various aspects of technology impact the pursuit of health care and health communication. In this chapter, I offer a snapshot of a continually emergent area of health communication by describing the implications of such innovations for gaining information, seeking support, enhancing relationships, facilitating independence, sharing expertise, and increasing care capabilities.

Gaining Information

During a summer session class on women and health communication, my students and I engaged in a spirited discussion about pursing information about health care concerns. As a relative novice to the Internet at the time, I naively inquired whether any of them had "surfed the net" for health care information. The jaw of one of the female student jerked open, and she blurted, "how could you *not*?" We continued our conversation, and she disclosed the *hours* that she invested in researching before visiting her doctor. She proudly claimed that "by the time that I walk in the door, I make darn sure that I know more than that doctor does."

Listening to her, I wondered how she approached her doctor with her wealth of data. Did she present it as confrontationally as she reported in class? However, even more so, I marveled over her time commitment, and I asked her—"How do you find the time?" With a most puzzled expression, she replied, "You can't afford *not* to."

Contemporary health care seekers have become discontent with singularity of perspective, traditional answers, and trust in professional wisdom and knowledge. For many, the Internet constitutes an invaluable vehicle for diverse sources of information, especially for those who deliberately weigh the validity of "facts" and claims.

Value of Information from the Internet

For health care participants, both seekers and professionals, technology constitutes a liberating resource with regard to information. From calling toll-free numbers to reach health-related organizations (see People's Medical Society, 1993) to tapping keyboard keys to summon websites to a screen, individuals may access information about important health-related concerns.

Thousands of Internet locations provide health care participants with seemingly infinite bits of information about health, wellness, disease, and doctors (see Duetsch, 1995; Fogel, 1998; Gustafson, Hawkins, Boberg, et al., 1999; Mallory, 1997; Miller, July 14, 1999; Robinson, Patrick, Eng, & Gustafson, 1998; Sharp & Sharp, 1998; Slack, 1997, 1999; Street, Gold, & Manning, 1997).

General websites on health-related issues abound (see Appendix B). In addition, websites also highlight issues pertaining to specific diseases or people, such as HIV/AIDS (see Dutcher, 1998), cancer, or women's issues.

Individuals can learn about managed care (see http://www.managedhealth.com; http://www.ncqa.org/) or obtain a comprehensive medical reference through a "virtual hospital" (see http://www.vh.org/). Health care seekers can "visit" an online doctor (see Gorman, November 16, 1998) or, according to Davis (November 6, 1998), even access a comprehensive online medical textbook, enabling seekers to obtain the same type of data that doctors use. According to Davis, as of November 1998, the online textbook had already been employed by "2.5 million in hospitals and homes worldwide" (p. 4A).

The Internet permits people to gather their own information, to prioritize those perspectives, and to chart their own course through mazes that health care professionals previously steered. Miller (July 14, 1999) reports that "two years ago, about 7 million searches a year were done on the National Library of Medicine's Medline" (p. 5D). Ever since the database of medical abstracts became available to Internet users in general (rather than reserved for members of the medical community), though, "the figure has skyrocketed to 180 million a year" (Miller, July 14, 1999, p. 5D). According to Davis and Miller (July 14, 1999), "By next year, experts expect more than 33 million to have researched health issues on line" (p. 1A).

For example, Davis (September 7, 1999) details the plight of Julie and Alex Armas. After a prenatal sonogram, their obstetrician informed them that their unborn child suffered from spina bifida. Because of their religious beliefs, the couple did not consider abortion. Instead, they sought a way to reduce the possible disabling consequences of the affliction. Davis reports:

> Like millions of others, the couple and their family quickly turned to the Internet to find out what the disorder was and to read about the latest medical advancements in the field. Julie's mother found Bruner's [a Nashville surgeon] www.fetal-surgery.com. (p. 8D)

Challenges of Information on the Internet

As with all good things, though, some can be too good to be true (see AP, April 28, 1998). As Elliot (November 28–30, 1997) argues, "some families even blame the Web for deaths of family members" (p. 18). Dr. John C. Wolf, a faculty member at the Ohio University College of Osteopathic Medicine, explains:

> There is a great deal of accurate and helpful information out there, but there also is an astounding amount of misleading "junk." Some web sites are run by "cyberquacks." Their material is not written by legitimate medical experts, but rather by people trying to sell products or health-related gimmicks. (January 6, 1999, p. 5)

To safeguard against inaccurate information, health care seekers need to rely on their healthy skepticism of single sources, searching instead for multiple perspectives of the issue in question or sticking to strictly monitored websites (such as the federal consumer health website—www.healthfinder.gov—or www.fda.gov) (see AP, June 24, 1999b; Miller, July 14, 1999).

Seeking Support

As Hafner (1996) acknowledges, "electronic mailing lists, online support forums and World Wide Web sites devoted to every conceivable disease have turned the Internet into a trove of medical information" (p. 280). Certainly, individuals can identify a plethora of perspectives and reports of research findings on the Internet. However, through that information and those interactions with like-others, health care seekers can gain significant social support (see Hafner, 1996; Street et al., 1997, and related work by Baym, 2000; Jones, 1995; Yanni, 1997). Hafner (1996) continues, ". . . the information and emotional support found online can be invaluable" (p. 280).

As I discussed in detail in the chapter on social support, support groups permit individuals with common illnesses or afflictions to connect. Despite the fragmentation and frenzy of contemporary society, online support groups offer health care seekers (and their loved ones) an opportunity to visit with others from around the world, negating barriers of time and distance (see Bly, July 14, 1999, Hafner, 1996; Jones, 1995; Nichols, 1999; Oldenburg, July 7,

1999; Weinberg et al., 1996). As Jones (1995) argues, computer-mediated communication has become important for ". . . community formation in a postmodern world. CMC allows us to customize our social contacts from fragmented communities" (p. 16).

Dolly Campbell started a website for Creutzfeldt-Jakob, an incurable brain disease, after her husband suffered and died from the disease. Campbell notes that "there is a tremendous satisfaction in being able to help others on this walk through hell. And the Internet has allowed us to reach out to people we never would have found otherwise" (Bly, July 14, 1999, p. D1).

Enhancing Health Care Participant Relationships

I couldn't stop shaking. I eyed the opening in the curtains and tried to plot some way to leave. Yet, I couldn't escape. I couldn't even stand. I felt trapped and helpless, like a tiny caged animal.

Whispering . . . I strained to listen, but I could only hear the murmur of what seemed to be side conversations in other little curtained areas. Where was Roger? What if those guys came back before he did? I could only wait and pray that they would tarry.

"Okay, this is the situation," Roger said as he finally re-entered and returned to my bedside. "They think that the PICC line has popped out of the vein and popped back into it, causing internal bleeding, so they have to do something. Their question is what."

I can only imagine the look on my face. How had I come to this? What was going to happen?

Roger continued, "Nobody's going to do anything unless you give the permission to do it. Now, there is another person here who's going to come in and take a look at you in a few minutes, and she's a surgeon. They're talking to her right now, and they'll be in in a few minutes."

He had barely finished when a woman in surgical garb entered, followed by the internal medicine resident, and that Attitude guy, and then four or five little resident groupies. I have become quite the attraction, I thought. Hey, I should sell tickets—come see the lady who has surpassed medical odds in having the most things go wrong with her in two months . . . step right up . . . get your . . .

". . . and so let me take a look at you," the woman doctor finished. I breathed deeply. I have to concentrate . . . I have to pay attention. Her name tag said, "associate professor." This lady might just know something . . . I prayed that she would know something as I glared at Attitude across the room.

"I'm not a PICC-line doctor, but let's see what we have going on here. I have worked with PICC lines. I'm a surgeon. I was on call tonight. I was working in surgery, and I just came down here to hang out, and they told me there's quite the interesting case down here. So I decided to come over and see what it was all about," she kind of rambled, but I liked her. She seemed very confident. SHE knew what she was doing. SHE recognized the importance of maintaining my line.

"Mmm, by golly, it does seem to pop out of the vein. What are the odds?" she said as she fingered my neck.

I cringed and pulled away. "Well, what can we do?" I asked. "If I lose this PICC line, then I'm not going to get the medicine I need."

"Well," she said. "you'll get the medicine you need. You'll just get it in another way."
I cowered. Please don't let them hurt me, please don't let them hurt me, I prayed.

She smiled reassuringly. "But I don't think we need to pull the line. It seems to me
that if we pull . . ." she reached down and referred to my chart briefly. "This is Ansef. Ansef
isn't anything that is going to be so upsetting to you that it's going to be bad if it goes into
your body and not directly near your heart."

Cautiously, I said, "Okay."

"Because of the nature of the medicine, your line doesn't have to go in as far as it
does. So we have some flexibility. We could pull the line back. Not out but back. So it is out
of the damaged area, thus letting that vein have a chance to heal," she looked at me and
then at Roger.

"Oh," I tried to process. Her idea seemed to make sense, certainly less extreme than
hot-headed Attitude. I glared at him again—no reason, it just made me feel better.

"Now, that's going to increase the possibility of infection because we're fiddling with
the PICC line, or irritation, but this will be a way of preserving the line and giving it
another chance," the doctor continued.

"You mean we're not pulling the line? What about dye? Do you want to inject dye to
see where it is?" Attitude asked. He wanted to do something fancy. Go get another toy,
I thought. Play with someone else. You can't have me as your science project anymore—
it's not a game.

"No, we don't need to dye to see where it is," the doctor dismissed him. "Why don't
we do this, and we'll do a follow-up x-ray to make sure it's in the right place." She smiled
and looked at me. "Before I proceed, though, why don't I give Dr. T. a call and let him
know what's going on and get his input on the situation." She patted my leg and left. The
hoard of residents exchanged glances. None of the residents had even considered consult-
ing Dr. T. Attitude stormed out. The male nurse noted that he was "looking forward to
sticking" me before leaving. What a terrible, terrible nightmare. I leaned back and started
to relax. The bad people were gone; the good people had triumphed. As my burst of adren-
aline faded, I began to drift as I waited for the surgeon to return.

She didn't claim to have all of the answers, but she sought creative solutions, not the
first one or the most obvious one. I admired that . . .

For contemporary health care participants, the combination of time limitations for
consultations and overwhelming amounts of possible information calls for "creative solutions." Indeed, as Davis and Miller (July 14, 1999) explain, health care professionals cannot keep up with the virtual explosion of research findings on a vast number of topics, nor
do they necessarily possess the time to pursue options with health care seekers. Although
some professionals may be threatened by health care seekers (such as my student) who
storm into offices armed with information, the Internet can facilitate health care relationships as partnerships between health care professionals and seekers.

Internet as Vehicle for Increased Interactions

Satava (1997) asserts that ". . . we can indeed dissolve time and space to electronically
bring patient and physician together, to empower the physician to provide better and more
humane care . . ." (p. 100). Some doctors encourage email interactions with their patients

(see Coiera, 1997; McKenzie, 1997). My doctor, Dr. S., routinely emails me, checking on my progress and encouraging me to touch base with him. When one of my test results raised a serious health concern during an unrelated issue, he sent me an email, urging me not to worry.

To be honest, I'm always a little surprised to receive an email from Dr. S. I know that he invests considerable hours in his job and his family, and emailing takes time. However, as I also understand from my own work, emailing takes less time than making telephone calls or writing letters, and it doesn't require busy people to coordinate schedules to converse. As such, email constitutes an excellent means through which health care professionals and seekers may interact efficiently (i.e., in a time- and money-preserving manner).

Technology as Co-Monitor

Some medical centers and practitioners employ technology even further to enhance health care relationships and to facilitate health outcomes. Baby CareLink, a program initiated by Beth Israel Deaconess Medical Center in Boston, permits parents of babies in a neonatal care unit to reach doctors and nurses electronically (see Frase-Blunt, 1998). After discharge, communication continues, facilitated by state-of-the-art technology. Frase-Blunt explains:

> This connection of the home, clinician, and tertiary care hospital allows for the episodic needs of high-risk newborns by continuously monitoring their progress, managing therapeutic treatments, and systematically following multiple medication plans. (p. 10)

Notably, technology enables care to occur at home, reducing cost and allowing more parental involvement. Davis and Miller (July 14, 1999) conclude:

> . . . some doctors and other experts believe that the Internet's biggest impact on the future of medicine will be its ability to instantly connect patients and doctors, letting them begin to solve problems before they get out of control. (p. 4D)

Relational Concerns

As I discussed in the chapters on industry relationships, the institutional environment has changed radically for health care professionals. With the advent of managed care and organizational cost-cutting measures, they lack the control, authority, and legitimacy that they once treasured as guardians of their patients' care. With the advent of consumerism and then the Internet, the carefully crafted relational system of professionals and seekers has been disrupted by changes in the rules and roles, changes in "what you are supposed to do/know" as a "real" doctor, a "real" patient.

Given the plethora of information on the Internet, the differential between health care professional and seeker knowledge has diminished in some instances and, in the cases of particularly persistent health care seekers, shifted from "doctor knows more" to "seeker knows more," as I will further detail in the closing chapter on decision making. According to Davis and Miller (July 14, 1999), "A motivated patient who wants to learn about just one condition easily can surpass a doctor's knowledge of its latest developments after just a few days on line" (p. 2A). Davis and Miller (July 14, 1999) argue that the rampant availability of information to nonmedical professionals ". . . is causing a dramatic shift in the balance of power between doctor and patient, changing how medicine is practiced more profoundly than anything since the advent of managed care" (p. 1A).

As health care seekers, like my student, come to health care encounters, the ways in which they introduce their Internet findings indicate their preferences for individual and relational identities for themselves and their health care professionals. Although individuals can certainly alter the artfully accomplished relational system with their health care counterparts, deviations in roles, changes in the rules of the game, necessarily impact face concerns. For health care professionals—individuals who have already experienced significant face threats due to managed care—the advancement of seeker knowledge may implicitly indicate seeker questions about professional knowledge, competence, and credibility (see my discussion in the chapter on decision making about knowledge and power relationships). Such indications, even though unstated overtly, can jeopardize face wants and contribute to defensiveness.

Should health care seekers avoid bringing their information and insights to the table during health care discussions? No, because single individuals (whether professional or seeker) cannot possibly keep up with the virtual flood of facts and claims about health issues, health care participants should share perspectives and knowledge bases. However, in light of consumerism and institutional changes, both health care participants should remain aware of respective relational and individual identity preferences as they engage in the process of deliberating about a situation.

Facilitating Independence

Contemporary individuals seek technological advances that can empower them and enable them to act as individuals. On-line medicine appeals to our contemporary preference for consumerism, for seeking the "best deal" and for accomplishing health care on our own time and terms. However, with that self-control, we assume responsibility for mistakes that we could formerly attribute to someone else.

Increasing Flexibility

More than ever before, individuals may conduct self-testing and obtain treatments without ever visiting an actual health care professional. For example, with their products like portable ultrasonic nebulizers for asthma patients and instant ear thermometers, Omron Healthcare, Inc. markets products that people can use in their homes to deal with health care situations (see www.omron.com/ohi). Home pregnancy tests also permit individuals to gain quick and convenient results when and where they want (see http://www. 4women.org/faq/pregtest.htm).

Health care seekers can order prescriptions online (see Gallagher, July 29, 1999; Rubin, November 2, 1998; January 21, 1999; Zuckerman, July 14, 1999), a practice that has raised eyebrows and concerns among members of the medical community. Gallagher (July 29, 1999) argues that "the good health news of the day is that, throughout the Internet, hundreds of Web sites exist that dispense low-cost prescription drugs without you having to drive to the druggist" (p. 12A). For individuals who desire assistance in identifying valid, legal online pharmacies, the Food and Drug Administration offers a web link called "Buying Medical Products Online?" (see www.fda.gov).

Especially in the case of individuals with disabilities, the Internet provides the potential for independence. In her review of literature on people with disabilities and computer-mediated communication (CMC), Fox (2000) suggests that the World Wide Web ". . . gives people with disabilities resources to increase their independence and lessens their reliance on professional agencies for assistance" (p. 321). In addition, according to Fox, "the numerous listservs, electronic bulletin boards, and newsgroups allow people with disabilities communicative access to other people with whom they would otherwise have little chance to interact" (p. 322).

While the informational and supportive resources on the Internet enable individuals, with or without disabilities, to avoid reliance on professionals and geographical boundaries, computer-mediated communication poses a special social advantage to those who have a potentially stigmatizing disability. As Fox (2000) explains, ". . . advantages exist for people with disabilities within the context of CMC that do not exist in face-to-face communication" (p. 327).

Possible Hazards of Self-Care

Although CMC remains compelling to health care seekers, self-care can be isolating and dangerous. When individuals pursue Internet support groups for companionship, as opposed to family and friends who live nearby, they risk social isolation and loss of physical support. When they engage in self-diagnosis and treatment without appropriate input from health care professionals, they jeopardize their health. In the case of on-line pharmacies, Gallagher (July 29, 1999) contends:

> The bad health news of the day—and it's far worse than the good news—is that scores of those sites supply both prescriptions and potentially dangerous prescription drugs to online visitors without first performing an exam and making a reliable diagnosis. (p. 12A)

As Rubin (November 2, 1998) notes, "Viagra, for example, by far the drug most commonly prescribed online, can lead to fatally low blood pressure if taken with nitroglycerin, a widely used heart medication, or other drugs" (p. 1A). Yet, individuals who thirst for convenience and accessibility of drugs can tap into the unregulated domain of online pharmacies with minimal questions.

Further, when untrained health care seekers trust at-home tests and equipment, they risk errors due to their inexperience and, perhaps, ignorance. After two at-home pregnancy tests showed that she wasn't expecting, one woman went to the doctor. According to Howard (1999), "A blood test gave her conclusive answers: She was 10 weeks into her first trimester, and though she didn't have a life-threatening disease, she *did* have to cope with an unwanted pregnancy" (p. 37).

The National Women's Health Information Center website notes that "although most manufacturers claim 99 percent accuracy in laboratory tests, inaccurate results may be more frequent in actual use." As Howard (1999) reasons, ". . . for a woman who may already be nervous and distracted by the possibility of a pregnancy, mistakes are all too easy to make" (p. 37).

Sharing Expertise

Telemedicine has reshaped the ways in which education, care, and communication occur in the health care industry (see Bashshur, Sanders, & Shannon, 1997; Berek & Canna, 1994; Field, 1996; Kolodner, 1997; Reid, 1996; Viegas & Dunn, 1998). As resources have expanded (in terms of funding for training and technological support), highly integrated systems of computer-mediated health care now span the United States and industrial areas of the world, linking health care professionals and seekers in the pursuit of proactive and cost-effective care discussions.

Building Connections

With telemedicine, health care professionals may share rich information about their patients and resources with other professionals (see Coiera, 1997; Davis, August 5, 1998; Frase-Blunt, 1998; Gustafson et al., 1999; Harris, 1995; McKenzie, 1997; Saba, Pocklington, & Miller, 1998; Slack, 1997; Street et al., 1997; Viegas & Dunn, 1998; Weghorst, Sieburg, & Morgan, 1997). In their historical overview of the development of telemedicine, Barrett and Brecht (1998) explain that the advent of the Internet, the deregulation of the telephone industry, and the development of compression technology and multimedia computers spurred the growth of telemedicine as a resource for connecting networks of physicians.

In brief, "telemedicine" refers to ". . . all occasions by which pertinent healthcare data are shared among authorized parties electronically through networks" (Purcell, 1998, p. 32). Through email or compressed video, health care professionals can converse about cases, develop skills, and even provide care. As Purcell (1998) continues, ". . . the ability to consult with a physician remote from the patient through two-way teleconferencing can improve the quality of decisions made by healthcare providers and hopefully lead to better outcomes" (p. 32).

Enhancing Access

When geographical or other physical barriers deter access to care, telemedicine offers an innovative means of linking health care participants and affording access. The availability of connections between physically dispersed professionals promotes patient care and continuing education of health care personnel.

Enhancing Patient Care

Especially in rural populations in the United States, health care seekers and professionals lack specialists for consultations about health care concerns. Delays in access to specialists hinder further testing and treatment, thus impacting health outcomes (see Bashshur et al., 1997; Reid, 1996; Viegas & Dunn, 1998). Reid (1996) contends:

> Rural patients are the greatest beneficiaries of telemedicine technology. . . . Telemedicine reduces the previously described geographic, social, and potentially cultural barriers to accessing care. Patients gain more timely access to the most appropriate level of care. Earlier intervention results in decreased morbidity and mortality. (p. 45)

Turner, Gailiun, Caruso, Murray, and Warren (1998) argue that telemedicine can also be integral to treatment in corrections environments. As the authors detail, when inmates travel to alternate locations for consultations with specialists or to obtain care beyond the capabilities of the prison facility, the process incurs cost and hinders communication between the consulting specialist and the primary care physician. By employing telemedicine, however, the primary care physician can observe the specialist's examination, interact with him or her directly, and offer insights to the specialist about the peculiarities of the inmate's situation (see Turner et al., 1998).

Although most examples of telemedicine include consultations, telemedicine can include teledermatology (wherein a specialist actually interviews and recommends treatment for a health care seeker (see Lowitt, 1998) and even telesurgery (Bowersox, 1998). In telesurgery, a specialist can observe and offer input during surgical procedures or, as indicated in some experimental cases, employ computer-controlled robotics to perform surgeries (see Bowersox, 1998).

The American Society of Plastic and Reconstructive Surgeons even highlighted the hope for robotics in plastic surgery in an advertising supplement to *USA Today*, thus enabling specialists to operate on patients in distant areas. Although the notion of robotic surgeries may sound like something from a science fiction movie, Davis (October 6, 1999) reports that Canadian surgeons have already employed a robot to perform the first endoscopic bypass surgery in the world. According to Davis, the head of the surgical team, Dr. Douglas Boyd, contends that someday "it will be possible for a surgeon to be hundreds of miles away while performing the surgery" (October 6, 1999, p. 1D).

Enhancing Continuing Education

A second important function of telemedicine features continuing education for health care professionals in relatively isolated areas (see Viegas & Dunn, 1998). In the case of rural medicine, for example, Bashshur and colleagues (1997) suggest:

> In current practice, telemedicine is utilized for two-way educational experience for primary care physicians in rural areas and consulting physicians in academic centers. Rural physicians gain from interacting directly with specialists on a case-by-case basis, as well as by having greater access to and participating in formal continuing education courses. Academic physicians, in turn, learn about the types of health problems facing rural practitioners. (p. 23)

Increasing Capabilities

Advances in technology permit faster and more efficient screenings, innovative treatments, and exciting health outcomes. However, with the ever-increasing capabilities, health care participants face challenging ethical choices about life and death issues.

Enhanced Possibilities

Experimental cancer drugs may lengthen life for cancer patients. Faster brain scans can help prevent strokes (Haney, February 6, 1999). An insulin pump for people with diabetes permits a continual flow of insulin, rather than periodic injections (see Sherman, July 9–11, 1999). Airports and shopping malls have installed defibrillators to revive people who suffer heart attacks in public places (see Davis, December 28, 1999). Laser surgery can correct corneas, shelving the need for eyeglasses (Estrich, June 25, 1998; Gorman, October 11, 1999; Lewis, 1998).

In a variety of arenas, research dollars have resulted in a plethora of new ways to detect and defeat disease and to enhance physical quality of life. For example, Peggy Smith, of Nashville, claims that the new ThinPrep Pap smear "saved her life by highlighting cancerous cells that a regular Pap didn't find" (see AP, November 29, 1998).

Earlier, I mentioned Julie and Alex Armas. Through a prenatal test, they learned that their unborn child suffered from spina bifida, and they sought someone to help. The Armases contacted Dr. Bruner and pursued the option of a fetal surgery in which the exposed portion of the baby's spinal cord would be closed. If left unaltered, the baby would suffer some uncertain amount of brain damage.

According to Davis (September 7, 1999), "The couple knew the experimental surgery might limit such brain damage, but to get the benefit they had to act fast" (p. 8D). According to Davis, Vanderbilt University ethicist Mark Bilton suggests:

> . . . the families who have decided to have the surgery share two "robustly American" characteristics: a strong religious faith and an equally strong faith in technology. He sees in each of them a hunger for a medical breakthrough though he cautions that the technique has not been proved as a breakthrough. (p. 8D)

Ethical Choices

In case after case, individuals pursue technology with the hope that it will enable them to live (and, perhaps, better) or to help a loved one. Estrich (June 25, 1998, p. 15A) noted that she treated her PRK (photorefractive keratectomy—a laser surgery for eyes) as "a trip to the beauty parlor" that would permit her to see without glasses. She viewed the high-tech, elective surgery as largely cosmetic, not a surgical procedure with inherent risks. Yet, as she discovered, some people have even lost their vision due to the procedure (Estrich, June 25, 1998).

The Armases' decision involved a surgery that could help their baby to be born "normal" and that could cause its premature death. They proceeded with the surgery, and the baby did survive the procedure and seems to have benefited from the operation. However, the tough reality is that Mrs. Armas could have miscarried the baby on the operating table. The benefits of technology truly come with the cost of tough ethical choices.

Guillemin and Holmstrom (1986) detail the emotional and physical challenges for parents of premature babies (see also Anspach, 1997; Layne, 1996). In her personal narrative about experiences with a child in a neonatal intensive care unit, Layne (1996) suggests that we tend to view technology as linear and progressive; however, such a conception countered the prevalent lived reality of neonatal intensive care unit parents, which mirrored a roller coaster more than a straight line. Layne's baby lived, yet not all babies do, and their battles resemble cyclical struggles rather than marches toward progress.

Although technology permits us to preserve life at younger and younger ages, such heroic efforts must be weighed with the sacrifice—in this situation, potentially life-long disabilities and pain. However, as Schneiderman and Jecker (1995, p. 4) caution, "The impact of all this technology extends well beyond the innovations themselves; indeed, their most important impact may be on the way doctors think." I would go further than Schneiderman and Jecker to suggest that many health care seekers concur. If little Brianna or Caitlyn had survived to be born alive, I would have moved the stars to seek solutions for them. I wouldn't give up on them either.

Schneiderman and Jecker (1995) continue, "*Technological imperative* [implies that] if a means or instrument of medication exists that can produce an effect, then medicine must use it" (p. 4), no matter what the cost. At what point do we determine that an effort is futile? At what price do we draw the line, in terms of emotional distress, financial expense, or physical suffering? At what instance do we declare enough has to be enough (see related work by Little, 1995; Zussman, 1992)?

Cultural and religious foundations underlie such ethical discussions of technological alternatives (see Schneiderman & Jecker, 1995; Sargent & Bascope, 1996). For example, if one adheres to a biomedical model of medicine, with a focus on a particular problem rather than a more holistic view, that stance flavors approaches to technological resources. Sargent and Bascope (1996) explain that "ways of knowing" about birth, from various cultural perspectives, influences adherence to biomedical orientations to technology or to resistence to technological interventions.

Yet, in addition to culture and religion, issues of identity, power, pride, affection, and a plethora of quite human emotions sprinkle through medical decisions. Until robots remove the requirement for humans to intervene in medical care, individual people make decisions within the context of their very complicated lived realities. No matter how "objective" one attempts to be, one cannot truly isolate out the variables of humanity; one can merely deny them.

In one episode of *ER* entitled, "Love's Labor Lost," Dr. Greene fervently fights to save a pregnant woman. The riveting episode features a wonderfully engaging woman who came to the ER with a complaint of recurrent urination. Greene examined her quickly, wrote her a prescription, and sent her on her way with her adoring husband. She collapsed as she departed. Greene reevaluated her case and called for a consult with her obstetric doctor.

Throughout the episode, Dr. Greene depended on his understanding of tests and measurements to assess the woman's situation. I could not sit down as I watched him try, again and again, to reach her doctor. Yet, the doctor did not come, and the woman's condition deteriorated.

Greene attempted an emergency c-section, which he blundered. He delivered a baby boy as the woman's doctor arrived. Together, they tried to stop the bleeding and to revive the woman. However, tragically, ultimately, the woman's doctor pronounced the woman dead. Greene refused to give up. He continued CPR for a long time, even though one of his colleagues looked at him compassionately and acknowledged that the woman had died. At what point should he have stopped trying? At what time did she really die, did the part that made her a lovable wife and an enthusiastic prospective mom seep away?

Even though Greene adhered to the biomedical model, his attachment to the woman and his guilt over medical mistakes compelled his answer to those questions to differ from the woman's doctor. His choice to persist and his eventual decision to stop trying stemmed from a plethora of perplexing perspectives, not a single viewpoint that rigidly dictates black and white.

In my case, the wrist reconstruction of screws and bone graft and a metal plate constituted a medical marvel. I joked prior to the surgery that I would emerge as a "bionic woman" with my new "high-tech" wrist. Before my illness, no one in my family had ever heard of a PICC line, and I certainly never believed that I could manage and maintain my own drug intake via the line. Yet, as soon as the first nurse came to my home on that Friday evening, she announced that the home health team goal was to teach me to administer my own drugs and to handle my own PICC line.

With the technological resources of the Internet and medical equipment, contemporary individuals gain their freedom, but they also acquire the burden and responsibility of self-care and tremendously burdensome choices. Health care seekers are expected to know more and do more than ever before. Paradoxically, the rampant explosion of information and equipment offers us more to learn than we can possibly comprehend. For those of us who fear the unknown, the raising of Pandora's lid blasts us with much that we cannot grasp and, perhaps, much to dread.

Even though science brought forth technology, the employment of technology by health care participants involves a balance of belief in scientific strengthes and creative artistry in considering alternatives about their use. In the six ways that I have detailed throughout this chapter, technology prompts praise while continuing to generate questions about its application by and for humans.

CLOSING THOUGHTS

The surgeon came back into my little curtained cubby. Dr. T. had approved the plan to pull the PICC line back into my upper arm. She measured the path of the line in order to know how much line to draw from my body.

My eyes followed her as she donned gloves and removed the tape from my arm. Tensely, I watched her as she began the procedure. I clung to Roger's hand and held my breath.

I closed my eyes. I could feel the line moving out of my vein—no additional pain, but also no immediate relief from the now constant throbbing in my neck. The entire effort took only a few minutes. Would it help?

She snipped the leftover line and rebandaged my arm. The surgeon smiled at me and said, "Okay, I think that we've solved the problem. I think you're good to go."

I just stared at her for a moment. Go? Just like that? Yet, I couldn't think well enough to ask additional questions. I felt far too fatigued and drained to care about much more. I directed my energy into relief . . .

My eyes drifted to the clock in the car . . . 4 A.M. Roger started the car, and we pulled out of the hospital parking lot. The science experiment was over. Yet, as we drove away, I wondered about how she knew that the bleeding would stop and that the vein would heal. Can't worry about that now, I told myself. She obviously understands this stuff . . . she just knows how it works . . . For now, I didn't have to understand. I slipped into sleep as we drove onto the highway.

CHAPTER

8 Diversity and Health Communication— Traditional Concerns

The cold wind whistled around my head as I walked from the car to the open gym door. Warmth embraced me as I passed through the door, and the smell of sweat quickly replaced the crisp chill of the winter air. Parents and players pushed past me in the tiny passageway between the parking lot and the basketball court, but I stood still just inside the door, savoring the scene before me.

Nine- and ten-year-old girls were dribbling and shooting basketballs on the court while a few younger children played on the stage at the end of the elementary school gym floor. I turned my head upward and to my right, noting the bleachers that were filled with adults. I realized the most incredible rush of familiarity. How amazingly wonderful to be with people who are alive, who are running and jumping and playing and watching, I thought. How wonderful to be alive . . . to be here . . . to just be another mom in a crowd of moms and dads who delight in their daughters' basketball triumphs . . .

I shifted my gaze back to the court. I knew so many of the girls, and I felt strangely surprised. How many games had I missed, I wondered. Too many, I answered myself. I had never known that such joy could come from attending a fifth- and sixth-grade girls city rec basketball game. I will never take this for granted again, I vowed.

"Hey, Mom," Britti said as she stripped off her coat and started to head for the court. "Take my coat."

"What do I look like, a human coat hanger?" I chided her. Oh, it was so good to be treated as a living, breathing, functioning, human coat hanger again. I felt so marvelously normal.

"Britti, why don't you lay it over by the bench?" Roger suggested.

"Okay," she shrugged, and she heaved her coat onto the bench and headed for the nearest basketball.

I felt the strongest urge to dive out there with her, to guard her, to try to steal the ball and put up a shot. As I always told her, you can take the girl out of Indiana, but you can't take Indiana basketball out of the girl. I was never any good, but as an Indiana native, I certainly inherited the state's passion for playing and watching hoops.

"Do you need help?" Roger asked.

"Huh?" I said as I cringed watching Britti miss a pretty easy shot.

"Do you need some help getting up the bleachers?" he inquired again.

I froze. For a moment, a blissful, beautiful moment, I forgot. I forgot about the cast on my right arm. I overlooked the IV in my left one. For that moment, I wasn't the invalid who needed IV therapy three times a day. For that instant, I had just been a mom who loves basketball and being in the community, simply a normal person on a clear Saturday morning in February in Athens, Ohio.

"No," I replied, trying to eye a hole in the crowded stands. "I can do it."

"Sure?" he persisted.

"Yes," I affirmed. Well, I am nothing if not a bit stubborn and proud. I wanted to be normal. I insisted upon accomplishing normality.

Roger gave me a "please be careful" look and headed for the bench. I watched as he pulled out his roster and prepared to coach Britti's team, and I started to edge my way through the parents and players who stood near the stands. However, I couldn't bound up the bleachers like before. As I climbed up the first step, I could no longer discard the reality that my body could not keep pace with my mind and my goals. Overtaken by a wave of dizziness and fatigue, I yearned to sit down, but I could not simply plop down any place. I had to have space to protect my IV and my cast. I couldn't be bumped. My smile faded, along with my fantasy of being my old self.

I paused on that first step, suddenly very conscious of my tattered sweatshirt with the ripped sleeves to accommodate the huge cast and the sensitive PICC line on my arms, very cognizant of the coat that covered only my shoulders, very aware that I lacked my trademark energy and zeal for life.

I glanced around the sea of many familiar faces, and I wondered if any of them could recognize the frail, pale shadow as the vibrant person who I used to be. They sat in pairs and groups, gossiping and visiting about school and community activities. I longed to join them, to catch up on events, to behave like I did before. Yet, if I sat with them, I couldn't slide effortlessly into their world of everyday talk about everyday events. They would no doubt address the elephant in the room and, in a quite concerned yet curious way, concentrate on me and my cast and IV and the circus that my wrist repair had become. I was so sick of being sick and focusing on treatments and prognoses. I bowed my head and turned away.

I chose a spot near Britti's team yet distant from others who came to cheer. As I surveyed the gym once more, I noticed several people whom I knew from scouts and school and softball. I attended to the action on the court, careful to avoid eye contact. I wanted to be at the game, yet I desired to be left alone. I wondered what people thought, what they knew, what they assumed. How did I look from their eyes, I pondered. I had been thin before my illness, but my weight loss from the hospital showed in my face and my bony shoulders. I thought that I looked gaunt in the mirror, but did I appear as frail as I felt? Could they see my IV? What were they thinking?

Focus, I thought. Just watch the game. Relax and enjoy the game, I challenged myself. Britti's team dropped back on defense, and Britti worked on the other team's top scorer. Britti swarmed the poor girl. I glanced at the ref—no foul. How could there not be a foul for that, I thought? The other girl started to make a drive for the basket, but suddenly, Britti had the ball. I wanted to stand up and jump and scream and cheer. My body chained my spirit. I wanted to cry. Others in the stands went on as usual—calling out encouragements and applauding efforts—while I sat motionlessly on the cold, hard bleacher.

Okay, I lectured myself. It's only been four days since the PICC-line incident. Look what you have accomplished in that time, I told my reluctant self. You learned to give yourself medicine through the IV, and you even mastered the art of garbage-bagging your arms and hip so you can shower. You can walk from one room to another without hugging the walls. You left the house and came to a game.

I didn't want to listen to my internal voice of reason. Instead, I looked wistfully at the others in the room, and I begrudged their collective energy and apparent good health. I couldn't keep up. Would I ever be able to regain what had once been normal?

"How you doin'?" a male voice inquired behind me.

I tried to smile as I twisted my head to the side. "Hi," I said, greeting our pediatrician.

"How's the arm?" he asked. We had visited at a previous basketball game soon after the reconstruction so he knew about the original two surgeries but not about the complications.

"It's good, I think." I hesitated, not certain about sharing more details. The account seemed too long, too involved, to detail while trying to keep pace with the game. I searched for Britti on the floor. Oh, there she was, under the basket going for a rebound. She missed it, and a girl from the other team grabbed the ball and scored. Britti scowled at her. We have to work on sportsmanship, I thought.

"When will you get the cast off?" he inquired.

"Ummm . . . I'm not really sure." One of the coaches called for a time-out, and the teams headed to the sidelines. I decided to give the doctor the sports-highlight condensed version of my saga. "I found out that I had a staph infection in my hip, and I was in the hospital, but now I'm getting outpatient IV antibiotics with a PICC line. I had some problems with it, but I think that I'm okay now."

"What happened?" he continued.

I took a deep breath. "Well, in a nutshell . . ." I summarized the main points, leaving out the trauma, omitting the twists and turns and strain of the seemingly endless saga. As I finished, I watched the teams return to the floor, and the doctor acknowledged that I had "had a time of it." The telling of the PICC-line drama resembled a commercial as we both shifted our attention back to the primary programming—our daughters' game.

My gaze drifted over to the other adults in the bleachers. How well do we really know each other? I wondered. We come to these games, and we share in this event and perhaps others. Whether we're talking about our health or our children or a school function, we do what I just did—we offer highlights. We give each other brief peeks at our lived realities, just enough to commiserate with each other or to engage in polite conversation, just enough to get by so that we can rush on to our next activity, the next stop in our packed day.

The ref blew his whistle, marking the end of the game. The children ran to their coaches and prepared to congratulate the opposing team on a good game. The adults readied themselves to depart. We had collaboratively engaged in the social event of city rec basketball. The adults and girls collected their belongings, donned their coats, and headed for that narrow passageway back into winter and their lives beyond the gym. All of us are in so many places, I thought. Yes, we live in the Athens area, and we connect through the commitments of our children. Yet, our connectedness relies upon tightly compacted, thirty-second summaries of events and emotions. Our fractured and chaotic lives hinder deeper attachments and affinities.

"Hey, Mom." Britti climbed up to my bleacher.

"Hey, you did great." I smiled at her as she pulled on her coat while rubbing sweat off her forehead with her hand. "How much did you pay the ref to keep him from calling fouls?"

"I didn't foul. I just went for the ball." Britti grinned.

I stood, hesitating for a moment to make sure that I had my balance. One of the other moms from the team passed by as she climbed down from a higher bleacher.

"How you doin'?" she asked as she moved on to the step below mine.

"Fine," I said. "I'm fine."

"Good," she responded as she continued toward the door. She didn't pause to see me struggling as I tried to drape the coat around my shoulders—she greeted me on the run, just like normal.

In that tiny elementary school gymnasium, people gathered to watch youth basketball, as they gather to watch youth softball in the summer and youth soccer in the fall. Although I usually think of those individuals as "just moms and dads" and "just girls," truly, each person encompasses much more than a family role or a gender or an age.

For example, on that day in the gym, I was, as I am now, a mom who loves basketball, a passion promoted by a childhood in Indiana and a stint as a cheerleader when my high school girl's basketball team won the state championship. I enact the role of "mom" in a manner consistent with my Type-A personality and high-energy professional lifestyle—I love to be involved, connected, prepared, and "together." Thus, I felt dissonance about my illness because I wanted to behave (and to be treated as) normal and yet, paradoxically, I appreciated support when people recognized that something was wrong. Although I didn't think that it was important to the particular social occasion, I also happen to be a white, thirty-something, well-educated, middle-class, Baptist female who voted for Clinton. Each of the other individuals who entered that gymnasium on that cold February morning could offer his or her own unique self-descriptions.

As we participated in the game (as parents and players), we did so in a manner that was consistent with our individual and collective understandings of ourselves, each other, and the social requirements for the event, understandings so ingrained and embedded that we take them for granted until someone acts inconsistently. Beyond mundane everyday interactions (such as a common focus on a basketball game), our backgrounds, attitudes, beliefs, and characteristics flavor more significant events, such as health care interactions.

As I discussed in Chapter 3, health care professionals, health care seekers, and support system members need to understand each other in order to facilitate the co-accomplishment of medical, educational, and relational goals during health care encounters. However, perhaps more than at any other time in history, health care participants recognize that one professional cannot be assumed to be the same as others; one health care seeker is not the same as others, and one support system may not resemble others in terms of structure or depth.

Increasingly, scholars, practitioners, and health care seekers argue that diversity makes a difference in terms of how we approach health, wellness, disease, and social interactions with others in the health care context (see Baker, 1997; Helman, 1984; Huff & Kline, 1999; Kavenagh & Kennedy, 1992; Kreps & Kunimoto, 1994; Purnell & Paulanka, 1998; Spector, 1996a; Whaley, 2000). In this chapter, I describe three categories that constitute core concerns in traditional treatments of diversity. Specifically, I explore the implications of ethnicity/race, sex/gender, and age for health communication.

Traditional Categories

In my book, *Partnership for Health*, I detail a health care encounter that I had with an overweight, middle-aged, Caucasian obstetrics specialist in high-risk pregnancies who happened to be substituting while my doctor attended a conference. The man swept into the room and proceeded to interrupt me and to disregard my answers to his questions. I grew increasingly frustrated and distressed. After two previous miscarriages, I needed for this doctor to help me, to make sure that this pregnancy was on track, to ensure that my medication seemed to be facilitating the pregnancy. However, he kept cutting off my responses and talking at the chart, with his back turned to me as I sat on the examining room bed.

Finally, I could no longer control my anger and my urgent desire for him to truly listen to me. I sat up as tall as I could on the cold table, straightening my thin hospital gown. "Look," I said loudly. "I don't know who you think you're dealing with, but I am not some hick from southeastern Ohio. I have a Ph.D. in communication; I specialize in doctor-patient communication, and frankly, you suck." I didn't take the time to compose my outburst in advance, but in retrospect, I realize that I automatically addressed attributes that could generate stereotypical reactions. I couldn't let him dismiss me or my baby by lumping me into some category—just another woman, possibly uneducated, from a rural and generally impoverished region.

As I have noted previously, I am a tiny person and, at the time, I had long blonde hair that was scooped up in a ponytail. Like always, I wore no makeup, and I usually look younger than I am. At that moment, I could do nothing about my physical appearance to gain authority—I couldn't slip out to put on a business suit, hose, and heels. I couldn't fix my hair. I could only try to sit up straighter.

However, I could attempt to rectify potential big city perceptions of a small town "girl." I worked to invoke status by countering possible a priori conceptions about my address—southeastern Ohio, a part of rural America known as Appalachia—a region that can prompt visions of poverty, poor education, and low social status. I noted that I wasn't a "hick" (a negative word that I abhor but that others often use in order to depict people from my region). I supported that claim by referring to my education—a Ph.D., and I tried to sound superior to him by arguing that I specialize in doctor-patient communication, thus advancing the claim that I could tell him a thing or two about communication in this context (i.e., that he "sucked").

Nearly six years after that incident, I remain surprised by the tack that I took in the conversation. Instead of sticking to the core issues at hand (as a good former college debater should do), I felt the need to gain some sort of legitimacy in order to get the man to listen to me. In so doing, I relied upon a very traditional conception of diversity by assuming that stereotypes (i.e., education, social status, location, gender, age, income level, etc.) influenced the doctor's style with me during our interaction. To this day, of course, I have no idea if the doctor treated all of his patients in the same manner or if his perception of me flavored the meeting.

Regardless of that particular doctor's beliefs and biases, though, research indicates that scholars, practitioners, health care educators, health care seekers, and support system members do routinely turn to sociodemographic categories such as race, culture, gender, age, religion, education, income level, and physical appearance as they approach and explain health care interactions (see, e.g., Hall & Dornan, 1990; Helman, 1984; Huff & Kline, 1999; Kreps & Kunimoto, 1994; Like, 1991; Purnell & Paulanka, 1998; Spector, 1996a; 1994; Whaley, 2000). In so doing, such categories permit individuals to bracket others and to contextualize interactions in light of assumptions about groupings of people. Although, as I will detail later, such bracketing can be problematic for individual interactions and even some policy decisions on organizational and government levels, the categories can serve as an initial way of adapting information and directing resources.

For example, the U.S. Department of Health and Human Services developed its set of substance abuse resource guides to target a wide range of specific populations of individuals, offering individual books for, among others, pregnant/postpartum women and their infants (1997), rural communities (1994), and Asian and Pacific Islander Americans (1996). Each publication contains lists of prevention materials, studies, articles and reports, groups, organizations and programs, and Internet access; however, those lists contain resources for people who fit the label of the publication. Ideally, those resources match the needs of that particular population. The *Healthy People* documents, in particular, exemplify the usefulness of sociodemographic categories for addressing general health care needs, especially in terms of health disparities:

> The demographic changes that are anticipated over the next decade magnify the importance of addressing disparities in health status. Groups currently experiencing poorer health status are expected to grow as a proportion of the total U.S. population; therefore, the future health of America as a whole will be influenced substantially by our success in improving the health of racial and ethnic minorities. While disparities among racial and ethnic groups especially between whites and African Americans have received considerable attention over the last decade, differential access to social and health care resources most often reflect occupational, educational, and income and wealth differences among Americans. Differences in the life circumstances of those with less income and those with more income in the United States are substantial. Furthermore, education is a major determinant of earnings potential. These differences in access to economic and social resources appear to drive many of the health disparities found across America. (http://web.health.gov/healthypeopl...ripts/p1.cfm?secname=goal2&pnum=p1)

The *Healthy People* documents point to significant societal programs with regard to sociodemographic differences and the opportunity for quality health care. In some cases, those differences stem from biological characteristics; in other situations, disparities emerge from social factors. Such distinctions between populations of people constitute important considerations for health care participants.

Ethnicity

As I noted at the beginning of the chapter, I happen to be a Euro-American from the state of Indiana. From what I have heard in random family stories, my ancestors left Ireland and Germany for the United States over a century ago. Apparently, the Becks even owned a castle on the Rhine River at some point. However, other than being able to share that piece of information with anyone who happens to ask the right question, I have little insight about traditions or rituals from Irish or German cultures. Mostly, I consider myself to be from Indiana, and my vision of the state steps right out of the movie, *Hoosiers*—farmkids shooting baskets on barns amid the cornfields, an image in my mind spun from folklore, a decade as a 4-Her, and three decades as a devoted fan of "Hoosier Hysteria" (the annual high school basketball tournament).

Gans (1999) suggests that my fifth generation distancing from European ancestors is not uncommon for individuals who live beyond the ethnic communities within larger cities in the United States. Although he contends that some individuals of long-standing European descent opt to include aspects of ancestral traditions into parts of their lives (for political or social reasons), Gans (1999) maintains that such endeavors constitute "symbolic ethnicity" that facilitates individual identity with a group, rather than actual participation in a community (see related work by Royal, 1995).

Other researchers oppose this assimilation-oriented depiction of American culture (see especially, Blommaert & Verschueren, 1998; Spector, 1996a, 1996b; van Dijk, Ting-Toomey, Smitherman, & Troutman, 1997). According to such scholars, for many, images of self and ethnicity can stem from roots far deeper than where one happens to grow up (see Blommaert & Verschueren, 1998; Kim, 1997; Spector, 1996a, 1996b). Kim (1997) argues:

> . . . the impact of ethnicity in shaping identities and interethnic communication behavior varies from situation to situation. Ethnicity can be critical, totally insignificant, or have a whole range of effects in between. (p. 264)

In my case, of course, ethnicity would not seem to have been a major influence in my life. I became a Christian when I was in my mid-twenties, as a result of personal exploration rather than ethnic allegiance. I never took the time to learn about rituals, traditions, or even the language and food from my Irish and German heritages. I rarely considered my race (Caucasian) or my language (American English) to be primary influences on my decision making or on my interactions with others, especially in health care situations.

However, in addition to my failure to connect with my Irish and German heritage, perhaps I did not reflect about my ethnicity because I happen to be Caucasian/Euro-American in a predominantly Caucasian/Euro-American society (the United States). I can speak American English with other native speakers, and I can assume at least an openness to Christian beliefs. Perhaps, I did not consider my ethnicity because the similarity of others did not make that ethnicity problematic for me as I went about my daily life. Consistent with Blommaert and Verschueren's discussion (1998) of "abnormality" and culture, by virtue of my status in the majority, I could legitimately interact with others as "just another normal" person, a person who happens to be Caucasian, a person who happens to speak American English, a person who happens to behave according to Christian values (see related work by Martin, 1997).

Ironically, if I had invested myself more in my Irish or German roots and lived in another time, I might well have not been able to slip into that deceptively homogenous majority so easily. If I had been born to African American or Native American parents, I could likely not slip into that majority at all (see Hord & Lee, 1995; L. Robinson, 1998).

Madrid (1997) maintains that ". . . despite the lip service given to the goal of the integration of minorities into institutional life, what has frequently occurred instead is ghetto-ization, marginalization, isolation" (p. 508). L. Robinson (1998) asserts:

> . . . racial identity does not imply acceptance of "race" as real, but acknowledges the social and political reality that people live in societies in which "race" identities are attributed to them, and that these attributions have real consequences for their experience of life. (p. 8)

In the health care context, ethnic identifications can become a significant consideration for potential health care outcomes, especially in the ways that health care participants explain and understand the health care situation (see Whaley, 2000). Core issues include health-related beliefs/traditional practices and biological differences/tendencies.

Notably, the very diversity of orientations to health and health care practices and of health care tendencies and outcomes between various ethnic groups precludes more than a quick glimpse of them in this section. Individuals who are interested in these fascinating and diverse health care traditions should pursue four books, in particular. These books delve into distinctions between dissimilar ethnic populations in great depth (Lassiter, 1995; Purnell & Paulanka, 1998; Spector, 1996a, 1996b), and they delineate differences in health beliefs and behaviors in far more detail than I can accomplish within the space constraints of this book.

Health-Related Beliefs/Traditional Practices

For individuals who adhere to particular ethnic-based beliefs and traditions, the commitment to certain health care practices may reflect and reify their core values and views of the world (see, e.g., Altenberg, 1992; Ambler, 1994; Bates, Rankin-Hill, & Sanchez-Ayendez, 1997; Cavender, 1988; Coreil, 1988; Finkler, 1985, 1994b; Hare, 1993; Helman, 1984; Huff & Kline, 1999; Jackson, 1993; Kelm, 1998; Lassiter, 1995; Lock, 1990; Logan, 1991; Nichter & Nichter, 1987; Purnell & Paulanka, 1998; L. Robinson, 1998; Romanucci-Ross et al., 1991; Spector, 1996a, 1996b; Waldram, Herring, & Young, 1995; Whaley, 2000; Zane, Takeuchi, & Young, 1994). Such traditions include religious beliefs, dietary habits, and language.

Religious Beliefs

Religious beliefs can serve as a prevailing influence on health care beliefs and practices (see Ambler, 1994; Krupat, 1994; Lassiter, 1995; Miner, 1997; Spector 1996a, Waldram et al., 1995). The desire to appeal to God and to reject evil forces extends to a number of ethnic communities. For example, Tripp-Reiner and Sorofman (1998, p. 315) reveal that members of Greek immigrant communities widely uphold the Greek Orthodox religion and that "problems are seen as originating outside the individual's control and are attributed to God, the devil, spirits, and envy or malice of others . . . often the forces of evil are believed to cause illness" (p. 315).

AbuGharbieh (1998) also notes that Arab Americans tend to be Muslim and that religious beliefs greatly flavor their approach to health and wellness. AbuGharbieh (1998) explains:

Many Muslims believe in combining spiritual medicine, performance of daily prayers, and reading or listening to *Qur'an*, with conventional medical treatment. The devout patient may request that his or her chair or bed be turned to face Mecca and that a basin of water be provided for ritual washing or ablution before praying. Providing for cleanliness is particularly important because the Muslim's prayer is not acceptable unless the body, clothing, and place of prayer is clean. (p. 153)

Other religions and health-related religious practices may not be so easily reconciled with Western medicine. Especially with colonialism in North American, Native Americans, Alaska Natives, and Aboriginals face the challenge of juxtaposing Western medicine with their traditional (and very spiritually grounded) health care practices (see Ambler, 1995; Indian Health Service, 1997; Kelm, 1998; Warry, 1998).

Waldram and colleagues (1995) describe one traditional healing practice that occurred (and still does, to a much more limited extent) in aboriginal cultures as well as Russia and Scandinavia—the sweat lodge. According to Waldram and colleagues (1995), the sweat lodge "was used for purposes of prayer, to maintain health, and to address particular health problems or social concerns. It was also used as a precursor to other religious and healing ceremonies" (p. 110). While an individual sits naked in the tiny and contained space, amid steaming rocks (perhaps treated with herbs) and his or her own sweat, others (especially an elder or a medicine pipe man) pray publicly and recite religious songs. Waldram and colleagues (1995) contend that "the therapeutic benefits of the sweat lodge have obviously been recognized widely, as evidenced by its global presence" (p. 110).

Notably, the influx of Western influences through missionaries and government interventions has impacted traditional Aboriginal healing processes. Warry (1998) contends that colonialism (the attempts by others to influence and alter native practices) has contributed to:

> . . . the rapid erosion of indigenous medicine, including herbalism and forms of spiritual healing. In many parts of the country [Canada] the conversion to Western medicine occurred very early after contact, simultaneous with the loss or decline of Aboriginal religious leaders, shamans, who can be thought of as indigenous spiritual doctors. (1998, p. 85)

Ironically, those same missionaries and government liaisons inadvertently transmitted new diseases to the Aboriginal people as well. Although they introduced new medicines, people died as they struggled to juxtapose old and new ways of responding to illness (see Warry, 1998). According to Warry, "In communities that lost between 20% and 40% of their families to disease, there was a crisis in faith—both with traditional religious beliefs and traditional medicinal practices" (p. 85).

Especially for individuals from diverse ethnic backgrounds who reside in the United States, the dominance of biomedicine and managed care, combined with limited mainstream support for religious health traditions, can hinder access to care. As Mayeno and Hirota (1994) note, the fragmentation of the contemporary health care system in the United States ". . . is even more formidable for those who possess different conceptions of health care and healing, use different care-seeking practices, and lack prior experience in dealing with such systems" (p. 355).

Dietary Habits / Traditions

Dietary habits/traditions can reflect and reify religious commitments as well as orientations to health and wellness. Spector (1996a) suggests, for example, that practicing Muslims view some foods as "filthy and are taught that a 'person is what he eats'" (p. 195).

Dietary traditions can stem from long-standing cultural traditions within a particular community. Spector (1996a) writes, for example, that " 'geophagy,' or eating clay and dirt occurred among the slaves, who brought the practice to this country [the United States] from Africa" (p. 196). She continues to note that "when clay was not available, dirt was substituted. In more modern times, when people were no longer living on farms and no longer had access to clay and dirt, Argo starch became the substitute" (1996a). In other cultures, Spector reports:

> People from many ethnic backgrounds eat raw garlic or onions in an effort to prevent illness. Garlic or onions also may be worn on the body or may be hung in the Italian, Greek, or Native American home. *Chachayotel*, a seed, may be tied around the waist by a Mexican person to prevent arthritic pain. Among traditional Chinese people, thousand-year-old eggs are eaten with rice to keep the body healthy and to prevent illness. (p. 142)

Beyond the eating (or avoidance) of particular foods, some ethnic groups adhere to philosophies that guide the selection and consumption of food. According to Helman (1984), "In Latin American folk medicine, the humoral theory—often called the 'Hot-Cold Theory of Disease'—postulates that health can only be maintained (or lost) by the effect of hot or cold on the body" (p. 12). Clark (1970) suggests:

> The "hot and cold" theory of disease is derived from the Hippocratic theory of pathology, which postulated that the human body in a state of health contained balanced quantities of the four "humours" (phlegm, blood, black bile, and yellow bile). Some of the four "humours" were thought to be innately "cold." A disproportion of hot and cold body essences was reflected in illness. This body of belief was brought to the New World by sixteenth-century Spanish explorers and colonists and was widely diffused among the native inhabitants of Spanish-America. (p. 164)

Similarly, the guiding philosophy of "yin or yang" common to Asian Americans focuses on two oppositional yet unified forces in the body, the yin and the yang (see Spector, 1996a). In the case of Japanese Americans, in particular, Lassiter (1995) details:

> The yin state is associated with symptoms of "internal cold" and reduced body function. In contrast, symptoms of the yang state are generalized hyperactivity with external manifestations such as a "warm" sensation and/or elevated temperature. (p. 141)

This hot-cold dichotomy extends to the categorizing of food as hot or cold, yet those distinctions remain unrelated to actual temperature of the food. For example, "yin foods are usually bland; yang foods are often spicy" (Lassiter, 1995, p. 141).

Language

Language constitutes another cultural artifact that reflects ethnic connections and that can impact health-related behaviors and practices (see, e.g., Huff & Kline, 1999; Pauwels, 1995; Samovar & Porter, 1997 as well as related work by Basso, 1990; Carbaugh, 1990; Fitch, 1998; van Dijk et al., 1997). In fact, according to Ellis (1999), "Language is the most elemental quality of the discourse of ethnic identity and group formation" (p. 158).

Language does not just involve uttering words that mean something to another. Language and linguistic and nonverbal patterns indicate and reify cultural preferences and orientations to the world. As van Dijk and colleagues (1997) contend, ". . . group members culturally produce and reproduce their own identity—and hence their group—by using the group's own language variety and special discourse forms . . ." (p. 164).

Saville-Troike (1992) offers an account of a Navajo man who came to his child's kindergarten classroom. Although the teacher greeted the man, he remained silent while his son quickly picked up his crayons and prepared to leave the room. Saville-Troike explains:

> From a Navajo perspective, the man's silence was appropriate and respectful. The teacher, on the other hand, expected not only to have the man return her greeting, but to have him identify himself and state his reason for being there. This would have required the man to break not only Navajo rules of politeness but also a traditional religious taboo that prohibits individuals from saying their own name. The teacher engaged in small talk in an attempt to be friendly and to cover her discomfort in the situation, as appropriate in her own speech community, while the man continued to maintain the silence appropriate in his. (p. 151)

Especially because language and linguistic/nonverbal patterns often stem from deeply embedded cultural and religious roots, they can flavor how individuals participate in health care discussions (a process that may well also be framed by religious orientations). Yet, in the United States, Hispanic Americans, Asian Americans, and members of other ethnic minorities may be forced to communicate with health care practitioners who do not share their native language or dialect and who do not demonstrate an understanding of the symbolism of their linguistic choices, not to mention the meaning of their words (see Huff & Kline, 1999; Pauwels, 1995; Spector, 1996a).

Health Tendencies and Outcomes

However, beyond diverse orientations to health care, research indicates that individuals in certain ethnic communities are more prone to particular diseases than others in the general population (see Henkel, 1998; Lassiter, 1995; Shelton, 1998; Spector, 1996b; Sugarman, Warren, Oge, & Helgerson, 1992; West, 1999; Zane et al., 1994). Spector's (1996b) booklet on health care assessments outlines a number of biological variations between populations such as African Americans, Asian/Pacific Islander Americans, American Indians, Aleuts and Eskimos, Hispanic Americans, and European-origin Americans. According to Spector (1996b) and Lassiter (1995), African Americans struggle with sickle cell anemia and lactose intolerance more than others in the general population, while European Americans face a unique battle with breast cancer. Henkel (1998) also stresses the diversity in death rates from prostate cancer in the African American community, in particular. The Healthy People 2010 website offers the following summary of health disparities:

> African American men under 65 suffer from prostate cancer at nearly twice the rate of whites. Vietnamese women suffer from cervical cancer at nearly five times the rate of whites. African-American men suffer from heart disease at nearly twice the rate of whites. Native Americans suffer from diabetes at nearly three times the average rate, while African Americans suffer 70 percent higher rates than whites and prevalence of diabetes in Hispanics is nearly double that of whites. (http://web.health.gov/healthypeopl...ripts/p1.cfm?secname=goal2&pnum=p1)

Notably, as the Healthy People 2010 website acknowledges, differences in socio-economic status (such as income and education) also impact health outcomes. If a person is poor, then that person usually lacks the same type of access to health care as his or her wealthier and/or more educated counterpart, and some ethnic populations tend to be poorer than others. Further, socioeconomic conditions, combined with diverse cultural traditions, may prompt more high-risk health behaviors or deter proactive health-seeking behaviors in some populations than in others (see Huff & Kline, 1999; Mayeno & Hirota, 1994).

For instance, in an Indian Health Service round table on cancer and Indian women, participants stressed a variety of cultural and socioeconomic issues that impede Indian women from obtaining adequate preventive care (Kauffman, 1991). Round Table participants recommended consideration of poverty, lifestyle choices, and accepted health prevention practices in terms of possible health consequences.

Although cultural and socioeconomic issues certainly impact ability and willingness to seek care, possible biological differences cannot be ignored with regard to health outcome disparities. As such, both socioeconomic and biological differences in physical responses to disease continue to be worthy of attention as researchers continue to explore explanations for disparities in disease tendencies and health outcomes.

Gender/Sex Differences

When I was working on *Partnership for Health*, I read a book entitled, *Outrageous Practices*, a book dedicated to detailing injustices to women in the health care system. As I read one section in particular, though, I grew a bit skeptical. According to the authors, Leslie Laurence and Beth Weinhouse, women had experienced chest pain, were rushed to the ER, and received mistaken diagnoses (such as indigestion or gallbladder trouble) and/or instructions to return home and "just relax." Some of those women traveled to their home and promptly died from myocardial infarction—a heart attack (see related work by Keyser, 1984; Laurence & Weinhouse, 1997; Nechas & Foley, 1994). According to Laurence and Weinhouse (1997), "Though it has been the leading cause of death in American women since 1908, heart disease is one of the best-kept secrets of women's health" (p. 85). In fact, according to Browder (1998), "cardiovascular disease kills more women than all forms of cancer combined" (p. 42).

Why would a doctor discount the possibility of an apparent heart condition, or worse, a heart attack, I wondered skeptically? I pursued original research articles and discovered strong empirical support for the Laurence and Weinhouse claim (see Aaronson, Schwartz, Goin, & Mancini, 1995; Altman, 1995; Legato, 1994; Steingart, Packer, Hamm, et al., 1991; Tobin, Wassertheil-Smoller, Wexler, et al., 1987). Even in 1999, a research report in the *New England Journal of Medicine* revealed that doctors referred 40 percent fewer women (and African Americans) for heart catheterization than their male (and Euro-American) counterparts (see Schulman, Berlin, Harless, Kerner, et al., 1999). Still, no clear explanation emerged, except the belief in an apparent old-school myth that women do not have heart attacks, a belief shared by many health care practitioners and seekers (see Laurence & Weinhouse, 1997; Starr, 1982).

I was working on this chapter when I took a break to go to my daughter's soccer game. As one of the coaches of the team of five-year-old kindergartners, I walked up and down the sidelines, yelling encouragements and suggestions to the children as they battled over the ball. One of the little girls, Lori, eked out the ball and started to make a run for the goal, but unfortunately, she headed straight for the opposing team's goal. I tried to yell to stop her, but she couldn't hear me. I quickly darted after her on the sidelines to save her from possible embarrassment.

As I did so, my heart started racing and pounding against my chest, and I started to feel dizzy and weak. I had experienced such palpitations before, usually during similar quick bursts of energy—like dashing for a ball in a remote corner of the tennis court. The palpitations usually stop within a few minutes so I try to relax and to take deep breathes until the symptoms ease. On this occasion, though, my calming efforts did not work.

I finished the game, and the pounding ceased. Yet, the pain in my chest continued to escalate. After about an hour, the pain started to shoot down my left arm, and I grew more concerned. "Oh," I tried to quiet my fears, "I can't be having a heart attack. I run five miles a day. I'm in great shape." I thought about this book and this chapter, and I shook my head. "What are the odds that anything else would happen to me, especially now, as I'm writing this book? What are the odds?"

The pain intensified, and I finally agreed to go to the emergency room. The nurse rushed me back into an examining area and hooked me up to a monitor immediately. Within minutes, a technician came in and conducted an EKG. "Gosh," I thought, "these people are taking this very seriously." Thus far, my experience did not resemble the descriptions of other women who struggled to gain legitimacy with their complaints.

After a few more minutes, an ER doctor entered. He felt my chest and my upper right arm.

"Ouch," I responded.

"That hurts?" he asked.

"Yeah," I said, trying to relax my body.

"Can I reproduce the pain?" he queried as he continued to tap at my chest and the upper arm region.

"No, it just hurts, but not like the pain that shoots down my arm," I answered.

"Okay, that's important. So, what happened?" he questioned.

I told him about chasing Lori down the sidelines and about getting the palpitations during quick bursts of energy. Sheepishly, I explained that I had had these palpitations for over ten years but that I had never really pursued an explanation before. I treated episodes as momentary interruptions of my activity. Other than isolated occasions, I didn't have a problem. I quickly interjected that I run and that I'm very active.

"I couldn't possibly be having a heart attack, right?" I probed.

"I very much doubt it. You're active; you don't smoke or drink; you're not overweight; you don't have a family history of heart disease; you don't have any of the risk factors. I'd like to get a chest x-ray to check out your lungs, but I would bet that we can get you on your way pretty quickly," he asserted.

I wanted to leave; I yearned for nothing to be wrong, but yet, I couldn't help feeling unsatisfied with the depth of explanation.

"I'm wondering why my chest still hurts," I asked.

"I would bet that it's just chest wall pain from exerting yourself," he said.

"What about the palpitations?" I inquired.

"I would suggest that you follow up with your doctor, but some people just get them. I don't think that you have a heart problem; you don't have the risk factors," he shrugged.

"Okay," I said, not wanting to press him. I didn't feel like arguing with him. I went for the chest x-ray and soon got released with a recommendation to take ibuprofen for "chest wall pain."

When I followed up with Dr. S. the next week, I expressed surprise at the ER doctor's dismissal of the possibility that my complaint could be heart-related. He laughed and noted that one of his supervisors in med school had even told him "women don't get heart attacks. Don't even check for it." Heart attacks are a "man's disease," health care practitioners and even health care seekers commonly reason (see Laurence & Weinhouse, 1997).

Would the ER doctor have treated a man differently? If I were a man, would I have handled the situation differently? A few years ago, a national news magazine received a lot of grief for its cover, which stated that "men and women are different." Even with trends toward equality in the workplace and family roles, the common reaction, from late night comedians to co-workers at water fountains, was "duh, of course."

As Verbrugge (1985) observes, though, "The far reaching differences between men and women have inspired curiosity, poetry, romance, and polemics for centuries, but they have only recently prompted scrutiny by social scientists" (p. 156). Especially for participants in health care encounters, sociocultural and biological differences with regard to sex and gender roles can impact how individuals interact and work to achieve health care outcomes (see Beck with Ragan & duPre, 1997; Beck & Ragan, 1995; Bishop, 1992; Conkling, 1996; Dan, 1994; duPre & Beck, 1997; Faelten, 1997; Gabbard-Alley, 1995; Gallant, Keita, & Royak-Schaler, 1997; Guttman, June 11-13, 1999; Laub, Somera, Gowen, & Dfaz, 1999; Lerner, 1995; Majeroni, Karuza, Wade, et al., 1993; McBride & BcBride, 1981; *Men's Health* editors, 1999; Mitchell, 1996; Muller, 1992; Porter, 1990; Ragan et al., 1995; Rahman, Strauss, Gertler, et al., 1994; Roter & Hall, 1997; Roter, Lipkin, & Korsgaardt, 1991; Tannen, 1990, 1992, 1993, 1997; Todd, 1989; Walsh, 1997; Weintraub, 1993; West, 1993; West & Fenstermaker, 1997; Wooddell & Hess, 1998; Wyckoff, 1987).

Sociocultural Differences

On New Year's Eve in 1991, Wade woke up with an awful toothache. He whined, and he grumbled, and he grouched around the house for a few hours. I suggested that we call the dentist and try to obtain some assistance. He refused, but kept on complaining about his tooth. Another hour of miserable commentary on his tooth ensued, and finally, I walked into the kitchen, called the dentist, pleaded for a last minute appointment, and re-entered the living room with a time in hand.

"You go to the doctor for every little thing," he said.

"I go when I need help," I responded.

He went to the dentist, who fixed the problem and gave him a prescription for the pain. To me, going to the dentist made complete sense. To him, going to the dentist wasted time and money (that is, until he took his first dose of the pain medication). We oriented to the health care situation from vastly diverse perspectives.

Through a multiplicity of influences, such as the media and our interactions with gender role models and peers, men and women gain insight into ways of enacting their respective gender roles (see, e.g., Belenky, Clinchy, Goldberger, & Tarule, 1973; Gilligan, 1982, 1988; Gilligan, Ward, & Taylor with Bardige, 1988; Guttman, June 11–13, 1999; Rakow, 1992 as well as related work by Apostolos-Cappadona & Ebersole, 1995) and, to some extent, how those roles get performed in the health care context (see, e.g., Hibbard & Pope, 1983; Wood, 1997). Wood (1997) explains that "from birth on, individuals are besieged with communication that presents cultural prescriptions for gender as natural and right . . ." (p. 165).

As Garfinkel (1967) details in his classic description of "Agnes" (a man who worked to learn how to be a woman as a necessary precursor to a sex change operation), the accomplishment of gender involves artful, symbolic communication practices that impact interactions with others, both male and female. In fact, West, Lazar, and Kramarae (1997, p. 119) assert that prevalent feminist scholars argue that "gender is accomplished *in* discourse" (see also, Rakow, 1992; West, 1993b).

Such enactments frame how men and women approach each other during health care encounters, especially in terms of face concerns and identity construction (see related work by Goffman, 1959). Particularly in the case of sex-related health issues, health care participants must carefully negotiate how one presents oneself as a "real" woman or man, in light of preferences to achieve health care services while avoiding displays of private body areas and conducting oneself in a manner consistent with desired gender performances.

Linguistic/Nonverbal Preferences

Linguistic/nonverbal preferences constitute an important part of how individuals present themselves as "real" men or "real" women (see Beck with Ragan & duPre, 1997; duPre & Beck, 1997; Fisher, 1993; Tannen, 1986, 1990, 1992, 1993; Tannen & Wallat, 1993; West & Fenstermaker, 1997; West et al., 1997; Wood, 1997). For example, Tannen (1993) argues that women tend to be more indirect more than their male counterparts, regardless of their position of authority. *Indirectness* can facilitate face-saving and politeness yet it can also be construed as a lack of assertiveness.

In *Partnership*, I mention Ellen, a pregnant woman who attempted to gain assistance for her cough by initially describing her symptoms but stopping short of requesting medication. When she noted that she had tried her former mother-in-law's medicine but that it had not worked, the nurse practitioner did not challenge Ellen on her behavior or admonish her for taking (a) someone else's prescription medication and (b) doing so while pregnant. Instead, the nurse practitioner suggested a natural alternative to the cough medicine, thus avoiding a more direct exchange about the potential dangers of the medication.

In this case, the indirectness permitted the nurse practitioner to redirect the health care seeker without threatening her face (i.e., implying that she had been "stupid" or "ignorant" or "irresponsible"). Yet, the indirectness may not have been strong enough to clear up possible misconceptions about dangers (or lack thereof) of taking someone else's prescription medication while pregnant.

The nurse practitioner also implicitly *downplayed* her *authority* during this encounter. She framed her suggestion as "you might want to try," instead of "do this." As Tannen (1994) explains, "If they [women] have to tell others what to do, give information, and correct errors . . . they will expend effort to assure others that they are not pulling rank, not trying to capitalize on or rub in their one-up position" (p. 177).

Fisher (1993) offers the example of "Katherine," a nurse practitioner, who ". . . assiduously refrained from imposing either her medical expertise or her definition of the situation" (p. 105) in such a way as to encourage the health care seeker to tell her story. Fisher wrote in her analysis of Katherine's exchange with a woman health care seeker that "what emerges is a richly textured narrative in which the patient, not the provider, locates her present complaint in her domestic arrangements and diagnoses herself" (p. 108).

In an article that I co-authored with Athena duPre (duPre & Beck, 1997; see also, Beck with Ragan & duPre, 1997), we detail the interactions between a female medical doctor and her patients. Throughout her conversations with health care seekers, the doctor engaged in a collaborative style that encouraged the health care seekers to participate and to contribute in collaborative decision making. When one health care seeker (a professional woman) asked the doctor for a particular type of medication (in a distinctly direct manner), the doctor explained why she did not like to prescribe that particular brand, but she then acknowledged that the health care seeker knew her experiences and her body better and agreed to write the requested prescription (see duPre & Beck, 1997). In so doing, the doctor prioritized the health care seeker's knowledge base, thus implicitly downplaying her own authority as the only legitimate perspective (as opposed to traditional biomedical paternalism).

A way of invoking power beyond outright assertions of authority involves *interruptions* (see Tannen, 1990, 1993). As West (1984b) observes, doctors tend to interrupt patients much more, unless "the doctor is a lady." When health care seekers interact with female health caregivers, according to West (1984b), "their interruptions seem to subvert physicians' authority" (p. 88).

As I detailed earlier, my male obstetrician's constant interruptions during our conversation alienated me because I felt dismissed. Importantly, I oriented to the doctor talking at the same time as I was as an "interruption" (and, thus, a power play), rather than an "overlap" (an eager desire to participate with me in the accomplishment of a health care discussion). Tannen (1993) maintains:

If one speaker repeatedly overlaps and another repeatedly gives way, the resulting communication is asymmetrical, and the effect (though not necessarily the intent) is domination. But if both speakers avoid overlap, or if both speakers overlap each other and win out equally, there is symmetry and no domination, regardless of speakers' intentions. (p. 176)

The female MD in our research dove enthusiastically into conversations, sometimes overlapping, but nearly always encouraging her counterparts to complete their thoughts. However, interestingly, health care seekers rarely initiated overlaps with health care professionals, perhaps attesting to the perceived role differential even when interacting with someone of the same gender. I interrupted the male obstetrician; however, I sat shaking on the table as I did so. I blurted out my indignant response to him as a means of getting him to attend to the need of my unborn child—in my view, my daughter's life literally depended on his willingness to listen, and a critical previous mistake drove me to override my socially ingrained preference to remain silent.

Tannen (1993) argues that women prefer *silence* to argument. As a former debater, I never really considered myself to be reluctant to share my perspective on anything. Yet, I have remained silent during health care encounters, despite my desire to speak and to assert myself.

After my first miscarriage, my obstetric specialist ran tests to pinpoint the problem with my pregnancy. He determined that I needed progesterone supplements in order to sustain a pregnancy and encouraged me to request supplements as soon as I discovered that I was expecting again. However, shortly after the miscarriage, I moved to a new area and obtained a new doctor, Dr. Z. Blessedly, I became pregnant quickly, and I immediately asked for the needed supplement. Doctor Z. told me to wait and see if my body required the supplements this time. I shared what my previous doctor had uncovered on the tests, but Dr. Z. brushed aside my concerns. I asked about the supplements on future visits, but he continued to dismiss my quietly spoken suggestions—"What about the supplements?" I left each time in tears, yet silent.

I miscarried again on September 16, 1993, and I cringe as I reflect on those exchanges. I never demanded; I never asserted. If I persisted, I did so indirectly. I didn't call Dr. Z. on his dismissal of my needs. Instead, I implicitly accepted the doctor's recommendation that we "wait and see" and remained quiet, although I grew increasingly frustrated and angry. As I read reports of my near-weekly blood counts, I stood by helplessly as the baby's levels dwindled until I ultimately miscarried.

Thus, after becoming pregnant on my very next cycle (much against Dr. Z.'s advice), I obtained a referral to a specialist, Dr. I. Dr. I. acknowledged my concerns and prescribed medication immediately. When I later met with Dr. I.'s substitute, I knew that I could not passively accept his definition of the encounter. I would not be dismissed. I vowed to make that day in November of 1993 very different from my days of indirectness and silence in September. I felt like Shirley MacLaine's character during the hospital scenes in *Terms of Endearment*, a mother lioness who would leap from her den to claw, fight and yell at anyone to get the best care for her child.

As a mom, I finally indulged my lioness impulses to serve as an advocate for my child. As a health care seeker on my own behalf, I often find myself retreating back against the wall of my cave. When my home health care nurse, Pam, told me that I needed to go to the hospital, I said "okay," but I knew that I didn't intend to go. When the ER doctor at the hospital said that I suffered from stress-induced chest wall pain, I said "okay," even though I still lacked a good explanation of the palpitations and the lingering pain.

For a normally assertive person who routinely expresses opinions, my silence during health care encounters does not fit with the way in which I usually prefer to conduct myself. In the highly institutionalized context of health care interactions, in which my interactional counterparts clearly and forcefully assert "how we are going to do business here," though, lack of agreement gets marked as dispreferred, if not disdained. Perhaps in this context, the face risks of opposition tend to outweigh the perceived risks of silence. In the case of my miscarried baby, Caitlyn, though, the silence cost much more than the face risk ever would have.

A combination of these linguistic preferences (indirectness, silence, etc.) can prove deadly for health care seekers, especially with regard to preventive care. As Iverson (1993) contends, "the three reasons most frequently cited by women for not having a mammogram are not believing it is necessary, their physician did not recommend having one, and never having thought about it" (p. 41). If health care seekers fail to ask important questions (or feel that they might offend their health care professional by asking or that they must wait for health care professionals to raise important issues), they put their health in jeopardy.

To what extent can linguistic preferences be generalized according to gender? Although substantial support has emerged for gender distinctions, other factors must be considered. For example, individuals in our health care interviews referred to the desire to visit with a woman health care professional because "she would be more caring or more open or more supportive or spend more time talking" (see also Bensing, Brink-Muinen, & De Bakker, 1993; Kerssens, Bensing, & Andela, 1997; Roter et al., 1991; Waller, 1988). However, as Fisher (1993) notes, women doctors may be more influenced by their status as a medical doctor than by gendered tendencies. The roles and training of health care professionals (MDs versus DOs versus chiropractors versus nurses versus nurse practitioners, etc.) and the socioeconomic, educational, occupational status, gender, and type of medical condition of health care seekers may flavor the extent to which they demonstrate linguistic preferences that match gender research (see related work by Bensing et al., 1993; Levinson, McCollum, & Kutner, 1984).

Role Expectations

Role expectations can also influence approaches to health care interactions. Notably, the enactment of roles has become difficult, especially as we enter the new millennium. With the increasing prevalence of women in the workplace and the demands of families with aging parents, women and men struggle to define roles and workloads at the office and within the immediate and extended families (see chapter on social support for additional information). At a minimal level, given increasing role demands, how can individuals preserve health by gaining enough sleep, exercise, and nutrition (see Abel & Nelson, 1990; Gallant et al., 1997)?

Those roles become even more complicated during health-related difficulties—Who takes care of the family? Who provides for the family? Who cares for ailing elderly parents?

Who cares for the baby? How can important aspects of gender and relational identities be balanced with health issues?

In their book about women and cancer survival, Runowicz and Haupt (1995) describe Clara and Herb as happily married for twenty-two years. Although they enjoyed a loving sexual relationship prior to Clara's bout with breast cancer, Clara revealed that her mastectomy left her without "the desire for closeness and sex." As Clara claimed sadly, "I just didn't feel like a woman any more" (p. 89). Although Runowicz and Haupt (1995) stress the potential for pursuing intimacy in spite of the battle scars common in wars with cancer, they acknowledge that societal emphasis on an "ideal" body image deters some female cancer survivors from such relationships. In so doing, those women set aside an important part of themselves and their gendered identity.

Because of gendered role expectations, some women may even jeopardize wellness by avoiding disclosure of important health-related information?. Would a "real" woman—a "devoted" wife—prioritize husband over health and refuse to report incidents of domestic violence? Would a "real" woman—a "good" mom—have a drinking problem or a violent temper? Would a "real" man—an "on-the-ball" father/professional—experience depression? Perceptions about "ideal" enactments of gendered roles may flavor the extent to which individuals opt to reveal such concerns and seek help.

Biological Differences

If the notion that men and women are different prompts a "duh" response from everyday Americans, that idea has been less evident to medical scientists. For years, "women's health" referred narrowly to the sex organs that most distinctly distinguish them from their male counterparts (see, e.g., Healy, 1991; Keyser, 1984; Laurence & Weinhouse, 1997; Muller, 1992; Nechas & Foley, 1994; Smith, 1992). Differences between male and female reactions to drugs or responses to treatment plans for other organs remained unclear due to a major inadequacy of research designs (see Kase, 1991; Khaw, 1993).

According to Laurence and Weinhouse (1997), women were routinely left out of medical trials until the 1990s. Laurence and Weinhouse argue:

> In June 1990 [with the release of an audit of the National Institutes of Health], American women got a rude shock. For all of the complaints leveled against the health care system—most having to do with insensitive male doctors and dissatisfaction with gynecological and obstetric care—the majority of women still assumed that at least they were included in America's state-of-the-art medical research. But they were wrong. For at least the past several decades women in this country had been systematically excluded from the vast majority of research to develop new drugs, medical treatments, and surgical techniques. (p. 60)

Although scientists pointed to problems with including women as research subjects (primarily due to expense, recruitment challenges, complications of hormonal cycles, and ethical considerations due to possibility of pregnancy—see Laurence & Weinhouse, 1997, pp. 69–71), they could not deny the results. Because of the exclusion of women in medical research, doctors had no scientific data about how women might respond to various drugs and therapeutic options (see, e.g., Neergard, May 16, 1999).

With the development of the Office of Research on Women's Health at the National Institutes of Health, researchers have been forced to address those problems and to include women as subjects, even concentrating on women in certain studies (see, e.g., McDonald, 1999; Rimm, Willett, Hu, Sampson, et al., 1998, as well as Appendix A). Notably, women's health now focuses more on nonreproductive organs and diseases (especially breast cancer and heart disease) than on reproductive organs (see, for example, http://www.nci.nih.gov/bci.html#14).

The acknowledgment (or dismissal) of potential sociocultural and biological differences between males and females impacts how individuals participate in health care encounters, either as health care practitioners or as health care seekers. Even when health care participants share the same sex, the enactment of gender roles and/or the amount of available medical information may hinder (or enhance) the participants' abilities to discuss health care concerns and gain effective and appropriate care.

Age

In the late 1990s, the U.S. Food and Drug Administration and the Nonprescription Drug Manufacturers Association distributed a booklet entitled, "Kids Aren't Just Small Adults." Similarly, the ever-growing population of graying individuals cannot be assumed to be "just old people." As the baby boom moves into its senior years, in particular, the need for age-appropriate health care and related behavioral recommendations has grown stronger (see Abel, 1991; Adelman, Greene, & Charon, 1987; Adelman, Greene, Charon, & Friedmann, 1992; Bull, 1993; Coupland & Nussbaum, 1993; Dickson-Markman & Shern, 1990; Gibson, 1998; Greene, Adelman, & Majerovitz, 1996; Haug, 1996; Haug & Ory, 1987; Hummert, Wiemann, & Nussbaum, 1994; Maynard, 1996; McPherson, 1994; Napier, 1994; Nussbaum & Coupland, 1995; Nussbaum, Thompson, & Robinson, 1989; Prohaska & Clark, 1997; Rakowski, 1997; Rosenwaike & Dolinsky, 1987; Williams, 1998; Woodruff, 1995). The advent of pediatrics and geriatrics as medical specialities affirms the strong consideration of age during health care interactions, especially in terms of acceptable treatments, relationships with health care professionals, and the need for social support.

Acceptable Treatments

In their book, *The Doctors' Book of Home Remedies for Seniors*, Doug Dollemore and the Editors of *Prevention: Health Books for Seniors* (1999) write to their senior readers:

> Older Americans are bombarded with news about heart disease, stroke, cancer, and other catastrophic ailments. Yet these probably aren't the problems that you and your friends talk about when someone mentions aging. You're concerned about the things you're facing now—the hundreds of little big things that make getting older so difficult. Things like arthritis, bunions, corns, calluses, memory loss, morning aches, shingles, dry mouth, hearing loss, and cold feet and hands. You're concerned about the things that nip away at self-reliance, independence, and self-confidence and threaten to make you feel older than your years. (p. xi)

Suffering from extreme arthritis, my grandfather's knees ache as he walks, making everyday tasks difficult (not to mention his job as a greeter at Walmart). He struck up a conversation recently with a representative from one of the orthopedic companies in my home town, and he learned about a new product that can strengthen cartilage in knees. During a subsequent visit with a specialist, Grandpa learned that the best option would be a knee replacement surgery; however, the specialist acknowledged that Grandpa would not be a good candidate for the surgery, given his health history and age. Thus, he agreed to allow Grandpa to receive the experimental treatments via three rounds of shots per knee (even though such treatments have not been approved for knees yet). Importantly, Grandpa's age impacted the type of treatment that would be suitable for responding to a non-life-threatening concern—his knees.

Notably, the experimental treatment has not really helped Grandpa's knees to date. As a very active man who still works outside the home and attends to his own lawn and home maintenance, he certainly hoped that the treatments could restore some of the mobility that has been lost to arthritis. As Napier (1994) notes, senior citizens who hope to counter the devastating effects of aging (such as through arthritis) increasingly place their faith in experimental (and often unproven) treatments. As Napier (1994) explains, "all types of unproven therapies can be economically harmful, often draining precious dollars from older Americans' limited resources" (p. 1). Additionally, seniors must consider treatment options in light of possible drug interactions with other necessary medications and the skyrocketing expense of most prescriptions (see Beisecker, 1988; Williams, 1998).

At the other end of the life span, children and adolescents face health challenges that are unique to them (see, e.g., Hulka, 1999; Twycross, 1998). Given their developing bodies, the amount of medication, the appropriateness of vaccinations, the availability of particular surgical procedures and other medical decisions must be juxtaposed with risks and benefits.

Impact on Health Care Relationships

An advertisement for Children's Hospital in Columbus, Ohio labels the doctor as a "pediatric anesthesiologist and storyteller." As the ad argues, "he understands why kids react differently to anesthesia," concluding with "after all, we don't just focus on the parts of a child that are sick, we also care for the parts that are healthy." Especially for younger or older health care seekers, age of health care participants can shape degree of commitment to particular roles as well as the level of participation during health care visits (see Beisecker, 1988; Cox & Waller, 1991; Edwards & Noller, 1998; Hasselkus, 1992; Haug, 1996; O'Hair, Behnke, & King, 1983; Thorne & Robinson, 1988; Woodward & Walltson, 1987).

Children and seniors may legitimize traditional institutional roles because of indoctrination about acceptable behaviors and beliefs about appropriate authority—that is, out of respect, individuals should refer to others by title, defer to presumed authority figures, and adhere to a perceived (and institutionalized) interactional format for the conversation. For example, my grandparents usually defer to professional recommendations rather than promote their own plan of action, mirroring the findings of Woodward and Wallston (1987).

In their study, Woodward and Wallston (1987) found that "individuals over 60 years of age desire less health-related control than do younger adults" (p. 6). Notably, as the more educated and skeptical babyboom generation reaches that age, such tendencies may certainly shift. Certainly, understandings of "appropriateness" and, as I shall discuss later, age-related stereotypes fluctuate according to generations and even local accomplishments of generation membership.

Social Support

In the case of younger and older individuals, social support becomes critical to the accomplishment of adequate health care (see Abel, 1991; Bull, 1993; Edwards & Noller, 1998; D. Gibson, 1998; Hasselkus, 1992; Litwin, 1996; Nussbaum & Coupland, 1995; Nussbaum et al., 1989). From drives to the doctor to assistance with activities of daily living to support during health care examinations, social support networks constitute a critical component of health care for younger and older individuals.

Dickson-Markman and Shern (1990) surveyed adults, one group consisting of people who were between the ages of 18 and 65 and another group of people who were over the age of 65. Dickson-Markman and Shern (1990) contend that the need for social support intensifies as individuals grow older. Dickson-Markman and Shern maintain:

> . . . age has a greater effect on health status for older people than younger [adult] people, therefore making the elderly group more susceptible to physical health problems. However, when social relations are absent or few, lack of social support may exacerbate existing health problems. (p. 60)

Ironically, in their more fragile years, both children and seniors become more vulnerable to abuse from would-be social support members. Far from being protected and upheld, all too often younger and older individuals face additional health risks as a result of abuse or neglect (see, e.g., Allan, 1998; Lett, 1995).

CLOSING THOUGHTS

I exhaled slowly and closed my eyes as Pam plucked the sutures from the skin around my hip incision. Saturday had been so wonderful. I got to watch Brittany at her basketball game, and I even talked Roger into driving us to the Ohio University (OU) game that afternoon. By tip-off at the OU game, I had started to feel tired, but I loved being out of the house. I stopped caring about the stares at my arms and the whispers as we walked by the crowded concession stand at the game. I felt free—free to get caught up in the excitement of dunked balls and three-point baskets. I observed the cheerleaders performing acrobatic feats and the dance team moving in ways that I couldn't even manage when healthy. I listened as the band played pep songs to energize the crowd. I sat in my seat and soaked in the scene like a sponge.

"Ouch," I said, as Pam twisted a particularly stubborn suture from the middle of my hip incision.

"Sorry," she responded. Pam paused and then moved on to the next suture.

Saturday had been great, but perhaps I exerted myself more than I should have, I thought. On our way home from the game that day, we picked up take-out Mexican food, and we chatted over dinner, reflecting on a perfectly normal day. Yet, before I could finish my burrito, my body yearned for sleep. As soon as the time arrived for my medication, I administered my regiment of saline solution, Ansef, and ten more cc of saline solution, and I fell asleep as soon as my head hit the pillow.

"Does it look healed?" I asked Pam, referring to the hip incision.

"Mmhmm, the incision looks great. I'm almost done. Okay, one last suture. All right, that's all over. You're done," Pam announced.

I rolled over from my side onto my back and adjusted myself in my pink chair. Because I had mastered my IV equipment, I could inject my own medication. I only needed Pam to visit once per day to replace the hip dressing, and I wondered how much longer that she would come to check on me. I felt so safe with her. She always checked my vitals and ensured that I was progressing okay. She had certainly served as my advocate during my scare with the PICC line. How odd to think that I had only been under her care for around ten days, I thought.

Pam picked up the materials for the hip dressing that I had assembled by the chair, and I closed my eyes again as she covered the incision. A mere two weeks ago, I had entered the hospital for the staph infection—it seemed more like an eternity than fourteen days. Strangely, I couldn't remember when my hip stopped hurting. I just felt so tired. I must have really worn myself out on Saturday, I thought.

"What did you do yesterday?" Pam inquired. "You look beat."

"Yeah, well, I must have done it on Saturday. I really didn't do anything yesterday but lie around the house," I noted. In fact, Sunday had been the first day without food from friends at work, and I lacked the energy to get up and cook anything. Britti lived on peanut butter sandwiches that she prepared for herself. I wondered, How could I keep from draining myself? Chelsea Meagan would be back from her grandmother's house tomorrow (Tuesday), and she needed her mother. I would have to summon the strength to care for her and to deal with Wade.

Pam finished the hip dressing and started her general examination. She placed the blood pressure cup around my leg. (I didn't have a spare arm so we had to get creative.) The air seeped out of the blood pressure bag, and Pam removed the cup, carefully marking my levels on the chart. As usual, she examined my eyes and felt the sides of my neck.

"OUCH!" I said, jerking away.

"What?" Pam asked. "What's wrong?"

"My collarbone area hurts," I acknowledged hesitantly, "when you touch it." I looked quickly at Pam and then slowly sank back against the back of the chair. Oh no, I thought, not again. Please, God, please, I prayed. Please don't let me go back downhill. Please . . . please, I kept repeating silently in my mind.

"Christie, this isn't good," Pam warned.

"I'm sure that it's nothing," I assured her. It had to be nothing. It couldn't not be nothing. Chelsea would be home the next day. I had to get better. I had to be better. I had just been to a basketball game—two of them, in fact! I WAS better.

"You need to go back to Columbus," Pam said softly.

I just learned how to do my medication. I just started to feel self-sufficient again. I couldn't go back. I couldn't.

"Let's see how I am tomorrow," I said. I refused to promise to go to Columbus. I couldn't push blindly through another maze of telling my story to countless people in the ER before finally hooking up with someone who actually knows something about PICC lines or infections. Pam paused, staring at me, and I could see the disapproval in her eyes. Yet, she turned silently to reach for a thermometer and then placed it in my mouth. We sat quietly as the clock ticked until the thermometer beeped.

"It's going back up," she said.

"What?" I shook my head. *Not again,* I thought, *not again.*

Pam flipped through her book and pressed the buttons on the phone. She didn't wait to ask my permission or try to change my mind about getting help.

What are the odds? What are the odds of anything else going wrong, I thought. Pam had definitely shifted into military mode, I reflected as I peeked over at her on the phone. She once told me that she had served in the military, but I wasn't quite certain about what she did. Judging from her crisis management style, she likely led the charge, I smiled to myself—definitely good to keep her on my side.

"Dr. T. is out of town," she reported. After she said it, I remembered that he had told me about his trip. *Good,* I thought, *I'm off the hook. I don't have to go. No one could see me anyway.* "However, Dr. S. and Dr. T.'s staff think that you need to go back up to Columbus to see what's going on," she continued.

"Where?" I asked.

"They want you to go to the ER," she answered.

Tears filled my eyes. *I couldn't do it.* I nodded to satisfy Pam, but I knew that I could not drive up to the ER. I could not talk to person after person who did not know me or my situation. I could not tell my story to person after person who did not even have expertise with my problem area.

Okay, I thought, *I can't be getting sick again—there must be some other explanation. I could be imagining this. Of course, I must just want attention. Surely, nothing could really be wrong anyway. If I just get some sleep, I will be better in the morning,* I assured myself.

"The ER has been contacted, and the staff is waiting for you to arrive," she noted as she collected her supplies. I moved my head up and down again.

I can't fight with you now, I thought, *but I can't go up there again.* I searched the ceiling again for answers, but they still eluded me. *I can't be the complacent patient now,* I thought. *I can't just fit in your mold and do what I'm supposed to do,* I informed all of "them" silently. *I know myself best, and I understand what I need—sleep, only sleep, lots of sleep,* I asserted without uttering the words.

Pam left, thinking that I would be a "good" patient, an obedient patient (okay, perhaps also, a logical patient) in terms of following instructions to obtain further care. She did not know me well enough to understand that I could not, would not, go down that road again.

9 Diversity and Health Communication— Postmodern Considerations

"Ugh," I grunted as I tried to shift to a more comfortable position on my pink chair.

"Mom," Britti darted from her bedroom into the living room. "Are you okay?"

I looked at her face, into her eyes, and I hated to see the fear once more. She's terrified, I realized, and I felt far too exhausted to muster the energy to eleviate her concerns.

"Honey, I'm fine," I lied as I leaned slightly toward the IV equipment. "I'm just trying to get organized . . . I need to take my medicine." Awkwardly, I fumbled with the syringes to fill them with saline solution and Ansef. I know how to do this, I admonished myself. Why can't I make my hands work? Why can't I concentrate? I closed my eyes and exhaled loudly.

"Mom," Britti moved closer. "Let me help. What can I do?"

She's just a little girl, I thought. Just a sweet little girl who has no business seeing her mom hooked up to tubes . . . just a sweet little girl who should not have to worry if her mom is going to collapse or even die. I searched her beautiful blue eyes, and I prayed for the words to comfort her.

"No, honey, really, I can do this. Please just go back to bed, and everything will be all right," I saw a flicker of doubt in her eyes. She didn't know what to believe—she knew what she was seeing, but she wanted to trust my words.

"I'm just tired," I continued. "Let me get back to the medicine so I can crash."

She flinched, and I yearned to slurp the word back into my mouth. Brittany didn't want me to crash. My body already appeared too broken.

"Mom," Brittany asked hesitantly, "do you promise that you're going to be all right?"

I could barely lift my head from the back of the pink chair without inducing waves of pain around my shoulder and down my left arm. Out of the corner of my right eye, I spotted my cast and the materials for my last injection of the evening. I couldn't move . . . couldn't think . . . couldn't think . . .

"Yes," I said simply. I prayed that I spoke truth as she turned and walked back to bed. She didn't believe me; I didn't believe me. Could I feel this weak and still live? Was this what it felt like to start dying? Would I slowly drift until I'm not here at all anymore?

I closed my eyes. If I died now, would Chelsea remember me? Years from now, would strangers pass my grave in the cemetery and comment on my young age, wondering whether I collided with something in my car or could not conquer cancer? From the dates on the headstone or the line on the family tree, could others come to comprehend who I was, who I still wanted to be?

"Open your eyes," I commanded myself. "Take your medicine, go to bed, and wake up less morbid."

I strained to sit up, and I pried one eyelid open. Good . . . good . . . You can do it, I cheered myself. Don't give up . . . don't stop . . . My eye slowly slid shut.

They would know that I was a woman, that I lived in the late twentieth century. Pictures could reveal my race, but what else could they know? I wished that I had kept a journal, some record of my hopes and dreams and passions for posterity, some lasting legacy.

Perhaps I should go back to the ER . . . perhaps someone there could help . . . Yet, I detested the lobbying for legitimacy, the struggles to be taken seriously. I wasn't an ignorant "nut"; I didn't cry wolf. I didn't invent the infection or prompt the PICC line to pop out of and into my vein. I didn't conjure up my current complaint. Why did I need to be the one to convince others that my situation, like my self, was vastly complex, not simple?

Although traditional diversity-related categories offer some insight into how and why health care participants make particular choices, in this chapter, I work to expand the conception of diversity by pursuing the complexity of individuals in contemporary society. After discussing additional socioeconomic categories of diversity, I detail the consequences of essentializing those categories, and I conclude with an argument for a person-centered approach to wellness.

Beyond Ethnicity, Gender, and Age

To what extent do the many categories in which we fit flavor how we orient to health care, health care interactions, and other health care participants? In addition to ethnicity/race, gender/sex, and age, individuals come to health care interactions as people with economic and educational constraints and resources, as spiritual creatures, as sexual beings, and as geographically situated individuals.

Economics/Education

Individuals come to health care interactions as people who happen to be more or less educated, who hold particular types of jobs, and who earn more or less money (often as a result of educational level and occupation) (see, e.g., Pendleton & Bochner, 1980; Rogers & Ginzberg, 1993; Wiggers & Sanson-Fisher, 1997). Although few health care participants peek at pay stubs before commencing conversations, they share what they do for a living (health care seeker occupation and type of health care practitioner—doctor, nurse, resident, medical student, technician, therapist, etc.). Through their choice of words and nonverbal style, they indicate co-cultural memberships and, through implication more than overt disclosure, possible socioeconomic status and "class" (see related discussion by Burke, 1995; Ellis, 1999).

For homeless individuals, the economic barrier to health care gets exacerbated by suceptibility to disease as well as stigma related to homelessness. Jezewski (1995) notes that many homeless individuals cannot gain Medicaid or other health insurance because they lack a permanent address. Jezewski details:

> Even when homeless persons do have Medicaid, the coverage does little to overcome barriers such as transportation, cultural differences between patient and providers, clinic hours that do not meet the needs of homeless persons, and the stigma that members of the health care delivery system often attach to the label "homeless." (p. 204)

Religion

Individuals enter the examining room with the comfort and social support of their respective religious convictions and communities (which may or may not be connected with ethnic traditions) (see, e.g., Dossey, 1996; Duckro, Magaletta, & Wolf, 1997; Ellison & Levin, 1998; Fintel & McDermott, 1997; Fuller, 1989; Koenig, George, Hays, Larson, Cohen, & Blazer, 1998; McAllister, 1998; McRae, Carey, & Anderson-Scott, 1998; Peterson, April 12, 1999). As Ellison and Levin (1998) report, medical scholars and health care seekers increasingly recognize the importance of the "religion–health connection," noting links between religion and healthier personal lifestyles, social integration and support, self-esteem and personal efficacy, coping mechanisms, and healthy beliefs. For many, health care dilemmas resemble the terror of spiraling through the eye of a storm, and they clutch their religion as a treasured life preserver.

Inspiration

Through their religious beliefs, health care seekers can find meaning in their health-related situations. In their book about faith in God and struggles with cancer, Fintel and McDermott (1997) acknowledge that people differ in their approach to spirituality in the face of a critical condition such as cancer. Fintel and McDermott (1997) explain that some seek explanations from God while others interpret cancer as a test, a punishment, or even an honor. Moreover, faith and prayer can enable individuals to draw closer to God and to feel peace with health outcomes, even those that do not result in healing.

For example, Stein (1985) describes a married couple who struggled with their infant's illness. Although both husband and wife are medical practitioners and well-schooled in biomedicine, they turned to their Catholic faith as a means of understanding and coping. According to Stein (1985), "They persisted in their anguished search for an explanation outside medicine because the medical explanation (or lack of one) did not satisfy them" (p. 13). Stein concludes that "they began to invoke such an explanation as 'the will of God' to give them peace . . . they came to accept the child as a 'gift from God,' 'a test of our faith,' for which they were perhaps selected (or elected) by God" (p. 14).

Empowerment

For years, the minister of Christian Education at my church and his wife yearned for a child. Yet, after a series of fertility tests, their doctor diagnosed them as infertile. Scott and Susan considered adoption, but they could not bring themselves to be comfortable with that solution. They believed that God might be telling them to devote themselves to their work in the ministry instead of becoming parents until Susan's mother saw a television report about a new fertility procedure.

Scott and Susan prayed about the procedure and decided to invest their savings in the possibility. They found a doctor who could perform the procedure, and Susan became pregnant. They were thrilled, praising God for this new technology and for the expensive fertility drugs that became available to them for free through an anonymous donor.

Although Susan miscarried one of her babies early in the pregnancy, she progressed normally with the two remaining babies until her doctor scanned her cervix and discovered that she had an incompetent cervix. Immediately, Susan had emergency surgery to close her cervix, and she found herself hospitalized for the remainder of the pregnancy, unable to move except for a roll to her side. Her twin daughters would die if she failed to follow the strict instructions.

Despite the dire circumstances, Susan remained upbeat, largely due to a large poster that Scott constructed and placed on the wall of her room. The poster emphasized: "This is the day that the Lord has made. We will rejoice and be glad in it" (Psalms 118:24, NIV). The calendar on the poster enabled Susan to focus on each day that God gave to the girls to grow inside her and to pray that He would grant even more precious days of development to her daughters, Sydney and Taylor.

One day, a hospital staff member stopped by and asked them how they could be so positive when the rest of the women on the floor were distraught about their situations. Scott and Susan credited the poster. The case worker asked where she could purchase the poster, and Scott offered to make additional posters for the other rooms in the unit. Due to an enthusiastic response, volunteers constructed permanent wooden signs with the verse in calligraphy, and each room in the obstetric unit at Riverside Hospital in Columbus, Ohio features the uplifting message.

Although Koenig and colleagues (1998) report mixed findings in their analysis of religious activity and blood pressure, religion can empower individuals to approach health care situations positively and proactively. For example, available in all fifty states of the United States and in thirteen other countries, a Houston-based program, First Place, describes itself as a "Christ-Centered Health Program" that emphasizes total wellness. According to a program brochure, participants seek to develop healthier dietary practices and, ultimately, "to help participants focus on giving Christ 'first place' in every area of life." As one woman stressed in her testimonial, "During the special prayer time the Holy Spirit spoke to me and I realized that I had allowed this weight problem to remain MY PROBLEM and I had never given it to the Lord. God began to impress on me that my body is the dwelling place of His gracious Spirit" (First Place, 1998). As another woman emphasized, "I am the queen of diet programs. I have dieted the last 35 years of my life and have finally found there's a higher power to help me control my weight" (Holbert, January 18, 1999).

Relational and Medical Implications

Notably, religious beliefs do not just impact individuals; they flavor health care interactions between health care professionals and seekers as dialogues about health care ensue. For example, as Duckro and colleagues (1997) note, ". . . members of religious communities may also be concerned about, and want to know, the provider's [or patient's] spirituality and religious commitment, especially when the health matter involves psychological or sexual issues" (p. 308).

Ethically, to what extent can individuals invoke their religious beliefs with regard to health care? When some religious factions believe only in prayer, they deny care to themselves and to members of their families. For example, Dean and Susan Heilman, members of the Faith Tabernacle Congregation Church in Pennsylvania, allowed their 22-month-old son, Dean Michael, to bleed to death. According to an Associated Press wire service report (February 19, 1999), Dean Michael, a hemophiliac, ". . . cut his toe on a piece of glass while playing in their backyard. His parents . . . bandaged his foot, rocked the child, and prayed." The parents were ultimately sentenced to seventeen years probation for the involuntary manslaughter of their son and ordered by the court to obtain a doctor for their remaining children (see AP, February 19, 1999).

When I read this account, I felt stunned that a parent would refuse to seek help for his or her child. However, as I reflect more, these parents likely trusted that they *were* seeking help—God's help. As a Christian, I believe that God can heal; however, I have been taught that God provides earthly vehicles for us as well as more divine interventions. Obviously, this couple does not share my belief. Should they be forced to do so? Should individuals who do not want a particular surgical intervention or blood transfusion or other medical procedure be forced to do so because it makes sense in terms of biomedical standards? Especially when we think about deeply rooted cultural traditions that stem from religious beliefs and practices, the line between religious freedom and criminal negligence becomes less clear.

Sexuality

Individuals initiate health care interactions as implicitly sexual beings, and sexual orientations and practices can flavor health care needs, expectations, and prejudices (see Andrews & Novick, 1995; Furin, 1997; Platt, 1996; Ponticelli, 1998; Ray, 1996; Roth & Fuller, 1998). As Sedgwick (1990) suggests, however, sexual preferences (and related identity issues) encompass more than a heterosexual/homosexual diochotomy. Especially in this era of AIDS and other sexually transmitted diseases and unwanted pregnancies, the enactment of sexuality (for all individuals, regardless of age, preferences, gender) has emerged as an important consideration with regard to overall health and wellness (see, e.g., Andrews & Novick, 1995; Ponticelli, 1998; Roth & Fuller, 1998). For example, Platt (1996) offers the example of a physician who attempts to press his patient into a birth control prescription. Although the woman politely declines her need for birth control, the doctor counters with "yeah, that's what they all say" before proceeding with his physical examination. Platt (1996) explains that "this patient doesn't need birth control because she is a lesbian and has sex only with other women" (p. 190). The interaction fails because the doctor does not seek—and the woman does not share—vital information. Without the knowledge that the woman is a lesbian, the doctor cannot address the woman's specific concerns—nor offer pertinent health insights—nor understand her perspective in the encounter (Platt, 1996). As White and Dull (1998) conclude from their research, lesbians "who were out to their primary care providers were more likely to seek early and preventative care, more likely to have Pap smears, and were more comfortable in discussing difficult issues" (p. 107).

Yet, if the woman did voluntarily reveal her sexual preference to the doctor, she faced possible bias because of her sexuality (see Platt, 1996; Stevens, 1998). Unfortunately, reactions to sexual preference can be as negative as one described by Stevens (1998). Dinah, an African American woman, felt comfortable with a new health care provider, a nurse-practitioner, and decided to disclose her sexual preference:

> She was doing a history on me and she was asking about pregnancies, so I thought it was a good time to tell her I was lesbian. When I said lesbian, it just took this nurse completely off guard. She started spelling it out loud as she wrote it on my chart, l-e-s-b-i-a-n. A nervous smile came over her face and she could not recompose herself. (p. 85)

According to Stevens (1998), the woman "was alarmed to realize that she had 'undressed' emotionally and physically before someone who could not cope with her as who she was" (p. 85). The stigma of sexual orientation deterred the health care process and the health care seeker's ability to accomplish her preferred medical, relational, and informational goals. In light of stigma about types and frequencies of sexual activities, important aspects of health care seeker identities and potential health risks may be left unexplored during health care encounters.

Geographical Location

Individuals interact about health care issues amid the larger landscape of their geographical regions of the world (see Bull, 1993; Findley, October 15, 1997; Giarchi, 1990; http://www.dartmouth.edu/~atlas/index.html). Even though organ donations and transplants have become common in the United States, for example, they occur far less in some other places in the world. According to an Associated Press wireservice report (March 1, 1999), "Transplants have long been a rarity in Japan for a number of reasons— cultural taboos oppose the cutting up of corpses and people have resisted becoming donors amid fears of doctors letting donors die to harvest their organs." The report emphasizes that "resistance to transplants is deeply rooted. Even some doctors and nurses oppose transplants, saying that they will lead to half-hearted treatment for potential donors."

Especially in developing countries, health care and health practices vary greatly (see AP, September 26, 1999; http://www.unfpa.org/swp/1999/chapter1c.htm). As I detail in Chapter 1, the United Nations State of the World Population 1999 report reveals the devastating impact of unwanted pregnancies, sexually transmitted diseases (in particular, HIV/AIDS), and poor access to resources and medical supplies in many developing countries.

However, according to a study conducted by scholars at the Dartmouth Medical School, individuals in the United States also receive different types of care depending on their geographical region, although even the most impoverished regions of the United States bear no resemblance to the plight of developing countries. Jack Lord, a representative of the American Hospital Association, which sponsored the Dartmouth study, contends that "geography is destiny in medicine. There are striking patterns of variability across the country which simply can't be explained by difference in disease rates" (see

Findlay, October 15, 1997, p. 19A). Giarchi argues (1990) that barriers to rural populations, in particular, include:

> . . . housing, the provision of health/medical services and welfare/social services; accessibility; information deprivation and sometimes local reluctance to utilize the "outsider" resources when the locals have to cross cultural boundaries to reach them. (p. 69)

However, the impact of geographical region on quality of care remains under dispute. In contrast to Giarchi (1990), Thorson and Powell (1993) assert, "Urban versus rural differences in satisfaction with health care services and usage seemingly have greater anecdotal than empirical support" (p. 145). In fact, Thorson and Powell argue that "income and education differences seem to have more influence on health care received than does residence" (p. 145).

Addictions

When I visited with my doctor about my heart concern, he asked me about caffeine consumption. I joked about needing to survive while finishing my book. He pressed me on the amount of caffeine that I consume daily, and finally, I told him that I drank around twelve cans of Diet Coke per day. Like other people who know about my pop intake, he reacted with "wow" and then told me to quit—immediately. I cringed and wondered how he would have responded if I would have told him that the number was possibly higher still on most days.

My doctor scared me into quitting cold turkey. My head hurt so much that I felt nauseous, and I couldn't think or move. I just sat in a chair and stared at my soap operas. I never want to go through that kind of withdrawal again. Yet, as pressures have mounted with the book deadline and other work and family obligations, I've turned back to the caffeine. I don't drink as much as I used to, but I can't escape it entirely.

We live in an addictive society. Some can stare for hours at televisions or video games, while others cannot stop gambling. Our fascination with body image prompts people to diet, and many become addicted to dieting and exercise as a means of maintaining control over their weight. Alcohol, tobacco, caffeinated beverages, and an array of prescription, over-the-counter, and illegal drugs attract countless individuals around the world to a web of addiction that cannot be easily escaped.

Addictions, whether to television or exercise, to Diet Coke or vodka, impact the physical and mental health of people who are addicted and their families. My father was addicted to alcohol and cigarettes, and I fear that the physical consequences of second-hand smoke may one day match the emotional scars of living with an alcoholic. I worry that my own addiction to caffeine may have harmed my heart.

Yet, even though our societal "bad habits" may lead to negative health problems, we persist in the behaviors, as well as the denial of their existence and implications (see, e.g., Denzin, 1991, 1993). Despite the prevalence of support structures for overcoming addictions, the necessary first step of acceptance and acknowledgment of an addiction opens an individual up to possible criticism and even social stigma (see, e.g., Cooper-Gordon, 1987; Curran, 1987; Denzin, 1993; Smith, 1993). Unfortunately, the combination of the addiction and stigma of addiction traps many in a vicious cycle of addiction and guilt, a cycle that impacts the potential of health care interactions for addressing health care needs.

Multiplicity of Categories

Considering the impact of a sole socioeconomic variable in isolation seems difficult and unrealistic; however, perhaps for political or pragmatic reasons, groups have attempted to argue the needs of "women" and "children" (see Bartolomeo, 1994; Burke, 1992) and minorities (see Office of Minority Health Resource Center—http://www.omhrc.gov). In the case of women alone, the women's health movement features the advent of Women's Health Month (usually in September) and numerous women's resource centers (including *Women's Health America Info-log*; National Women's Health Information Center—http:// www.4woman.org; Women's Health Access—http://womenshealth.com; Women's Health Initiative).

However, health care participants in the late 1990s could not simply be defined by their race/ethnicity or their sex/gender or their sexual orientation or their age or their education, income, or job, or their religion or their addictions or their geographical location or their disabilities or their afflictions (see related works on diversity of traditional groupings by Anseld & Angel, 1997; Braithwaite, 1996; Fraithwaited & Thompson, 2000; Joyce, 1994; Kavanagh & Kennedy, 1992; Ng, Chin, Moy, & Okihiro, 1995; Ray, 1996; Skolnick, 1992; Weintraub, 1993). To acknowledge the complexity a bit more, health care participants can be part of the rural aging population (see Bull, 1993). They can be African American lesbians (see Mason-John, 1995; Stevens, 1998), minority senior citizens (see Angel & Angel, 1997; Ball & Whittington, 1995), and older women (see Barry, Gooding, Harris, Hazzard, & Winograd, 1993; Culpepper, 1993; Fox, Siu, & Stein, 1994; D. Gibson, 1998; McKeever & Martinson, 1986; Ward-Griffin & Ploeg, 1997). In the case of older women, especially, Culpepper (1993) contends:

> Ageism and sexism intersect in women's lives with terrible force, accelerating and intensifying our marginalization. Hardships caused by race, class, sexual orientation, lack of education, and disability all increase with aging. (p. 192)

Dangers of Essentialism

In a riveting episode of the television drama, *ER*, the compassionate attending physician, Dr. Greene, springs into action when emergency technicians rush two young men into the emergency department of his inner-city hospital. Apparently, according to the technicians, one of the young men shot and injured the other one during an attempted robbery. The gunman was hit by a police bullet during his attempted escape. Tragically, the technicians described the young man who had been working at the convenience store as a "good kid," trying to earn extra money for college while the other young man was a "bad seed," who had been in trouble before.

Dr. Greene quickly scanned both of the young men (who were barely more than boys), and he decided to concentrate on one of them, leaving the other to less experienced residents. As the episode ensues, Dr. Greene comments on his desire to save the innocent victim, implicitly downplaying the importance of helping the attacker. Dr. Greene stabilizes and then hurries his patient to surgery. The other patient fares less favorably and ultimately dies near the end of the episode.

Although, ethically, Dr. Greene should have left judgment to the court system and fought equally to save both young men, his actions did not even work toward his initial goal. If he wanted to prioritize the victim, he made a critical mistake. As he discovered soon after sending his patient to surgery, Dr. Greene, a Caucasian male, had jumped to the conclusion that the Caucasian young man was the victim and that the African American young man was the assailant. He guessed wrong.

In reality, the African American young man held a job, earned strong grades, and hoped that his high school basketball stardom would result in a top college basketball scholarship. The Caucasian young man had drifted in and out of trouble for years.

Health care practitioners and health care seekers come to health care encounters in terms of their own lived realities and a priori expectations and assumptions about the workings of the world. We tend to "essentialize" types of others, often relying on categorizing people according to the traditional categories that I have just shared. As Fuss (1989) explains, "Essentialism is most commonly understood as a belief in the real, true essence of things, the invariable and fixed properties which define the 'whatness' of a given entity" (p. xi).

Indeed, essentialism fits consistently with modernist tendencies, the desire to orient to an absolute reality, a concrete foundation of facts (see Fuss, 1989; Shi, 1995). In fact, early feminist theories relied on essentialism or standpoint epistemology to assert women's experiences (as opposed to male experiences), implicitly promoting commonality of the female experience (see Fuss, 1989; Harding, 1991; Kemp & Squires, 1997).

Although Fuss (1989) argues that essentialism cannot be avoided, at least to some extent, the very nature of essentialism can deter comprehensive understandings of individuals, given the diversity of characteristics within traditional socioeconomic categories and the mix of categories (and other co-cultural attributes) by individual people. Indeed, according to Blalock and Devellis (1986,), ". . . our expectations that certain characteristics are associated with certain kinds of people can bias the way we process information, making it unlikely that new information will be evaluated fairly" (p. 19).

Although Dr. Greene had treated African Americans previously without a problem and he did not use derogatory words to reveal racist tendencies, his actions in that particular episode reflected his apparent take-for-granted assumption that African Americans were more likely to engage in criminal behavior than Euro-Americans. Further, his belief that the African American male shot the Caucasian young man fueled his anger about violence and gangs and "people like that." Dr. Greene's stereotyping of his patients impacted how he cared for the two young men who struggled for life in the ER that night.

For both health care practitioners and health care seekers, such essentialism frames health care interactions (see related works by Adelman et al., 1992; Blalock, & Devellis, 1986; Fisher & Groce, 1985; Forsythe, 1996; Nazario, 1993; Verghese, 1999). Especially in terms of socioeconomic categories, taken-for granted assumptions influence orientations to health care counterparts (see Adelman et al., 1992; Anderson, Rakowski, & Hickey, 1988; Beck, 1990; Greene, Hoffman, Charon, & Adelman, 1987; Healy, 1991; Jackson, 1993; Kurtz et al., 1985; Lamas, Pashos, Normand, & McNeil, 1995; Rubinstein, 1995; Schulman et al., 1999; Spector, 1996a; Weisman & Teitelbaum, 1985).

Medical Services

Essentialism can hinder the seeking and offering of medical services. When my mother called to tell me about my grandfather's admission to the hospital for pneumonia, she emphasized that they were not excited about "that squinty-eyed doctor in the ER." Even though he spoke "pretty good English," his appearance as "an Oriental guy" sent up red flags in their minds, hindering their ability to trust his opinion.

From the doctor's perspective, though, Grandpa's age may have been a similar "red flag," depending on the essentialistic stereotypes of his health care professionals (see Adelman et al., 1992; Anderson et al., 1988; Greene et al., 1987; Lamas et al., 1995; Meuleman, Davidson, & Caranasos, 1988; Nussbaum et al., 1989; Rubinstein, 1995; Turpie, Bloch, Edwards, et al., 1992). Rubenstein (1995) collected narratives from individuals who confronted the deaths of their elderly parents and noted frustration from those survivors about the treatment of their parents by health care practitioners. According to Rubenstein (1995), "In some cases the ageist treatment of an elderly parent by a physician was clear and overt. Some daughters described physicians and others as telling them nothing could be done for a parent *because she was old*" (pp. 260–261).

Indeed, Anderson and colleagues (1988) found that "physicians' beliefs about preventive activities for older patients may influence their perceptions of clinical encounters." Further, in their review of literature on elderly patients and cardiovascular interventions, Lamas and colleagues (1995) note:

> Physicians may treat older patients less aggressively due to concerns about the elderly being more prone to adverse effects of therapies, absence of data specifically addressing the elderly, and physicians' attitudes that lifesaving interventions are of limited use in the aged. (p. 1067)

Kay, an interview participant, offers another disturbing account of ageism that impacted her ability to obtain desired medical services. Kay recalls that she wanted to obtain some form of birth control. Too embarrassed to contact her mother or to use familiar health care practitioners, Kay picked a gynecologist from the telephone book. Kay describes her visit with the doctor:

> The man was quite elderly. The nurse kept calling me honey and sweetie which was fine but it was not the kind of setting that I wanted for this kind of doctor. I guess I wanted something not, just more personal. I didn't want to be treated like a child . . . I almost felt like he was disappointed in me because I was so young and interested in seeking birth control. After the examination, he took me into a room and started questioning me about my sexual history, how many partners, how old I was, which was really embarrassing, but I guess I went through a formality. Well, then he decided that because I was so young and it was just one partner that I had been with that he didn't think I should get birth control. And that really, really upset me because I had gone out of my way to protect myself and I was in a monogamous relationship. I thought I was doing the responsible thing, and to be denied by the doctor made me feel just really, really irresponsible.

In Kay's situation, her age (and, potentially, the physician's age) became a factor in a request for a medical service that, if denied, could result in significant health consequences (i.e., an unwanted pregnancy). For other health care seekers, essentialism can be life-threatening (see Beck, November 29, 1990; Council on Ethical and Judicial Affairs, 1991; Healy, 1991; Hendrick, 1994; Weisman & Teitelbaum, 1985 as well as transcripts of *CBS This Morning*, July 24, 1991; *World News Tonight with Peter Jennings*, April 13, 1994; *Today*, May 9, 1990).

Schulman and colleagues (1999) detail a research project in which 720 doctors were shown four pictures of patients. The only actual differences between the cases were race, sex, and age, yet the doctors offered diverse treatment plans. Schulman and colleagues suggest:

> Bias may represent overt prejudice on the part of physicians or, more likely, could be the result of subconscious perceptions rather than deliberate actions or thoughts. Subconscious bias occurs when a patient's membership in a target group automatically activates a cultural stereotype in the physician's memory regardless of the level of prejudice the physician has. (p. 624)

Notably, the Schulman study received widespread press as well as a critical subsequent rebuttal in the *New England Journal of Medicine* (where the original article appeared) (Fackelmann, September 16, 1999). Yet, as Poirier (1997) explains, essentialistic assumptions about socioeconomic status can open or close doors to medical services. For example, Poirier (1997) notes that women from higher socioeconomic groups confront domestic violence like their lower economic counterparts yet may not be considered "at risk." Poirier (1997) contends that "domestic abuse extends into all neighborhoods. . . . Clinicians should implement universal screening and educating of all women, not just those who present symptoms of abuse or fill the stereotypical picture of an abused woman" (p. 122).

Relational Development

Essentialism can also impact emergent relationships between health care professionals and health care seekers. Marguerite elaborated on an experience with one health care practitioner who commented directly on her nationality:

> Finally, I got in with the doctor, and he was talking, and he said my name, and then he started saying something like, my nationality and how they were good people, just like people of his nationality were, and how, he went on and on and on. And then he said that, like how we weren't like some other nationalities who would, as he put it, "sell their mother for a piece of gold."

Marguerite acknowledged that the exchange made her feel "a little intimidated and a little . . . uncomfortable." She continued, ". . . I really didn't understand what it had to do with me being sick, and why he was saying it. I mean, there are a lot of things to have conversations about, but that just didn't seem to be appropriate at all." Although Marguerite's experience was uncomfortable, Althea Alexander's interaction with a resident exemplifies much more offensive stereotyping. Nazario (1993) offers the following account:

> When Althea Alexander broke her arm, the attending resident at Los Angeles County-USC Medical Center told her to "hold your arm like you usually hold your can of beer on Saturday night." Alexander, who is black, exploded, "What are you talking about?" she demanded. "Do you think I'm a welfare mother?" The white resident shrugged: "Well, aren't you?" Wrong. Alexander was a top official at the USC School of Medicine, where the resident was studying. (p. A1)

Essentialism and Trust

In addition to critical errors in assessments, such stereotyping of health care counterparts hinders trust and mutuality. For example, Julia recalled a visit with a particularly young-looking doctor:

> I think at first I was very nervous because he looked so young and had to be just out of school, and yeah, I was nervous because he was in control, but I just thank God I didn't have that serious of an illness. If he didn't treat what I had correctly, then it could have led into something else.

When her interviewer inquired if she would have been more comfortable with an older doctor, Julia replied:

> Yes, which is funny because it is stereotyping a doctor by his age and the way he looks. But, I think I would have felt more comfortable if I had gotten an older doctor because, you know, you kind of compare their age to the experience they have. But, it was good my mom was in there with me because I think if I was in there by myself with this young, new doctor, I think I would have felt even more uncomfortable.

In my case, when I first met Dr. T., I thought that he looked young, but we are so similar in age that I didn't think much about his experience. He had been presented to me as an expert, and I fervently desired to believe that he would know what to do. Further, he spoke with such authority that I did not ask about how long he had been in practice or how much experience that he had with such procedures. Roger referred to Dr. T. as "Doogie" (from the television show about a teen doctor, *Doogie Howser, M.D.*) almost from the start, though. As time passed and complications ensued, I started to see the youth from behind the confident mask as my blinders of hope gradually cracked. Throughout the saga, though, I viewed Dr. T. as my guide for getting better, and I kept highlighting the "expert" part of his identity and burying possible implications of his age and experience. To categorize him that way after the initial surgery would have been far too frightening.

Essentialism and Empowerment

For Zelda, being categorized as a "child" by her health care professionals actually enabled her to gain extra comfort during a difficult health care event. Interestingly, Zelda was not really a "child" at the time; she was 19 years old, and yet, the staff at Children's Hospital oriented to her as a child. Zelda remembers:

> I was at the Children's Hospital, and my pediatrician recommended this doctor, children's surgeon, and quite frankly, I had never been under, other than getting my wisdom teeth out, and um, the first time I was out I was completely scared because I had no idea what was going on. I didn't know this doctor; I'd only met him a few times prior, and I was going under, and there were doctors and nurses all over. I didn't know what was going to happen. It wasn't a major surgery, but the fact that I was out cold . . . I mean, I was, I had an IV and everything like that, and the drugs were really strong. I was just really scared. But he [the children's surgeon] was overwhelmingly nice. He's like one of the top doctors in the *** area, I guess, and the nurses [were great]. I mean, I was 19 years old, one of the oldest people at the Children's Hospital, and the doctors treated me like a little ten year old, and at the time, I needed that. I needed someone to pamper me and baby me. I was scared. They didn't make me feel out of place or anything. They made me feel totally comfortable, before and after the surgery.

I know just how Zelda feels. My obstetrician, Dr. I., hurried me to the hospital on the evening before Chelsea Meagan was born because all of the water had drained from around the baby. (We still don't know how—or even when—that happened.) He scheduled a c-section for the next day, and I checked into the hospital for observation until the surgery. During the night, a very nice resident arrived to discuss my anesthesia for the surgery. Although I hesitated about the possibility of a spinal anesthesia, the resident assured me that "if you were my wife, I wouldn't let you do a general anesthesia—it's too risky." Ultimately, I agreed.

Around seven in the morning, another guy bopped into my room. "Hi, I'm going to do your anesthesia," he said, starting to set up. I looked at him.

"Where's the other guy? The fellow that I spoke with last night?" I asked as I watched him prepare.

"He left. Don't worry—I'll just whip it in, you'll be fine," he said in an annoyingly cocky manner.

"I don't think so," I replied.

"What?" he responded.

"You're not whipping anything in my back. I've changed my mind," I asserted, definitely not trusting the arrogance of this young man.

"Well, you can't do that," he said as he moved his materials.

"Like heck, I can't. You get out. I want a real doctor," I demanded.

"I am a real doctor," he said, beginning to grow red in the face.

"I WANT TO TALK TO YOUR SUPERVISOR," I said more loudly.

"Look, I'm the only one here," he noted.

"I WANT TO TALK TO THE PERSON IN CHARGE RIGHT NOW," I yelled, figuring that women in OB have a reputation for being obnoxious. I just knew that I didn't trust this doctor with my spine and that I refused to take chances with him. The resident stormed out.

A few minutes later, an elderly doctor walked into my room. He smiled at me and picked up my chart. He moved to the head of the bed and put his hand on my shoulder.

"Hi, honey, my name is Dr. D. I am the head of the anesthesiology department here, and I understand that you wanted to see me?" he introduced himself.

"This resident came in here and said that he was going to whip the IV into my spine, and I don't trust him, and I don't want him fiddling with my back. I don't want anyone fiddling with my back," I blurted.

"Okay, honey, you don't have to have anyone do anything that you don't want for them to do," he reassured me. At that moment, Dr. I. entered, looked at the elderly doctor and then at me.

"What do you want, dear?" Dr. D. asked.

"I want to get a general anesthesia and go to sleep and wake up with a baby," I stated.

"Okay," he said, turning to Dr. I. "Can this little lady just have a general? She seems to be quite upset about the idea of a spinal."

Dr. I. agreed, and Dr. D. continued to console me by noting that he would administer the anesthesia himself during the surgery. Although I usually experience problems with anesthesia, I woke up wonderfully after Dr. D.'s attention in the operating room.

Usually, I would hate for anyone but my spouse to call me "honey" or "dear," words that can be very patronizing for a grown woman. However, like Zelda, I felt frightened and confused, and I yearned for someone to care for me and to tell me that everything would be okay. To this day, I thank God that Dr. D. helped me through a traumatic time. Whether he sensed that he needed to respond to me that way or he simply spoke to all of his female patients in that potentially condescending manner, though, I'll never know. However, relationally, the doctor's orientation to me (as Zelda's doctor to her) as well as our respective responses worked to position all of us into distinct categories—adults versus children (even though neither Zelda nor I could legitimately be classified as "children"), people who provided care versus people who wanted someone else to care for them (even though both Zelda and I could have chosen to participate more proactively in our health care discussions).

Essentialism and Organizational Relationships

Essentialism can also cloud the relational dynamic within certain health care organizations when individuals label them according to preconceived biases. In Athens, for example, students from more urban areas routinely bash our local hospital because they consider it to be "just a rural hospital." When I moved to Athens, a colleague informed me that a person can't do two things here—shop or get really sick.

Sam explained that ". . . there's some kind of stereotype that goes along with Athens and the rural area being backwoods." Even people who grew up in the area seem to accept the common belief that the doctors lack experience to evaluate cases and perform procedures as in the more major cities. Marcie acknowledged:

> Being that we are in southern Ohio and in a rural area, I don't know how good the doctors are, but I have heard stories of misdiagnoses and things like that. I just would not feel comfortable going to them. I have used them for colds and things like that, but if I ever had something more serious come up, I would definitely go somewhere else.

Summary of Essentialism

The assumption that people (or even entire regions) are simply a particular way due to some socioeconomic category hinders an awareness of the complexity of individuals and of types of health care professionals and organizations, with serious potential medical and relational consequences. Yet, in a very modernist way, society seems to yearn for the simplicity of dubbing people as this or that, professionals as this way or that way. When I told a friend that my present research featured an orthopedic surgeon, he argued that "orthopedic surgeons aren't like the rest of health care professionals. They are all obnoxious and arrogant." Can we truly say that everyone in one group, by virtual of that group membership as part of their complicated identities, fits a singular mold?

Yet, as Forsythe (1996) explains, such modernist, essentialistic preferences guide current trends toward involving computers in assessing health-related symptoms. Although the prevailing logic (by health care professionals and health care seekers) may be that computers make impartial calculations without human prejudices, even computer assessments stem from programer biases about people and treatment. In fact, far from "unbiased," Forsythe (1996) argues that, in the health care context, computers get programmed by individuals (usually health care professionals) who view the world in a particular way, flavored by their orientations to health care seekers and to medical decision making (usually, with a heavy emphasis on patient compliance rather than involvement). Forsythe (1996) offers the following conclusion about a computer system that was designed to assist in treatment of migraines:

> The designers [of the system] intend to adapt the migraine system to individual neurologists by encoding in its knowledge base each doctor's personal preferences in medical and treatment. While one might assume such preferences to be "strictly medical," in fact some of them seem distinctly cultural. For example, one physician we observed consistently recommended one particular migraine drug to male patients and another to females. When queried about this, he said that the medication he suggests to men is his true drug of choice for migraine. But because the drug can also cause weight gain, he does not recommend it to his female patients. Believing that women either should not or would not wish to gain weight, he makes a choice on their behalf that they might prefer to make for themselves. (p. 567)

A Postmodern Conception of Diversity

Feminist scholars have recognized the dangers of essentialism, arguing instead that experiences vary. For example, one person's experience as a woman may differ from another woman's experiences (see, for example, Collins, 1990; Fonow & Cook, 1991; Garry & Pearsall, 1996; hooks, 1981; Rakow, 1992; Trinh, 1989).

Blurring Boundaries

Trinh (1989) explains, "Despite our desperate, eternal attempt to separate, contain, and mend, categories always leak" (p. 94). Amid our modernist desires for absolutism, the blurring of boundaries muddies distinctions between types of people. As Rosaldo (1989) asserts, "More often than we usually care to think, our everyday lives are crisscrossed by border zones, pockets, and eruptions of all kinds" (p. 207). To be sure, as the globalization of world cultures, economies, power bases, and even health systems ensues, the result may not be complete cultural hybridity, even if such global hybridization could emerge (see Moore-Gilbert, 1997).

However, as individuals participate in society, they become their own hybrids as a result of their disparate activities, cultural allegiances, and unique choices (see Benhabib, 1992; Gergen, 1991, 1994). As Gergen (1991) suggests, individuals become "socially saturated," overwhelmed by options in terms of mediated messages, relationships, geographical location, and overall ways of approaching life. Gergen contends:

> Social saturation furnishes us with a multiplicity of incoherent and unrelated languages of the self. For everything we "know to be true" about ourselves, other voices within respond with doubt and even derision. This fragmentation of self-conceptions corresponds to a multiplicity of incoherent and disconnected relationships. These relationships pull us in myriad directions, inviting us to play such a variety of roles that the very concept of an "authentic self" with knowable characteristics recedes from view. (pp. 6–7)

Gergen (1991) continues, "Under postmodern conditions, persons exist in a state of continuous construction and recontruction . . ." (p. 7). Although Gergen seems to leave little room for consistency in his view of the postmodern self, I would argue that individuals choose to carry parts of their backgrounds and cultural roots with them as they travel through their lives and as they accumulate new experiences, new values, new customs, new beliefs, and new practices. The process of continual metamorphis as a complex, multifaceted individual involves the ongoing struggle to juxtapose multiple simultaneous (and potentially conflicting) identities, some older, some newer.

All of the health care experiences that I have described thus far in this volume contribute to who I am now; however, I am no more defined by those health care experiences than I am by all of the relationships, educational opportunities, and civic, church, professional, and family commitments that I have had (and will have) in my life. As I move from episode to episode, from minute to minute, in my daily life, I highlight (sometimes consciously, sometimes unconsciously) assorted aspects of my ever-emergent, multiple identities.

In his work on hermeneutics, Gadamer (1976, 1988, 1997) emphasizes the episodic or temporal nature of interpretation. As social actors, we interpret texts (whether physical texts bound in books or mediated moments in motion pictures or interactional texts of verbal and nonverbal actions) within the context of our lived reality at a given time, in a given place. The critical difficulty for health care participants stems from discerning how to interpret others and the utterances and actions of those others within the context of our respective, complicated, multifaceted lived realities.

We can no longer view health care participants as just health care professionals or just health care seekers, simply women or men, people of a given age or race. Until we consider diversity beyond categorization, we lack a comprehensive understanding of how others make meaning from our interactions and how they, as unique, multifaceted individuals, orient to challenging equally unique health care situations.

Person-Oriented Wellness

Roger helped me into the car and then walked around to the driver's side. After a difficult night of increasing pain in my shoulder and left arm, I finally decided near dawn to drive back to Columbus. I administered my antibiotics and then called to bum yet another ride to the hospital. I glanced over at Roger as he started the car, and I leaned back against my headrest and sighed. I felt numb.

We sat in silence for most of the ride. What could we really say except "what are the odds that something else would happen?" or "what do you think will happen now?" However, both of us knew enough now to know that we couldn't calculate the odds or speculate the future. So, we watched the road and the other cars of people on their way to places in their busy days, and we put ourselves on auto-pilot for the ever-so-familiar drill at the emergency room—"Same address? Insurance?", the admissions clerk would inquire. "Reason for visit?" the triage nurse would ask, while taking vitals and preparing my chart.

I entered the emergency room waiting room and scanned others who sat in chairs as they awaited their turn in triage, admissions, and examining areas. Unlike evenings, only a few people were scattered around the room—a Caucasian woman with a child and a young African American man. I put down my purse and eased myself down into my own chair. I shook my head and sought to summon patience for participating in the now rote routine of clunking my way through the medical maze.

"Beck?" the nurse called from the triage area.

I stood, steadied myself, and then moved toward the nurse.

"What brings you here?" she asked as I sat in the familiar "patient's" chair.

I couldn't be "good" and complacent anymore. I leaned toward her and tried to seek her assistance in circumventing the system.

"Here's the deal," I began, proceeding to tell her my story. I told her about my wrist and then the infection and then the PICC line and my problems with it. I explained that no one seemed to know anything about PICC lines and that I needed to talk to someone in infectious diseases as well as someone who directs the PICC line nurses. I emphasized that I didn't want to talk to any more medical students nor even more residents—I wanted to speak with people who had all of their training. Even if the hospital was a teaching hospital, I no longer desired to be an example or an experiment. I remembered the awful resident from the last visit who kept advocating extremist measures, and I cringed.

I reached out and touched the nurse's arm. "Please, please, help me," I begged in a whisper. It had come to that, really. I was ready to beg for help, all too ready to plead with someone to just lift me out of the narrow, rigid passages of the maze.

The nurse stared at me, and I saw compassion in her eyes. She wants to help me, I realized, as she said, "Let me see what I can do" and turned to the phone.

To accomplish people-oriented wellness, both health care professionals and health care seekers must overcome two difficult barriers—perceptions of preordained institutionalized roles (type of health care professional and type of patient) and perceptions of stereotypical categories of people (by age, race/ethnicity, gender/sex, geographical location, income, occupation, religion, etc.). Instead of highlighting roles or stereotypes, the people who talk with each other during health care encounters need to emphasize the pursuit of wellness in the context of individual health care participants (see related work by Mishler, 1984).

Desire to Understand

Person-oriented wellness involves, first, a sincere desire to understand how the other person is orienting to the health care encounter. A health care professional should concentrate on determining what aspects of a seeker's multifaceted identities impact that seeker's comprehension of health-related issues. For example, the professional should seek (and the seeker should share) *if* (and then *how*) ethnic traditions or religious practices or sexual orientation influence the specific medical situation. Further, the professional should seek (and the seeker should share) how the pursuit of wellness gets juxtaposed with other, simultaneous dimensions of that seeker's lived reality (i.e., in terms of family and career responsibilities, ideologies, possible addictions, lack of financial resources, possible physical or emotional abuse, medical history, etc.). In my case, ethnic traditions, religious practices, and sexual orientation had little to do with my plea to the nurse. My plea stemmed from my terror, frustration, and fervent desire to get better so that I could resume my identities as a mother, as a professional, as an energetic contributer to my community.

For my own part, as a health care seeker, I desired to treat the triage nurse as an advocate, not simply as a nurse who had the limited responsibility of performing initial assessments in the emergency room. I reached out to her as a fellow human being who might also be afraid and discouraged, if the tables were turned. Was she a mom? Did she understand that I had two little ones at home who depended on me? Had she ever been through anything remotely like my situation? I couldn't know. Unspoken rules prohibit such queries.

The institutionalization of medical roles (i.e., types of professionals versus patients) works to lock individuals into set roles without an acknowledgment of them as multifaceted people with emotions. When health care seekers gaze at professionals and see only roles (and vice versa), they fail to link with fellow human beings who have their own pressures (especially time and responsibility), emotional reactions, and fallibilities.

Person-oriented wellness constitutes a *dyadic process* that requires health care professionals and health care seekers to avoid assumptions and to engage each other in dialogues about how they can offer and gain help within the context of their respective lived realities. What issues are relevant (and why) to health care professionals? What issues are relevant (and why) to health care seekers?

Desire to Build Common Ground

As I discussed in Chapter 2, person-oriented wellness involves, second, a sincere desire to facilitate a common ground between health care professionals and health care seekers as people, rather than as members of a category. If both health care participants focus on ways to enact wellness within the context of multiple individual realities, they can build toward mutual understanding. By avoiding "cookie cutter" approaches to learning about each other, health care participants can grapple with individual perspectives, needs, and identities, not stereotypes of groupings.

Notably, in my case, the nurse never would have picked up the phone to try to contact an internist for me if I had not stepped out of my role as a generic patient. If we had relied on our usual, modernist conceptions of our roles and categories, we would have played out another rote interaction that would not have permitted me to express my multi-faceted concerns nor for the nurse to respond to them. Each health care participant, both professional and seeker, needs to introduce his or her orientations to and expectations of health care encounters for patient-centered wellness practices to ensue.

CLOSING THOUGHTS

The nurse returned the telephone to its cradle and sighed. "I'm sorry," she said. "The internal medicine clinic is closed today, and the receptionist didn't know who to contact about PICC lines."

Tears filled my eyes, and I looked up at Roger and then back at the nurse. "What am I going to do?" I asked, almost rhetorically. "Isn't there anyone in the hospital who knows anything about this?" I couldn't believe that the hospital would not have anyone on staff on a given day in the area of infectious disease.

"Well, there's no one who is available for a consult in the ER. To get an appointment with an internist, you would need an appointment in the clinic, and it's closed today," the nurse responded. "I'm really sorry."

"What should I do?" I inquired again.

"Well, I can send you back, and one of the doctors back there should know what to do," she answered, but she didn't sound confident. "I am truly sorry."

I thought about leaving as I stood to return to my seat. I looked at the lady with a child, and I hoped that the child had something easy to fix—like a broken arm. Wait a second, I remembered. A broken arm from so long ago started this saga for me. As I stared at the child, with her blonde curls on her mother's lap, I could no longer think of what might be simple to cure.

Time passed . . . I answered the admission lady's questions. Yes, I still live in the same place. Yes, I still have the same insurance and employer. I responded dutifully at first and then grew edgy with the redundant inquisition. "Nope, things haven't changed since I was here only SEVEN DAYS AGO," I interjected at one point. I glanced up at Roger, and he gestured for me to calm down. I realized that the admission lady was just doing her job, but for me, it constituted one more exemplar of people going through the motions—case after case, different yet seemingly treated the same in a static system.

Please look at me, I thought, really, truly, look at me. Please see beyond my cast . . . please see the person who wants to cheer at one daughter's game and to cradle the other daughter while reading her bedtime stories at the end of the day . . . the person who wants to do so much that she burns the candle at both ends of her life . . . the person who wants to succeed . . . the person who wants all of the kids in her life to savor her chocolate chip cookies and to enjoy her fun parties . . . the person who wants to serve God and to be a part of his work on Earth . . . oh yes, the person who wants to live . . .

The admission lady busied herself by typing my information into the computer as I stared at her. She would not look at me. I was just another person on just another day with just another complaint. I would not be able to make her raise her eyes to see me, nor could I make her understand that I wasn't just another patient with a problem. I am me, far too complicated to pigeonhole, yet with every press of a key, I got coded as female (click), 30-something (click), Caucasian (click), Athens County (click), Baptist (click), professional (click).

The woman finished and instructed me to return to my seat, and I did so silently. I'm not a click, I retorted to her in my head. I'm all of those categories, yes, but I'm much more. Rage swelled inside me, and I yearned to scream, perhaps more to disrupt the organizationally mandated order than to accomplish anything. In spite of my anger, at that point, I really could do little more than wait for another chance to tell my story and to pray for someone who could help.

10 Public Dialogues About Health

I reached into my bookbag and pulled out a USA Today *with my left hand as my right arm lay on the table, blanketed by a large heating unit. I glanced around as the two occupational therapists busied themselves with other individuals with various injuries, and I smiled to acknowledge a young man who entered the room. I had visited with the young man during a previous occupational therapy session, and he had told me about how his broken finger threatened his career as a college gymnast. He seemed like a nice guy who was fighting hard to battle back in time for a major competition. I made a mental note to watch him on television, and I wondered if the commentators would mention his dramatic recovery from a potentially career-ending injury.*

I watched as the gymnast walked over to a large container, carefully raised a heating unit from steaming water, moved to a table, and masterfully positioned a towel and the heating unit over his hand to prepare for therapy. It doesn't take long, I thought, for the process of therapy to become routine, like something that a person has always done and known.

I turned back to the USA Today *and tried to concentrate on the headlines, but my mind drifted to the realization that therapy had just recently replaced my struggle with the infection as the focal point of my life. I heard Connie, one of the occupational therapists, ask another client about an appointment later in the week. Wow, I thought, the second week of March. Just a month ago, I had been in and out of the hospital, trying to figure out all of the problems with the PICC line and the infection, trying to survive.*

I stared ahead. I had wanted so much for someone to give me answers, for someone to help me who possessed some degree of expertise with my situation. After Pam sent me to the ER with the second PICC line-problem, I felt like a pregnant Mary searching for room in the inn. Like Mary, I desired a particular type of help. Like Mary, who ultimately rested in a bed of hay in a stable instead of a hotel bed, I had to settle for a less than optimal option. As opposed to someone who specialized in infections or PICC lines, I met with the orthopedic resident, Dr. D., who happened to be on call.

A gruff woman, Dr. D. tersely examined me as I closed my eyes in despair. This doctor is certainly no Marcus Welby, I observed. Even when doctors on ER *get busy, they display some degree of empathy. Hmmm, I'm a doctor of communication, I thought; perhaps, I should prescribe a good dose of television to facilitate friendliness. Despite my despair, I couldn't help twisting the corners of my mouth upward, and I opened my eyes. Roger looked at me quizzically, and I softly said "nothing." I shifted my gaze to the*

resident, to her frowning face and distracted manner, and decided against recommend-
ing my prescription.

Dr. D. concluded that the line had gone bad because it had been moved the previous
week. "It happens sometimes," she shrugged, "We'll need to pull it now." As Dr. D. donned
gloves and prepared to remove the line, she treated the removal as routine and nonconse-
quential, commenting that, as a patient, I "had never believed in it anyway." She was
wrong; I had believed in it, clung to it, trusted that it could enable me to gain the drugs that
I needed to recover.

As I lay on the hospital bed that day, I implored her to tell me how I could beat the
infection without IV antibiotics. Dr. D. changed the story that I had heard since the beginning
of my illness. "You've had IV antibiotics for three weeks. That should be good enough," she
noted as she wrote my prescription for a strong antibiotic pill, 800 mg per dose of Aug-
mentin. "Should be?" I thought. Does she know, I wondered? How does she know? What
happened to the need for at least six weeks of IV antibiotics to defeat the infection?

I ran my hand through my hair, inhaled deeply, and scanned the others in the ther-
apy room. The weeks after that trip to the ER had been rough—filled with more visits to my
general doctor and the surgeon and even two more trips back to the ER, more blood tests
to monitor the infection and anemia, more concerns about my progress. Yet I'm here now,
I thought. After a month of uncertainty and frustration and, at times, sheer terror, I no
longer needed to worry about survival. I survived. I could concentrate on rehabbing my
wrist and growing strong again without pain.

Connie caught my eye and mouthed the words "You're next." I returned my unread
paper to my bookbag and waited. I watched Connie as she finished with another client, an
elderly man. The man had been injured in a robbery at his small store. The gunman had
fired several shots into the man's arm. After emergency surgery, the man faced months of
occupational therapy to regain some use of his arm. How sad, I thought. His arm will never
be the same as before that awful night.

We all have our stories, I thought, with individual histories and plot complications.
From so many different roads and life circumstances, we converge in this room at this time,
I mused. I looked at the man as his wife helped him to his feet. We intersect here, I thought,
but even with our common need for OT, our afflictions and treatment run the gamut of
rehabbing a finger to salvaging an entire arm.

As I observed Connie with the man and his wife, I remembered viewing and reading
reports of the robbery and the arrest of the gunman on the news and in the local paper.
How odd to be in the same room as a person on the news, I thought. Observing the recov-
ery efforts of the victim of violence and the gymnast in the occupational therapy room per-
sonalized the robbery of a small store and the training of an athlete. As the man and his
wife left, Connie greeted the gymnast on her way to my table, and I marveled at the oppor-
tunity to peek at their respective human dramas, "up close and personal."

In this chapter, I explore public dialogues about health. First, I detail the trend
toward active participation in the public sphere, and second, I discuss how individuals
and organizations construct public narratives that resonate with others. I conclude by
reflecting on the ethical implications of the plethora of public dialogues about health care
concerns.

Participating in the Public Sphere

During one of my occupational therapy sessions, I sat near Linda, a woman who struggled with chronic pain. As my wrist warmed in preparation for therapy, I observed how Connie carefully flexed Linda's wrist to the right, stretching and releasing it and then bending her wrist to the left. Linda moaned with every move, and I wanted to reach out to her. Fortunately, I did not suffer as much with therapy as she apparently did, and I thought that I could distract her through conversation.

I told her about my reconstruction and referred only briefly to the infection. Connie caught my eye and slightly dropped her jaw when I said that I'd had a few minor setbacks— she knew about my lengthy saga to get well. Somehow, though, my story didn't seem important right then; instead, I invited Linda to tell me about her own situation. I wondered why Connie closed her eyes and then reopened them to stare intently at Linda's forearm.

Linda noted that she had been diagnosed with carpal tunnel and that her doctor had performed two carpal tunnel release surgeries on her, but to no avail. Therapy offered little relief for the pain, and the pain blocks did not seem to work. After telling me about her situation and complaining about the ineffectiveness of her treatment, Linda grew loud and abrasive, despite Connie's efforts to calm her down. Angry and disillusioned, Linda continued to vent about her inability to work at a job and her frustration with worker's compensation.

"They tell me that I should be able to go back to work, that I should be okay. I want to be okay. I want to work. I want to be normal, but no one believes me that I'm not and that all of this stuff isn't working. Why won't anyone believe me?" Linda exploded.

Stunned, I couldn't think of a response, and I fixed my gaze on Connie's gloved hands, which continued to flex Linda's wrist. Connie slowly inhaled and replied, "I believe you, Linda. I know that you're hurting. Maybe your doctor will be able to think of something different to try today."

Linda shouted, "There isn't anything else! Meanwhile, I have to keep fighting for my benefits so that my kids won't starve, and I have to deal with this pain. I can't take it any more. I can't stand this pain." She took a breath and shook her head. "Maybe someone would believe me if I just went over and blew up the whole *@* place. If I just blew up the whole place, someone might just take me seriously."

I started to get very nervous. What if Linda was making a real threat? I stared at Connie, but she didn't seem bothered by Linda's outburst.

"If you see the whole place in flames on the news, think of me," Linda said. "I'll be in the front of the crowd, cheering. They'll take me seriously then."

After Linda left, I asked Connie if we should report Linda's utterance to someone as a threat.

"Oh no," Connie said. "She's said that so many times now. She just gets frustrated when her checks are late or someone challenges her pain as a disability. She just needs to spout off and then she's fine."

Reluctantly, I decided to trust Connie's judgment, especially since I overheard the comments in the context of the confidential OT room. However, for the months to follow, I warily watched the news and hoped that Linda would not act on her desperate desire for her pain to be legitimized by health benefits officials.

Discussions about health-related issues abound, on television, radio, and the Internet, in newspaper and magazine articles. From formalized and funded public health campaigns to individual appeals for attention to a cause, competing health narratives battle to be heard by a public deafened by an unending bombardment of multiple and mixed messages.

As we begin the twenty-first century, the most intimate of health issues seem to be legitimate public concerns, from personal struggles with illness to the very public positioning of quite personal products. A woman gives birth to sextuplets, sparking headlines, talk show and news program coverage, and a national media debate about the ethics of fertility drugs and multiple births (see Rubin, November 18, 1999). A public figure (such as Christopher Reeve, Ronald Reagan, Michael J. Fox, Walter Payton, or Dudley Moore) experiences injury or illness, and reporters relentlessly pursue information for all of the "inquiring minds who want to know." A pharmaceutical company, hospital, medical association, or individual doctor launches public relations and advertising campaigns to "inform consumers about choices of drugs or services." A health-related foundation funds a campaign to promote "safe sex," family planning, or "healthy lifestyle practices." Television dramas, soap operas, and talk shows highlight health concerns and the work of health care professionals, from the plights of fictional characters to the trials of actual people.

With each of these endeavors into the public eye, individuals and organizations bring a multiplicity of agendas, ranging from personal to political to economic. From advancing a perspective to preserving a reputation, from encouraging charitable donations to promoting health care practices, from selling newspapers or advertising spots to increasing market share, the public dialogue about health constitutes a fascinating interplay between what should be of private or public domain.

Invitational Media

Mediated messages pervade contemporary society (see, e.g., Cerulo, Ruane, & Chayko, 1992; Gergen, 1991; Meyrowitz, 1985). Whereas typical families in the previous generation owned one television and accessed the three major networks, many families in the United States acquire multiple televisions and pay for cable or satellite as a means of reaching fifty or more stations. With the pressing of a button on our remote controls, we can flip through soap operas, legal trials, Congressional hearings, sporting events, news headlines, old movies, classic television shows, and increasingly, television talk shows. Special interest magazines abound, and the Internet has enabled newspapers and radio stations to reach worldwide audiences.

However, those messages may no longer be viewed as simple, unidirectional tools for informing a silent and passive audience. As Meyrowitz (1985) explains, boundaries between personal and public domains continue to blur. Aden (1999) suggests that individuals can transcend static places (such as fixed positions in geographical areas or socioeconomic status) through symbolic pilgrimages into popular culture stories. From their armchairs, voyagers can venture into public places, and through playful interpretations, they can reconfigure the public domain as quite personal and accessible.

However, the graying of distinctions between what counts as "private" and "public" has transformed beyond an imaginary merging of private and public domains. In 1985, Meyrowitz argued that viewers/readers enact parasocial relationships with characters or personalities that promote a sense of intimacy and connection (see also related work by Schickel, 1985). According to Meyrowitz (1985), "Viewers come to feel they 'know' the people they 'meet' on television in the same way they know their friends and associates" (p. 119). Indeed, one participant in a class-action lawsuit claims that celebrity ads persuaded him to start smoking in the 1950s. Frank Amodeo trusted the famous athletes, thinking "they smoked, so how could it be bad?" (AP, December 3, 1999, p. 15A).

Although I would not argue with Meyrowitz's description of parasocial relationships, I would suggest that the invitational nature of contemporary mediated resources encourages and enables actual dialogues between people who would not likely have interacted some fifteen years ago. Mediated messages increasingly involve interaction between "everyday" people and talk show hosts, celebrities, media producers, and even politicians (see, e.g., Cerulo et al., 1992). Television fans influence plot and character development through their telephone calls, letters, and emails to fan magazines and networks and through their participation on show websites. Individuals may call on-air radio or television personalities to share insights or seek advice. For example, Dr. Laura (Schlessinger), a radio talk show host and pop psychologist, inspires some 60,000 people per day to call, hoping to gain her advice on air (see AP, July 29, 1998). The Internet permits individuals to "chat" with professionals, celebrities, and like-others about health and other concerns as well as to offer their own perspectives via personal web sites.

More than ever before, "ordinary" people *can* legitimately claim public space as their own, as a forum for their ideas and interests. The advent of the Internet and the explosion of competing television networks and programs provide people—from an array of social situations and with a host of agendas—with a chance to be speak out, an opportunity to be heard, that might not otherwise occur in the frenzy of contemporary life. The pervasive media invites individuals, such as Linda, to tell (or draw attention to) their stories and to view the public sphere as a place to pursue personal plights, especially if, as in Linda's case, individual situations seem to lack salience to local bureaucrats.

Idealizing Public Discussions

Contemporary mediated resources have the potential to lift a multiplicity of voices into the public "sphere," a publicly situated forum for debate and persuasion; however, the emotional emphasis of those voices raise red flags about the value of such contributions (see Calhoun, 1992; Goodnight, 1982; Goodnight & Hingstman, 1997; Habermas, 1989, 1992, Phillips, 1996, as well as related work by Meyrowitz, 1985). Ideally, according to some theorists, the public sphere constitutes an open and impartial place for deliberations and discussions, a place for logical disputes that lead to consensus about public issues (such as funding for research about diseases or identifying health and wellness practices) (see Calhoun, 1992; Goodnight, 1982; Goodnight & Hingstman, 1997; Habermas, 1989, 1992; Phillips, 1996).

Goodnight (1982) differentiates the public sphere from personal and technical spheres by suggesting that diverse types of evidence and logic pertain to argumentation in each of the spheres. According to Goodnight (1982), the personal appeals and technical jargon and artistry that pervade personal and technical spheres should diminish during deliberative approaches to public concerns. Goodnight (1982) bemoans ever-expanding media coverage of events that emphasizes personal sagas rather than deliberative argumentation, noting that "instead of expanding public forums, these devices seem to be geared to producing either refined information or compelling fantasy" (p. 226). For both Habermas (1987, 1992) and Goodnight (1982), the fragmentation of the public sphere with competing commercial, personal, and technical interests clouds the potentiality of the public sphere to facilitate public consensus (see Calhoun, 1992; Phillips, 1996).

However, as Phillips (1996) observes, both Habermas and Goodnight envision an idealized public dialogue about issues in which all individuals can openly participate, in which everyone possesses an equal voice, in which all share common assumptions about what constitutes "fair," "reasonable," and "equitable." In an increasingly diverse society, Phillips (1996) questions the likelihood of achieving consensus on core assumptions, not to mention members' application of assumptions to complicated and challenging issues which confront contemporary citizens.

Despite debate on the "decay" or the "viability" of the public sphere for decision making when "nonrational" personal concerns become factors in public deliberations (see particularly, reviews by Goodnight & Hingstman, 1997; Phillips, 1996), the invitational nature of mediated resources promotes "getting personal" in the positioning of what should be public problems. Further, an emphasis on personal perspectives fits with a fragmented society wherein individuals lack static ties and a sense of connectedness—a one-size-fits-all public good does not implicitly match disparate people with individualized life experiences and priorities. As such, the highlighting of personal experiences cannot be ignored as an increasingly prevalent force in public dialogues about health.

Yet, diverse and competing perspectives get jumbled in the overwhelmed, chaotic, and confusing public sphere. As people and organizations fight to the forefront for their "five minutes" of attention, they face the challenge of positioning their personal struggles so they become matters of mainstream public concern.

Narratives as Argument

Although I would like to become numb to continual news flashes about what item or behavior will kill/hurt/maim us this week, I find myself wanting to watch the television shows that feature people who are afflicted with diseases or movies that highlight injured people who triumph over all. I pick up magazines and newspapers with dramatic stories of individuals (especially children) who have fought illness, breathed or consumed something harmful, or perhaps, happened to be in the wrong place at the wrong time. Human dramas intrigue me. Fisher (1984, 1987) presents an alternate view to prioritizing rational deliberation in decision making. Fisher (1984) asserts that "humans are essentially storytellers" (p. 7) and that narrative ". . . is meaningful for persons in particular and in general, across communities as well as cultures, across time and place" (p. 8). Importantly, Fisher (1987) suggests that his emphasis on narrative as a means of argumentation ". . . does not disregard the roles of reason and rationality; it expands their meanings, recognizing their potential presence in all forms of human communication" (p. 58).

Thus, drawing on Burke's notions of identification and consubstantiality, Fisher (1984, 1987) proposes that individuals tell stories as a way of connecting with others and, in so doing, persuading those others about a given cause or situation. In the cases of the gymnast and the elderly man in the occupational therapy room, as well as Linda, I found myself drawn to their stories, to their very human dramas of hardship and recovery.

Their stories provided me with a way of understanding their respective plights that "just the facts" (man shot during robbery; gymnast broke finger) could not produce. For me, a focus on "just the facts" depersonalizes inherently personal situations. However, as Fisher (1984, 1987) stresses, narratives do not simply provide the counter to "facts"; instead, stories merge fact and values, reason and emotion. According to Fisher (1987), "Stories are enactments of the whole mind in concert with itself" (p. 68).

Notably, as Fisher (1987) contends, "obviously some stories are better stories than others." Fisher explains:

> Rationality is determined by the nature of persons as narrative beings—their inherent aware-ness of *narrative probability*, what constitutes a coherent story, and their constant habit of testing *narrative fidelity*, whether or not the stories they experience ring true with the stories they know to be true in their lives. (p. 64)

As I will detail in the next section, contemporary contributions to the public dia-logue about health care issues tend to highlight stories about human struggles with illness and industry-wide bureaucracies. Those narratives represent rhetorical efforts to persuade, perhaps only to care about an individual person, but increasingly, to inspire support for a cause or health-related behaviors. If they ring true, if they strike media consumers as consistent with what they know/understand, they may succeed with such persuasion (see Fisher, 1987). Although such stories can facilitate discussions of important public health concerns, the personal, economic, political, and social ramifications of public and personal health decisions raise ethical questions about narrative-driven public dialogues, an issue to be pursued further at the end of the chapter.

Public Narratives

Slowly, I pried the prongs of the black clothespin apart and positioned it closer to the sil-ver rod. I needed to keep the sides separated just long enough to put the prongs around the rod. I neared the rod and pressed the prongs to the outer rim. Concentrate . . . hold on . . . just a sec longer . . . I cheered myself toward the goal. Do it . . . just do it . . . YES, it hooked. I leaned back against my chair and exhaled loudly. A middle-aged woman at the table behind me clapped. "Is that the first time that you've done a black one?" she asked. "Yeah," I smiled, looking at the black clothespin on top of the other colors. How odd to feel such a sense of accomplishment over a clothespin, I marveled.

I reached to pick up another black clothespin. In a few short weeks of occupational therapy, I had made incredible progress. I had improved my ability to flex and to bend my wrist, and I hoped to rid myself of the protective wrist cover soon. I smiled at the clothes-pin in my palm. I wish that I could get toys like this at home, I thought. I carried my "thera-putty" and "thera-band" in my purse already, doing repetitions as many times a day as I could tolerate, and I just started to use the one pound weight that I purchased at Target. Yet, I also really liked the stretches and strengthening from exercises like the clothespins and other OT "toys." Rehabbing gave me a sense of ownership and empowerment. I loved being able to do something in order to help myself to recover.

Once again, I concentrated on pushing the prongs apart with my fingers—push, push, I thought. "Ugh," I said as I dropped the clothespin on the table. Keri, one of the OTs, glanced over at me from her work with another person. "How you doin'?" she asked.

I glared at the clothespin and snapped, "Fine." I felt grumpy. I had been doing so well and then I had to drop the stupid pin. How could I let go?

"Why don't you call it a day?" Keri suggested. I sighed. I wanted to be able to put all of the pins on the rod at one sitting. How annoying that my wrist started to throb before I could do it . . .

"Yeah, I guess I'd better. Dr. T. wants me to go for a consultation with another doctor today because I've felt so tired," I responded. I was so tired of being tired and of hurting, but I didn't know what this doctor could tell me that others had been unable to find.

"That'll be good," Keri suggested. I rolled my eyes. I doubted that the new doctor would tell me anything other than I was anemic and that infections take a while to shake off. I had just finished my prescription of Augmentin the previous week. I'd be better soon, I thought, again considering canceling the appointment.

"Yeah," I grunted, as I stood up and prepared to leave. I dreaded retelling my story to one more person. For a new nurse, and then the new doctor, I would need to detail all of the problems with my wrist and then the infection and then the PICC line and then the PICC line again and then the lingering exhaustion. Reconstructing my case for each new health care practitioner required me to delve into minute detail. Each peculiarity consti-tuted a core component of my ongoing health care puzzle.

The public presentation of personal narratives also involves critical parts. I would argue that public narratives can accomplish coherence and consistency—factors in narra-tive rationality that were identified by Fisher—through the description of some personal trauma, the assertion of connectedness with multiple like-others, and the "natural" appeal for assistance/prevention outreach.

Personal Trauma

When I visited Chicago for a conference in early November 1999, the timing of my trip coincided with a tragedy in the world of sports and the city of Chicago. As I walked from one conference hotel to another in the early evening, I saw the lights on one building shap-ing the number 34, and I knew that the lighting tribute heralded the life and death of Chicago Bear football great Walter Payton.

Payton had suffered from a rare liver disease, primary sclerosing cholangitis (PSC). Payton remained silent about his illness until a Chicago sports commentator referred to Payton as "the Raisin Man" and noted his dwindling frame. Payton felt compelled to "set the record straight" (Howlett, February 3, 1999, p. C2). Because he was very active in the Chicago community, news of Payton's illness, need for a transplant, and subse-quent death dominated television and radio stations in Chicago as well as sports-related programming across the United States.

Like Payton, Michael J. Fox spoke out about his struggle with Parkinson's disease when his symptoms became a burden to hide (see Davis, November 27, 1998, December 1, 1998; Schneider & Gold, December 7, 1998). Originally, according to Moore (1999), "Fox and Pollan (Tracy, his wife) made the decision that they would fight the disease in private, confiding in only their families and a few close friends" (p. 16). However, Schneider and Gold (December 7, 1998) report that "after so many years of keeping his condition private, Fox now feels at ease, and relieved, at going public with it" (p. 130).

Like Arthur Ashe, a tennis great, and Ronald Reagan, a former United States president, Payton and Fox were "outed" when the struggle to conceal symptoms and treatment grew too difficult. Their choice to call a news conference and to acknowledge their respective battles with an illness came as a consequence of their fame. Reporters started to sniff out a problem, and each seized the opportunity to tell his story rather than staying silent and deferring to tabloid speculation. For their behaviors/symptoms to "make sense" to others, they needed to reveal their personal traumas.

Situating the Trauma

The writing team of *Murphy Brown* concentrated on depicting the personal trauma of illness when they wrote Murphy's breast cancer storyline. As in the case of Nancy, the woman who battled ovarian cancer on *thirtysomething*, the *Murphy Brown* writers illustrated how illness intersected with the character's lived reality. For the narrative to be coherent and consistent, the writers needed to situate the story within the framework of Murphy's multifaceted identities, what she believes and values, what she holds as responsibilities, perspectives, and so on—much as individuals in "real life" find themselves wrestling to juxtapose illness with the rest of their lived realities (see related work by Tulabut, July 18, 1999).

With regard to Nancy on *thirtysomething*, Sharf and Freimuth (1993) observed that "the story of Nancy's ovarian cancer was sprung on the viewership with no warning, much like the onset of the disease itself" (p. 147). Further, Sharf and Freimuth suggested, "Reflecting the chronicity of the ailment, in almost every show that followed, there was some mention of cancer. . . . In short, the experience of illness became part of the ongoing 'reality' in the lives of the friends featured on the program" (p. 147).

Pursuing "Why?"

One of the most compelling aspects of the *Murphy Brown* and *thirtysomething* stories involved the question "why?". As in everyday life, the introduction of illness seems inconsistent with everything else that a person has to manage. In Nancy's case, the character had separated from her husband during the previous season, and she was raising her two young children and trying to start a career as a book illustrator. In fact, she received the ovarian cancer diagnosis just before her book (based on a story that she created with her son, Ethan) was released. Just when life started to turn around for Nancy, cancer struck—what are the odds? Surely, such inopportune timing must be the result of cruel fiction, as opposed to "real life."

Unfortunately, the intriguing part about personal traumas is that truth is often stranger than fiction. What are the odds that Christopher Reeve, a gifted rider and handsome, athletic man, would be thrown from his horse and left paralyzed? What are the odds that bubbly dancer and actress Annette Funicello would develop multiple sclerosis? What are the odds that professional athletes, such as Magic Johnson and Arthur Ashe, would contract AIDS? In these instances, diseases clash with individuals' public personas as well as a priori conceptions about "who gets" such a disease or suffers a twist of fate—however, perhaps no more so than with Payton and Fox.

Payton had been called invincible on the playing field. As Howlett (February 3, 1999) explains, "teammates and others who knew Payton recall a player who, while not always the strongest or the swiftest, was always the toughest and best-conditioned" (p. C2). How could *he* develop such an affliction? How could such a tough, healthy guy require an organ transplant? For Fox, the diagnosis of an "old person's disease" conflicts with his youthful appearance and actual age; he was diagnosed around age 30. How could an incredibly youthful man like Fox, a guy who loved to skate and play hockey, a guy who portrayed energetic teenagers well into his late twenties, develop an "old person's disease"?

Their respective status as public figures catapulted them into a situation where each ultimately had to reveal a quite personal problem—something that "happened to me." However, the dissonance between the public persona and the implications of the particular disease catapulted me (and others) into a pursuit of sense-making—How could this be? How could this happen? How could this fit? As Fisher (1987) explains, a story must be coherent and "ring true." Given the inconsistency of the disease with the public persona, the story seemed insufficient only with the disclosure of illness.

Connectedness with Multiple Like-Others

Fortunately, I have frightened my teenage daughter from piercing her ears or any other body part. (Such persuasion wasn't hard—I just said the words "blood" and "pain." Britti dropped the discussion pretty quickly!) However, countless men and women engage in body piercing. Other than the possibility of pain and a bit of blood (and biases about the impact on appearance), little harm seems to come from piercing a range of body parts.

"It" Could Happen to You
Leeann Winner would beg to differ. A 14-year-old from Westerville, Ohio, Leeann visited a shop at a mall and requested an upper ear piercing. According to Leeann, "A lot of my friends have done it. I thought it would look good" (Somerson, October 23, 1999, p. 1A). After developing a bacterial infection, though, Leeann faced two surgeries and over a month of IV antibiotics. Somerson reports that "her doctors say the best she can hope for is a cauliflower ear and cosmetic surgery; the worst, losing part of her ear and having the infection spread" (p. A1).

Although Leeann suffered the personal trauma of the infected ear, her story necessitated more than simply a recounting of her visit to the mall and her trips to the hospital. For the story to ring true, readers needed to know that Leeann's desire for the earring and Leeann's struggle with the infection were not "unreasonable" or "flukes"; the story had to contain her connectedness to like-others.

Notably, Leeann emphasized that "a lot" of her friends had their upper ears pierced. In fact, Somerson (October 23, 1999) observes that Leeann's older sister obtained a similar piercing, without consequence. Leeann had no reason to suspect that the procedure might be dangerous.

Despite Leeann's perception that "everybody does it," the procedure exposed her to a highly risky (but unpublicized) type of infection. An article about Leeann's situation included interviews with doctors who verify the potential for infection through piercing of the ear cartilage (Somerson, October 23, 1999). For example, Dr. Cliff Hood notes that "any time you pierce the cartilage, there is a high risk for infection. And fixing the problem is not an innocuous procedure" (Somerson, October 23, 1999, p. 2A).

Like others, Leeann thought that the process was "no big deal." Like others, Leeann unknowingly put herself at risk for a dangerous infection—she wasn't "stupid" or "careless." Like at least a few others, Leeann developed a serious infection.

For individuals or organizations who ultimately want to step beyond the public sharing of personal traumas to promote some sort of awareness or prevention outreach (like Leeann's angry mother), a critical mid-step involves identification, illustrating a clear connection between the stricken person/people and others and their respective behaviors, in order to construct a coherent and consistent narrative.

Personalizing the Potential for Illness

Michael J. Fox's illness did not match the stereotype that Parkinson's disease strikes only the elderly. To counter that perception, news reports that featured Fox's disclosure pointed to the reality that "15% of patients are diagnosed below the age of 50—some as young as 13" (Davis, December 1, 1998b, D1). By making Fox's disclosure consistent with a little known (but now publicized) fact, readers can make sense of Fox's news—Parkinson's disease is not just an elderly person's disease. In fact, Fox has now been positioned as a highly public example of a much more youthful group of individuals who are afflicted with Parkinson's disease.

Nicole Johnson, Miss America 1999, seized the opportunity to engage in a public dialogue about diabetes during her reign. However, five years earlier as a college sophomore, diabetes was the farthest thing from her mind, something that did not enter her realm of possibility, not something that would happen to her. Fackelmann (December 14, 1998) explains:

> Like most college sophomores, Nicole Johnson started the school year with great expectations. But soon, the normally vivacious 19-year-old found she could barely drag herself through the day. At first, Johnson blamed her lack of zip on a heavy load at the University of South Florida in Tampa. Johnson's fatigue, weight loss, and edginess got worse. She began to suspect something was seriously amiss and sought help from several doctors. One told her she had anemia. Another said she had the flu. (p. 6D)

Like most sophomores, Johnson had a busy life. Neither Johnson nor her doctors considered a test for diabetes. In her "Search for the Missing Millions" tour, where she visited seventeen cities, Johnson asserted that millions of people, like her, do not suspect nor seek testing for diabetes yet they may be in the preliminary stages of the disease.

An emergency room test ultimately enabled doctors to diagnose Johnson as a diabetic. Fackelmann (December 14, 1998) notes that "Johnson considers herself lucky. Had her diagnosis been delayed longer, she could have slipped into a coma" (p. 6D).

Outreach for Assistance/Awareness/Action

Because public narratives constitute purposeful, rhetorical efforts, appeals for assistance/ prevention extend naturally from disclosures of personal traumas and connections of that trauma with like-others (people who have a disease or people who lack awareness that they may be at risk, people who lead "ordinary" lives until some tragedy strikes). When Michael J. Fox first disclosed his Parkinson's disease diagnosis, he did not make overt pleas on behalf of funding for Parkinson's disease research or awareness. However, he expressed a belief that he could "help people by talking" (Schneider & Gold, December 7, 1998, p. 128).

Especially in terms of celebrities, references to some larger public good include the more specific (yet general) hope of inspiring or supporting like-others. When Montel Williams, a talk show host, revealed that he has multiple sclerosis, he stressed that "I want to inspire people and show them that they can live and prosper with MS . . . I want others affected by this disease to know that you can get out of bed" (Fackelmann, August 24, 1999, p. 2D). After his stroke, actor Robert Guillaume (October 11, 1999) explained why he accepted an opportunity to present at the 1998 Emmy Award ceremony and, in part, to return to work at *Sports Night*:

> I hope that people who have had strokes will see me and take a positive approach toward their own recoveries. That was the reason I decided to do the Emmys. I welcomed the chance to let people know your life isn't over. I was especially anxious to reach black Americans, since stroke. (p. 80)

However, the dominant push in public narratives stems from an outreach toward some concrete goal, such as fund-raising for research, raising health safety questions, promoting particular health care practices, alerting the public to some disease or danger. For example, Abraham Lieberman, the medical director for the National Parkinson Foundation, told an interviewer that he wanted to solicit Fox's help. "I would say, 'I applaud you for announcing that you have it. Now you should take the next step and help us find a cure for the disease by lending your energy and your spirit and your good ideas to us' " (Davis, December 1, 1998b, p. D1).

On January 18, 2000, Lieberman got his wish. Michael J. Fox announced his plans to leave his sitcom, *Spin City*, in order to concentrate on his family and fighting for a cure for Parkinson's disease (see Bazell, January 19, 2000; Graham, January 19, 2000; Levin & Johnson, January 20, 2000; Rubin, January 20, 2000). "As I saw the outpouring of love and support from so many corners," Fox explained, "I realized that I could mobilize that and hopefully make a difference" (Bazell, January 19, 2000).

Lieberman heralds the importance of a spokesperson who has personal experience with an illness as well as public attention beyond the illness, contending that "the greatest thing for polio was when Franklin D. Roosevelt had polio and chaired the March of Dimes. He was the driving force" (Davis, December 1, 1998b, p. D1). In his article on prostate cancer, Henkel (1997, p. 1) refers to public figures such as Don Ameche, Bill Bixby, Teddy Savalas, and Frank Zappa, noting that "if there's a silver lining to be found amid the clouds of these tragic deaths, it is that the fame of these men has helped spotlight a disease that now ranks as the second most common cancer men get—after skin cancer." Based on research after Magic Johnson's announcement that he tested HIV-positive, Brown and

Basil (1995) argue that ". . . the celebrities we identify with can have an important impact on our health and, in a more general sense, on what we think, what we talk about, and how we act" (p. 366).

As Piver wrote in his book about Gilda Radner's battle with ovarian cancer, "For the first time ever, ovarian cancer had *come out of the closet* because of who Gilda Radner was and what she meant to so many people. Apparently, the days of no newspaper or magazine articles or television specials on ovarian cancer were over" (Piver & Wilder, 1996, p. 20).

After Gilda Radner's death, her husband Gene Wilder recorded a public service announcement, "Please Don't Be Afraid, Just Do It," promoting the use of the blood test CA125. According to Piver and Wilder (1996), "Literally tens of thousands of telephone calls (27,000 the first month) were received from people around the country asking questions about ovarian cancer" (p. 21).

As I will suggest in the following examples, individuals offer personal pleas in a public forum in a variety of ways and for a host of reasons. Whether individuals are primarily lobbying for legislation, pursuing punitive damages, appealing for research and awareness, or raising questions, they voice their stories in the public sphere and make their issues part of the public dialogue about health.

Appeals for Legislation
When he fell from his horse on May 27, 1995, Christopher Reeve's world took an unthinkable turn; the actor who portrayed Superman left the hospital as a ventilator-dependent quadriplegic. Since that fateful day, Reeve has focused on regaining his health—through diligent exercise and through public lobbying for spinal research funding (see Gerosa, 1999). According to Gerosa (1999), Reeve ". . . urged Congress to increase funding for biomedical research by $2 billion at the National Institutes of Health" (p. 240).

Television's *Dr. Quinn, Medicine Woman*, actress Jane Seymour, also exemplifies celebrities who appeal to Congress for legislative support of health-related causes. According to Williams (February 24, 1999), Seymour spoke on behalf of alternative medicines that benefited her father in his struggle with cancer. However, public efforts to enact legislation include "everyday," "ordinary" people who want to prevent others from suffering their fate and to gain help for their own situations.

When Lydia and Ed Bogan could not persuade their health insurance company to cover the cost of a special formula for their daughter, Kaitlynn, they appealed to their state legislator (see Somerson, October 10, 1999). Kaitlynn suffers from food allergies. Somerson (October 10, 1999) reported that "nearly every meat, fruit and vegetable causes blisters, vomiting, bloody diarrhea and weight loss" (p. C1). Following their doctor's recommendation, the Bogans tried Neocate, and according to Mrs. Bogan, "It worked so fast. Within three days we had a new baby" (Somerson, October 10, 1999, p. C1).

Unfortunately, at $40 per day, the expense of Neocate adds up, and the Bogans believe that the health insurance company should pay because it is medically necessary. Mrs. Bogan emphasizes that "we appealed five times. They said no to the wrong person. We are facing Big Brother head-on and we will change the law" (Somerson, October 10, 1999, p. C1). Ohio State Representative Gene Krebs agrees, and he has proposed legislation to require insurance companies to cover prescription formulas (Somerson, October 10, 1999).

Becky Schoonover, an 18-year-old senior in high school, became pregnant during her junior year. After giving birth to her daughter, Taylor, the former honor student and cheerleader learned that Taylor became infected with Group B strep sometime during the birthing process. According to Edwards (February 14, 1999, p. 1E), "Within days, little Taylor developed meningitis that ravaged her brain and left her permanently handicapped."

Although doctors predicted that Taylor would die within a few days, the young mother never gave up. Schoonover told an interviewer that "I read her books, I sang her songs—I was trying to cram everything that you're supposed to do with a child into two days" (Edwards, February 14, 1999, p. 1E).

Remarkably, Taylor lived, albeit with serious disabilities. Through subsequent research, Schoonover discovered that three major medical groups—the American College of Obstetrics and Gynecology, Centers for Disease Control, and the American Academy of Pediatrics—recommend testing for Group B Strep. If a woman tests positive, then she can be given antibiotics that can prevent infection.

Schoonover wants legislation that mandates the test. Although detection of Group B Strep is tricky—a woman could test negative a few weeks prior to birth and then become positive in the interim, as Schoonover did—Schoonover believes that the information is vital to protecting mothers and children, like her daughter Taylor.

Appeals for Justice

While individuals like Schoonover strive to persuade legislators, others launch public battles in the court system as a means of gaining voice and enacting change. For example, a *USA Today* article discussed the series of pending lawsuits against automobile manufacturers for deaths of children from automobile air bags (O'Donnell, July 13, 1998). The article featured the smiling pictures of little ones who perished in air bag-related accidents, including one particularly heart-wrenching photograph of six-year-old Kelsey Trent who lived for nine months as a ventilator-assisted quadriplegic before succumbing to her injuries. O'Donnell (July 13, 1998) reports that cases may be settled out of court because "automakers are particularly skittish about the publicity that will result from having a child-death case go to trial" (p. 3B).

The motion picture, *A Civil Action* (starring John Travolta) featured the efforts of a group of townspeople to obtain justice and action after the illnesses and, in some cases, deaths of children in Woburn, Massachusetts. Apparently, the major employer in the small town, a factory that had ties to two major corporations, routinely dumped chemicals that contaminated the water source.

A mother of one of the ill children, Anne Anderson, persisted in documenting leukemia cases, organizing other parents, and appealing for assistance to local authorities (DiPerna, February 4, 1999). After watching *A Civil Action*, my friend Roger suggested that the producers missed the real story, the story of the townspeople, and DiPerna (February 4, 1999), an environmental policy writer, agrees, noting that "perhaps most unfortunate, the film has depicted the parents as forlorn victims with no choice but to put themselves in the hands of a legal system that supposedly never could render justice" (p. 15A).

After trying to get help from the local authorities, Anderson and the other Woburn parents did seek legal assistance. As DiPerna (February 4, 1999) acknowledged, "Although the courts are not the ideal forum for the resolution of pollution cases, they are for the moment the only forum" (p. 15A). Yet, Jan Schlictmann, the lawyer portrayed by Travolta in the film, explains the challenge of such a legal effort:

> On behalf of the families, my firm waged an extensive legal battle against two of the world's largest corporations, Beatrice Foods and W.R. Grace, implicated in the pollution. However, years of litigation brought more heartache than justice. Only after the war ended, with no clear-cut winners and losers, did federal and state officials acknowledge that the contaminated water was responsible for the city's blight of childhood cancer. The two companies are now part of a $70 million, 50-year cleanup. (p. 15A)

Appeals for Research and Awareness

I grew up watching the CBS soap opera, *Guiding Light*. For over a quarter of a century, the character of Roger Thorpe fluctuated between romantic lead and ruthless villain. Portrayed artfully by Michael Zaslow, Roger Thorpe captivated audiences as a strong, handsome, tough, and irrepressible anti-hero. Brought back from the dead more times than I can remember, his revivals always made sense to me because I could never quite believe that Thorpe could perish—he seemed invincible.

Zaslow's presentation of Thorpe as invincible ultimately cost Zaslow his job. According to a web site that was created by a group of fans named "United in Support of Michael Zaslow" (http:// america.net/~gwp.usmz/), "In April 1997, Michael Zaslow was forced by Procter and Gamble, *Guiding Light*'s parent company, to take a sabbatical from the show and was immediately replaced because his speech had become impaired."

When *Guiding Light* forced Zaslow to take the "sabbatical," Zaslow did not know the source of his symptoms. In November 1997, Zaslow discovered that he suffered from amyotrophic lateral sclerosis (ALS), commonly known as Lou Gehrig's Disease (http://america.net/~gwp/usmz/z-on-als.html). However, even before Zaslow received the fateful diagnosis, Mickey Dwyer-Dobbin, the Procter and Gamble day time head, told *TV Guide*:

> We did *not* fire him. We asked him to take a sabbatical and, during this time, we have been paying him a small stipend. . . . Roger is a powerful, active, sexual, multicolored villain. That's who we need him to be on the GL canvas. We do not need a wizened little old man. And that's what he would have to play in his condition." (Logan, August 9, 1997, p. 25)

Zaslow filed suit against Procter and Gamble (which was subsequently settled out of court), and he began a very public fight to find a cure for ALS (see "Late breaking news," December 29, 1998; Lipton & Wang, December 21, 1998; http://america.net/~gwp/usmz/proj-als.html; http://america.net/~gwp/usmz/z-on-als.html; http://america.net/~gwp/usmz/som519. html). According to a May 19, 1998 article titled "A Call to Arms" in *Soap Opera Magazine*, "ever since he was diagnosed with ALS last year, Michael Zaslow and his wife, Susan Hufford, have been planning to use his 'celebrity' status to create awareness . . . and raise much needed money for research" (http://america.net/~gwp/ usmz/som519.html). Zaslow emphasized that "my friends, colleagues, and I have created ZazAngels to raise funds for ALS research. I want people to see the disease, to see how debilitating it is, and then jump into the fight . . ." (http://america.net/~gwp/usmz/som 519.html).

In May, 1998 Zaslow accepted an opportunity to return to *One Life to Live* as David Renaldi, a striking concert pianist whom he portrayed for six years after one of his "deaths" on *Guiding Light*. Like the actor, the character returned with ALS, increasingly wheelchair-bound and limited to speaking through a keyboard-activated synthesized voice (see Lipton & Wang, December 21, 1998).

Zaslow's return to daytime television generated a groundswell of support for Zaslow as an actor and as a crusader for ALS. As Zaslow stressed, "The show doesn't pull any punches. . . . Once enough people understand what ALS sufferers go through, we will put an end to this rotten disease" (Lipton & Wang, December 21, 1998, p. 72). Fans flooded the United in Support of Michael Zaslow website with praises (http://www.america.net/~gwp/usmz/zaznotes.html):

- The staff on OLTL is to be commended for having the courage to bring Michael Zaslow back as David. The vignette on last Friday's 20/20 was so moving; I was in tears. I remember Michael as the powerful Roger Thorpe on GL, and now he is just as powerful as David on OLTL, only more so.

   Thank you OLTL for giving Michael the chance to show his great acting skills again. Guiding Light should be ashamed of themselves. They are truly cowards in every sense of the word. Michael . . . you are truly an inspiration to all.
- Thank you OLTL for creating such a wonderful story around Michael Zaslow. I have to admit that I knew very little about this disease before it was addressed by OLTL. MZ's courage in what I call the role of his life has reminded me just how near and dear those loved ones are in my life and how very fortunate we are to have our health.
- Thank you so much for giving Michael Zaslow a chance to shine on One Life to Live. I am thrilled that he is back on OLTL & I am now an OLTL fan. As a disabled person and a 17-year Guiding Light viewer, Mr. Zaslow's brutal dismissal from GL in April 1997 was devastating to his many fans and supporters. I saw the 20/20 profile and I was thrilled to see him on TV again. It was heartwrenching to see the hurt in his eyes and on his face when asked about the GL situation, but Mr. Zaslow is a true professional and a class act. I adore him and wish him & his family the best. Thank you, Mr. Zaslow, for hanging in there & being you. You are an inspiration to me.

On December 6, 1998, Zaslow died. However, his wife, Susan Hufford, continues to lobby for ALS research. At the *Soap Opera Digest* award ceremony on February 26, 1999, Zaslow received a posthumous recognition for his incredible work on daytime television, the Editor's Choice Award.

While expressing gratitude for the award, Hufford embraced the opportunity to appeal again to the millions of viewers in the international television audience and the hundreds of individuals in the theater, especially Zaslow's fans. Hufford stressed that "it was you, the fans, who kept him going during his darkest hours. You did not desert him, and I know that you will not desert him now." She persisted urgently, "ZazAngels continues raising funds for ALS research so that this *dreadful, horrible* disease, amyotrophic lateral sclerosis, can finally be eradicated" (*Soap Opera Digest Awards*, February 26, 1999).

In a multiplicity of ways, Zaslow, his family, and his close friends pursued funding for ALS research in the public sphere. Through his interviews and, especially, his work on

One Life to Live, Zaslow offered a raw peek into the human drama of a person with ALS. In contrast with his former image of invincibility (on *Guiding Light* and *One Life to Live*), Zaslow illustrated that anyone can develop ALS, and he connected with those who felt distanced from the disease and those who were already stricken.

Moreover, through his continual, overt, intimate, mediated appeals for contributions to ALS research (as well as his optimism about the potentiality of a "cure by 2000"), Zaslow personalized activism, stressing that "*you* can help." As his co-star, Brynn Thayer emphasized, "ALS can strike anybody . . . [Michael is] making what could have been a very negative thing that has happened to him and his family . . . into an extremely positive thing. We all want to be a part of it and we want you to join us" (http://america.net/~ gwp/ usmz/hotline.html).

Notably, Walter Payton did not take on the fight for increasing organ donations—he quietly awaited a transplant until he developed cancer and became ineligible to receive a donation. However, as one Chicago television station noted, Payton's illness thrust the need for organ donations into the public spotlight, even rekindling a related public debate about the system for distributing available organs (see, e.g., Oldham, February 24, 1999; Weir, February 24, 1999). Some of Payton's family and former teammates capitalized on that spotlight by referring to their own decisions to become organ donors as a result of Payton's wait for a transplant and by urging others to make a similar choice in honor of Payton.

Raising Questions
Our multifaceted media resources permit us to raise public questions about health-related products and recommendations, rather than assuming that FDA approval guarantees safety. Unfortunately, those questions usually get posed after "horror stories" start to emerge.

The Case of the Silicone Breast Implants   In their compelling book, *The Silicone Breast Implant Story*, Vanderford and Smith (1996) describe a public dialogue about the safety of silicone breast implants in Tampa Bay, Florida. Frightened and confused, women observed and participated in the construction of a public narrative about the potential negative consequences of implants. Vanderford and Smith report:

> Women in the Tampa Bay area concerned about the safety of their implants were quite outspoken. They had been featured in some of the early national TV coverage, they were visible in the local press, and they willingly accepted the title Silicone Sisters for their support groups. (p. 15)

Searching for answers, women turned to television programs (such as *Face to Face* with Connie Chung and *Geraldo*) as well as sought outlets to express their personal stories and anxieties (Vanderford & Smith, 1996). According to Vanderford and Smith (1996), women employed mediated reports as ways of introducing their own fears to health care professionals and searching for additional assistance and support. Vanderford and Smith observed, "In the case of silicone breast implants, the news media appear to have played an especially powerful role. We know many women are receiving most, if not all, of their information about implants from the media" (p. 111).

Notably, the public raising of questions about silicone implant safety primarily emerged through the telling of "horror stories" from women who experienced difficulties. According to Vanderford and Smith (1996), "Many women featured in the news reports indicated that their motives to 'go public' with their implant story were to prevent other women from suffering what the storyteller had endured" (p. 112).

Despite the lack of press from women who did not have problems with their implants, Vanderford and Smith (1996) asserted that the narratives rang true, instead of seeming reactionary or poorly reasoned. As I will detail in the next chapter, individuals in contemporary society struggle to sort through rampant, competing messages in our efforts to prioritize information and to make decisions. In this case, especially because the narratives tended to cast the physicians in the villain role (as opposed to the women as trusting heroines), they resonated with media audiences. Consistent with the postmodern distrust of science and scientific "experts" (see Chapter 2), even if women could not understand the desire to get an implant, they *could* believe that health care professionals might not take time to listen or be equipped to offer the best advice. Vanderford and Smith (1996) stressed that "the horror stories combined not only with other media illness stories, but also with many patients' personal experiences."

Case of Vaccinations   Tiny Sarah Frances weighed less than three and a half pounds when she was born two months premature. Like most babies (including my own Chelsea Meagan), Sarah received a Hepatitis B vaccination prior to her release from the hospital at three weeks of age. When her parents, Natalie and Deven Korzine, took her to the doctor for a two-month checkup, they expressed concern about further vaccinations because Sarah only weighed around six pounds. After reassuring the Korzines, the doctor administered the usual round of vaccinations for a two-month old baby, despite the fact that Sarah was only a few days older than her original due date (Manning, August 3, 1999). Manning reports that "twelve hours later, the baby was dead. . . . The cause of death was ruled 'undetermined,' but Natalie says a pathologist told her it was a 'vaccine-related death. Her little system was bombarded too much' " (p. 2A).

Stories like Sarah's have gained considerable coverage in the media, filled with heartbroken parents' pleas for authorities to reexamine immunization practices, escalating fears similar to one of my interview participants whom I discussed earlier in Chapter 1. According to Manning (August 16, 1999), "A stunning increase in the number of children diagnosed with autism has schools straining to provide services and health officials urgently seeking answers" (p. D1). Importantly, Manning continued, "And the increases are fueling a grassroots movement of parents determined to expose what they believe is a connection between autism and vaccines" (p. D1).

However, as in the case with silicone breast implants, the public dialogue about the safety of vaccinations raises more questions than poses answers. According to Manning (August 16, 1999), "Linked through Internet chat rooms and Web sites, parents of kids with autism are . . . demanding research into origins and treatments for the neurological disorder" (p. 2A), pleading for evidence that counters their collective hunch that vaccinations (the MMR one, in particular) can cause autism. Some parents even testified before a congressional committee that was formed by Representative Dan Burton after his own grandson developed autism (see Manning, August 3, 1999).

However, the lobby in support of vaccinations appears more vocal in the public sphere than the proponents of silicone breast implants, a lobby that includes a formal, organized push to persuade parents to immunize their children (see Smith, 1997). Notably, the individuals and organizations that herald the safety of vaccinations harken to "scientific proof," treating the tragic narratives as "random stories" and "isolated instances" of problems.

Merck & Co., the company that produces the MMR vaccines, denies a link between autism and its product (see Manning, August 16, 1999). Pediatricians, such as Dr. Mark Rosenberg of Illinois, acknowledge that "these individual situations are obviously tragic." However, he considers them to be tragic anomalies that do not warrant widespread policy change (see Manning, August 3, 1999, p. 2A).

Fellow parents have even joined the public dialogue in favor of vaccinations. After the death of their son, Corey, Ben and Pam Jackson of New Orleans believe that a vaccination for pneumococcus bacteria (which causes meningitis) should be added to the list of requirements. Ben Jackson emphasizes the benefits of vaccination, despite reports of possible negative side effects, arguing "If there is a vaccine out there that can save a child from dying, I will be lining up anybody I can to let them know the risks of [meningitis]" (Manning, November 23, 1999, p. 11D). As Trish Parnell, Director of Parents of Kids with Infectious Diseases, wrote in a letter to the editor of *USA Today* (August 11, 1999):

> As parents of children who have died or have been made ill from infectious diseases, we understand the pain that comes when it's your child who's affected. Should science prove that this or any other vaccine is causing more harm than good, we will stand with all those concerned with children's health and demand that the vaccine be removed from the market. At this point there is not science to back up such assumptions, and we must not leave children unprotected from vaccine-preventable diseases. (p. 14A).

Regardless of possible policy outcomes, the public raising of questions about vaccinations, a taken-for-granted necessity of visits to the doctor by preschool children, has stirred a public debate. Given the pervasiveness of support for vaccinations, the storytellers needed to start with questioning vaccination practices, rather than beginning with an appeal for policy change. By positioning their cause as "concerned parents who want answers," they can more easily identify with other parents and lovers of children who want the best for kids without seeming like extremists. Reasonable people want to ensure safety, and additional research and verification seems like a more logical next step than encouraging parents not to vaccinate their children.

However, every day, children go to the doctor to receive vaccinations—what happens in the interim, between the raising of questions and the offering of answers? As in the case of "mad cow disease" in England, people wait and uncertainly—or perhaps, ignorantly— consume products without a clear understanding of possible risks.

Promoting Accountability

In their book, *Mad Cows and Mother's Milk: The Perils of Poor Risk Communication*, Powell and Leiss (1997) chronicle concern over British beef products, beginning in the mid-1980s. Throughout the saga, British officials asserted that cows that were infected with

BSE [bovine spongiform encephalopathy], also known as "mad cow disease," posed no risk to humans because the disease could not be transmitted between species. In 1995, stories of unexplained fatalities started to slip into the news, generating alarm and responses of continued denial from authorities. Noting the example of a teenage girl from Wales who fell into a coma, Powell and Leiss (1997) reported:

> Her relatives blamed her illness on eating hamburgers contaminated with beef from cattle with BSE [bovine spongiform encephalopathy]. The story also quoted prominent scientists who said anything unusual—like two teenagers [the Wales girl and a British boy] dying from CJD [Creutzfeldt-Jakob disease]—was cause for concern. In response, the government said there would be no inquiry into the death of the boy and insisted, "We continue to believe there's no evidence that BSE can cause CJD in humans." (p. 7)

More cases of deaths from CJD started to appear in the British press, mostly of teenagers and farmers. However, the Ministry of Agriculture continued its adamant assertion that beef products bore no danger to British citizens. According to Powell and Leiss (1997), however, ". . . the debate bounced back and forth, with industry and government saying there was no scientific evidence that BSE could cross the species barrier into humans, and the public saying, in effect, 'we don't believe you'" (p. 8).

When an advisory committee finally conceded a "most likely" link between consumption of beef that was contaminated with BSE and human affliction with CJD in 1996 (Powell & Leiss, 1997, p. 12), the Ministry of Agriculture persisted in damage control efforts, despite a concurrent estimate by a researcher that ". . . by 2010 as many as ten million Britons might have CJD, assuming high infectivity" (Powell & Leiss, 1997, p. 13).

Unlike representatives of Jack-in-the-Box restaurant in the United States, who admitted responsibility for E. coli–related deaths within a week, the British government hedged on acknowledging health risks from infected beef for over a decade (Powell & Leiss, 1997). As Powell and Leiss (1997) explained, "The Jack-in-the-Box outbreak had all the elements of a dramatic story—at least in the United States. Children were involved; the risk was relatively unknown and unfamiliar" (p. 96), resulting in rampant public indignation over apparent bumbling of food safety issues. Amid such public wrath, in that case, government and industry officials responded swiftly to improve beef inspection practices, lessening the likelihood of diminished consumer confidence in beef products.

Powell and Leiss (1997) pointed to a "vacuum" between the scientific assessment of a risk and the public assessment of a risk. That vacuum can prove alarming as people raise questions about items or practices, especially common ones, that may have the potential to jeopardize health. Powell and Leiss contended:

> Society as well as nature abhors a vacuum, and so it is filled from other sources [than science]. For example, events reported in the media (some of them alarming) become the substantial basis of the public framing of these risks; or an interest group takes up the challenge and fills the vacuum with its own information and perspectives; or the intuitively based fears and concerns of individuals simply grow and spread until they become a substantial consensus in the arena of public opinion; or the vacuum is filled by the soothing expressions beloved of politicians: "there is no risk of . . . (fill in the blank)." (pp. 31–32)

Funded Health Promotion Campaigns

When public officials recognize a health threat, though, health promotion campaigns enable them to share information with at-risk individuals and to advocate "safe" health behaviors. Unlike personally driven appeals to gain assistance or awareness, health promotion campaigns constitute structured, organized, funded efforts to promote some sort of health care practice (see, e.g., Atkin & Wallack, 1990; Backer & Rogers, 1993; Backer, Rogers, & Sopory, 1992; Clift & Freimuth, 1995; Downie, Tannahill, & Tannahill, 1996; Huff & Kline, 1999; Maibach & Parrott, 1995; McKenzie & Smeltzer, 1997; Piotrow, Kincaid, Rimon II, & Rinehart, 1997; Ratzan, 1994a, 1994b; Rogers, 1994; Salmon, 1989; Singhal & Rogers, 1999; Webb, 1994). Clift and Freimuth (1995) suggest that health communication, in this sense, involves " . . . an approach which attempts to change a set of behaviors in a large-scale target audience regarding a specific problem in a predefined period of time" (p. 68).

As such, health campaigns focus on identifying some need, setting goals and objectives of the campaign effort, planning ways of addressing that need, implementing communication strategies to accomplish goals and objectives, and evaluating impacts of the campaign (see, e.g., Atkin & Wallack, 1990; Backer et al., 1992; Clift & Freimuth, 1995; McKenzie & Smeltzer, 1997; Piotrow et al., 1997; Rogers, 1994; Salmon, 1989; Singhal & Rogers, 1999; Webb, 1994). Although health campaigns adhere to a variety of models and theoretical frameworks (such as social marketing or diffusion of innovations), they share a focus on goal-oriented persuasion by some agency or organization—health campaigns emphasize a preferred behavioral change by a predefined group of people (see Clift & Freimuth, 1995).

Notably, similar to personal appeals for assistance, health campaigns depend on highlighting personal traumas and demonstrating connectedness with multiple like-others as part of their persuasive effort. Whether referring to fictional characters or actual people, campaigns facilitate the personalization of a health-related problem or practice by viewers/readers as a basis for possible decisions to enact different health behaviors.

Entertainment–Education

Thus far in this chapter, I have referred to Nancy's bout with ovarian cancer on *thirtysomething*, Murphy's struggle with breast cancer on *Murphy Brown*, and David's affliction with ALS on *One Life to Live*. These storylines exemplify health-related plots that routinely unfold on television shows and, in countries beyond the United States, on radio and television (see related work by Glik, Berkanovic, Stone, Ibarra, et al., 1998; Neuendorf, 1990; Signorielli, 1990). As Singhal and Rogers (1999) detail in their excellent review of entertainment–education, mediated stories constitute an important resource for disseminating information about health concerns.

Goal

Singhal and Rogers (1999) define entertainment–education as "the process of purposely designing and implementing a media message to both entertain and educate, in order to increase audience knowledge about an educational issue, create favorable attitudes, and change overt behavior" (p. xii). As the fan postings about Michael Zaslow indicate, story-lines in conventional soap operas (such as those in the United States) can facilitate under-standing and empathy about a disease. Usually, within the United States, plots about health-related issues stem from a producer's desire to tell a particular story as well as to generate commercial success—that is, a story that will captivate an audience. *All My Children*, however, does routinely promote health practices within storylines and even in pub-lic service announcements following select episodes (see Klingle & Aune, 1994).

Unlike most of the shows that air in the United States, though, Singhal and Rogers (1999) claim that entertainment–education soap operas include education as a primary goal (along with commercial and entertainment success). Frequently funded and assisted by agencies such as Population Communication Services (PCS), based at Johns Hopkins Uni-versity (see Piotrow et al., 1997; Singhal & Rogers, 1999), writers/producers overtly focus on ways of inspiring audience change after observing media role models.

For example, Singhal and Rogers (1999) stress that "the history of the entertain-ment–education strategy in television is inextricably linked with the work of Miguel Sabido, a writer–producer–director of theater and television in Mexico" (p. 47). In his soap opera, *Acompaname* (Come Along With Me), Sabido employed the tenants of social learning theory as he encouraged family planning, a difficult topic in a predominantly Catholic country. The soap opera featured three sisters and the implications of family planning (and lack thereof) in their married lives. Singhal and Rogers (1999) report:

> Data provided by Mexico's national family planning program showed that during the 1976–1977 year when *Acompaname* was on the air, 562,464 individuals adopted family planning at government health clinics, an increase of 33% over the previous year. The num-ber of phone calls per month to the national family planning program increased from zero to 500. Most callers said they were motivated by *Acompaname* to seek such information (the telephone number was shown at the end of each episode). (p. 57)

India's soap opera, *Tinka Tinka Sukh*, also emphasized family planning and other pro-social issues (see Singhal & Rogers, 1999, as well as related work by Piotrow et al., 1997). Fan correspondence to All India Radio (AIR), which broadcast the show, from villagers in Lutsaan echoed the show's standpoint that "as the cost of living rises, having more children than one can afford is inviting trouble. . . . This message of *Tinka Tinka Sukh* comes across very clearly" (Singhal & Rogers, 1999, p. 1).

Parasocial Identification

Viewers of entertainment–education arrive at epiphanies about health and wellness prac-tices through engagement with the characters as well as interactions with others about the show; the process of persuasion involves a more complicated, circular process than a uni-directional one. Papa, Singhal, Law, Sood, and Rogers (1998) point to the evolution of parasocial relationships between viewers and characters, noting that "parasocial interac-tion can promote strong levels of identification between media characters and audience members who then reflect carefully on the educational content of the E-E program" (p. 24). As audience members turn to each other for discussions of content, Papa and col-leagues (1998) explain that "these conversations create a socially constructed learning environment in which people evaluate previously held thoughts and behaviors, consider new behavioral options, and identify steps to initiate social improvement" (p. 25).

Notably, entertainment–education also fits neatly within the narrative frame. Characters struggle with plot-driven personal trauma, and through parasocial interactions between viewers and characters, viewers connect with characters. If writers script the characters well, their lives, choices, utterances, and relationships ring true to viewers; viewers can identify with them. Even if those viewers might not have made the same choices as the characters, the characters' decisions make sense because of their consistence with the essence of the particular character and with the character's specific situation. Although characters on soap operas never speak directly to viewers with clear-cut "do this" or "do that" messages, viewers can learn "preferred" behavior as they observe the consequentiality of actions for their beloved characters. Because viewers often feel a bond with characters, they can truly "feel their pain."

Informational Persuasion

A storyboard for a Bayer aspirin commercial titled, "EKG Revised," illustrates the EKG of someone who might be having a heart attack. The narrator of the commercial encourages the person to summon an ambulance, take a Bayer aspirin, and call a doctor. According to the commercial, "It's now been proven that aspirin can do more than help prevent second heart attacks. Now Bayer may actually help stop you from dying if you take it during a heart attack."

A magazine advertisement for PAPNET shows a picture of a smiling woman with this quotation: "I never questioned my Pap smear results. Then my doctor told me PAPNET found missed precancerous cells and said don't panic, be thankful we caught it early." According to the ad, "PAPNET is the only test that double-checks your Pap smear and displays suspect cells on a video monitor for detailed expert analysis."

Following the narrative format, these advertisements tell the stories of two individuals while offering information. Although appealing because of the stories, the ads do not constitute entertainment–education because readers gain little else beyond a persuasive presentation of informative material.

Corporations, such as pharmaceutical companies and professional laboratories, engage in considerable informational persuasion through print, media, and Internet advertising as well as product displays, special promotions, and direct appeals to physicians and consumers. Beyond the advertising efforts of companies, however, health-related foundations also rely on informational persuasion as a means of encouraging individuals to make healthy life choices (see Atkin & Wallack, 1990; Bracht, 1990; Edgar, Fitzpatrick, & Freimuth, 1992; Freimuth et al., 1989; Hussein, 1998; Maibach & Parrott, 1995; Piotrow et al., 1997; Ratzan, 1993; Ratzan, Payne, & Massett, 1994; Rogers, 1994; Svenkerud & Singhal, 1998; Witte, 1994; Witte, Cameron, Lapinski, & Nzyuko, 1998).

Goal
With the global population escalating per second, family planning exemplifies a private decision with significant personal *and* societal consequences (see Piotrow et al., 1997). In their book, Piotrow and colleagues describe fifteen years of program development and

evaluation for family planning and reproductive health initiatives, sponsored by Population Communication Services [PCS] in the Center for Communication Programs at Johns Hopkins School of Hygiene and Public Health. Notably, the PCS does not stand alone in its work to bring awareness and action with regard to reproductive and sexual health practices and population control; citing a study by the United Nations Population Fund, Piotrow and colleagues (1997) stated, "by the mid-1990s more than 168 countries had adopted national population development policies" (p. 8).

Stressing a theoretically driven, goal-oriented approach to promoting behavioral change, Piotrow and colleagues (1997) note that "PCS works in close partnership with dozens of government agencies, private nongovernmental organizations, and commercial firms in more than 50 countries" (p. 13), contributing support for assessing needs, producing effective communication materials, offering technical aid, implementing programs, and evaluating impacts. According to Piotrow and colleagues, "Population Communication Services has become an acknowledged leader in family planning communication. Annual budgets have increased from about $2 million in 1983 to more than $20 million in 1997" (pp. 12–13).

Strategies

In order to reach target audiences in diverse cultures, Piotrow and colleagues (1997, p. 73) stress that "a good strategy always employs a multichannel, mutually reinforcing approach appropriate to the audience and prevailing conditions," including interpersonal, group, and mass media efforts. In addition to entertainment–education efforts, examples of communication strategies include:

- The *jiggasha* approach in Bangladesh wherein workers educate village opinion leaders who then hold discussion groups with other women. According to Piotrow and colleagues (1997), "Research finds that, where highly influential women are active in *jiggashas*, modern contraceptive use is generally high" (p. 35).
- A video and comic book with the theme "Street-smart youth can stay strong without AIDS" for street youth in Brazil, targeted to youth who ". . . faced death every day. Immediate survival, not future disease, was their concern" (Piotrow et al., 1997, p. 36).
- The Gold Star campaign in Egypt in which government family planning clinics can earn and display a Gold Star as a mark of quality and excellence in care. According to Piotrow and colleagues (1997), "It is the first nationwide family planning communication strategy in a developing country focused on promoting quality of care and positioning government clinics as a source of high-quality care" (p. 65).

Related to sexual health and family planning initiatives, several health campaigns involve awareness about personal ways to limit the risk of HIV infection (see, e.g., Chay-Nemeth, 1998; Edgar et al., 1992; Morisky & Coan, 1998; Ratzan, 1993, Ratzan et al.; Svenkerud & Singhal, 1998; Witte, 1991–1992; Witte et al., 1998; as well as a related article by Hussein, 1998). Notably, as with the related family planning campaigns, HIV/AIDS awareness/action initiatives require sensitive discussion of very personal choices (e.g., sexual practices, drug use, number and type of interpersonal relationships) by individuals in diverse sociocultural-economic situations.

Promoting the "Better Choices"

However, all health campaigns truly deal with "personal" issues and choices. We make our life choices based on our array of (potentially conflicting) spiritual, cultural, relational, institutional, political, and economic allegiances, beliefs, traditions, and values. We may not always do something that seems "logical," "practical," "reasonable," or "no big deal" to others.

Although cancer screening might be a "logical" practice, some still avoid it, necessitating campaigns to encourage people to seek testing for various forms of cancer. For example, according to Davis (March 3, 1999), "of the 56,000 people who will die from [colorectal cancer] this year, federal officials think 30,000 could have been saved with screening" (p. D1). Thus, the Centers for Disease Control and Prevention, the Health Care Financing Administration, and the National Cancer Institute have teamed for a new campaign to promote colorectal cancer screenings (see Davis, March 3, 1999).

Although many people love to play outdoors during sunny weather, the dangers of even casual exposure to the sun may not be actively considered, in spite of increased attention skin cancer. In an advertisement supplement to *USA Today*, the American Academy of Dermatologists emphasized the need for "sun safety 101" and regular skin exams. More formal campaigns with regard to skin cancer also focus on prevention practices in general as well as during recreational activities (see, e.g., Buller & Borland, 1999; Parrott, Duggan, Cremo, Eckles, Jones, & Steiner, 1999).

Although the dangers of drugs and cigarette smoking get preached from the very early elementary school grades (as well as in a host of television shows and movies), people still use illegal drugs and smoke cigarettes, thus necessitating the need to attempt new means of persuasion through innovative health campaigns (see, e.g., Elwood & Ataabadi, 1996). In one campaign, the Office of National Drug Control Policy encourages grandparents to talk to their grandchildren about the hazards of drug use (see AP, December 27, 1998). Campaigns that discourage smoking include combinations of interpersonal influences, informational literature, and support resources for resisting peer pressure and for ending addiction (see, e.g., Hafstad & Aaro, 1997; Perry, 1996).

Like personal appeals for assistance and action, organized public health campaigns strive to involve individuals in the enactment of proactive health behaviors. As I will detail in the next chapter, issues of self-efficacy and individual empowerment have emerged as critical aspects of persuasive attempts. Through artful rhetorical efforts, health concerns get positioned for the reader or viewer as "my" or "our" problem, not "someone else's," something that other reasonable good people in similar situations need to address as well. Good health promotion campaigns enable individuals to participate in health narratives, if only in their reflections about the implications of problems for them in their own lived realities.

Ethical Implications of Public Dialogues about Health

The sun spilled in the window of the internal medicine doctor's office. What a beautiful March afternoon, I thought, a wonderful beginning of spring break. I chuckled to myself—some break. I hadn't worked in nearly ten weeks so I could hardly "take a break." Wait,

I thought quickly, what about a break from being sick, a break from the ER, a break from the hospital? I had managed to drive up to Columbus for two consecutive weeks without a trip to the hospital; I must be setting some sort of record for myself. I started to visualize my continued break from ill health by thinking about all of the things that I could do for the next week before the start of the new quarter and a return to work—going to a movie, going to a mall, ahhh, going shopping without getting tired. I looked longingly out of the window and yearned to play tennis . . . soon, I thought, very soon.

"Well, you're in a good mood," Dr. L. said as she came in the door and introduced herself.

"It's sunny out," I responded.

Dr. L. bemoaned the fact that we were both stuck in a doctor's office on such a pretty day, and she asked questions about my medical history, commiserating with me about the original wrist break, the inadequate break reset, the surgery, the staph infection. She began to examine my eyes, my throat, my lungs. I told her that I continued to suffer from fatigue. She inquired about my wrist, and I complained that I must have worked it too hard during OT that morning. She picked up my wrist and studied it from side to side.

"You have an infection here," she said.

"What?" I responded, sitting up straighter and searching my arm myself.

"You have cellulitis here," Dr. L. noted, pointing to a thin red streak from the start of my wrist and running up my forearm. "We need to find out what kind it is and get you started on antibiotics again."

I couldn't speak. My jaw dropped, and I shook my head, but I couldn't force words to come. My fever had been elevated when the nurse took my temperature, but I never suspected that the infection had returned. When my wrist had throbbed that morning, I had attributed the pain to the stress of a hard rehab session, not infection, never infection, not again. "Why?" I finally managed to ask.

Dr. L. sighed and tried to explain, "Well, orthopedics is a primary area for infection. Because your bones are being moved around, and your bones don't like being moved around, if there is any chance for infection, it will happen around where the bones shifted. In your case, the staph infection must have lain dormant and then re-emerged when you went off the Augmentin. It resurfaced around an area where you were very vulnerable, around the metal plate and where you've been working the wrist."

Dr. L. informed me that I would either need another prescription of Augmentin or more IV therapy and then left to send in the nurse to draw a blood sample. She closed the door behind her, and tears filled my eyes. I hadn't anticipated a sudden thunderstorm; nothing in the forecast even hinted at such a cloudy turn of events.

The girls were in Virginia for spring break, but I had to get home to let our Sheltie, Sunni, out. I tried to imagine how I could call Roger and ask him to walk Sunni without telling him about the infection. I wanted to be done with being sick. I glanced down at the all-too-familiar hospital smock that I had to put on for the examination, and wet splashes spilled to my cheeks.

When the nurse finally returned to collect the blood sample, she needed an instruction sheet to guide her through collecting blood—another rookie. What are the odds, I thought? Why?

A quick analysis of one of the blood samples indicated that my white blood cell count was a 4, even a bit below normal range and certainly not elevated. Good, I thought, I could go home. I wanted to get home, to shut the blinds, to close out the sounds of thunder from yet another storm. I walked out from Dr. L.'s office into the brightness and warmth of the sun, but I could only sense gray and cold. Winter had returned.

As I drove back to Athens, I began to feel worse. I ached. I felt dizzy. I felt drained. My wrist looked swollen and increasingly redder, and my hip even hurt. Am I a nut, I wondered? Is this psychosomatic? Am I imagining all of this? Upon my return, I phoned Keri, the OT, who apologized for not catching the red streak. I called Dr. D., the gruff orthopedic resident (who had pulled the PICC line) who was covering again for Dr. T. The man only leaves town when something else goes wrong with me, I thought. Hmm, maybe something only goes wrong with me because he leaves town—it's a plot, I speculated. Dr. D. arrogantly assured me that Dr. L. did not know what she was talking about, that I couldn't have another infection, and that Dr. L. wouldn't know an infection if it bit her. I didn't know what to think; I'm not sure that I could think—my body and brain had been numbed by an emotional stun gun.

The next day, Roger and I drove back up to Columbus to meet with Dr. D. As soon as they saw me walk into the reception area, Keri and Connie summoned me back to the OT room, eager to evaluate my arm and to see what had been detected. Keri, Connie, and then Dr. T.'s nurse, Katie, Dr. T.'s secretary, Lois, and one of Dr. T.'s colleagues' secretary, Joyce, hovered around my arm. All agreed on redness, but none could see a streak. Perhaps it's gone away, I thought. Perhaps, Dr. L. did not know what she was seeing after all. Hope, I thought, there's hope that I can get out of here and see a movie. Hmmm, I wondered if Connie would let me do an OT session since we had obviously driven all of the way to Columbus for nothing.

Before I could ask, though, Katie noticed the clock. Dr. D. was still at the hospital, and the time neared 5 P.M. Joyce suggested that we pull my lab reports up on the computer to see if I needed to stick around to talk with Dr. D. If I had an infection, then I should go to the ER because all of the other doctors in Dr. T.'s practice were leaving soon for the day, and Dr. D. would not have anyone to consult for help. If I didn't really have an infection, then I could go home.

"What are the odds?" Katie said as she looked over the report.

"What?" I asked, as I moved closer to her and scanned the report for relevant information.

"Preliminary report of positive staph. I'll be darned. I could have sworn that you didn't have an infection," Katie noted, shaking her head.

I sat down quickly, and Katie kneeled by me. "Okay," she asserted, "here's what we need to do. We'll have the resident meet you in the ER—"

"No, I don't want to go back there," I interrupted.

"You don't have a choice. Stress your history. Tell her that you've been an outlier. Emphasize your history with infection," Katie directed.

Roger pulled me to my feet, and we headed down the corridor, down the steps, through the entrance way and into another beautiful, bright afternoon outside. I didn't know what to believe. Even more than during my original struggles with my wrist and then my hip and then the PICC line, I felt incredible dissonance. Should I believe Dr. L.? Should I believe the second blood test that would seem to conflict with the white blood cell count from the previous day? Should I believe the resident? Should I believe all of the OTs and people in Dr. T.'s office? The disparate perspectives swirled through my head as we hit hectic rush-hour traffic in a now-routine commute to the hospital.

Multiplicity of Public and Personal Perspectives

Although to a much lesser extent, my confusion about the possible recurrence of the staph infection resembles the plethora of clashing and clambering perspectives in the public sphere. From paid promotions by pharmaceutical companies to PR campaigns for hospitals and managed care organizations to personal appeals for assistance and awareness to public health campaigns that advocate preferred health practices, competing public dialogues about health mirror overgrown thickets more than clear paths. How can a person figure out which way to proceed or where to turn without tripping or getting miserably lost? What can one believe or trust as true?

Habermas and his colleagues would dub the jumbled and confusing public sphere a muddled mess, yet the invitational media, combined with appeals to consumerism, provides everyone with some sort of mediated stump as a soap box and virtually yanks them to their feet. How can we listen when the combined shouts deafen us?

Fisher offers us a way of understanding how we assess the narrative rationality of narratives; however, his paradigm cannot shine light on how we prioritize conflicting narratives that all ring true with various aspects of our multifaceted identities. While I will discuss decision-prioritizing practices in the next chapter, the almost frantic activity in the public sphere over health care issues raises an important ethical question that I pose to conclude this chapter: To what extent do people/organizations have the obligation or right to participate in the public sphere in their preferred way?

Right to Privacy Versus Obligation to Serve

After learning that a tabloid newspaper planned to release the news that his wife, Kathy, has been diagnosed with multiple sclerosis, Kevin Newman, anchor of *Good Morning America*, made the difficult decision to disclose the news himself. In his statement, Newman closed by noting that "I thank you for respecting my family's privacy in this matter" (Johnson, October 26, 1998, p. 2D). According to Johnson (October 26, 1998), "Newman is bound to find support from his colleagues. These days, medical conditions that used to be considered private often become public" (p. 2D).

Even in the post–Princess Diana era, a time of criticism of the press for relentlessly pursuing the personal lives of celebrities, few, if any, issues seem off-limits or too personal. For example, despite her refusal to discuss her affliction with Parkinson's disease, the press continues to focus on U.S. Attorney General Janet Reno's illness, even to the point of quoting doctors who disagree with her course of treatment without examining her firsthand (see Johnson & Willing, June 17, 1999). According to Johnson and Willing (June 17, 1999), "All of the attention rankles Reno, who just wants to put in her 12-to-18 hour workdays with a minimum of bother . . . " (p. D1).

However, satisfying "inquiring minds" sells, and the willingness of some public figures to talk intimately about private concerns blurs the boundary between topics that may or may not legitimately be probed—some people bare their souls while others bar their doors. For example, Cathy Hainer, a reporter for *USA Today*, chronicled her tragic battle with breast cancer for the paper (e.g., see Hainer, December 6, 1999; Wilson, December 16, 1999). After a two-year struggle, she succumbed to the illness on December 14, 1999. As Tom Curley, president and publisher of *USA Today* argues, "Cathy's story moved a nation" (Wilson, December 16, 1999, p. 1D). One reader wrote that Hainer's death ". . . is so gut wrenching" (Feral, December 17, 1999, p. 30A). Another reader praised Hainer's ability "to share her most intimate thoughts and feelings about [cancer's] affect on her life" (Cleveland, December 9, 1999, p. 18A).

Johnson (October 26, 1998) notes other news reporters who have jumped into the public dialogue about health as a result of personal health traumas:

> ABC's Sam Donaldson and NBC's *Today* producer Jeff Zucker have talked at length about their battles with cancer. *Today* co-anchor Katie Couric has become a crusader for cancer awareness since January, when her husband, Jay Monahan, died of colon cancer. *Dateline NBC* anchor Stone Phillips and his wife, Debra, have talked publicly about her battle with MS. (p. 2D)

Ethically, though, when should public figures be afforded a right to privacy on health issues? Conversely, given the potential public health benefits of celebrity examples, when should public figures consider such health disclosures to be a civic obligation, something that they "should do" for the public good? For example, a cover story on Montel Williams' diagnosis of MS prompted conflicting reader reactions. One reader criticized the space given to celebrity afflictions while others retorted that the story could raise awareness and inspire individuals. As one defender of the Williams story recalled, ". . . I was extremely ill at the time Christopher Reeve had his accident. Your stories about him made me feel that if he could deal with his problems, I could certainly deal with mine" (De Stafano, January 17, 2000, p. 4).

Media Mistakes and Media Literacy

From staging the work world of health care professionals (see e.g., Lupton & McLean, 1998; Turow, 1989) to showcasing illness (see e.g., Hilton, October 22, 1999; Sharf & Freimuth, 1993; Sharf, Freimuth, Greenspon, & Plotnick, 1996), the mass media, television in particular, offers a plethora of images about health care. Even setting aside the array of paid advertisements for products and services, mediated messages from television shows, magazine articles, and newspaper headings bombard us with suggestions, criticisms, horror stories, and heart-wrenching dramas. What should one trust? If something appears on television, whether positioned as fact or fiction, should it count as "isolated instance" or "compelling proof" of a health risk or benefit? For example, I mentioned the Bayer aspirin campaign earlier. On January 11, 2000, the FTC ordered Bayer to buffer its claim by acknowledging publicly that "frequent aspirin use isn't right for everyone" (Appleby, January 12, 2000, p. 2B). According to Appleby, "Bayer went too far touting the drug's benefits" (p. 2B).

Ang (1996) and others argue that contemporary consumers of mediated messages wrestle with interpreting and contextualizing meanings in terms of their disparate lived realities. Although we can no longer conceptualize audiences as passive receivers, readings of mediated messages can range from face value acceptance to critical, perhaps cynical, skepticism about the believability of a claim to sheer confusion about how to interpret or act on a message, depending on the fear, confidence, prior knowledge, desperation, cultural/political/religious perspectives, and so on, of individual audience members (see, e.g., Chew, Palmer, & Kim, 1998; Hall & Ward, February 23, 1999; McMahan, Witte, & Meyer, 1998).

The hit television drama, *ER*, highlights the fallibility of the medical profession. In the 1999 Thanksgiving episode, nurse Carol Hathaway went into labor with her twins. After a few minor plot twists, she gave birth to the first baby, a little girl. Following a few more major plot twists, doctors whisked Hathaway into the operating room for an emergency c-section. Her doctor, a substitute for her obstetrician of choice, noted heavy bleeding and prepared to begin a hysterectomy. Urged by a desperate Hathaway, her friend, breathing partner, and colleague, ER doc Dr. Mark Greene, pleaded with the doctor to reconsider. Ultimately, Hathaway awakened in her room to find her twin baby girls, and she joyously discovered that Mark prevented the hysterectomy. Her delivery nurse noted that "while I wouldn't admit this outside of this room, you owe your ovaries to your friend here," implying that the doctor mistakenly wanted to perform the hysterectomy without exhausting efforts to stop the bleeding in another manner.

In cases such as this birthing sequence, physician error in judgment under pressure rings true with contemporary skepticism of the medical profession—all-too-human doctors make mistakes. *ER* likely did not misrepresent something that could not legitimately occur (although the portrayal of such error could work to reify public fears about unnecessary procedures). However, according to Hilton (October 22, 1999), *ER* did commit an error during a different episode that ". . . could mislead millions of people about their most basic right as patients" (p. 4).

Depictions of Medical Accuracy

In their dramatization of health care, media sources characterize health care professionals as certain types of people, usually with varying degrees of fallibility and compassion, to health care seekers (see, e.g., Pfau, Mullen, & Garrow, 1995; Wober & Gunter, 1985-86). As one of our interview participants, Alex, noted, "A lot of [ideas about health care] is stereotyping from the television. What you see on television are not the actual doctors' mistakes; it is the stereotype about the doctor that scares people."

On *ER*, a young woman entered with her father. Suffering from terminal cancer, the woman fought to breathe. Apparently, according to the account of her father, the woman experienced a similar attack earlier and decided to sign an advance directive that expressed her desire to refuse life-saving measures such as ventilation (see Hilton, October 22, 1999). However, the advance directive only comes into play when the patient can no longer voice his or her interests. In this case, the patient woke after her father left the room and begged Dr. Greene to assist her. After verifying her request, Greene hooked the woman up to a ventilator. When the father returned and objected strenuously to Greene's intervention in his daughter's process of dying, Greene stated that the young woman changed her mind.

Critically, the show did not emphasize that the young woman had the right to renege her decision at any point and that the beligerent father did not have the right to invoke the advance directive when his daughter consciously revoked it. Greene's superior sided with the father, but little could be done since the ventilator had been started.

In fairness to *ER*'s handling of the ethical dilemma, the young woman only spoke while Greene was alone with her in the room. Thus, he lacked witnesses that the young woman regained consciousness long enough to ask for the ventilation. However, the show did not clarify that the patient has a legal right to change her mind, whether she has witnesses or not. In so doing, the show could have left doubt in viewers' minds about their rights in similar situations.

As Sharf and Freimuth (1993) and Sharf and colleagues (1996) note in their analyses of Nancy's struggle with ovarian cancer on *thirtysomething*, the details of ovarian cancer on the show did not always mirror usual patterns in "real life." Even though most shows utilize health consultants to advise stories, the most well-intended plots and scripts or reporting of issues in the news can suffer from single perspectives, oversimplification of procedures or complications, overlooked details, and/or political and/or economic bias (see, e.g., Cohen & Solomon, 1995; Moyer, Greener, Beauvais, & Salovey, 1995). For example, in their analysis of reports about breast cancer and mammography in the popular press, Moyer and colleagues (1995) found ". . . substantial inaccuracy in the translation of health research into popular print," although such "inaccuracies appear unintentional" (p. 157).

Based on a Rodale press survey (November, 1998), "Approximately one-quarter of the nation's adults—or an estimated 41,740,841 people—think there is too much conflicting or confusing information in at least half of the health stories they see in the media" (p. 4). Yet, despite that confusion, according to the survey, "More than one-half (54%) of the nation's adults—or an estimated 98,000,236 adults—say they changed a behavior . . . because of a health story that appeared in the media."

Catalyst for Conversation

At the very least, such stories prompt questions that health care seekers then direct to health care practitioners (see, e.g., Carey & Merrill, January 12, 1999; Rodale press survey, November, 1998). In some cases, medical practitioners even push popular press articles as educational resources. In a letter to the editor in *Cosmopolitan*, Dr. Hernan Reyes (December, 1998) contends:

> I'm an OB-GYN (all OB-GYNs worth their salt read Cosmo—especially male ones). I keep articles like "Cosmo Health's Unprotected Sex SOS" (September) on hand for colleagues and patients to read. Thank you, and keep up the great work explaining such useful information in terms patients can understand. (p. 40)

The Chairperson of the Utah Breast Cancer Coalition congratulated the publication *Life Extension* on its web site development. Gerald McCoy (May, 1999) wrote the following letter to the editor:

> Thank you for the great web site! I have been involved with the fight against breast cancer ever since being diagnosed in 1992. For years, I have reprinted and recited from your magazine articles and references. Now I can lead people directly to your web site. The information

is invaluable: It has aided many of the women I have worked with in overcoming the effects of both the disease and the discomforts of conventional treatment therapies. Your articles on supplements and their ability to accomplish self-healing has helped and, perhaps, even saved many. (p. 69)

How can we know what is "real"? Can we ascertain a static "real" or "truth" that can be "real" or "truth" for all media participants, regardless of vantage on the world? According to Engstrom (October 12, 1998), "the ability to gauge truth and accuracy in media reports about medical developments may never have been more crucial than it is now . . . and in this media-saturated age there are mountains of both good and bad information."

Engstrom (October 12, 1998) suggests that readers/hearers examine the statistical support for claims (i.e., in terms of sample size, duration of study, replications of research, funding sources, publication information, etc.). While those tips can help, individuals also need to contextualize media representations of research, health care professionals, and illnesses within their own life script, their own unique lived reality. To what extent can we do so as multiple, mixed media messages swirl around us as part and parcel of the frenzy of our daily lives? To what extent does the media (and individuals and organizations who employ mediated resources) possess the right to bombard us with so many health-related messages? To what extent should the media (and individuals and organizations who employ mediated resources) feel an obligation to place those messages into the public sphere?

Partiality, Colonialism, and the "Common Good"

In their depiction of the idealized public sphere, Habermas and others herald deliberative decision making that features socially oriented, not personally motivated, contributions to public discussions (see Calhoun, 1992; Goodnight, 1982; Goodnight & Hingstman, 1997; Habermas, 1989, 1992; Phillips, 1996). Consensus could then reflect the common societal good, rather than the championing of individual agendas. Even though Fisher (1984, 1987) suggests that narratives (which are implicitly personal) can provide a valuable alternative to deliberative decision making, he argues against "manipulative rhetoric" in which ". . . the audience is being 'played,' 'worked,' or otherwise used for the communicator's ends rather than for their own ends" (Fisher, 1987, p. 117). Fisher maintains:

> Among the evidences of this kind of "manipulation" are: (1) uses of technical knowledge of rhetorical strategies and tactics, of issues, argumentative forms, tests of arguments, and so on in a self-serving way; (2) indications that the communicator's aim is not to perpetuate dialogue, to encourage an authentic bilateral exchange, to further deliberation, to invite true criticism, or to advance the truth of the matter; and (3) clues that the function of the communication is to serve personal ambition rather than self-discovery or social knowledge or public action. (pp. 117–118)

Inherent Biases
As people participate in the public sphere about health care issues, whether as contributors or interpreters, I would argue that we implicitly interact as biased participants. Earlier, I discussed how our diverse and multifaceted orientations flavor how we approach health care

and health care interactions. We cannot escape our fears and frustrations; we cannot transcend our sociocultural-political-economic-related preferences and values. We cannot set aside our previous experiences with illnesses, health care professionals, support system members, and mediated messages. We cannot avoid contextualizing our reactions in terms of where we have been, where we are now, and where we hope to be one day.

How, then, can we contribute as impartial participants, or can we? Certainly, when individuals or organizations pay for advertising or receive money for endorsements, they cannot be deemed as impartial. For example, although people learn about doctors and HMOs in some manner, physician and HMO promotional efforts through advertising or public relations campaigns raise ethical questions for some (see Leventhal, 1995; Smith & Schaaf, 1995–1996). When medical associations (such as the American Medical Association or the American Dental Association) endorse products or practices, they offer credibility to such products and practices, for a price, and with great potential for conflict of interest (see Jurgensen, August 21, 1997; Young, August 21, 1997). In one case, Jurgensen (August 21, 1997) reports that "the American Cancer Society sold its logo to the Florida orange juice industry for $1 million a year. It has a similar deal with a company making nicotine gum and patches" (p. 14A).

When individuals or organizations make public pleas for assistance or action, they also cannot be deemed to be impartial. Whether a person who is sick or an agency with the goal of preventing illness, that person or agency communicates with a predetermined agenda and some sort of persuasive goal. Whether litigation or damage control, the person or agency approaches the persuasive situation with communication strategies that promote actions that are preferred by the contributor to the dialogue.

Determining a "Common Good"

However, even though contributions to the public sphere lack impartiality, I would suggest that the primary problem with such contributions is not the lack of bias; it is the failure of communicators to acknowledge inherent partiality with regard to issues as well as the potential of alternate perspectives. When people advertise, savvy consumers recognize the ad as a paid endorsement. However, when agencies engage in communication campaigns that overtly target behavioral change, partiality may not appear as evident, primarily because campaigns get couched as promoters of the "public good."

In 1998, I wrote a review of the Piotrow and colleagues' book on family planning campaigns. As I noted in the review, ". . . the authors provide a well-tested recipe for communication campaigns that can be adapted to suit specialized needs and preferences" (Beck, 1998, p. 379). However, extending from Witte (1994) and Salmon (1989), I questioned the assumption that campaign planners and target audiences of persuasive efforts necessarily share definitions of the "common" or "public" good (see related argument by Jewkes & Murcott, 1998; Milewa, Valentine, & Calnan, 1998).

Salmon (1989) suggested that definitions of the "common good" emerge "disproportionately [from] government, corporations, and other institutions possessing legitimacy, social power, and resources and access to the mass media" (p. 25), as opposed to marginalized people without power and resources, people who get cast as the targets of persuasive efforts. Although I cannot argue with the motivations of health campaign organizers, I wonder about the implication of campaigns that encourage people to change their cultural, social, and sometimes even intimate, beliefs and practices for some larger "good" that they may not concur with—seemingly, " 'we' (i.e., health communication scholars from developed nations in conjunction with the political-religious-economic-cultural elite in fractured, developing societies) know the 'common good' and how best to achieve it," unlike "you" who should act as "we" say (Beck, 1998, p. 380, as well as related arguments by Jewkes & Murcott, 1998; Walker, 1995).

To play both sides of the fence, though, how do we alert people to the dangers of unprotected sex, unwanted pregnancies, cigarette smoking, drug and alcohol abuse, and domestic violence? Should we not encourage people to wear seat belts and to avoid driving while intoxicated? Aren't some issues just common sense that we should promote to protect us all—for the "common good"?

I would suggest that, especially in terms of structured and funded public health initiatives, much could be gained by a dialogic approach to co-constructing what counts as "common goods" that acknowledges the rich diversity of perspectives among individuals and communities (see related work by Anderson et al., 1994; Arnett, 1992). Rather than implementing a "top-down" approach that uses cultural information only as a means of developing persuasive communication strategies to accomplish predefined goals, I would encourage campaign organizers to involve individual people in the co-determination of health goals, goals that include and reflect the values, beliefs, and priorities of otherwise marginalized people in "target audiences." At the very least, as people and organizations continue to participate actively in the public sphere, we need to ask the important question—what right or obligation do all of us have to impose our beliefs, values, and priorities. on others through persuasive communication efforts?

CLOSING THOUGHTS

"Name?" I truly believe that overall unhappiness must be a criterion for getting a job as an admissions person in the ER. I tried to command patience.

"Christina S. Beck," I responded.

"So what is your maiden name?" she asked.

"My name is Beck. I kept my name," I answered again.

"Well, what is your married name?" she probed.

"Beck, my name is Beck. It always has been Beck, always will be Beck," I could not be the only person who this woman has ever experienced who kept her name.

"Are you married?" she persisted.

"Well, technically, but that's a long story," I said, not meaning to throw her off, but I couldn't just force myself to fit an a priori assumption that all married people change names. I could not cram myself into that mold.

According to Dr. D., who met me at the admissions desk, the marks on my arm didn't match the classic characteristics of infection. "If anything," she said, "I'd say this is RSD, reflex sympathetic dystrophy." However, she shrugged and stressed that "we'll get to the bottom of this." She ordered blood work, instructed a nurse to start an IV, and admitted me to the hospital for observation and IV antibiotics, "just in case."

I searched for familiar faces as I walked back to a curtained examining area. I looked at the faces of people who looked far too young to be in medical school, and I felt old. What are their stories, I wondered? I closed my eyes and sighed loudly as the nurse handed me a hospital gown and told me to change. Why did I have to be the "interesting case" in Number Eight? Why did I agree to stay when no one even knows if the tests are accurate or if IV antibiotics are truly necessary? I complied because I "should," just like the good little patients on television, while I fought to quell my anger, my frustration, my exhaustion with yet another stay in yet another hospital room for yet another complication.

The patient care associate wheeled me to my room, even though I felt that I could walk. I crawled into bed, and Roger handed my bookbag to me. I sighed loudly as I pulled a notebook out of my bag. I wanted to go to a movie; I didn't want to spend my spring break in the hospital. How could I be back here, I thought as I looked at the ceiling. Hhhhhhhhhhhh, I exhaled, searching for a pen amid the clutter of the bottom of my bag. I stopped. My fingers touched the tiny microrecorder that Roger had lent to me for journaling my experience.

"I want to tell my story," I said to Roger.

"You should," he responded.

"What would I say? Why would anyone be remotely interested?" I questioned. Everything seemed so redundant and tedious and frustrating at that moment. What could I contribute that had not already been said?

"I think that people would be fascinated," he contended before stepping out of the room to make a phone call.

I leaned back, exhaled again, clicked on the tape recorder, and paused. I closed my eyes and started to talk, "Tonight, I'm trapped in a terrible cycle of feeling better, getting sick, feeling better, getting sick. It's just like that movie, Groundhog Day, where that guy, oh, darn, what's his name? hmm—"

I heard a hand on the door, and I shoved the recorder under the covers as the patient care associate entered. He surveyed the room. "Who were you talking to?"

"No one," I answered.

"I could have sworn that I heard you talking to someone," he asserted.

I shrugged as he suggested, albeit playfully, the possibility of a psych consult. For now, at least, my journal and my story had to be my own, I thought, as I held out my arm toward the blood pressure cup.

CHAPTER

11

Making Decisions About Health—An Epilogue

I never watch NYPD Blue. *I'm more of a* thirtysomething, *sappy, romantic comedy type of person. However, I stumbled onto publicity about Jimmy Smits' character's illness (see Bianco, November 24, 1998; Graham, November 25, 1998). One review caught my attention in particular. Speaking of Smits' character, Bobby Simone, Bianco (November 24, 1998) wrote, "We're used to seeing him sexy and vital; watching him be subjected to the indignities and battles of modern medicine is a traumatic reminder of the fragility of life" (p. D1).*

I thought that the episode might be a useful example for this book so I decided to watch the conclusion of a storyline that focused on Simone's heart problems and ultimate heart transplant. Known for its raw examination of human experiences, the show struggled with the complexities of contemporary health care and communication—clashes in orientation to health care participants, clashes in perspectives, clashes in trust of high-tech medical capabilities, confusion about what to do or where to turn and who to believe.

I paced for much of the episode. I couldn't bear to sit down. My own heart ached for the desperately ill man and his devastated wife, Diane, who just wanted to do the right thing.

The show began as the couple prepared to leave the hospital after the heart transplant. Diane noticed something amiss on her husband's chest. After considerable urging (because the doctor refused to admit that something could be wrong), Diane finally convinced the doctor to examine Bobby, and he discovered signs of an infection.

Riveted, I couldn't twist my eyes away from the screen. The doctor didn't believe her . . . "Everything's okay" . . . "He's fine" . . . "It's nothing" . . . "Don't worry" . . . The words sounded hauntingly familiar. I wanted to click the television off; I didn't need to watch this. I never watch NYPD Blue; *I don't even like the show. I don't even know the characters. Yet, I couldn't move away.*

The heart specialist ordered tests and then operated to clean out the infection. Diane didn't know who to trust or where to turn. Her gut told her to distrust the heart specialist, but her head told her to listen—he's the expert, after all. He must *know what he's doing. Yet, did the doctor really possess the best answers for her husband, or was he growing frustrated with the case due to complications? He specialized in heart transplants, not infections. I couldn't move out of the room. Goosebumps popped out of my arms. A chill slivered down my spine.*

Diane turned to another doctor, not a high powered-heart expert, but the doctor who referred them to the transplant surgeon in the first place. She begged him to help her. What was real? What was true? What was possible? What could be done? Could he help? The doctor hesitated; should he go against the expert? Could he risk the professional consequences of "speaking out of turn" against such a powerful man?

"Just tell her," I said to the man on the screen. "Please just help her anyway."

Gently, the doctor told her that Bobby was going to die, that the proposed procedure by the expert was a way of shifting the fatality from his department to another one, that they couldn't treat the infection without causing Bobby's body to reject the transplant. Yet, if they left the infection untreated, it would kill him. She had to decide what to do.

What to do . . . what to do . . . she hadn't slept; she hadn't eaten; she was emotionally and physically drained, and now, now of all times, now, she had to make the most important decision of her life—should she try the procedure that this doctor said would not work? Or, should she try nothing at all, ensuring that Bobby would die? She couldn't make this kind of decision now, nor could she delay. She looked at her life partner in the bed, and tears streamed down her face.

She'd go with her instincts; she'd make him comfortable, and she'd always let him know that he was loved. She had to love him enough to let him go without a painful fight— no more pain, more more battles, just a peaceful escape.

Tears filled my eyes as I backed up to my couch and put my head in my lap. Oddly, I wasn't crying for Bobby and Diane as much as I was crying for me. As I tried to stifle my sobs, I fought to get perspective. It's been almost two years since the first surgery, I reasoned to myself. I'm better now. Why are the demons back?

My shoulders shook as all of the frustration and anger and exhaustion came rushing back. I couldn't flee from it; I couldn't shake it off. Amid my tears, I saw Dr. T., and I could hear him saying, albeit ever so respectfully, "It's nothing; you're fine." Yet, I wasn't "fine." I wasn't fine when my hand was paralyzed in the hospital, and I had to have the second surgery. I wasn't fine when I had the staph infection. I wasn't fine when I was alone, all alone in the hospital, and that terrible woman kept jabbing me with a needle. I wasn't fine when the nurses screwed up when they installed the PICC line, and my neck was swelling up with blood. I wasn't fine when no one knew what to do, and I had to make decisions when I was in no condition to make decisions. I wasn't fine when I was exhausted, and no one could figure out why. I wasn't fine when my wrist started to swell and—

I fought to get a breath. My throat clogged with the residue of too-long repressed tears. I had buried these emotions for so long, but they hadn't decayed. I looked up at the television, but I cared little about the weatherman or the forecast on the 11 P.M. news. I lived, I thought as I tried to reconcile my reaction to the fictional characters and their harrowing experience. I lived . . .

In his edited book, Whaley (2000) explores the explanation of illness. Although answers elude us about medical miracles and mysteries, we inherently attribute meaning to our individual health care experiences. Through our interactions with other health care participants and social support system members and through our examination of mediated material about given health care concerns, we co-construct individual and relational definitions of who we are, how we want to be taken, and importantly, how we wish for events to unfold during particular portions of our life journey. Our orientations to ordeals reflect, reify, and sometimes, reconfigure our outlooks on life. My medical mazes became meaningful as I positioned myself in relation to my health care trials and to others that I tapped in the tunnels.

Throughout this book, I have detailed much of my physical and emotional saga with the wrist surgeries and subsequent complications. As I consider that trying time in my life, I realize that much of my fear and frustration surfaced from confusion. I simply didn't know what to do at some points, what decision to make, what perspectives to prioritize. Thus, I decided to close the book with an examination of the complexities of decision making in this challenging, confusing contemporary era.

This chapter begins by revisiting one of the core reasons for that confusion—the multiplicity of mixed messages, from a vast variety of sources, about health care. I then explore the link between power, knowledge, and control in light of health care interactions. I close the chapter with the conundrum that all health care participants confront—communicating amid the chaos of contemporary health care issues and relationships.

Multiple Messengers with Mixed Messages

I will never know when or how I acquired the staph infection. After my second wrist surgery, I landed in a room with a woman who turned out to have an infectious disease, and I caught my nurse coming over to me without washing her hands between patients. Did I contract something from that other patient via the nurse who did not take the time to scrub possible germs away before attending to my hip? Did the infection begin because of some unclean equipment in the operating room or because someone happened to be careless as they removed the bone from my hip to rebuild the wrist?

However or whenever it happened, I know that I am not the only one who ever contracted a staph infection nor who suffered due to a misdiagnosis or some other error in medical care. According to a report by the Institute of Medicine, "Medical errors kill more Americans than traffic accidents, breast cancer or AIDS" (Davis & Appleby, November 30, 1999, p. A1).

I also know that I am not the only one who has ever encountered confounding contradictions during health care experiences. As I contemplate my quest for wellness, I'm struck by the disturbing disagreements between health care professionals about my situation and possible courses of action. In the previous chapter, I described the possible recurrence of my staph infection. Numerous health care providers (an internal medicine doctor, an orthopedic resident, an orthopedic nurse, two occupational therapists) weighed in with their own opinions about what could (or could not) be the trouble with my wrist—an infection, RSD, nothing. As experts argued, I begrudged my lost time and stolen spring break due to yet another misdiagnosis, more mixed messages, more missteps through my medical maze.

Who Is an "Expert"?

We come to our health care encounters amid vast amounts of information about health care, health care professionals (even in terms of their mistakes), health resources, and medical perspectives and approaches. from more sources than ever before (see, e.g., Connell &

Crawford, 1988; Howze, Broyden, & Impara, 1992; Johnson & Meischke, 1991; Reagan & Collins, 1987; Tardy & Hale, 1998). We can tap an unending tide of tips from friends, relatives, support group members and aquaintances, news updates and special reports, advertisements, Internet websites, and, of course, insights from health care professionals.

Howze and colleagues (1992) trained hair stylists to serve as informal advocates for mammography. According to Howze and colleagues (1992), interactions between women clients and the hair stylists about breast cancer enhanced the women's understanding of risks and screening benefits. Tardy and Hale (1998) discovered that members of a mothers' and toddlers' playgroup sought and shared information about health issues and resources that impacted dietary decisions and physician selection.

As Wickham-Searl (1994) explains, discouragement with distant health care professionals can direct health care seekers toward others, people who possess a personalized perspective of a particular health care situation or concern. In her investigation of mothers of disabled children, Wickham-Searl (1994) learned that the mothers came to depend on themselves and like-others more and traditional "experts" to a lesser extent. According to Wickham-Searl (1994), the women seemed to move ". . . the focus of authority from those presumed to be knowledgeable on account of their professional status, to themselves, women vested with the authority of raising children who were disabled" (p. 180).

As health care participants grow ever aware of medical fallibility and uncertainty, the careful consideration of contributions escalates in importance (see related work by Allman, 1998; Calnan, 1984; Little, 1995; Zussman, 1992). For example, Browner and Press (1996) examined women's orientation to information about prenatal care (see also related work by Sesia, 1996). Browner and Press (1996) conclude:

> In the case of our pregnant informants, embodied knowledge and everyday life exigencies proved to be pivotal in their selective designation of certain biomedical knowledge as authoritative. The women challenged biomedical authority in prenatal care specifically when they saw it as based solely on clinician's judgments, and balanced these judgments against their own embodied knowledge and their ability to accommodate their lives to the recommendations being proposed. (p. 152)

However, both Tardy and Hale (1998) and Wickham-Searl (1994) acknowledge that health care seekers do not restrict themselves to a single source, a singular "authority." Tardy and Hale (1998) note that the women in the playgroup referenced family members and health care professionals as they offered and responded to peer health insights. Wickham-Searl (1994) stressed that the mothers of disabled children did not disregard professional input; they just considered it within the context of their own lived realities.

As Joanne Palmer (1999) discovered, the multiplicity of possible mediated and interpersonal sources can overwhelm and frustrate. When Palmer disclosed her desire to get pregnant to friends and family, they proffered plenty of free advice to complement her own search of the Internet for useful information. The lay authorities' advice ranged from acupuncture to consuming herbs to timing of intercourse to renting the movie *Body Heat* to taking a cruise. As Palmer (1999, p. 184) noted, "in my small town, you can get a hot tip anytime, anywhere. 'Hey, how's it going?' a friend calls across the banana bin at the grocery store." That friend, by the way, suggested the movie and "sexy underwear." Claims the friend, "it worked for us" (Palmer, 1999, p. 184).

What Counts as a "Fact"?

Through interpersonal interactions, professional consultations, and a vast array of mediated outlets, individuals encounter a flood of "the latest" "facts" and research findings. However, the deluge of data can be discouraging to individuals as they juxtapose conflicting reports and complicated issues.

- Some studies suggest that thalidomide, a drug linked to birth defects in the 1950s and 1960s, could be a valuable treatment for some forms of cancer (see Fackelmann, August 24, 1999a).
- Although some health care professionals in obstetrics have suggested that walking speeds the progression of labor, recent research indicates that it may not (see Painter, July 9, 1998).
- "Shower therapy" can purportedly prevent the common cold (see Nordenberg, 1998).

How can one keep up with what might emerge as "dangerous" when research keeps emerging, changing what counts as "safe" or "effective"? For example, in good faith, people consumed the diet drugs Pondimin, Redux, and Fen-Phen. According to an advertisement promoting a class action settlement for damages, angry customers now claim that the drugs may have contributed to "lesions or abnormalities in the heart valves of some people."

Searching for solutions, individuals increasingly seek nontraditional resources, yet the usefulness and safety of products and procedures remain under dispute. Books and articles abound on alternative medicine, ranging from charges of "quackery" (see, e.g., Barrett & the editors of *Consumer Reports*, 1990; Barrett & Herbert, 1994; Barrett & Jarvis, 1993; Hellmich, July 13, 1998; Magner, 1995; Raso, 1993; Young, 1992) to praises for health benefits (see, e.g., Butler, 1992; Eisenberg et al., November 11, 1998; Fink, 1997; Hellmich, July 13, 1998; Lerner, 1994; Weil, 1995). One article, "Homeopathy: Real Medicine or Empty Promises," ended equivocally: "Even professionals who practice homeopathy warn that nothing in medicine—either conventional or alternative—is absolute" (Stehlin, 1998, p. 4; see also Ernst & Hahn, 1998).

Summary—Mixed Messages

Amid the plethora of contradicting sources and claims, how can health care seekers sort through the issues? How can they decide how to proceed?

Cathy Hainer, the *USA Today* reporter who chronicled her fight with breast cancer, learned that she was "disease-free" after six months of treatment (Friend, June 22, 1998). However, as Friend (June 22, 1998) noted at the time, "Cathy has beaten huge odds . . . as a result, she faces the most perplexing decision since her diagnosis: What to do next?" (p. 6D).

Unlike the majority of women with Stage 4 breast cancer, Hainer responded "dramatically." Friendexplains, "Whatever option Cathy chooses is a step into uncharted territory . . . the options from which she can choose span the spectrum" (p. 6D) of no additional treatment to high-dose chemotherapy. The difficulty of the decision derived from inconclusive data. As Friend (June 22, 1998) reports, "none of these options, however, has been shown to be better than another" (p. 6D).

Stressing the absence of scientific support, two of her doctors recommended the high-dose chemotherapy. Hainer sought the opinion of yet another professional who suggested the standard-dose chemotherapy, recognizing the risk of death with the high-dose alternative (Friend, June 22, 1998). According to Friend, "the best the experts can do . . . is spread a hand of cards with the options and ask Cathy to pick one" (p. 6D).

Despite the wealth of scientific studies and technological capabilities, we still lack conclusive information about many health-related issues. Yet, we have no deficiency in perspectives, vistas that health care participants must somehow juxtapose and then accept or discard. As I will now detail, that process of legitimizing expertise, knowledge, and authority is central to how individuals co-construct health care decision making and prioritize information.

Power, Knowledge, and Control

Click, click, click, click . . . I flipped through the channels of the hospital television. Talk show, talk show, cartoon, infomercial, talk show, Price Is Right. *I paused, watching to see if the large, white-haired lady would win $1000 on the wheel—click, click . . . click . . . No, she missed it by a hair; still, she gets to be in the showcase. Oh man, I told her in my mind, stop kissing up to Bob (Barker) like you've known him all of your life.*

I turned off the television and leaned back against the pillow. What a way to spend spring break . . . I had screwed around with the staph infection possibility all week so far—reeling from the diagnosis on Monday and getting admitted to the hospital on Tuesday evening. Now, I was also wasting Wednesday. I'd planned to come up to Columbus for therapy and then shop, maybe even take a long walk along the river . . . something that normal people do because they're not stuck in the hospital.

"Aaaaaagh," I said aloud, "Why am I here?" I stood up, dragging my IV pole with me to the window. Great, I thought. My grand view consists of the hospital courtyard.

I awaited the result of my blood work. Dr. T.'s resident reiterated that she rejected the possibility that my infection had recurred when she met with me during rounds that morning, yet she insisted that I stay until the afternoon, "just in case."

I'm an "outlier," Kate had instructed me to emphasize. I ambled from the window back to the bed. Pressing the call button, I requested a Diet Coke and sat on the bedside, staring at my bare toes. What does that mean, to be an "outlier"? Have I been labeled as someone who beats the odds or gets defeated by them? How did I get to be one?

A patient care associate entered with a can of pop and the prerequisite straw and cup of ice. I thanked her and tugged at the tab of the can. I never use ice at home, but in the hospital, I automatically open the can and pour the warm soda over the ice. I halted, holding the can atop the cup. Oh my goodness, I thought. I've been here so much that I have a pattern with my pop.

"Ma'am?" I stopped the woman on her way out of the door.

"Yes?" she answered.

"Could I get dressed and walk around?" I asked. She looked hesitant so I continued. "Really, it would mean a lot to me. I'm just waiting on a test result, and I'm kind of bored." I don't belong here, I reasoned. If I stay in this room for a second more, I might

fizz over like a can of pop that's been dropped or jarred or shaken just one too many times. "Please?"

"Are you on strict bed rest?" she inquired.

"No, I'm here for a test result, just a precaution . . . Please," I said. It's spring break, and I want to be on a tennis court. The sun shone through my window, and I pined to pry open the forbidding bars of my sterile cage and slip into the brightness of a spring afternoon.

"I'll check with the nurse," she said as she departed.

Deflated, I shuffled to the chair by the window and picked up the pair of shorts that I wore on the previous day. Shorts . . . spring . . . it had been such a long haul since the cold night of the first surgery. Slowly, I pulled my IV pole with me as I returned to the bed and picked up the cup of Diet Coke. I sipped the drink and realized again how much I hate watered-down soda.

I craved the freedom of drinking out of a cold can, chasing a tennis ball in the back-court, reading a book in the sunshine. I sat back against the pillow, closed my eyes, and fantasized about getting dressed and moving around without permission . . . about knowing who to believe . . . about enjoying some control over my existence . . . about knowing what in the world was going on with my body this time.

Accomplishing "Power"

In essence, I wanted power. I craved the legitimacy, the authority, to direct my course, but at that moment, I couldn't grasp it. Why, I wondered? My steaks have to completely cooked (practically burned), my daiquiris completely frozen, with just the right mix of strawberries (lots) and rum (minimal), my Diet Cokes always without ice yet cold. If not, I send them back and demand new. I'm the ultimate "Sally" (from *When Harry Met Sally*) when I'm eating in a restaurant, no matter how simple or fancy, no matter who happens to join me for dinner. I feel that I *can* order at restaurants, but unless a dire circumstance arises, I do not react the same in health care settings. I don't behave as though I possess the legitimate "right" to do so.

The issue of power in health care interactions has fascinated scholars, from early works on the institutionalization implicit in the biomedical model of health care (see, e.g., Parsons, 1951) to more contemporary examinations of the impact of gender on power in health care settings (see, e.g., Davis, 1993; Davis, Leijenaar, & Oldersma, 1991; Fisher, 1986, 1993, 1995; Todd, 1993), ways of enacting power (see Ainsworth-Vaughn, 1998; Kritek, 1981; Rinehart, 1991) and legitimacy (see Roberts, 1999), and current complexities of power and health care roles (see Beisecker, 1990; Wiener, Fagerhaugh, Strauss, & Suczek, 1980). Indeed, power pervades health care interactions. However, the nature of that power can no longer be viewed simplistically in terms of a formalized, static, institutionalized hierarchy, especially in light of managed care, team-based care, consumerism, diverse orientations to health care, and fragmented medical roles.

"Owning" Power

I stared at the hospital door, and I yearned to leave. Looking down at my thin hospital smock, I hated feeling naked, not just physically. I felt stripped of myself. I couldn't really be me, the person who usually asserts and argues . . . I walked to the bathroom with my IV pole in tow, and I caught my impression in the mirror—defeated, dejected.

I closed my eyes and remembered the long ago morning when I learned that my second hospital roommate carried some communicable disease. The nurse had come to relocate her, and I demanded to know what was going on. The nurse nonchalantly said that the roommate had a contagious disease and must be isolated. Terrified, I struggled out of bed and yanked my IV pole into the hallway. Bare under the scant gown, I refused to go back into the room.

"Please, go back into bed," the nurse requested.

"No," I said strongly. I felt weak and a little embarrassed about the fact that anyone could see my butt who walked up from behind. I couldn't care. I thought of Chelsea and Britti. What if I had contracted some terrible disease? What if . . . ?

"What does she have?" I demanded.

"I can't tell you," the nurse said. "Look, you can't stand out here."

"I AM NOT GOING BACK IN THERE," I stressed. "I need to know what I've been exposed to. I want to talk to a doctor NOW."

"No doctors are available now. You have to go back in the room," the nurse spoke quickly. I could tell that she was frustrated, and I felt a little bad for her. She had been quite nice to me, but I could not comply. I would not comply.

I hobbled toward the nurse's station. Someone would understand my perspective. Someone would get a doctor. My head started to swim. I hadn't been out of bed since the second surgery, and my hip hurt, and my arm felt heavy.

Another nurse at the nurse's station saw me approach. "What are you doing?" she asked.

I explained that I needed information about the woman in my room. I just wanted a doctor to tell me about the disease. Why couldn't someone find a doctor in a hospital? Why was my request so odd, so difficult? How could they treat my reaction as unreasonable? Yet, the nurses simply stared at me as I stood in my open gown with my IV pole, pathetic yet assertive.

Increasing skepticism about science and medical authority, exacerbated by quakes in the health care industry and the constant deluge of information through the Internet and other mediated sources, have worked to fragment traditional power structures. Many no longer accept a doctor's opinion as "gospel." MCOs can constrain coverage of care, but consumer activists challenge coverage limitations. From social support system members to celebrities, personal and public advocacy abounds, pursuing power with regard to particular people and predicaments. Given that I subscribe to social constructionism, I do not believe that individuals ever really could "own" power. However, in these chaotic contemporary times, even assumptions about power have become increasingly problematic.

Preferences for power reflect embedded understandings of legitimate identities, roles, rules, and relationships, stemming from medical and societal acculturations, personal perspectives and priorities, and interpersonal influences. Even though some medical students might get indoctrinated in the traditions of biomedicine, the advent of alternative medicine, the awareness of psychosocial influences, consumerism, and collaborative care cracks rigid role descriptions that prescribe "a" way of interacting with health care seekers. For health care seekers, even those who have been raised by the rules of biomedicine or other models of health care, the multiplicity of messages about how health care can and should ensue clutters vistas on viewing roles.

My a priori perceptions of who I should be and what I should and could do during particular health care situations arose from my taken-for-granted assumptions about "how things work here" and what a "legitimate patient" or a "legitimate consumer" might do. As in my situation, though, the postmodern enactment of power in health care situations constitutes a fluctuating construction rather than a commitment to static roles and role performances. As I noted earlier, I didn't want to be a "difficult patient," an "Elaine" (from *Seinfeld*), but I also could not shelve my desire to participate, my frustration with inefficiency, and my urge to serve as my own best advocate.

Requiring Legitimacy

I splashed water on my face. I grew tense just remembering the pleading for information, the huddling of nurses who whispered about my request and refusal to return to my room. Yet, I held my ground and demanded to talk with someone in charge.

One nurse stepped forward and handed me a robe. "Let's go somewhere and talk," she suggested.

"I am not going back in that room," I asserted.

"That's fine," she said. "We can go in a conference room."

"I want to consult with a doctor about this," I continued.

"I've contacted a staff member who specializes in infectious diseases. She'll be with us in a few minutes, but right now, we need to get you off of your feet," she said.

We walked slowly toward a tiny conference room, and I felt the stares of the other nurses as we moved away from the nurses' station. How could they perceive my desire for information as so extreme, I wondered? Who would not *want to know? I felt exhausted, but I needed to persist.*

I slowly sat in a conference room chair and fought to look alert. A professionally dressed woman entered, identifying herself as a patient care advocate. She greeted me. "Miss Beck?" she asked.

"Actually, it's Doctor Beck," I asserted. "I'm not a 'miss,' " and I hoped for some credibility points.

"Really?" she responded.

"Yes," I continued before she could pursue exactly what type of doctor I am. "I need to know about this illness."

"As you know, we are not at liberty to disclose another patient's condition," she asserted.

"Okay, well, I am at liberty to call my lawyer and to call the press and to call the head of this whole hospital to get some answers. Now, you can tell me, or we can have the whole city of Columbus reading about what you're hiding," I blurted, trying not to sound desperate, but I needed some niche, some way of getting this lady to take me seriously. How could I be so tired? Yet, I couldn't show my fatigue, my fear, my frustration. "Never let them see you sweat," the classic commercial commands . . .

"We are confident that you're not at risk," she said.

"Then why is she being moved to isolation?" I demanded. From the look in her eye, I knew that I had hit her battleship. She couldn't answer that one. I nailed the critical question. I proved that I wasn't stupid and that I refused to back down.

"Okay, okay . . ." the woman paused, looking at the nurse in charge. She sighed. "We're not supposed to divulge this information, but given the circumstances . . . "

She told me about the woman's illness and the warning signs. She attempted to reassure me that the odds of catching anything were incredibly remote. I cared little for her efforts at comfort, only for the information. Yet, I felt dismayed at the strength that I had to expend to attain it, to make the claim that I had the legitimate right to facts that could impact my life.

I stared at my reflection in the mirror and shook my head. It's been nearly four months, I marveled. I'm amazed by what I've been through, I thought as I walked toward my bed and the watered-down Diet Coke. I glanced at my shorts on the chair and back again at the door. Screw it, I thought. There's no reason that I shouldn't wear clothes, I reflected. Grinning, I slid off the gown and started to get dressed.

In her compelling description of a health care experience, Kritek (1981) describes the process of becoming a "patient" who needed a gall bladder surgery. Although she was a nurse who knew the staff and the protocol, she "felt forced to relinquish personal views, knowledge, and expertise" (Kritek, 1981, p. 29).

My efforts to gain control and assert power required my successful positioning as a "legitimate" participant. Yet, paradoxically, that legitimacy depended upon knowledge that I could not acquire due to an inherent differential in access to information. As Kritek discovered, becoming "the patient" involved the relinquishing of her self as a knowledgeable expert, thus decreasing her legitimate authority to contribute and to control medical activities. As long as I had to beg for information, the staff could implicitly treat me as a lesser participant—not a true player who could "really" comprehend all of the ethical, legal, and medical considerations.

Asserting Legitimacy Through Knowledge

After Dr. D. released me that afternoon, I banished the staph infection in my mind, determined not to revisit the possibility of another infection, resolved not to return to the hospital. I wanted to get better; I thirsted to play tennis. I sought to live. Yet, I desired to do more than live. I had paid too high a price to just exist; I vowed to do everything that I could to maximize my recovery so that all of the needles and pain and fatigue could be justified. I resumed occupational therapy with renewed vigor.

When I met with Dr. T. about a week later, he inquired about my hospital stay and assured me that I did not have an infection (which I already knew) or RSD. "I'm not sure what happened," he claimed, "but I know that you're fine." He smiled, "Things sure do happen to you when I leave town, don't they?"

As I drove back to Athens that spring day, I wondered how he knew that I was "fine." Should I believe him? Yet, I shoved the skepticism aside. The tennis courts awaited, and I embraced his encouragement to increase the rehab. "Work it, work it, work it," he had instructed. I vowed to do just that. This whole nightmare would be worth it if I could whip a cross-court backhand by the end of the summer, I smiled to myself.

In the biomedical model of medicine, the knowledge differential between health care professionals and seekers perpetuates the power gap—doctors know; patients don't. The very fact that professionals struggle over what to share and when to remain silent reflects the patriarchial tendencies of the profession (see work on informed consent and medical risk by Barry, 1999; Bogardus, Holmboe, & Jekel, 1999; Haas, 1991; Schuck, 1994; Waitzkin, 1985). As Waitzkin (1985) concedes, "How much information to give to patients, and how much to withhold, are questions of never ending speculation in medicine" (p. 81).

However, the plethora of sources and the glut of information about health care issues cloud the absolutism of professional authority (see related work on fragmentation of knowledge and postmodernism—Appleby, Covington, Hoyt, Latham, & Sneider, 1996; Flax, 1990). The positioning of knowledge requires health care participants to engage in an artful construction about what counts as legitimate knowledge, what should be shared in health care interactions, and how assertions of knowledge impact emergent health care roles (see, e.g., Arney & Bergen, 1984; Browner & Press, 1996; Cicourel, 1986; Gadamer, 1996; Peters, Stanley, Rose, & Salmon, 1998; Sarick, February 23, 1999; Sesia, 1996; Waitzkin, 1989).

As I tried to convince Dr. T. that I had a problem with my hip, as I worked to get the nurses to tell me about my roommate's disease, as I pleaded with the one nurse to get someone to help her with my IV, their collective reactions resembled Foucault's notion of "disciplinary power" (see Foucault, 1972; McHoul & Grace, 1993). Because of the inherent legitimacy of their position as health care professionals—that is, due to their training and their status as accepted professionals with viable levels of expertise—they could negate my assertions—that is, I didn't really know anything; I didn't really need to know anything. Such negations worked interactionally to slot us in specific roles and to reify the unspoken rules about the legitimacy of our respective contributions.

However, as I emphasized that I *did* know something, I made the perceived legitimacy of our respective positions problematic. I *did* have an infection; I *did* have a problem with my PICC line; I *did* know my body. Yet, I don't *always* know *best*. How do we discern who does know better and when? Given such uncertainties about who should assert power and who possesses "the best" information and knowledge, how do we determine who should claim control of complex health care decisions?

The Quest for Control

My frustration festered from an inability to control the uncontrollable. Even though we can eat right, get plenty of sleep, drink water, and pop vitamins, we can't completely prevent the onset of illness. Although the staph infection could have likely been avoided, once the bacteria invaded my hip, I couldn't will my body to simply be well. Similar to a fair-goer in a funhouse, disease forced me to fight through the twists and turns, to mash against mirrors and dart through the darkness, as I struggled to surface on the other side. I couldn't stop, and I couldn't escape.

Yet, health care participants *can* control choices about the course of treatment—how they will proceed and what they will do. In fact, the quest for control stems from philosophical assumptions about power-based medical roles, orientations that undergird health care encounters and outcomes. Health care participants (seekers, professionals, and social support system members) enter health care interactions with a priori under-standings of who possesses the legitimate authority, the power, to control the decision-making process.

Through their overt treatment of each other, health care participants display their preferences for who should take the lead and how individuals should contribute, implicitly reflecting views of power and control. Yet, as I will argue, those taken-for-granted assumptions are not necessarily static or shared by health care participants. In fact, individuals might well have very different conceptions of control depending on specific circumstances and interactional partners.

Perceptions of Control

When I entered the hospital for the suspected staph recurrence, I did so grudgingly. Nonetheless, I consented to checking into another hospital room, submitting to another IV and rounds of blood tests, and deferring to staff members with regard to my activities. I yielded control to the hospital staff just as I had done during the ER visits and the trips to Dr. T.'s office. As Taylor (1979) argues, "the hospital is one of the few places where an individual foreits control over virtually every task he or she customarily performs" (p. 157).

Perceived control impacts the nature of interactions between health care seekers, pro-fessionals, and support system members (see, e.g., Brenders, 1989; Calnan, 1989; Haug & Lavin, 1981; Hughes, 1982; Hunt, Arar, & Larme, 1998; Kayser-Jones, 1995; Mahler & Kulik, 1990; Montbriand, 1995; Naber, Halstead, Broome, & Rehwaldt, 1995; Northouse & Northouse, 1987; O'Hair, 1989; Pepler & Lynch, 1991; Sankar, 1986; Street, Piziak, Carpentier, Herzog, Hejl, Skinner, & McLellan, 1993; von Friederichs-Fitzwater, Callahan, Flynn, & Williams, 1991). As I explained in the chapter on professional-seeker relationships, the very structure of conversation, especially in terms of questions and answers, reflects and reifies who possesses legitimate control of the interaction (see, e.g., Ainsworth-Vaughn, 1998; Brenders, 1989; Hughes, 1982; O'Hair, 1989; Pepler & Lynch, 1991; Roberts, 1999; von Friederichs-Fitzwater et al., 1991).

With the advent of home care (see, e.g, Sankar, 1986), alternative medicine (see, e.g., Montbriand, 1995), and encouragement of health care seeker ownership of proactive health care behaviors (see, e.g., Calnan, 1989; Hunt, Arar, & Larme, 1998; Mahler & Kulik, 1990) in this era of consumerism and managed care, perceived control may fluctuate dramatically. Although I yielded much control in the hospital, *I* ultimately demanded that another nurse try to start the IV when the original nurse failed to accomplish the task. I fought trips to the emergency room when *I* thought that I knew better. After I learned how to give myself med-ication with the IV machine, *I* assumed responsibility for remembering to inject my anti-biotics at the right time and in the correct manner. Each assertion of perceived control, by myself and the health care professionals, reflected assumptions of power—that is, who had the legitimate authority to command control—as well as our emergent definition of how decision making may occur.

Models of Medical Decision Making

In their examinations of health care interactions, scholars who study health communication suggest an array of models of medical decision making. As one of those scholars, I have reflected on various models, and because of my own philosophical biases, I argued earlier for a partnership approach to health communication (see Beck with Ragan & duPre, 1997). Although the various models emerge from strong theoretical assumptions about how health care ought to work, for various reasons, each ultimately disappoints in its ability to capture the complexities that are implicit to contemporary health care decisions.

Compliance-Gaining Models   At one end of the continuum, adherence to traditional biomedicine coincides with models that promote professional control and seeker compliance (see Burgoon, Pfau, Parrott, Birk, Coker, & Burgoon, 1987; Eraker et al., 1984; Falvo, 1985; Fisher, 1992; Hunt et al., 1989; O'Hair et al., 1987; Paskett et al., 1990; Phillips & Jones, 1991; Shumaker, Schron, & Ockene, 1990; Steele et al., 1990; Stone, 1979). The view that professionals possess specialized knowledge that should be prioritized pervades this perspective of decision making. Because the professional "knows best," the seeker should comply with recommendations, consistent with my comments in Chapter 2 about scientific authority and institutionalized roles.

Emphasis on compliance gaining permeates efforts on behalf of public health (e.g., in terms of promoting proactive health choices such as practicing safe sex, obtaining vaccinations, and discouraging substance abuse) (see discussion in chapter on public dialogues as well). For example, based on the desire to gain patient compliance, proponents of the Health Belief Model strive to persuade individuals that each person possesses the power to enact proactive health care practices, such as disease prevention (see Becker, 1974; French, Kurczynski, Weaver, & Pituch, 1992; Janz & Becker, 1984; Mattson, 1999; see also work on the Transtheoretical Model of Behavior Change by Grimley, Prochaska, Velicer, & Prochaska, 1995). This model stresses self-efficacy (or individual ability to engage in preferred behaviors); however, the crux remains on compliance, rather than choice—individuals gain assurance that they can behave in a manner preferred by a health care professional and/or public officials.

Although I would not dub efforts to promote wellness and healthy behaviors as "bad," by any means, an emphasis on compliance gaining discourages attention to the lived reality of health care participant, to what constitutes "healthy" or "proactive" wellness practices for them as unique, multifaceted individuals. What can people actually accomplish in their daily lives? How does the health concern fit in their respective lived realities?

To determine the source of my chest pain, Dr. S. recommended a series of tests. Obligingly, I adhered to a first round of tests, but my symptoms subsided as days passed. I've rescheduled blood work at least four times because I don't have the time right now. Because I'm no longer hurting, I lack the desire to carve precious minutes for going to the doctor and waiting in line—I have the book to finish, papers to grade, kids to transport, a new house to unpack.

Many of the studies that feature compliance gaining as a goal bemoan "patient" failure to comply. Perhaps, the "failure" truly constitutes the unwillingness to listen, to prioritize another perspective, to avoid unidirectional commands that ignore the plethora of issues beyond a studied opinion. Especially in this era of lay experts, access to diverse information, and consumerism, health care seekers and their social support system members often lack the willingness to "just accept." Even when they do comply, the professional recommendation likely parallels other information as well as what rings true in their own lived realities.

I didn't want to go to the ER or stay in my hospital room, but I ultimately did so because it made sense to me. Conversely, I resisted removal of the PICC line because that recommendation clashed with my understanding of previous information, my perception of what I needed to get well.

Consumerism Models   At the other end of the continuum, a consumer-oriented approach highlights consumer control and professional compliance with requests for information or resources (see Annandale & Hunt, 1998; De Ridder, Depla, Severens, & Malsch, 1997; Johnson, 1997; Kelner & Wellman, 1997; Kolata, 1994; Lupton, 1997; Makoul, Arntson, & Schofield, 1995; Meerabeau, 1998; Minkler, 1999; Nonprescription Drug Manufacturers Association, 1992; Peters et al., 1998; Risker, 1995; Shaffer & Sherell, 1995; Steptoe & Appels, 1989). Consumer-oriented models highlight the market demands of contemporary health care—if we want it, we'll research it and buy the "best" option. In this perspective, quality health care can be purchased by individuals with the resources and shopping savvy to select the most efficient option.

Notably, the accent on consumer selectivity implies that, with the right resources and research, individuals without medical training can diagnose and treat themselves, relying on professionals as "rubber stamps" who write prescriptions and respond to concerns. The advent of the Internet and other mediated sources continues to fuel the fire for consumer orientations to health care services.

As I noted in the chapter on technology, such self-care can be dangerous. When consumerism continues to its logical extreme, individuals lose the benefits of consulting with an expert. After talking with multiple professionals in the ER, I grew cynical and skeptical. None of them knew anything, I concluded. I could spout off my case, touting my test results. I could dismiss theories because I thought that I possessed a better grasp of the situation—I *knew* better, and they seemed to know nothing. In my effort to be an efficient and discerning consumer, I nearly rebuffed the one doctor who finally figured out the PICC-line problem.

Partnership-Oriented Models   In the middle of the continuum between doctor control/ patient deference on one hand and seeker control/professional deference on the other lie various partnership-oriented models. These models encourage collaboration between health care participants about the best course of action (see Broom & Woodward, 1996; Charles, Gafni, & Whelan, 1997; Greenfield, Kaplan, & Ware, 1985; Smith, 1996; Stewart et al., 1995). Such models include the informed consent decision model (see Braddock, Edwards, Hasenberg, Laidley, & Levinson, 1999; Gafni, Charles, & Whelan, 1998; Ubel & Loewenstein, 1997), participative decision making (see Ballard-Reisch, 1990), dialogue medicine (see Hellstrom, 1998), patient-as-citizen (see Arntson, 1989; Danis & Churchill, 1991; Rimal et al., 1997), mutual persuasion (see Smith & Pettegrew, 1986), and partnership (Beck with Ragan & duPre, 1997).

Because these models, as ideals, do not privilege one type of participant (professional or seeker) over another, health care participants must orient to the sharedness of responsibility similarly. Such partnership models require preparation by all participants as well as a willingness to listen, to question, to understand, to identify.

I truly enjoy such a working relationship with Dr. S. However, I can't remember ever calling him by his first name, even when I see him at a children's music concert or the softball fields. Most of the time, I defer to his instructions, despite my openness to ask questions and offer opinions. When we talk about work or family, we seem to stand on common ground. When he starts to examine me or offer his analysis, he talks and I listen, and our roles emerge as unusually generic. Although I advocate a partnership model, I find such a dynamic difficult to enact due to deeply embedded cultural and social notions of doctor and patient roles.

Power, Knowledge, and Control—A Summary

Revisiting these models now, including my own, I am struck by two realizations. First, our existing models of medical decision making do not account for the complexity of multiple voices for control in health care situations. Although some of the models account for seeker participation in conversations with health care professionals, they do not address the role of social support system members in decision making (even though such individuals might well engage in the discussion, especially with older or younger seekers). Further, they do not discuss the challenge of diverse professional perspectives for the decision-making process. Especially in complicated health care situations (like discussion of cancer treatments or other surgical options), health care decisions do not occur as a result of one interaction or even one health care professional. How do individuals display their respective knowledge and preferences for power amid the layers of multiple participants? How does control get enacted in such scenarios? Who gets to exert or assert control?

Second, our existing models of medical decision making do not account for fluctuations in roles due to changing circumstances. When health care seekers get increasingly frustrated, when health care professionals need to admit mistakes, when social support system members step in as advocates for critically ill friends or relatives, the dynamic of health care interactions necessarily shifts, particularly in terms of control. Yet, within the artfully and delicately constructed system of role definitions and individual identities, disruptions in roles, breaking of taken-for-granted rules, and abandoning of assumptions create relational and individual identity complications. Who gets to decide what happens next? How can trust be restored? Who gets to enact control, or who (if anyone) must defer?

Power, knowledge, and control constitute important considerations in health communication, perhaps even more so than ever before. Increasingly, power, knowledge, and control may best be characterized as complex, emergent, and temporal, something to be achieved within the broad context of the system of the seeker in conjunction with various health care professionals and support system members. Because of the plethora of influences in contemporary health care, enactment of power, knowledge, or control cannot be confined to a doctor and a health care seeker, nor can they be bound to rigid role performances. As such, decision making is difficult to diagram or depict in a static model.

The Complexities of Contemporary Decision Making

I rubbed my face with my left hand and worked on wrestling the sides of the clothespin apart and closer to the rod. Waves of pain shot down through my arm. Don't let go, I coached myself . . . Hang on. Closer . . . "Uuuuuuugh," I grunted as I dropped the pin. Slowly, I lifted my forearm and examined it. Red streaks resonated through my skin. I felt nauseous and dizzy as the pain pulsated through my wrist and up my arm. I closed my eyes.

How had I come to May, I thought? After the last infection scare, I had stressed rehab, strictly heeding Dr. T.'s recommendation to strengthen my wrist. Exercise after exercise, thrice-weekly drives to Columbus, more pain, more frustration—I almost died for this? I wondered.

Keri re-entered the rehab room, and I concentrated on concealing my pain. I didn't desire to detect their dissention today. Keri and Connie disagreed with Dr. T.'s dismissal of my discomfort and with my determination to continue the rehab.

Almost a month after my last hospital stay, the pain in my wrist intensified, and the red marks grew more pronounced. Connie and Keri observed the anguish in my eyes, surpassed only by my fierce passion to press on with my rehab per Dr. T.'s recurrent instructions. They suggested that "something's not right," that I "shouldn't be in this much pain," that the red flares on my wrist reflected "something wrong." They encouraged me to consult with Dr. T. Connie even asked him to "take a quick peak" at me as he passed by the OT room one day.

"Keep working it," he cheered, "Your flexibility is improving. You're doing fine." Connie and Keri exchanged glances, but they said nothing, except briefly acknowledging his time.

Connie and Keri care a lot for me, I thought, as I remembered their efforts to get an off-the-record second opinion of my situation. One of Dr. T.'s colleagues had sauntered into the OT room during my previous OT visit, and Connie had asked him to "do her a favor" by looking at my wrist. Connie downplayed the consultation by framing it as a "quick question" about something curious. The doctor noted that my symptoms mirrored RSD, but he backed away as soon as he learned that I was Dr. T.'s patient.

"Given the symptoms, I think that RSD is a strong possibility, but I can't really say. Talk to Dr. T.," the doctor responded.

I could take the pain, I thought. I could be tough, but I can't stand for anything else to be wrong, not now, not after everything else. Dr. T. denied a problem, and I yearned to believe him.

"Christie, I think that you've had enough for today," Connie said.

I nodded, discouraged, dizzy, disgruntled. I stood, but the world spun. I want to play tennis, I thought . . . I want to play outside . . . I want to be well . . . I want . . . to get . . . home . . . home.

I leaned down and picked up my purse. My feet felt wobbly as I headed toward the stairwell.

RSD, RSD, I had heard that term before . . . Oh yes, Dr. D. had mentioned it during my hospital stay. "What's that?" I had asked.

"Basically, your body responds poorly to pain," she had explained.

Poor reactions to pain . . . pain . . . Man, I feel so wiped out, I thought as I reached the landing of the stairwell. I paused, considering the two-hour drive back to Athens in rush hour traffic. I turned back to the OT room.

"I don't feel well," I admitted as I re-entered the OT room.

Connie called Katie, Dr. T.'s nurse, and the two helped me up on an examining table. Katie took my blood pressure.

"Christie, your blood pressure is incredibly low," she said.

"It's always low," I slurred. How could I feel this way? What was going on?

"Not this low," Katie said. "You are on the borderline of going into shock. We need to get you to the ER."

"NO," I refused loudly. "I'm not going back there. Look, I'm fine, really. I'm making a big deal out of nothing."

Yet, my pain was no more "nothing" then than it had been back in October and November. Denying did not diminish it.

I tried to climb down from the table, but I lacked balance and nearly fell.

"No, you're not," Connie said.

"Okay," Katie conceded, "Let's try to stabilize your blood pressure here in the office, if we can. If we can't do it in half an hour, though, I'm calling an ambulance."

Connie brought me a glass of water. "Drink," she instructed.

"What does water have to do with anything?" I asked. Connie babbled something about hydration, pain, blood pressure . . . I really didn't want understand all of the terms, the implications. I wanted to go home.

My thoughts drifted to the upcoming celebrity auction that I was coordinating. The Girl Scout troop planned to visit DisneyWorld in July. I closed my eyes and saw images of envelopes and flyers and lists, to do lists . . . so much to do . . . too much to do . . .

"Okay," Katie returned, and I forced my eyelids to open. "I'm going to start an IV so that we can get some more fluids in you."

I was trapped in a huge nightmare. I couldn't bear any more needles, no more IVs. I had just driven up for OT, harmless OT, no-needles OT. How could this be happening?

"No, please," I begged. "I don't want an IV. I'm fine. I just want to be better and drive home. Please just let me go home."

"Look," Katie asserted firmly. "We can do this here, or we can get you to the ER."

Tears welled up in my eyes, and I yearned to throw a fit—a good, old-fashioned, temper tantrum. Surely, someone owed me that. I knew that Connie and Katie were staying late to try and help me, but why more IVs? Picking, prodding, more prodding, more picking, more problems, more pain—why now? Why?

Katie made two stabs at starting the IV and missed on both attempts. My blood pressure dipped further, and she decided not to try again.

"Drink one more glass of water, and let's see if that helps," she directed after apologizing for her inability to start the IV promptly. I slumped back against the wall as I lifted the glass to my lips. Maybe my veins do roll, I thought. I shuddered as I envisioned another trip to the ER, another telephone SOS to Roger and the girls, another miserable round of residents, more questions, more . . . "Please let me go home," I prayed. "Please let me . . ."

I injected so many words in that blank—live, thrive, work, play, escape. Over five months post-op, my horror continued in a tiny office as everyone else climbed in their cars, ventured through rush-hour traffic, made dinner for their children, helped with homework, and went to bed after taking vitamins and brushing teeth. I had not yet manipulated my way through the medical maze.

Juxtaposing Role Enactments and Knowledge Bases

Ultimately, God answered my prayers. My blood pressure moved upward, but Connie refused to let me drive home immediately. Instead, she insisted that I join her for dinner in her home until she could be certain that my pressure stabilized. As we dined later, she dropped her noncommital guard and encouraged me to seek a second opinion. "I'd get in a lot of trouble for saying this, but you almost went into shock," she noted. "What will it take to convince him that something's wrong?"

Connie searched her file and offered me an article on Reflex Sympathetic Dystrophy (RSD) (see Watson & Carlson, 1987; related work by Kirkpatrick, July 13, 1999). "I know that you're really smart," she said, "Read this and see what you think. I'm not a doctor or anything, but I think that you should know the possibilities."

As I drove home that evening, I reflected on Connie's comment—"I'm not a doctor or anything." Clearly, she knew enough to know that something was amiss, and her knowledge included research articles on a possible consequence of my surgical procedure. Yet, the perceived institutional structure (perhaps perpetuated by organizational rules, policies, "ways of doing things here" that I could not access as a "patient") influenced her willingness to challenge Dr. T. directly and, to some extent, to contribute to my decision-making process. Connie's hesitation reminded me of the PICC-line nurse who refused to respond clearly to queries about the PICC line, something within her purported realm of expertise.

As I continued toward Athens, my thoughts also drifted to Pam, my home health care nurse. What happened to her, I wondered? After Dr. D. pulled my PICC line, my need for home care ceased. I saw her once more, but never again. She served as such an incredible advocate for me, I remembered. Both Pam and Dr. S. interceded on my behalf numerous times during the PICC-line saga. Neither of them permitted possible status or role differences (i.e., general practitioner and home care nurse versus surgeon, specialist, expert; case manager versus health care team participants) restrain them from questioning, asserting, and in a few cases, demanding. Notably, they didn't necessarily know *what* was wrong, but they readily admitted a lack of knowledge, *not* a lack of authority or responsibility, by pursuing answers from Dr. T.

Even though Dr. T. held the roles of expert and case manager through virtue of his surgery on my hand, he lacked responses to important questions. All others on the "team" (including me) empowered him as the legitimate authority, and he accepted that position. Only twice in my case did Dr. T. refer me to someone else, thus relinquishing some of that power and control over the health care decision-making process.

I would never expect Dr. T. to know everything; he couldn't. Yet, when he maintained his role by not referring me to someone else (and by dismissing concerns from me and others), he placed the rest of the "team" in an awkward interactional position. If we usurped his authority by going over his head or questioning his conclusions, we risked a variety of organizational, identity, and even liability consequences. As Goffman (1959) notes, team members are obliged to present themselves in particular ways during public presentations. When Roger and I went to the hospital to consult with the PICC-line nurse without Dr. T.'s knowledge, I feared that he might resent me for somehow "disobeying" by indicating to others that I preferred another authority. Connie and Keri held their tongues, careful not to show disrespect or disregard for Dr. T.'s position as "expert."

Yet, failure to question cracked the door to further health problems for me. I wouldn't be surprised if Katie cornered Dr. T. privately after my PICC-line visit, mentioning the potential of stroke, which he might have overlooked. If Pam had not insisted that I return to the hospital, I might well have died in my home, assuming that everything was "okay." Dr. T. and the "authorities" at the hospital pushed other possibilities aside, denying my pain and incoherence.

After the near-shock incident in the OT office, I sought second opinions, but no one would accept my case. I had been through too much. I returned to Dr. T., resolved to obtain answers. Although he continued to contradict a RSD diagnosis, he admitted that I might be on the borderline for developing the syndrome. "Back off of rehab," he directed. "You don't want to get RSD; strength isn't worth it. Just take it easy for a few months and rest the wrist. You've been working it too hard."

For months, he had been commanding me to work it, work it, work it, and now, Dr. T. passed the buck to me—I had been "working it too hard." For months, he had been telling me that I needed intense rehab if I wanted to attain the benefits from the reconstructive surgery, and now, he told me to "just take it easy."

Stunned, I persisted, "Will my wrist get better?"

"You've made excellent progress. You have considerable movement. Maybe you've reached your rehab potential," he asserted. "See me in a few months."

Why had he flipped 180 degrees? Had someone spoken to him? Did Connie, Keri, or Katie talk to one of his superiors? Why did he change his tune?

I will never gain an explanation for his reversal in position. However, as a health care seeker, I do know that the combination of multifaceted role enactments and diverse bases of knowledge prompted significant conundrums for my pursuit of wellness—How could I access all of the rich perspectives when some felt restricted in their ability to share important insights? How should I prioritize that information when it became available?

Prioritizing Information and Devising a Plan

As I left Dr. T.'s office for Athens that day, I struggled to sort through a next step. I still could not hold a tennis racket without feeling a twinge, and I experience pain upon the touch of my wrist. How could this outcome be the best that I could do? How could I have gone through everything that I had experienced only to return to square one? How could I know who and what to believe?

I rejected the notion of living with chronic pain. I had no good reason to think that my situation would differ from millions of others who fight through pain every day (see, e.g., http://www.ampainsoc.org/). I had no plan for how to proceed, except that I yearned to move on with my life.

A woman emailed me recently. She heard about my book from speaking to one of my students, and she hoped to gain information about recovering from carpal tunnel and chronic pain. I read and reread her story. She lives in constant pain, trying to hold a job that requires keyboarding, caring for her children, and living a quality life. I referred her to the Reflex Sympathetic Dystrophy Syndrome Association website and a few other sources that I discovered on the Internet, and I offered my good wishes. I could do little else.

Although some interventions exist for chronic pain, solutions depend strongly on individual reactions, as in all other medical circumstances. I got pretty lucky. I stopped therapy, and after time, the pain began to subside over the summer. Drives to Columbus no longer involved trips to OT or the ER. When the side of my wrist started to throb again in September 1997, I revisited Dr. T. for the first time since May. He prescribed an anti-inflammatory drug, and when the redness didn't disappear, he determined that one of the screws in my wrist had gone bad. He recommended that he remove it surgically. In December 1997, I had my third wrist surgery of the year. Fortunately, no complications ensued.

Yet, for the woman who emailed me, the waves of pain continue in a debilitating manner. She struggles to maintain her relationships at work and at home, and she battles her doctor for additional resources and treatment. "People just can't understand the pain," she notes, "until they feel it themselves."

Precisely because all situations and health care participants are unique, health care seekers, professionals, and social support system members must treat health care challenges as emergent, temporal, diverse, and multifaceted. Health care information, options, and relationships should be considered in light of the lived reality of health care participants, especially the health care seeker.

Throughout this book, I have discussed the value of identification in health care interactions. The extent to which health care participants identify (or do not identify) with each other impacts the sharing of information, viewpoints, and ideas for action. Further, as health care seekers sift through the plethora of perspectives from professionals and an array of other sources, I contend that their respective ability to identify with materials and suggestions can guide their decision making. In my case, I juxtaposed comments from friends, family, nurses, occupational therapists, a general practitioner, an orthopedic specialist, and a hand specialist. When I sat at Don Pablo's, trying to decide about the original surgery, no one told me what to do. I had to reflect upon what coincided with my version of "reasonable" and "acceptable."

Notably, as I grew more and more entrapped in my medical maze, I couldn't always gain perspective or rationale. Although I maintained my ability to give or deny consent for various versions of care, in retrospect, I question my qualifications to prioritize information at some points. When I was sliding in and out of consciousness, I made decisions that might have resulted in serious problems. I was very fortunate.

My experience crystalizes for me the importance of a strong social support network, particularly in terms of a friend or loved one who shares a similar perspective, someone who can be entrusted to assess input and make decisions that stem from a common framework of the world and medicine. Without such an individual or network, health care seekers must rely on themselves when they lack the physical and emotional capacities to sort through already complicated and confusing recommendations.

CLOSING THOUGHTS

As a health communication scholar, the wrist reconstruction/staph infection saga enabled me to comprehend the complexities of contemporary health communication. Having relatively good health throughout my life, I conceptualized health communication in the limited sense of doctor–patient communication, rather than the complicated, tangled web of bureaucracies, professionals, support systems, and mediated resources that it can be. I did not even imagine the challenges of working with multiple health care professionals or attempting to juxtapose serious illness on to an already chaotic life.

I never considered how support systems could be stretched in an effort to care for children, accomplish work and civic obligations, and manage necessary daily routines when illness renders a family member unable to contribute as well as in need of support. Given my lived reality as a white, middle-class, Baptist woman on the brink of the new millennium, I had only experienced negative consequences from my sociocultural-economic background one time. Although I cannot claim to know discrimination, I have had at least a taste of frustration with being labeled and categorized.

Chelsea Meagan, now five, remembers the time when "Mommy had a big boo boo on her arm." Brittany, now thirteen, wishes that I would never write another book. She associates *Partnership* with the staph infection and this project with my chest pain as well as the renewal of more suffering due to my wrist. Gilda Radner's book title sums it up—"It's always something."

As I close this book, I want to emphasize, though, that the "something," the health care concern, always occurs within the context of a life. For most of us, that life constitutes an increasingly complicated and multifaceted existence. We can't just stop to be "sick."

Further, we cannot disregard the implicativeness of the swirl of activity around us for our reactions to health care relationships and health care decisions. We seek (and perhaps offer) health care amid our individualized philosophies of medicine, our multiplicity of interactions with diverse health care professionals within the fragmented, emergent, chaotic health care industry, our temporal and splintered social support networks, rampantly expanding technology, and deafening public dialogues about health.

I bookmarked the chapter on my wrist reconstruction as I ended my first marriage. Although I wanted complete closure with each painful event, I know now that remnants of both will remain with me forever. Wade and I have moved on, creating a new, pretty positive relationship based on what can be rather than on what never will be again. I'm able to nail a crisp, cross-court backhand again, but my tennis games usually terminate when I drop my racket in pain after about an hour of play. Like my first marriage, the wrist saga merges with my other life experiences, the other scraps of encounters that shape me and how I respond to situations, especially health care concerns.

As I move on into new medical mazes, I feel wiser in the world of managed care and team-based approaches to health care; I know more about interacting with diverse types of professionals; I grasp the grip that technology holds on accomplishing and communicating about health care. Perhaps most importantly, though, I feel stronger due to substantially more social support.

On July 24, 1999, I married Roger. (Okay, who didn't see that one coming?) I could gush about him, but I'll refrain, except for this—I now understand the beauty and richness of spousal support in times of health crisis. He couldn't stop my heart palpitations, but he compelled me to seek help. He can't stop my wrist from throbbing as I type these final pages, but he can give me the extra time that I need to accomplish the task . . .

Medical mazes can mind-boggle us, frustrate us, discourage us, confuse us. Whether we're deciding about an annual flu shot, considering vaccinating our children, or seeking help for a broken arm, cracked tooth, or serious illness, we sometimes know only that we can't know *for certain* what may transpire. I'm glad that I now have a life partner to comfort me when I get scared in the darkness of a terrifying tunnel. However, managing our way through the medical mazes of the new millennium depends on the communication between all health care participants—seekers, professionals, and support system members—as they co-construct what counts as the "best" course.

Throughout the book, excerpts will be shared from interviews with health care participants. Students in interviewing classes at Ohio University served as co-researchers by talking with health care participants about their health care experiences. The primary reason for conducting the interviews was pedagogical. I hoped that my students would practice their information-gathering skills while learning more about participants' experiences during health care interviews.

In all, 287 individuals were interviewed by students over a two-year period. Each interview participant signed a release form, acknowledging that s/he consented to be audiotaped, to allow the interview to be transcribed by the student interviewer, and to allow the transcript to be used in my research data set. Because the interview participants were guaranteed confidentiality, the student interviewers were instructed to exclude the names of participants from transcripts. For the purpose of this book, I have created names for each of the interview participants that are not their own. Neither the interview participants nor the student interviewers received payment for their involvement in the study. The interviews were to take approximately ten minutes.

Each student interviewer could develop his or her own interview schedule as long as it fulfilled the primary goal of attaining information about health care experiences. Each student interviewer could select anyone as a participant. Because this project lacks consistency in terms of interview schedules and sample selection methods, the comments by the interview participants are not intended to be generalizable. I have selected excerpts as a means of illustrating points only.

APPENDIX

B

These internet references constitute just a small sample of the many internet sources of information about health care issues.

http://www.healthyculture.com
http://dartmouth. edu
http://galenet.gale.co...ir-nohits.html&r=O&f=S
http://www.wsu.edu:8080/~wrc/links.htm
http://www.netwellness.org
http://www.yahoo.com/health/
http://www.infoseek.com/topic/health
http://www.excite.com/health
http://medscape.com
http://www.healthscout.com/
http://www.aol.com/webcenters/health/
http://www4.ccf.org/health/
http://www.betterhealth.com/
http://www.hotbot.com/health/
http://www.bewell.com/
http://www.mayohealth.org
http://www.einstein.edu/
http://www.healthy.net/
http://www.nih.gov/
http://nhic-nt.health.org/
http://www.healthfinder.gov
http://www.healthtalk.com/
http://www.mylifepath.com/
http://www.americas doctor.com
http://www.healthanswers.com
http://www.onhealth.com
http://www.amhrt.org

http://www.ama-assn.org/special/womh/womh.htm
http://www.womenconnect.com
http://www. managedhealth.com
http://www.ncqa.org
http://www.vh.org/
http://www.dartmouth.edu/~drisin/about_ site.html

REFERENCES

AAMC STAT. (1998, July 5). Pitt establishes nation's first endowed chair in patient-centered care.

Aaronson, K., Schwartz, J., Goin, J., & Mancini, D. (1995). Sex differences in patient acceptance of cardiac transplant candidacy. *Circulation, 91*(11), 2753–2761.

Aaronson, L. S. (1989, January/February). Perceived and received support: Effects on health behavior during pregnancy. *Nursing Research, 38,* 4–9.

Abel, E. K. (1991). *Who cares for the elderly? Public policy and the experiences of adult daughters.* Philadelphia, PA: Temple University Press.

Abel, E. K., & Nelson, M. K. (Eds.). (1990). *Circles of care: Work and identity in women's lives.* Albany, NY: State University of New York.

Abercrombie, N. (1994). Authority and consumer society. In R. Keat, N. Whiteley, & N. Abercrombie (Eds.), *The authority of the consumer* (pp. 43–57). New York: Routledge.

AbuGharbieh, P. (1998). Arab Americans. In L. Purnell and B. Paulanka (Eds.), *Transcultural health care* (pp. 137–162). Philadelphia: F.A. Davis.

Adams, P. (1998). *House calls: How we can all heal the world one visit at a time.* San Francisco: Robert D. Reed Publishers.

Adams, P., with Mylander, M. (1998). *Gesundheit! Bringing good health to you, the medical system, and society through physician service, complementary therapies, humor, and joy.* Rochester, VT: Healing Arts Press.

Adelman, M. B. (1991). Play and incongruity: Framing safe-sex talk. *Health Communication, 3,*139–155.

Adelman, M. B. (1992). Sustaining passion: Eroticism and safe-sex talk. *Archives of Sexual Behavior, 21,* 481–494.

Adelman, M. B., & Frey, L. R.(1997). *The fragile community: Living together with AIDS.* Mahwah, NJ: Lawrence Erlbaum Associates.

Adelman, R., Greene, M., & Charon, R. (1987, December). The physician–elderly patient–companion triad in the medical encounter: The development of a conceptual framework and research agenda. *The Gerontologist, 27*(6), 729–734.

Adelman, R., Greene, M., Charon, R., & Friedmann, E. (1992, June). The content of physician and elderly patient interaction in the medical primary care encounter. *Communication Research, 19* (3), 370–380.

Aden, R. (1999). *Popular stories and promised lands: Fan cultures and symbolic pilgrimages.* Tuscaloosa, AL: University of Alabama Press.

Ainsworth-Vaughn, N. (1998). *Claiming power in doctor-patient talk.* New York: Oxford University Press.

Airhihenbuwa, C. (1995). *Health and culture: Beyond the western paradigm.* Thousand Oaks, CA: Sage.

Albrecht, T. L., & Adelman, M. B. (1987). Communication networks as structures of social support. In T. L. Albrecht, M. B. Adelman, & associates (Eds.), *Communicating social support* (pp. 40–63). Newbury Park, CA: Sage.

Albrecht, T. L., Adelman, M. B., & associates (Eds.). (1987). *Communicating social support.* Newbury Park, CA: Sage.

Allan, M.A. (1998). Elder abuse: A challenge for home care nurse. *Home Healthcare Nurse, 16 (2),* 103–110.

Allman, J. (1998). Bearing the burden or baring the soul: Physicians' self-disclosure and boundary management regarding medical mistakes. *Health Communication, 10,* 175–197.

Altenberg, H. (1992). *Holistic medicine: A meeting of east and west.* Tokyo: Japan Publications.

Altman, L. (1995, February 15). Study finds sexual biases in doctors' choice of pacemakers. *The New York Times National,* p. A16.

Ambler, M. (1994, Winter). Making room for tradition: *Tribal College Journal of American Indian Higher Education, 5* (3), 17–19, 37.

American Osteopathic Association. (1991). *What is a DO?* Chicago: American Osteopathic Association.

Anderson, L., Rakowski, W., & Hickey, T. (1988, June). Satisfaction with clinical encounters among residents and geriatric patients. *Journal of Medical Education, 63,* 447–455.

Anderson, R., Cissna, K., & Arnett, R. (1994). *The reach of dialogue: Confirmation, voice, and community.* Cresskill, NJ: Hampton Press.

Anderson, W. (Ed.). (1995). *The truth about the truth: De-confusing and re-constructing the postmodern world.* New York: G.P. Putnam's Sons.

Andrews, L., & Novick, L., & associates (1995). *HIV care: A comprehensive handbook for providers.* Thousand Oaks, CA: Sage.

Ang, I. (1996). *Living room wars: Rethinking media audiences for a postmodern world.* New York: Routledge.

Angel, R. J., & Angel, J. L. (1997). *Who will care for us? Aging and long-term care in multicultural America.* New York: New York University Press.

Angell, M., & Kassirer, J. P. (1996). Quality and the medical marketplace—following elephants. *The New England Journal of Medicine, 335,* 883–885.

Annandale, E., & Hunt, K. (1998). Accounts of disagreements with doctors. *Social Science and Medicine, 46*(1), 119–129.

Anspach, R. (1997). *Deciding who lives: Fateful choices in the intensive-care nursery.* Berkeley, CA: University of California Press.

AP. (1998, April 28). Health facts on the web are not always reliable. *Athens Messenger,* p. 6.

AP. (1998, July 1). Caregiving a health risk for daughters. *Athens Messenger,* p. 6.

AP. (1998, July 29). Dr. Laura is priestess of airwaves. *Athens Messenger,* p. 8.

AP. (1998, November 29).Doctors debate benefits of new pap test. *Athens Messenger,* p. 10C.

AP. (1998, December 27). Grandparents enlisted as troops in war on drugs. *Athens Messenger,* p. 4A.

AP. (1999, February 19). Faith-healing parents get probation, fines. *Athens Messenger,* p. 5.

AP. (1999, February 28). Will there be enough nurses? *Athens Messenger,* p. 2D.

AP. (1999, March 1). Organs transplants are welcome news in Japan. *Athens Messenger,* p. 6.

AP. (1999, April 9). Democrats kick off campaign for patients' rights. *Athens Messenger,* p. 1.

AP. (1999, April 11). A compromise is prescribed in health care debate. *Athens Messenger,* p. A1.

AP. (1999, June 10). New mothers staying in hospital longer, reversing trend of "drive-by deliveries." *Athens Messenger,* p. 1.

AP. (1999, June 21). Support important if you want to stay with an exercise program. *Athens Messenger,* p. 11.

AP. (1999, June 24a). AMA: Forming union a matter of autonomy. *Athens Messenger,* p. 1.

AP. (1999, June 24b). FTC aims at health products making false claims on the web. *Athens Messenger,* p. 16.

AP. (1999, July 12). Fight for "patients' bill of rights" focuses new interest on the nation's uninsured. *Athens Messenger,* p. 5.

AP. (1999, July 13). Senate HMO debate highlights political philosophies. *Athens Messenger,* p. 1.

AP. (1999, September 26). U.N. report calls for better health care for women. *Athens Messenger,* p. 11A.

AP. (1999, October 9). Lawmaker pushes bill requiring state to post physician profiles. *Columbus Dispatch,* p. 5B.

AP. (1999, December 3). Cancer survivor recalls celebrity ads. *USA Today,* p. 15A.

AP. (1999, December 7). Clinton, Congress take aim at deadly medical mistake. *Athens Messenger,* p. 1.

Apostolos-Cappadona, D., & Ebersole, L. (1995). *Women, creativity, and the arts: Critical and autobiographical perspectives.* New York: Continuum.

Appleby, J. (1999, July 14). Study stirs health care tiff. *USA Today,* p. 2B.

Appleby, J. (1999, July 29). Health-plan hassles called threat to care. *USA Today,* p. 1A.

Appleby, J. (1999, August 24). Kaiser plan widely watched. *USA Today,* pp. 1–2A.

Appleby, J. (1999, October 29). HMO image driving patients to other plan. *USA Today,* p. 3B.

Appleby, J. (1999, November 9). Health plan eases doctor oversight. *USA Today,* p. 1A.

Appleby, J. (2000, January 12). Bayer must spend $1M to clarify claims about aspirin's benefits. *USA Today,* p. 2B.

Appleby, J., Covington, E., Hoyt, D., Latham, M., & Sneider, A. (Eds.). (1996). *Knowledge and postmodernism in historical perspective.* New York: Routledge.

Archer, J. (1973). *The prodigal daughter.* New York: Pocket Books.

Area Health Education Centers. (1999). *Consortium for health education in Appalachian Ohio* (Annual report). Athens, OH: Ohio University.

Armour, S.(1998, August 19). Elder care challenges employers. *USA Today,* p. 6B.

Arnett, R. (1992). *Dialogic education: Conversation about ideas and between persons.* Carbondale, IL: Southern Illinois University Press.

Arney, W. (1982). *Power and the profession of obstetrics.* Chicago: The University of Chicago Press.

Arney, W., & Bergen, B. (1984). *Medicine and the management of living: Taming the last great beast.* Chicago: The University of Chicago Press.

Arntson, P. (1989). Improving citizens' health competencies. *Health Communication 1(1),* 29–34.

Aronsson, K., & Satterlund-Larsson, U. (1987). Politeness strategies and doctor-patient communication: On the social choreography of collaborative thinking. *Journal of Language and Social Psychology, 6*(1), 1–26.

Aroskar, M. (1991). Caring—another side. *Journal of Professional Nursing, 7* (1), 3.

Aston, G. (1997). Your right to talk to patients. *American Medical Association News, 40*(10), 1 & 36.

Atkin, C., & Wallack, L. (Eds.). (1990). *Mass communication and public health.* Newbury Park, CA: Sage.

Atkinson, P. (1995). *Medical talk and medical work: The liturgy of the clinic.* Thousand Oaks, CA: Sage Publications.

Atkinson, P. (1997). *The clinical experience: The construction and reconstruction of medical reality* (2nd ed.). Aldershot: Ashgate.

Austin, E. W. (1995). Direct and indirect influences of parent-child communication on adolescents' prevention behaviors for AIDS and drug abuse. In G. L. Kreps & D. O'Hair (Eds.), *Communication and health outcomes* (pp. 163–184). Cresskill, NJ: Hampton Press.

Backer, T., & Rogers, E. (Eds.). (1993). *Organizational aspects of health communication campaigns: What works?* Newbury Park, CA: Sage.

Backer, T., Rogers, E., & Sopory, P. (1992). *Designing health communication campaigns: What works?* Newbury Park, CA: Sage.

Baer, H. (Ed.). (1987). *Encounters with biomedicine: Case studies in medical anthropology.* New York: Gordon and Breach.

Baer, H. (1995). Medical pluralism in the United States: A review. *Medical Anthropology Quarterly, 9* (4), 493–502.

Baer, H., Singer, M., & Susser, I. (1997). *Medical anthropology and the world system: A critical perspective.* Westport, CT: Bergin & Garvey.

Baider, L., Cooper, C. L., & De-Nour, A. K. (Eds.). (1996). *Cancer and the family.* New York: John Wiley & Sons.

Baker, B. (1998, January/February). Rx: Friendship. *Common Boundary,* pp. 37–41.

Baker, C. (1997, September). Cultural relativism and cultural diversity: Implications for nursing practice. *Advances in Nursing Science, 20*(1), 3–11.

Ball, M. M., & Whittington, F. J. (1995). *Surviving dependence: Voice of African American elders.* Amityville, NY: Baywood Publishing Company.

Ballard-Reisch, D. (1990). A model of participative decision making for physician-patient interaction. *Health Communication, 2*(2), 91–104.

Barnlund, D. (1997). Communication in a global village. In L. A. Samovar & R. E. Porter (Eds.), *Intercultural communication* (pp. 27–35). Belmont, CA: Wadsworth Publishing Company.

Barr, O. (1997, September 25–October 8). Interdisciplinary teamwork: Consideration of the challenges. *British Journal of Nursing, 6*(17), 1005–1010.

Barrett, J., & Brecht, R. (1998). Historical context of telemedicine. In S. Viegas & K. Dunn (Eds.), *Telemedicine: Practicing in the information age* (pp. 9–15). Philadelphia: Lippincott-Raven Publishers.

Barrett, L. L. (1998, November). *Independent living: Do older parents and adult children see it the same way? An AARP survey.* Washington, DC: AARP.

Barrett, S., & editors of Consumer Reports (1990). *Health schemes, scams, and frauds.* Mount Vernon, NY: Consumers Union.

Barrett, S., & Herbert, V. (1994). *The vitamin pushers: How the "health food" industry is selling America a bill of goods.* Amherst, NY: Prometheus Books.

Barrett, S., & Jarvis, W. (Eds.). (1993). *The health robbers: A close look at quackery in America.* Buffalo, NY: Prometheus Books.

Barry, M. (1999, December 22–29). Involving patients in medical decisions. How can physicians do better? *JAMA, 282*(24), 2356–2357.

Barry, P., Gooding, J., Harris, T., Hazzard, W., & Winograd, C. (1993). Older women's health. *Journal of American Geriatrics Society, 41,* 680–683.

Bartolomeo, C. (1994, April). Women and children last. *American Teacher, 78,* 16–17.

Bashshur, R., Sanders, J., & Shannon, G. (Eds.). (1997). *Telemedicine: Theory and practice.* Springfield, IL: Charles C. Thomas.

Bass, D. (1990). *Caring families: Supports and interventions.* Silver Spring, MD: NASW Press.

Basso, K. (1990). *Western Apache language and culture: Essays in linguistic anthropology.* Tucson: University of Arizona Press.

Bates, M., Rankin-Hill, L., & Sanchez-Ayendez, M. (1997). The effects of the cultural context of health care on treatment of and response to chronic pain and illness. *Social Science and Medicine, 45* (9), 1433–1447.

Bateson, G. (1951). Information and codification: A philosophical approach. In J. Ruesch & G. Bateson (Eds.), *Communication: The social matrix of psychiatry* (pp. 168–211). New York: Norton.

Bateson, G. (1972). *Steps to an ecology of mind.* New York: Ballantine.

Batiuk, T. (1999, January 31). Funky Winkerbean. Batom, Inc. Distributed by North America Syndicate.

Batiuk, T. (1999, February 7). Funky Winkerbean. Batom, Inc. Distributed by North America Syndicate.

Batiuk, T. (1999, February 21). Funky Winkerbean. Batom, Inc. Distributed by North America Syndicate.

Batiuk, T. (1999, March 21). Funky Winkerbean. Batom, Inc. Distributed by North America Syndicate.

Batt, S. (1994). *Patient no more: The politics of breast cancer*. Charlottetown, Canada: Best Gagne.

Baxter, L., & Montgomery, B. (1996). *Relating: Dialogues and dialectics*. New York: The Guilford Press.

Baym, N. (2000). *Tune in, log in: Soaps, fandom and online community*. Thousand Oaks, CA: Sage.

Bazell, R. (2000, January, 19). Fox to aid in Parkinson's awareness. *MSNBC* [On-line]. Availability http:www.msnbc.com/news/359570.asp

Beach, W. (1995). Preserving and constraining options: "Okays" and "official" priorities in medical interviews. In G. Morris & R. Chenail (Eds.), *The talk of the clinic: Explorations in the analysis of medical and therapeutic discourse* (pp. 259–290). Hillsdale, NJ: Lawrence Erlbaum Associates.

Beach, W. A. (1996). *Conversations about illness: Family preoccupations with bulimia*. Mahwah, NJ: Lawrence Erlbaum Associates.

Beck, C. (1998). [Review of the book *Health Communication: Lessons from family planning and reproductive health*]. *Journal of Health Communication, 3*(4), 379–382.

Beck, C., & Ragan, S. (1995). The impact of relational activities on the accomplishment of practitioner and patient goals in the gynecologic examination. In G. Kreps & D. O'Hair (Eds.), *Communication and health outcomes* (pp. 73–86). Cresskill, NJ: Hampton Press.

Beck, C. with Ragan, S., & duPre, A. (1997). *Partnership for health: Building relationships between women and health caregivers*. Mahwah, NJ: Lawrence Erlbaum Associates.

Beck, J. (1990, November 29). Doctors' attitudes can be hazardous to women's health. *Chicago Tribune*, p. 1:23.

Beck, J. K., Dries, T. J., & Cook, E. C. (1998, March 1). Development of an interdisciplinary, telephone-based care program. *American Journal of Health-System Pharmacy, 55,* 453–457.

Becker, G. (1994). Metaphors in disrupted lives: Infertility and cultural constructions of continuity. *Medical Anthropology Quarterly, 8* (4), 383–410.

Becker, M. (1974). The health belief model and sick role behavior. *Health Education Monographs, 2,* 409–419.

Beisecker, A. (1988). Aging and the desire for information and input in medical decisions: Patient consumerism in medical enounters. *The Gerontologist, 28*(3), 330–335.

Beisecker, A. (1989). The influence of a companion on the doctor-elderly patient interaction. *Health Communication, 1*(1), 55–70.

Beisecker, A. (1990). Patient power in doctor-patient communication: What do we know? *Health Communication, 2*(2), 105–122.

Beisecker, A., & Beisecker, T. (1990). Patient information-seeking behaviors when communicating with doctors. *Medical Care, 28* (1), 19–28.

Belenky, M., Clinchy, B., Goldberger, N., & Tarule, J. (1973). *Women's ways of knowing: The development of self, voice, and mind*. New York: Basic Books.

Bellah, R., Madsen, R., Sullivan, W., Swidler, A., & Tipton, S. (1985). *Habits of the heart: Individualism and commitment in American life*. New York: Harper & Row.

Bellandi, D. (1998, April 13). Designed for growth: Catholic megasystem CHI set to take off. *Modern Healthcare*, 36–38.

Benedetto, R. (1998, July 7). Nancy Reagan's work is still not done, article says. *USA Today*, p. 11A.

Benhabib, S. (1992). *Situating the self. Gender, community and postmodernism in contemporary ethics*. New York: Routledge.

Bensing, J., Brink-Muinen, A., & De Bakker, D. (1993). Gender differences in practice style. A Dutch study of general practitioners. *Medical Care, 319* (3), 219–229.

Berek, B., & Canna, M. (1994). *Telemedicine on the move: Health care heads down the information superhighway.* Chicago, IL: American Hospital Association.

Berg, M. (1997). *Rationalizing medical work: Decision-support techniques and medical practices.* Cambridge, MA: The MIT Press.

Berger, P., & Luckmann, T. (1966). *The social construction of reality: A treatise in the sociology of knowledge.* Garden City, NY: Doubleday.

Best, S., & Kellner, D. (1991). *Postmodern theory: Critical interrogations.* New York: Guilford Press.

Bianco, R. (1998, November 24). Smits departs with a stirring salute. *USA Today,* p. 1D.

Biegel, D. E., Tracy, E. M., & Corvo, K. N. (1994, August). Strengthening social networks: Intervention strategies for mental health case managers. *Health & Social Work, 19*(3), 206–216.

Bishop, J. (1992, February). Guidelines for a nonsexist (gender sensitive) doctor-patient relationship. *Canadian Journal of Psychiatry, 37,* 62–65.

Blalock, S., & Devellis, B. (1986). Stereotyping: The link between theory and practice. *Patient Education and Counseling, 8,* 17–25.

Blaxter, M., & Paterson, E. (1982). *Mothers and daughters: A three-generational study of health attitudes and behaviour.* London: Heinemann Eductional Books Ltd.

Blommaert, J., & Verschueren, J. (1998). *Debating diversity: Analysing the discourse of tolerance.* New York: Routledge.

Bloom, J. R., Alexander, J. A., & Nuchols, B. A. (1997). Nurse staffing patterns and hospital efficiency in the United States. *Social Science and Medicine, 44*(2), 147–155.

Blot, D., Vandewoude, K., & Colardyn, F. (1998). Letter to editor. *New England Journal of Medicine, 339* (27), 2025.

Bly, L. (1999, July 14). A network of support: Patients find emotional, practical advice—and each other. *USA Today,* pp. 1–2D.

Boden, D., & Zimmerman, D. (Eds.). (1991). *Talk and social structure: Studies in ethnomethodology and conversation analysis.* Berkeley, CA: University of California Press.

Bodenheimer, T., Lo, B., & Casalino, L. (1999, June 2). Primary care physicians should be coordinators, not gatekeepers. *JAMA, 281*(21), 2045–2049.

Bogardus, S., Holmboe, E., & Jekel, J. (1999, March 17). Perils, pitfalls, and possibilities in talking about medical risk. *JAMA, 281,* 1037–1041.

Bogner, M. (Eds.). (1994). *Human error in medicine.* Hillsdale, NJ: Lawrence Erlbaum Associates.

Boorstein, M. (1995, January 1). Cancer patient gives future doctors lesson in compassion. AP News Service.

Booth, A. (Ed.). (1991). *Contemporary families: Looking forward, looking back.* Minneapolis, MN: National Council on Family Relations.

Booth, C. (1999, August 30). Taking care of our aging parents. *Time,* pp. 48–51.

Bosk, C. L. (1979). *Forgive and remember: Managing medical failure.* Chicago: The University of Chicago Press.

Bosk, C. (1981). *Managing medical failure.* Chicago: The University of Chicago Press.

Bourhis, R. Y., Roth, S., & MacQueen, G. (1989). Communication in the hospital setting: A survey of medical and everyday language use amongst patients, nurses, and doctors. *Social Science and Medicine, 28*(40), 339–346.

Bowersox, J. (1998). Telerobotics in surgery. In S. Viegas & K. Dunn (Eds.), *Telemedicine: Practicing in the information age* (pp. 107–114). Philadelphia: Lippincott-Raven.

Bowles, S. (1999, March 29). Amid diabetic agony, a friend's selfless offer. *USA Today,* p. 5D.

Boyd, E. A. (1997). *Constructing histories and negotiating care: Professional discourse during medical peer review.* Unpublished doctoral dissertation, University of California, Los Angeles.

Bracht, N. (Ed.). (1990). *Health promotion at the community level.* Newbury Park, CA: Sage.

Braddock, C., Edwards, K., Hasenberg, N., Laidley, T., & Levinson, W. (1999, December 22–29). Informed decision making in outpatient practice. *JAMA, 282*(24), 2313–2320.

Braithwaite, D. (1996). "Person first": Expanding communicative choices by persons with disabilities. In E. B. Ray (Ed.), *Communication and disenfranchisement* (pp. 449–464). Mahwah, NJ: Lawrence Erlbaum Associates.

Braithwaite, D., & Thompson, T. (Eds.). (2000). *Handbook of communication and people with disabilities.* Mahwah, NJ: Lawrence Erlbaum Associates.

Brandenburger, A., & Nalebuff, B. (1996). *Co-opetition.* New York: Doubleday.

Brenders, D. A. (1989). Perceived control and the interpersonal dimension of health care. *Health Communication, 1*(2), 117–135.

Briar, K. H., & Kaplan, C. (1990). *The family caregiving crisis.* Silver Spring, MD: National Association of Social Workers.

Brink, S. (1997, March 10). Medicine: Innovative programs prepare students for managed care. *U.S. News and World Report,* 84–85.

Bronstein, J. M. (1996). The politics of U.S. health care reform. *Medical Anthropology Quarterly, 10*(1), 20–28.

Bronzino, J. D., Smith, V. H., & Wade, M. L. (1991). *Medical technology and society: An interdisciplinary perspective.* Cambridge, MA: Massachusetts Institute of Technology Press.

Brooks, N., & Matson, R. (1987). Managing multiple sclerosis. In J. Roth & P. Conrad (Eds.), *Research in the sociology of health care: The experience and management of chronic illness* (pp. 73–106). Greenwich, CT: JAI Press.

Broom, D., & Woodward, R. (1996). Medicalisation reconsidered: Toward a collaborative approach to care. *Sociology of Health & Illness, 18*(3), 357–378.

Browder, S. E. (1998, December 17). A woman's heart. *Woman's Day,* 42, 44, 46.

Brown, K. (1990). Connected independence: A paradox of rural health? *Journal of Rural Community Psychology, 11*(1), 51–64.

Brown, P., & Levinson, S.(1987). *Politeness: Some universals in language use.* Cambridge: Cambridge University Press.

Brown, W., & Basil, M. (1995). Media celebrities and public health: Responses to "Magic" Johnson's HIV disclosure and its impact on AIDS risk and high-risk behaviors. *Health Communication, 7*(4), 345–370.

Browner, C., & Press, N. (1996). The production of authoritative knowledge in American prenatal care. *Medical Anthropology Quarterly, 10*(2), 141–156.

Bulechek, G. M., & McCloskey J. C. (Eds.). (1992). Nursing interventions. *The Nursing Clinics of North America, 27*(20).

Bull, C. (Ed.). (1993). *Aging in rural America.* Newbury Park, CA: Sage.

Buller, D.B., & Borland, R. (1999). Skin cancer prevention for children: A critical review. *Health Education and Behavior, 26*(3), 37–343.

Burdi, M. D., & Baker, L. C. (1997). Market-level health maintenance organization activity and physician autonomy and satisfaction. *The American Journal of Managed Care, 3*(9), 1357–1366.

Burgoon, J., Pfau, M., Parrott, R., Birk, T., Coker, R., & Burgoon, M. (1987). Relational communication, satisfaction, compliance-gaining strategies, and compliance in communication between physicians and patients. *Communication Monographs, 54,* 307–324.

Burke, K. (1969). *A rhetoric of motives.* Berkeley, CA: University of California Press.

Burke, M. (1992, August 5). Women's, children's groups say reform debate ignores needs. *Hospitals, 66,* 28–30.

Burke, M. J. (1995). *The conundrum of class.* Chicago: The University of Chicago Press.

Burleson, B. R., Albrecht, T. L., & Sarason, I. G. (Eds.). (1994). *Communication of social support: Messages, interactions, relationships, and community.* Thousand Oaks, CA: Sage.

Bursztajn, H., Feinbloom, R., Hamm, R., & Brodsky, A. (1981). *Medical choices, medical chances. How patients, families, and physicians can cope with uncertainty.* New York: Merloyd Lawrence.

Bury, M. (1986). Social constructionism and the development of medical sociology. *Sociology of Health and Illness, 8* (2), 137–169.

Butler, K. (1992). *A consumer's guide to "alternative medicine."* Buffalo, NY: Prometheus Books.

Butterill, D., O'Hanlon, J., & Book, H. (1992, April). When the system is the problem, don't blame the patient: Problems inherent in the interdisciplinary inpatient team. *Canadian Journal of Psychiatry, 37*(3), 168–172.

Cain, N. (1996). *Healing the child: A mother's story.* New York: Rawson Associates.

Calhoun, C. (Ed.). (1992). *Habermas and the public sphere.* Cambridge, MA: The MIT Press.

Calnan, M. (1984). Clinical uncertainty: Is it a problem in the doctor-patient relationship? *Sociology of Health and Illness, 6*(1), 74–85.

Calnan, M. (1989). Control over health and patterns of health-related behavior. *Social Science and Medicine, 29*(2), 131–136.

Cancer claims life of Pryce's daughter. (1999, September 5). *Columbus Dispatch,* p. D1.

Capitanio, J., & Herek, G. (1999). AIDS-related stigma and attitudes toward injecting drug users among black and white Americans. *American Behavioral Scientist, 42* (7), 1148–1161.

Capron, A. M. (1996, September–October). Between doctor and patient. *Hastings Center Report,* 23–4.

Carbaugh, D. (1990). *Cultural communication and intercultural contact.* Hillsdale, NJ: Lawrence Erlbaum Associates.

Carbaugh, D. (1996). *Situating selves: The communication of social identities in American scenes.* Albany, NY: SUNY Press.

Carey, A., & Merrill, D. (1999, January 12). Drug ads bring in patients. *USA Today,* p. 1B.

Carter, R., with Golant, S. K. (1994). *Helping yourself help others: A book for caregivers.* New York: Times Books.

Cassell, E. (1991). *The nature of suffering and the goals of medicine.* New York: Oxford University Press.

Cassell, E. (1999). Diagnosing suffering: A perspective. *Annals of Internal Medicine, 131,* 531–534.

Cassell, J. (1991). *Expected miracles: Surgeons at work.* Philadelphia: Temple University Press.

Cavender, T. (1988). The professionalism of traditional medicine in Zimbabwe. *Human Organization, 47* (3), 251–256.

Cawyer, C. S., & Smith-Dupré, A. (1995). Communicating social support: Identifying supportive episodes in an HIV/AIDS support group. *Communication Quarterly, 43*(3), 243–358.

Cegala, D., McNeilis, K., McGee, D., & Jonas, A. (1995). A study of doctors' and patients' perceptions of information processing and communication competence during the medical interview. *Health Communication, 7* (3), 179–203.

Cerminara, K. L. (1998). The class action suit as a method of patient empowerment in the managed care setting. *American Journal of Law and Medicine, 24*(1), 7–58.

Cerulo, K., Ruane, J., & Chayko, M. (1992). Technological ties that bind: Media-generated primary groups. *Communication Research, 19*(1), 109–129.

Charles, C., Gafni, A., & Whelan, T. (1997). Shared decision-making in the medical encounter: What does it mean? (Or it takes at least two to tango). *Social Science and Medicine, 44*(5), 681–692.

Charmaz, K. (1997). Identity dilemmas of chronically ill men. In A. Strauss & J. Corbin (Eds.), *Grounded theory in practice* (pp. 35–62). Thousand Oaks, CA: Sage.

Charon, R. (1986). To render the lives of patients. *Literature and Medicine, 5,* 58–74.

Chay-Nemeth, C. (1998). Demystifying AIDS in Thailand: A dialectical analysis of the Thai sex industry. *Journal of Health Communication, 3*(3), 217–232.

Chew, F., Palmer, S., & Kim, S. (1998). Testing the influence of the health belief model and a television program on nutrition behavior. *Health Communication, 10*(3), 227–246.

Cichon, E., & Masterson, J. (1993). Physician-patient communication: Mutual role expectations. *Communication Quarterly, 41* (4), 477–489.

Cicirelli, V. G. (1992). *Family caregiving: Autonomous and paternalistic decision making.* Newbury Park, CA: Sage.

Cicourel, A. (1970). Basic and normative rules in the negotiation of status and role. In H. P. Dreitzel (Ed.), *Recent sociology No. 2.* New York: Macmillan Co.

Cicourel, A. (1986). The reproduction of objective knowledge: Common sense reasoning in medical decision making. *The Knowledge Society,* 87–122.

Clark, J., & Mishler, E. (1992). Attending to patients' stories: Reframing the clinical task. *Sociology of Health and Illness, 14* (3), 344–372.

Clark, M. (1970). *Health in the Mexican-American culture.* Berkeley, CA: University of California Press.

Clear, J. B., Starbecker, M. M., & Kelly, D. W. (1999). Nursing centers and health promotion: A federal vantage point. *Family and Community Health, 21* (4), 1–14.

Cleveland, A. (1999, December 9). Hainer's experience, journal bring gift of love. *USA Today,* p. 18A.

Clift, E., & Freimuth, V. (1995, March/April). Health communication: What is it and what can it do for you? *Journal of Health Education, 26*(2), 68–74.

Cline, R., Johnson, S., & Freeman, K. (1992). Talk among social partners about AIDS: Interpersonal communication for risk reduction or risk enhancement? *Health Communication, 4*(1), 39–56.

Clinton, H. (1996). *It takes a village.* New York: Simon & Schuster.

Clipp, E. C., & George, L. K. (1990). Caregiver needs and patterns of social support. *Journal of Gerontology: Social Sciences, 45*(3), S102–111.

Cohen, J., & Solomon, N. (1995). *Through the media looking glass: Decoding bias and blather in the news.* Monroe, ME: Common Courage Press.

Coiera, E. (1997). *Guide to medical informatics, the internet, and telemedicine.* New York: Chapman & Hall Medical.

Coile, R. C., Jr. (1997a). *The five stages of managed care: Strategies for providers, HMOs, and suppliers.* Chicago, IL: Health Administration Press.

Coile, R. C., Jr. (1997b). Managed care in the millennium. *Russ Coile's Health Trends, 9*(12), 1, 3–5.

Coile, R. C., Jr. (1998). Top 10 health care trends for 1998. *Russ Coile's Health Trends, 10*(3), 1–12.

Cole, R. E., & Reiss, D. (Eds.). (1993). *How do families cope with chronic illness.* Hillsdale, NJ: Lawrence Erlbaum Associates.

Collins, P. (1990). *Black feminist thought: Knowledge, consciousness, and the politics of empowerment.* Boston: Unwin Hyman.

Committee on Labor and Human Resources (1998). *Global health: U.S. response to infectious diseases.* Washington, DC: U.S. Government Printing Office.

Conkling, W. (1996, July/August). Are women the weaker sex? *American Health,* 54–58.

Connell, C., & Crawford, C. (1988, March-April). How people obtain their health information— A survey in two Pennsylvania counties. *Public Health Report, 103*(2), 189–195.

Conrad, P. (Ed.). (1997). *The sociology of health and illness: Critical perspectives* (5th ed.). New York: St. Martin's Press.

Coontz, S. (1992). *The way we never were.* New York: BasicBooks.

Cooper, L. (1999, September). Coping with miscarriage. *Parents, 74* (9), p. 25.

Cooper-Gordon, B. (1987, May-June). Women and the stigma of addiction. *Alcoholism & Addiction,* p. 20.

Corea, G. (1977). *The hidden malpractice.* New York: William Morrow.

Coreil, J. (1988). Innovation among Haitian healers: The adoption of oral rehydration therapy. *Human Organization, 47* (1), 48–57.

Cott, C. (1997). "We decide, you carry it out": A social network analysis of multidisciplinary long-term care teams. *Social Science and Medicine, 45*(9), 1411–1421.

Coulehan, J., & Block, M. (1992). *The medical interview: A primer for students of the art* (2nd ed.). Philadelphia: F.A. Davis Company.

Council on Ethical and Judicial Affairs (1991, July 24–31). Gender disparaties in clinical decision making. *JAMA, 266*(4), 559–562.

Coupland, N., & Nussbaum, J. (Eds.). (1993). *Discourse and lifespan identity.* Newbury Park, CA: Sage.

Cousins, N. (1988). Intangibles in medicine: An attempt at a balancing perspective. *Journal of the American Medical Association, 260* (11), 1610–1612.

Cox, B. J., & Waller, L. L. (1991). *Bridging the communication gap with the elderly.* American Hospital Association.

Craig, D. (1987). Hospital culture: Change and challenges. *Journal of Healthcare Education and Training, 2*(1), 19–22.

Craig, D. (1997). *The five stages of managed care: Strategies for providers, HMOs, and suppliers.* Chicago: Health Administration Press.

Cristofer, M. (1977). *The shadow box.* New York: Drama Book Specialists.

Culpepper, E. (1993). Ageism, sexism and health care: Why we need old women in power. In G. Winslow & J. Walters (Eds.), *Facing limits: Ethics and health care for the elderly* (pp. 191–210). Boulder, CO: Westview Press.

Cunningham, M. A., & Wilcox, J. R. (1984). "When an M.D. gives an R.N. a harmful order: Modifying a bind." In R. N. Bostrom (Ed.), *Communication yearbook 8* (pp. 764–778). Beverly Hills, CA: Sage.

Cupach, W., & Metts, S. (1994). *Facework.* Thousand Oaks, CA: Sage.

Curran, E. (1987, May-June). Working with alcoholic mothers. *Alcoholism & Addiction,* p. 22.

Curtin, J. (1994). Gynecologic cancer: Prevention and screening strategies for the 1990s. In J. Sechzer, A. Griffin, & S. Pfafflin (Eds.). *Forging a women's health research agenda: Policy issues for the 1990s* (pp. 140–146). New York: New York Academy of Sciences.

Cyr, D. (1998, June). How to manage your doctor. *US Airways Attache,* 40–43.

Dan, A. (Ed.). (1994). *Reframing women's health: Multidisciplinary research and practice.* Thousand Oaks, CA: Sage.

Danis, M., & Churchill, L. (1991, January-February). Autonomy and the common weal. *Hastings Center Report,* 25–31.

Davis, F. (1993, March). Who should doctor women? *Working Woman, 18,* 81–82.

Davis, K., Leijenaar, M., & Oldersma, J. (1991). *The gender of power.* Newbury Park, CA: Sage.

Davis, N., Cole, E., & Rothblum, E. (1993). *Faces of women and aging.* New York: The Haworth Press.

Davis, R. (1998, August 5). Health database appears to be in the "cards." *USA Today,* p. 6D.

Davis, R. (1998, October 19). Medicine's flying lessons. *USA Today,* pp. 1–2D.

Davis, R. (1998, October 19). Tracking near-misses in the field of medicine. *USA Today,* p. 4D.

Davis, R. (1998, November 6). Web searcher heal thyself? New site touted. *USA Today,* p. 4A.

Davis, R. (1998, November 27). Fox one of few under 40 with Parkinson's. *USA Today,* p. 3A.

Davis, R. (1998a, December 1). A fantastic voyage to soothe cerebral chaos. *USA Today,* p. 6D.

Davis, R. (1998b, December 1). Actor Fox could spur Parkinson's funding. *USA Today,* p. D1.

Davis, R. (1999, February 16). Medicine's dirty little secret. *USA Today,* pp. 1–2D.

Davis, R. (1999, March 3). Forces unite for colorectal cancer fight. *USA Today,* p. 1D.

Davis, R. (1999, September 7). Spinal surgery in womb tests faith, technology. *USA Today,* p. 8D.

Davis, R. (1999, October 6). First "keyhole" surgery bypasses big heart incision. *USA Today,* p. 1D.

Davis, R. (1999, December 28). Cheating heart attacks. *USA Today,* pp. 1–2D.

Davis, R. (2000, January 14). 2 new organs in 1 diabetic's fight. *USA Today,* p. 10A.

Davis, R., & Appleby, J. (1999, November 30). Medical mistakes 8th top killer. *USA Today,* p. 1A.

Davis, R., & Miller, L. (1999, July 14). Millions scour the web to find medical information. *USA Today,* pp. 1–2A.

Davis-Floyd, R., & Davis, E. (1996). Intuition as authoritative knowledge in midwifery and home-birth. *Medical Anthropology Quarterly, 10* (2), 237–269.

Dawson, A. (1997). Parent-to-parent link program. *Canadian Journal of Rehabilitation, 10,* 333–334.

Denzin, N. (1991). *Hollywood shot by shot: Alcoholism in American cinema.* New York: Aldine De Gruyter.

Denzin, N. (1993). *The alcoholic society: Addition and recovery of the self.* New Brunswick: Transaction Publishers.

De Ridder, D., Depla, M., Severens, P., & Malsch, M. (1997). Beliefs on coping with illness: A consumer's perspective. *Social Science and Medicine, 44*(5), 553–559.

Derlega, V., & Barbee, A. (Eds.). (1998). *HIV & social interaction.* Thousand Oaks, CA: Sage.

De Salvo, L. (1999). *Writing as a way of healing: How telling our stories transforms our lives.* New York: HarperSanFrancisco.

De Stafano, R. (2000, January 17). Mailbag. *People,* p. 4.

Devine, P., Plant, E., & Harrison, K. (1999). The problem of "us" versus "them" and AIDS stigma. *American Behavioral Scientist, 42* (7), 1212–1228.

Dickson-Markman, F., & Shern, D. L. (1990). Social support and health in the elderly. *Journal of Applied Communication Research, 18* (1), 49–63.

Dievler, A., & Giovannini, T. (1998, December). Community health centers: Promise and performance. *Medical Care Research and Review, 55,* 405–431.

Dindia, K. (1998). "Going into and coming out of the closet": The dialectics of stigma disclosure. In B. Montgomery & L. Baxter (Eds.), *Dialectical approaches to studying personal relationships* (pp. 83–108). Mahwah, NJ: Lawrence Erlbaum Associates.

DiPerna, P. (1999, February 4). Author remember mother as central figure. *USA Today,* p. 15A.

Dollemore, D., & the editors of Prevention Health Books for Seniors (1999). *The doctors' book of home remedies for seniors: An A-Z guide to staying physically active, mentally sharp, and disease-free.* Emmaus, PA: Rodale Press.

Dossey, L. (1996). *Prayer is good medicine.* New York: HarperSanFrancisco.

Dossey, L. (1998, July 21). Options fit doctors' beliefs. *USA Today,* p. 6D.

Downie, R. S., Tannahill, C., & Tannahill, A. (1996). *Health promotion: Models and values* (2nd ed.). New York: Oxford University Press.

Drass, K. A. (1988). Discourse and occupational perspective: A comparison of nurse practitioners and physician assistants. *Discourse Processes, 11,* 163–181.

Dreitzel, H. (1970). Introduction: Patterns of communicative behavior. In H. Dreitzel (Ed.), *Recent sociology #2* (pp. vii–xxi). New York: Macmillan Company.

Drew, P., & Heritage, J. (Eds.). (1992). *Talk at work.* Cambridge: Cambridge University Press.

Duck, S., with Silver, R. C. (Eds.). (1990). *Personal relationships and social support.* Newbury Park, CA: Sage.

Duckro, P. N., Magaletta, P., & Wolf, A. (1997). Health behavior in religious communities. In D. S. Gochman (Ed.), *Handbook of health behavior research III: Demography, development and diversity* (pp. 305–322). New York: Plenum Press.

Duetsch, H. (1995, August). The medical information superhighway. *Journal of Florida Medical Association, 82,* 545–548.

duPre, A. (1998). *Humor and the healing arts: A multimethod analysis of humor use in health care.* Mahwah, NJ: Lawrence Erlbaum Associates.

duPre, A., & Beck, C. (1997). "How can I put this?" Exaggerated self-disparagement as alignment strategy during problematic disclosures by patients to doctors. *Qualitative Health Research, 7* (4), 487–503.

Durant, J. (1998). Alternative medicine: An attractive nuisance. *Journal of Clinical Oncology, 16* (1), 1–2.

Dutcher, G. A. (1998). HIV/AIDS information resources and services from the National Institute of Health. In J. T. Huber (Ed.), *HIV/AIDS internet information sources and resources* (pp. 91–98). Haworth Press.

Edelstein, L. (1943). *The bulletin of the history of medicine, no. 1.* Baltimore, MD: Johns Hopkins University Press.

Eden, J. (1993). *Energetic healing: The merging of ancient and modern medical practices.* New York: Plenum Press.

Edgar, T., Fitzpatrick, M., & Freimuth, V. (Eds.). (1992). *AIDS: A communication perspective.* Hillsdale, NJ: Lawrence Erlbaum Associates.

Edwards, H., & Noller, P. (1998). Factors influencing caregiver-care receiver communication and its impact on the well-being of older care receivers. *Health Communication, 10*(4), 317–341.

Edwards, M. (1999, February 14). Her baby's rare illness inspires teen's crusade. *Columbus Dispatch,* p. 1E.

Ehrenreich, J. (Ed.). (1978). *The cultural crisis of modern medicine.* New York: Monthly Review Press.

Eisenberg, D., Davis, R., Ettner, S., Appel, S., Wilkey, S., Rompay, M., & Kessler, R. (1998, November 11). Trends in alternative medicine use in the United States, 1990–1997. *Journal of the American Medical Association, 280* (18), 1569–1617.

Eisenberg, L. (1988, March). Science in medicine: Too much or too little and too limited in scope? *The American Journal of Medicine, 84,* 483–491.

Eisenberg, L., & Kleinman, A. (Eds.). (1981). *The relevance of social science for medicine.* Boston: D. Reidel Publishing.

Eisler, P. (1998, December 7). Care, control at center of unique labor dispute. *USA Today,* p. 1A.

Elkind, D. (1994). *Ties that stress: The new family imbalance.* Cambridge, MA: Harvard University Press.

Ell, K., & Northen, H. (1990). *Families and health care: Psychosocial practice.* New York: Aldine de Gruyter.

Elliot, C. (1997, November 28–30). Is "cyber medicine" safe? *USA Weekend,* p. 18.

Elliott, P. (1992, January 20). How to get patients to really listen to you? *Medical Economics,* 65–69.

Ellis, B. H., & Miller, K. I. (1994). Supportive communication among nurses: Effects on commitment, burnout, and retention. *Health Communication, 6* (2), 77–96.

Ellis, D. (1999). *Crafting society: Ethnicity, class, and communication theory.* Mahwah, NJ: Lawrence Erlbaum Associates.

Ellison, C. G., & Levin, J. S. (1998). The religion-health connection; Evidence, theory, and future directions. *Health Education and Behavior, 25* (6), 700–720.

El nasser, H. (1999, December 30). Parents of disabled kids relate to "breaking point." *USA Today,* p. 4A.

Elwood, W., & Ataabadi, A. (1996). Tuned in and tuned off: Out-of-treatment injection drug and crack users' response to media intervention campaigns. *Communication Reports, 9*(1), 49–60.

Emanuel, E., & Dubler, N. (1997). Preserving the physician-patient relationship in the era of managed care. In G. Henderson, N. King, R. Strauss, S. Estroff, & L. Churchill (Eds.), *The social medicine reader* (pp. 495–509). Durham, NC: Duke University Press.

Emerson, J. (1970). Behavior in private places: Sustaining definitions of reality in gynecological examinations. In H. Dreitzel (Ed.), *Recent sociology no. 2* (pp. 74–97). New York: Macmillan.

Engel, N. (1980). Confirmation and validation: The caring that is professional nursing. *Image, 12* (3), 53–56.

Engstrom, P. (1998, October 12). How to read news on health. *Onhealth* [On-line]. Available http: onhealth.com/ch1/in-depth/item/item, 25780_1_1.asp

Eraker, S., Kirscht, J., & Becker, M. (1984). Understanding and improving patient compliance. *Annals of Internal Medicine, 100,* 258–268.

Erbe, B., & Shiner, J. (1999, July 16). Do we want better or cheaper health care? *The Athens Messenger,* p. 4.

Ernst, E., & Hahn, E. (Eds.). (1998). *Homoeopathy: A critical appraisal.* Woburn, MA: Butterworth Heinemann.

Escaf, M. (1995, July-August). Communication system facilitates integrated patient-centred care. *Leadership in Health Services,* 19–23.

Estrich, S. (1998, June 25). Staring up close at eyeball surgery. *USA Today,* p. 15A.

Eubanks, P. (1992, July 5). Patients at the center: CEO discusses national project to refocus patient care delivery. *Hospitals,* 56–58.

Evans, B., Stanley, R., & Burrows, G. (1992). Communication skills training and patients' satisfaction. *Health Communication, 4* (2), 155–170.

Evans, D., Block, M., Steinberg, E., & Penrose, A. (1986). Frames and heuristics in doctor-patient discourse. *Social Science and Medicine, 22* (10), 1027–1034.

Fackelmann, K. (1998, December 14). Search is on for "missing millions" with diabetes. *USA Today,* p. 6D.

Fackelmann, K. (1999a, August 24). Desperate cancer patients try thalidomide. *USA Today,* p. 7D.

Fackelmann, R. (1999b, August 24). Montel Williams promises to prosper in spite of MS. *USA Today*, p. 2D.

Fackelmann, K. (1999, September 16). Does unequal treatment really have roots in racism? *USA Today,* p. 10D.

Faelten, S. (Ed.). (1997). *The doctors book of home remedies for women.* Emmaus, PA: Rodale Press.

Fagin, C. M. (1992, September). Collaboration between nurses and physicians: No longer a choice. *Nursing and Health Care, 13*(7), 354–363.

Falvo, D. (1985). *Effective patient education: A guide to increased compliance.* Rockville, MD: Aspen.

Farquhar, J. (1994). *Knowing practice: The clinical encounter of Chinese medicine.* Boulder, CO: Westview Press.

Faulkner, A. O. (1985, Spring). Interdisciplinary health care teams: An educational approach to improvement of health care for the aged. *Gerontology and Geriatrics Education, 5*(3), 29–39.

Feinberg, J. (1988). The effect of patient-practitioner interaction on compliance: A review of the literature and application in rheumatoid arthritis. *Patient Education and Counseling, 11,* 171–187.

Feldman, D., Novack, D., & Gracely, E. (1998, August 10/24). Effects of managed care on physician-patient relationships, quality of care, and the ethical practice of medicine. *Archives of Internal Medicine, 158,* 1626–1632.

Felton, S., Cady, N., Metzler, M. H., & Burton, S. (1997). Implementation of collaborative practice through interdisciplinary rounds on a general surgery service. *Nursing Case Management, 2*(3), 122–126.

Feral, P. (1999, December 17). Farewell, Cathy Hainer [Letter to the editor]. *USA Today,* p. 30A.

Fernandez, D. (1982). Correction of post-traumatic wrist deformity in adults by osteotomy, bone-grafting, and internal fixation. *Journal of Bone and Joint Surgery, 64-A* (8), 1164–1178.

Field, M. (Ed.). (1996). *Telemedicine: A guide to assessing telecommunications in health care.* Washington, DC: National Academy Press.

Finck, K. (1986). The potential health care crisis of hysterectomy. In D. Kjernik & I. Martinson (Eds.), *Women in health and illness: Life experience and crisis* (pp. 200–217). Philadelphia: Saunders.

Findlay, S. (1997, October 15). Study finds medical care influenced by geography. *USA Today,* p. 19A.

Fink, J. (1997). *Third opinion* (3rd ed.). Garden City Park, NY: Avery Publishing Group.

Finkler, K. (1985). *Spiritualist healers in Mexico: Successes and failures of alternative therapeutics.* Salem, WI: Sheffield.

Finkler, K. (1991). *Physicians at work, patients in pain: Biomedical practices and patient response in Mexico.* Boulder, CO: Westview Press.

Finkler, K. (1994a). Sacred healing and biomedicine compared. *Medical Anthropology Quarterly, 8* (2), 178–197.

Finkler, K. (1994b). *Women in pain: Gender and morbidity in Mexico.* Philadelphia: University of Pennsylvania Press.

Fintel, W. A., & McDermott, G. R. (1997). *Dear god, it's cancer* (rev. ed.). Dallas, TX: Word publishing.

First Place. (1998). A Christ-centered health program [brochure]. Houston, TX: Author.

Fischer, E. A., & Coddington, D. C. (1998, January). Integrated health care: Passing fad or lasting legacy? *Healthcare Financial Management,* 42–48.

Fisher, R. (1992). Patient education and compliance: A pharmacist's perspective. *Patient Education and Counseling, 19,* 261–271.

Fisher, S. (1986). *In the patient's best interest: Women and the politics of medical decisions.* New Brunswick, NJ: Rutgers University Press.

Fisher, S. (1993). Is care a remedy?: The case of nurse practitioners. In S. Fisher & K. Davis (Eds.), *Negotiating at the margins: Women and the gendered discourses of power and resistance.* New Brunswick, NJ: Rutgers University Press.

Fisher, S. (1995). *Nursing wounds: Nurse practitioners,doctors, women patients and the negotiation of meaning.* New Brunswick, NJ: Rutgers University Press.

Fisher, S., & Groce, S. (1985). Doctor-patient negotiation of cultural assumptions. *Sociology of Health and Illness, 71*(3), 343–374.

Fisher, W. (1984). Narration as a human communication paradigm: The case of public moral argument. *Communication Monographs, 51*(1), 1–22.

Fisher, W. (1987). *Human communication as narration: Toward a philosophy of reason, value, and action.* Columbia, SC: University of South Carolina.

Fitch, K. L. (1998). *Speaking relationally: Culture, communication, and interpersonal connection.* New York: Guilford Press.

Flax, J. (1990). *Thinking fragments: Psychoanalysis, feminism,and postmodernism in the contemporary west.* Berkeley, CA: University of California Press.

Flocke, S., Stange, K., & Zyzanski, S. (1997, August). The impact of insurance type and forced discontinuity on the delivery of primary care. *Journal of Family Practice, 45*(2), 129–135.

Fogel, S. C. (1998). HIV-related internet news and discussion groups as professional and social support tools. In J. T. Huber (Ed.), *HIV/AIDS internet information sources and resources* (pp. 79–90). Haworth Press.

Fonow, M., & Cook, J. (Eds.). (1991). *Beyond methodology: Feminist scholarship as lived research.* Bloomington, IN: Indiana University Press.

Forsythe, D. (1996). New bottles, old wine: Hidden cultural assumptions in a computerized explanation system for migraine sufferers. *Medical Anthropology Quarterly, 10*(4), 551–574.

Foster, S. D. (1998, May 21). Changing rules won't affect safety. *USA Today,* p. 14A.

Foucault, M. (1972). *The archaeology of knowledge and the discourse on language.* New York: Pantheon Books.

Foucault, M. (1980). *Power/knowledge: Selected interviews and other writings—1972–1977.* New York: Pantheon Books.

Foucault, M. (1994). *The birth of the clinic: An archaeology of medical perception.* New York: Vintage Books.

Fox, N. (1992). *The social meaning of surgery.* Philadelphia: Open University Press.

Fox, S. A. (2000). The uses and abuses of computer-mediated communication for people with disabilities. In D. O. Braithwaite & T. Thompson (Eds.), *Handbook of communication and people with disabilities* (pp. 319–336). Mahwah, NJ: Lawrence Erlbaum Associates.

Fox, S., Siu, A., & Stein, J. (1994, September 26). The importance of physician communication on breast cancer screening of older women. *Archives of Internal Medicine, 154*(18), 2058–2068.

Frahm, A. (1993). *Cancer battle plan: Six strategies for beating cancer from a recovered "hopeless case."* CO: Pinion.

Frahm, A. (1998). Maintaining hope after the doctors give up. In M. Woodell & D. Hess (Eds.), *Women confront cancer: Choosing alternative and complementary therapies* (pp. 80–90). New York: New York University Press.

Frank, A. (1995). *The wounded storyteller: Body, illness, and ethics.* Chicago: University of Chicago Press.

Frankel, R. (1984). From sentence to sequence: Understanding the medical encounter through microinteractional analysis. *Discourse Processes, 7,* 135–170.

Frankel, R. (1990). Talking in interviews: A dispreference for patient-initiated questions in physician-patient encounters. In G. Psathas (Ed.), *Interactional competence* (pp. 231–262). Washington, DC: University Press of America.

Frankel, R. (1993). The laying on of hands: Aspects of the organization of gaze, touch, and talk in a medical encounter. In A. Todd & S. Fisher (Eds.), *The social organization of doctor-patient communication* (2nd ed.; ppp. 71–106). Norwood, NJ: Ablex.

Franks, P., Campbell, T. L., & Shields, C. G. (1992). Social relationships and health: The relative roles of family functioning and social support. *Social Science and Medicine, 34*(7), 779–788.

Frase-Blunt, M. (1998). Telemedicine: Across the miles and right next door. *Hospital Topics: Research and Perspectives on Healthcare, 76,* 9–13.

Freeman, V., Rathore, S., Weinfurt, K., Schulman, K., & Sulmasy, D. (1999, October 25). Lying for patients. *Archives of Internal Medicine, 159,* 2263–2270.

Freidson, E. (1975). *Doctoring together: A study of professional social control.* New York: Elsevier.

Freimuth, V., Stein, J., & Kean, T. (1989). *Searching for health information: The cancer information service model.* Philadelphia: University of Pennsylvania Press.

French, B., Kurczynski, T., Weaver, M.,& Pituch, M. (1992). Evaluation of the health belief model and decision making regarding amniocentesis in women of advanced maternal age. *Health Education Quarterly, 19*(2), 177–186.

Frenchmeyer, M. (1999, October 20). Don't call her midwife: Doula's job is to cater to women giving birth. *Athens Messenger,* p. 5.

Frey, L., Query, J., Jr., Flint, L., & Adelman, M. (1998). Living together with AIDS: Social support processes in a residential facility. In V. J. Derlega & A. P. Barbee (Eds.), *HIV & social interaction* (pp. 129–146). Thousand Oaks, CA: Sage.

Friedman, M. M. (1992). *Family nursing: Theory and practice* (3rd ed.). Norwalk, CT: Appleton & Lange.

Friend, T. (1998, June 22). After cancer: Therapy choices boggle the mind. *USA Today,* p. 6D.

Fuller, R. C. (1989). *Alternative medicine and American religious life.* New York: Oxford University Press.

Furin, J. (1997). "You have to be your own doctor": Sociocultural influences on alternative therapy use among gay men with AIDS in west Hollywood. *Medical Anthropology Quarterly, 11*(4), 498–504.

Fuss, D. (1989). *Essentially speaking: Feminism, nature & difference.* New York: Routledge.

Gabbard-Alley, A. S. (1995). Health communication and gender: A review and critique. *Health Communication, 7* (1), 35–54.

Gabe, J., Kelleher, D., & Williams, G. (Eds.). (1994). *Challenging medicine.* London: Routledge.

Gabriel, J. (1935). *Through the patient's eyes: Hospitals-doctors-nurses.* Philadelphia: J. B. Lippincott Company.

Gadamer, H. (1976). *Philosophical hermeneutics.* Berkeley, CA: University of California Press.

Gadamer, H. (1996). *The enigma of health: The art of healing in a scientific age.* Stanford, CA: Stanford University Press.

Gadamer, H. (1997). Rhetoric and hermeneutics (J. Weinsheimer, trans.). In W. Jost & M. Hyde (Eds.), *Rhetoric and hermeneutics in our time: A reader* (pp. 45–59). New Haven, CT: Yale University Press.

Gafni, A., Charles, C., & Whelan, T. (1998). The physician-patient encounter: The physician as a perfect agent for the patient versus the informed treatment decision-making model. *Social Science and Medicine, 47*(3), 347–354.

Gage, M. (1998, April). From independence to interdependence: Creating synergistic healthcare teams. *JONA, 28*(4), 17–26.

Gaines, A., & Hahn, R. (1985). Among the physicians: Encounter, exchange and transformation. In R. Hahn & A. Gaines (Eds.), *Physicians of western medicine: Anthropological approaches to theory and practice* (pp. 3–22). Dordrecht: D. Reidel.

Gallagher, B. (1999, May 4). Patients face big bills as insurers deny emergency claims. *USA Today,* p. 12A.

Gallagher, B. (1999, June 11). Congress dawdles as deadline for guarding medical data nears. *USA Today,* p. 25A.

Gallagher, B. (1999, June 25). Doctors' union move exposes managed care's flaws. *USA Today,* p. 14A.

Gallagher, B. (1999, July 13). Why should law protect HMOs that injure patients? *USA Today,* p. 14A.

Gallagher, B. (1999, July 29). On-line presciption services leave patients pleased but at risk. *USA Today,* p. 12A.

Gallagher, B. (1999, November 30). FDA exposes patients to risks of medical recycling. *USA Today,* p. 18A.

Gallagher, B. (1999, December 3). Candor on errors is the cure, but medical professional recoils. *USA Today,* p. 28A.

Gallagher, B. (1999, December 21). Suit aims to put patients first. *USA Today,* p. 15A.

Gallant, S., Keita, G., & Royak-Schaler, R. (Eds.). (1997). *Health care for women: Psychological, social, and behavioral influences.* Washington, DC: American Psychological Association.

Gans, H. (1999). *Making sense of America: Sociological analyses and essays.* New York: Rowman & Littlefield.

Garfinkel, H. (1967). *Studies in ethnomethodology.* Cambridge: Polity Press.

Garry, A., & Pearsall, M. (1996). *Women, knowledge, and reality: Explorations in feminist philosophy* (2nd ed.). New York: Routledge.

Geertz, C. (1973). *The interpretation of culture: Selected essays.* New York: Basic Books.

Geist, P., & Dreyer, J. (1993). The demise of dialogue: A critique of the medical encounter. *Western Journal of Communication, 57* (2), 233–246.

Gelber, S. (1998). Is managed care the way to go? Deciding whether to embark. In G. Schamess & A. Lightburn (Eds.), *Humane managed care?* Washington, DC: NASW Press.

Gergen, K. (1991). *The saturated self: Dilemmas of identity in contemporary life.* New York: Basic Books.

Gergen, K. (1994). *Realities and relationships: Soundings in social construction.* Cambridge, MA: Harvard University Press.

Gerhardt, U. (1987). Parsons, role theory, and health interaction. In G. Scambler (Ed.), *Sociological theory and medical sociology* (pp. 110–133). New York: Tavistock Publications.

Gerosa, M. (1999, November). In sickness: Message of love. *Ladies' Home Journal,* pp. 182–185, 236–240.

Gerrity, P., & Kinsey, K. K. (1999). An urban nurse-managed primary health care center: Health promotion in action. *Family and Community Health, 21* (4), 29–40.

Gerteis, M. (1993). Coordinating care and integrating services. In M. Gerteis, S. Edgman-Levitan, & J. Daley (Eds.), *Through the patient's eyes: Understanding and promoting patient-centered care* (pp. 45–71). San Francisco: Jossey-Bass.

Gesler, W., & Gordon, R. (1998). Alternative therapies: Why now? In R. Gordon, B. Nienstedt, & W. Gesler (Eds.), *Alternative therapies* (pp. 3–12). New York: Springer.

Gevitz, N. (1982). *The DOs: Osteopathic medicine in America.* Baltimore, MD: The Johns Hopkins University Press.

Gevitz, N. (Ed.). (1988). *Other healers: Unorthodox medicine in America.* Baltimore, MD: The Johns Hopkins University Press.

Gevitz, N. (1996). The history of osteopathic medicine. In C. M. Sirica (Ed.), *Osteopathic medicine: Past, present, and future* (pp. 25–48). New York: Josiah Macy, Jr. Foundation.

Giarchi, G. (1990). Distance decay and information deprivation: Health implications for people in rural isolation. In P. Abott & G. Payne (Eds.), *New directions in the sociology of health* (pp. 57–69). New York: The Falmer Press.

Gibson, A. (1998, July 9). Home health on life support. *The Athens News,* pp. 1–3.

Gibson, D. (1998). *Aged care: Old policies, new problems.* New York: Cambridge University Press.

Gilligan, C. (1982). *In a different voice: Psychological theory and women's development.* Cambridge, MA: Harvard University Press.

Gilligan, C. (1988). Remapping the moral domain: New images of self in relationship. In C. Gilligan, J. V. Ward, & J. M. Taylor with B. Bardige (Eds.), *Mapping the moral domain* (pp. 3–20). Cambridge, MA: Harvard University Press.

Ginzberg, E., & Ostow, M. (1997, April 3). Managed care: A look back and a look ahead. *The New England Journal of Medicine, 336*(14), 1018–1020.

Giovannetti de Jesus, J., & Bergamasco, R. B. (1998). When the housewife is missing. *Journal of Family Nursing, 4* (4), 387–393.

Gjerdingen, D., Froberg, D., & Fontaine, P. (1991, July). The effect of social support on women's health during pregnancy, labor and delivery, and the postpartum period. *Family Medicine, 23*(5), 370–375.

Glatzer, R. (1998). A breast surgeon battles cancer. *American Health, 17* (4), 78–81.

Glik, D., Berkanovic, E., Stone, K., Ibarra, L., Jones, M., Rosen, B., Schreibman, M., Gordon, L., Minassian, L., & Richardes, D. (1998). Health education goes Hollywood: Working with prime-time and daytime entertainment television for immunization promotion. *Journal of Health Communication, 3*(3), 263–284.

Goffman, E. (1959). *The presentation of self in everyday life.* Garden City, NY: Doubleday Anchor Books.

Goffman, E. (1963). *Stigma: Notes on the management of spoiled identity.* Englewood Cliffs, NJ: Prentice-Hall, Inc.

Goffman, E. (1967). *Interaction ritual: Essays on face-to-face behavior.* New York: Pantheon Books.

Goffman, E. (1974). *Frame analysis: An essay on the organization of experience.* Boston: Northeastern University Press.

Gold, M. (Ed.). (1998). *Contemporary managed care: Readings in structure, operations, and public policy.* Chicago, IL: Health Administration Press.

Goldberg, R., Guadagnoli, E., Silliman, R., & Glicksman, A. (1990). Cancer patients' concerns: Congruence between patients and primary care physicians. *Journal of Cancer Education, 5* (3), 193–199.

Goldsmith, D. (1992, April). Managing conflicting goals in supportive interaction: An interactive theoretical framework. *Communication Research, 19* (2), 264–286.

Goldsmith, D. (1994). The role of facework in supportive communication. In B. Burleson, T. Albrecht, & I. Sarason (Eds.), *Communication of social support: Messages, interactions, and community* (pp. 29–49). Thousand Oaks, CA: Sage.

Good, B. (1994). *Medicine, rationality, and experience: An anthropological perspective.* Cambridge: Cambridge University Press.

Good, B., & Good, M. (1993). "Learning medicine": The constructing of medical knowledge at Harvard Medical School. In S. Lindenbaum & M. Lock (Eds.), *Knowledge, power, and practice: The anthropology of medicine and everyday life* (pp. 81–107). Berkeley, CA: University of California Press.

Goodman, E., Tipton, A., Hecht, L., & Chesney, M. (1994, December). Perseverance pays off: Health care providers' impact on HIV testing decisions by adolescent females. *Pediatrics, 94*(6), 878–882.

Goodnight, G. (1982). The personal, technical, and public spheres of argument: A speculative inquiry into the art of public deliberation. *Journal of the American Forensic Association, 18,* 214–227.

Goodnight, G., & Hingstman, D. (1997). [Review of the book *Studies in the public sphere*]. *Quarterly Journal of Speech, 83,* 351–370.

Goodwin, N. R., Ackerman, F., & Kiron, D. (Eds.). (1997). *The consumer society.* Washington, DC: Island Press.

Gordon, J. (1996). *Manifesto for a new medicine: Your guide to healing partnerships and the wise use of alternative therapies.* Reading, MA: Addison-Wesley.

Gordon, R., Nienstedt, B., & Gesler, W. (Eds.). (1998). *Alternative therapies: Expanding options in health care.* New York: Springer Publishing Company.

Gordon, T., & Edwards, W. (1995). *Making the patient your partner: Communication skill for doctors and other caregivers.* Westport, CT: Auburn House.

Gorman, C. (1998, November 16). Need a fast answer to a medical question? AOL now lets you talk to physicians for free. *Time,* p. 128.

Gorman, C. (1999, October 11). R U ready to dump your glasses? Laser surgery can work wonders but there are risks. *Time,* pp. 58–63.

Gottlieb, B. H. (Ed.). (1988). *Marshaling social support: Format, process and effects.* Newbury Park, CA: Sage.

Graham, J. (1998, November 25). Smits' exit leaves "NYPD Blue" cast grieving. *USA Today,* p. 1D.

Graham, J. (2000, January 19). Fox says he'll quit "Spin City" at end of season cites Parkinson's, time with family. *USA Today,* p. 4D.

Grainger, K. (1993). "That's a lovely bath, dear": Reality construction in the discourse of elder care. *Journal of Aging Studies, 7* (3), 247–262.

Graves, G. (1999). "Is my baby normal?" Plenty of parents worry about their baby's development. *Parents, 74* (6), 165–166.

Gray, B. H. (1991). *The profit motive and patient care: The changing accountability of doctors and hospitals.* Cambridge, MA: Harvard University Press.

Greene, M. G., Adelman, R. D., & Majerovitz, S. D. (1996). Physician and older patient support in the medical encounter. *Health Communication, 8* (3), 263–279.

Greene, M. G., Hoffman, S., Charon, R., & Adelman, R. (1987). Psychosocial concerns in the medical encounter: A comparison of the interactions of doctors with their old and young patients. *The Gerontologist, 27*(2), 164–168.

Greenfield, S., Kaplan, S., & Ware, J. (1985). Expanding patient involvement in care. *Annals of Internal Medicine, 102,* 520–528.

Greenwald, J. (1999, August 30). Elder care: Making the right choice. *Time,* pp. 52–56.

Grieco, A. J. (1998, February 15). Home care helps patients and families. *The Roanoke Times,* p. D3.

Grimley, D., Prochaska, J., Velicer, W., & Prochaska, G. (1995, February). Contraceptive and condom use adoption and maintenance: A stage paradigm approach. *Health Education Quarterly, 22*(1), 20–35.

Grodin, D., & Lindlof, T. (Eds.). (1996). *Constructing the self in a mediated world.* Thousand Oaks, CA: Sage.

Grodner, M. (1991, November). Using the health belief model for bulimia prevention. *Journal of American College Health, 40,* 107–112.

Grueninger, U., Duffy, F., & Goldstein, M. (1995). Patient education in the medical encounter: How to facilitate learning, behavior change, and coping. In M. Lipkin, Jr., S. Putnam, & A. Lazare (Eds.), *The medical interview: Clinical care, education, and research* (pp. 122–133). New York: Springer-Verlag.

Grumbach, K., Osmond, D., Vranizan, K., Jaffe, D., & Bindman, A. (1998, November 19). Primary care physicians' experience of financial incentives in managed-care systems. *The New England Journal of Medicine, 339*(21), 1516–1521.

Grumbach, K., Selby, J., Damberg, C., Bindman, A., Quesenberry, C., Jr., Truman, A., & Uratsu, C. (1999, July 21). Resolving the gatekeeper conundrum: What patients value in primary care and referrals to specialists. *JAMA, 282*(3), 261–266.

Guillaume, R. (1999, October 11). Role of a lifetime. *People,* pp. 77–80.

Guillemin, J., & Holmstrom, L. (1986). *Mixed blessings: Intensive care for newborns.* New York: Oxford University Press.

Gustafson, D. H., Hawkins, R., Boberg, E., Pingree, S., Serlin, R. E., Graziano, F., & Chan, C. L. (1999). Impact of a patient-centered, a computer-based, health information/support system. *American Journal of Preventive Medicine, 16* (1), 1–9.

Guttman, M. (1999, June 11–13). Why more men are finally going to the doctor. *USA Weekend,* p. 10.

Haas, L. (1991). Hide-and-seek or show-and-tell? Emerging issues of informed consent. *Ethics & Behavior, 1*(3), 175–189.

Habermas, J. (1989). *The structural transformation of the public sphere.* Cambridge, MA: The MIT Press.

Habermas, J. (1992). Further reflections on the public sphere. In C. Calhoun (Ed.), *Habermas and the public sphere* (pp. 421–461). Cambridge, MA: The MIT Press.

Hadlow, J., & Pitts, M. (1991). The understanding of common health terms by doctors, nurses and patients. *Social Science and Medicine, 32* (2), 193–196.

Hafner, K. (1996). The doctor is on. *Women's Health Digest, 2*(4), 280–281.

Hafstad, A., & Aaro, L. E. (1997). Activating interpersonal influence through provocative appeals: Evaluation of a mass media-based antismoking campaign targeting adolescents. *Health Communication, 9*(3), 253–272.

Hagland, M. (1996, October 20). The patient. *Hospitals & Health Networks,* 25–30.

Hahn, R., & Gaines, A. (Eds.). (1985). *Physicians of western medicine: Anthropological approaches to theory and practice.* Dordrecht: D. Reidel.

Hainer, C. (1999, December 6). "In effect, I am a virtual prisoner in my body." *USA Today,* p. 6D.

Haldeman, S. (1992). *Principles and practices of chiropractic* (2nd ed.). Norwalk, CT: Appleton & Lange.

Hall, A. E. (1997, January). Coping resources and self-perceived well-being of college students who report a parental drinking problem. *Journal of American College Health, 45,* 159–164.

Hall, B. (1997). Theories of culture, communication and context. In J. Owen (Ed.), *Context and communication behavior* (pp. 111–132). Reno, NV: Context Press.

Hall, C., & Ward, S. (1999, February 23). Confusing health news. *USA Today,* p. 1D.

Hall, J. (1993). Physicians' liking for their patients: More evidence for the role of affect in medical care. *Health Psychology, 12* (2), 140–146.

Hall, J., & Dornan, M. (1990). Patient sociodemographic characteristics as predictors of satisfaction with medical care: A meta-analysis. *Social Science and Medicine, 30* (7), 811–818.

Hallstein, D. (1999). A postmodern caring: Feminist standpoint theories, revisioned caring, and communication ethics. *Western Journal of Communication, 63* (1), 32–56.

Halm, E., Causino, N., & Blumenthal, D. (1997, November 26). Is gatekeeping better than traditional care? A survey of physicians' attitudes. *JAMA, 278*(20), 1677–1681.

Halvorson, G. C. (1993). *Strong medicine.* New York: Random House.

Haney, D. Q. (1999, February 6). Developing faster brain scans improves treatment of strokes. *The Columbus Dispatch,* p. 5A.

Haraway, D. (1995). Fractured identities. In P. Joyce (Ed.), *Class* (pp. 95–98). New York: Oxford University Press.

Harding, S. (1991). *Whose science? Whose knowledge? Thinking from women's lives.* Ithaca, NY: Cornell University Press

Hare, M. L. (1993). The emergence of an urban U.S. Chinese medicine. *Medical Anthropology Medicine, 7* (1), 30–49.

Harris, L. (1995). *Health and the new media: Technologies transforming personal and public health.* Mahwah, NJ: Lawrence Erlbaum Associates.

Harris, L., & Associates, Inc. (1998). *The future of health care.* New York: Author.

Hart, K. L. (Ed.). (1998, Spring). The black bag: Multiethnicity and health. *Journal for Minority Medical Students, 10*(3).

Hasselkus, B. R. (1992). The family caregiver as interpreter in the geriatric medical interview. *Medical Anthropology Quarterly, 6* (3), 288–304.

Hatch, J., & Voorhorst, S. (1992). The church as a resource for health promotion activities in the black community. In D. Becker, D. Hill, J.Jackson, D. Levine, F. Stillman, & S. Weiss (Eds.), *Health behavior research in minority populations* (pp. 30–34). Bethesda, MD: US Department of Health and Human Services.

Haug, M. R. (1996). The effects of physician/elder patient characteristics on health communication. *Health Communication, 8* (3), 249–262.

Haug, M. R., & Lavin, B. (1981, September). Practitioner or patient—Who's in charge? *Journal of Health and Social Behavior, 22,* 219–229.

Haug, M. R., & Ory, M. G. (1987). Issues in elderly patient-provider interactions. *Research on Aging, 9* (1), 3–44.

Havas, E. (1998). Managed care: Business as usual. In G. Schamess & A. Lightburn (Eds.), *Humane care* (pp. 75–84). Washington, DC: NASW Press.

Healy, B. (1991, July 24/31). Women's health, public welfare. *JAMA, 266* (4), 566–568.

Healy, M. (1997, September 15). STDs still taboo during doctor visits: Silence may lead to lack of treatment. *USA Today,* p. D1.

Healy, M. (1998, October 5). Doctors to probe patients for depression. *USA Today,* p. 4D.

Heath, C. (1986). *Body movement and speech in medical interaction.* Cambridge: Cambridge University Press.

Hellmich, N. (1998, July 13). Popularity of herb sprouts from publicity. *USA Today,* p. 4D.

Hellstrom, O. (1998). Dialogue medicine: A health-liberating attitude in general practice. *Patient Education and Counseling, 35,* 221–231.

Helman, C. (1984). *Culture, health and illness: An introduction for health professionals.* Boston: John Wright & Sons.

Helman, C. (1985). Communication in primary care: The role of patient and practitioner explanatory models. *Social Science and Medicine, 20* (9), 923–931.

Hendrick, B. (1994, May 15). Male-oriented medicine ignores women's midlife woes, study says. *The Atlanta Journal and Constitution,* p. 1A.

Henkel, J. (1997). *Prostate cancer: New tests create treatment dilemmas* [Brochure]. Rockville, MD: U.S. Food and Drug Administration.

Henkel, J. (1998). *Prostate cancer* [Brochure]. Rockville, MD: U.S. Food and Drug Administration.

Hensbest, R., & Stewart, M. (1990). Patient-centeredness in the consultation. 2: Does it really make a difference? *Family Practice, 7* (1), 28–33.

Herek, G. (1999). AIDS and stigma. *American Behavioral Scientist, 42* (7), 1106–1116.

Herek, G., & Capitanio, J. (1999). AIDS stigma and sexual prejudice. *American Behavioral Scientist, 42* (7), 1130–1147.

Herzlinger, R. E. (1997). *Market-driven health care: Who wins, who loses in the transformation of America's largest service industry.* Reading, MA: Perseus Books.

Hibbard, J. H., & Pope, C. R. (1983). Gender roles, illness orientation and use of medical services. *Social Science and Medicine, 17* (3), 129–137.

Hibbard, J. H., & Weeks, E. C. (1987, November). Consumerism in health care: Prevalence and predictors. *Medical Care, 25*(11), 1019–1032.

Hilton, B. (1997, January 29). What does managed health care really mean? *The Athens Messenger,* p. 4.

Hilton, B. (1997, August 27). Making your hospital stay smoother and safer. *The Athens Messenger,* p. 4.

Hilton, B. (1998, July 8). Changes in medicine—only some for the better. *The Athens Messenger,* p. 4.

Hilton, B. (1999, October 22). "ER" flubs medical issue. *The Athens Messenger,* p. 4.

Hittner, P. (1992). What to ask before you go to the hospital. *Better Homes and Gardens, 70* (11), 48–53.

Hjortdahl, P., & Laerum, E. (1992). Continuity of care in general practice: Effect on patient satisfaction. *British Medical Journal, 304,* 1287–1290.

Hogan, J. M. (Ed.). (1998). *Rhetoric and community: Studies in unity and fragmentation.* Columbia, SC: University of South Carolina Press.

Holbert, J. (1998, July 6). Albany's family doctor maintains personal touch. *Athens Messenger,* p. 5.

Holbert, J. (1998, October 26). Albany boy's heart condition makes his family grow stronger. *The Athens Messenger,* p. 5.

Holbert, J. (1999, January 18). Fighting fat with faith. *The Athens Messenger,* p. 5.

Holleman, W. L., Holleman, M. C., & Moy, J. G. (1997, February 1). Are ethics and managed care strange bedfellows or a marriage made in heaven? *The Lancet, 349,* 350–51.

hooks, b. (1981). *Ain't I a woman: Black women and feminism.* Boston: South End Press.

Hord, F. L., & Lee, J. S. (1995). *I am because we are: Readings in black philosophy.* Boston: University of Massachusetts Press.

Hornblow, A., Kidson, M., & Ironsides, W. (1988). Empathic processes: Perception by medical students of patients' anxiety and depression. *Medical Education, 22,* 15–18.

Hospice helps keep families together. (1998, Spring). *Horizons, 6* (3), 1,3.

Howard, B. (1999, May). "Am I pregnant?" How not to flunk your home pregnancy test. *New Woman,* p. 37.

Howlett, D. (1999, February 3). Payton has liver disease. *USA Today,* pp. 1–2C.

Howze, E., Broyden, R., & Impara, J. (1992). Using informal caregivers to communicate with women about mammography. *Health Communication, 4*(3), 227–244.

Hruby, R. (1996). Contemporary philosophy and practice of osteopathic medicine. In C. M. Sirica (Ed.), *Osteopathic medicine: Past, present, and future* (pp. 49–88). New York: Josiah Macy, Jr. Foundation.

Hubbard, K., O'Neill, A., & Cheakalos, C. (1999, April 12). Out of control: Weight-obsessed, stressed-out coeds are increasingly falling prey to eating disorders. *People*, 52–69.

Huff, R., & Kline, M. (Eds.). (1999). *Promoting health in multicultural populations: A handbook for practitioners.* Thousand Oaks, CA: Sage.

Hughes, D. (1982). Control in the medical consultation: Organizing talk in a situation where co-participants have differential competence. *Sociology, 16*(3), 359–376.

Hulka, F. (1999). Pediatric traum systems: Critical distinctions. *Journal of Trauma, 47* (3), S85–89.

Hultman, J. (1995). *Here's how, doctor.* Los Angeles, CA: Medical Business Advisers Publishing.

Hummert, M., Wiemann, J., & Nussbaum, J. (Eds.). (1994). *Interpersonal communication in older adulthood: Interdisciplinary theory and research.* Thousand Oaks, CA: Sage.

Hunt, L., Arar, N., & Larme, A. (1998, December). Contrasting patient and practitioner perspectives in type 2 diabetes management. *Western Journal of Nursing Research, 20*(6), 656–682.

Hunt, L., Jordan, B., Irwin, S., & Browner, C. (1989). Compliance and the patient's perspective: Controlling symptoms in everyday life. *Culture, Medicine and Psychiatry, 13*, 315–334.

Hunter, K. (1991). *Doctors' stories: The narrative structure of medical knowledge.* Princeton, NJ: Princeton University Press.

Hussein, A. (1998). Highlights of activities from 1974 to 1988. *World Health Forum, 19,* 219–233.

Ignagni, K. (1998, June 28). Managed care helps patients. *The Athens Messenger,* p. A9.

Illich, I. (1976). *Medical nemesis: The exploration of health.* New York: Pantheon Books.

In the blink of an eye. (1998, December). *Ronald McDonald House Charities, 4*(2), 1–2.

Independent living: Do older parents and adult children see it the same way? (1998, November). Washington, DC: AARP.

Indian Health Service (1997, January). *Fact sheet* (IHS/OD/OC-January 1997, Rev 6). Rockville, MD: Author.

Iverson, D. C. (1993, August 1). Involving providers and patients in cancer control and prevention efforts. *Cancer, 72* (3), 1138–1143.

Jackson, E. M. (1993). Whiting-out difference: Why U.S. nursing research fails black families. *Medical Anthropology Quarterly, 7*(4), 363–385.

Janz, N., & Becker, M. (1984). The health belief model: A decade later. *Health Education Quarterly, 11*(1), 1–47.

Jewkes, R., & Murcott, A. (1998). Community representatives: Representing the "community"? *Social Science and Medicine, 46*(7), 843–858.

Jezewski, M. A. (1995). Staying connected: The core of facilitating health care for homeless persons. *Public Health Nursing, 12*(3), 203–210.

Jezierski, M. (1994, October). Abuse of women by male partners: Basic knowledge for emergency nurses. *Journal of Emergency Nursing, 20*(5), 361–372.

Johnson, J. (1997). *Cancer-related information seeking.* Cresskill, NJ: Hampton Press, Inc.

Johnson, J., & Meischke, H. (1991, July/August). Women's preferences for cancer information from specific communication channels. *American Behavioral Scientist, 34*(6), 742–755.

Johnson, K., & Willing, R. (1999, June 17). Disease is Reno's daily trial. *USA Today,* pp. 1–2D.

Johnson, P. (1998, October 26). GMA host reveals wife's illness before tabloid can. *USA Today,* p. 3D.

Johnston, M. A. (1992, April). A model program to address insensitive behaviors toward medical students. *Academic Medicine, 67*(4), 236–7.

Jonas, W. (1998, November 11). Alternative medicine—Learning from the past, examining the present, advancing to the future. *JAMA, 280*(18), 1616–1617.

Jones, J. A., & Phillips, G. M. (1988). *Communicating with your doctor: Rx for good medical care.* Carbondale, IL: Southern Illinois University Press.

Jones, S. (Ed.). (1995). *Cybersociety: Computer-mediated communication and community.* Thousand Oaks, CA: Sage.

Joos, I., Nelson, R., & Lyness, A. (1985). *Man, health, and nursing: Basic concepts and theories*. Reston, VA: Reston Publishing Company.

Jordan, B., & Irwin, S. (1987). A close encounter with a court-ordered cesarean section: A case of differing realities. In H. Baer (Ed.), *Encounters with biomedicine: Case studies in medical anthropology* (pp. 185–200). New York: Gordon Breach.

Joyce, M. (1994). The graying of America: Implications and opportunities for health marketers. *American Behavioral Scientist,38*(2), 341–350.

Jurgensen, K. (1997, August 21). Endorsements aside, buyer beware still best policy. *USA Today,* p. 14A.

Jurgensen, K. (1998, May 21). Medicare, medicaid may soon let nurses do anesthesia. *USA Today,* p. 14A.

Jurgensen, K. (1998, July 13). Privacy? At most HMOs you don't have any. *USA Today,* p. 12A.

Jurgensen, K. (1998, October 23). Workers' health care costs rise, as costs to employers drop. *USA Today,* p. 10A.

Jurgensen, K. (1998, November 11). Doctors fudge truth to avoid HMO care denials. *USA Today,* p. 24A.

Jurgensen, K. (1998, December 7). HMOs restrict treatment using flawed guidelines. *USA Today,* p. 24A.

Kahana, E., Biegel, D. E., & Wykle, M. L. (Eds.). (1994). *Family caregiving across the lifespan*. Thousand Oaks, CA: Sage.

Kaniasty, K., & Norris, F. (1995, June). Mobilization and deterioration of social support following natural disasters. *Current Directions in Psychological Science,* pp. 94–98.

Kaplan, S. (1998, October). Health care beware. *George, 58.*

Karas, S. (1998). *Changing the world: One relationship at a time*. Freedom, CA: The Crossing Press.

Kase, L. M. (1991, September). What doctors don't know about women's health. *McCall's,* 22–24, 144.

Kassirer, J. P. (1997, April 3). Is managed care here to stay? *The New England Journal of Medicine, 336*(14), 1013–1014.

Katovich, M. (1986). Temporal stages of situated activity and identity activation. In C. Couch, S. Saxton, & M. Katovich (Eds.), *Studies in symbolic interaction: A research annual: The Iowa School, supplement 2 (Part B)* (pp. 329–352). Greenwich, CT: JAI Press.

Katz, P., & Kirkland, F. (1988). Traditional thought and modern western surgery. *Social Science and Medicine, 26* (12), 1175–1181.

Katzman, E. M., & Roberts, J. I. (1988). Nurse-physician conflicts as barriers to the enactment of nursing roles. *Western Journal of Nursing Research, 10*(5), 576–590.

Kauffman, J. (1991, January). *Indian women's health care: Consensus statement*. Washington, DC: U.S. Department of Health and Human Services.

Kavanagh, K., & Kennedy, P. (1992). *Promoting cultural diversity*. Newbury Park, CA: Sage.

Kayser-Jones, J. (1981). *Old, alone, and neglected: care of the aged in the United States and Scotland*. Berkeley, CA: University of California Press.

Kayser-Jones, J. (1995). Decision making in the treatment of acute illness in nursing homes: Framing the decision problem, treatment plan, and outcome. *Medical Anthropology Quarterly, 9*(2), 236–256.

Keat, R., Whiteley, N., & Abercrombie, N. (Eds.). (1994). *The authority of the consumer*. New York: Routledge

Kelm, M. (1998). *Colonizing bodies: Aboriginal health and healing in British Columbia, 1900–50*. Vancouver, BC: UBCPress.

Kellner, D. (1998). Foreword. In M. Alfino, J. Caputo, & R. Wynyard (Eds.), *McDonaldization revisited* (pp. vii–xiv). Westport, CT: Praeger.

Kelner, M., & Wellman, B. (1997). Health care and consumer choice: Medical and alternative therapies. *Social Science and Medicine, 45* (2), 203–212.

Kelsey, K., Earp, J., & Kirkley, B. (1997, October). *Is social support beneficial for dietary change? A review of literature* [On-line]. Availability http:web.lexis-nexis...bb7a00d22a8c809dfb65d2

Kemp, S., & Squires, J. (Eds.). (1997). *Feminisms.* New York: Oxford University Press.

Kennell, J., Klaus, M., McGrath, S., Robertson, S., & Hinkley, C. (1991, May 1). Continuous emotional support during labor in a US hospital. *JAMA, 265*(17), 2197–2201.

Kerr, E., Hays, R., Mittman, B., Siu, A., Leake, B., & Brooke, R. (1997, July 23–30). Primary care physicians' satisfaction with quality of care in California capitated medical groups. *JAMA, 278*(4), 308–312.

Kerssens, J., Bensing, J., & Andela, M. (1997). Patient preference for genders of health professionals. *Social Science and Medicine, 44*(10), 1531–1540.

Keyser, H. (1984). *Women under the knife.* Philadelphia: George F. Stickley.

Keyser, H. (1993). *Prescription for disaster: Health care in America.* Austin, TX: Eakin Press.

Khan, S., Nessim, S., Gray, R., Czer, L., Chaux, A., & Matloff, J. (1990). Increased mortality of women in coronary artery bypass surgery: Evidence for referral bias. *Annals of Internal Medicine, 112,* 561–567.

Khaw, K. (1993, May 1). Where are the women in studies of coronary heart disease? *British Medical Journal, 306*(6886), 1145–1146.

Kim, Y. (1997). The behavior-context interface in interethnic communication. In J. Owen (Ed.), *Context and communication behavior* (pp. 261–294). Reno, NV: Context Press.

Kinsey, K. K., & Gerrity, P. (1999). Foreword. *Family and Community Health, 21*(4), vii–ix.

Kirkpatrick, A. (Ed.). (1999, July 13). *Reflex sympathetic dystrophy syndrome association of America: Clinical practice guideline* [On-line]. Available http:www.rsds.org/cpgeng.htm

Kirschner, M. H. (1998, July 1). HMO crisis shows need for national health care [Letters]. *USA Today,* p. 11A.

Kisken, T. (1999, November 9). Stretching the truth may extend patients' lives. *Athens Messenger,* p. 4.

Klass, P. (1987). *A not entirely benign procedure.* New York: G.P. Putnam's Sons.

Kleinman, A. (1978). Concepts and a model for the comparison of medical systems as cultural systems. *Social Science and Medicine, 12,* 85–91.

Kleinman, A. (1980). *Patients and healers in the context of culture: An exploration of the borderland between anthropology, medicine, and psychiatry.* Berkeley: University of California Press.

Klingle, R., & Aune, K. (1994). Effects of the daytime serial and public service announcement in promoting cognitions, attitudes, and behaviors related to bone-marrow testing. *Health Communication, 6*(3), 225–245.

Knorr-Cetina, K., & Cicourel, A. (1981). *Advances in social theory and methodology: Toward an integration of micro-and macro-sociologies.* Boston: Routedge & Kegan Paul.

Koenig, H., George, L., Hays, J., Larson, D., Cohen, H., & Blazer, D. (1998). The relationship between religious activities and blood pressure in older adults. *International Journal of Psychiatry in Medicine, 28*(2), 189–213.

Kolata, G. (1993, May 5). Why do so many women have breast removed needlessly? *New York Times,* p. C13.

Kolata, G. (1994, April 24). Their treatment, their lives, their decisions. *New York Times Magazine,* pp. 66, 100, 105.

Kolodner, R. (Ed.). (1997). *Computerizing large integrated health networks.* New York: Springer.

Koren, T. (1997a). *When will I get better?* Philadelphia: Koren Publications.

Koren, T. (1997b). *Chiropractic: Bringing out the best in you! An introduction* (4th ed.). Philadelphia: Koren Publications.

Kosberg, J. I. (Ed.). (1992). *Family care of the elderly: Social and cultural changes.* Newbury Park, CA: Sage.

Kreps, G. (1988). Relational communication in health care. *Southern Speech Communication Journal, 53,* 344–359.

Kreps, G., & Kunimoto, E. (1994). *Effective communication in multicultural health care settings.* Thousand Oaks, CA: Sage.

Kreps, G., & O'Hair, D. (Eds.). (1995). *Communication and health outcomes.* Cresskill, NJ: Hampton Press.

Kreps, G., & Query, J. (1990). Health communication and interpersonal competence. In G. Phillips & J. Wood (Eds.), *Speech communication: Essays to commemorate the 75th anniversary of the Speech Communication Association* (pp. 293–323). Carbondale, IL: Southern Illinois University.

Kristjanson, L., & Chalmers, K. (1990). Nurse-client interactions in community-based practice: Creating common ground. *Public Health Nursing, 7* (4), 215–223.

Kritek, P. (1981, June). Patient power & powerlessness. *The Journal of Nursing Leadership and Management, 12*(6), 26–34.

Krupat, A. (Ed.). (1994). *Native American autobiography.* Madison: University of Wisconsin Press.

Kurtz, M., Johnson, S., Tomlinson, T., & Fiel, N. (1985). Teaching medical students the effects of values and stereotyping on the doctor/patient relationship. *Social Science and Medicine, 21*(9), 1043–1047.

Lamas, G., Pashos, C., Normand, S., & McNeil, B. (1995, February 15). Permanent pacemaker selection and subsequent survival in elderly medicare pacemaker recipients. *Circulation, 91*(4), 1063–1069.

Lamb, G. S., & Napodano, R. J. (1984, January). Physician-nurse practitioner interaction patterns in primary care practices. *American Journal of Public Health, 74*(1), 26–29.

Lambert, R., Street, R., Cegala, D., Smith, D., Kurtz, S., & Schofield, T. (1997). Provider-patient communication, patient-centered care, and the mangle of practice. *Health Communication, 9* (1), 27–43.

Lantos, J. (1997). *Do we still need doctors?* New York: Routledge.

Larsson, U., Johanson, M., & Svardsudd, K. (1994). Sensitive patient-doctor communications relating to the breasts and prostate. *Journal of Cancer Education, 9* (1), 19–25.

Laschinger, H. K., & Weston, W. (1995, March-April). Role perceptions of freshman and senior nursing and medical students and attitudes toward collaborative decision making. *Journal of Professional Nursing, 11*(2), 119–128.

Lassiter, S. (1995). *Multicultural clients: A professional handbook for health care providers and social workers.* Westport, CT: Greenwood Press.

Late-breaking news: Emmy-winner Zaslow dies. (1998, December 29). *Soap Opera Digest,* p. 4.

Latham, C. (1996). Predictors of patient outcomes following interactions with nurses. *Western Journal of Nursing Research, 18* (5), 548–564.

Laub, C., Somera, D., Gowen, L., & Diaz, R. (1999, April). Targeting "risky" gender ideologies. Constructing a community-driven, theory-based HIV prevention intervention for youth. *Health Education and Behavior, 26*(2), 185–199.

Laurence, L., & Weinhouse, B. (1997). *Outrageous practices: The alarming truth about how medicine mistreats women.* New York: Fawcett Columbine.

Lawrence, D. (Ed.). (1991). *Fundamentals of chiropractic diagnosis and management.* Baltimore, MD: Williams & Wilkins.

Lawrence, J. (1998, November 17). For Ohio lawmaker, ill child puts politics in its place. *USA Today,* p. 8A.

Layne, L. (1996). "How's the baby doing?" Struggling with narratives of progress in a neonatal intensive care unit. *Medical Anthropology Quarterly, 10*(4), 624–656.

Lazare, A., Putnam, S., & Lipkin Jr., M.(1995). Three functions of the medical interview. In M. Lipkin Jr., S. Putnam, & A. Lazare (Eds.), *The medical interview: Clinical care, education, and research* (pp. 3–19). New York: Springer-Verlag.

Leahey, L. (1999, April 27). Editor's note. *Soap Opera Digest,* p. 18.

Leavitt, M. B., Lamb, S. A., & Voss, B. S. (1996). Brain tumor support group: Content themes and mechanisms of support. *Oncology Nursing Forum, 23*(8), 1247–1256.

Legato, M. (1994). Cardiovascular disease in women: What's different? What's new? What's unresolved? In J. Sechzer, A. Griffin, & S. Pfafflin (Eds.). *Forging a women's health research agenda: Policy issues for the 1990s* (pp. 147–157). New York: New York Academy of Sciences.

Leib, M. (1998, May 29). Care team safest approach [Letters]. *USA Today,* p. 14A.

Lenhart, J. (1999, February 28). A dose of good will. *Washington Post,* p. 1.

Lerner, M. (1994). *Choices in healing: Integrating the best of conventional and complementary approaches to cancer.* Cambridge, MA: MIT Press.

Lerner, R. (1995, August). What does being female have to do with it? *Professional Counselor,* p. 20.

Lester, R. (1997). The (dis)embodied self in anorexia nervosa. *Social Science and Medicine, 44* (4), 479–489.

Lett, J. (1995). Abuse of the elderly. *Journal of the Florida Medical Association, 82* (10), 675–678.

Leventhal, R. (1995). The marketing of physicians' services: Should doctors advertise? *Health Marketing Quarterly, 12*(4), 49–57.

Levin, G., & Johnson, K. (2000, January 20). Fox made choice "while I could." *USA Today,* p. 4D.

Levinson, R., McCollum, K., & Kutner, N. (1984). Gender homophily in preferences for physicians. *Sex Roles, 10*(5/6), 315–325.

Levy, D. (1997, October 10). Medical mistakes happen to many, AMA poll finds. *USA Today,* p. 3A.

Lewinsohn, R. (1998). Medical theories, science, and the practice of medicine. *Social Science and Medicine, 46* (10), 1261–1270.

Lewis, C. (1998, September). *Laser eye surgery* (FDA Publication No. 98–1293). Rockville, MD: Department of Health and Human Services.

Lewis, J. E., Malow, R. M., & Ireland, S. J. (1997, January). HIV/AIDS risk in heterosexual college student: A review of a decade literature. *Journal of American College Health, 45,* 147–158.

Lewis, L. (1994). A challenge for health education: The enactment problem and a communication-related solution. *Health Communication, 6*(3), 225–245.

Lieberman, T. (1999, August). How does your HMO stack up? *Consumer Reports,* pp. 23–29.

Like, R. (1991, March-April). Culturally sensitive health care: Recommendations for family practice training. *Family Medicine, 23*(3), 180–181.

Limbacher, P. B. (1998, April 6). Off the beaten path: More for-profit hospital companies traveling to rural markets. *Modern Healthcare,* pp. 67–72.

Liner, R. S. (1997). Physician deselection: The dynamics of a new threat to the physician-patient relationship. *American Journal of Law and Medicine, 23*(4), 511–537.

Lipkin Jr., M., Putnam, S., & Lazare, A. (Eds.). (1995). *The medical interview: Clinical care, education, and research.* New York: Springer-Verlag.

Lipton, M., & Wang, C. (1998, December 21). One life to give. *People,* pp. 71–72.

Little, M. (1995). *Humane medicine.* New York: Cambridge University Press.

Litwin, H. (Ed.). (1996). *The social networks of older people: A cross-national analysis.* Westport, CT: Praeger.

Lochman, J. (1983). Factors related to patients' satisfaction with their medical care. *Journal of Community Health, 9* (2), 91–109.

Lock, M. (1990). Rationalization of Japanese herbal medication: The hegemony of orchestrated pluralism. *Human Organization, 49* (1), 41–47.

Logan, M. (1991). Locus of illness control beliefs among Brazilian herbalists: Findings and methodological recommendations. *Human Organization, 50* (1), 82–88.

Logan, M. (1997, August 9). He's down but not out. *TV Guide, 45* (32), 25.

Lore, D. (1997, July 15). Managing medicine. *The Beacon Journal,* p. 1A.

Lorig, K. (1992). *Patient education: A practical approach.* St. Louis, MO: Mosby-Year Book.

Losee, R. (1998, Spring). Caught in the crossfire: Stress in healthcare settings and ways to address it. *Hospital Topics: Research and Perspectives on Healthcare, 76*(2), 5–8.

Lowitt, M. (1998). Teledermatology. In S. Viegas & K. Dunn (Eds.), *Telemedicine: Practicing in the information age* (pp. 115–122). Philadelphia: Lippincott-Raven.

Lundeen, S. P. (1999). An alternative paradigm for promoting health in communities: The Lundeen Community Nursing Center model. *Family and Community Health, 21* (4), 15–28.

Lupton, D. (1994). *Medicine as culture: Illness, disease and the body in western societies.* Thousand Oaks, CA: Sage.

Lupton, D. (1996). Your life in their hands: Trust in the medical encounter. In V. James & J. Gabe (Eds.), *Health and the sociology of emotions* (pp. 157–172). Oxford: Blackwell Publishers.

Lupton, D. (1997). Consumerism, reflexivity, and the medical encounter. *Social Science and Medicine, 45* (3), 373–381.

Lupton, D., & McLean, J. (1998). Representing doctors: Discourse and images in the Australian press. *Social Science and Medicine, 46*(8), 947–958.

Lury, C. (1996). *Consumer culture.* New Brunswick, NJ: Rutgers University Press.

MacStravic, S. (1994). Patient loyalty to physicians. *Journal of Health Marketing, 14* (4), 53–55.

MacStravic, S., & Montrose, G. (1998). *Managing health care demand.* Gaithersburg, MD: Aspen Publishers.

Madrid, A. (1997). Being "the other": Ethnic identity in a changing society. In J. Henslin (Ed.), *Down to earth sociology: Introductory readings* (9th ed.; pp. 73–77). New York: The Free Press.

Maffei, C., Lingiardi, V., & Orlandini, A. (1991). How we teach the doctor-patient relationship. *Medical Teacher, 13* (4), 339–347.

Magner, G. (1995). *Chiropractic: The victim's perspective.* Amherst, NY: Prometheus Books.

Mahler, H., & Kulik, J. (1990). Preferences for health care involvement, perceived control and surgical recovery: A prospective study. *Social Science and Medicine, 31*(7), 742–751.

Maibach, E., & Parrott, R. (Eds.). (1995). *Designing health messages.* Thousand Oaks, CA: Sage.

Majeroni, B., Karuza, J., Wade, C., McCreadie, M., & Calkins, E. (1993, July/August). Gender of physicians and patients and preventive care for community-based older adults. *The Journal of the American Board of Family Practice, 6*(4), 359–365.

Makoul, G., Arntson, P., & Schofield, T. (1995). Health promotion in primary care: Physician-patient communication and decision making about prescription medications. *Social Science and Medicine, 41*(9), 1241–1254.

Mallory, C. (1997). What's on the internet? Services for women affected by HIV and AIDS. *Health Care for Women International, 18,* 315–322.

Manning, A. (1997, September 22). Patients' pleas yield rash of unneeded prescriptions. *USA Today,* p. 1D.

Manning, A. (1999, August 3). Kids in USA get 21 shots before start of 1st grade. *USA Today,* p. 1A.

Manning, A. (1999, August 16). Vaccine-autism link feared. *USA Today,* p. 1D.

Manning, A. (1999, November 23). Baby's death drives couple to embrace vaccine. *USA Today,* p. 11D.

MAP. (1998). *The status and trends of the HIV/AIDS epidemics in the world.* Boston: Monitoring the AIDS Pandemic (MAP).

Marshall, N., Barnett, R., Baruch, G., & Pleck, J. (1990). Double jeopardy. In E. Abel & M. Nelson (Eds.), *Circles of care* (pp. 266–277). Albany: State University of New York.

Martin, J. (1997). Understanding whiteness in the United States. In L. A. Samovar, & R. E. Porter (Eds.), *Intercultural communication* (pp. 54–62). Wadsworth.

Marwick, C. (1996, September 11). Effect of managed care felt in every medical field. *Medical News & Perspectives, 276*(10), 768–769.

Maseide, P. (1981). Sincerity may frighten the patient: Medical dilemmas in patient care. *Journal of Pragmatics, 5,* 145–167.

Mason-John, V. (Ed.). (1995). *Talking back: Lesbians of African and Asian descent speak out.* New York: Cassell.

Mathews, J. (1983). The communication process in clinical settings. *Social Science and Medicine, 17* (18), 1371–1378.

Mattson, M. (1999, September). Toward a reconceptualization of communication cues to action in the health belief model: HIV test counseling. *Communication Monographs, 66,* 240–265.

May, C. (1990). Research on nurse-patient relationships: Problems of theory, problems of practice. *Journal of Advanced Nursing, 15,* 307–315.

Mayeno, L., & Hirota, S. (1994). Access to health care. In N. Zane, D. Takeuchi, & K. Young (Eds.), *Confronting critical health issues of Asian and Pacific Islander Americans.* Thousand Oaks, CA: Sage.

Mayer, M. (1993). *Examining myself: One woman's story of breast cancer treatment and recovery.* Boston: Faber and Faber.

Maynard, M. (1996). Promoting older ethnic minorities health behaviors: Primary and secondary prevention considerations. *Journal of Primary Prevention, 17*(2), 219–229.

McAllister, E. (1998). Family therapy with conservative Christian families. *Family Therapy, 25*(3), 169–180.

McBride, A., & McBride, W. (1981). Theoretical underpinnings for women's health. *Women and Health, 6*(1/2), 37–55.

McCoy, G. (1999, May). Great web site. *Life extension,* p. 69.

McDonald, K. (1999, June 25). Studies of women's health produce a wealth of knowledge on the biology of gender differences. *The Chronicle of Higher Education,* pp. A19, A22.

McHann, M. (Ed.). (1994). *What every home health nurse needs to know: A book of readings.* Memphis, TN: Consultants in Care.

McHoul, A., & Grace, W. (1993). *A Foucault primer: Discourse, power and the subject.* Washington Square, NY: New York University Press.

McKeever, L., & Martinson, I. (1986). Older women's health care. In D. Kjernik & I. Martinson (Eds.), *Women in health and illness: Life experiences and crises* (pp. 34–45). Philadelphia: W.B. Saunders Company.

McKenzie, B. (1997). *Medicine and the internet: Introducing online resources and terminology* (2nd ed.). Oxford: Oxford University Press.

McKenzie, J., & Smeltzer, J. (1997). *Planning, implementing, and evaluating health promotion programs* (2nd ed.). Boston: Allyn & Bacon.

McKinlay, J., & Stoeckle, J. (1997). Corporationization and the social transformation of doctoring. In P. Conrad (Ed.), *The sociology of health and illness* (pp. 182–193). New York: St. Martin's Press.

McMahan, S., Witte, K., & Meyer, J. (1998). The preception of risk messages regarding electromagnetic fields: Extending the extended parallel process model to unknown risk. *Health Communication, 10*(3), 247–260.

McNamee, S. (1992). Reconstructing identity: the communal construction of crisis. In S. McNamee & K. Gergen (Eds.), *Therapy as social construction* (pp. 186–199). Newbury Park, CA: Sage.

McNamee, S. (1996). Therapy and identity construction in a postmodern world. In D. Grodin, & T. Lindlof (Eds.), *Constructing the self in a mediated world* (pp. 141–155). Thousand Oaks, CA: Sage.

McPherson, B. (1994). Sociocultural perspectives on aging and physical activity. *Journal of Aging and Physical Activity, 2*(4), 329–353.

McRae, M., Carey, P., & Anderson-Scott, R. (1998). Black churches as therapeutic systems: A group process perspective. *Health Education and Behavior, 25*(6), 778–789.

Meerabeau, L. (1998). Consumerism and health care: The example of fertility treatment. *Journal of Advanced Nursing, 27,* 721–729.

Mengel, M., & Fields, S. (Eds.). (1997). *Introduction to clinical skills: A patient-centered textbook.* New York: Plenum Medical Book Company.

Menikheim, M. L., & Meyers, M. W. (1986). Communication patterns of women and nurses. In D. Kjernik & I. Martinson (Eds.), *Women in health and illness: Life experiences and crises* (pp. 80–87). Philadelphia: W. B. Saunders Company.

Men's Health Editors. (1999). *The complete book of men's health.* Emmaus, PA: Rodale Press.

Merger consolidates home health care services. (1997, Fall). *The Health Advocate, 6,* 1–3.

Merline, J. (1996, November). The backlash against managed care. *Consumer's Research,* 15–19.

Messner, R. L. (1993, August). What patients really want from their nurses. *American Journal of Nursing, 93,* 38–41.

Meuleman, J., Davidson, R., & Caranasos, G. (1988, February). A comparison of attitudes toward geriatrics among medical residents. *Journal of Medical Education, 63,* 135–137.

Meyer, M. (1997, March 17). Bound and gagged: HMOs need to be transformed—but in the right way. *Newsweek,* 45.

Meyrowitz, J. (1985). *No sense of place: The impact of electronic media on social behavior.* New York: Oxford University Press.

Michels, R. (1999, March 25). Medical education and managed care. *The New England Journal of Medicine, 340*(12), 959–961.

Mihalik, G., & Scherer, M. (1998). Fundamental mechanisms of managed behavioral health care. *Journal of Health Care Finance, 24*(3), 1–15.

Milewa, T., Valentine, J., & Calnan, M. (1998). Managerialism and active citizenship in Britain's reformed health service; Power and community in an era of decentralisation. *Social Science and Medicine, 47*(4), 507–517.

Millenson, M. (1997). *Demanding medical excellence: Doctors and accountability in the information age.* Chicago: University of Chicago Press.

Miller, D. (Ed.). (1995). *Acknowledging consumption: A review of new studies.* New York: Routledge.

Miller, K. (1998). The evolution of professional identity: The case of osteopathic medicine. *Social Science and Medicine, 47* (11), 1739–1748.

Miller, L. (1999, July 14). Guidelines, libraries offer cures for web confusion. *USA Today,* p. 5D.

Miller, T. W. (Ed.). (1989). *Stressful life events.* Madison: International Universities Press.

Miner, H. (1997). Body ritual among the Nacirema. In J. Henslin (Ed.), *Down to earth sociology: Introductory readings* (9th ed.; pp. 73–77). New York: The Free Press.

Minkler, M. (1999, February). Personal responsibility for health? A review of the arguments and the evidence at century's end. *Health Education & Behavior, 26*(1), 121–140.

Mishler, E. (1984). *The discourse of medicine: Dialectics of medical interviews.* Norwood, NJ: Ablex.

Mitchell, B. (1999, August 19). "It's cancer!" *The Athens News,* pp. 1, 10 & 11.

Mitchell, B. (1999, August 23). A lesson learned: Early detection best cure for cancer. *The Athens News,* pp. 16–17.

Mitchell, F. (1996). *Case hysteries.* Lewiston, NY: Mellen Poetry Press.

Mitchem, A. (1998, June 28). Managed care hurts patients. *Athens Messenger,* p. 9A.

Montbriand, M. (1995). Alternative therapies as control behaviors used by cancer patients. *Journal of Advanced Nursing, 22,* 646–654.

The Montel William Show. (1999, January 28). Is health care in America killing us? Paramount Pictures Corp.

Montgomery, C. (1993). *Healing through communication: The practice of caring.* Newbury Park, CA: Sage.

Moore, M. (1999, September). The fight of their lives. *McCall's,* pp. 16–18, 20.

Moore-Gilbert, B. (1997). *Postcolonial theory: contexts, practices, politics.* New York: Verso.

Morisky, D., & Coan, D. (1998). Asia—The new epidemic zone for HIV/AIDS. *Journal of Health Communication, 3*(3), 185–192.

Morse, B. W., & Piland, R. N. (1981). An assessment of communication competencies needed by intermediate-level health care providers: A study of nurse-patient, nurse-doctor, nurse-nurse communication relationships. *Journal of Applied Communication Research, 9*(1), 30–41.

Moyer, A., Greener, S., Beauvais, J., & Salovey, P. (1995). Accuracy of health research reported in the popular press: Breast cancer and mammography. *Health Communication, 7*(2), 147–161.

Mulholland, J. (1994). Multiple directives in the doctor-patient consultation. *Australian Journal of Communication, 21* (2), 74–94.

Muller, C. (1992). *Health care and gender.* New York: Russell Sage Foundation.

Muller, W. (1999, April 2–4). Remember the Sabbath? *USA Weekend,* pp. 4–5.

Naber, S., Halstead, L., Broome, M., & Rehwaldt, M. (1995). Communication and control: Parent, child, and health care professional interactions during painful procedures. *Issues in Comprehensive Pediatric Nursing, 18,* 79–90.

Napier, K. (1994). *Unproven medical treatments lure elderly* [Brochure]. Rockville, MD: FDA.

National Committee for Quality Assurance (NCQA). (1999). *The state of managed care quality.*

Navaroli, R. (1997). Panelist discuss managed health care. *Athens Messenger,* p. 8.

Nazario, S. (1993, December 20). Treating doctors for prejudice. *Los Angeles Times,* p. A1.

Nechas, E., & Foley, D. (1994). *Unequal treatment: What you don't know about how women are mistreated by the medical community.* New York: Simon & Schuster.

Neergaard, L. (1999, May 16). Patient's gender might affect results of prescription drugs. *The Columbus Dispatch,* p. 4A.

Nettleton, S. (1992). *Power, pain and dentistry.* Philadelphia: Open University Press.

Nettleton, S. (1995). *The sociology of health and illness.* Cambridge: Polity Press.

Neuendorf, K. (1990). Health images in the mass media. In E. B. Ray & L. Donohew (Eds.), *Communication and health: System and applications* (pp. 111–135). Hillsdale, NJ: Lawrence Erlbaum & Associates.

Ng, W., Chin, S., Moy, J., & Okihiro, G. (Eds.). (1995). *Reviewing Asian American locating diversity.* Pullman, WA: Washington State University Press.

Nichols, J. L. (1999). *Women living with multiple sclerosis.* Alameda, CA: Hunter House.

Nichter, M., & Nichter, M. (1987). Cultural notions of fertility in South Asia and their impact on Sri Lankan family planning practices. *Human Organization, 46*(1), 18–28.

Nieves, J. (1998). Foreword. In G. Schamess & A. Lightburn (Eds.), *Humane managed care?* Washington, DC: NASW Press.

Nonprescription Drug Manufacturers Association. (1992, May). *Self-medication in the '90s: Practices and perceptions.* Washington, DC: Author.

Nordenberg, T. (1997, January-February). Overcoming infertility. *FDA Consumer Magazine.*

Nordenberg, T. (1998, March). *Colds & flu* (FDA Publication No. 98-1264). Rockville, MD: Department of Health and Human Services.

Northouse, L. L. (1988, March/April). Social support in patients' and husbands' adjustment to breast cancer. *Nursing Research, 37*(2), 91–95.

Northouse, P., & Northouse, L. (1987). Communication and cancer: Issues confronting patients, health professionals, and family members. *Journal of Psychosocial Oncology, 5*(3), 17–46.

Nurse anesthetists are specialists, not just "nurses." (May 29, 1998). [Letters]. *USA Today*, p. 14A.

Nussbaum, J., & Coupland, J. (Eds.). (1995). *Handbook of communication and aging research.* Mahwah, NJ: Lawrence Erlbaum Associates.

Nussbaum, J., Thompson, T., & Robinson, J. (1989). *Communication and aging.* New York: Harper & Row.

Oberst, M. (1995). Editorial: The naked emperor revisited. *Research in Nursing & Health, 18,* 383.

O'Connor, K. F. (1996). Ethical/moral experiences of oncology nurses. *Oncology Nursing Forum, 23*(5), 787–794.

O'Donnell, J. (1998, July 13). Child-death cases say automakers failed to act. *USA Today,* p. 3B.

Ogles, B. M., Trout, S. C., Gillespie, D. K., & Penkert, K. S. (1998). Special section: Public/private collaboration in managing behavioral health services: Managed care as a platform for cross-system integration. *The Journal of Behavioral Health Services & Research, 25*(3), 252–268.

O'Hair, D. (1989). Dimensions of relational communication and control during physician-patient interactions. *Health Communication, 1*(2), 97–115.

O'Hair, D., Behnke, R., & King, P. (1983). Age-related patient preferences for physician communication styles. *Educational Gerontology, 9,* 147–158.

O'Hair, D., O'Hair, M., Southward, G., & Krayer, K. (1987). Physician communication and patient compliance. *The Journal of Compliance in Health Care, 2* (2), 125–129.

Oldenburg, A. (1999, January 7). Something clicks when dieters share struggles on line. *USA Today,* p. 6D.

Oldham, P. (1999, February 24). Current system fair to all awaiting organs. *USA Today,* p. 13A.

Olmsted, M. (1994). A doctor's story. In K. Hicks (Ed.), *Misdiagnosis: Woman as a disease* (pp. 71–82). Allentown, PA: People's Medical Society.

Olson, J. (1995). Relationships between nurse-expressed empathy, patient-perceived empathy and patient distress. *Image: Journal of Nursing Scholarship, 27* (4), 317–322.

Ong, L., DeHaes, C., Hoos, A., & Lammes, F. (1995). Doctor-patient communication: A review of the literature. *Social Science and Medicine, 40* (7), 903–918.

Orem, D. (1995). *Nursing: Concepts of practice.* St. Louis, MO: Mosby.

Orodenker, S. Z. (1991). *Family caregiving in a changing society: The effects of employment on caregiver stress.* New York: Garland.

Ostasiewski, P., & Fugate, D. L. (1994, Winter). Implementing the patient circle. *Journal of Health Care Marketing, 14*(4), 20–26.

Oxman, T. E., & Berkman, L. F. (1990). Assessment of social relationships in elderly patients. *International Journal of Psychiatry in Medicine, 20*(1), 65–84.

Page, S. (1999, December 7). Medical errors targeted. *USA Today,* p. 1A.

Paget, M. A. (1988). *The unity of mistakes: A phenomenological interpretation of medical work.* Philadelphia: Temple University Press.

Painter, K. (1998, July 9). Walk don't speed childbirth. *USA Today,* p. 1D.

Painter, K. (1999, July 13). Adrift in Alzheimer's sea of forgetfulness. *USA Today,* p. 6D.

Painter, K. (1999, August 11). Doctors of same race get patients involved. *USA Today,* p. 1D.

Palmer, J. (1999, February). What to expect when you're not expecting. *Parents,* p. 184.

Palomo, J. R. (1999, March 8). A tax credit to care for mom wouldn't have helped my sisters. *USA Today,* p. 13A.

Papa, M., Singhal, A., Law, S., Sood, S., Rogers, E. (1998). *Entertainment-education and social change: An analysis of paradoxical communication.* Paper presented at the Development Communication Division, International Communication Association, Jerusalem, Israel.

Papa, M., Singhal, A., Law, S., Sood, S., Rogers, E., & Shefner-Rogers C. (1998, July). *Entertainment-education and social change: An analysis of parasocial interaction, social learning, and para-*

doxical communication. Paper presented at the International Communication Association, Jerusalem, Israel.

Parle, M., Maguire, P., & Heaven, C. (1997). The development of a training model to improve health professionals' skills, self-efficacy and outcome expectancies when communicating with cancer patients. *Social Science and Medicine, 44* (2), 231–240.

Parnell, T. (1999, August 11). [Letters]. *USA Today,* p. 14A.

Parrott, R. (1994). Exploring family practitioners' and patients' information exchange about prescribed medications: Implications for practitioners' interviewing and patients' understanding. *Health Communication, 6*(4), 267–280.

Parrott, R. L., & Condit, C. M. (Eds.). (1996). *Evaluating women's health messages.* Thousand Oaks, CA: Sage.

Parrott, R., Duggan, A., Cremo, J., Eckles, A., Jones, K., & Steiner, C. (1999, June). Communicating about youth's sun exposure risk to soccer coaches and parents: A pilot study in Georgia. *Health Education and Behavior, 26*(3), 385–395.

Parsons, T. (1951). *The social system.* New York: The Free Press.

Paskett, E., Carter, W., Chu, J., & White, E. (1990). Compliance behavior in women with abnormal pap smears. *Medical Care, 28* (7), 643–656.

Pauwels, A. (1995). *Cross-cultural communication in the health sciences: Communicating with migrating patients.* Melbourne, Australia: Macmillan Education Australia.

Pear, R. (1999, August 15). Courts more receptive to patients suing HMOs. *The Columbus Dispatch,* p. 3A.

Pearson, J. (1995). *Marriage after mourning: The secrets of surviving couples.* Dubuque, IA: Kendall/Hunt Publishing Co.

Pendleton, D., & Bochner, S. (1980). The communication of medical information in general practice consultations as a function of patients' social class. *Social Science and Medicine, 14,* 669–673.

People's Medical Society. (1993). *Dial 800 for health.* New York: Wings Books.

Pepler, C., & Lynch, A. (1991). Relational messages of control in nurse-patient interactions with terminally ill patients with AIDS and cancer. *Journal of Palliative Care, 7*(1), 18–29.

Perry, C. (1996, October). Education and prevention. *CARHP Clinical proceedings,* 20–21.

Peters, S., Stanley, I., Rose, M., & Salmon, P. (1998). Patients with medically unexplained symptoms: Sources of patients' authority and implications for demands on medical care. *Social Science and Medicine, 46*(4–5), 559–565.

Peterson, K. S. (1998, November 9). Minding the patient: Teams listen to hearts, minds. *USA Today,* p. 6D.

Peterson, K. S. (1999, January 28). 36% of seniors say their kids don't help. *USA Today,* p. 1A.

Peterson, K. S. (1999, April 12). Psychology sharing spirit with shamans. *USA Today,* p. 4D.

Peterson, K. S. (1999, December 16). Thank you, Cathy, for all you taught us. *USA Today,* p. 9D.

Peterson, L. W., Halsey, J., Albrecht, T. L., & McGough, K. (1995, June). Communicating with staff nurses: Support or hostility. *Nursing Management, 26*(6), 36–38.

Pfau, M., Mullen, L., & Garrow, K. (1995). The influence of television viewing on public perceptions of physicians. *Journal of Broadcasting and Electronic Media, 39,* 441–458.

Philipsen, G. (1992). *Speaking culturally: Explorations in social communication.* Albany: State University of New York Press.

Phillips, G., & Jones, A. (1991). Medical compliance: Patient or physician responsibility? *American Behavioral Scientist, 34* (6), 756–767.

Phillips, K. (1996). The spaces of public dissension: Reconsidering the public sphere. *Communication Monographs, 63*(3), 231–248.

Pilisuk, M., & Parks, S. H. (1986). *The healing web: Social networks and human survival.* Hanover, NH: University Press of New England.

Pinkerton, S., & Schroeder, P. (1988). *Commitment to excellent: Developing a professional nursing staff.* Rockville, MD: Aspen.

Piotrow, P., Kincaid, D., Rimon II, J., & Rinehart, W. (1997). *Health communication: Lessons from family planning and reproductive health.* Westport, CT: Praeger.

Piver, M., & Wilder, G. (1996). *Gilda's disease: Sharing personal experience and a medical perspective on ovarian cancer.* Amherst, NY: Prometheus Books.

Pizzini, F. (1991). Communication hierarchies in humour: Gender differences in the obstetrical/gynaecological setting. *Discourse & Society, 2* (4), 477–488.

Platt, F. (1995). *Conversation repair: Case studies in doctor-patient communication.* Boston: Little, Brown and Company.

Platt, F. (1996, March 15). Why don't you use birth control? *Patient Care,* 189–190.

Poirier, L. (1997, May). The importance of screening for domestic violence in all women. *The Nurse Practitioner, 22*(5), 105–122.

Ponticelli, C. (Ed.). (1998). *Gateways to improving lesbian health and health care: Opening doors.* New York: Harrington Park Press.

Porter, M. (1990). Professional-client relationships and women's reproductive health care. In S. Cunningham-Burley & N. McKeganey (Eds.), *Readings in medical sociology* (pp. 182–212). New York: Tavistock/Routledge.

Porter, P. (2000, January 16). Prognosis: Ugly. *Columbus Dispatch,* pp. 1–2G.

Posner, K. L., Gild, W. M., & Winans, E. V. (1995). Changes in clinical practice in response to reductions in reimbursement: Physician autonomy and resistance to bureaucratization. *Medical Anthropology Journal, 9*(4), 476–492.

Potter, J. (1996). *Representing reality: Discourse, rhetoric and social construction.* London: Sage.

Powell, D., & Leiss, W. (1997). *Mad cows and mother's milk: The perils of poor risk communication.* Buffalo, NY: McGill-Queen's University Press.

Price, R. (1999, September 26). Widower prevails big over insurer. *Columbus Dispatch,* p. 1E.

Prohaska, T., & Clark, M. (1997). Health behavior and the human life cycle. In D. Gochman (Ed.), *Handbook of health behavior research III: demography, development and diversity* (pp. 29–48). New York: Plenum Press.

Psathas, G. (1990). The organization of talk, gaze, and activity in a medical interview. In G. Psathas (Ed.), *Interaction competence* (pp. 205–229). Washington, DC: International Institute for Ethnomethodology and Conversation Analysis & University Press of America.

Puddifoot, J. E., & Johnson, M. P. (1997). The legitimacy of grieving: The partner's experience at miscarriage. *Social Science and Medicine, 45*(6), 837–845.

Purcell, C. (1998). Telemedicine: The perspective of one state. In S. Viegas, & K. Dunn (Eds.), *Telemedicine: Practicing in the information age* (pp. 31–36). Philadelphia: Lippincott-Raven Publishers.

Purnell, L., & Paulanka, B. (Eds.). (1998). *Transcultural health care: A culturally competent approach.* Philadelphia, PA: F. A. Davis.

Putnam, S., Stiles, W., Jacob, M., & James, S. (1985). Patient exposition and physician explanation in initial medical interviews and outcomes of clinic visits. *Medical Care, 23* (1), 74–83.

Putting managed care in its place. (1998, January 5). *Hospital & Health Networks,* pp. 34–35.

Query, J. L., & James, A. C. (1989). The relationship between interpersonal communication competence and social support among elderly support groups in retirement communities. *Health Communication, 1*(3), 165–184.

Quindlen, A. (1994). The human touch. *New York Times,* p. 21A.

Radner, G. (1989). *It's always something.* New York: Avon Books.

Ragan, S. (1990). Verbal play and multiple goals in the gynaecological exam interaction. *Journal of Language and Social Psychology, 9* (1-2), 67–84.

Ragan, S., Beck, C., & White, M. (1995). Educating the patient: Interactive learning in an Ob-Gyn context. In G. Morris & R. Chenail (Eds.), *The talk of the clinic: Explorations in the analysis of medical and therapeutic discourse* (pp. 185–208). Hillsdale, NJ: Lawrence Erlbaum Associates.

Ragan, S., & Pagano, M. (1987). Communicating with female patients: Affective interaction during contraceptive counseling and gynecologic exams. *Women's Studies in Communication, 10*, 46–57.

Rahman, O., Strauss, J., Gertler, P., Ashley, D., & Fox, K. (1994). Gender differences in adult health: An international comparison. *The Gerontogist, 34*(4), 463–469.

Rakow, L. (Ed.). (1992). *Women making meaning: New feminist directions in communication.* New York: Routledge.

Rakowski, W. (1997). Health behavior in the elderly. In D. Gochman (Ed.), *Handbook of health behavior research III: Demography, development and diversity* (pp. 97–117). New York: Plenum Press.

Raso, J. (1993). *Mystical diets.* Buffalo, NY: Prometheus Books.

Raso, J. (1994). *Alternative healthcare: A comprehensive guide.* Amherst, NY: Prometheus Books.

Ratzan, S. (Ed.). (1993). *AIDS: Effective health communication for the 90s.* Washington, DC: Taylor & Francis.

Ratzan, S. (1994a). Editor's introduction; Communication—The key to a healthier tomorrow. *American Behavioral Scientist, 38*(2), 202–207.

Ratzan, S. (1994b). Health communication as negotiation: The healthy America act. *American Behavioral Scientist, 38*(2), 224–247.

Ratzan, S., Payne, J., & Massett, H. (1994). America responds to AIDS campaign. *American Behavioral Scientist, 38*(2), 294–309.

Ray, E. B. (Ed.). (1996). *Communication and disenfranchisement.* Mahwah, NJ: Lawrence Erlbaum Associates.

Reagan, J., & Collins, J. (1987). Sources for health care information in two small communities. *Journalism Quarterly, 64*(2-3), 560–563.

Redman, B. (1997). *The practice of patient education.* St. Louis, MO: Mosby.

Reed, M. (1999, Winter). Health a concern to many in Athens county. *Rural Report, 18*(1), 1, 4.

Reeve, D. (1999). *Care packages.* New York: Random House.

Reid, J. (1996). *A telemedicine primer: Understanding the issues.* Billings, MT: Innovative Medical Communications.

Reid-Wallace, C. (1992). National policy perspectives: Medical schools and America 2000. *Academic Medicine, 67* (6), 380–381.

Resnick, C., & Tighe, E. G. (1997). The role of multidisciplinary community clinics in managed care systems. *Social Work, 42*(1), 91–98.

Reyes, H. (1998, December). Doctor's orders. *Cosmopolitan,* p. 40.

Rhodes, L. (1990). Studying biomedicine as a cultural system. In T. Johnson & C. Sargent (Eds.), *Medical anthropology: Contemporary theory and method* (pp. 159–173). Westport, CT: Praeger.

Rimal, R., Ratzan, S., Arntson, P., & Freimuth, V. (1997). Reconceptualizing the "patient": Health care promotion as increasing citizens' decision-making competencies. *Health Communication, 9* (1) 61–74.

Rimm, E., Willett, W., Hu, F., Sampson, L., Colditz, G., Manson, J., Hennekens, C., & Stampfer, M. (1998, February 4). Folate and vitamin B6 from diet and supplements in relation to risk of coronary heart disease among women. *JAMA, 279*(5), 359–364.

Rinehart, N. (1991). *Client or patient? Power and related concepts in health care.* St. Louis, MO: Ishiyaku EuroAmerica.

Risker, D. C. (1995). A segmentation analysis of consumer uses of health information. *Health Marketing Quarterly, 12*(4), 39–48.

Ritchey, F., Yoels, W., Clair, J., & Allman, R. (1995). Competing medical and social ideologies and communication accuracy in medical encounters. *Research in Sociology of Health Care, 12,* 189–211.

Ritzer, G. (1996). *The McDonalization of society* (rev. ed.). Thousand Oak, CA: Pine Forge Press.

Ritzer, G. (1997). *Postmodern social theory.* New York: McGraw Hill.

Roberts, F. D. (1999). *Talking about treatment.* New York: Oxford University Press.

Robinson, J. (1998). Getting down to business: Talk, gaze, and body orientation during openings of doctor-patient consultations. *Human Communication Research, 25* (1), 97–213.

Robinson, L. (1998). *"Race," communication and the caring professions.* Philadelphia, PA: Open University Press.

Robinson, T., Patrick, K., Eng, T., & Gustafson, D. (1998). An evidence-based approach to interactive health communication. *JAMA, 280*(14), 1264–1268.

Rodale Press Survey. (1998, November). *Survey of public opinion regarding health news coverage.* Emmaus, PA: Rodale Press.

Rogers, D., & Ginzberg, E. (Eds.). (1993). *Medical care and the health of the poor.* Boulder, CO: Westview Press.

Rogers, E. (1994). The field of health communication today. *American Behavioral Scientist, 38*(2), 208–214.

Roman, L. A., Lindsay, J. K., Boger, R. P., DeWys, M., Beaumont, E. J., Jones, A. S., & Haas, B. (1995). Parent-to-parent support initiated in the neonatal intensive care unit. *Research in Nursing & Health, 18,* 385–394.

Romanucci-Ross, L., Moerman, D., & Tancredi, L. (Eds.). (1991). *The anthropology of medicine: From culture to method* (2nd ed.). New York: Bergin & Garvey.

Rondeau, K. V., & Wagar, T. H. (1998, Spring). Hospital chief executive officer perceptions of organizational culture and performance. *Hopital Topics: Research and Perspectives on Healthcare, 76*(2), 14–21.

Roots, C. (1998). *The sandwich generation: Adult children caring for aging parents.* New York: Garland Publishing.

Rorty, R. (1991). *Objectivity, relativism, and truth: Philosophical papers* (Vol. 1). New York: Cambridge University Press.

Rosaldo, R. (1989). *Culture and truth: The remaking of social analysis.* Boston: Beacon Press.

Rosenau, P. (Ed.). (1994). *Health care reform in the nineties.* Thousand Oaks, CA: Sage.

Rosenwaike, I., & Dolinsky, A. (1987). The changing demographic determinants of the growth of the extreme aged. *The Gerontologist, 27*(3), 275–280.

Rost, K., Roter, D., Bertakis, K., & Quill, T. (1990). Physician-patient familiarity and patient recall of medication change. *Family Medicine, 22* (6), 453–457.

Roter, D. (1984). Patient question asking in physician-patient interactions. *Health Psychology, 3* (5), 395–409.

Roter, D., & Hall, J. (1992). *Doctors talking with patients/patients talking with doctors: Improving communication in medical visits.* Westport, CT: Auburn House.

Roter, D., & Hall, J. (1997). Gender differences in patient-physician communication. In S. Gallant, G. Keita, & R. Royak-Schaler (Eds.), *Health care for women: Psychological, social, and behavioral influences* (pp. 57–72). Washington, DC: American Psychological Association.

Roter, D., Lipkin, M., & Korsgaard, A. (1991, November). Sex differences in patients' and physicians' communication during primary care medical visits. *Medical Care, 29*(11), 1083–1093.

Roth, N., & Fuller, L. (Eds.). (1998). *Women and AIDS: Negotiating safer practices, care and representation.* New York: Harrington Park Press.

Rother, J. (1997, March-April). Making sense of managed care. *Modern Maturity, 40*(2), 82,84.

Rothman, D., Marcus, S., & Kiceluk, S. (Eds.). (1995). *Medicine and western civilization.* New Brunswick, NJ: Rutgers University Press.

Rowland-Morin, P., & Carroll, J. (1990). Verbal communication skills and patient satisfaction. *Evaluation and the Health Professions, 13* (2), 168–185.

Royal, R. (Ed.). (1995). *Reinventing the American people: Unity and diversity today.* Grand Rapids, MI: Williams B. Eerdmans.

Ruben, B. (1993). What patients remember: A content analysis of critical incidents in health care. *Health Communication, 5* (2), 99–112.

Rubin, D. (1982). *Caring: A daughter's story.* New York: Holt, Rinehart, & Winston.

Rubin, R. (1998, June 22). A potent HMO issue: Pill vs. Viagra. *USA Today,* p. 1D.

Rubin, R. (1998, November 2). Industry's rapid growth, change defy regulation. *USA Today,* p. 1A, 2A.

Rubin, R. (1998, November 11). Info center means power for patients. *USA Today,* p. 4A.

Rubin, R. (1999, January 21). On-line viagra worries medical boards. *USA Today,* p. 1D.

Rubin, R. (1999, November 18). Songs full of heart. *USA Today,* p. 10D.

Rubin, R. (1999, December 21). Do mammograms pass the test? *USA Today,* p. 1A.

Rubin, R. (2000, January 20). Fox's exit returns Parkinson's to spotlight. *USA Today,* p. 9D.

Rubinstein, R. (1995). Narratives of elder parental death: A structural and cultural analysis. *Medical Anthropology Quarterly, 9*(2), 257–276.

Rundle, R., & Binkley, C. (1999, August 27). Hospitals now offer amenities that rival top-flight hotels. *The Wall Street Journal Interactive Edition* [online]. Availability http: interactive.wsj. com/archive/retr...721242459333.djm&template=printing.tmpl

Runowicz, C., & Haupt, D. (1995). *To be alive: A woman's guide to a full life after cancer.* New York: Henry Holt.

Saba, V. K., Pocklington, D. B., & Miller, K. P. (Eds.). (1998). *Nursing and computers: An anthology, 1987–1996.* New York: Springer.

Sadowski, W. (1996, August). Can you trust your doctor? *Prevention, 48*(8), 88–96, 134.

Salmon, C. (Ed.). (1989). *Information campaigns: Balancing social values and social change.* Newbury Park, CA: Sage.

Samovar, L., & Porter, R. (Eds.). (1997). *Intercultural communication* (8th edition). Belmont, CA: Wadsworth.

Samra, R. (1993). The image of the physician: A rhetorical perspective. *Public Relations Review, 19* (4), 341–348.

Sanders, R. (1995). A neo-rhetorical perspective: The enactment of role-identities as interactive and strategic. In S. Sigman (Ed.), *The consequentiality of communication* (pp. 67–120). Hillsdale, NJ: Lawrence Erlbaum Associates.

Sandlin, L. (1998, December 20). Crisis brings out best in two sons. *The Columbus Dispatch,* p. 1I.

Sankar, A. (1986). Out of the clinic into the home: Control and patient-physician communication. *Social Science and Medicine, 22*(9), 973–982.

Sarbin, T., & Kitsuse, J. (Eds.). (1994). *Constructing the social.* London: Sage.

Sargent, C., & Bascope, G. (1996). Ways of knowing about birth in three cultures. *Medical Anthropology Quarterly, 10*(2), 213–236.

Sarick, L. (1999, February 23). A case for "watchful waiting." *The Globe and Mail,* p. A 20.

Sass, J., & Mattson, M. (1999, May). When social support is uncomfortable. *Management Communication Quarterly, 12*(4), 511–543.

Satava, R. (1997). Medical virtual reality. In S. Weghorst, H. Sieburg, & K. Morgan (Eds.), *Medicine meets virtual reality: Health care in the information age* (pp. 100–106). Burke, VA: IOS Press.

Saunders, P. (1998). "You're out of your mind!": Humor as a face-saving strategy during neuropsychological examinations. *Health Communication, 10* (4), 357–372.

Saville-Troike, M. (1992). Cultural maintenance and "vanishing" languages. In C. Kramsch & S. McConnell-Ginet (Eds.), *Text and context: Cross-disciplinary perspectives on language study* (148–155). Lexington, MA: D.C. Heath and Company.

Sawa, R. J. (Ed.). (1992). *Family health care.* Thousand Oaks, CA: Sage.

Schamess, G., & Lightburn, A. (Eds.). (1998). *Humane managed care?* Washington, DC: NASW Press.

Schauffler, H., Brown, C., & Milstein, A. (1999, March-April). Raising the bar: The use of performance guarantees by the pacific business group on health. *Health Affiliation (Millwood), 18*(2), 134–142.

Schickel, R. (1985). *Intimate strangers: The culture of celebrity.* Garden City, NY: Doubleday & Company.

Schlichtmann, J. (1999, February 4). Lawyer promotes cooperation over lawsuits. *USA Today*, p. 15A.

Schneider, K., & Gold, T. (1998, December 7). After the tears. *People, 50*(21), 126–136.

Schneiderman, L., & Jecker, N. (1995). *Wrong medicine: Doctors, patients, and futile treatment.* Baltimore, MD: The John Hopkins University Press.

Schraeder, C., Lamb, G., Shelton, P., & Britt, T. (1997, January). Community nursing organizations: A new frontier. *American Journal of Nursing, 97*(1), 63–65.

Schrof, J. (1998, December 21). Required course: Bedside manner 101. *U.S. News & World Report*, p. 66.

Schuck, P. (1994). Rethinking informed consent. *Yale Law Journal, 103,* 899–959.

Schulman, K., Berlin, J., Harless, W., Kerner, J., Sistrunk, S., Gersh, B., Dube, R., Taleghani, C., Burker, J., Williams, S., Eisenberg, J., & Escarce, J. (1999, February 25). The effect of race and sex on physicians' recommendations for cardiac catheterization. *The New England Journal of Medicine, 340*(8), 618–626.

Schutz, A. (1962). *Collected papers I: The problem of social reality.* The Hague: Martinus Nijhoff.

Sedgwick, E. (1990). *Epistemology of the closet.* Berkeley: University of California Press.

Segalman, R. (Ed.). (1998). *Reclaiming the family.* St. Paul, MN: PWPA.

Seidman, S. (Ed.). (1994). *The postmodern turn: New perspectives on social theory.* New York: Cambridge University Press.

Seroussi, K. (2000, February). We cured our son's autism. *Parents,* pp. 118–120, 123–125.

Sesia, P. (1996). "Women come here on their own when they need to": Prenatal care, authoritative knowledge, and maternal health in Oaxaca. *Medical Anthropology Quarterly, 10*(2), 121–140.

Shaffer, T., & Sherrell, D. (1995). Exploring patient role behaviors for health care services: The assertive, activated and passive patient. *Health Marketing Quarterly, 13* (1), 19–35.

Shaller, D. V., Sharp, R. S., & Rubin, R. D. (1998, April 22/29). A national action plan to meet health care quality information needs in the age of managed care. *JAMA, 279*(16), 1254–1258.

Shapiro, M. (1995). Doctors learning their trade: The reproduction of professional power. In G. Lupton & J. Najman (Eds.), *Sociology of health and illness: Australian readings* (2nd ed.; pp. 217–235). South Melbourne: Macmillan Education.

SHARE. (1998). [brochure]. New York: Author.

Sharf, B. F. (1988). Teaching patients to speak up: Past and future trends. *Patient Education and Counseling, 11*, 95–108.

Sharf, B., & Freimuth, V. (1993). The construction of illness on entertainment television: Coping with cancer on thirtysomething. *Health Communication, 5*(3), 141–160.

Sharf, B., Freimuth, V., Greenspon, P., & Plotnick, C. (1996). Confronting cancer on thirtysomething: Audience response to health content on entertainment television. *Journal of Health Communication, 1,* 157–172.

Sharf, B., & Poirier, S. (1988). Exploring (un)common ground: Communication and literature in a health care setting. *Communication Education, 37*, 224–236.

Sharf, B., & Street, R. (1997). The patient as a central construct: Shifting the emphasis. *Health Communication, 9*(1), 1–11.

Sharp, R., & Sharp, V. (1998). *Webdoctor: Your online guide to health care and wellness.* St. Louis, MO: Quality Medical Publishing.

Sheer, B. (1996, July/August). Reaching collaboration through empowerment: A developmental process. *Journal of Obstetric, Gynecologic, & Neonatal Nursing, 25*(6), 513–517.

Shelton, D. (1998, April 6). Blacks' concern over HIV/AIDS rises as epidemic continues. *American Medical News,* 9–10.

Sherman, T. (1999, July 9–11). Millions of diabetics could get high-tech help. *USA Weekend,* p. 16.

Shi, D. (1995). *Facing facts: Realism in American thought and culture, 1850–1920.* New York: Oxford University Press.

Shilts, R. (1987). *And the band played on: Politics, people, and the AIDS epidemic.* New York: St. Martin's Press.

Shorter, E. (1992). Recent changes in family life and new challenges in primary care. In R. Sawa (Ed.), *Family health care* (pp. 9–17). Newbury Park, CA: Sage.

Shotter, J. (1984). *Social accountability and selfhood.* Oxford: Basil Blackwell Publishers.

Shotter, J. (1993). *Conversational realities: Constructing life through language.* London: Sage.

Shotter, J., & Gergen, K. (Eds.). (1989). *Texts of identity.* London: Sage.

Shumaker, S., Schron, E., & Ockene, J. (Eds.). (1990). *The handbook of health behavior change.* New York: Springer Publishing Company.

Siegal, B. (1988). *Love, medicine, and miracles.* New York: Harper & Row.

Signorielli, N. (1990). Television and health: Images and impact. In C. Atkin & L. Wallack (Eds.), *Mass communication and public health* (pp. 96–113). Newbury Park, CA: Sage.

Silverman, D. (1989). *Communication and medical practice.* Newbury Park, CA: Sage.

Silverman, M., & Huelsman, E. (1990). The dynamics of long-term familial caregiving. In J. F. Gubrium, & A. Sankar (Eds.), *The home care experience* (pp. 173–188). Newbury Park, CA: Sage.

Simon, S., Pan, R., Sullivan, A., Clark-Chiarelli, N., Connelly, M., Peters, A., Singer, J., Inui, T., & Block, S. (1999, March 25). Views of managed care. *The New England Journal of Medicine, 340*(12), 928–936.

Singhal, A., & Rogers, E. (1999). *Entertainment-education: A communication strategy for social change.* Mahwah, NJ: Lawrence Erlbaum Associates.

Sirica, C. (Ed.). (1996). *Osteopathic medicine: Past, present, and future.* New York: Josiah Macy, Jr. Foundation.

Skolnick, A. (1992, November 11). At third meeting, menopause experts make the most of insufficient data. *JAMA, 268*(18), 2483–2485.

Slack, W. V. (1997). *Cybermedicine: How computing empowers doctors and patients for better health care.* San Francisco: Jossey-Bass.

Slack, W. V. (1999). The patient online. *American Journal of Preventive Medicine, 16* (1), 43–45.

Smith, D. (1987). *The everyday world as problematic: A feminist sociology.* Boston: Northeastern University Press.

Smith, D., & Pettegrew, L. (1986). Mutual persuasion as a model for doctor-patient communication. *Theoretical Medicine, 7,* 127–146.

Smith, J. (1992). *Women and doctors.* New York: Atlantic Monthly.

Smith, L. M., & Godfrey, H. (1995). *Family support programs and rehabilitation: A cognitive-behavioral approach to traumatic brain injury.* New York: Plenum Press.

Smith, P., & Schaaf, R. (1995–96, Winter). How public relations techniques are used by medical practices in the managed health care marketplace. *Public Relations Quarterly.* 19–22.

Smith, R. C. (1996). *The patient's story: Integrated patient-doctor interviewing.* Boston: Little, Brown and Company.

Smith, R. T. et al. (1997). Resource support and heart patient recovery. *International Journal of Rehabilitation Research, 20,* 11–28.

Smith, S. (1996, June 12). Discharge planning: The need for effective communication. *Nursing Standard, 10*(38), 39–41.

Smith, S. (1997, November). The effective use of fear appeals in persuasive immunization strategies: An analysis of national immunization intervention messages. *Journal of Applied Communication Research, 25*(4), 264–292.

Smith, V. (1993, December). From the acting director of CSAP. In U.S. Department of Health and Human Services (Ed.), *Prevention in the workplace* (DHHS Publication No. [SMA] 94-2068). Rockville, MD: National Clearinghouse for Alcohol and Drug Information.

Snyder, M., Omoto, A. M., & Crain, A. L. (1999, April). Punished for their good deeds: Stigmatization of AIDS volunteers. *American Behavioral Scientist, 42* (7), 1175–1192.

Soap Opera Digest Awards (February 26, 1999).

Somerson, M. (1999, July 18). New moms rest easier. *Columbus Dispatch,* pp. 1–2D.

Somerson, M. (1999, October 2). Hospital labor to offer perks to moms-to-be. *Columbus Dispatch,* pp. 1–2A.

Somerson, M. (1999, October 10). Mom takes on health insurer. *The Columbus Dispatch,* pp. 1–2C.

Somerson, M. (1999, October 23). Teen pays dearly for pierced ear. *The Columbus Dispatch,* pp. 1–2A.

Sparta, C. (1999, January 28). Sending in the clowns is serious business. *USA Today,* p. 8D.

Spector, R. (1996a). *Cultural diversity in health and illness* (4th ed.). Stamford, CT: Appleton & Lange.

Spector, R. (1996b). *Guide to heritage assessment and health traditions.* Stamford, CT: Appleton & Lange.

Sperry, L. (1998, December 20). Women develop strength crossing bridges together. *The Columbus Dispatch,* p. 81.

Spiro, H. (1992). What is empathy and can it be taught? *Annals of Internal Medicine, 116* (10), 843–844.

Spragins, E. E. (1999, March 1). What are they hiding? *Newsweek,* p. 74.

Squire, E., Huss, K., & Huss, R. (1991). Letter to the editor. *Journal of the American Medical Association, 266* (19), 2702.

Stacey, M. (1996, July). How to talk to your doctor. *Town and country, 150*(5), 78–81, 111.

Stapleton, S. (1998, May 18). Stressed out? International meeting shows you're alone. *American Medical News, 41*(19), 1, 26.

Starr, P. (1982). *The social transformation of American medicine.* New York: Basic Books.

Steel, D. (1992). *Mixed blessings.* New York: Delacorte Press.

Steele, D., Jackson, T., & Gutmann, M. (1990). Have you been taking your pills?: The adherence-monitoring sequence in the medical interview. *Journal of Family Practice, 30* (3), 294–299.

Stehlin, I. (1998, February). *Homeopathy: Real medicine or empty promises?* (FDA Publication No. 97-1267). Rockville, MD: Department of Health and Human Services.

Stein, H. (1985). *The psychodynamics of medical practice: Unconscious factors in patient care.* Berkeley, CA: University of California Press.

Stein, H. (1990). *American medicine as culture.* Boulder, CO: Westview Press.

Stein, L. I., Watts, D. T., & Howell, T. (1990, November/December). The doctor-nurse game revisited. *Nursing Outlook, 38*(6), 264–268.

Stein, R. E. K., Bauman, L. J., & Jessop, D. J. (1994). Women as formal and informal caregivers of children. In E. Friedman (Ed.), *An unfinished revolution* (pp. 103–120). New York: The United Hospital Fund.

Steingart, R., Packer, M., Hamm, P., Coglianese, M., Gersh, B., Geltman, E., Sollano, J., Katz, S., Moye, L., Basta, L., Lewis, S., Gottlieb, S., Bernstein, V., McEwan, P., Jacobson, K., Brown,

E., Kukin, M., Kantrowitz, N., & Pfeffer, M. (1991, July 25). Sex differences in the management of coronary artery disease. *The New England Journal of Medicine, 235*(4), 226–230.

Steptoe, A., & Appels, A. (Eds.). (1989). *Stress, personal control and health.* New York: John Wiley & Sons.

Steptoe, A., Sutcliffe, I., Allen, B., & Coombes, C. (1991). Satisfaction with communication, medical knowledge, and coping style in patients with metastatic cancer. *Social Science and Medicine, 32* (6), 627–632.

Sternberg, S. (1998, November 23). Study: Consumers support legislative fix. *USA Today,* p. 1D.

Sternberg, S. (2000, January 12). Resistant HIV isn't only cause of drug failure. *USA Today,* p. 8D.

Stetz, K. M., McDonald, J. C., & Compton, K. (1996). Needs and experiences of family caregivers during morrow transplantation. *Oncology Nursing Forum, 23*(9), 1422–1427.

Stevens, P. (1998). The experiences of lesbians of color in health care enounters: Narratives insights for improving access and quality. In C. Ponticelli (Ed.), *Gateways to improving lesbian health and health care: Opening doors* (pp. 77–94). New York: Harrington Park Press.

Stewart, M. (1993). *Integrating social support in nursing.* Newbury Park, CA: Sage.

Stewart, M., Brown, J., Weston, W., McWhinney, I., McWilliam, C., & Freeman, T. (1995). *Patient-centered medicine: Transforming the clinical method.* Thousand Oaks, CA: Sage.

Stewart, M., & Roter, D. (Eds.). (1989). *Communicating with medical patients.* Newbury Park, CA: Sage.

Stone, G. (1979). Patient compliance and the role of the expert. *Journal of Social Issues, 35* (1), 34–59.

St. Peter, R., Reed, M, Kemper, P., & Blumenthal, D. (1999, December 23). Changes in the scope of care provided by primary care physicians. *The New England Journal of Medicine, 341*(26), 180–185.

Strauss, A., Fagerhaugh, S., Suczek, B., & Wiener, C. (1985). *Social organization of medical work.* Chicago: University of Chicago Press.

Street, R. L., Jr., Gold, W. R., & Manning, T. (1997). *Health promotion and interactive technology: Theoretical applications and future directions.* Mahwah, NJ: Lawrence Erlbaum Associates.

Street, R., Jr., Piziak, V., Carpentier, W., Herzog, J., Hejl, J., Skinner, G., & McLellan, L. (1993, May). Provider-patient communication and metabolic control. *Diabetes Care, 16*(5), 714–721.

Strofolino, M. (1999, February 23). A priority for our health care: Enough nurses. *The Globe and Mail,* p. A17.

Strong, P. M. (1979). *The ceremonial order of the clinic: Parents, doctors and medical bureaucracies.* Boston: Routledge & Kegan Paul.

Sugarman, J., Warren, C., Oge, L., & Helgerson, S. (1992, July-August). Using the behavioral risk factor surveillance system to monitor year 2000 objectives among American Indians. *Public Health Report, 107*(4), 449–456.

Sullivan, L. (1992). Skills necessary for contemporary health professionals. *Medical Education, 26,* 3–6.

Suominen, T., Leino-Kilpi, H., & Laippala, P. (1995). Who provides support and how? Breast cancer patients and nurses evaluate patient support. *Cancer Nursing, 18*(4), 278–285.

Svenkerud, P., & Singhal, A. (1998). Enhancing the effectiveness of HIV/Aids prevention programs targeted to unique population groups in Thailand: Lessons learned from applying concepts of diffusion of innovation and social marketing. *Journal of Health Communication, 3*(3), 193–216.

Swingle, C. (2000, January 12). Cooped-up moms-to-be get help coping. *USA Today,* p. 8D.

Tabak, E. (1988). Encouraging patient question-asking: a clinical trial. *Patient Education and Counseling, 12,* 37–49.

Taleisnik, J., & Watson, H. (1984). Midcarpal instability caused by malunited fractures of the distal radius. *Journal of Hand Surgery, 9A* (3), 350–357.

Tannen, D. (1986). *That's not what I meant.* New York: Ballantine Books.

Tannen, D. (1990). *You just don't understand: Women and men in conversation.* New York: Ballantine Books.

Tannen, D. (1992). Rethinking power and solidarity in gender and dominance. In C. Kramsch & S. McConnell-Ginet (Eds.), *Text and context: Cross-disciplinary perspectives on language study* (135–147). Lexington, MA: D.C. Heath and Company.

Tannen, D. (Ed.). (1993). *Gender and conversational interaction.* New York: Oxford University Press.

Tannen, D. (1994). *Talking from 9 to 5.* New York: William Morrow and Company.

Tannen, D. (1997). Women and men talking: An interactional sociolinguistic approach. In M. R. Walsh (Ed.), *Women, men, & gender: Ongoing debates* (pp. 82–90). New Haven, CT: Yale University Press.

Tannen, D., & Wallat, C. (1993). Doctor/mother/child communication: Linguistic analysis of a pediatric interaction. In A. Todd & S. Fisher (Eds.), *The social organization of doctor-patient communication* (pp. 31–48). Norwood, NJ: Ablex Publishing.

Tardy, R. W., & Hale, C. L. (1998, December). Getting "plugged in": A network analysis of health information-seeking among "stay-at-home moms." *Communication Monographs, 65*(4), 336–357.

Taylor, S. (1979). Hospital patient behavior: Reactance, helplessness, or control? *Journal of Social Issues, 35* (1), 156–184.

Taylor, S. E., Falke, R. L., Mazel, R. M., & Hilsberg, B. L. (1988). Sources of satisfaction and dissatisfaction among members of cancer support groups. In B. H. Gottlieb (Ed.), *Marshaling social support: Formats, processes and effects* (pp. 187–208). Newbury Park, CA: Sage.

ten Have, P. (1991). Talk and institution: A reconsideration of the "asymmetry" of doctor-patient interaction. In D. Boden & D. Zimmerman (Eds.), *Talk and social structure* (pp. 138–163). Berkeley, CA: University of California Press.

Thompson, C., & Pledger, L. (1993). Doctor-patient communication: Is patient knowledge of medical terminology improving? *Health Communication, 5* (2), 89–97.

Thompson, S., Nanni, C., & Schwankovsky, L. (1990). Patient-oriented interventions to improve communication in a medical office visit. *Health Psychology, 9* (4), 390–404.

Thompson, T. (1984). The invisible helping hand: The role of communication in the health and social service professionals. *Communication Quarterly, 32*(2), 148–163.

Thompson, T. (1998). The patient/health relationship. In L. Jackson & B. Duffy (Eds.), *Health communication research: A guide to developments and directions* (pp. 37–56). Westport, CT: Greenwood Press.

Thompson, T. (2000). The nature and language of illness explanations. In B. Whaley (Ed.), *Explaining illness: Research, theory and strategies* (pp. 3–40). Mahwah, NJ: Lawrence Erlbaum Associates.

Thorne, S., McCormick, J., & Carty, E. (1997). Deconstructing the gender neutrality of chronic illness and disability. *Health Care for Women International, 18,* 1–16.

Thorne, S., & Robinson, C. (1988, May). Legacy of the country doctor. *Journal of Gerontological Nursing, 14*(5), 23–26.

Thorson, J., & Powell, F. (1993). The rural aged, social value, and health care. In C. N. Bull (Ed.), *Aging in rural America* (pp. 134–145). Newbury Park, CA: Sage.

Ting-Toomey, S. (Ed.). (1994). *The challenge of facework: Cross-cultural and interpersonal issues.* Albany: State University of New York Press.

Tobin, J., Wassertheil-Smoller, S., Wexler, J., Steingart, R., Budner, N., Lense, L., & Wachspress, J. (1987). Sex bias in considering coronary bypass surgery. *Annals of Internal Medicine, 107*(1), 19–25.

Todd, A. (1989). *Intimate adversaries: Cultural conflict between doctors and women patients.* Philadelphia: University of Pennsylvania Press.

Todd, A. (1993). Exploring women's experiences: Power and resistance in medical discourse. In A. Todd & S. Fisher (Eds.), *The social organization of doctor-patient communication* (pp. 267–285). Norwood, NJ: Ablex.

Togno-Armanasco, V. D., Hopkin, L. A., & Harter, S. (1995, May). How case management really works. *American Journal of Nursing, 95*(5), 24I-L.

Toombs, S. (1995). Sufficient unto the day: A life with multiple sclerosis. In S. Toombs, D. Barnard, & R. Carson (Eds.), *Chronic illness: From experience to policy* (pp. 3–23). Bloomington: Indiana University Press.

Toombs, S., Barnard, D., & Carson, R. (Eds.). (1995). *Chronic illness: From experience to policy.* Bloomington: Indiana University Press.

Tracy, K. (1990). The many faces of facework. In H. Giles & P. Robinson (Eds.), *Handbook of language and social psychology* (pp. 209–223). London: Wiley.

Trinh, T. M. (1989). *Woman, native, other: Writing. Postcoloniality and feminism.* Bloomington: Indiana University Press.

Tripp-Reimer, T., & Sorofman, B. (1998). Greek Americans. In L. Purnell, & B. Paulanka (Eds.), *Transcultural health care* (pp. 301–322). Philadelphia: F.A. Davis.

Tulabut, E. (1999, July 18). 70 with breast cancer finally get voice in book. *The Columbus Dispatch,* p. 8C.

Turner, B. (1992). *Regulating bodies: Essays in medical sociology.* London: Routledge.

Turner, B., & Samson, C. (1995). *Medical power and social knowledge* (2nd ed.). Thousand Oaks, CA: Sage.

Turner, J., Gailiun, M., Caruso, K., Murray, O., & Warren, M. (1998). The corrections environment. In S. Viegas & K. Dunn (Eds.), *Telemedicine: Practicing in the information age* (pp. 61–68). Philadelphia: Lippincott-Raven Publishers.

Turow, J. (1989). *Playing doctor: Television, storytelling, and medical power.* New York: Oxford University Press.

Turpie, I., Bloch, R., Edwards, M., Rangachari, P., Patterson, C., & Tainsh, S. (1992, May). A program to sensitize students to issues of geriatric care. *Academic Medicine,67*(5), 304–305.

Tweet, A. G., & Gavin-Marciano, K. (1998). *The guide to benchmarking in healthcare: Practical lessons from the field.* New York: Quality Resources.

Twycross, A. (1998). Children's cognitive level and their perception of pain. *Paediatric Nursing, 10* (3), 24–27.

Ubel, P., & Loewenstein, G. (1997). The role of decision analysis in informed consent: Choosing between intuition and systematicity. *Social Science and Medicine, 44*(5), 647–656.

UNAIDS. (1998a). *Report on the global HIV/AIDS epidemic.* Geneva: Joint United Nations Programme on HIV/AIDS (UNAIDS) and World Health Organization (WHO).

UNAIDS. (1998b). *AIDS epidemic update: December 1998.* Geneva: Joint United Nations Programme on HIV/AIDS (UNAIDS) and World Health Organization (WHO).

Unger, D. G., Jacobs, S. B., & Cannon, C. (1996). Social support and marital satisfaction among couples coping with chronic constructive airway disease. *Journal of Social and Personal Relationships, 13*(1), 123–142.

U.S. Department of Health and Human Services. (1990, September). *Healthy people 2000.* Washington, DC: U.S. Government Printing Office.

U.S. Department of Health and Human Services. (1991, September). *Alcohol practices, policies, and potentials of American colleges and universities: A white paper.* (DHHS publication no. [ADM] 91-1842). Rockville, MD: Office of substance abuse prevention.

U.S. Department of Health and Human Services. (1993, August). *Children of alcoholics* (DHHS publication no. [SMA-93] 2023). Rockville, MD: Author.

U.S. Department of Health and Human Services. (1994, August). *Rural communities* (DHHS Publication No. [SMA] 94-2087). Rockville, ND: National Clearinghous for Alcohol and Drug Information.

U.S. Department of Health and Human Services. (1996, September). *Asian and Pacific Islander Americans.* Rockville, MD: National Clearinghouse for Alcohol and Drug Information.

U.S. Department of Health and Human Services (1997, September). *Pregnant/postpartum women and their infants.* Rockville, MD: National Clearinghouse for Alcohol and Drug Information.

U.S. Department of Health and Human Services (1998). Healthy People 2010. http://web.health .gov/healthypeople/2010 Draft.htm.

Uzelac, E. (1999, July 23–25). The doctor's in the house. *USA Weekend,* pp. 4–5.

Van Blerkom, L. (1995). Clown doctors: Shaman healers of Western medicine. *Medical Anthropology Quarterly, 9* (4), 462–475.

Van Buren, A. (1997, August 22). Dear Abby: Ovarian cancer, a silent killer. *Athens Messenger,* p. 5.

Van Buren, A. (1999, January 26). Dear Abby: Grieving. *Athens Messenger,* p. 5.

Van Buren, A. (1999, May 12). Dear Abby: Sister won't take "no" for answer. *Athens Messenger,* p. 5.

Van Buren, A. (1999, March 31). Dear Abby: No news can sometimes be bad news. *Athens Messenger,* p. 5.

Vanderford, M., Jenks, E., & Sharf, B. (1997). Exploring patients' experiences as a primary source of meaning. *Health Communication, 9* (1), 13–26.

Vanderford, M., & Smith, D. (1996). *The silicon breast implant story: Communication and uncertainty.* Mahwah, NJ: Lawrence Erlbaum Associates.

van Dijk, T., Ting-Toomey, S., Smitherman, G., & Troutman, D. (1997). Discourse, ethnicity, culture and racism. In T. A. van Dijk (Ed.), *Discourse as social interaction* (pp. 144–180). Thousand Oaks, CA: Sage.

Veatch, R.M. (1991). *The patient-physician relation.* Bloomington, Indiana University Press.

Verbrugge, L. (1985, September). Gender and health: An update on hypotheses and evidence. *Journal of Health and Social Behavior, 26,* 155–182.

Vergano, D. (1999, December 13). Best of care or just at cost? *USA Today,* p. 7D.

Verghese, A. (1999, March 1). Showing doctors their biases. *The New York Times,* p. 21A.

Viegas, S. F., & Dunn, K. (Eds.). (1998). *Telemedicine: Practicing in the information age.* Philadelphia: Lippincott-Raven.

vom Eigen, K., Walker, J. D., Edgman-Levitan, S., Cleary, P. D., & Delbanco, T. L. (1999). Carepartner experiences with hospital care. *Medical Care, 37* (1), 33–38.

von Friederichs-Fitzwater, M., Callahan, E., Flynn, N., & Williams, J. (1991). Relational control in physician-patient encounters. *Health Communication, 3*(1), 17–36.

Wacker, R., Roberto, K., & Piper, L. (1998). *Community resources for older adults: Programs and services in an era of change.* Thousand Oaks, CA: Pine Forge Press.

Wadsworth, M. (1976). Studies of doctor-patient communication. In M. Wadsworth & D. Robinson (Eds.), *Studies in everyday medical life* (pp. 3–12). London: Martin Robertson & Co. Ltd.

Waitzkin, H. (1984). Doctor-patient communication: Clinical implications of social scientific research. *Journal of the American Medical Association, 252* (17), 2441–2446.

Waitzkin, H. (1985). Information giving in medical care. *Journal of Health and Social Behavior, 26,* 81–101.

Waitzkin, H. (1989, June). A critical theory of medical discourse: Ideology, social control, and the processing of social context in medical enounters. *Journal of Health and Social Behavior, 30,* 220–239.

Waitzkin, H. (1991). *The politics of medical encounters: How patients and doctors deal with social problems.* New Haven, CT: Yale University Press.

Waitzkin, H., & Stoeckle, J. (1976). Information control and the micropolitics of health care: Summary of an ongoing research project. *Social Science and Medicine, 10,* 263–276.

Waldram, J., Herring, D., & Young, T. (1995). *Aboriginal health in Canada: Historical, cultural, and epidemiological perspectives.* Buffalo, NY: University of Toronto Press.

Walker, R. (1995). The public's problem with public health research. *Health Promotion International, 10*(3), 229–237.

Waller, K. (1988). Women doctors for women patients? *British Journal of Medical Psychology, 61,* 125–135.

Walsh, M. (Ed.). (1997). *Women, men, & gender: Ongoing debates.* New Haven, CT: Yale University Press.

Walter, G. (1993). *Osteopathic medicine: Past and present.* Kirksville, MO: Kirksville College of Osteopathic Medicine.

Walters, R. (1992). *Options: The alternative cancer therapy book.* Garden City Park, NY: Avery Publishing Group.

Ward-Griffin, C., & Ploeg, J. (1997). A feminist approach to health promotion for older women. *Canadian Journal on Aging, 16*(2), 279–296.

Ware, J. E. (1994). Monitoring health care from the patients's point of view. *Hospital Practice, 29* (5), 12 & 17.

Warry, W. (1998). *Unfinished dreams: Community healing and the reality of aboriginal self-government.* Buffalo, NY: University of Toronto Press Incorporated.

Wartman, S., Morlock, L., Malitz, F., & Palm, E. (1983). Impact of divergent evaluations by physicians and patients of patients' complaints. *Public Health Reports, 98* (2), 141–145.

Watson, H., & Carlson, L. (1987). Treatment of reflex sympathetic dystrophy of the hand with an active "stress loading" program. *Journal of Hand Surgery, 12A*(2 Pt 1), 779–785.

Watzlawick, P., Bavelas, J., & Jackson, D. (1967). *Pragmatics of human communication: A study of interactional patterns, pathologies, and patterns.* New York: W. W. Norton and Company.

Webb, P. (1994). *Health promotion and patient education: A professional's guide.* New York: Chapman & Hall.

Webster, D. (1993). Tension and paradox in framing interstitial cystitis. *Journal of Women's Health, 2* (1), 81–84.

Webster, K. (1999, January 29). Doctors: Efforts to reduce c-sections dangerous. *Athens Messenger,* p. 10.

Weghorst, S., Sieburg, H., & Morgan, K. (Eds.). (1997). *Medicine meets virtual reality: Health care in the information age.* Burke, VA: IOS Press.

Weil, A. (1995). *Spontaneous healing: How to discover and enhance your body's natural ability to maintain and heal itself.* New York: Alfred A. Knopf.

Weinberg, N. Schmale, J., Uken, J., & Wessel, K. (1996). Online help: Cancer patients participate in a computer-mediated support group. *Health and Social Work, 21* (1), 24–29.

Weintraub, J. (1993). Gender differences in oral health research: Beyond the dichotomous variable. *Journal of Dental Education, 57*(10), 753–758.

Weir, G. (1999, February 24). Don't tie gift of life to recipient's location. *USA Today,* p. 13A.

Weisman, C., & Teitelbaum, M. (1985). Physician gender and the physician-patient relationship: Recent evidence and relevant questions. *Social Science and Medicine, 20*(11), 1119–1127.

Welch, W. M. (1998, June 19–21). 1974 pensions law sparks political fire. *USA Today,* p. 1A.

Welch, W. M. (1998, June 25). GOP leaders' HMO bill avoids giving patients suing power. *USA Today,* p. 6A.

Welch, W. M. (1998, July 17). HMO laws' hurdle: The ability to sue. *USA Today,* p. 5A.

Welch, W. M. (1999, July 12). "Medical necessity" is crux of health debate. *USA Today,* p. 14A.

Welch, W. M. (1999, July 14). Senate shoots down HMO reforms for women. *USA Today,* p. 5A.

Welch, W. M. (1999, October 8–10). House measure would allow lawsuit against HMOs: Senate showdown awaits. *USA Today,* p. 1A.

West, C. (1984a). Medical misfires: Mishearings, misgivings, and misunderstandings in physician-patient dialogues. *Discourse Processes, 7,* 107–134.

West, C. (1984b). When the doctor is a "lady": Power, status and gender in physician-patient encounters. *Symbolic Interaction, 7*(1), 87–106.

West, C. (1984c). *Routine complications: Troubles with talk between doctors and patients.* Bloomington: Indiana University Press.

West, C. (1993a). "Ask me no questions . . . " An analysis of queries and replies in physician-patient dialogues. In A. Todd & S. Fisher (Eds.), *The social organization of doctor-patient communication* (2nd ed.; pp. 127–160). Norwood, NJ: Ablex.

West, C. (1993b). Reconceptualizing gender in physician-patient relationships. *Social Science and Medicine, 36*(1), 57–66.

West, C., & Fenstermaker, S. (1997). Doing difference. In M. R. Walsh (Ed.), *Women, men, & gender: Ongoing debates* (pp. 58–72). New Haven, CT: Yale University Press.

West, C., & Frankel, R. (1991). Miscommunication in medicine. In N. Coupland, H. Giles, & J. Wiemann (Eds.), *"Miscommunication" and problematic talk.* Newbury Park, CA: Sage.

West, C., Lazar, M., & Kramarae, C. (1997). Gender in discourse. In T. A. van Dijk (Ed.), *Discourse as social interaction* (pp. 119–143). Thousand Oaks, CA: Sage.

West, J. (1999, February/March). National diabetes education program. *Closing the gap* (Office of Minority Health, U. S. Department of Health and Human Services), pp. 1–3.

West, M. A., & Wallace, M. (1991). Innovation in health care teams. *European Journal of Social Psychology, 21,* 303–315.

West, S. (1994). *The hysterectomy hoax.* New York: Doubleday.

Weston, W., & Brown, J. (1989). The importance of patients' beliefs. In M. Stewart & D. Roter (Eds.), *Communicating with medical patients* (pp. 77–85). Newbury Park, CA: Sage.

Whaley, B. (Ed.). (2000). *Explaining illness: Research, theory and strategies.* Mahwah, NJ: Lawrence Erlbaum Associates.

White, J., & Dull, V. (1998). Room for improvement: Communication between lesbians and primary care providers. In C. Ponticelli (Ed.), *Gateways to improving lesbian health and health care: Opening doors* (pp. 95–110). New York: Harrington Park Press.

Wickham, D. (1998, March 17). Mergers "stealth war" on reproductive rights. *USA Today,* p. 15A.

Wickham-Searl, P. (1994). Mothers of children with disabilities and the construction of expertise. *Research in Sociology of Health Care, 11,* 175–187.

Wieder, D. L. (1988). *Language and social reality: The case of telling the convict code.* Washington, DC: University Press of America.

Wieder, D. L., & Pratt, S. (1990). On being a recognizable Indian among Indians. In D. Carbaugh (Ed.), *Cultural communication and intercultural contact* (pp. 45–64). Hillsdale, NJ: Lawrence Erlbaum Associates.

Wiener, C., Fagerhaugh, S., Strauss, A., & Suczek, B. (1980, September/October). Patient power: Complex issues need complex answer. *Social Policy,* 30–38.

Wiener, C., Strauss, A., Fagerhaugh, S., & Suczek, B. (1997). Trajectories, biographies, and the evolving medical technology scene: Labor and delivery and the intensive care nursery. In A. Strauss & J. Corbin (Eds.), *Grounded theory in practice* (pp. 229–250). Thousand Oaks, CA: Sage.

Wiggers, J., & Sanson-Fisher, R. (1997). Practitioner provision of preventive care in general practice consultations: Association with patient educational and occupational status. *Social Science and Medicine, 44*(2), 137–146.

Wiles, R., & Higgins, J. (1996). Doctor-patient relationships in the private sector: Patients' perceptions. *Sociology of Health & Illness, 18* (3), 341–356.

Wilkins, C. (1996). *An ethnographic study of the emergence of culture in two merging health care organizations.* Unpublished doctoral dissertation. Athens, OH: Ohio University.

Wilkins, C. (1998). [Untitled guest lecture]. Presented at Ohio University, Athens, Ohio.

Williams, G., Gabe, J., & Kelleher, D. (1994). Epilogue: The last days of Doctor Power. In J. Gabe, D. Kelleher, & G. Williams (Eds.), *Challenging medicine* (pp. 181–187). London: Routledge.

Williams, J. (1999, February 24). Crystal's diamond dreams dashed. *USA Today,* p. 4D.

Williams, R. (1998, July). *Medications and older adults* (Publication No.[FDA]98-3225). Rockville, MD: FDA consumer.

Williams, S. (1987). Goffman, interactionism, and the management of stigma in everyday life. In G. Scambler (Ed.), *Sociological theory and medical sociology* (pp. 134–164). New York: Tavistock Publications.

Williams, S., & Calnan, M. (Eds.). (1996). *Modern medicine: Lay perspectives and experiences.* London: UCL Press.

Williamson, C. (1992). *Whose standards? Consumer and professional standards in health care.* Philadelphia: Open University Press.

Wilson, C. (1999, December 16). A final farewell, but forever a friend. *USA Today,* p. 1D.

Winett, R. A., Anderson, E. S., Moore, J. F., Sikkema, K. J., Hook, R. J., Webster, D. A., Taylor, C. D., Dalton, J. E., Ollendick, T. H., & Eisler, R. M. (1992). Family/media approach to HIV prevention: Results with a home-based, parent-teen video program. *Health Psychology, 11* (3), 203–206.

Witte, K. (1991–92). The role of threat and efficacy in AIDS prevention. *International Quarterly of Community Health Education, 12*(3), 225–249.

Witte, K. (1994). Ethical issues and guidelines. *American Behavioral Scientist, 38*(2), 285–293.

Witte, K., Cameron, K., Lapinski, M., & Nzyuko, S. (1998). The theoretically based evaluation of HIV/AIDS prevention campaigns along the Trans-Africa highway in Kenya. *Journal of Health Communication, 3*(4), 345–366.

Wloszczyna, S. (1999, January 4). The real Patch, practicing the best medicine. *USA Today,* p. 4D.

Wober, M., & Gunter, B. (1985–86, Winter). Television and beliefs about health care and medical treatment. *Current Psychological Research and Reviews,* 291–304.

Wolf, J. C. (1999, January 6). Quackery hasn't died—it's on the internet. *Athens Messenger,* p. 5.

Wolinsky, F. (1980). *The sociology of health: Principles, professions, and issues.* Boston: Little, Brown and Company.

Wolinsky, F., & Wolinsky, S. (1981). Expecting sick-role legitimation and getting it. *Journal of Health and Social Behavior, 22,* 229–242.

Wood, J. T. (1994). *Who cares? Women, care and culture.* Carbondale and Edwardsville, IL: Southern Illinois University Press.

Wood, J. T. (1997). Gender, communication, and culture. In L. A. Samovar, & R. E. Porter (Eds.), *Intercultural communication* (pp. 164–173). Belmont, CA: Wadsworth Publishing Company.

Wooddell, M, & Hess, D. (Eds.). (1998). *Women confront cancer.* New York: New York University.

Woodruff, L. (1995, December). Growing diversity in the aging population. *Caring Magazine, 14*(12), 4–10.

Woodward, N., & Wallston, B. (1987). Age and health care beliefs: Self-efficacy as a mediator of low desire for control. *Psychology and Aging, 2*(1), 3–8.

Wooten, P. (1998a). An interview with Vera Robinson, EdN, RN. wysiwyg://152http://www.neta.com/~laffinrn/44jest.html.

Wooten, P. (1998b). Making humor work. wysiwyg://149/http://www.neta.com/~laffinrn/34jest.html.

World News Tonight with Peter Jennings. (1994, April 13). American agenda—Double standards in medicine.

Wright, P., & Treacher, A. (Eds.). (1982). *The problem of medical knowledge.* Edinburgh University Press.

Wyatt, N. (1991). Physician-patient relationships: What do doctors say? *Health Communication, 3* (3), 157–174.

Wyckoff, E. (1987, May-June). Women have special treatment needs. *Alcoholism and Addiction,* p. 24.

Yanni, D. (1997). Shifts in identity: The contextualizing function of communication technologies. In J. Owen (Ed.), *Context and communication behavior* (pp. 457–465). Reno, NV: Context Press.

Yelsma, P. (1995). Husband and wife intimacy: Attributes of physiological recovery of myocardial infarction patients. In G. L. Kreps, & D. O'Hair (Eds.), *Communication and health outcomes* (pp. 107–122). Cresskill, NJ: Hampton Press.

Yoffe, E. (1999, November 14). Few doctors wash hands, data show. *Columbus Dispatch,* p. 6E.

Young, J. H. (1992). *American health quackery.* Princeton, NJ: Princeton University Press.

Young, Q. (1997, August 21). AMA deal is a big mistake. *USA Today,* p. 14A.

Zane, N., Takeuchi, D., & Young, K. (Eds.). (1994). *Confronting critical health issues of Asian and Pacific Islander Americans.* Thousand Oaks, CA: Sage.

Zarit, S. H., Pearlin, L. I., & Schaie, K. W. (Eds.). (1993). *Caregiving systems; Formal and informal helpers.* Hillsdale, NJ: Lawrence Erlbaum Associates.

Zimmermann, S. (1994). Social cognition and evaluations of health care team communication effectiveness. *Western Journal of Communication, 58* (Spring), 116–141.

Zimmermann, S., & Applegate, J. L. (1992). Person-centered comforting in the hospice interdisciplinary team. *Communication Research, 19* (2), 240–263.

Zola, I. (1983). *Socio-medical inquiries: recollections, reflections, and reconsiderations.* Philadelphia: Temple University Press.

Zuckerman, M. J. (1999, July 14). Shopping online for drug? Take a big dose of caution. *USA Today,* p. 4D.

Zussman, R. (1992). *Intensive care: Medical ethics and the medical profession.* Chicago: The University of Chicago Press.

INDEX